MICHIGAN

A History of the Wolverine State

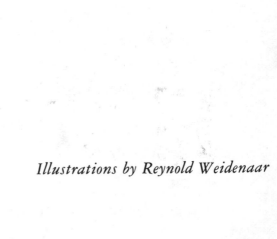

Illustrations by Reynold Weidenaar

MICHIGAN

A History of the Wolverine State

by

WILLIS F. DUNBAR
Western Michigan University

Revised Edition
by

GEORGE S. MAY
Eastern Michigan University

WILLIAM B. EERDMANS PUBLISHING COMPANY
GRAND RAPIDS, MICHIGAN

© Copyright 1965, 1970
Revised Edition Copyright © 1980
by William B. Eerdmans Publishing Company
255 Jefferson, S.E.
Grand Rapids, Michigan 49503
All rights reserved
Library of Congress Catalog Number 64–8579

Library of Congress Cataloging in Publication Data

Dunbar, Willis Frederick, 1902–
    Michigan: a history of the Wolverine State.

    Bibliography: p. 731
    Includes indexes.
    1. Michigan—History.   I.   May, George Smith,
1924–   joint author.   II.   Title.
F566.D84 1980   977.4   79–17750
ISBN 0–8028–7043–0

WILLIS F. DUNBAR, 1902–1970

"Every community has its roots in the past. Its people live in the present and look to the future, but their way of life and their patterns of thought are conditioned by their heritage. A widespread understanding of that heritage is essential in order that progress may be planned wisely."

    Willis F. Dunbar, Kalamazoo and how it grew *(1959)*

CONTENTS

PREFACE

Michigan is perhaps the least typical of all the original forty-eight states in the union. It is unique geographically because it consists of two large peninsulas, whose shores are washed by the waters of four of the five Great Lakes. In few other states does one find such striking differences between the soils, climate, vegetation, and the development of an area as there is between southern Michigan and the lands north of Saginaw Bay. The highly industrialized southeastern region is in sharp contrast to the sparsely settled Upper Peninsula and the northern half of the lower peninsula. Today, Michigan is heavily dependent on a single industry: automotive manufacturing. In the past, Michigan experienced boom periods in the fur trade, land speculation, farming, mining, and lumbering. Politically, it was a stronghold of the Republican party for three-quarters of a century, only to become, in more recent years, a state where party rivalry is intense and elections hotly contested.

Michigan is a state with a colorful past. The French voyageurs, missionaries, and empire builders were the first Europeans to come to this part of the country, which was then thinly populated by a few thousand Indians. In due time, the British replaced the French, and for a few hours the Spanish flag flew over one of the forts. The early American settlers included a preponderance of Yankees from western New York and New England. From Europe came immigrants, such as the Finns, the Cornish, the Swedes, and the Italians, to work in the mines and lumber camps. Germans, Irish, and Dutch settled in the cities and the rich agricultural area of southern Michigan. The automobile industry attracted large numbers of immigrants from southern and eastern Europe in the early years of the twentieth

ix

century, while the industrial expansion of later years brought a large influx of southern blacks and whites. The intermingling of these many nationalities and racial stocks, their quest for greater economic opportunity, their exploitation of the state's natural resources, their constructive efforts to achieve social justice, their sacrifices to provide educational, religious, and cultural institutions, and their contributions to the nation and to the world constitute the warp and woof of Michigan's history.

In Michigan and elsewhere in the United States there has been a remarkable growth of interest in state and local history since the Second World War. It is not a little ironical that just at the time our nation has been more deeply involved than ever before in world affairs we should take such a keen interest not only in our national past but also in the history of our communities, neighborhoods, and states. This interest perhaps reflects a comprehension that here are the grass roots of our history as a nation. If one spent all his life in Washington, D.C., for example, he would gain a rather illusory picture of American life. The kind of people we are, our outlook on life, our ways of doing things, and our faults and foibles as well as our strengths can best be understood by carefully examining our cities, our rural areas, and our states. This is why state and local history is important, and it is in this sense that this history of Michigan is presented—to further an understanding of a nation's history through a study of one of its major components.

*   *   *   *   *

The history that follows is a new version of an earlier work written by Willis F. Dunbar and originally published in 1965. Dr. Dunbar was born in 1902 in Hartford, Michigan, and he described, in charming fashion, the life he knew as a boy in that southwestern Michigan town in one of his last books, *How It Was in Hartford* (1968). His adult years, however, were primarily associated with Kalamazoo. He was a graduate in 1924 of Kalamazoo College, where he taught history and later served as dean between 1928 and 1942. During this time he also earned a doctorate in history from the University of Michigan in 1939. As a program director and news analyst with the Fetzer Broadcasting Company in Kalamazoo from 1943 to 1951, his voice became familiar to thousands of radio listeners in western Michigan. In 1951 he returned to teaching as a member of the history department at what is now Western Michigan University in Kalamazoo, although he continued to make regular appearances on radio and television throughout the years that followed.

It was while he was at Western, where he became the head of the history department in 1960, that Dr. Dunbar, through his immensely popular courses in Michigan history, his service on the Michigan Historical Commission, his active role in the Historical Society of Michigan, and especially through his books, became the best-known authority on the state's history. *Michigan: A History of the Wolverine State,* published in 1965 and reissued in a revised edition in 1970, a few months before Dr. Dunbar's death, climaxed a lifetime of study and writing. It was immediately recognized as the most satisfactory and complete one-volume history of Michigan ever produced.

In the present edition I have tried to maintain Dr. Dunbar's high standards, but readers who are familiar with the earlier editions will note numerous ways in which they differ from the book in hand. An obvious difference is apparent in the organization of the material, resulting primarily from my desire to retain a modified chronological approach throughout, rather than the topical approach that Dr. Dunbar employed in dealing with the decades since the Civil War. As for the text itself, in addition to the inclusion of new material that covers events and developments since the last edition was published, a good many changes have been made that reflect new information and interpretations that appeared in articles and books on the state's history that have been published in the past decade. Other changes, however, reflect the differences that always exist among historians as to the importance that should be attached to certain subjects. Dr. Dunbar's interest in the history of education, cultural activities, and politics was evidenced in the emphasis that he gave to these topics, and I have retained much of his sections on these topics in the present edition. On the other hand, the major additions or changes that I have made in the treatment of the Indians and other groups that later settled in Michigan, the accounts of the War of 1812 and the Civil War, and economic activities—particularly the growth of manufacturing—reflect some of my own interests. Overall, it is my hope that the changes I have made will strengthen, as well as update, this highly successful and well-received work.

In conclusion, I wish to thank Bill Eerdmans for entrusting me with the task of revising one of his publications, and to his editorial staff, especially Marlin Van Elderen and Sharon J. Anderson, for their work on the manuscript I submitted; to my colleagues at Eastern Michigan University, for the answers they were always willing to provide to questions on matters that fell into their area of expertise; to my students, who have taught me so much about the aspects of Michigan history that most interest the average person; and to Tish, who, as always, encouraged me to complete this latest of numerous historical projects that we have seen through together.

George S. May
Eastern Michigan University

LIST OF MAPS

THE PHYSICAL ENVIRONMENT

In the early 1600s, French explorers reached the lands we now call Michigan and began to keep written records of their activities and observations in the area. Such written materials are what the historian studies. The history of Michigan, however, was conditioned by forces at work long before the seventeenth century, and without a knowledge of these forces there can be no real understanding of the developments of the past 350 years.

Time, as reckoned by the geologist, has little meaning to the ordinary person. He is unable to conceive of a million years, to say nothing of a billion years, yet these are the time units that mark geological ages. During these dark recesses of time when the earth was cooling, volcanic eruptions in northern Michigan brought deposits of copper to the earth's surface that would be mined by the Indians several thousand years before the arrival of the white man. During these ages, deposits of iron, petroleum, and other mineral resources were also formed which would later lead to other mining activities in Michigan.

Relatively late in geological time, great icecaps covered the northern part of North America. As the climate warmed and cooled, these icecaps, or glaciers, retreated and advanced. The advance and recession of the glaciers occurred not once but four times. The underlying rock over which these great glaciers spread varied in character. A formation known as the Laurentian Shield (also called the Canadian Shield) is the most dominant feature of eastern and central Canada and extends as far south as Michigan's Upper Peninsula. It was the earliest land mass of North America. It consisted of crystalline rocks and granites, which did not easily erode. South of the

Laurentian Shield the predominant rocks were sandstone, limestone, and shale, which were much softer, and hence more vulnerable to erosion. The advancing glaciers swept the Laurentian Shield bare of soil, depositing it helter-skelter over the area as far south as the Ohio River. Combined with this soil was the soil which was formed by the erosion of the limestone and shale to the south of the Shield. This resulted in the formation of a belt of fertile land for agriculture in southern Michigan and other parts of the lower Middle West, while leaving sandy soils ill-suited to farming in the region that embraces the northern portions of Wisconsin and Michigan. Thus, while the glaciers were responsible for providing the basis for a prosperous agricultural economy in southern Michigan, they were also responsible for creating the conditions that have greatly retarded the development of much of the northern two-thirds of the state.

The configuration of the land of Michigan, the size and location of the lakes, islands, and peninsulas, resulted from varying degrees of resistance to erosion by different strata of rocks. The Great Lakes mark the location of weak rocks, such as limestone and shale, that were easily eroded in pre-glacial ages to form river valleys that drained into this region. These valleys ran parallel to the direction in which the great masses of ice in the ice ages flowed down from the north. These glaciers not only further eroded the existing river beds but the immense weight of the ice, which reached a maximum depth of nearly two miles, depressed the earth's surface. While the position of the lakes conformed to the established drainage patterns of the pre-glacial period, their shape was also affected by the gradual rebounding of the earth's surface, after the glaciers disappeared. The islands in the lakes are features that are both the result of this rebounding action and of the fact that the islands generally rest on stronger rocks that were more resistant to the preceding eroding force of water and ice.[1]

The lakes that emerged after the last Ice Age and assumed their present shapes approximately 2500 years ago have been the single greatest influence on Michigan's historical development. In every period of Michigan history, the existence of water on all sides save one has influenced the activities of the inhabitants of these lands. The Great Lakes have provided invaluable transportation from the time of the Indian and fur trader canoes to present-day giant ore boats. The opening of the St. Lawrence Seaway on April 25, 1959, made Michigan ports on the Great Lakes available to large ocean-going vessels despite Michigan's location deep in the interior of the North American continent, hundreds of miles from any ocean. Although the lakes have been an avenue of commerce, they also have been a barrier to commerce since they have severely limited the construction of short and efficient highways and railroad networks on adjacent lands. The lakes affect the climate and therefore the agriculture. Prevailing westerly winds blowing across Lake Michigan nurture Michigan's fruit belt along the west coast of the lower peninsula. Because they are cool in the spring, these winds prevent the premature development of the fruit buds, and warmed by the lake in the autumn, these winds prolong the growing season. In addition, the lakes have been an important food source with their abundant supply of fish.

Glacial activity also scooped out the areas now covered by Michigan's many thousands of inland lakes. The largest of these is Houghton Lake, in Roscommon County, with an area of nearly thirty-one square miles. Six others have areas of twenty or more square miles, with approximately 15,800 lakes covering two acres or more.[2] The number of lakes is so great that it has been difficult to find distinctive names for all of them. Thus, Long Lake, Little Lake, Big Lake, Round Lake, Bass Lake, Mud Lake, Crooked Lake, and Silver Lake are among the names that have been used repeatedly. These inland lakes, as well as the Great Lakes, constitute one of the foundations upon which Michigan's tourist industry is based because they offer limitless opportunities for fishing, swimming, and boating.

As the glaciers retreated the present river system of Michigan was created. Michigan rivers are unusual in that they are extended rivers. The surfaces of the Great Lakes originally rested at a higher sea level than at present, but after the glacial period they receded to their present levels and the rivers extended in order to flow to a lower lake outlet. The Huron River once flowed westward into other rivers that led to the body of water that later became Lake Michigan, but when the lake levels receded, it exited by way of the Raisin River to Lake Erie, and finally through its own outlet to that lake. On the western side of the lower peninsula nearly all the rivers have outlets that are partially dammed by sand dunes, and hence rivers such as the Kalamazoo, Black, Muskegon, and Manistee form lakes before flowing into Lake Michigan. During the great lumber boom of the nineteenth century these lakes were ideal locations for sawmills, and provided excellent sheltered harbors for various types of lake craft. Many Michigan rivers have rapids, around which many early towns originated. There are many waterfalls, nearly all of them on the rivers of the Upper Peninsula where the most famous are the Tahquamenon Falls. The rivers were used extensively by the French fur traders and missionaries for transportation, and before the coming of the railroads they were invaluable to the American settlers. They have also been important in powering mills and at one time were a major source of electric power. In 1934, forty Michigan rivers were producing electric power at 217 sites. The greater efficiency of other methods of producing power, however, have made hydroelectric plants the size of those in Michigan an insignificant source of power, with the remaining plants of this type accounting for only one and a half percent of Michigan's electric energy in 1976.[3] On the other hand, Michigan's rivers are second only to its lakes in the promotion of the vacation and tourist industry.

Particularly important are the three rivers that connect the Great Lakes adjacent to Michigan. The St. Mary's River connects Lake Huron with Lake Superior, which lies twenty-two feet above the level of the lower lakes. In order for ships to pass through this waterway a canal with locks was built in the 1850s. The Soo Canal at one time carried a greater tonnage of shipping than either the Panama or Suez canals, despite the fact that it is normally closed to traffic from December to April. The St. Clair River, connecting Lake Huron with Lake St. Clair, and the Detroit River, connecting the latter with Lake Erie, are similarly among the busiest waterways in the world. The importance of these rivers was recognized by the early French explorers as well as the British who followed them, for both built fortifications to control these strategic rivers and the Straits of Mackinac which link the waters of Lake Huron and Lake Michigan.

Other Michigan rivers deserve mention because of their historic associations. The St. Joseph, which rises in Hillsdale County and flows westward until it reaches St. Joseph County and then makes a southerly bend into Indiana, only to return northward and find its outlet at St. Joseph, was one of the major routes of travel for Indians, explorers, missionaries, and fur traders. Forts and a mission were built along its banks. Only a short portage had to be made to pass from the St. Joseph to the Kankakee River, whose waters flow into the Mississippi. Fur trading was also active on the Kalamazoo and Grand rivers, the latter of which is, at 225 miles, Michigan's longest river. The Muskegon and the Manistee on the western side of the lower peninsula, the Saginaw and its tributaries on the eastern side, and the Menominee in the Upper Peninsula were the most important rivers for the lumbermen.

The state of Michigan, as nature made it and as it has been set off as a separate political unit, comprises an area of 96,675 square miles. This includes 38,459 square miles of Great Lakes waters, since the boundaries of the state extend out into the lakes and encompass much of Lakes Michigan, Superior, and Huron, and a small portion

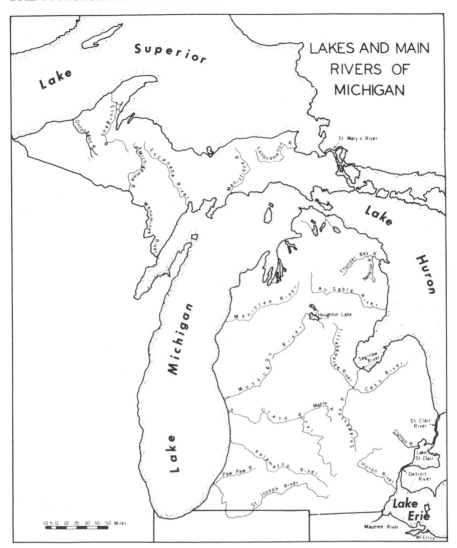

LAKES AND MAIN RIVERS OF MICHIGAN

of Lake Erie. Michigan ranks twenty-third among the states in land area, with 56,817 square miles of land and 1,399 square miles of inland water.[4] The shoreline of Michigan measures 3,121 miles, more than that of any other state except Alaska.

The name "Michigan" is an Indian word generally interpreted to mean "great water" and was first applied by the French to one of the Great Lakes which had earlier been called the "Lake of the Illinois." Thomas Jefferson designated one of the future states that were to be created by the Ordinance of 1784 as "Michigania," but its location was not where Michigan is today. This ordinance never went into effect, being superseded by the Northwest Ordinance of 1787. In 1805, under the provisions of this act, Congress created the Territory of Michigan, with boundaries considerably different from those of the state that eventually evolved from this territory. Political considerations resulted in the addition of the western portion of the Upper Peninsula and changes in the southern boundary of the lower peninsula. Thus the present shape and size of Michigan have been determined by a combination of natural and man-made factors.

The soils within the boundaries of Michigan are extremely diverse. They range in texture from plastic, compact clays to sands so loose that they are constantly shifted by the winds. The range of humus and soils containing essential elements of nutrition (nitrogen, phosphorus, potassium, and lime) is also very great. In addition to mineral soils there is a large acreage of organic soils (peat and muck) which vary widely in character. Deforestation, drainage, overcropping, and other changes wrought by man over many centuries have greatly altered the character of the land. The sand dunes along Lake Michigan and the many swamps in the interior may have given some early visitors a false impression of the true nature of the land. Later exploration, however, revealed many areas of rich and fertile soils. Perhaps no state has such a wide variety of soils. For this reason, an unusually wide variety of farm operations came to be characteristic of Michigan agriculture.

Before any farming could take place, the land had to be cleared, because except for the open grassland or prairie in the southern, particularly the southwestern part of the lower peninsula, the land was covered with dense forests that constituted, together with the waters of the lakes, Michigan's most visible resource. Although these forests were composed of numerous varieties and species of trees, the wooded areas lying south of a line extending roughly from the Saginaw Bay to the mouth of the Grand River included predominately hardwoods, while north of that line the forests were most commonly composed of soft, coniferous trees. The same line also roughly divided the most fertile soils of southern Michigan which could support successful agricultural operations from the increasingly sandy soils of northern Michigan which generally were not suited to farming activities. Fortunately for the economic development of the northern two-thirds of the state, the trees that flourished in that area's thin soils were those that supported a great boom in lumbering in the last half of the nineteenth century.

Michigan's greatest concentration of mineral wealth was also found in these same northern areas. Although the French demon-

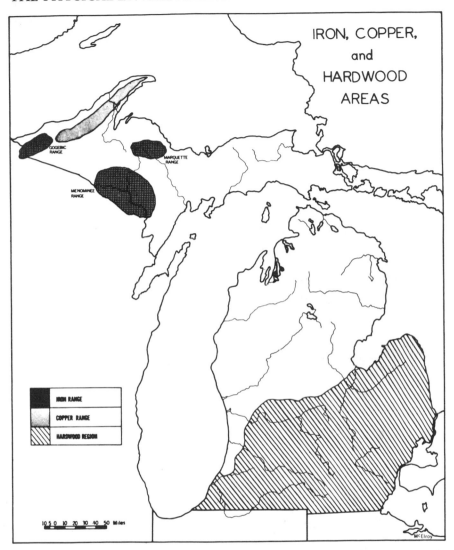

IRON, COPPER, and HARDWOOD AREAS

GOGEBIC RANGE

MARQUETTE RANGE

MENOMINEE RANGE

IRON RANGE

COPPER RANGE

HARDWOOD REGION

10 5 0 10 20 30 40 50 Miles

McElroy

strated interest in the copper that the Indians had earlier dug out of Michigan's soils, no large-scale effort was made to exploit this vast mineral resource until the mid-nineteenth century. The Copper Country, stretching through the Keweenaw Peninsula and southward, is located in what are now Keweenaw, Houghton, and Ontonagon counties. The three Michigan iron ranges, likewise found in the western part of the Upper Peninsula, are the Marquette, Menominee, and Gogebic ranges. Michigan also has major deposits of salt, gypsum, limestone, sand and gravel, petroleum, and coal. All would contribute to the growth of a highly diversified economy in the state.

Finally, Michigan's climate must be mentioned as a factor in the state's history. Michiganians,[5] unlike residents of Florida or California, are not likely to boast of their climate. The weather is notoriously changeable. Though this may be unpleasant at times, one school of geographers holds that changeable weather conditions stimulate greater physical vigor and mental alertness.[6] Climatic conditions, combined with thin soils, militate against profitable agriculture in northern Michigan. On the other hand, as noted earlier, the westerly winds that moderate the climate on the western side of the lower peninsula are an asset to agriculture in that area. The cool breezes of summer attract many vacationers to Michigan, and the heavy snowfall and cold weather in the winter have made Michigan a major skiing and winter resort center. Thus the state's climate, like so much of that which has resulted from Michigan's physical environment, has been a liability in some respects, but on the whole it has proven to be an even greater asset to the state and its people.

Dome-shaped dwellings of early Michigan Indians

MICHIGAN'S FIRST RESIDENTS

Before the white man came to Michigan the land was inhabited by people who became known as Indians. This name resulted from a gross miscalculation made by the European discoverer of the New World. Columbus firmly believed that he had reached the Indies, which was the name given by the Europeans to the dimly known Far East. Hence Columbus called the native peoples in this land Indians. Like so many misnomers, this one has persisted through the centuries.

The Indians found by the French in Michigan over a century after Columbus were descendants of peoples that had arrived here at an earlier time. Where they came from, when they arrived, and who they were have been and will continue to be subjects of controversy. Although all of these questions may never be answered in an entirely satisfactory manner, much of what passed for answers in the past has had to be discarded or greatly revised by recent findings. With regard to the first question, the most common assumption remains that the native peoples of the Western Hemisphere originally came from Asia by way of the Bering Straits, where at times in the past the two hemispheres have been joined by a land bridge. Even today the present narrow waterway is not great enough to prevent Eskimos on either side from travelling back and forth in their comparatively primitive vessels.

The development of new, more accurate methods of determining the age of certain kinds of archaeological discoveries, beginning with the radiocarbon method perfected in the 1940s, has resulted in important changes in the dating of known prehistoric Indian sites and has pushed farther back in time the period in which these peoples were first thought to have arrived in this hemisphere. In the 1970s new discoveries suggested that even these revised estimates were far too conservative as finds in California and Mexico and elsewhere raised the possibility that mankind had been found in those areas at least as far back as 100,000 or even 250,000 years ago, rather than the 20,000- to 40,000-year range that previously had been assumed.[1]

In the case of Michigan, and much of the northern part of North America, however, the possibilities for discovering evidence of human existence are limited by the fact that approximately 18,000 years ago these areas were largely covered by the glaciers of the last great ice age which made the region entirely uninhabitable. Furthermore, the immense weight of these glaciers, thousands of feet thick, ground out all surface evidence of prior life in these lands. In approximately 11,000 B.C., a warming trend initiated a significant northward retreat of the ice which led in turn to a restoration of life to the uncovered surfaces. Animals moved in to feed from the vegetation that now grew up again, and soon after people, who lived by hunting these animals, also arrived.

Although conditions in the extreme southern part of Michigan might have supported human life as early as 13,000 years ago, the earliest uncovered evidence of such life is a site in the Detroit area that archaeologists believe is perhaps 11,000 years old, or, in other words, that dates from about 9,000 B.C. The archaeological evidence from this and other early sites is pitifully meager—a few broken stone tools, a spear point, an animal bone or two, the remains of a fire hearth—but, nevertheless, by working with geologists and botanists who can tell them of the changes in land forms, water levels, climate, and vegetation, archaeologists have been able to piece together a picture of the gradual movement into the area of peoples of different levels of cultural development, and how they adapted themselves to a changing environment.

The first inhabitants of Michigan in these post-glacial years lived by hunting the big animals that were then found here, such as the mastodons, which would become extinct, and the caribou, now found only much farther north, where they migrated in search of the cold climate that no longer was found in Michigan as, by approximately 6,000 B.C., the glaciers had disappeared from the area south of Canada.

During the next four thousand years, as the climate became warmer and drier than it has been at any time in the past 20,000 years, other peoples moved into these thickly forested lands, hunting the animals that were now largely similar to those that a modern hunter would expect to find in Michigan. These peoples also increas-

ingly took advantage of the abundant food supply available in the Great Lakes. Although their water levels were much lower than they have been in recent times, these lakes, which in the immediate post-glacial era were more directly linked to the oceans and had thus harbored whales and walrus, now became predominately the home of varieties of small marine life.

The increasing variety of the man-made objects that are found at the sites dating from these years, in contrast with those from earlier periods, has led archaeologists to conclude that these objects are evidence of cultural progress. The most startling advance of these ancient Michigan inhabitants was the use made of the copper found in the Upper Peninsula. This metal was being mined as far back as 5,000 B.C., leaving shallow pits that are still discernible today. By alternately heating and chilling the chunks of ore that they dug out, these Old Copper Indians, as they have been termed, removed the surrounding rocks in order to reach the soft pure copper which they then hammered into tools and weapons to replace or to supplement their stone implements. These Indians were apparently the first peoples anywhere in the Western Hemisphere to work with metals. They still lived by hunting and fishing, but they appear to have been the first in the area to have domesticated the dog—the only domestic animal of the prehistoric peoples of Michigan. They also developed and built dugouts or canoes to reach the islands where some of their mine pits were located. They buried their dead in cemeteries, indicating an increased degree of community identity and organization, and they traded with other peoples, as evidenced by the discovery of some of these early Michigan copper products at sites in New York, Illiniois, and Kentucky.

In the last two thousand years of the pre-Christian era, major cultural changes occurred in the area. At the same time land forms, the dimensions and depths of the lakes, and the flora and fauna assumed the general characteristics that are visible today. The first burial mounds were built during this period, and their existence today is a visible reminder of these early Michigan residents who were the contemporaries of or who preceded the far better known civilizations of the ancient Mediterranean world or the Mayan, Aztec, and Incan civilizations. Over a thousand Indian mounds have been identified in Michigan, chiefly in the southern part of the lower peninsula. Although the very large number of bodies that were buried in the largest of these mounds (which pioneers in the River Rouge area found and subsequently leveled in the nineteenth century) were probably the result of deaths caused by some disaster, it is generally presumed that burial in a mound was an honor accorded only to a select few. This fact, together with the placement of artifacts and other treasured possessions with the dead person's remains, suggests again a degree of tribal organization, a respect for those in authority, and a prescribed ceremonial life that would have less likely existed in earlier, more primitive cultures.

Another evidence of cultural progress in this period is found in the appearance of pottery, which marked a major advance over earlier, laboriously-fashioned stone or wooden vessels. But an even more important step toward the development of a culture was taken around 100 B.C. when some of the peoples in Michigan began growing their own food.

Agriculture is one of several features of what archæologists have called the Hopewell Indian culture which emerged in the lower Midwest around 500 B.C. Within a few hundred years this culture, the most advanced to be found among any Indians in the region at any time prior to the historic era, had spread to sites along the rivers of southwestern Michigan. For the first time, some Michiganians ceased to be dependent on food they obtained by hunting, fishing, and gathering activities. They began to grow some of their own food, raising corn, squash, beans, and also probably some tobacco, which Indians of the region already had been smoking for several years.

In addition to introducing agriculture to Michigan, the Hope-

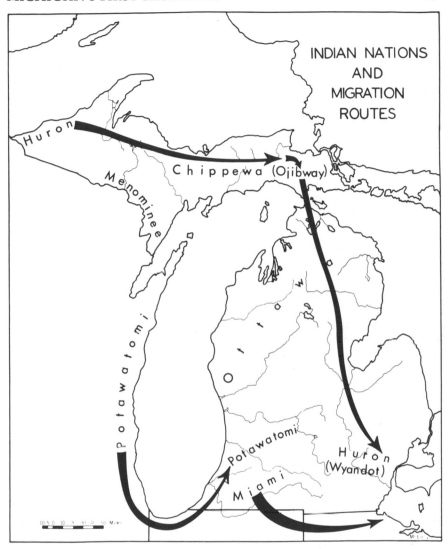

well Indians also produced artistically decorated pottery, which also led to the production of small sculptured human and animal figures, elaborately carved pipe bowls, jewelry, and other objects. These were made from a variety of materials, including shells from the coastal regions, obsidian from the Rocky Mountains, mica from the Middle Atlantic area, and lead from Missouri. To obtain this material, the Hopewell Indians obviously had developed extensive trade with other peoples, and some of their copper objects have been found at sites as far away as the Gulf of Mexico.

The diversity of the Hopewell culture is further indicated by their use of musical instruments, their development of fabrics using finger-weaving techniques, and their construction of large earthen wall inclosures around groups of burial mounds. In addition, the so-called garden beds, found by pioneers in the nineteenth century in parts of southern and western Michigan, may date from the Hopewell period. Among the most curious of all North American antiquities, these garden beds, covering as much as 120 acres, consisted of low ridges of soil approximately eighteen inches high, arranged in a variety of nearly perfect geometrical patterns which resembled formal gardens. What function they were intended to serve remains a mystery. Except for a few reported in Indiana and Wisconsin, they have been found only in Michigan but all of them were destroyed by modern farming operations. A few Indian mounds have survived, however, including a small one in Bronson Park, Kalamazoo, and a group of about fifteen mounds, known as the Norton Mounds, located along the Grand River southwest of Grand Rapids.

Some time after A.D. 700 the Hopewell culture declined and the remaining years before the onset of the historic period in the early seventeenth century saw a diversity of cultures in the area, some of which coexisted with the earlier Hopewell culture, while others existed outside the Hopewell culture. None of these cultures, however, reached the levels of Hopewell. Toward the end of the prehistoric years the number of these early residents of Michigan appears to have declined considerably for reasons that are not clear. Their culture also appears to have retrogressed because they seem to have ceased using the copper that earlier peoples had been utilizing for several thousand years.

Suddenly in the early 1600s the innumerable and glaring gaps in the archaeological knowledge and evidence of Michigan's first peoples began to be filled in from the written records of European observers who entered these areas and reported what they found and saw.

In all of Michigan, which did not then exist, of course, as a separate, politically defined area, these outsiders found relatively few Indians. There is little doubt that Michigan today contains far more Indians than it did at the start of the historic period. In the entire upper Great Lakes region the estimated Indian population in the early 1600s is believed to have numbered approximately 100,000. Compared to later population standards for this same area, this figure is small, but on a larger scale these Indians comprised a tenth of the total Indian population for all of North America north of Mexico when Europeans first began to have extensive contact with this continent.

The French were the first to explore the upper Great Lakes, and they would eventually identify nine tribes which would play a role in Michigan's development. Although the French had difficulty in distinguishing between tribes and the bands or clans into which the tribes were divided, the names that now identify these different groups are names that were actually used at the time and are not terms arbitrarily assigned by later investigators, as is the case with such prehistoric names as the Old Copper and Hopewell Indians.

The nine upper Great Lakes tribes fall into three linguistic groupings, while at least three levels of cultural development are also apparent. On the east, living in the Georgian Bay area, were the Huron Indians and the closely related Tionontati or Tobacco Huron. There is uncertainty, in fact, as to what was the exact relationship between these two groups; however, as a result of wars the two groups were forced to merge, and the term Wyandot became the more common name for the merged group. These Indians were the only representatives of the Iroquoian linguistic group in this region. Other tribes that spoke this language, including the several tribes known collectively as the Iroquois, were located southeast of the Hurons. The Hurons and Tobacco Hurons are believed to have been the most numerous of the upper Great Lakes tribes, with a population estimated between 45,000 to 60,000. Culturally, they were also the most advanced according to European standards, since they were relatively sedentary people, living in large villages with a high degree of community and tribal organization. This resulted from the fact that they were the most agriculturally oriented of all these Indians, growing a substantial amount of their food. Gardening, rather than farming, might be more descriptive of the Huron agriculture which was primarily the job of the women; however, in view of the almost total lack of farm equipment and the complete absence of work animals, the size of the fields that were cultivated was surprisingly large. The Hurons did not need to move about a great deal searching for food. The hunting they did was not so much for meat as it was for the skins and hides of the animals which they used as items of clothing or to cover their dwellings. The Hurons continued, however, to take advantage of the area's abundant supply of fish, which constituted a major part of their diet.

To the north of the Hurons and living among the islands and on the shores of northern Lake Huron was the Ottawa tribe, a small group of approximately 3,000 people. They were members of the Algonquian linguistic group, which geographically is the most widely distributed Indian language group in North America and is represented among seven of the nine upper Great Lakes tribes. Despite their language differences with the Hurons and the fact that they were still much more dependent on hunting and fishing for food than they were on farming, the Ottawas were on good terms with the Hurons and their histories would be closely linked for nearly two centuries.

To the north of the Ottawa was the second most numerous of these tribes, the Chippewa, numbering approximately 30,000 but scattered over a vast area around Lake Superior and far to the north in Canada. Their name is often spelled Ojibwa, which simply illustrates the problem that Europeans had in agreeing on a phonetic spelling of the Indian term they heard, because the Indians had not yet developed a written language. The Chippewas were Algonquian in their language but culturally they were different from all the other tribes in that they did almost no farming but were nearly as dependent on hunting, fishing, and gathering activities as were the Indians of the pre-agricultural era. One Chippewa group lived in what became the Sault Ste. Marie area and was highly skilled in fishing the fast-moving waters of the St. Mary's River. Another group was found along the Lake Michigan shore of the Upper Peninsula near present-day Escanaba. Other groups were scattered around Lake Superior outside of what is now Michigan. Because these nomadic Indians were so widely dispersed there is some belief that they may not have considered themselves one tribe until later in the historic period when outside pressures compelled them to draw together.

Westward across the Upper Peninsula, the Menominee Indians, numbering approximately 3,000, lived in the valley of the river which bears their name and which forms part of the Michigan-Wisconsin boundary. An Algonquian-speaking tribe, the Menominee, like the Ottawa and the remaining five tribes, were in the middle of the scale relative to how they obtained their food, not growing as much as the Hurons but not as dependent on hunting and fishing as the Chippewa. One distinguishing feature of the Menominee, however, was the extent to which they harvested the wild rice that grew so abundantly in their area and which was more important in their diet than in that of any other tribe in the region.

South of the Menominee in central Wisconsin were the Fox and the Sac or Sauk Indians, each with populations of approximately 3,000. They were linguistically related to the Menominee, but culturally the latter were much closer to their neighbors in the Green Bay area—the Winnebago Indians—who may have numbered close to 4,000, even though this tribe was the sole representative this far east of the Siouan linguistic stock that was most commonly associated with tribes much farther west. The Sac and the Fox, on the other hand, sometimes hunted in the open prairie country to the south, and the different techniques used in hunting the buffalo that were found on those prairies brought these two tribes closer culturally to the Miami, an Algonquian tribe of approximately 4,500 people that lived in southern Wisconsin at the start of the historic period. The prairie hunting forays of the Miami were conducted by an entire village, in contrast to the hunts of the northern tribes in which smaller, family-size groups scoured regional forests.

The ninth of the tribes in the upper Great Lakes at the beginning of the historic period was the Potawatomi, with a population of approximately 4,000. They were first reported by the French in the mid-seventeenth century as living in Wisconsin near Green Bay, but there is evidence that earlier in that century some of them were living in the western part of Michigan's lower peninsula. This peninsula seems to have become largely deserted, however, because of the attacks of the fierce Iroquois tribes from New York, which caused the Indians living in southern Michigan to flee to Wisconsin. Late in the seventeenth century, population pressures in Wisconsin helped to bring about an eastward movement of both the Potawatomi and Miami tribes who now began to make their homes in parts of northern Indiana, southern Michigan, and northern Ohio.

Overall, the Indians whom the French found in the upper Great Lakes region do not seem to have been as warlike as were some of the tribes in other areas, and thus, with certain notable exceptions, Michigan's history is largely free of accounts of violent confrontations between Indians and whites such as are commonly associated with the relationship of these races in some other parts of the country. In other ways these Michigan Indians do not fit the stereotyped images that have been perpetuated by many writers and film-makers; images that generally, if they have any factual basis, are more likely to relate to the Plains Indians of the West. The Indians of the forested Great Lakes area had few if any horses at the start of the historic period. They did not normally live in tepees, but instead built dome-shaped dwellings with a framework of saplings lashed together and covered with bark and skins. Nor did the members of these several tribes wear the elaborate feathered headdress of the Plains Indians, although in recent times some Indian residents of Michigan have adopted this costume in order to satisfy tourists.

That so many tourists expect Indians to conform to their images of them is only one evidence of the general lack of understanding of the Indians. This is no new phenomenom, however, for the French and other Europeans who first encountered these natives were startled and perplexed by the glaring differences between the western European and Indian cultures. Some of the more open-minded out-

siders commented favorably on some aspects of the Indian lifestyle, such as their hospitality towards strangers, their courage and stamina, and the love shown by the parents towards their children. But for the most part the Indian culture was looked upon as decidedly inferior to that of the Europeans. The term which the French used to refer to these people, *sauvages* (although it does not have quite the same negative connotations as the English word "savages"), expressed what they felt was the uncivilized nature of the Indians, if not their innate inferiority to the French. Thus, the best and most enlightened policy that the French, and later the British and the Americans, could think of in dealing with the Indians was to try to "civilize" these primitive people.

The Indians readily agreed that the white man's gun, iron kettle, blankets, and many other products were indeed superior to anything that the Indian had developed, and when the opportunity arose, the Indian quickly added these items to his culture. But he did not agree that his way of life itself was inferior, and he therefore resisted efforts that were aimed at Europeanizing or Americanizing him. As he became increasingly dependent on the white man for the material objects which had become so desirable, he found it more and more difficult to stand aloof from the white man's influence in other aspects of his culture. For two centuries, however, the Indians of the Michigan area were able to hold out quite effectively because during that time their services were regarded as useful and essential to the kind of development that outsiders were interested in pursuing.

Today, although some Indians in northern Michigan still try to preserve the ways of their ancestors, there is little to remind the uninitiated of that time until the 1600s when the Indians were the only residents of the area. Perhaps the most obvious evidence lies in the many words the Indians contributed to the language of those who followed them into the area. Particularly notable are the number of Indian terms and names used as geographical place names, including Michigan, Saginaw, Washtenaw, Kalamazoo, Mackinac, Pontiac, Tecumseh, Muskegon, Ottawa, Chippewa, Gogebic, Osceola, Topinabee, Pokagon, and many more. It must be noted, however, that in most instances these words of Indian origin have undergone considerable alteration and modification in the course of many different approaches to phonetic spellings of the spoken term. In some cases, such as Mackinac, the changes have been so great that it is impossible for Indian language scholars to agree upon the original meaning of the term since even the word or expression that the present spelling is supposed to represent cannot be exactly determined.[2] Thus even this remnant of Michigan's Indian heritage is in danger of being lost.

THE FRENCH EXPLORERS

Frenchmen were the first Europeans to see Michigan, arriving at approximately the same time the Pilgrims were landing in New England, nine hundred miles to the east.[1] The background of this development illustrates the ways in which the course of history has been influenced by geography. The Spanish, who colonized Mexico in the sixteenth century, explored far to the north of that country into what is now the United States, but their settlements reached only as far north as Texas and New Mexico as they found the Great Plains area of the West toilsome and unpromising. The English and the Dutch, who founded colonies along the Atlantic, were barred from the interior by formidable ranges of mountains and by the strength of the Iroquois Indians who occupied the Mohawk Valley, the one major route offering easy access to the West. But the French, whose explorers discovered the St. Lawrence River, were lured into the interior through lakes and rivers which eventually flowed into the Atlantic by way of the St. Lawrence. Because the French king gained title to the St. Lawrence valley by reason of discovery, his subjects were the first Europeans to follow this route into the interior to the shores of Michigan.

Jacques Cartier, a Breton pilot from the port of St. Malo, found the mouth of the St. Lawrence and explored it as far as the site of the city of Montreal in the course of three voyages for the king of France between 1534 and 1542. King Francis I had directed Cartier to search for a route through this land that would provide the French with a new and shorter way of reaching the riches of the Orient, while at the same time looking for some of the same kind of wealth in these lands that the Spanish were finding in the land that Columbus discovered in the south. Cartier's hopes of finding the desired water route to the Orient were frustrated when he encountered the Lachine Rapids in the St. Lawrence above Montreal. In addition, the riches he thought he had found in this area proved not to be gold and diamonds, but fool's gold (iron pyrite) and quartz. The resulting disillusionment partially explains why the French failed to follow up on Cartier's discoveries for some sixty years. At this time France also was engulfed in a long series of disastrous civil wars. Peace was finally restored in 1598, and a remarkably able monarch, Henry IV, now was once more able to encourage exploration and colonization in America. Lacking funds of his own to establish colonies, the king granted a monopoly of the fur trade to a successful promoter, Pierre du Gua, the Sieur de Monts, as a means of developing his American possessions. Among those associated with de Monts was a French navigator and mapmaker, Samuel de Champlain. This was the man whose initiative would eventually push French explorers to the far west.

Champlain persuaded de Monts that a post up the St. Lawrence would be desirable for the fur trade, and on July 3, 1608, he founded Quebec. The death of Henry IV in 1610 resulted in the cancellation of de Mont's monopoly, but Champlain was retained by the new company formed by a group of French noblemen.

The direction that Champlain's explorations took and the route to the West that the French would follow for many years was determined the year after Quebec was founded. In order to cultivate the friendship of the Algonquian tribes who lived in the vicinity of Quebec, Champlain and several other Frenchmen accompanied these Indians on a war party against their dreaded enemies, the Iroquois, in what is now New York. The Indians and the French went up the Richelieu River to the lake that now bears Champlain's name, where on July 30, 1609, they encountered a band of two hundred Mohawk Indians, one of the Iroquois tribes. The firearms used by the French in the ensuing struggle threw the Mohawks into panic-stricken flight and incurred the lasting enmity of these Indians and their fellow Iroquois toward the French. This powerful Indian confederation occupied lands along the southern shores of Lake Ontario and hence was in a position to block the use of this portion of the Great Lakes waterway by the French. It is by no means certain that Champlain would have conducted his explorations of the West along the route of today's St. Lawrence Seaway had it not been for the enmity of the Iroquois, but there can be no doubt that throughout the remainder of the seventeenth century the Iroquois consistently prevented the French from conducting explorations that might have taken them into southern Michigan and the areas to the south of the Great Lakes.

The mighty Ottawa River, which pours the waters accumulated along its 696-mile course into the St. Lawrence at Montreal, must have presented an inviting route to the West, which Champlain and other French explorers quite likely would have taken in preference to the southern route via Lake Ontario, regardless of the attitude of the Iroquois. Paddling against the Ottawa's current presented no great difficulty to the experienced canoemen who accompanied Champlain in 1613 on his first trip up the river. Two years later Champlain reached Georgian Bay by the Ottawa route. He and his men traveled up the Ottawa and into its tributary, the Mattawa, carrying their canoes and supplies through rapids, around waterfalls and over portages until they reached Lake Nippising, where they followed the French River into Georgian Bay. At the head of this bay Champlain found Father Joseph Le Caron, a Recollet who had recently arrived to begin a mission among the Huron Indians. Joining a Huron war party, Champlain traveled to the northern shore of Lake Ontario. The party then crossed the lake into New York where they fought a battle with some Iroquois. Champlain was badly wounded and was taken back to the Huron country where he spent the winter of 1615–16. While there, the Indians told him tales of a great lake forty days' journey to the west. Although intrigued by this, Champlain returned to Quebec in the spring and left further explorations in the hands of younger men. One of these men, Etienne Brulé, ventured further west from Huron country and around 1620 reached the St. Mary's River—the first European to set foot on Michigan soil.

*   *   *   *   *

Curiosity about the unknown and the itch for adventure were the traits of the intrepid Frenchmen who braved the dangers and privations of the wilderness in order to discover what lay beyond the horizon. In addition, however, there were specific goals that continued to motivate these explorations. One of these was the persistent search for a water route through the continent to the Far East. A century after Cartier had failed to find this route via the St. Lawrence, Champlain heard of a people called "People of the Sea" who dwelt beside the "Stinking Water" (which he assumed meant salt water). Champlain jumped to the conclusion that these people were Oriental or that they traded with the Orient; thus, he equipped Jean Nicolet, before Nicolet left for an expedition westward in 1634, with a gorgeous robe of China damask "all strewn with flowers and birds of many colors" to put on when he arrived among these people. After passing through the Straits of Mackinac, Nicolet reached his destination at Green Bay. We may imagine Nicolet's disappointment when the only peoples he found were some Winnebago Indians. The latter were even more startled by the sight of Nicolet, who announced his arrival by firing two pistols in the air. They quickly recovered and accommodated Nicolet until his return to Quebec with the news that the route to the Orient had still not been found.[2]

But this was not the end of the quest; it was only the beginning. When the French heard of a great river further west, they jumped to the conclusion that this would lead them to the western sea. A prime objective of the famous expedition of Jolliet and Marquette in 1673 was to explore this river, the Mississippi, in the hope that it would flow westward into the Pacific. Still later, in 1720, the Jesuit, Pierre Francois Xavier de Charlevoix, passed through the Michigan area in yet another futile effort to substantiate new rumors of an existing route to the Orient. It is amazing how long Europeans persisted in pursuing this will-o'-the-wisp. Long after they knew that rapids and falls blocked the inland water routes, necessitating laborious portages, the search went on. Indeed, one wonders how useful such a waterway would have been if it had been found.

Along with this desire to find a way through the continent to the wealth of the East, was the desire to find wealth in the new land itself. By the early decades of the sixteenth century, a thousand vessels or more were visiting the northern coasts of America each year and returning with valuable cargoes of fish. When the fisherman landed in the Gulf of St. Lawrence area to dry their fish in preparation for the return trip, they encountered the native peoples of the area as well as others who had come down the St. Lawrence to fish these same waters in the summer. At a time when furs were in great demand in Europe, the French fishermen discovered that these peoples were using furs for clothing. A haphazard trade began between the Indians and the French, with the former obtaining some of the products of the European civilization in exchange for furs which the Indians could readily replace and which were about the only product of their culture regarded as having much economic value to the French. By the end of the sixteenth century, a growing awareness in France of the existence of this immense, virtually untapped, reservoir of furs initiated efforts to organize the full-scale exploitation of this source of wealth.

The fur trade that developed in the seventeenth and eighteenth century became the mainstay of the economy of New France and the great prize for which Great Britain and France contended in the long series of wars they fought in America during those years. The French kings saw in the fur trade a source of revenues badly needed for ventures both in France and in war against other nations. French businessmen, attracted by the enormous profits that were potentially available to those who could control this trade, sought and were granted a monopoly of the business by the king in return for handsome donations to the royal treasury. Henry IV began this practice at the end of the sixteenth century. Those who were granted the monopoly also had to promise that they would help in the colonization of the king's lands in the New World. When the company's preoccupations with exploiting its trade rights led to its neglect of these assigned responsibilities, the French government did not hesitate to rescind the monopoly and grant it to others, as Cardinal Richelieu did in 1627 when, on behalf of Louis XIII, he awarded the fur trade monopoly to the Company of One Hundred Associates in return for a definite commitment by that group to transport a stated number of settlers to New France over a set period of time. Later, in 1663, Louis XIV became dissatisfied with the slow growth of the colony under private development and converted New France into a royal colony and took personal charge of its development. He and his successor, Louis XV, however, continued to sell the rights to the fur trade to a succession of companies.

To understand the crucial importance of the fur trade in determining the destiny of the interior of North America, including Michigan, it is necessary to realize that the commerce of early modern times, unlike that of the twentieth-century industrial world, dealt largely in luxury items. The trade in foodstuffs, textiles, and other necessities was less important because such a predominant proportion of the European population produced and processed the necessities of life for themselves and their families. The trade in furs, while no small business even today, does not exert as much powerful influence as it did in the seventeenth and eighteenth centuries. Furs at that time were worn by the French aristocrats and the members of the wealthy middle class, which aped the styles and manners of the lords and their ladies. Since France became the fashion center of Europe under Louis XIV, the wearing of furs spread to other European countries. The limited supply of furs that could easily be obtained in Europe soon made the control of the vast fur resources of North America essential in meeting this growing demand for furs.

The pelts that were shipped to Europe from North America included bear, elk, deer, martin, raccoon, mink, muskrat, opossum, lynx, wolf, fox, and an occasional wolverine pelt, although none of the latter, strangely enough, came from the future Wolverine State because the natural habitat of this contentious animal was much farther north in Canada.[3] Far more important than any of these, or all of them together, was the beaver. In fact, the North American fur trade in the seventeenth and eighteenth centuries might more accurately be termed the beaver trade because of the over-riding importance that this one animal pelt achieved as the broad-brimmed beaver hat came into vogue in Europe. It is estimated that there were about ten million beavers in America when the Europeans arrived. The number was depleted rapidly in the years that followed. The beaver's habits made it impossible for him to escape his enemies because he was not a migratory animal and lived in lodges that could be attacked at any time in all seasons. The beaver is not a very prolific creature; if left alone the beaver population increases only about twenty percent annually; thus, as the beavers were exterminated in one region after another, the traders and trappers were forced to advance farther and farther inland to find them. Even before the close of the seventeenth century, Cadillac reported that beaver was very rare in the vicinity of the Straits of Mackinac.

The fur of the beaver consists of two parts: the guard hair, up to two inches in length, and the underhair or fur, at most an inch long. The pelts that commanded the highest prices were those that had been worn or slept in by the Indians and were known as *castor gras* or greasy beaver. The grease and sweat of the Indian's body and the smoke in their lodges made these used pelts supple and loosened the long, coarse guard hairs, which were then easily removed, leaving the soft, high quality underfur. The beaver weighs from thirty to sixty pounds, and the pelt weighs from one and a half to two pounds. The flesh of the beaver was relished by the Indians, but with their primitive weapons they could kill only a limited number of them. However, at the same time that the white man came and created a sudden demand for large numbers of beaver pelts he provided the Indians with iron weapons and guns, and subsequently the beavers were slaughtered so rapidly that they soon virtually disappeared from an area. Thus, the need to find new sources of furs to maintain the continued growth of the fur trade exerted an almost irresistible expansionist demand that the boundaries of the French colony be extended farther inland to encompass fresh stocks of fur-bearing animals.

For many years, those in control of the trade sought to confine the actual trade to selected posts in the St. Lawrence to which the Indians brought their furs and exchanged them for the French trade goods. But as the main sources of furs became farther and farther removed from these posts, practical considerations forced the authorities to license a few traders to go into the interior to trade with these more distant Indians in their villages, even though this made it less certain that the company would end up with all the furs that the traders obtained than when the trade was conducted entirely under the watchful eyes of company officials at the St. Lawrence settlements.

The trade, however, was by no means confined to those who were licensed by the authorities. The famed *coureurs de bois* scorned all regulations and all restraint. Although the term is often mistakenly applied to all the Frenchmen who went into the woods to engage in the fur trade, the *coureurs de bois* were actually the bootleggers in the business, the unlicensed traders who sold the furs they obtained to the highest bidders, who often turned out to be the rival Dutch and English trading companies in New York. In a further attempt to control the trade, the French in the latter part of the seventeenth century began to establish outposts in the interior as advance bases for the fur trade. It was then that the special importance of Michigan in the fur trade became obvious, for in addition to the furs that could be obtained in these lands, the French established three posts in Michigan which gave them command of the main travel routes in the upper Great Lakes regions and a vast area beyond these lakes. These posts became the principal gathering places of traders venturing into or returning from this immensely rich, fur-producing land. The French establishment at the Straits of Mackinac, whether on the north side at the present site of St. Ignace or the later post on the south side at what is now Mackinaw City was the point of rendezvous for traders who had secured furs hundreds of miles to the north and northwest. Fort St. Joseph, near the present city of Niles, was the center of trade for the Illinois country to the southwest, while Detroit was strategically placed to control the trade routes leading into other parts of the lower Middle West. In addition, the French intermittently had a post at Sault Ste. Marie at the entrance into Lake Superior, which ultimately developed, however, into a kind of dependency of the more important post at the Straits of Mackinac.

To these posts came a host of individuals involved in all aspects of the fur trade. The most colorful and certainly the best known were the *voyageurs,* the hardy men who paddled hundreds of miles up swift streams and across lakes, carrying their canoes and cargoes on their backs over portages from one body of water to another. A hundred miles was a day's journey, but when competition was keen their paddles would dip on through the night. Sometimes out on the Great Lakes they did not put ashore for several days and nights, chewing pemmican (dried meat) for food and keeping themselves awake by singing. Because of this singing, the *voyageur* commonly has been depicted as a happy-go-lucky type who loved his work, which is probably no more accurate an image of all of these workers than any other effort to stereotype a large group of people.[4]

The fur trade was not the only source of profit that the French sought to develop in their American colony. Champlain, before coming to New France, had become personally familiar with the vast harvests of gold and silver that the Spanish were reaping in their colonies. This stimulated him and other Frenchmen before and after him to find similar wealth in New France. Of course, they never found it. Father Claude Allouez in the 1660s did find specimens of the copper in Michigan's Upper Peninsula which Cartier had heard of from Indians in the east in the 1530s. The French were briefly intrigued by this discovery but soon abandoned any thought of exploiting this resource. Other efforts of French authorities to encourage the growth of such economic activities as farming aroused only limited interest among potential French colonists. Among the residents of New France itself the lure of the fur trade, with the excitement and possible riches associated with it, held an almost fatal fascination for young men, drawing them into the wilds of the interior and further weakening the growth of a more diversified economy in the St. Lawrence settlements and the newer ones that ultimately grew up in areas such as Michigan.

In addition to the search for economic gain, another impelling force behind French explorations farther into the interior was the vision of imperial glory. Champlain must have hoped to build up a vast empire for his king comparable with that which he had seen belonging to the Spanish monarch. For many years under private developers New France remained a relatively minor colony when compared with those that several other European nations had built up, but once Louis XIV took over direction of the colony in the 1660s the primary motivation behind the explorations and colonial developments in the following years and decades was increasingly less economic than it was related to a desire to enhance the imperial image of France.

Still another force that drove some Frenchmen into the interior was the flaming zeal of the French missionaries, particularly the Jesuits, to save the souls of the Indians. It did not matter to these men how difficult or even hopeless it might seem to convert the Indians to Christianity and to persuade them to accept civilized ways. The missionary's job was to carry out the will of God, to forego all bodily pleasures, and to labor unceasingly to convert the Indians, as much for the sake of his own soul as for that of the Indian. When a man has not the slightest desire to live any longer than God ordains, he is not only unafraid to brave danger but he welcomes it. Thus we find men like Father Menard, Allouez, and Marquette blazing the trails that led to Michigan and other areas of the west. Among these missionaries were rascals and men who were not above seeking a little worldly fame and wealth for themselves, but for the most part the French missionaries were intensely devoted to their religious cause.

The degree to which the French succeeded in achieving their varied goals in the New World was usually determined by their success in dealing with the Indians, who for many decades far out-numbered the French. The enmity of the Iroquois, which Champlain had incurred early in his career in New France, partially accounts for the preference of the French for the northern route by way of the Ottawa River and Lake Nippising in their early explorations of the West. The Iroquois soon became allies of the Dutch, who settled in the Hudson River Valley, and of the English, who took over the Dutch colony in 1664. Furnished by the Dutch with iron axes, awls, traps, and other implements, the Iroquois quickly passed from the Stone Age to the Iron Age. The Dutch also provided them with guns and ammunition. Thus equipped, the Iroquois became a powerful foe of the French and an equally powerful ally of the Dutch and later of the English in their efforts to wrest control of the Great Lakes Indian trade away from the French.

In addition to the problems created by the Iroquois, conditions in the homeland affected the exploration of the West. Champlain's work was made difficult by the misgovernment that followed the assassination of Henry IV in 1610. The great nobles who dominated the scene were interested only in personal profit and opposed expansion and settlement as injurious to the fur trade, which yielded them gains as high as forty percent. Cardinal Richelieu, who came to power in 1624, emphasized colonization and to some degree encouraged expansion. During his regime, however, England and France were at war, and the English captured and held Quebec for three years. Although the French regained their colony in 1632, Richelieu, in the closing years of his career, became deeply engrossed in European power struggles and had little time to devote to the interests of New France. Cardinal Mazarin, who was master of France between 1643 and 1661 when young Louis XIV was growing into manhood, was also forced to devote most of his attention to domestic and European concerns.

At Mazarin's death in 1661, Louis XIV assumed personal rule. He relied heavily, however, on the advice of his brilliant finance minister, Jean-Baptiste Colbert, whose interest in the colony lay primarily in assuring the security of the French settlements along the St. Lawrence. He consistently opposed the establishment of posts in the interior on the ground that this would weaken the settlements along the St. Lawrence. This definitely handicapped western exploration and explains why so much of that exploration was carried on by missionaries and by illicit fur traders, rather than by official expeditions sent out by the governor. Colbert was only willing to sanction exploration that was aimed at finding the elusive waterway through the continent and at finding mineral wealth. As for the fur trade, he wanted the Indians to continue to bring their peltry to Montreal and the other St. Lawrence trading centers. But experience demonstrated that this was impractical, chiefly because the Iroquois and their English allies penetrated the West and threatened to divert the flow of furs to New York. Had it not been for this threat to the backbone of New France's economy, the exploration of the West and the establishment of trading posts and settlements in the interior might have come about more slowly than it actually did.

*   *   *   *   *

Because of the route that they followed to reach the West, the French became acquainted with northern Michigan long before they were aware of the areas to the south. The discoveries of Brulé and Nicolet gave them some knowledge of the St. Mary's River and the Straits of Mackinac. Brulé apparently ventured for some distance into Lake Superior, providing information that Champlain used in maps of the area that he published by the early 1630s. The next known visitors to Michigan, however, were two Jesuit priests, whose appearance in 1641 resulted not from explorations initiated by Champlain but by the work of Catholic missionaries.

This work was begun by Father Joseph Le Caron, a Recollet priest who started a mission among the Huron Indians at the head of Georgian Bay in the summer of 1615. He was one of three members of that order who came to New France at the invitation of Champlain. Le Caron soon felt that the task was beyond the limited resources available to him and his fellow Recollets and, as a result, requested the assistance of the more powerful Jesuit order. The first Jesuits arrived in 1625. The missionary work was interrupted during the period from 1629 to 1632 when the colony was occupied by the English, but when Champlain returned in 1633 he was accompanied by four Jesuits who were returning to the missionary work among the Hurons that they had abandoned four years earlier. They were joined by other priests and by lay brothers who undertook the task not only of converting the Hurons, the most numerous and, from the French standpoint, the most advanced of all the Indians they had thus far encountered, but also of teaching them the ways of European civilization. Blacksmiths, bakers, farmers, and other artisans were brought in and a fortified headquarters was built to serve as a safe retreat for the missionaries and their converts. Located near present-day Midland, Ontario, it was named Sainte Marie, in honor of the mother of Christ. A church and shrine are maintained at the restored site today which thousands visit annually.

From Ste. Marie, the Jesuits by the end of the 1630s were looking for other areas into which they might expand their work. Thus, in 1641, Fathers Isaac Jogues and Charles Raymbault traveled to the banks of the river that links Lake Superior and Lake Huron, a river that they named St. Mary's. Along the rapids ("sault" in French) in this river they met with the Chippewas who gathered there to obtain the whitefish that abounded in these waters. After conducting the first Christian religious services ever held in Michigan, the missionaries returned later that summer to the Huron mission, having christianed the future communities of Sault Ste. Marie in Michigan and Ontario.

Although the Jesuits' work in what they called Huronia was enjoying increasing success by the 1640s, it was doomed to destruction. A long-standing feud existed between the Huron and the five Iroquois tribes in New York. Supplied by the Dutch with guns and gunpowder, the Iroquois suddenly descended on the Huron villages in 1642. The attacks continued year after year with devastating effects for the Hurons, many of whom were killed, along with several of the Jesuit missionaries, including Isaac Jogues. Driven from Ste. Marie in 1648, the Jesuits sought to establish a new base, also called Ste. Marie, on one of the Christian Islands in Georgian Bay. Thousands of Indians followed them, but there was no means of feeding such a multitude. In despair, the Jesuits abandoned the Huron mission in 1650 and returned to the St. Lawrence, while the pitiful remnant of the once powerful Huron tribe, together with the neighboring Ottawas, fled to Wisconsin to escape annihilation by the triumphant Iroquois. Later, in 1653, a great Iroquois war party was almost totally destroyed by the Chippewa when it ventured westward into Lake Superior. Iroquois Point near Sault Ste. Marie is traditionally said to be the site of this great Iroquois defeat.

The destruction of Huronia threatened also to destroy much of the French fur trade, since the French had relied on the Hurons to serve as middlemen who conveyed the furs from the Great Lakes area to the trading posts in the St. Lawrence. For some years, all contact between those posts and the Indians of the West was cut off by the Iroquois, who now controlled all the travel routes and who hoped to take over the important role in the fur trade with the Europeans that had previously been assumed by the Hurons. However, chastened by their defeat in 1653, the Iroquois signed a truce which enabled the French to reopen contact with the western tribes. In 1654 a great fleet of Indian canoes laden with furs ventured down the Ottawa to Montreal and was warmly welcomed by the French.

When these Indians returned to the West, they were accompanied by two young Frenchmen, generally believed to have been Medart Chouart, Sieur de Groseilliers and his brother-in-law, Pierre Esprit, Sieur de Radisson. Groseilliers had spent several years in Huronia as an assistant to the Jesuits, while Radisson, a mere youth, had experienced several harrowing adventures among the Iroquois. Some years later, Radisson wrote an account of his "third voyage" (the first two being those to the Iroquois), which probably refers to the one begun when he and Groseilliers returned with the western Indians in 1654. In 1659, three years after their return from the West, the two adventurers were off to Lake Superior and more distant areas to the northwest. They returned in 1660 with large quantities of furs, but were heavily fined by the governor of New France for having undertaken this expedition without his permission. In disgust, the two men went to England, where Radisson wrote an account of these journeys and convinced the English that great wealth in the fur trade lay in the areas to the north and west of Lake Superior. Ultimately, in 1670, the English king, Charles II, chartered the Hudson's Bay Company, which has endured to the present day and is the greatest fur company of all time.

The extent of the discoveries of Radisson and Groseilliers is difficult to determine because the account that Radisson wrote was written in a language unfamiliar to him. He also seems to have deliberately obscured the narrative, rendering it difficult to follow. It seems certain, however, that the two Frenchmen followed the southern shore of Lake Superior and ventured into the interior of Michigan's Upper Peninsula in the course of their trip. In his description, Radisson clearly identifies the Pictured Rocks near Munising, and notes the presence of copper in the Keweenaw Peninsula.[5]

Their explorations had important consequences for French developments in Michigan. Their discovery of vast new sources of furs eventually caused the French authorities to begin the practice of licensing traders to go into the interior and of establishing new posts in the West as advance bases for this trade, rather than continuing to insist that the Indians bring the furs to the St. Lawrence and risk the danger of having these furs diverted to the rival posts of the Dutch and English in New York or, later, those of the Hudson's Bay Company to the north.

In addition, Groseilliers and Radisson were instrumental in persuading the Jesuits to resume their missionary work in the West. Whey they returned from their first western trip in 1656, they reported finding the remnants of the Hurons living in Wisconsin. When the Indians who accompanied the two Frenchmen in 1656 left to return to their villages, two Jesuits went with them, hoping to resume their work with the Hurons. This party, however, was attacked by the Iroquois, once again on the warpath, and one Jesuit was killed while the other managed to escape to Quebec. In 1660, Radisson reported upon his return from the Lake Superior area that some of the Hurons were now living at the western end of that lake. This fired the zeal of Father René Menard, who had ministered to these people in the halcyon days of Huronia. He went west with an Indian party, accompanied, it would appear, by a number of fur traders, determined to restore the Huron mission. Near the present site of L'Anse, along Michigan's Lake Superior shore, Menard wintered among the Indians with whom he had traveled west, although he strained his welcome when he rebuked the tribal chief for what the Jesuit regarded as depraved conduct. Finally, in the spring of 1661 Menard found his way to Chequamegon Bay, at the head of which today stands the city of Ashland, Wisconsin. The Indians he found there were friendly. They may or they may not have been Hurons, but in any event Menard almost at once went inland in search of other Hurons who were said to be there. He was never seen again.

Events transpiring in France and in the St. Lawrence valley now further escalated the exploration of Michigan and the West. In 1661, the year that the young and ambitious monarch, Louis XIV, became ruler of France in fact as well as in name, the French court read in the *Jesuit Relations* words addressed to the king: "When you consider, Sire, what the French name signifies, you will know that a great king who makes Europe tremble ought not to be held in contempt in America." The young king was being challenged to alleviate the desperate situation in New France. The Iroquois were threatening the very bastions of French authority: Montreal and Quebec. Other warnings reached the king, and in 1663 he took drastic action. Up to this time New France had been little more than a preserve of the Company of New France, which was interested only in the profit it might gain from the fur trade. Now the king deprived the company of its rights and made New France a royal colony, under a governor appointed by the king and a sovereign council. Two years later an official called an intendent was added, ranking with the governor and the bishop in importance and reporting to the king of the activities of the former. A new company was created to receive the monopoly of the fur trade.

For several years, Louis XIV and his minister, Jean-Baptiste Colbert, devoted much time, precious manpower, and other resources in attempting to build New France into a more respectable representative of French power in America. In addition to sending out shiploads of settlers, a French military force was dispatched to the St. Lawrence in 1664 under the command of the Marquis de Tracy. Within three years, the Iroquois were humbled and defeated, and in 1667 they agreed to peace terms and gave hostages to the French as a guarantee that the New York tribes would keep the peace.

The stage was thus set for a much more vigorous and sustained French advance westward. After 1664, the Iroquois were forced to meet the threat and onslaught of large French forces and no longer blocked the way west by the old Ottawa River route. This enabled the Jesuits to seek out the surviving Hurons and undertake the task of spreading Christianity to other tribes in the interior. Their wanderings revealed much of the nature of present-day Michigan. The French now were able to search further for the water route by which they hoped to reach the Indies and also to pursue that equally illusory hope of discovering a source of precious metals. But so far as the fur traders were concerned, Colbert was determined that the Indians should bring the furs to the St. Lawrence, and was firmly opposed to the establishment of settlements in the interior. The traders, however, tended to be a lawless lot, seldom obeying rules laid down in distant France, and officials in New France frequently connived with them to permit trading in the West in return for a share of the rich profits. Thus the fur traders, too, in this period of increased activity in the West would bring back information about Michigan's land, waters, resources, and peoples.

On the morning of August 8, 1665, Indians who had come down the Ottawa to Three Rivers in the St. Lawrence valley began their return trip west. They were followed by six Frenchmen manning a canoe bearing a Jesuit priest, Father Claude Allouez. He had set out to retrace the route of Father Menard and to resume the work among the Indians of the West. Allouez was, at the time, forty-three years old. He had been a Jesuit since he was seventeen. His absolute devotion to the cause of Christ, his willingness and ability to suffer sustained privation and hardship, and his undaunted spirit made him an ideal missionary. Until his death a quarter of a century later, he was the most active of all the missionaries who now appeared in the upper Great Lakes region. Allouez reportedly instructed more than one hundred thousand Indians in the Christian teachings during these years and baptized more than ten thousand. A cross marks the supposed location of his burial site at what is now Niles, Michigan, where he was active in the mission that had been established on the St. Joseph River in the late 1680s.

In 1665, Allouez reached the site of L'Anse, where he found two Indian women who remembered the instruction given them five years before by Menard. Late that autumn Allouez arrived at Chequamegon Bay and established a mission at a place he called "La Pointe du Saint Esprit," or Holy Spirit Point. He erected a small bark chapel and adorned its sides with pictures of the infernal regions and the judgment day. Large numbers of Ottawas and a few Hurons listened to his teachings. He returned to Quebec in 1667, seeking help to carry on his work, and also informing the French that he had found copper in his travels along Michigan's Lake Superior shore.

Allouez returned to the Holy Spirit Mission in 1668 with another priest to assist him. The two men were followed west by two other Frenchmen, Brother Louys Le Boême and Father Jacques Marquette who, by the end of the year, had established the first mission in Michigan. Marquette, the most famous of these Jesuit missionaries, had arrived in New France two years before to begin the missionary work for which he had trained and dreamed of for so long, although he was then only twenty-nine years old. After carefully studying the languages and dialects of the Indians with which he would be working, Marquette was assigned to the West where he established a mission among the Chippewa at Sault Ste. Marie, and where Fathers Jogues and Raymbault had appeared briefly twenty-seven years before. Brother Le Boême, a skilled carpenter, erected a small enclosure of cedar posts twelve feet high, within which was built a chapel and a house. Outside the enclosure some land was cleared and grain was sown. The mission was maintained by the Jesuits until just prior to 1700. After the mission was abandoned there were for some years no permanent, year-round residents at Sault Ste. Marie, but the spot was too strategic to be long abandoned, and in the middle of the eighteenth century it was again the site of an established French outpost. These developments are the basis for the claim that Sault Ste. Marie is the oldest settlement of European origins in Michigan and, indeed, in the entire Middle West.[6]

By 1668 what is now Michigan's Upper Peninsula had become

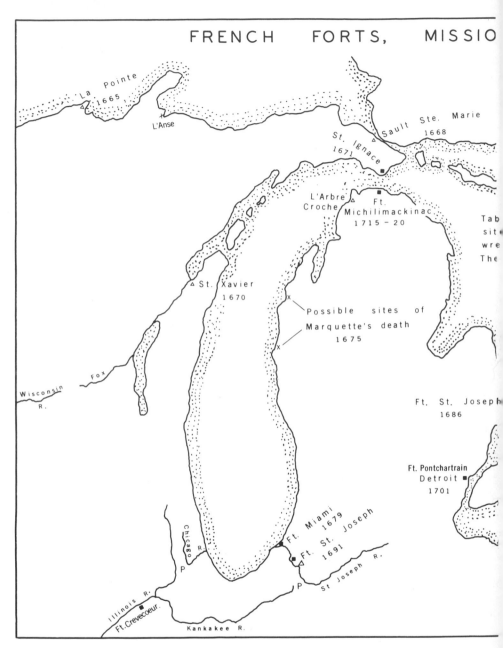

La Pointe
1665

L'Anse

Sault Ste. Marie
1668

St. Ignace
1671

L'Arbre Croche
Ft. Michilimackinac
1715 – 20

Tab
sit
wre
The

St. Xavier
1670

x

Possible sites of
Marquette's death
1675

x

Fox

Wisconsin R.

Ft. St. Joseph
1686

Ft. Pontchartrain
Detroit
1701

Chicago R.

P

Ft. Miami
1679

Ft. St. Joseph
1691

P   St Joseph R.

Illinois R.
Ft.Crevecoeur.

Kankakee R.

well known to the French, but as yet they knew little of the great peninsula to the south. Jean Nicolet must have caught a glimpse of the lower peninsula as he passed through the Straits of Mackinac on his trip to Green Bay in 1634. It had been a popular Indian hunting ground and the site of a few villages, but earlier in the seventeenth

L. NIPISSING

Many Portages

Montreal

Ottawa R

GEORGIAN BAY

amore x
of
ck of
Griffin?

HURONIA

△ Ste. Marie

- - - Route Followed By French Explorers

■ Forts

△ Missions

P Portages

Stan Smeed

century it appears to have been deserted by these Indians, who fled westward during the Iroquois wars. In 1669, as far as can be definitely determined, its eastern shoreline was followed for the first time by a European. In the spring of that year, an experienced trader and explorer, Adrien Jolliet, was sent on a mission by Jean Talon, the

37

intendent of New France, and the ablest of the officials appointed in the early years of the colony under royal control. Talon, who was interested in creating a more diverse economy in the colony, was intrigued by the reports that Allouez had brought back of copper in the Lake Superior region. In 1668, therefore, he had sent out an expedition under Jean Péré to see what could be done to exploit this resource. A supporting expedition under Jolliet followed in the spring of 1669. It is doubtful whether Jolliet went beyond the Sault. He may have received word that the Péré expedition had decided that the mining of copper at this point was not a practical idea. At any rate, Jolliet decided to return to Montreal that same year. He appears to have rescued an Iroquois prisoner from his Indian captors, and this Indian, in gratitude, offered to guide Jolliet home by an easier route than that which the French had followed for many years. Accordingly, Jolliet and the Iroquois paddled southward along the Lake Huron shore of the lower peninsula, through the St. Clair River, Lake St. Clair, and the Detroit River to the northern shore of Lake Erie. Here they abandoned their canoe and proceeded overland across southern Ontario. Near the present city of Hamilton they encountered a party of French and Indians on their way west.

The principal members of this party were Father François Dollier de Casson, Father René Bréhant de Galinée, and Robert Cavelier de la Salle. La Salle, who later enters the stage of Michigan history, was on his way to search for a river to the south that might be the long-sought waterway to the Indies. The two priests were members of the Sulpician order, bound westward to start a mission among a band of Indians that had not yet heard the gospel. Jolliet told them of a large tribe called the Potawatomi living to the south of the Sault among whom no missionary had yet gone. Dollier and his companion immediately became determined to seek out this tribe. La Salle, wishing to press the search for the river of which he had heard, parted company with the priests and proceeded southward; Dollier and Galinée, together with about seven other men, continued along the shore of Lake Erie until winter caught up with them. They spent about five months near Port Dover in a snug retreat, which they built somewhat inland from the lake. Late in March they resumed their journey. But the journal of Galinée relates that a storm arose during the night while the party was sleeping on shore, and swept away most of their packs, including those that contained the altar service. Without the sacraments the priests could not start their missionary work among the Potawatomi. Rather than return to Montreal for another service, they determined to proceed to Sault Ste. Marie and return with the Ottawa when the latter journeyed eastward with their furs.

Fur trader's building on Mackinac Island

As the priests and their companions were paddling up the Detroit River, they beheld on shore a stone idol that the Indians worshipped in order to assure themselves a safe journey across Lake Erie. Since that lake had been anything but kind to the Sulpicians, and because the idol was an object of heathen worship, Galinée demolished it with a consecrated axe, and the party carried the pieces of stone out into the middle of the river in their canoes to sink them. So far as is known, this was the occasion of the first visit of white men to the land of the Detroit area. The party then proceeded swiftly up the channel into Lake Huron and from there to the Jesuit mission at Sault Ste. Marie. Thus in 1669 and 1670 the eastern shore of Michigan's lower peninsula was traced by the journeys of Adrien Jolliet and Dollier and Galinée.[7]

During 1670 and 1671 there was intense activity in the upper lakes area. Early in 1670, Father Allouez journeyed to Green Bay, where he established the St. Francis Xavier mission. He was replaced at the mission on Chequamegon Bay by Father Marquette, who, in turn, was replaced at Sault Ste. Marie by Father Claude Dablon, a veteran of nearly fifteen years' work in New France. In addition to his work at Sault Ste. Marie, Dablon was placed in charge of all the burgeoning missionary work in the upper Great Lakes region, a job that he held for a number of years. In the summer of 1670, the Indians at the Holy Spirit Mission in the west killed a visiting Sioux chief and four of his companions. Fearing retaliation by the Sioux, the Hurons and Ottawas living around the mission fled eastward, the Ottawas taking refuge on Manitoulin Island, at the head of Lake Huron, and the Hurons settling in the Straits of Mackinac area, where many Ottawas later joined them. Father Marquette followed his charges east to Sault Ste. Marie, where in the spring of 1671 he met with Dablon, who instructed Marquette to establish a new mission at the straits. The previous winter, Dablon had conducted a mission on Mackinac Island among the Indians who had already begun to arrive in the area. His experience convinced him that the island was not a suitable site for a mission, and thus, in the summer of 1671, he instructed Marquette to locate the new mission on the north side of the Straits of Mackinac. Marquette named the mission St. Ignace, after the founder of the Jesuit order.[8]

That same summer also witnessed the enactment of "the Pageant of the Sault," an impressive ceremony designed to establish French title to the North American interior. This was another of the projects of the Intendant Talon, who recently had returned from a visit to the French court. It is possible that Talon had heard of the formation of the Hudson's Bay Company in England and chose this way of asserting France's title to an area whose vast fur resources the English might attempt to tap from Hudson Bay. In the fall of 1670, therefore, Talon sent out an expedition commanded by Simon Francois, Sieur de St. Lusson, to impress Indian tribesmen with the might and majesty of France. St. Lusson's expedition wintered on Manitoulin Island, and in the spring he sent runners to summon the Indian tribes of the entire upper lakes area to Sault Ste. Marie. Here, on June 14, 1671, surrounded by perhaps twenty of his fellow countrymen and a vast assemblage of Indians, he fulfilled his mission. First the *Te Deum* was chanted and a huge cross with the escutcheon of France above it was raised. Hymns and prayers for the king followed, with Father Allouez addressing the Indians in a manner that would impress them with the power of the French monarch, warning them, none too subtly, of the fate that would befall them if they incurred that monarch's wrath by trading with other than French nationals. St. Lusson then made a solemn declaration that all the lands "bounded on the one side by the Northern and Western Seas and on the other side by the South Sea including all its length and breadth" belonged to the king of France, that all its people were the king's subjects, and that no other nation might intrude therein. Raising a piece of sod three times, he cried: *"Vive le roi."* A great bonfire concluded the ceremony.[9]

The year after this ceremony, Talon determined to send out an expedition to discover the river west of the Great Lakes, which the French had heard of from the Indians and which they referred to as the Messipi. One purpose of the mission would be to determine whether the river flowed westward into the Pacific and would thus be the long-sought waterway through the continent. As leader of the expedition, he selected Louis Jolliet, a fur trader skilled in navigation and map-making, and younger brother of Adrien Jolliet, to whom Talon might have assigned this task had he not died in the latter stages of his return trip from the Sault in 1669. Before departing for the West, Louis Jolliet talked with Father Dablon, who suggested that Father Marquette be included on the expedition. Marquette may, in fact, have earlier discussed with Jolliet his interest in exploring the western river to learn more about the people living there for future missionary efforts.

On May 17, 1673, Jolliet and Marquette, together with five other Frenchmen, departed from St. Ignace. Following the Lake Michigan shore of the Upper Peninsula into Green Bay, they ascended the Fox River, portaged to the Wisconsin, and on June 17, a month after the start of the trip, they entered the Mississippi, "with a joy which I am unable to make known," Marquette later declared. They were then borne southward by the great river, but by the time they reached the mouth of the Arkansas River it was clear to them that this waterway led into the Gulf of Mexico, not the Pacific, as the French had hoped. Furthermore, they were entering an area where it was clear that the Indians were influenced by the Spanish. Jolliet and Marquette had thus discovered the extent to which the French might hope to extend their authority in this central continental region before encountering difficulties with prior claims asserted by the Spanish from the south or the English from the east. Jolliet and Marquette decided, then, to turn around and retrace their course northward. When they reached the mouth of the Illinois River, however, they diverged from their outgoing route and proceeded on up through Illinois and by way of the Des Plaines and Chicago rivers reached the western shores of Lake Michigan. They then proceeded north along that shore to Green Bay where Marquette spent the winter while Jolliet proceeded back to the east.

Marquette remained at Green Bay until the fall of 1674. He sought and received permission to return to the Illinois country to resume contacts that he had made with the peoples there the previous year. In Illinois, however, the illness that had seriously weakened Marquette the previous summer became worse, until Marquette, who was only thirty-seven years old, realized he did not have long to live. Hoping to see his beloved mission of St. Ignace before dying, Marquette set out from Illinois in the spring of 1675 with two *voyageurs* as canoemen. They traveled up along the western shore of Michigan's lower peninsula until they reached the mouth of a river flowing into Lake Michigan. Marquette became so ill at this point that they had to stop and put ashore. Within a few hours, on May 18, 1675, Marquette was dead. The contemporary records of this event are not sufficiently detailed and the site of this most famous Jesuit missionary's death cannot be absolutely determined. Most authorities, however, assume that he died at the present site of Ludington at the mouth of the river that has long been called the Pere Marquette.[10]

In a boating accident on his way back to Quebec, Jolliet had the misfortune of losing the journal he had kept and the maps he had drawn on the journey. Copies that he had left at Sault Ste. Marie were destroyed in a fire. From memory he drew new maps of the country he had explored. Marquette may also have drawn a map that, along with Jolliet's, ultimately reached France. By 1681, a map published in Paris, obviously based on this new information, shows the Mississippi River and the western shore of Lake Michigan. Earlier maps had called the lake *Lac des Illinois*; however, this was the first to call it *Lac de Michigami*, thus introducing an early variation of the future state's name. By the end of the 1680s, the shores of Lake Michigan, which as late as the previous decade had been incompletely shown on published maps, were shown in their entirety on both French and British maps. These improvements were based not only on the findings of Jolliet and Marquette but on those of another explorer, Robert Cavelier de la Salle.

La Salle was a protege of Louis de Buade, Comte de Frontenac, who served as governor of New France from 1672 to 1682 and again from 1689 to his death in 1698. Francis Parkman, the distinguished American historian of New France, regarded Frontenac as the greatest of the French governors. This opinion has been greatly modified by modern writers, particularly Canadians, on the basis of more recent research,[11] but whatever the final verdict may be, there is no question that Frontenac did much to encourage French exploration and French fur trade in the West. He did so in the face of great difficulties. After 1672, Louis XIV was spending large sums of money on wars and subsidies to his allies. Little could be spared for New France. Expansion westward was therefore discouraged in order to keep down the costs involved in maintaining the colony. Frontenac did his best to evade these instructions. He realized that unless the French were active in the West the Great Lakes tribes would likely shift their trading activities to the British in New York, in part because the British traders often offered more for the Indians' furs than the French did, and also because the Indians had fears of attacks from the Iroquois allies of the British if they did not shift their loyalties from the French. But in addition to Frontenac's desire as governor to maintain the stability of the colony's major economic activity there is no doubt that his actions were also the result of his desire to recoup his depressed finances by sharing in the profits of the fur traders.

Although Louis Jolliet was refused permission by the king to establish a fort in the Illinois region, La Salle was more fortunate in winning approval for his expansionist schemes. With Frontenac's support, La Salle went to France in the fall of 1674 and obtained approval from the king for a settlement and fort named Fort Frontenac, which he had already built on Lake Ontario. La Salle received a large grant of land and special fur trading rights so that he might finance this development. Had he been content with this award, La Salle's fortune would have been assured, but he had greater plans, based on his earlier pioneering explorations down the Ohio River which he may have followed as far as its juncture with the Mississippi, and which had led him to see some of the potential that lay in the development of this area of the lower Middle West. In 1677 he returned to France and received permission to establish a colony in Illinois. He was to accomplish this at his own expense, and to enable him to do this he was awarded a grant of land and given a monopoly of the trade in buffalo hides. He was forbidden, however, to trade in furs with any of the Great Lakes tribes that brought their furs to Montreal. The bait La Salle used to obtain the king's approval was his promise to explore the lower Mississippi, to seek the waterway to the Pacific, and to locate valuable minerals.

La Salle quickly violated this agreement by sending an advance party of fifteen men to trade with the Illinois Indians in order to accumulate a cargo of furs. In 1679 he built a shipyard above Niagara Falls, and there workmen constructed the first sailing vesssl to sail the upper Great Lakes. La Salle named this vessel the *Griffin,* after the legendary beast that appeared on Frontenac's coat-of-arms. On August 7, 1679, La Salle and his men set sail from Niagara. This maiden voyage of the *Griffin* is described in the account of a French priest, Father Louis Hennepin, who accompanied La Salle and subsequently wrote a popular book on his experiences in the service of

La Salle in the West. Hennepin provided his European audience with the most detailed description to that time of the lands along lower Michigan's eastern shore, including a famous passage in which he predicted a great future for any settlement that might be built on the banks of the Detroit River because of the volume of traffic it would eventually carry between the upper and lower lakes.

When La Salle arrived at St. Ignace he discovered that his advance party had stopped there and that some had deserted. However, a considerable quantity of furs had been collected at an Indian village in Green Bay, which were loaded onto the *Griffin.* The ship set sail on September 18, 1679, on the return voyage to Niagara, with instructions from La Salle to return with all speed to a rendezvous at the mouth of the St. Joseph River, or the River of the Miami, as that river in southwestern Michigan was then called.

With a party of fourteen men and four canoes, La Salle proceeded south down the Wisconsin shore to the southern end of Lake Michigan and arrived at St. Joseph on November 1. Here, on a bluff overlooking the lake in what is now the city of St. Joseph, La Salle built a stockaded fort. The first non-Indian outpost in the lower peninsula, the fort was called Fort Miami, after the Indian tribe which by that time had moved into the area. On November 20 a party of twenty men arrived from St. Ignace, led by Henri de Tonty, an Italian who had been reared in France. He was known as "The Man with the Iron Hand" because his right hand had been mangled in a naval engagement and he had amputated it and replaced it with one made of iron. He had become La Salle's most faithful and trusted aide. He now brought word that the *Griffin* had not returned to St. Ignace, but it was hoped that the ship would still show up, despite the lateness of the year. However, no one would ever see the *Griffin* again. The vessel was lost in a storm, somewhere in the northern lakes, and strangely enough the French would make little use of sailing vessels on the upper lakes during the remaining eighty years of their control of that area.[12]

On December 3, La Salle left Fort Miami with thirty-two men and went up the St. Joseph to the present site of South Bend, where they followed the portage route five miles to the Kankakee, whose waters flowed into the Illinois. At an Indian village along the Illinois, La Salle built Fort Crevecoeur[13] and also set his men to work on the construction of a ship which would presumably be used to explore the Mississippi. Upon returning to Fort Miami, La Salle found that there was still no sign of the *Griffin* with its much needed supplies. Realizing that he must now return to the east for supplies, La Salle sought the quickest way of making the journey. He determined that it would save time to cross the peninsula on foot. Therefore, on March 25, 1680, La Salle and three or four of his men set out from Fort Miami. So far as is known, they were the first white men to see any considerable portion of the interior of southern Michigan. They crossed the prairies of southwestern Michigan, setting the grass on fire at one point to hinder hostile Indians who were following them. They continued on through present Kalamazoo, Calhoun, Jackson, and Washtenaw counties until they reached the Huron River, probably in the area where the village of Dexter now stands. Here they built a canoe, but when the border of present Wayne County was reached they found the river blocked by trees. The canoe was abandoned and they continued on by foot to the Detroit River, and from there finally back to Fort Frontenac, which La Salle reached on May 6.[14]

La Salle was confronted with many difficulties in carrying out his plans, of which the loss of the *Griffin* was but one. When he returned to Fort Crevecoeur in 1681, he found the fort, which he had left in charge of Tonty, deserted and in ruins, the victim of an Iroquois raid. Tonty had survived, however, and he worked with La Salle in the building of a new fort—Fort St. Louis. In addition, La Salle descended the Mississippi to its mouth on April 9, 1682, and now devoted most of his attention to his new schemes for the development of Louisiana, as La Salle dubbed the new French possessions in the lower Mississippi valley. Eventually, his single-minded pursuit of his plans led to his assassination by his own men in 1687. His earlier work, however, had helped to round out the French knowledge of the Michigan area that had been acquired in the course of the explorations of the seventeenth century. What the French did with the information they had gained would comprise much of the history of the following decades.

Voyageurs

4

MICHIGAN UNDER FRENCH DEVELOPMENT

The events that transpired in Michigan in the latter years of the seventeenth century reflected a vacillating French policy with respect to the West. It hinged on whether to build forts and to encourage trading in the West or to concentrate as far as possible on the peltry trade in the St. Lawrence settlements and make those settlements stronger. Colbert earlier had consistently favored the latter policy and had sent the governor repeated orders to implement it. Frontenac managed to evade Colbert's directives by issuing special licenses to trade in the West and by supporting La Salle's schemes. On occasion the French court had departed from Colbert's policy, but basically it remained in effect. In 1682 Frontenac was recalled to France and relieved as governor, in part because of his quarrelsome nature but also because of his persistent efforts to disperse the strength of New France in defiance of orders.

Frontenac's successor as governor, Lefebvre de la Barre, quickly came under the influence of Frontenac's enemies and instituted new policies. He seized Fort Frontenac from La Salle's agents, and when the great explorer returned from his journey to the mouth of the Mississippi to obtain supplies for his Illinois settlement, La Barre blocked his path, forcing La Salle to go to France for help. In France La Salle met with unexpected success. Colbert died in 1683, and his son, Seignelay, backed La Salle's plan to establish a colony at the mouth of the Mississippi. In addition, La Barre was ordered to restore Fort Frontenac and Fort St. Louis, which he had also seized, to

47

La Salle. The policy of concentration, which appeared to have won out with Frontenac's recall, thus was modified within a year.

Still another modification of this policy is more closely related to Michigan history. Daniel Greysolon, Sieur de Duluth, who had traded for furs extensively in the region around Lake Superior and the Upper Mississippi Valley, went to France in 1683 and returned with a license that empowered him to trade with the Sioux. He came back to Lake Superior, building forts on the northwest shores of this lake and taking possession of the portage between the St. Croix and Brulé rivers across which the furs were carried on their long journey from the Northwest.[1]

But developments elsewhere would force Duluth and other fur traders, as well as *voyageurs* and missionaries, to concentrate in the St. Lawrence settlements. The Iroquois were on the warpath again. As early as 1680 they had devastated Fort Crevecoeur in the Illinois country. In 1684, aided and supported by British fur traders and goaded into action by the aggressive governor of New York, Thomas Dongan, they boldly attacked the French. Striking far to the north and west against the Indians allied with the French, they forced the Frenchmen to flee for refuge. Concentration ceased to be a question of policy; it became a matter of necessity. The Iroquois carried the war to the very gates of Montreal.

Alarmed by these developments, the French court replaced La Barre as governor in 1686, sending out as his successor the Marquis de Denonville, a much abler and more energetic man. Denonville struck boldly into the Iroquois country, destroying a number of their villages. And he took steps to save the West from the domination of the Iroquois and their English allies. Word had reached Montreal that in 1685 English fur traders from Albany had reached the Straits of Mackinac with fifteen canoes laden with goods for trade with the natives. Denonville countered by making three moves. Nicholas Perrot, known as a skilled forest diplomat, was sent to build two forts along the route from Green Bay to the Mississippi to impress the Indians of that area with French power and to hearten them to resist the Iroquois. To maintain the ties with the French of the Miami and Potawatomi Indians who had now drifted eastward into the St. Joseph River valley, Denonville sought the aid of the Jesuits. On October 1, 1686, he granted to the Jesuit order an area of land a little less than a mile square along the St. Joseph River at any point they might select. It is probable that Father Claude Allouez was carrying on missionary work in the area as early as 1683 and that Iroquois depredations had forced his withdrawal to St. Ignace. Denonville apparently hoped by his grant to encourage the Jesuits to resume their missionary activity in this strategic area. The St. Joseph mission was established near the site of the present city of Niles. The exact date of its founding has been the subject of much speculation; it certainly existed as early as 1690.[2]

Denonville's third project also involved activity in what is now Michigan. Duluth, the experienced northwest fur trader, was commissioned to build a fort between Lakes Erie and Huron to block the passage of such English fur traders as had reached Michilimackinac the preceding year. Duluth chose the site of the modern city of Port Huron for the fort, which was constructed in 1686 and named Fort St. Joseph. The following year Denonville sent orders west to assemble a force of French and Indians at the new fort to move from there to Lake Ontario and to join his expedition against the Iroquois. In obedience to his command some two hundred Frenchmen involved in the western fur trade and about five hundred Indians assembled at Fort St. Joseph in 1687. Henri de Tonty, La Salle's former lieutenant, brought in a party, and Nicholas Perrot came from Wisconsin with another force. Olivier Morel de La Durantaye brought in from St. Ignace, not only a contingent of fighting men, but also an English trader and his party that had been captured. La Durantaye had been sent to St. Ignace in 1683 with thirty soldiers, who constituted the first French garrison at the great trading rendezvous and mission station. There was much rejoicing and wild demonstrations before Duluth and the other leaders could get the unruly force started for the meeting with Denonville's troops. On the way another English trading party was captured. Although Denonville's expedition did not bring the Iroquois to bay, it gave the French a psychological lift. Duluth returned to his fur trading in the Northwest, and Louis Armand de Lom d'Arce, Baron de Lahontan, was appointed as commandant at Fort St. Joseph.

The first French fort in the lower peninsula—Fort Miami at the mouth of the St. Joseph River—had been abandoned following the departure of La Salle. Fort St. Joseph at Port Huron likewise had a short history. Lahontan, its commandant, was a young noblemen with well-developed and sophisticated interests who soon wearied of this lonely outpost and decided in the summer of 1688 to abandon it, which he did, making his way up to St. Ignace.

The war with the Iroquois was by no means over. The St. Lawrence settlements were repeatedly raided, with the Iroquois terrorizing the area right to the gates of Montreal. Then in 1689 the conflict was intensified as France and England began the first of a series of wars with one another that was to last, off and on, for a century and a quarter. When the Stuart king, James II, was driven off his English throne in 1688, his place was taken by William III, who, as stadholder of Holland, had been an implacable foe of Louis XIV. The war that resulted in Europe was known as the War of the League of Augsburg, after one of the allied groups that opposed Louis XIV, but in American history the war is known as King William's War.

In this emergency, Louis XIV recalled Frontenac from retirement and sent the former governor back to resume his old post and to save New France. Frontenac had lost none of his quarrelsome propensities, but even his severest critics grant that he must be given credit for rescuing New France at this very perilous juncture. In his fight to save the West, the aging count depended heavily on those Frenchmen already in the area and experienced in dealings with the Indians: Nicholas Perrot in Wisconsin, Henri de Tonty in Illinois, and Pierre le Sueur, who had built forts at Chequamegon Bay and on the Mississippi near the mouth of the St. Croix River. What chiefly worried Frontenac was the strong possibility that the western Indians, lured by the prospect of cheap English goods and despairing that their French friends would protect them from the Iroquois, would make peace with the New York tribes. Frontenac's strategy, therefore, was to demonstrate French strength, promote the fur trade, and cultivate all the ties of friendship that had existed through the years.

The center of French influence in the Great Lakes area was St. Ignace. Near the Jesuit mission established there in 1671 the Hurons and Ottawas had their villages. The settlement had become a logical center of the fur trade, and the Jesuits complained that the brandy that the traders used in their barter debauched the Indians. Only the Jesuits referred to the place as St. Ignace. Fur traders and official documents invariably called it Michilimackinac. La Durantaye, military commandant since 1683, was recalled in 1690 by Frontenac, possibly because he was regarded as too friendly with the Jesuits. To replace him, Frontenac sent out Louis de la Porte, Sieur de Louvigny, with 150 soldiers to impress the Indians at this all-important post. A fort was constructed and given Frontenac's family name, De Buade, though this name was rarely used, the fort usually being called the fort at Michilimackinac.[3]

In southwestern Michigan, Frontenac took steps to demonstrate French power in this region, going beyond Denonville's earlier action in establishing a mission. Probably because of his experience among the Potawatomi in Wisconsin, Nicholas Perrot was sent by Frontenac in May, 1690, to carry messages to the Potawatomi and the Miami who were now living in the St. Joseph River valley. In 1691, Augustin le Gardeur, Sieur de Courtemanche, was sent to build a fort on the St. Joseph. The site selected was near the mission, just south of the present city of Niles, and upstream some twenty-five miles from the site of Fort Miami, which had been destroyed after it was no longer needed by La Salle. The new fort was named Fort St. Joseph, but it is not to be confused with the temporary fort the French had built five years earlier on the other side of the lower peninsula. In the spring of 1694, the new Fort St. Joseph withstood an attack by three to four hundred Iroquois, an action that helped to blunt the enthusiasm of the Iroquois for further invasions of the Middle West. At the same time, this victory provided a boost to the morale of the Michigan Indians and strengthened their feelings of loyalty to the French, who had fought with them to help repel this Iroquois attack. Thus the energetic measures of Frontenac to save the West for France began to bear fruit.

In 1693 and again in 1695 huge flotillas of canoes heavily laden with furs arrived at Montreal. In 1694, Frontenac sent one of his proteges, Antoine de la Mothe Cadillac, to take command at Michilimackinac. This young man, a native of Gascony, had been born of middle-class parents (his claims to nobility were one of his later fabrications) in 1658 and came to Acadia (now Nova Scotia) when he was twenty-five. For a time he was a privateer. After a sojourn in France he returned to America in 1690. He met Frontenac, who made him a lieutenant in the colonial troops. He was later promoted to captain. Cadillac served as commander at Michilimackinac for three years. Near the fort were sixty houses occupied by Frenchmen, with the villages of the Hurons and Ottawas and the Jesuit mission rounding out the settlement. Father Henry Nouvel, in charge of the mission, was also the Jesuit Superior of all the western missions, while Cadillac also had general supervision of the scattered forts in Michigan, Illinois, and Wisconsin. In addition to serving as the military and missionary headquarters in the West, Michilimackinac was the most important center in the area for the fur trade, with thousands of Indians and hundreds of fur traders and their employees flocking to the settlement in the summer months. During the short time he was there, Cadillac, following the practice of most French officials from the governor on down, made a small fortune from the fur trade.

Cadillac soon became bitterly antagonistic toward the Jesuits, and they toward him. It arose in part because of the effects of the brandy furnished by Cadillac to the Indians whom the Jesuits were trying to convert to Christianity. To celebrate an Ottawa and Potawatomi foray against Iroquois hunters, which netted thirty scalps and as many prisoners, Cadillac gave the victorious Indians enough brandy for an all-night orgy. Father Pinet, who denounced Cadillac as the cause of the disorders, was threatened by the commandant. Another Jesuit, Father Carheil, was described by Cadillac as the most violent and seditious person he had ever known. Frontenac staunchly backed Cadillac, but the story was different at the French court where the Jesuits received a sympathetic hearing.

Meanwhile, Frontenac, determined to bring the Iroquois to terms once and for all, led an army into their country. The principal village of the Onondaga, one of the Iroquois tribes, was destroyed, and a fort, together with several villages of the Oneida, another Iroquois tribe, was burned. Returning to Quebec in September, 1696, the seventy-six-year-old governor, weary from his exertions but no doubt convinced that he had at last overcome the immense difficulties that had faced him when he had arrived there six years before, found a decree waiting for him from the French king. The decree was dated May 21, 1696, and it directed Frontenac to abandon and destroy the forts that had been built in the West, save for one in Illinois. He was to issue no more licenses to traders that would authorize them to trade in the West. Instead he was to recall all soldiers, settlers, and traders from the West. Only the Jesuits were allowed to continue their work in the area. He was also ordered to make peace with the Iroquois, even if it did not include the western Indians whose allegiance Frontenac had fought so hard to retain.

This decree meant a return to the policy of concentration that Colbert had upheld for so long and that Frontenac had never been willing to accept. Several reasons have been advanced for the court's action. The Jesuits had great influence at court, which had been struck by a wave of austerity when Louis married his mistress, Madame de Maintenon, who had many friends among the clergy. They pleaded for a chance to carry on the work among the Indians, unhindered by the demoralizing influence on the natives of the fur traders and soldiers. There were other influences, however, that were more important in inducing the court to issue the decree. Due to an oversupply of beaver skins, the European market had collapsed almost completely. The decree had been sought by French fur merchants as a means of cutting off the supply of furs at its source, thereby permitting the forces of supply and demand to allow the price of furs in Europe to rebound from the disastrously low levels to which they had been driven by the glut of pelts coming out of New France.

To Frontenac the decree of May, 1696 must have seemed a repudiation of everything for which he had fought. But he had never taken seriously orders from the distant French capital with which he did not concur, and this decree was no exception. He made no peace with the Iroquois. He still gave licenses to trade in the West, and the *fleur de lis* still waved over the western forts. The crusty old governor even prepared two new military expeditions to be sent to the West. He was gratified when Cadillac arrived in Montreal accompanied by three hundred Ottawa, Huron, and Potawatomi warriors who, under the leadership of a Huron known as "The Rat," had defeated an Iroquois war party and were now prepared to lay before the governor their demands for arms and ammunition. Frontenac promised that such goods would soon be forthcoming. Whether he could have fulfilled his pledge cannot be known, for on November 28, 1698 the old governor died.

Although French troops were withdrawn from Michilimackinac and Fort St. Joseph by Frontenac's successor, Chevalier de la Calliers, French fur traders continued to carry on their activities. The Iroquois tribes, who had suffered terrible losses during the past decade, were at length ready to make peace. Since the western Indian tribes had to be included in the negotiations, messages were sent summoning them to Montreal. Between seven and eight hundred warriors, representing tribes from the West and Northwest, arrived on July 22, 1701, under the leadership of Courtemanche, who had been sent to collect them and bring them east. On the preceding day three hundred Iroquois delegates had arrived. The signing of the peace on August 4, 1701, was celebrated with a feast at which three roasted oxen were consumed and with the firing of cannon and fireworks. A Huron chieftain, already stricken with a fatal disease, delivered a passionate, two-hour speech that so exhausted him that he died the same night. Other orators declared that they had now buried their instruments of war in a pit so deep that they should never be found, that the Iroquois were brothers of the other tribes, that the past should be forgotten. The Iroquois, in turn, solemnly agreed to remain neutral in any future war between the French and the British, and they kept their promise.

The Treaty of 1701 with the Iroquois ushered in a new era for the West. The menace of the Iroquois, which had so long been an obstacle to French activity in Michigan and the remainder of the West, was now at last removed. As the great ceremony at Montreal was in progress, an expedition, led by Cadillac, already was enroute to the West to establish the French in a new area and to lay the foundations of the great Michigan city, Detroit.

In 1699 Cadillac had gone to France with the purpose of convincing the court that the abandonment of the western country would be disastrous to New France. He attracted the attention of Count Pontchartrain, the king's chief minister, and convinced him that a new start in the West was essential if that great region were to be saved from English domination. The attitude of the court had undergone a change from that which had helped to bring on the decree of 1696. The Spanish king died in 1700, and Louis XIV was determined that his grandson should succeed to the Spanish throne. He realized that this would mean war since the other European powers, including Great Britain, would surely resist seeing Bourbons on both the French and Spanish thrones. Increasingly, now, the colonies were viewed by the king and his advisers relative to how they might advance these larger imperial objectives. Cadillac proposed that a French colony be established somewhere along *Le Detroit,* a term used by the French for some years to refer to the waterway linking Lake Erie and Lake Huron, which, despite the fact it consists of two rivers and a small lake, was regarded as one waterway or narrows. This was a strategic point from which to control access to the upper lakes, and Cadillac warned that if the French did not act at once, the English from New York would seize this point, as in fact they were planning to do. Cadillac's proposal, together with others that shortly led to French strongholds being established in southern Illinois and at the mouth of the Mississippi, was regarded in France to be more important from a military standpoint than for the economic reasons that had earlier dictated the establishment of fur trading centers. From these new centers the French could control a vast interior region, driving a wedge between the colonies of France's enemy, Great Britain, on the east, and France's anticipated ally, Spain, to the southwest.

In addition, Cadillac envisioned Detroit becoming an authentic settlement, inhabited not simply by soldiers, traders, and missionaries temporarily assigned to the area, but by French civilians and their families who would make this their permanent home. Around this colony the Indians were to be invited to come and live, trading their furs and receiving instruction from the priests. Through daily contact with the French, the natives would gradually adopt French customs and culture, Cadillac asserted. As for Cadillac himself, he would receive the rights of a landlord, and would be authorized to make grants of land to French settlers, to charge them rentals, and collect other fees characteristic of the French feudal system. He would also profit by the fur trade. He entered into a contract with the Company of the Colony of Canada—the organization to which the king had granted the control of the fur trade—to buy the furs traded at Detroit. In 1705, Cadillac bought out the company's rights in the Detroit fur trade.

Cadillac travelled to the site of his new colony by the old Ottawa River route, since the peace settlement with the Iroquois, which would make the Lake Ontario-Lake Erie route safe to use, had not yet been signed when he departed for the West. With him were fifty soldiers and fifty workmen with provisions and tools. He carefully explored the water route between Lake Huron and Lake Erie and chose the present site of Detroit for several reasons. The river at this point was relatively narrow and unobstructed by islands, making it possible for guns in the fort to command the entire width of the river. A short distance from the banks of the river the ground rose approximately forty feet above the water, and to the rear, a small river—the Savoyard—ran diagonally southwest. These conditions meant that this place would be easy to fortify.

Cadillac and his men landed on July 24, 1701, the date which now marks the founding of Detroit. Workmen immediately started felling trees for use in building a palisade twelve feet high and two hundred feet square in the heart of what is now Detroit's Civic Center. The fort was called Fort Pontchartrain, in honor of the king's minister who had responsibility over the colonies and had been influential in gaining support for Cadillac's project. Inside the palisade, houses were built of logs set upright, in the manner of the palisade. Subsequently here and at other French settlements in Michigan, buildings of the type developed in Quebec with walls constructed of logs laid in a horizontal fashion became more common. One of the early constructions was a church for the new settlement; a church called St. Anne's, inaugurating a parish which has continued under that name in Detroit to the present day.

That fall, Cadillac's wife and the wife of Henri de Tonty's brother, Alphonse, who was second in command, were brought out to Detroit. An impelling reason for this action was Cadillac's desire to convince the Indians that Detroit was intended to be a permanent settlement. In the years that followed, Cadillac sought to encourage the development of a body of permanent residents at Detroit through the granting of sixty-eight small lots to settlers within the fort's confines and seventy-five grants of farm land outside the fort on both sides of the river. All of the farm grants fronted on the river, and in order to provide as many river-front grants as possible, the farms were narrow, some of them only two hundred feet in width, but extending inland as far as three miles. Because of their elongated shapes, these land grants are often referred to as the French ribbon farms.

The recipients of these grants, known as *habitants,* were required to honor Cadillac much in the manner that feudal tenants paid homage to the lord of the manor. In addition to showing him respect, the *habitants* were required to pay Cadillac annual fees, and their grain was to be ground in his mill, for which service Cadillac received a certain percentage of the grain. The habitants also were required to work a certain number of days each year on his farm, and craftsmen or traders were to agree to certain conditions as to the way in which they could carry on their work.

Although only a limited number of Frenchmen responded to Cadillac's efforts to promote settlement at Detroit, he was much more successful in the appeals he made to the Indians, his efforts leading to what was probably the biggest change in Indian settlement patterns in the upper lakes since the Iroquois attacks on Huronia sixty years earlier.Soon after Detroit was established, approximately two thousand Indians reportedly moved to the area, with the Huron, Miami, Ottawa, and Chippewa Indians establishing villages along the river, above and below the fort. The departure of the Ottawas and Hurons from St. Ignace forced the Jesuits in 1705 to abandon their mission at that site, further adding to the enmity that the members of this order had already developed toward Cadillac.

Cadillac remained in command at Detroit for nine years. In 1710 he was appointed governor of Louisiana, the French colony in the lower Mississippi, and he left to assume that post in 1711. He returned to France in 1717 and died there in 1730. During his stay at Detroit Cadillac had made many enemies. He had extracted the last possible penny from the *habitants*. The Company of the Colony of Canada had hated him because he diverted so much of the fur trade to Detroit. And last but not least, he had encountered the hostility of the Jesuits, who were opposed to the concentration of the Indians around Detroit, in the belief that they would be debauched by brandy and exploited by the fur traders.

The opinions of historians and others on Cadillac vary widely. Detroit historical groups have honored the memory of the city's founder, making pilgrimages to his homeland, and eventually, in 1972, even assuming the considerable expense of preserving Cadillac's birthplace in the village of St. Nicolas de la Grave, as a memorial. Others, however, have not been so favorably inclined toward Cadillac. Even his patron in France, Count Pontchartrain, wrote to Cadillac the year before his removal from Detroit that he showed "too much greed" and too little moderation in his dealings with the residents of Detroit. In Cadillac's favor it can be observed that there was little drunkenness and debauchery at Detroit because he placed all liquor in a central warehouse and charged a high price for it. There can also be no denying that he had the ability to establish good rapport with the Indians. And it must not be forgotten that his enemies consistently blackened his character and on many occasions did so quite unfairly. But recent studies have supported those who have been critical of Cadillac. The Canadian historian, W. J. Eccles, a leading student of New France, has described Cadillac as "one of the worst scoundrels ever to set foot in North America."[4]

Scarcely had Cadillac left Detroit than a crisis involving Indian relations arose. More than a thousand Fox Indians from Wisconsin arrived in response to an earlier invitation from Cadillac that they settle in the Detroit area. The other Indians at Detroit were hostile to the newcomers, and the acting French commandant, Jacques-Charles Renaud Dubuisson, ordered the Fox to leave. They refused to do so, and a fierce conflict between the Fox and the French and the other Indians broke out. Detroit was under siege for nineteen days. At length the Fox retreated, only to be overtaken by Huron, Ottawa, and Potawatomi warriors who nearly annihilated them. Those Fox Indians who escaped to Wisconsin aroused anti-French feelings among the Fox who had remained there with the account of how the French at Detroit had treated them. For many years, the Fox in Wisconsin successfully prevented the French from passing through their lands to reach the Mississippi valley. They defeated a number of expeditions sent out to chastise them, before they finally were defeated and forced to flee across the Mississippi into Iowa in 1734.

The war against the Fox may have been the motivating force behind the reestablishment of a French fort at the Straits of Mackinac. Another explanation may be the fear of inroads by British fur traders operating out of Hudson Bay. A fort at the Straits of Mackinac would more effectively check possible incursions from the north into the area which France regarded as its own. Exactly when the French reestablished a garrison at the Straits is not certain. A veteran officer, the Marchand de Lignery, was sent to Michilimackinac in 1715 to enlist *coureurs de bois* for the Fox campaign. The following year, the Sieur de Louvigny came out to the Mackinac area with 225 soldiers, and at this point he was joined by two hundred fur traders and a considerable number of Indians for a campaign into Wisconsin against the Fox. This was an example, along with the raid against the Iroquois in 1687 that was organized at Fort St. Joseph, of the role that Michigan would play in these colonial wars. Rarely would Michigan be the site of actual combat, but it would serve as the major staging area in the West where forces that would be employed in other areas were mobilized. De Louvigny may have left some of the soldiers at the Straits when he returned to Montreal. Father Charlevoix, who traveled through the area in 1721, reported that the fort and mission at that time were occupied, but by only a handful of Frenchmen. It is not entirely clear what part of the Straits he was referring to. The older settlement on the north side of the Straits was still the site of some activity, but the main center of settlement was now transferred to the south side, where the present city of Mackinaw City now stands. There, sometime around 1715, a new fort was constructed which became not only a military outpost but also the trading center of the northern lakes, with a growing number of Frenchmen making it their permanent place of residence. The Jesuits returned to the area and maintained a parish church for these residents as well as continuing their missionary work among the Indians. By the early 1740s, these missionary activities were concentrated among the Ottawas who settled in the L'Arbre Croche area, some thirty miles to the southwest, where members of this tribe still reside today.

The Jesuits also continued their work for several years at the St. Joseph mission near the present city of Niles following the withdrawal of the military garrison from that point in the late 1690s. Although there appears to have been no missionary there for a time, the mission was manned again by 1718, and in 1719 soldiers were also sent out to reoccupy the fort.

*   *   *   *   *

In 1713, after the conclusion of the war with Great Britain that is known in American history as Queen Anne's War (which had begun five years after the conclusion of King William's War in 1697), France was at peace with the British for three decades. Aside from problems with Indians, particularly the desultory conflicts with the Fox Indians, this was one of the longest relatively trouble-free periods that New France ever enjoyed. But in spite of this, the population of the colony grew very slowly. Few Frenchmen came to the colony, and non-Catholics were forbidden to settle there. Unlike the British, the French authorities refused to encourage other nationalities to emigrate to the colony.

The same disappointingly slow growth rate of the colony as a whole carried over to the settlements in Michigan. Detroit never lived up to the expectations of its founder. Although some of Cadillac's successors continued to have hopes that Detroit would become an agricultural center capable of supplying the needs of the outposts in the upper lakes, these hopes were not realized. The town's small population actually declined after Cadillac's departure as confusion reigned as to the status of the land grants that Cadillac had made. By the 1720s, after these questions were largely resolved, the population climbed back to the figure of approximately two hundred that it had reached a decade earlier, and in the following years it reached a peak, according to one estimate, of over two thousand by 1760. The accuracy of the latter figure, however, is by no means assured. A governmental proclamation in 1749 that promised to supply tools, seed, livestock, and other assistance to any man going to Detroit for the purpose of farming stimulated some activity for several years. However, in 1757, a governmental report listed only "about two hundred habitants" as living in the area, and although they were said to be enjoying considerable success with their farming operations, they were not a large enough group to make Detroit the supply center for the Great Lakes. Instead, great amounts of money, time, and labor still had to be expended to transport food from the main settlements in the St. Lawrence to these western areas.[5]

English and American observers and writers in later years depicted the French *habitants* as a happy-go-lucky, irresponsible, essentially lazy lot, more interested in playing than in working, thereby casting most of the onus for Detroit's lack of progress in the French period on the *habitants'* shoulders. In actuality, the *habitants* were, as a group, hard-working, conservative folk of good, solid peasant stock. The failure of Detroit to develop according to plan was less the fault of its inhabitants than it was the failure or inability of the French authorities to shift the emphasis in New France away from the fur trade, which undoubtedly attracted the more enterprising individuals since no other activities held out to the colonial resident similar prospects for profit.[6] Thus, Detroit's importance continued to be not that of an agricultural center but that of a fur-trading center, particularly of the trade to the south into the Maumee and Wabash river valleys.

There were occasional troubles with the Indians, but they did not take on an immediately menacing aspect for the residents of Detroit, or any of the other settlements in Michigan, once the Fox had departed. A Jesuit missionary, Father Armand de la Richardie, ministered to the Hurons at Detroit, transferring his mission to Bois Blanc Island in 1742. Schools were not regularly kept, and most of the *habitants* were illiterate. There were no democratic institutions, so politics (as that term is usually understood) was absent from the life of the community. And there were only occasional travelers to bring news of the outside world. All in all, Detroiters lived an isolated and, in a sense, idyllic life during this period.

At the Straits of Mackinac, Indian encampments and traders' houses clustered around and within the new fort on the south side of the water route. During the first few years after the fort's construction, the fur trade seems to have languished because so many Indians had gone to live in the Detroit area. But by the 1730s and 1740s activity had increased markedly as traders by the hundreds assembled there in the summer months with the fruits of the previous year's trading activities in Indian villages stretching far to the west and north. There also was a lively, though much smaller trade at Fort St. Joseph, the center of the Potawatomi country in southwestern Michigan. A small French garrison and the Jesuit mission continued to be maintained here, along with the homes of a handful of French civilians involved with the fur trade who lived there year-round.

Thus during the years of peace from 1713 to 1744, a degree of stability and permanency previously unknown characterized the French settlements in Michigan. In the Great Lakes region, the French now occupied eleven major posts. In what is now Michigan, there were forts at Detroit, Michilimackinac, and Niles, with the addition of a small post at Sault Ste. Marie in 1750. In what is now Wisconsin, there were small forts at Green Bay and in the north on Chequamegon Bay. On the Mississippi River in Illinois, the French constructed Fort Chartres, an elaborate military post and the only one in the area that departed from the wooden stockade in favor of European stone fortification. Also in southern Illinois were the small agricultural settlements of Cahokia and Kaskaskia. In what is now Indiana were Fort Ouiatenon and Fort Vincennes on the Wabash River and Fort Miamis on the Maumee.

Of these outposts, Michilimackinac and Detroit were the most important. From these two points the influence of France radiated, the fur traders carried on their business, and the missionaries went out to convert the large numbers of Indians living close by. A census taken in 1736 revealed that around Detroit two hundred Ottawa, two hundred Huron, and one hundred Potawatomi warriors lived with their families. There were 180 Ottawa braves at Michilimackinac, who moved with their families to L'Arbre Croche in 1742. About a hundred Potawatomi warriors, with their families, resided near Fort St. Joseph, while a handful of Chippewas lived at Sault Ste. Marie. The Miami Indians had for the most part moved out of Michigan, with approximately two hundred Miami braves residing near Fort Miamis. Apparently the largest number of Chippewa lived in villages close to La Pointe, in northern Wisconsin.[7]

All these Indians were nominally attached to the French. But some of them had learned that they could make a better bargain for their peltry with the British than with the French. The Miami had been trading secretly with the British for years. In 1738 a band of

Huron, fearful of the enmity of the Ottawa and Chippewa toward them and not satisfied with the way the French at Detroit treated them, moved their village down to Sandusky Bay in northern Ohio, where British traders operating out of Albany had little difficulty reaching them. Unlike the French traders, the British were not hampered by monopolies and by having to pay license fees. This was the situation when King George's War broke out in 1744. The following year Chief Nicolas of the Huron band living on Sandusky Bay allowed the British to build a "strong-house" near his village, and the Iroquois, at the instigation of the British, urged the Huron warriors to attack Detroit. Five French traders returning to Detroit were captured and killed in June, 1747. This incident and a timely warning received by the French commandant at Detroit from a squaw alerted him to the danger. He called the nearby French *habitants* into the fort for protection, but the Indians living near Detroit promptly disavowed any connection with the plot. Even though the proposed foray against Detroit was thus foiled, several more French traders were killed or plundered during the summer of 1747. There was also trouble at Michilimackinac, but when reinforcements arrived the rumblings among the Indians died away. Deserted by his fellow Indians, Chief Nicolas moved his village southward and the British had to abandon their trading place on Sandusky Bay.[8]

The peace that came in 1748 was hardly more than a truce. The fourth and decisive war between France and Great Britain for the possession of North America did not break out along the border between New France and New England, nor on the borderland between the Carolinas and Georgia on the one side and Spanish Florida on the other, where most of the fighting had taken place in the earlier wars. Instead, it was in the valley of the Ohio River that the rivalry between the two powers brought about the clash that started the French and Indian War.

Conflicting claims for the Ohio Valley were not of recent origin. As early as 1671 at the famous "Pageant of the Sault," St. Lusson had claimed for the King of France all the lands drained by the lakes and rivers of the interior. British claims went back even further. In 1606 King James of England had granted to the London Company a charter for Virginia, which included "all that Space and Circuit of Land, lying from the Sea Coast of the Precinct aforesaid, up into the Land, throughout from Sea to Sea, West and Northwest." The description, though vague, was later to be interpreted as giving Virginia title to Kentucky and the territory north of the Ohio River including most or all of the future states of Ohio, Indiana, Illinois, Wisconsin, and Michigan. When King James dissolved the London Company in

1624, the crown assumed this claim. Subsequent charters, granted to Massachusetts and Connecticut, also ran from sea to sea and partially overlapped the Virginia claim, including areas in the southern third of Michigan.

Although both Britain and France had laid claim to the Ohio Valley in the seventeenth century, it was not until after King George's War that much attention was given to the fact that these claims were in conflict. Few British colonists had ventured west of the Allegheny Mountains up to that time. But in 1747 a group of Virginians formed an association to promote settlement in the Ohio Valley. And at about the same time Pennsylvania fur traders were boldly venturing westward into the Ohio Valley and were challenging the French control over the fur trade with the Indians of that region. These two developments aroused the French to action.

In 1748, the association of Virginians, called the Ohio Company, obtained a grant of 200,000 acres of land along the Ohio River, with the provision that an additional 300,000 acres would be granted if one hundred families were settled on the land within seven years. Although the effort to secure settlers failed, the French were alarmed at the prospective intrusion into a region they considered to be outside the limits of the English colonies. Several other land companies were formed in Virginia and Pennsylvania during this same period, with the purpose of seeking land grants for speculative purposes.

The Pennsylvania fur traders found a golden opportunity to benefit when, during King George's War, the British navy disrupted French trade to the extent that Montreal merchants were unable to obtain adequate supplies of trading goods required to secure peltry from the Indians. A tough Irish trader from Pennsylvania, George Croghan, was operating trading centers on the Upper Ohio by the close of 1744. From these bases trading expeditions were travelling as far west as the Illinois country. Other traders ventured up the rivers flowing into the Ohio. And in 1748, Croghan had a palisaded fort constructed at the Miami Indian village of Pickawillany, the site of the present Piqua, Ohio. With the help of Conrad Weiser and with the approval of the Pennsylvania Assembly, Croghan lured chieftains of several Indian tribes of the Ohio Valley to Logstown, Pennsylvania, where they signed a treaty pledging their allegiance to Great Britain rather than France.

In 1749, the French reacted to these challenges to their claims on the Ohio Valley by sending Pierre-Joseph Céleron de Blainville with two hundred soldiers into the region. He did not have a sufficient force to attack Pickawillany and, instead, planted lead plates proclaiming that the land belonged to the King of France at the mouths of several of the rivers flowing into the Ohio.

Another move made by the French to check British inroads had a more direct connection with Michigan. This involved the building of a fort and the establishment of a settlement on the St. Mary's River long inhabited by a band of Chippewa. The site of the earliest mission in Michigan, the Soo had been a natural stopping place for fur traders during and after the time when the Jesuits maintained a mission there. The passage through the St. Mary's River afforded a means whereby Indians from the far North could avoid Michilimackinac and carry their peltry to British traders. To forestall this the governor of New France in 1750 granted a seignory eighteen miles square bordering on the St. Mary's River to Louis le Gardeur de Repentigny, who had proved his prowess by conducting a successful raid into New York. The grant was to be shared by Captain Louis de Bonne, a nephew of the governor, but the latter never visited the property, so far as is known. Repentigny erected three buildings enclosed in a stockade, and established Jean-Baptiste Cadotte and his Indian wife as tenants. He had horses and cattle brought from Michilimackinac for their use. Repentigny gave the Chippewa a belt of wampum and persuaded them to deliver to him a belt that had been sent them by the British.[9]

Although Repentigny's fort and the symbol of French authority that it provided probably served to maintain the allegiance of the Chippewa to the French cause, it had little significance in the impending struggle. Much more important was the fact that a long succession of incompetent governors of New France was broken in 1752 when the Marquis Duquesne assumed that position. He was a capable naval officer who imposed firm discipline and took decisive action to strengthen New France. Lacking sufficient French personnel, he enlisted France's remaining Indian allies to meet the British threat. Under his orders, a war party of approximately 240 Ottawas and Frenchmen, which was organized at Detroit in June, 1752, attacked Pickawillany. The fort was utterly destroyed and the local chieftain, who was among those who had gone over to the British and had been nicknamed "Old Britain," was killed, boiled, and eaten by the Ottawa. Five English traders in the village were taken prisoner and their trade goods were confiscated. This attack served as a warning for the British to keep out of the French preserves, and for the Indians to remain loyal to the French. The Indians were impressed, and most of those in Ohio who had been favoring the British now returned to the French fold.

The British fur traders were not as grave a threat to the French in the West as were the farmers from Virginia and other British colonies coming into the Ohio Valley. Fur traders, regardless of their nationality, wanted these lands to remain a wilderness, where the Indians could continue to obtain the furs that the traders needed. Farmers, on the other hand, wanted to drive out the Indians and clear the forests, thus destroying the fur trade. The conflict that now began marked not only the renewal of the long struggle between the French and the British for political dominance in North America but also the beginning of a war between two competing economic systems—the fur trade and farming—which would not be settled in Michigan until the 1820s.

The forts that the French had built at Detroit, Michilimackinac, Sault Ste. Marie, and other strategic points had been designed to control fur trade routes, but these posts would be of little help in controlling the land routes that the farmers would take over the mountains into the fertile lands of the Middle West. Hence, in 1753, Duquesne ordered a string of new forts built farther to the east. Presqu'Isle, at what is now Erie, Pennsylvania, Le Boeuf, and Venango were all in western Pennsylvania, but the Quakers who dominated the Pennsylvania government refused to take any steps that

Fort Pontchartrain, first settlement, Detroit

might lead to war. Governor Robert Dinwiddie of Virginia had no such qualms. Clearly the French were seeking control of the Ohio Valley, which Virginia claimed under its charter. Dinwiddie sent the young Virginia surveyor, George Washington, to warn the French to get out. In the winter of 1753–54, Washington visited Venango and Le Boeuf, where he was received politely by the French commanders but was told that the French had no intention of leaving. When Dinwiddie received this news he decided that Virginia would seek to beat the French to the most strategic spot from which to control the Ohio, the point where the Allegheny and Monongahela rivers join to form the Ohio. The small force of Virginians that was dispatched in 1754 to begin work on this fort was soon driven off by the arrival of a great fleet of canoes carrying five hundred Frenchmen who proceeded to build a strong fort which they named Fort Duquesne.

Meanwhile, Washington had been sent with a force of approximately 150 militia to secure control of the fort that the Virginians were supposedly building at the future site of Pittsburgh. When the French commandant at Fort Duquesne, the Sieur de Contrecoeur, learned of Washington's approach, he sent a party of forty men to warn Washington that he was trespassing on French territory and that he should return forthwith to Virginia. Although this French force was supposed to be operating under a flag of truce, fighting broke out between the French and the Virginians, with both sides claiming the other fired the first shot. Several French soldiers were killed, including the commander of the detachment, and the rest of the party was captured.

The French officer killed in this engagement, Joseph de Villiers, surnamed Jumonville, had spent part of his youth in Michigan, where his father, the Sieur de Villiers, was the commander of Fort St. Joseph from 1724 to 1730. Joseph's brother, Louis, also a French officer, was at Fort Duquesne when news of his brother's death arrived. He quickly organized a large force to take revenge for what the French regarded as a massacre. After fighting an all-day battle against de Villiers' larger force, Washington was forced to surrender under terms that allowed his force to march out of their encampment with the honors of war, and return to Virginia. The articles of capitulation stated that Washington had wrongly invaded the territory of France and had attacked and killed Joseph de Villiers and his men in violation of the recognized rules of warfare. Washington would claim that he was not correctly informed by his interpreter as to the nature of the statements he had signed, although the interpreter was the same one he had employed in his meetings with the French the previous winter.[10]

These events marked the start of the fourth and last of the Anglo-French colonial wars that had begun with King William's War in 1689. But in this case the war was not an extension of a conflict that had begun earlier in Europe. Instead, it was a war that the colonists themselves had initiated, and rather than calling it by the name of the current monarch of Great Britain, the Virginians and the other English colonists referred to this war as the French and Indian War, after the two groups that were blocking their advance into the rich farm lands of the Middle West and thus threatening to stifle the further growth of these colonies. It was a war that was launched by two skirmishes in the summer of 1754 between forces led by the future first president of the United States and two officers who had grown up in Michigan. The outcome of the war would eventually determine that Michigan would develop as a member of the new nation headed by George Washington and not as a province or a portion of a province in the Dominion of Canada.

Officially, at least, France and Great Britain remained at peace until 1756, because they were in the process of reshaping their European alliances. When this had been carried out, the war that is known in European history—and in Canadian history, where the European ties were more long-lasting than they were in the United States—as the Seven Years' War broke out. But the fighting in America did not wait for the developments in Europe. Great Britain sent General Edward Braddock to take command of two regiments of redcoats and whatever colonial forces he could muster in a drive to capture Fort Duquesne in 1755. It was an ill-starred venture. When he set out, Braddock had a force of 1,400 regulars, 450 Virginians commanded by George Washington, and fifty Indian scouts. The French commander at Fort Duquesne intended to fight the more numerous forces of Braddock by remaining on the defensive within the walls of the fort. He was persuaded, however, to send out approximately 250 of his men, together with several hundred Indians, to harass the oncoming British force, hoping to delay the advance of the troops but not to defeat and turn them back. However, the Indians and the French, who adopted the Indian guerrilla style of warfare, poured a murderous fire into the ranks of Braddock's men. The British began to break in confusion, and Braddock, who was mortally wounded, ordered a retreat that soon turned into a rout. An even more disastrous outcome was averted by the action of Washington and his men, who were somewhat more familiar with the wilderness battle tactics and fought a rear-guard action that enabled the forces finally to regroup and retreat with some dignity.

A native of Michigan played perhaps the decisive role in defeating Braddock. He was Charles Langlade, who was born about 1732 at the French settlement at Michilimackinac. His father was a Frenchman, reportedly of an aristocratic family, who had come to Michilimackinac to recoup the family fortune in the fur trade. Langlade's mother was an Ottawa woman, the sister of a chief. There is a story that when Langlade was a boy of five his mother's brother had a dream in which the Great Spirit directed him to take a little boy with him on a war party and promised him victory if he did so. The chief did as he was told, and the victory that was won was attributed to the presence of the little boy, Charles Langlade. For whatever cause, Langlade had a powerful influence over the Indian tribesmen who were allied with the French, and this, combined with his talents as a military leader, led to his constant use by the French to mobilize and lead Indian forces in support of French interests. Langlade had carried out the devastating raid on Pickawillany in 1752, and now, in 1755, Langlade was directed to lead a force of Ottawas and Chippewas from northern Michigan to assist in the defense of Fort Duquesne. Langlade and his men were among those who went out to attack the British, and according to one source it was his repeated urgings that finally persuaded the commander of this French force to strike the superior British army where the latter was at a great disadvantage. Two British officers later testified that the defeat of Braddock could be attributed to Langlade.[11]

Following the defeat of Braddock, Langlade and his Indians returned to Michigan. Indian warriors traditionally did not like long campaigns, and insisted upon returning to their villages each fall in order to provide for their families. Men like Langlade continually had to organize new war parties to replace those that had disbanded at the end of a summer's fighting. Langlade carried out these assignments with distinction throughout the French and Indian War. Later, this remarkable Michiganian was persuaded to serve in the same capacity for the British during the American Revolution. He had an uncanny way of turning up at crucial moments in these wars, and by the end of his long career had reportedly fought in ninety-nine battles. As an old man he is said to have expressed disappointment that he could not have fought in one more so he could have retired with an even hundred engagements to his credit.

During the two years after Braddock's defeat, results of the fighting in the colonies continued to be dismal for the British. Late in 1757, however, the tide began to turn. A new British ministry, headed by William Pitt, injected fresh vigor and ideas into the British cause. Pitt was one of the first British statesmen to realize the true value of the British colonies. He decided that it was more important to British interests to secure a decisive victory in North America than on the continent of Europe. Therefore, while he provided subsidies to Frederick the Great to help him keep the French armies occupied in Europe, Pitt concentrated the British forces in the colonies. He rid the military ranks of many of its incompetent officers, replacing them with able young commanders. The British navy was strengthened with the addition of more ships and within a short time had succeeded in virtually cutting off New France from any further contact with the home country, forcing the French commander there, the Marquis de Montcalm, to make do with the men and materials that were available in the colony.

By 1758, the measures that Pitt had taken began to bear fruit. In July, the French stronghold of Louisburg, which guarded the approaches into the Gulf of St. Lawrence, was captured. About the same time, another British force in the west captured Fort Frontenac, cutting the main route between Detroit and the St. Lawrence settlements. Finally, later that year, General John Forbes succeeded in capturing Fort Duquesne, which he promptly renamed Fort Pitt.

When news of Forbes' advance toward Fort Duquesne reached Detroit, a force of Michigan Indians was assembled to go to the defense of that post. The Michigan warriors arrived at Fort Duquesne while Forbes was still proceeding slowly westward. He moved slowly because he knew that the longer he delayed, the more impatient the Indian allies of the French would become to return home. But an advance British force under Major James Grant virtually invited attack, and on September 14 it was surprised and cut to pieces, with losses of over four hundred men. Forbes and his main detachment still delayed their advance, however, and his tactics paid off. By November, the Indian allies of the French had dispersed in such numbers that the French commander at Fort Duquesne knew he could not withstand a British attack, and on November 24 he blew up the fort and retired up the Allegheny River to Fort Venango.

The evaporation of the Indian forces that led to the abandonment of Fort Duquesne may have resulted in part from a cunning deal made with the Indians. At Albany in 1754, the Iroquois confederacy had ceded the lands occupied by the Delaware west of the Susquehanna River to the British. Now to pacify these Indians a treaty was signed at Easton, Pennsylvania, promising the Delaware and other Indians that the lands west of the mountains would be respected as Indian property. This concession on the part of the British may have helped persuade the Indians to leave Fort Duquesne in its hour of need. On November 25, 1758, the British flag flew over the gateway to the Ohio for the first time.

In 1759, the British moved in for the kill. Crown Point and Ticonderoga in the Lake Champlain route from the south into the St. Lawrence were captured, while in the west Niagara fell into British hands. Then on September 17, the military stronghold of New France, the supposedly impregnable citadel of Quebec, surrendered after the most celebrated battle of the war. This battle was fought on September 13 on the Plains of Abraham, and both of the opposing commanders, General James Wolfe and the Marquis de Montcalm, lost their lives. Among the defenders of Quebec were Charles Langlade and four hundred of his Indian warriors. Langlade already had been of inestimable aid to the French. In 1757 he had won a battle from Major Robert Rogers and his famous rangers on Lake Champlain. That same year, Langlade and his Indian followers helped Montcalm capture Fort William Henry on Lake George in New York. He had now become a lieutenant in the French army. At one stage in the siege of Quebec Wolfe landed 3,000 of his men in an exposed position, separate from the rest of his army. Langlade quickly saw that this was a golden opportunity to inflict a stinging defeat on the British expedition and he sent an appeal to the commander to come to his support. It went unheeded, and although Langlade's Indians attacked anyway and inflicted considerable loss on the British force, the chance for a knockout blow was lost. Later Wolfe moved his forces above Quebec, crossed the river, and scaled the cliffs in front of the city by using a narrow, unguarded pathway. The battle that followed resulted in a British victory and Quebec was surrendered.[12]

Earlier the same year, when the British were attacking Fort Niagara, Indians from Detroit and the Illinois country came to the relief of the fort. This time, however, it was the French and Indian forces that were ambushed by the British. After sustaining heavy losses the Detroit Indians fled across Lake Erie back to their villages. With the tide of the war turning, the Indians now began to waver in their support of the French. A delegation of Huron, Ottawa, and Chippewa went to Fort Pitt and smoked the pipe of peace with George Croghan, representing the British. Even so, the majority of the tribesmen co-operated with the French commandant at Detroit, who, after the fall of Fort Niagara and Quebec, prepared for a last ditch stand against what he thought might be a British foray against Detroit.

The French cause was not without hope in the spring of 1760.

The British in Quebec faced near-starvation before the ice went out of the St. Lawrence, enabling a British supply fleet to rescue them. At the very time the British fleet arrived, Quebec was under attack by the Chevalier de Lévis, Montcalm's successor as commander of the French forces, and a stinging defeat had been inflicted upon the British at the battle of Sainte-Foy. But the coming of the British fleet with men and supplies completely reversed the situation. Lévis retreated to Montreal where three British armies converged early in September. It was the Marquis de Vaudreuil, last governor of New France, who decided to surrender. Most of the Indian allies of the French already had melted away and even some of the regulars had deserted. All of the remaining areas of New France still under French control were surrendered. General Jeffrey Amherst, the British commander, promised that the French people might continue to live in their homes, be secure in their property, engage in trade on equal terms with the British, and enjoy religious freedom as far as British law would permit. Lévis and his men laid down their arms on September 8, 1760.

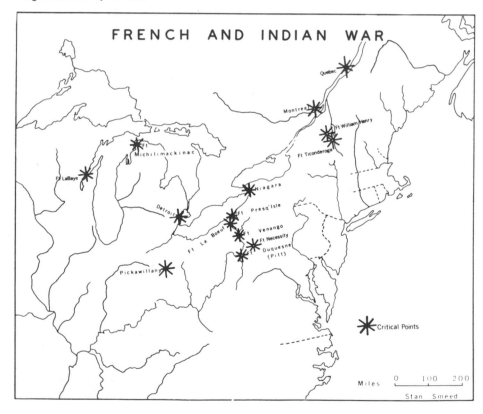

Four French posts in the Great Lakes area remained garrisoned at the time of the surrender: Detroit, Michilimackinac, St. Joseph, and the fort at Green Bay. Charles Langlade, sorrowfully returning from the East, brought word of the surrender to Captain Louis Beaujeu, commandant at Mackinac. The terms of the capitulation stipulated that the officers and soldiers of the garrisons were to be allowed to go to the nearest seaport to take ship for France. Beaujeu, to avoid the humiliation of surrendering his post to the British, departed from Michilimackinac late in 1760, crossed Lake Michigan to Green Bay, picked up the small garrison there, and proceeded southward to Louisiana, the separate French colony in the lower Mississippi valley, which had not been included in the surrender. On his way southward, in the Illinois country, he made contact with another French force of two hundred men from Detroit. This force had been sent to reinforce Montreal but, hearing of the surrender, it had returned to Detroit and had been permitted to proceed to the same destination as Beaujeu had chosen: New Orleans.[13]

General Amherst selected Robert Rogers, leader of the celebrated Rogers' Rangers, to hurry westward after the surrender and to take over the Great Lakes posts from the French. He was instructed to go to Fort Pitt first to pick up a company of British regulars to garrison Detroit. General Robert Monckton at Fort Pitt assigned the duty to a company of the 60th Regiment of Royal Americans, under Captain Donald Campbell. Rogers' responsibility was chiefly that of dealing with the Indians and winning them over to the British side. Along the shore of Lake Erie, the expedition made contact with the pro-English band of Ottawa that already had smoked the pipe of peace with George Croghan. Rogers wrote an account in later years in which he told of meeting Pontiac, leader of the Ottawa Indians at Detroit, on this occasion. He gave a careful description of Pontiac and the ceremony, which was accepted as authentic by Parkman and later writers, but which now appears to have been a mere figment of Rogers' imagination.[14] Pontiac was probably among the chiefs who welcomed the British force when it reached the mouth of the Detroit River. The formal surrender took place on November 29, 1760, when the French commandant, Captain François de Bellestre, gave up his arms and his men. The *fleur-de-lis* of France came down and the British colors were raised.

Captain Campbell and George Croghan, who accompanied the expedition, thought Fort Pontchartrain was the finest they had ever seen. Pickets were twelve to fifteen feet in height, and the area they enclosed was very large. Inside the stockade were houses and shops, Ste. Anne's Church, and a barracks. The commandant's house stood on a stone foundation measuring forty-three by thirty-two feet and all the rooms were plastered. The other houses had sharply sloping roofs, dormer windows, and board siding over hewn logs. The *habitants* witnessed the ceremony of surrender with seeming indifference. The Indians, in contrast, appeared to be happy with the change, probably anticipating cheaper goods and better trading conditions. However, they reminded the British that "this country was given by God to the Indians" and expressed the hope that "you would preserve it for our joint use." Rogers secured the release of a total of fifty-seven English prisoners held by the natives. Having thus secured Detroit, Rogers ordered a small party of Rangers to proceed southward to take possession of Forts Miamis and Ouiatenon. He led another party northward to take over Fort Michilimackinac. He was turned back by ice, however, and returned to Detroit, then marched overland to Fort Pitt, which he reached on January 23, 1761.[15]

Captain Campbell and his men spent a pleasant winter in Detroit. The *habitants* willingly furnished them with foodstuffs, and accounts indicate that there was a good deal of dancing, card playing, and conviviality at the commandant's house. But Captain Campbell had his worries. The Indians were demanding more and more; there even were hints of a plan to attack the fort, which was now called Fort Detroit by the British. Campbell did not feel that he could weaken his garrison by sending an expedition to take over the forts in the north. English traders, arriving in the spring, did not bring the goods the Indians wanted, and their prices were high. Furthermore, Campbell forbade the sale of rum to the natives. Finally, Campbell learned that the Seneca, one of the Iroquois tribes, had hatched a conspiracy to unite all the western Indians in an attack on the British posts at Detroit, Fort Pitt, Presqu'Isle, and Niagara. Although they were becoming unhappy with the British, the western tribes were not yet ready to revolt, and the Seneca plot failed. Campbell sent word of the situation to General Amherst. It was decided that a large reinforcement of British regulars would be sent to strengthen Detroit and to take over the other French posts, and that Sir William Johnson and Croghan would accompany the troops and hold a grand council in Detroit to pacify the Indians.

Sir William Johnson was a man of immense influence among the Indians. A native of Ireland, he had come to America in 1737 to manage a tract of land in the Mohawk Valley of New York that had been acquired by his uncle. He later added a tract of his own, traded with the Indians, erected a store and a mill as well as a beautiful Georgian mansion. The fort and the house still stand. He was adopted by the Mohawk and learned their language. It was his influence that held the Iroquois allegiance to the British during the French and Indian War. For his victory over the French in the Battle of Lake George he received the thanks of Parliament and was created a baronet. In 1756 he was appointed as Indian agent for all the tribes living north of the Carolinas and the Ohio River. The expedition to Detroit was under the command of a thirty-two-year-old man who had won his laurels in the war just ended: Henry Gladwin. The arrival of Johnson, Croghan, Gladwin, and his men at Detroit early in September was the occasion of much festivity. Johnson related that there were frequent balls where dancing continued on one occasion until five in the morning, and on another until seven. Johnson was especially attracted to a handsome young woman named Angelique Cuillerier dit Beaubien, daughter of a prosperous French trader. The grand council with the Indians opened September 9. There was a great deal of speech making on both sides. Johnson did not mention an alarming communication he had received from General Amherst en route, instructing him that henceforth there would be no more presents for the Indians. Spokesmen for the Indians proclaimed their loyalty to the British, reminded the British of the services to their cause rendered by the Indians in the late war, and confessed to some shortcomings. One chief admitted some horse stealing, but said it had been done "by some of our idle young men, who you know are very difficult to restrain." All in all, the conference appeared successful, though Johnson must have had misgivings for the future in view of the new policy of Amherst on presents, to which the Indians had become accustomed during the war. And he may have been concerned that Chief Pontiac of the Ottawa took no part in the council; at least there is no record indicating that Pontiac spoke. The council was topped off by an exchange of wampum belts and a huge feast, at which the *pièce de résistance* was an immense roasted ox provided by Johnson.[16]

Gladwin sent Captain Henry Balfour to take possession of the northern posts on September 9. Arriving at Fort Michilimackinac on September 28, he found that the home-town military hero, Lieutenant Charles Langlade, had been left in command by the departed garrison. Langlade officially handed the fort over to Balfour. At the post were a number of French half-breed traders and a few hardy English traders who had arrived in advance of the soldiers. Balfour left Lieutenant William Leslye and twenty-eight men to garrison the fort. The fort at the time was described as being roughly square, containing five long barracks for soldiers and traders, a few houses and storerooms, a church, a priest's house, a powder magazine, a guard house, and a few other buildings.

Balfour then crossed to Green Bay, where he left a small garrison to occupy Fort La Baye. From there he proceeded southward to the mouth of the St. Joseph River, and up that stream to Fort St. Joseph. Here he left fifteen men under the command of youthful Ensign Francis Schlosser and returned overland to Detroit with the remainder of his small force. The following year, Lieutenant John Jamet, with a small contingent, was sent to occupy Repentigny's fort at the Sault, which had been abandoned by the French.

This completed the British occupation of the French posts throughout the West, except for the Illinois country. Forts Vincennes and Chartres were included within the jurisdiction of New Orleans and were considered part of French Louisiana. They were not included within the surrender by Lévis in 1760. Hence the British made no attempt to occupy them until after the conclusion of peace in 1763, with Fort Chartres not being taken over by the British until 1765.

Although the fighting in America ended with the surrender of Montreal in 1760, the war in Europe continued until 1763. This meant that the situation in America remained uncertain for three years. France had surrendered her empire along the St. Lawrence and around the Great Lakes, but there was always the possibility that it might be restored if victory could be won in Europe. This, however, was not to be the case. Frederick the Great and his Prussian army held their own against an alliance consisting of most of the other European powers, and when the Peace of Paris was signed in 1763 the loss of the French empire in America was confirmed. Great Britain received all the French possessions east of the Mississippi, while Spain, by an earlier treaty, had been given New Orleans and all the lands claimed by France west of the Mississippi. The sole remnants of the great empire that had been created by Champlain and his successors were the tiny islands of St. Pierre and Miquelon in the Gulf of St. Lawrence, which have remained French possessions to the present day.

Although the period in which Michigan was under French control ended with the occupation of the area by the British in 1760–61 and the final cession of these lands by the French in 1763, one should not fall into the rather common error of forgetting about the French after this time. Even though the soldiers departed from Detroit, Michilimackinac, and other posts, nearly all of the French civilians stayed. Until the early 1820's, the majority of Michigan's non-Indian population was French in background, exerting a powerful influence on Michigan's economy, society, and politics, despite the fact that political power now rested with others. Many of Michigan's residents today can trace their ancestry back to the pioneer French settlers of the early eighteenth century, and although little in the way of physical remains survives from those days, innumerable place names, such as Detroit, Au Sable, Presque Isle, Isle Royale, and Grand Traverse Bay, are a reminder of the *voyageurs,* the *habitants,* and the *coureur de bois.* Oddly enough, the Marquis de Montcalm, who lost the decisive battle for control of the French colony, is the namesake of a Michigan county, while the victor in that battle, James Wolfe, remains unhonored in the state that became British largely because of Wolfe's actions.

Fort Mackinac

5

MICHIGAN UNDER THE BRITISH FLAG

The British flag flew over Michigan for thirty-six years, from 1760 to 1796. The early years of this period, however, were a time in which British control was by no means firmly established. No one could be sure until the news arrived in the fall of 1763 of the peace settlement that had been signed in Paris in February of that year that Michigan would remain in British hands. But even before that decision was known, the British garrisons had to confront the most formidable Indian uprising in American history.

For almost a century, the British had endeavored to gain the favor of the western tribes. They had sold the Indians liquor at a time when the French authorities were trying to stop this practice by French fur traders. The British had sought to buy the Indians' friendship through the lavish distribution of presents, and the traders had paid the Indians more for their furs than the Indians could get from the French. After the British took over control of these interior lands, the Indians expected these past practices to be continued, but were soon dismayed to learn that this was not to be the case. General Jeffrey Amherst, commander of the British forces in America at the end of the French and Indian War, was largely responsible for these changes in Indian policy. He was opposed to any further coddling of the Indians. The war had been an enormously expensive burden on Great Britain, and with the fighting in America at an end, Amherst was under pressure to reduce all unnecessary military expenses including gifts to the Indians in time of peace. The Indians thus found themselves cut off from a major source of the white man's goods upon which they had come to depend. They could still obtain these goods, but only through dealing with the fur traders. Amherst also ordered rigid restrictions on the sale of liquor to the Indians, and declared that no more leniency should be shown towards the Indians who were guilty of misbehavior. Amherst lacked any real comprehension of the problems involved in dealing with these proud native peoples.

The abolition of the French fur-trading monopoly gave independent traders free rein and opened the way for an orgy of cheating, fraud, and dishonest dealings that quickly infuriated the Indians. Shoddy goods were dispensed at high prices and the natives were taunted for their gullibility. In spite of restrictions, whisky or rum were offered as an inducement, but were diluted with water, tobacco being added to give it the desired "kick." The new rules compelled the Indians to come to the forts to sell their furs where the soldiers and some of the British traders were haughty and scornful to them. Another development that alarmed the Indians was the entrance into Kentucky, western Pennsylvania, and Tennessee of settlers from the East. If this kept up, how long would it be before they would be crowded out of their hunting grounds? And finally, the French *habitants* and fur-trading personnel in the West were sympathetic with the disgruntled natives, and assured the Indians that the king of France was asleep and would presently awake and scatter these usurpers. The possibility of the resumption of French control was substantiated by the fact that at the time the Indian uprising was in the making, no treaty of peace had yet been signed by Britain and France.

It appears quite likely that both the French in the Illinois country and those living along the St. Lawrence were involved in encouraging the Indians to strike back against the British. In the fall of 1762, George Croghan at Fort Pitt learned from a Detroit Indian that during the preceding summer there had been a secret war council at the Ottawa village along the Detroit River, attended by chiefs of the Ottawa, Huron, and Potawatomi tribes as well as the Chippewa from the Lake Superior region. The latter had brought with them two Frenchmen in Indian dress. The council plotted to attack the British, the informer related, and had sent deputies to the tribes on the Wabash and along the Ohio River to the south. Croghan later received another report that the Shawnee in the Ohio Valley had received a war belt from Detroit and that the tribes in that region were being stirred emotionally by a "prophet" among the Delaware nation, a psychotic who claimed to have had visions in which a spirit told him that the Indians, by purifying themselves and returning to their ancient ways, would be able to drive the white men out of their country. Meanwhile in the East, the Seneca, who had tried to make trouble for the British two years before, were hatching a definite conspiracy. There is reason to believe that the Seneca were inspired and encouraged by the French along the St. Lawrence. The Seneca passed a war belt on to the Delaware, who conveyed it to the Shawnee and the Miami. The Seneca sent another war belt to Detroit. The Detroit Indians thus were prompted from both west and east to attack the British.

There can be no question that Pontiac was the moving spirit in the plot devised to capture Detroit. Francis Parkman believed he was the instigator of the entire uprising of the western Indians against British rule, a belief that Parkman expressed in his *History of the Conspiracy of Pontiac,* published in 1851. A century later, however, Howard Peckham, in *Pontiac and the Indian Uprising,* convincingly refuted Parkman's conspiracy theory and demonstrated that Pontiac could only be credited with leading the attack against British authority in the Detroit area. In 1763, Pontiac was probably in his forties and had long since risen to leadership among his fellow Ottawa tribesmen because of his intellect, shrewdness, bravery, and oratorical prowess. His plan, as he outlined it to a conclave of Detroit Indians held in April, 1763, in what is believed to be the site of the present Council Park in the downriver Detroit community of Lincoln Park, called for gaining entrance into the fort on the pretext of desiring a parley, and then, at a given signal, attacking their enemies. Unfortunately for the Indians, the commandant of the fort had been forewarned. There are many stories about how Major Henry Gladwin, who had succeeded Captain Campbell in command, learned of Pontiac's plot. Gladwin never revealed the name of the person who warned him. The most persistent theory is that it was an Indian woman, named Catherine, who was romantically linked with Gladwin or one of the other British officers and who therefore wanted to save her lover from possible death. A famous painting by J. M. Stanley, an artist who came to Detroit in 1834, depicts a handsome Catherine delivering the warning to Gladwin. Aside from the fact that other versions of essentially the same story describe the woman as old and ugly, rather than young and beautiful, it is more likely that Gladwin was tipped off by one of the French residents, many of whom had close ties with the Indians and could have been privy to Pontiac's plans.[1]

Pontiac's strategy called for approximately sixty of his best warriors to accompany him into the fort, each concealing tomahawks, knives, or sawed-off muskets under their blankets. The rest of the Ottawa would be spread around, also carrying hidden weapons. Pontiac would speak to Gladwin and hold up a belt of green and white wampum. When he turned it over it would signal the Ottawa to fall upon the British. On Saturday morning, May 7, 1763, approximately three hundred braves and squaws, almost all of them wearing blankets, crossed the river to the fort. They were admitted through the gate, and small groups began to move through the town. They found that the merchants had closed and locked their shops, and on the parade ground they saw the soldiers drawn up with muskets ready. Gladwin and Campbell stood waiting, wearing pistols and sabers. Pontiac realized that Gladwin had learned of the plot and was prepared to deal with the Indians. Stripped of the element of surprise that was essential to the success of his plan, Pontiac, after expressing indignation at the unfriendly attitude the British were showing toward him, withdrew from the fort. Two days later, he tried again, but this time the Indians were not even admitted to the stockade. Meanwhile, Gladwin prepared for a siege and moved into the fort all the food supplies the French farmers would sell.

After a week in which the Indians killed or captured approximately thirty Englishmen outside the fort, Pontiac asked for a day's truce. Captain Campbell and Lieutenant George McDougall went out to meet him, hoping to restore peace, but Pontiac broke the truce and kept them prisoner. Later, during a sortie from the fort, one of the officers killed a nephew of Wasson, chief of the Chippewa who had joined Pontiac's forces, and then proceeded to scalp the young man and wave the bloody trophy insolently at the Indians. Wasson was so enraged that he killed Captain Campbell, tore off his scalp, cut out his heart, and ate it.

The siege of the fort was now on in earnest. Gladwin had only 123 soldiers, approximately twenty English traders, and a few Frenchmen who would aid him in the defense of the fort. Pontiac's forces probably numbered more than five hundred. Gladwin did not fear a direct assault on the stockade so much as he did fire from burning arrows. Every precaution was taken to make ready water supplies to extinguish such fires. Two ships with small cannon, the sloop *Michigan* and the schooner *Huron*—part of the fleet that the seafaring British began building up as soon as they gained control of the Great Lakes—could defend the fort from the river side, although it became necessary to use these vessels to bring in supplies and reinforcements. In response to a plea sent to Niagara for help, approximately one hundred men with barrels of meat and flour were sent out in ten small boats. Discovering this force moving along the north shore of Lake Erie, Indians attacked when the men landed for a night's sleep. Only forty of the men escaped, but still managed to bring some of the provisions through to Detroit. By using larger vessels, Gladwin could depend on securing troops and provisions from the east, and this was what enabled him to hold out.

Meanwhile, Pontiac's actions at Detroit helped to inspire Indians elsewhere to attack other British-held forts in the West. These efforts were so successful that by July only Detroit, Niagara, and Fort Pitt remained in British hands. The capture of the fort at Michilimackinac was accomplished by a clever stratagem worked out by Minavavana, chief of the Chippewa. He first sent away all of his followers who were not wholeheartedly against the British. He then cultivated a friendship with the post commander, Captain George Etherington. Charles Langlade warned Etherington that there was a plot to capture the fort, and Alexander Henry, a young English trader who had arrived at the Straits in 1761 ahead of the British troops, also warned the commandant of possible danger. Etherington, however, did not put any stock in the reports, having been completely duped by Minavavana. The chief proposed that they celebrate the birthday of King George III on June 2 (although the king's birthday was actually on June 4). As part of the festivities, the Indians would demonstrate their loyalty by staging a ball game between the Chippewa and some visiting Sauk Indians from Wisconsin, which Etherington thought was a fine idea. The spot chosen for the game was just outside the gates of the fort, along the shores of Lake Michigan. Near the gates, squaws squatted or stood, wrapped in their blankets, even though it was a hot day. Underneath their blankets, however, the women had concealed a variety of weapons. The ball game began much to the amusement of the soldiers and officers who watched idly without taking the precaution to arm themselves. The game, baggataway, was similar to lacrosse. A wooden ball was used and this was clouted by any member of the team in the general direction of a goal post by means of a four-foot bat terminating at one end in a circular curve, netted with leather strings. After the game had gone on for some time, the ball was worked toward the gate and finally was hit over into the fort. The players dashed to retrieve the ball, but as they reached the gates the Indian women passed them the weapons they had been hiding and the attack began. The French traders went to their homes and were not harmed, but within minutes twenty British soldiers and one English trader lay dead. One who escaped was Alexander Henry, who concealed himself in the attic of Langlade's house. Years later Henry wrote a vivid account of the frightful events:

> Through an aperture which afforded me a view of the area of the fort, I beheld, in shapes the foulest and most horrible, the ferocious

triumphs of barbarian conquerers. The dead were scalped and mangled; the dying were writhing and shrieking under the unsatiated knife and tomahawk; and from the bodies of some, ripped open, their butchers were drinking the blood, scooped up in the hollow of joined hands and quaffed amid shouts of rage and victory.[2]

With Captain Etherington at Michilimackinac were Lieutenant William Leslye, whom he had succeeded in command, and Lieutenant John Jamet. The fort at the Sault had burned the preceding December, and Jamet and his small force had sought refuge at Michilimackinac. Jamet was killed while defending himself with his sword. Leslye and Etherington were taken prisoner by the victorious Chippewa, along with fifteen soldiers and three English traders. Thus ended what has come down in history as the Massacre at Michilimackinac, a term used by white historians. The Indians regarded this as a victory for their cause, won by the only tactics which could have enabled them to capture a fortified post such as Michilimackinac.

Just why the Chippewa spared their prisoners is not known. It is probable, however, that most, if not all of the prisoners would have been killed were it not for the intercession of the Ottawa Indians from L'Arbre Croche. The latter had not been notified of the planned attack on Michilimackinac either by Minavavana, who prepared the plan, or by Matchekewis, who carried it out. Had they been notified, the Ottawa might not have chosen to participate in the attack, since they were not as anxious to battle the British as were some of the other Great Lakes Indians. Now, however, they were furious at not being able to share in the plunder. They set out at once for Michilimackinac, and arrived there on June 4. They immediately seized all the British prisoners, but after a conference allowed the Chippewa to keep five, while they retained custody of the other prisoners, including Etherington and Leslye. A Chippewa chief who arrived too late for the baggataway festivities killed four of the five prisoners held by the Chippewa. One body was cut up, boiled, and eaten.

The Ottawa carried their prisoners back to L'Arbre Croche. There they were joined by the garrison from Green Bay. The Sauk, Fox, Menominee, and Winnebago Indians in Wisconsin had long been at odds with the French and accordingly had made no trouble for Lieutenant James Gorrell and his garrison which had taken over the old French fort at Green Bay. Gorrell, however, had been sent word by Etherington, who now considered himself and his men safe among the L'Arbre Croche Ottawa, to join him. Gorrell and his men, together with a number of Wisconsin Indians, crossed Lake Michigan to L'Arbre Croche, where Gorrell successfully persuaded the Ottawa to take their prisoners to Montreal and collect a reward from the British authorities. In spite of the objections of the Chippewa, the Indians started for Montreal with their prisoners on July 18 and arrived at their destination less than a month later. Among the prisoners they delivered was Ezekiel Solomon, the first Jewish trader in Michigan. He had been among the first traders to arrive at Michilimackinac in 1761. After the suppression of the Indian uprising, he returned to Michigan and traded in the area for a number of years. His fellow trader during these same years, Alexander Henry, owed his life in 1763 not to the actions of the Ottawa, as Solomon did, but to Henry's friendship with a Chippewa leader, Wawatam, who successfully pleaded with Minavavana to release his friend.[3]

About a week before the Chippewa had captured the fort at Michilimackinac, Potawatomi warriors had overwhelmed the small garrison at Fort St. Joseph where Ensign Francis Schlosser was in command. He apparently paid no heed to the warning of Louis Chevalier, a French resident of the area for more than thirty years, that the Indians intended to attack the fort. On May 25 a group of approximately one hundred Potawatomi from Detroit appeared, saying they had come to visit relatives. They notified Schlosser that they wished to bid him good morning. A Frenchman warned the commandant that the Indians' intentions were not friendly, and Schlosser then hastened to put his men under arms. But it was too late. The fort was already swarming with Indians, and Schlosser was seized and eleven soldiers were killed. Only three soldiers were spared. They, along with Schlosser, were taken to Detroit, where they were handed over to Gladwin.

Even though the Indians were successful in capturing every British post west of Niagara except Detroit, Pontiac's inability to take this crucial outpost led to the failure of this great Indian uprising. Captain James Dalyell reached the besieged fort at the end of July with 260 redcoats to assist in the defense. Dalyell, contemptuous of the Indians, at once urged Gladwin to take the offensive and launch a surprise night attack on Pontiac's camp. Gladwin at first demurred but at length consented. The emergence of the British force at 2:30 a.m. on July 31 was quickly reported by Indian spies, and approximately two miles from the fort, Dalyell and his men were ambushed by Pontiac and more than four hundred Indians. The fighting raged along what was then called Parent's Creek but which was thereafter dubbed Bloody Run. Before the British could fight their way back to the fort, twenty of their number, including Captain Dalyell, were dead, forty-two were wounded, and an uncounted number taken prisoner.

In spite of this success, Pontiac was in trouble. Detroit continued to be supplied by ship, and there seemed to be no prospect that the siege could be successful since the Indians did not have the weapons and skills needed to cut off the flow of waterborne supplies to the British. Delegations of Indians from beyond Detroit began seeking peace with Gladwin. On September 9, seventy Potawatomi from the St. Joseph region arrived and asked for peace. Pontiac's forces began to melt away, particularly when news came from the east that Colonel Henry Bouquet had inflicted a defeat on the Indians at the Battle of Bushy Creek. During October, several Indian chiefs smoked the pipe of peace with Gladwin. As the first snows of winter fell, more of Pontiac's allies wanted to leave in order to provide their families' winter food needs. Finally, in desperation, Pontiac sent a messenger to the French commandant at Fort Chartres, Major Neyon de Villiers, seeking his help. De Villiers had just learned that the treaty of peace had been signed and that France had ceded all her lands east of the Mississippi to Great Britain. He was only interested in waiting for the British to assume control of the fort so he could return to France. He thus informed Pontiac that there was no longer any possibility of French assistance in the attack on Detroit, and advised him to give up the fight.

Therefore, on October 31, Pontiac accepted the fact that he had failed. He sent Gladwin a message, written down for him by a Frenchman, in which the Ottawa leader announced that he was abandoning the siege. He also expressed a wish to begin peace talks. A few days later, however, Pontiac and a few of his devoted followers slipped away to the Maumee River area, where they spent the winter. In March of 1764, Pontiac went to Illinois and talked of resuming the war against the British. He abandoned such ideas when it became obvious that he had little support even among his fellow Ottawas. Had he attempted to go ahead with his military plans it would have been a futile gesture. Colonel John Bradstreet was sent by General Thomas Gage, who had succeeded Amherst as British commander-in-chief, on an expedition across northern Ohio, and on August 26, 1764, Bradstreet reached Detroit, where representatives of the western tribes were assembled. They acknowledged the sovereignty of King George, agreed to surrender all their captives, and promised to make war on any tribe that turned against the British. Another expedition from Fort Pitt, under Colonel Bouquet, was necessary to finally pacify the western natives and convince them that further resistance was pointless.

At Oswego, New York, Sir William Johnson presided over a great peace council in July, 1766, that put the finishing touches on the peace arrangements hammered out earlier by Bradstreet and Bouquet. Pontiac himself was present at this council, and he, like the other leaders who were present, stood up and pledged to work for peace between the British and the Indians during the remainder of his life. The great Michigan Indian leader appears to have kept his word, as he went among the tribes of the Midwest and preached that the realities of the situation, if nothing else, made it impractical for the Indians to oppose the presence of the British among them. It was because of his pro-British attitude, apparently, that members of the Peoria tribe in Illinois murdered Pontiac in the spring of 1769. Others took his body across the Mississippi and buried him in St. Louis.

Following Colonel Bradstreet's arrival in Detroit in August of 1764, Henry Gladwin, having served his king most capably, returned to England, where he lived the life of a country gentleman until his death in 1791. Bradstreet sent Captain William Howard to reoccupy Michilimackinac. Charles Langlade, who had done what he could to save the British garrison, now carried out a plan he had made before the uprising to move his headquarters to Green Bay, where he had numerous relatives. Here he spent the remainder of his life, although during the American Revolution he fought with the British against the thirteen colonies. However, he became reconciled to American control and lived until early in the nineteenth century. He became known as the "father of Wisconsin," and a county in that state is named for him.[4]

The British did not reestablish permanent garrisons after the Indian uprising either at Sault Ste. Marie or at Fort St. Joseph. Around the latter place the Potawatomi villages continued to be occupied and it continued to be a rendezvous for fur traders. Louis Chevalier was given the responsibility of guarding British interests in the St. Joseph Valley following the suppression of the Indian outbreak. He was under the supervision of the commandant at Michilimackinac.

Having acquired a vast new territory from the French under the peace treaty signed at Paris on February 10, 1763, the British were confronted with the problem of how to govern it. The responsibility for formulating a policy was entrusted to the Earl of Shelburne, who was president of the Board of Trade. Unlike many of his contemporaries who spent their time drinking and gambling, Shelburne was industrious and well-read. On June 8, 1763, he proposed the policy that was adopted by the British government and announced in October, 1763. It is known as the Proclamation of 1763.

Shelburne drew up his plan before news of the Indian uprising led by Pontiac had reached England. Nevertheless, its provisions were based on considerations related to the Indian problem. During the French and Indian War the British, in order to secure Indian support, had signed the Treaty of Easton with several chiefs, pledging that the region west of the Alleghenies would be reserved for the natives. The British had also pacified the Cherokee in the south by making a pledge similar to the one they had made to the northern tribes at Easton. Hence the British government, if it was to keep its pledges to the Indians, had to reserve the trans-Allegheny region for them. The need to take steps to counter the menace of Indian revolt was underscored when news reached England of Pontiac's attack on Detroit and the Indian assaults on other British-held posts. This news hastened the issuance of the Proclamation by the British authorities.[5]

The Proclamation reserved all the lands west of the Alleghenies for the Indians, and no purchases of Indian lands were to be made except through imperial agents. Traders were required to take out licenses from the governor or commander-in-chief of the colony where they resided. The Proclamation provided for civil government in the Province of Quebec, but that province was to include only the French settlements along the St. Lawrence. This left the entire Great Lakes area under military rule.

Several of the thirteen colonies had claims under their charters on the region west of the Alleghenies. The Proclamation nullified these claims, and this nullification became one of the basic causes for the animosity against the mother country that led to the American Revolution. The Proclamation was not intended to be permanent, but rather was designed as a temporary expedient to quiet hostile Indians. The British appear to have contemplated a gradual and orderly acquisition of Indian lands through purchase by imperial agents, which lands would then be opened to settlement. By failing to provide civil government for Detroit, Michilimackinac, and other western posts, the Proclamation left the French people who resided at these places, as well as the British who came to them, under military rule until the passage of the Quebec Act in 1774.

The method of regulating the fur trade was a major problem facing the British after the defeat of Pontiac. As early as 1756 the British government had appointed two imperial agents, one in the

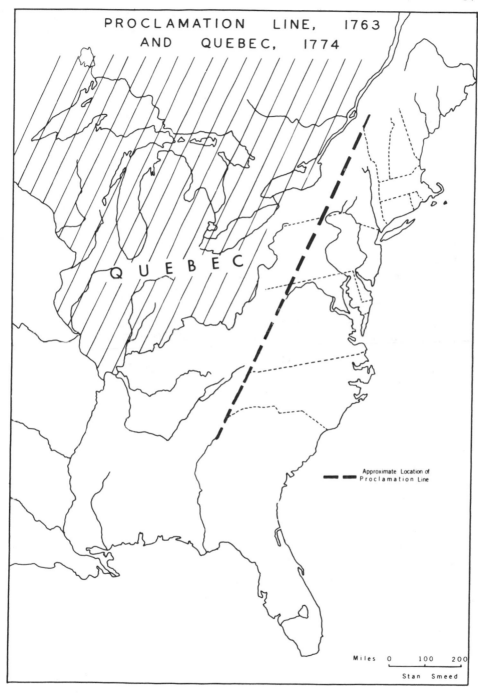

PROCLAMATION LINE, 1763
AND QUEBEC, 1774

Q U E B E C

Approximate Location of
Proclamation Line

Miles 0 100 200

Stan Smeed

North and the other in the South, to regulate the fur trade. The appointee in the North was Sir William Johnson, whose prestige and influence among the Indians made him particularly well suited to the task of developing policies that would assuage the Indians' fears and hostilities. In November of 1763, Johnson proposed a comprehensive plan to place Indian affairs entirely in the hands of the two imperial agents, himself in the North and Captain John Stuart in the South. The plan would be administered by their agents, who were called commissaries. These commissaries were to control prices, keep the traders from cheating the natives, and see that the rules of the trade were enforced. They were to act in cooperation with the military commandants at the various posts, who were subject to the orders of the commander-in-chief of the British forces in America. Johnson advised that all trade be confined to the posts and that each trader be licensed. This plan was received with favor by the Board of Trade in London, but it never received full approval. In January, 1765, General James Murray issued a proclamation declaring hostilities with the natives at an end and opening the fur trade at designated posts, including Detroit and Michilimackinac, to licensed traders. In spite of the fact that no authorization had been received from London, Johnson's plan was partially put into effect. It evoked a storm of protest from Montreal merchants, particularly that part of it that prohibited trade outside the posts. Spanish and French traders operating out of New Orleans and St. Louis would capture a large part of the peltry trade, it was feared, if the British traders were confined to the posts. At Michilimackinac, Captain Howard issued permits to a few individuals to conduct trade outside the post, an action for which he was harshly criticized by those who were denied the coveted permits.

One of the factors that created delay and uncertainty in America was the frequent changes in ministries at the British capital. Shelburne, who had been responsible for the Proclamation of 1763, was replaced by Lord Hillsborough even before the Proclamation was issued. But in 1767 Shelburne was back in office. He did not share Johnson's view that the West should be kept as a permanent reserve for Indians and fur traders. He had never intended that the Proclamation should be more than a temporary policy. He saw in the West a great area for future settlement and colonization, whereas Johnson thought of it only in terms of the fur trade and Indian relations. Shelburne suggested the formation of three new colonies: one around Detroit, another in the Illinois country, and a third on the Ohio River. He proposed to let the thirteen colonies control the fur trade, to withdraw the troops gradually, and to open the area for settlement in an orderly fashion. Before the talented Shelburne could press the plan upon the king there was another political overturn and Hillsborough once more replaced him. Hillsborough's plan was neither to follow a determined policy of imperial control nor to put the responsibility squarely on the colonies. The Indian agents were retained, but with reduced authority. The colonies were to pay the salaries of the lesser officials at the posts and were to supply presents for the Indians, a wholly impractical idea. No new colonies were to be authorized. The plan utterly failed to give the colonies any stake in the West, yet, for reasons of economy, it made imperial control ineffective.

The Proclamation of 1763 had virtually invalidated the claims and dashed the hopes of the land speculation companies that had been formed just prior to the French and Indian War in Virginia and Pennsylvania. But there was a rash of new schemes in the years following 1763, based on the expectation that the terms of the Proclamation would be modified or reversed. A Virginia group, which included on its roster of members the Washingtons and the Lees, and a Pennsylvania company that included Benjamin Franklin among its members, sought to induce the British government to grant large tracts of land for purposes of settlement. Several other such companies were formed in America. Major Robert Rogers, commandant at Fort Michilimackinac during part of the period, and Jonathan Carver, one of his subordinates, each made a proposal for new western colonies, including one centering around Detroit. Largely through pressure from land speculators and the companies they formed, the imperial agents negotiated with the Indians for an extension westward of the Proclamation line. Although the larger schemes of the land speculators seemed at times close to realization, they failed to materialize prior to the outbreak of the Revolution. The opposition of the great fur merchants in London, and the probability that any large-scale colonization would have sparked a new Indian revolt probably were the principal factors in bringing about the failure of the schemes of the land speculators.

Thus Michigan and the entire Great Lakes area remained Indian country, with the British asserting their authority only at a few isolated posts. In the interests of economy, garrisons were maintained after 1771 only at Detroit and Michilimackinac. Trade revived at Detroit, where Indians from the entire lower lakes region brought their annual catches to exchange for clothing, guns, ammunition, trinkets, and—whenever possible—intoxicating liquor. The French *habitants,* scattered along both banks of the Detroit River, appeared quite indifferent to the change in masters, so long as they could enjoy their small farms and orchards, have a hand in the fur trade, and worship in their beloved church. Although Detroit remained under military rule, a magistrate was appointed and petty disputes were settled by suits at law.

The most colorful figure appearing at Michilimackinac during the British regime was Major Robert Rogers. After he had successfully carried out his assignment to accept the surrender of Detroit to the British in 1760, he was sent to the Carolinas to help put down the revolt of the Cherokee. While there he met Governor Arthur Dobbs, the aging governor of North Carolina, who long had been fascinated by the lure of the imaginary Northwest Passage. He appears to have found an ardent disciple in Rogers, who accepted his belief that there was a waterway between Hudson Bay and the Pacific Ocean. In 1765 Rogers went to London in quest of authority and financial backing to make a search for this passage. He had resigned his military commission, having gotten into the ill graces of both General Gage and Sir William Johnson. But he made quite a hit in England, got some influential backers, and won an appointment as commandant at Michilimackinac. When he left England he was confident that his extravagant requests for financial backing, together with permission to undertake the search for a northwest passage, would be forthcoming, although he had no positive assurance of either. He assumed command at Michilimackinac in 1766. In the fall of that year he sent out an expedition to look for the passage. The expedition was led by Jonathan Carver, from whose pen we have vivid descriptions of the West of that day.[6] Carver got only as far as the Grand Portage, north of Lake Superior, when lack of supplies forced him to return.

Soon after the return of Carver, Rogers fell on evil days. Gage and Johnson, both distrustful of Rogers, sent a commissary to watch over his activities. The man chosen was Lieutenant Benjamin Roberts, with whom Rogers had already quarreled. Roberts found that the traders were very favorable to Rogers, for Rogers knew the Indians well and understood every aspect of the fur trade. Disregarding orders to confine the trade to an area near the fort, Rogers granted permission to the traders to venture in all directions. In 1767, thirty-two canoes carrying trade goods left Michilimackinac for Lake Superior, sixty canoes for Green Bay, and twenty-nine for other destinations in Lake Huron and Lake Michigan. Because he was heavily in debt, Rogers traded on his own account, which was forbidden, although this was essentially what officers since Cadillac's day had always done. Rogers also allowed liquor to be used in trading, another violation of his orders. Needless to say, he was soon involved in a bitter quarrel with Roberts. Although they managed to compose their differences temporarily, Rogers was accused of conspiring to join hands with the French traders operating out of St. Louis. For this he was arrested and taken in chains back to Montreal for trial. Despite the efforts of his powerful enemies to convict him on a charge of treason, he was acquitted and returned to England where he was again lionized for a time. Rogers' career, however, was ultimately ruined by the charges that had been made against him, and the remaining years of his life were increasingly tragic ones for him.[7]

The British also made an effort while Rogers was at Michilimackinac to exploit the mineral wealth of the Lake Superior region. Much earlier the French had discovered that the shores of this great lake abounded in copper, but they had not vigorously pursued mining the mineral. Apparently through his acquaintance with Rogers, Charles Townshend, a British official, became interested in the possibility of exploiting the mineral wealth of this region. He commissioned Rogers to investigate the possibilities, and Rogers responded in 1767 by engaging Henry Bostwick, a British trader, and Jean Baptiste Cadotte, who was acquainted with the Indian legends and the stories of the French attempts at mining, to make an exploratory trip. Alexander Baxter, Jr., son of the Russian consul at London, also appeared at Michilimackinac, probably because of his interest in the project. Baxter was a mining expert and upon examining the data and specimens collected by Bostwick and Cadotte became convinced there were great riches to be gained by exploiting the area. A company was formed for the purpose by a group of English noblemen and funds were subscribed. Alexander Henry, a fur trader, was also involved in the project. A shipyard was set up near Sault Ste. Marie, a fort was constructed, an assaying furnace was begun, and men were sent out to collect ores. It was confidently expected that gold and silver, as well as copper, would be found.

The fur traders disliked all this hubbub and looked askance at the establishment of a fort near the Sault. Meanwhile Lieutenant John Nordberg, another Russian mining expert, found a stone that assayed in London seventy-five percent silver. The promoters were elated and redoubled their efforts. Workmen were first taken to the mouth of the Ontonagon River, where some mining was attempted in 1771, but in 1772 prospecting was shifted to the northeast shore of Lake Superior, where a shaft thirty feet deep was sunk. The vein did not prove profitable, and the next year the project was suspended. Thus ended the British effort to exploit a source of wealth that one day was to prove far richer than the commerce in furs.

Persistent reports of disorder and even disloyalty in the West reached the British commander, General Gage, but nothing was done to meet repeated demands from Detroit, and even from the Illinois country, for civil government. An alternative, seriously considered and favored by Gage, was to deport the French residents of Illinois, and perhaps others in the West, in the manner in which the British had earlier uprooted the Acadians from Nova Scotia and sent them to Louisiana. "Let the savages enjoy their Deserts in quiet," advised Gage. But when the Earl of Hillsborough, who favored Gage's plan, was succeeded as president of the Board of Trade by the Earl of Dartmouth whose ideas were quite different, the policy of deportation was abandoned.

In 1774, Parliament passed the Quebec Act, which extended the boundaries of the Province of Quebec west to the Mississippi River and south as far as the Ohio River. French civil law was to be applied, but in criminal cases British law would prevail. Religious liberty was to be enjoyed by Roman Catholics, whereas only limited toleration was the rule in England at the time. Four lieutenant governors were to be appointed, one each for Detroit, Michilimackinac, the Illinois settlements, and Vincennes. The governor of Quebec was to have an appointed legislative council, but there was no provision for an elected assembly, since representative government was not part of the French inhabitants' cultural heritage. When the Revolution broke out, this act helped to retain the allegiance of the French people of Quebec to Great Britain, and caused them to turn a cold shoulder to proposals of the Continental Congress that they join in the revolt against the mother country. Their priests felt that the full freedom of worship accorded Roman Catholics in the Quebec Act might be more than they could expect were the Puritan New Englanders to have a voice in their affairs. But so far as the thirteen colonies were concerned, the Quebec Act was associated with the other "coercive laws" passed in 1774 to discipline the colonies. In fact it is the only British act specifically referred to in the Declaration of Independence. The omission of an elected assembly in the Quebec Act was cited in the Declaration as evidence of the intent of the king's government to impose tyranny on America. By extending the boundaries of the Province of Quebec, the Quebec Act was also viewed by Americans as invalidating the claims of Virginia, Massachusetts, and Connecticut to western lands even though the act contained a provision specifically denying this intent.

Sir Guy Carleton, who became governor of Quebec, appointed Henry Hamilton as lieutenant governor at Detroit the year following the passage of the Quebec Act. Inferior courts of jurisdiction were to be established both at Detroit and at Michilimackinac, with appeals possible to the superior courts at Quebec and Montreal. This was the extent of civil government in Michigan. The revolt of the thirteen colonies, which started in 1775, made it impractical to carry out the plans for civil government. Hamilton became the commander of the British forces around Detroit as well as the chief resident civil official; thus, there was little real modification of military rule, except that marriages could now be legally registered, petty disputes could be resolved by civil processes, and matters such as the inheritance of property could be handled in a legal manner.

*   *   *   *   *

The American Revolution, which delayed for more than a decade the full implementation of the Quebec Act, was, to a considerable extent, more the direct result of problems growing out of administering and developing Britain's new western lands, such as Michigan, than it was of the events around Boston that American historians traditionally have emphasized. It had cost the British taxpayer a pretty penny to pay for the French and Indian War. The British national debt more than doubled. After the war, the cost of maintaining garrisons and officials at places such as Detroit and Michilimackinac meant a further drain on the British treasury. It was about time, the British government concluded, that the colonies paid part of the bill. The Americans protested the taxes that Parliament proceeded to impose on them, partly because of their natural aversion to any taxes, and partly because they contended that they received no benefits from the maintenance of British garrisons in the West which the taxes were designed to pay for; rather, the profits from the fur trade which these garrisons protected went into the pockets of London merchants. The colonists were denied the legal right to settle on the western lands by the terms of the Proclamation of 1763, although these were not fully observed. The resentment of the Virginians in particular against the closing of the West to settlement persuaded them to join forces with the New Englanders, who were protesting the new taxes. This combination of forces from New England and Virginia made possible the American Revolution and victory for the patriots.

During the Revolution, as during the earlier colonial wars between Britain and France, no actual fighting between the principal combatants occurred on Michigan soil, but Michigan again played a major role in the war, this time as the center of British power in the West, just as it had been the center of French power in the earlier conflicts. The Indians, who only a dozen years before had fought to drive the British out of this region, now fought with them against the Americans. British policy after 1763 had been designed to assuage the Indians and to prevent encroachment on their lands by colonial farmers. Thus it was inevitable that the natives would side with the British, because an American victory would, Indian leaders quite correctly foresaw, have disastrous consequences for the Indians of the Middle West. The Continental Congress never entertained the hope that the Indians could be persuaded to support the patriot cause, but rather concentrated its efforts on keeping the Indian tribes neutral. Even with this limited objective, only the Shawnee and the Delaware tribes promised to remain neutral.

In the Michigan area, the veteran frontier soldier, Charles Langlade, organized and led Indian war parties in support of the British as he had done so many times on behalf of the French in earlier wars. In fact, on July 4, 1776, when the Declaration of Independence was being signed in Philadelphia, Langlade was departing from Michilimackinac on an assignment designed to prevent the revolutionists from achieving their goal of independence. Much of the attention of Langlade, the Michigan Indians, and the British authorities was directed at Kentucky, then part of Virginia, where a few settlements had been established in violation of the Proclamation of 1763. The Indians resented this invasion of their hunting grounds, and the Revolution afforded them an open invitation to attack these settlements. Indians around Detroit demanded that Governor Hamilton furnish them with arms, ammunition, and supplies for their forays against the Kentuckians, and pay them a bounty for the scalps they brought back. Although reluctant to let loose the barbarism of an Indian war, Hamilton had no alternative if he was to retain the loyalty of the Indians to the British cause. This was no excuse in the eyes of the Kentuckians, who nicknamed Hamilton "the hair-buyer"—a term that has stuck with Hamilton, despite the work of recent historians who have shown that the practice of taking scalps was not one that Hamilton actively encouraged. These historians have also shown that Hamilton's policy of turning the Indians loose was dictated by his superiors and carried out by other British officers as well, who have escaped Hamilton's fate of being branded an early-day war criminal.[8]

Tiring of the constant raids, George Rogers Clark, a young Kentuckian, determined that the best defense was to take the offensive. He journeyed to the Virginia capital of Williamsburg in the winter of 1777–78, where he obtained approval and some assistance from Governor Patrick Henry to attack the British-held posts in the

Illinois country and ultimately to advance north and attack the bases in Michigan from which the Indian attacks originated. By this time an alliance of the Americans with France had become a certainty and Clark hoped to use this as a lever to secure the backing of the French inhabitants in the West. His little army reached Kaskaskia in southern Illinois on July 4, 1778, approaching so stealthily that its defenders had little chance to resist. Nearby Cahokia was occupied without any resistance. The local priest, Father Pierre Gibault, was among those whom Clark won over to the American cause, after he promised the priest that the Americans would not interfere with Catholic worship. Gibault not only helped convert the local French inhabitants to the patriot cause, but also journeyed overland to Vincennes, where his persuasion was important in securing for Clark the support of the local French inhabitants. Ever after, Father Gibault was known as the "patriot priest." He had come to the Illinois country in 1768, and was for many years one of very few Catholic priests in the Middle West after the departure of the Jesuits, who had left in 1762 when they were expelled from France and French possessions by order of the king. On his way out to Illinois in 1768, Gibault stopped at Michilimackinac and Fort St. Joseph to hear confessions, to baptize, and to perform marriage ceremonies, and from his base in Kaskaskia he made at least two more missionary trips to Michigan. He was at Fort St. Joseph in 1773, where he made the last entry in the register of the mission begun over eighty years before, and at Michilimackinac in 1775, returning from the latter by way of Detroit.[9]

By August of 1778, Clark was in control of the Illinois country. The alliance of the Indians with the British threatened to come apart in the face of Clark's confidence, his blustering speeches, and his distribution of presents. When Hamilton in Detroit learned of Clark's actions, he hastened to take counter measures. He summoned the Indians, gathered supplies, and enlisted the militia for a retaliatory blow. He left Detroit on October 7 with approximately 250 men. Their route led them down the Detroit River to Lake Erie and into the Maumee River, which they followed to its source. Then they went over a short portage to the Wabash and down that river to Vincennes, which they reached after a journey of seventy-one days. Since Captain Leonard Helm, whom Clark had sent to take possession of the fort at Vincennes, known as Fort Sackville, had but one man to help him, he had no recourse but to surrender. The 621 inhabitants of Vincennes were summoned by Hamilton to renew their oaths of allegiance to Britain.

The capture of Vincennes by Henry Hamilton was the prelude

to one of the most heroic exploits in American history. When Clark learned that Vincennes had fallen to the British, he decided that since his own small force was no match for Hamilton's, the only hope he had of recapturing the Indiana outpost was by means of a surprise attack. Actually, only a third of Hamilton's attacking force remained with him as the Indians and most of the militia returned to their homes once Fort Sackville had been captured. In any event, Clark reasoned that Hamilton would not think the Americans would move on Vincennes in mid-winter, but that is precisely what Clark did. With 172 men, he proceeded overland on February 6, 1779, sending supplies by the water route down the Mississippi to the Ohio, and then up the Ohio to the Wabash and on to Vincennes. Clark's men, half-starved, waded through deep mud in driving, cold rains, often fording streams where they had to break the ice with their shoulders as they waded across. Hamilton was unaware of Clark's approach until Clark opened fire on the fort. The townspeople were easily won over and furnished the Americans with supplies of ammunition and food which they had hidden away. The Kentucky riflemen, with deadly accuracy, picked off the British defenders, and on February 25, Hamilton surrendered the fort and its seventy-nine defenders to Clark. Hamilton was then taken to Williamsburg, where he was confined for many months in the jail that is now one of the leading tourist attractions in the restored colonial city. He was never brought to trial for the atrocities for which he had been held responsible. Eventually, this ex-lieutenant-governor of Detroit was handed back to the British, and he finished out his career as governor of the British colony of Bermuda, the capital of which is named in his honor.[10]

Clark's victory created a new situation in the upper Middle West. The Indians began to waver in their support of the British. Colonel Arent Schuyler de Peyster, the commander at Michilimackinac, had called Charles Langlade from Green Bay and Charles Gautier, another who was, like Langlade, engaged in the fur trade when not on military assignment, to organize an Indian force to cooperate with Hamilton in the attack he had planned to make from Vincennes to recapture control of Kaskaskia and Cahokia. When the Indian war party arrived at what is now Milwaukee it learned of Hamilton's surrender. At once the Indians turned insolent and refused to go further. Already they had been somewhat affected by agents sent among them by Clark. De Peyster received reports that the Ottawa and Chippewa had promised American agents that they would remain neutral in the event of an attack on Michilimackinac.

At Detroit, Captain Richard Lernoult, who had succeeded Hamilton in command there, was told by the Wyandot that they intended to make peace with the Americans. At a council held in June of 1779, Ottawa, Chippewa, and Potawatomi chieftains in the Detroit area made similar declarations. Lernoult, anticipating that Clark would strike north at Detroit, hastened to strengthen the defenses of Detroit by building a new fort on a hill located behind the town, from which point an attacking enemy force, equipped with cannon, could have forced the surrender of the old French fort on the river. Designed to withstand an attack by a properly equipped army rather than to impress the Indians, the new bastion was named Fort Lernoult.[11]

Colonel De Peyster, who wrote verses that provide interesting insights into life in Michigan in these years and who eventually retired to Scotland where he became the close friend of another poet, Robert Burns,[12] was transferred from Michilimackinac to the command at Detroit. Major Patrick Sinclair replaced de Peyster at Michilimackinac, arriving there in the fall of 1779. Sinclair at once decided to relocate the fort at the Straits on Mackinac Island, where he would be in a better position for a defense against an American attack than he would be within the decaying walls of the old French fort along the shores of Lake Michigan. Between 1779 and 1781, a new fort was built on the south side of Mackinac Island. Materials from the old fort were used in the new post and in the adjacent settlement, with some buildings, including the Catholic church, being hauled in their entirety or in sections over the frozen surface of the Straits in the winter. What was left of the old fort was destroyed when the island fort was occupied in 1781. When Francis Parkman visited the site in 1845, there was little that was visible to help him recreate the scene of the Indian attack of 1763. However, much remained beneath the surface which archaeologists have uncovered since 1959, and which has enabled many of the fort's buildings to be reconstructed on their original locations.

As it turned out, neither Fort Lernoult nor the new Fort Michilimackinac would have had to have been built since George Rogers Clark was never able to organize the forces needed for an assault on the British bases in Michigan. Instead, in 1780, the British took the offensive, and planned an attack on the Illinois settlements, to be launched from Michilimackinac. An Indian force of more than seven hundred warriors was assembled by Charles Langlade and other traders, with supplies being provided from Michilimackinac. The force, which included several Sioux warriors, gathered at Prairie du Chien, where the Wisconsin River enters the Mississippi. The foray was directed against Spanish St. Louis as well as Kaskaskia and Cahokia, since Spain had joined the war against Great Britain in 1779. Langlade's forces assaulted both Cahokia and St. Louis on May 26, 1780, but without Langlade's customary success. Both places fended off the attacks, and in a short time counter-measures against the British were being planned.

Early in 1781, an emissary of the French government, Colonel Mottin de la Balme, arrived in Illinois to rally the French residents against Britain. As a result of his efforts an expedition was organized that captured the British post on the Maumee River near present-day Fort Wayne, Indiana. But Miami Indians under Chief Little Turtle pursued La Balme and killed almost all of the invaders, including La Balme. Of more interest to Michigan's history, an expedition of sixteen men from Cahokia had marched against Fort St. Joseph in December, 1780. There had been no garrison at that southwestern Michigan fort since the 1763 uprising, and the Indians who lived nearby were away on their winter hunt. Some fifty bales of goods were seized and several traders were taken prisoner. But as the raiders were retreating down the shore of Lake Michigan, they were overtaken near the present site of Michigan City, Indiana, by a pursuing band of British militiamen and traders. Four were killed, two were wounded, seven surrendered, and three escaped in the woods. The goods and captives they had carried off were confiscated.[13]

Fort St. Joseph, though not garrisoned, was a place of some importance to the British during the Revolution. In 1779, De Peyster had sent his second-in-command at Michilimackinac, Lieutenant Thomas Bennett, with a force of twenty soldiers and sixty traders and Indians to Fort St. Joseph to intercept an American detachment that, he had been informed, was coming up the Wabash to occupy the place. The rumor proved not to be based on fact. Bennett arrived at Fort St. Joseph, which apparently was in ruins, and is believed to have built a fortification on the western side of the river. His attempt to obtain pledges of support for the British cause from the neighboring Potawatomi ended in failure. Even the arrival of Langlade with a reinforcement of sixty Chippewa did not change the attitude of the natives, and Bennett returned to Michilimackinac. The following year Sinclair, who had succeeded De Peyster at Michilimackinac, decided it would be best for the British cause if the inhabitants at the site of Fort St. Joseph were removed. Louis Chevalier, the trader on whom the British had relied, was now suspected of secretly favoring the American cause. He and his wife were brought to Michilimackinac along with the others. He was subsequently taken to Montreal, where he was tried and acquitted of charges of disloyalty.

Apparently some traders were left at Fort St. Joseph, and they were the ones who were captured by the French raiding party from Cahokia, and later released by the force which overtook and broke up the raiding party. The British force was under the command of Lieutenant Dagneau de Quindre who had been sent from Michilimackinac by Sinclair to safeguard the place. He and his men appear to have been encamped some distance from the old fort when the raiding party arrived. As soon as the news of the disaster which had befallen the raiding party reached Cahokia and St. Louis across the Mississippi River, a retaliatory force was recruited. Don Eugenio Pouré, a militia captain at St. Louis, was given command by the Spanish commandant at St. Louis, Don Francisco Cruzat, who organized the expedition. It included sixty-five militiamen, both Spanish from St. Louis and French from Cahokia, and at least sixty Indians. Setting out in the dead of winter, the party arrived at Fort St. Joseph on February 12, 1781, after following the portage from the Kankakee to the St. Joseph River. One of the members of the party was Louison Chevalier, son of the trader now under suspicion by the British. The fort was taken and the Spanish flag was raised, giving Niles the distinction of being the only place in Michigan which has been under four flags. The Spanish control of the area was transitory at best, however, for after gathering all the loot it could carry, the expedition, after only twenty-four hours, took the flag down and left Fort St. Joseph to make its way back to Cahokia and St. Louis.

To this day, the motives behind this raid on Fort St. Joseph remain unclear. Older historians were inclined to believe that it was designed to give Spain a claim on the lands east of the Mississippi. Some of the more recent investigators, who have had access to the Spanish archives, reject this theory, declaring that although the Spanish did seek to use the raid to advance their claims to these areas, this was after the raid had taken place. There is no evidence that the raid was officially inspired or ordered by the Madrid government. Another suggestion is that it was planned to forestall another possible attack on Cahokia and St. Louis by destroying supplies that were presumed to have been deposited at Fort St. Joseph for such an expedition. Other writers, however, view the raid as having been inspired by the hope for loot, or a wish to revenge the defeat suffered by the raiding party of the preceding year, or that it was part of an effort by the Spanish to strengthen ties with certain Indian groups.[14]

The British in Detroit continued to plan expeditions against both Clark in Illinois and Fort Pitt, while Clark and the commander at Fort Pitt planned to attack Detroit. None of these plans succeeded, although there was a great deal of fighting in the Ohio valley area even after the surrender at Yorktown in the fall of 1781, which virtually ended hostilities in the East. Not until De Peyster received word in April of 1783 that a treaty of peace had been signed, did hostilities cease in the western country.

During the war there was an episode in Michigan history that demonstrated the plight of those who chose not to fight on either side. A religious group called Moravians, who came originally from Germany to settle at Bethlehem, Pennsylvania, had established some missions among the Indians near the present town of Tuscarawas in southern Ohio. The missionaries had taught the Indians arts and crafts, as well as their religion, which, like that of the Quakers, was opposed to war. When the Revolution broke out the Moravians and their Delaware charges attempted to stay neutral. This was difficult because the patriots regarded all the western Indians as openly or secretly disposed toward the British. In order to escape the tide of conflict, the settlement was moved northward to the neighborhood of Sandusky on Lake Erie. Late in 1781 some of the Delaware, called "Christian Indians," returned to their town of Gnadenhutten in southern Ohio to harvest the grain they had planted. While there, a party of Virginians and others deceived them into surrender by telling them they would be taken east for protection. Then the Americans murdered ninety of them in cold blood. David Zeisburger, leader of the mission, had conferred with De Peyster at Detroit regarding the removal of his community to Michigan. Hearing the news of the frightful massacre at Gnadenhutten, Zeisburger and his followers started for Detroit, with their possessions.

For a time the Moravians and their Delaware charges lived in or near Detroit. Zeisburger leaves us this description of the town in April, 1782:

> It is something wonderful here, and pleasant if anyone is found who shows a desire for God's word, for the place here is like Sodom, where all the sins are committed. The French have, indeed, a Church here and a Priest, who, however, is quite old, and never preaches, but merely reads mass. The English and Protestants have neither church nor preacher, and wish for neither, although they could have them if they would.[15]

Somewhat later the Moravians and their Delaware converts were allowed to build a community on the Clinton River near present-day

Mount Clemens. It consisted of twenty-seven log cabins and a meeting house. Land was cleared, crops were raised, and a road was built—the first inland road in Michigan—between the settlement and a mill situated within the present city of Detroit. The community prospered between 1782 and 1786. But when it became clear that Michigan would ultimately be taken over by the United States, most of the group moved to Canada, where they built a town called New Gnadenhutten on the Thames River. Here again a successful and thriving community developed, only to be destroyed once more as a result of war when the armies of William Henry Harrison swept through the area during the War of 1812.

* * * * *

The end of the Revolutionary War found the Americans in somewhat shaky control of Kentucky and the Illinois country and the British still in firm possession of the Great Lakes region, including Michigan. Therefore, had each side kept the territory it controlled at the close of the war, Michigan would have remained in British hands. That this did not happen was due largely to certain aspects of European politics at the time.

Several generations of historians held the belief that the conquests of George Rogers Clark saved Michigan and the Northwest for the United States. But a careful study of the peace negotiations has led the foremost authority on the subject and many other writers in recent years to deny that such was the case. They have concluded that Clark's hold on the Illinois country at the time the peace was negotiated was very weak; there even is some doubt about whether the negotiators were fully acquainted with Clark's earlier victories. And it now seems clear that, in any event, the principal reason the United States was able to obtain title to the area between the Alleghenies and the Mississippi was that Great Britain preferred to see the United States get all this region rather than allowing Spain to obtain a portion of it.[16]

The disaster the British suffered at Yorktown and a change in the ministry made the British government ready to negotiate for peace. A peace commission was appointed and proceeded to Paris, where it met the American negotiators, Benjamin Franklin, John Adams, John Jay, and Henry Laurens. The American commission had been instructed by Congress to negotiate jointly with the French. But when Jay learned that the French foreign minister, Count Vergennes, had sent an aide to London to confer with British officials, he suspected that the French were dealing separately with

Britain, and persuaded his fellow commissioners that this justified them in proceeding with separate negotiations as well. Franklin proposed to the British commission that it would be desirable for Britain to cede all of Canada and Nova Scotia to the United States. But news that the Franco-Spanish assault on British-held Gibraltar had failed, served to stiffen the British attitude, and it became evident that it was out of the question for the United States to secure Canada. The question then was how much territory south of Canada the United States would be able to acquire, and where the boundary lines would be drawn.

The Count of Aranda, Spanish minister at the French court, now attempted to persuade Vergennes to back a plan that would not only return Florida to Spain (it had been lost to Britain in 1763), but would also give Spain a large area east of the Mississippi, extending from the Ohio River to the Gulf of Mexico. Under Aranda's plan the United States would have retained parts of what are now the states of Kentucky, Tennessee, and Ohio. The remainder of the region north of the Ohio would have been allowed to remain in British hands while Spain would have received the area south of Tennessee. The British rejected this proposal, and instead agreed to cede all the region between Canada and Florida, east of the Mississippi to the United States.

But the question remained as to exactly where the boundary between Canada and the United States would be located. The Americans gave the British a choice of two lines: one, the 45th parallel from the St. Lawrence River to the Mississippi, the other, through the middle of Lakes Ontario, Erie, Huron, and Superior, and the rivers connecting these lakes. Had the British accepted the first option, the United States would have secured what is now southern Ontario, but the northern tip of lower Michigan, all of upper Michigan, northern Wisconsin, and northern Minnesota would have remained British. Great Britain would have had title to all the rich iron and copper deposits of the Lake Superior region. The British selected the boundary through the middle of the Great Lakes and their connecting waterways probably because this left them free to use these lakes and waterways for the fur trade and other commercial purposes.[17] This boundary was not surveyed for another forty years, and until that was done, disputes over the precise location of the line described in the treaty were an ever-present threat to peace between the British and their former colonies.

The Treaty of 1783 specifically gave Isle Royale in Lake Superior to the United States. It stated that the water boundary

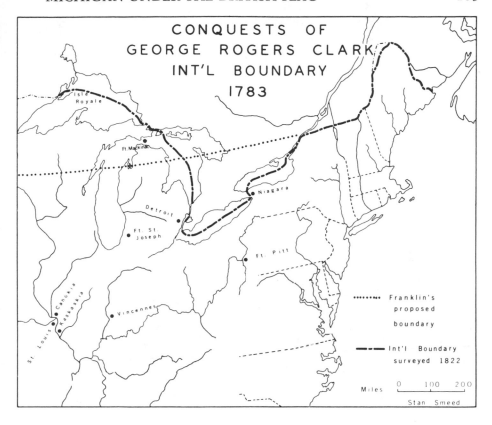

CONQUESTS OF
GEORGE ROGERS CLARK
INT'L BOUNDARY
1783

Franklin's
proposed
boundary

Int'l Boundary
surveyed 1822

Miles   0   100   200

Stan Smeed

should run "northward of the isles Royal and Phelipeaux." The latter
first appeared on a map prepared by the cartographer Bellin in 1744.
The island does not exist, but it continued to appear on maps of Lake
Superior for many years, including the Mitchell map used in the Paris
peace talks of 1783. Many writers and others, including park rangers
at Isle Royale National Park, have perpetuated the story that
Franklin, knowing of the existence of copper deposits on Isle Royale,
managed to include the island within the United States because of
that knowledge. This story, for the most part, has now been dis-
proved. Mitchell's map shows both Isle Royale and the mythical
island of Phelipeaux centrally located in Lake Superior, which was, in
the case of Isle Royale, considerably to the south of where that island
is actually located. According to Mitchell, therefore, the natural
water dividing line that the negotiators were attempting to describe
in the treaty would run north of Isle Royale, which is no doubt the
reason the island was placed on the American side of the line, where

it would ultimately fall within the boundaries of the state of Michigan.[18]

The preliminary articles of peace were signed on November 30, 1782, but they did not take effect until the Anglo-French treaty, settling the war between Britain and France, was signed on September 3, 1783. Even then, however, all provisions of the treaty with the new United States were not immediately carried out. Although Great Britain had agreed to withdraw all of its garrisons from the territory ceded to the United States, this promise was not kept. Until 1796, British soldiers continued to occupy Detroit, Mackinac Island, and other "northwest posts," including Niagara, Oswego, and several forts extending as far east as Lake Champlain. For thirteen years, British occupation of these areas, including Michigan, effectively delayed occupation by the Americans.

There were several reasons for this delay. Even before the treaty had been ratified, influential fur merchants in London were urging the British government to retain the posts for two or three years to give them time to readjust their trading operations. The day before George III proclaimed the treaty, an order went out to America to retain the posts. But instead of keeping the posts for two or three years, the British stayed on for thirteen years, offering as justification the claim that the United States had violated certain terms of the treaty. The United States had agreed to "earnestly recommend" to the states the return of confiscated properties belonging to loyalists who had fled the colonies during the Revolution. Congress made the recommendation but the states did nothing. The treaty also specified that debts owed by Americans to the British prior to the Revolution were obligations still to be honored. The implementation of this treaty provision was again one that was impeded by the actions of the individual states. Nevertheless, it is clear that the British had decided to retain the northwest posts before they knew whether or not the Americans were going to live up to all of their treaty pledges.

The British not only kept their troops at Detroit and the fort on Mackinac Island, they also took measures to establish institutions of civil government in Michigan—political actions which implied an intention to go beyond a mere temporary occupation of the area. Michigan was administered as a part of the province of Quebec, established by the act of 1774. During the Revolution, thousands of loyalists had settled in what is now southern Ontario. Almost at once they began to demand the traditional British rights, such as *habeas corpus,* trial by jury, British commercial law, and an elective assembly. To meet these demands, Sir Guy Carleton, now Lord Dorchester—the governor—established four administrative districts in the region. Detroit, with a population still predominantly French, was included within the District of Hesse. A court of common pleas, sheriff, and justices of the peace were provided for the district. William D. Powell presided over the court of common pleas, which held its sessions at Sandwich (present-day Windsor) on the Canadian side of the Detroit River.

In 1791, a more comprehensive plan for the government of Canada divided Quebec into two provinces: Lower Canada (so-called because it was on the lower reaches of the St. Lawrence River), with a predominantly French population, and Upper Canada, where the small number of French people in Michigan was far outnumbered by approximately twenty-thousand English-speaking loyalists now living in the region of Kingston and Niagara. Each province was to have an elected assembly. John Graves Simcoe, a British officer in the Revolution and an ardent imperialist, was appointed chief executive of Upper Canada with the title of lieutenant governor. Soon after his arrival in the capital of Kingston, counties were established from which representatives were to be chosen to the assembly. Simcoe chose good English names for the counties, as well as for the towns. The Detroit area was divided between the counties of Kent and Essex. In 1792, the first election in Michigan history was held to choose the area's members in the provincial assembly. The victors from the Detroit area were William Macomb, Francois Baby, and David W. Smith. In addition, another area resident, Alexander Grant, was appointed to the lieutenant governor's council. Laws were quickly passed for the introduction of trial by jury, a system of courts and English civil law, replacing the French civil law that previously had prevailed in the area. Another law legalized all marriages that had been contracted irregularly because of the absence of clergy in these remote settlements.

Aside from these political changes, life in Michigan went on much as it had before the war. The Indians continued to bring their furs from great distances, exchanging them for the usual trade goods and for liquor when they could get it. The value of the fur trade at Detroit in 1785 was estimated by one British official at £180,000, of which well over half came from territories within the boundaries of the United States. After 1785, however, the fur trade at Detroit declined, but at Michilimackinac the volume of trade continued to be high. The northern trade was largely in the hands of the North West Company, formed in 1783. Headquarters were on Mackinac Island

MICHIGAN DURING
THE AMERICAN
REVOLUTION

(which the British, however, still called Michilimackinac) adjacent to
the fort. By 1793, the French Revolution began to have an effect on
the fur trade. The French aristocrats, who had always been heavy
buyers of furs, were fleeing into exile or were falling victim to the
guillotine. Keeping the forts in repair and providing for the garrisons
began to be viewed as an increasingly heavy expense which, together
with the decline in the fur trade, was a factor in the British decision

to evacuate these posts. However, the involvement of Great Britain in a new war with France in 1793, and a brilliant victory over the Indians by the American general, Anthony Wayne, were the decisive factors in finally ending the British occupation of Michigan.

Wolverine

6

MICHIGAN AND THE OLD NORTHWEST, 1783–1805

While Michigan was still being governed as part of Canada, decisions that were to play a major role in its future were being reached by the United States. Five of the original thirteen states had claims on all or part of what was then the northwestern part of the country, including Michigan, an area that later became known as the "Old Northwest" when the American boundary was pushed westward beyond the Mississippi. The claims of New York and Pennsylvania were based on treaties they had signed with the Indians granting them certain lands in the West. The claims of Virginia, Massachusetts, and Connecticut arose from provisions in their colonial charters. The Carolinas and Georgia had claims to lands to the south of Kentucky.

The impetus for the surrender of these western land claims originated with Maryland, one of the states that had no such land claims. When the Articles of Confederation were adopted by Congress in 1777 and sent to the states for approval, Maryland announced that it would not ratify this loose bond of union until the landed states gave up their claims to the central government—and without Maryland's support the articles would not take effect since the unanimous approval of all thirteen states was required in the ratification process. Maryland argued that all states, not a favored group, should share in the benefits of the development of the West. Several circumstances gave support to Maryland's case. The fortunes of war were at a low ebb for the Americans and it was apparent that their only hope for success in their quest for independence was to agree upon the basis for a firm union of the states. Thus, in 1780, the Continental Congress made one of the most important policy decisions in American history in an effort to break the deadlock that was delaying the move for the unification of the states. A promise was made that the western lands, if ceded to the central government, would be "formed into separate republican states, which shall become members of the federal union, and have the same rights and sovereignty, freedom, and independence as the other states." This was an ingenious plan which would ultimately lead to the creation of virtually all the new states in the west, including Michigan.

New York ceded its western claims in 1780, and in the same year Pennsylvania agreed to a definite western boundary, including within the state a small outlet to Lake Erie. Virginia's situation was complicated by the rival claims of companies composed of land speculators which had received earlier grants or had bought land from the Indians. As early as 1781, Virginia agreed to cede a large portion of her claims if Congress would agree not to validate any of the claims of the companies whose rights to land were not recognized by Virginia. This was sufficient to persuade Maryland at last to ratify the Articles of Confederation, but it was not until 1784 that Congress finally agreed to Virginia's stipulations and her land cession was completed. This was the decisive step, and the other states ceded their lands soon afterward, including Massachusetts in 1785 and Connecticut in 1786, the two other states with claims to part of Michigan's land area.

Certain reservations were made in the cessions of Massachusetts, Connecticut, and Virginia, with that of Massachusetts being of special importance in the history of Michigan. When ceding her western claims, Massachusetts reserved that portion lying within the state of New York. The same year in which Massachusetts ceded its lands to the United States, its representatives, meeting with New York officials, secured an agreement that Massachusetts should retain title to all the land west of a line drawn south from Sodus Bay on Lake Ontario to the Pennsylvania border, except for a mile-wide strip along the Niagara. Massachusetts also was awarded a tract east of the Sodus Bay-Pennsylvania line, along the upper reaches of the Susquehanna River. New York retained sovereignty over all these lands, but Massachusetts retained title to the land. The Bay State proceeded to dispose of these lands to speculators, who, in turn, sold them to settlers. Most of the people who bought the lands were from the New England states, where a combination of rocky soils and growing population led to a mass exodus into western New York, which became a little New England. These transplanted New En-

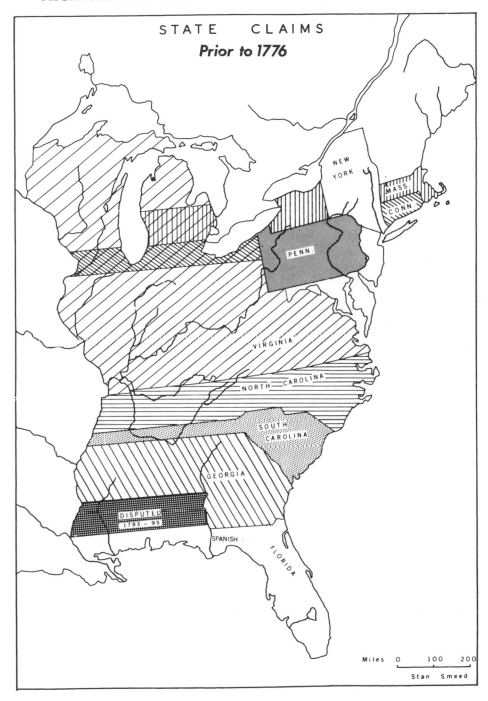

STATE   CLAIMS
Prior to 1776

NEW
YORK

MASS.

CONN.

PENN.

VIRGINIA

NORTH   CAROLINA

SOUTH
CAROLINA

GEORGIA

DISPUTED
1783 - 95

SPANISH

FLORIDA

Miles   0   100   200

Stan   Smeed

glanders and their sons and daughters were to constitute the largest segment of the great migration of settlers to Michigan that took place in the late 1820s and 1830s. The resulting dominance of the New England element in Michigan's population is one of the most significant influences on the state's development.[1]

Once the states had ceded the largest part of their lands to the United States, Congress was faced with the necessity of deciding what would be done with these lands. Its decision was embodied in the Land Ordinance of 1785, one of the most important actions in American history.

From the beginning there were several points of view on what policy should be adopted in disposing of the lands. One faction favored the "southern system," by which the purchaser would obtain a warrant, select the tract he wanted, and then have it surveyed. In contrast, the "New England system" called for a survey of the land in advance of its sale. The latter method was incorporated in the act of 1785. A more basic difference of opinion related to whether the land should be sold in large tracts to wealthy individuals and companies, who would then sell it to actual settlers, or whether it should be sold directly to settlers by the government. Related to this issue was the question of whether the land should be made available readily and on easy terms to promote settlement, or be regarded as a great national resource to be husbanded primarily for the income it would bring to the treasury. The Ordinance of 1785 represented a compromise on all these questions.

The Ordinance provided that the land belonging to the United States should be surveyed, in advance of sale, into townships six miles square, each containing thirty-six "sections" one mile square. A uniform system of numbering the sections was adopted. The townships were to be surveyed from an east-west line called a "base line," and a north-south line called a "prime meridian." The land was to be sold at auction, with a minimum price of $1.00 per acre. The least amount a buyer could purchase was 640 acres. Alternate townships were to be sold intact, while the others were to be sold by sections. Section sixteen in each township was to be reserved from sale for the benefit of schools. Although certain modifications were later made, the Ordinance of 1785 established the policy followed by the United States government for the disposal of virtually all its lands in the West, including those in Michigan.

The subsequent changes in the policy pertained mainly to the minimum amount that could be purchased, the minimum price, and the convenience of the purchaser. A land law passed in 1800 established the minimum price at $2.00 an acre, but made it possible to buy the land on the installment plan, with a down payment of one-quarter the purchase price, and with one-quarter due and payable at the end of one, two, and three years. Because this plan led many buyers to purchase more land than they could pay for, another change in 1820 provided for a cash price of $1.25 an acre. This is the price for which most of the United States government land in Michigan was purchased. In 1862 the Homestead law was enacted, which made it possible for a person to receive 160 acres of government land upon payment of a small fee, by residing on the land for five years. More than three million acres of land in northern Michigan were homesteaded under this law. The minimum amount of land that could be purchased from the government was lowered to 320 acres in 1800, to 160 acres in 1804, and to 80 acres in 1824. The Harrison land law, passed in 1800, provided for land offices in the West; until that time government land could be purchased only in the eastern states. Quite often settlers would build a cabin and start clearing land before it was surveyed, hoping to be able to purchase it when it was placed on the market. These people were called "squatters." In 1841 a "preemption law" gave a person who had settled on land, erected a dwelling, and made certain improvements, the right to purchase 160 acres at the minimum price when the land went on the market.

The reservation of four sections of land for future disposal, included in the act of 1785, was subsequently abandoned, but the reservation of section sixteen in each township for schools became a settled policy. Congress developed the practice of handing over the title of these sections to the states when they were admitted to the Union. These sections were then sold, the proceeds going, in some states, to the townships in which they were situated. Michigan was the first state to place these section sixteen proceeds into a state fund, the income from which was designed as a permanent endowment for schools.

Better known than the Land Ordinance of 1785 and equally important was the ordinance of 1787 which established policies with respect to the government of the western lands and which, because it applied specifically to the Old Northwest, is generally called the Northwest Ordinance. In 1784, Congress had adopted an ordinance, based on recommendations of Thomas Jefferson, that divided the Old Northwest into ten future states, to which Jefferson gave some rather fanciful names. One of these states, under Jefferson's plan, was to be called Michigania, marking the first appearance of this term for a political unit. Jefferson's Michigania, however, would have been located in a portion of what is now the state of Wisconsin. The area that became the present state of Michigan was divided up among

three other states which Jefferson called Metropotamia, Cherrone-
sus, and Sylvania. It was perhaps fortunate for the future residents of
these areas that they were not saddled with any of these names, since
the act of 1784 was never implemented. Instead, it was superseded
by the act of 1787.[2]

The impetus for the passage of the Northwest Ordinance came
from a group of Massachusetts veterans of the Revolution who had
formed an organization called the Ohio Company at a meeting in
Boston on March 1, 1786. The plan for the company originated with
General Rufus Putnam, and was based on the idea of using depreciated paper money, with which the veterans had been paid off, to
buy a tract of land in the West. The job of negotiating with Congress
for the purchase of this land was entrusted to the Reverend Manas-
seh Cutler, who proceeded to negotiate a shady deal with Colonel
William Duer, an official of Congress who handled land sales. The
scheme was to combine the request of the Ohio Company with a
petition for an option to purchase an enormous tract of land by the
Scioto Company, which Duer and several Congressmen had formed.
This arrangement was consummated, although the Scioto Company
never was able to make the payments to take up its option. The Ohio
Company, however, went forward, and in 1788 some of its members
established the first American settlement in the Old Northwest on
the tract it had purchased, founding the city of Marietta (named for
Marie Antoinette of France) on the Muskingum River in the southeastern portion of what is now Ohio.

While negotiating the Ohio Company's land purchase, Cutler
insisted that Congress take action to provide government for the
region in which the tract was located. The Northwest Ordinance was
the outgrowth of this demand. One of the most significant documents in American history, it appears to have been drafted and
passed principally to facilitate the deal made by Cutler and Duer. A
committee, formed on July 9, 1787, made its recommendations two
days later, and two days after this, on July 13, 1787, Congress passed
the ordinance. Although this act was rushed through so hastily, it
proved to be one of the most effective and enduring pieces of legislation any American Congress ever enacted. The 1784 ordinance was
available as a starting point, although Jefferson himself was now the
American minister to France. The greatest defect of Jefferson's plan
had been its failure to provide an orderly procedure for the evolution
of the new states. Congress had debated this matter for years, many
members distrusting the capacity of frontiersmen to govern themselves. The time had come for decision, and Cutler's proposal provided the stimulus for making a decision. A number of modifications

in the action taken in 1787 were made in later years. In the main, however, the outlines of the Northwest Ordinance were followed in providing for government not only in the Old Northwest, but also in the vast area west of the Mississippi that the United States acquired later.

The important provisions of the ordinance may be grouped under three headings: first, it provided for the division of the Old Northwest into not less than three nor more than five states and set forth the boundaries of these future states; second, it stipulated three stages of development through which these divisions would pass as they progressed towards statehood; and third, it contained a statement of rights guaranteed to the people who settled in the region.

With regard to the future states, the ordinance provided that the minimum of three states would be formed by drawing two north-south lines, one northward from Vincennes on the Wabash River, and the other north from the mouth of the Miami River, both lines continuing to the international boundary. These three states thus would have consisted roughly of the present states of Illinois, Indiana, and Ohio plus the areas due north of those three states. The ordinance also provided that Congress might create one or two additional states from the area lying north of a line drawn due east and west through the southernmost tip of Lake Michigan, which would then become the northern boundary of the first three states. This provision was to have special and unexpected consequences in the subsequent evolution of the state of Michigan.

The entire region of the Old Northwest was originally established as the Northwest Territory. The area was in effect a colony of the United States. It was to be governed by a governor, secretary, and three judges, all appointed by Congress.[3] The five territorial officials were empowered to adopt those laws of the original states which were best suited to the territory. Thus at first the people of the territory would not enjoy self-government. However, the ordinance went on to provide that when the territory had a population of 5,000 free, adult males, partial self-government would be inaugurated. At this second stage of territorial development, the voters of the territory (males who owned at least fifty acres of land) were to have the right to elect a house of representatives. In addition, there was to be a legislative council which was to consist of five men selected by Congress from a list of ten nominated by the territorial house of representatives. The laws of the territory were henceforth to be made by the house of representatives, the legislative council, and the governor, the consent of all three being required. The house of representatives and the legislative council were to have the right to choose by joint ballot a delegate to the Congress of the United States, who would have the right to participate in debates, but not the right to vote.

The right to eventual statehood was guaranteed. The ordinance stated that "whenever any of the said states shall have sixty thousand free inhabitants therein, such state shall be admitted by its delegates into the Congress of the United States, on an equal footing with the original states in all respects whatsoever; and shall be at liberty to form a permanent constitution and state government: provided the constitution or government so to be formed, shall be republican and in conformity to the principles contained in these articles. . . ." This right to statehood applied to each of the states into which Congress might eventually determine to divide the Northwest Territory. It was not clear from the ordinance whether each of the future states should pass through the three stages leading to statehood, but this became the accepted policy.

The rights guaranteed to the people who might settle in the Old Northwest conformed to those that had been regarded as the traditional rights of Englishmen. These included the benefit of the writ of *habeas corpus* to safeguard against arbitrary arrest, the right to trial by jury, security of property, and religious freedom. Slavery was prohibited, but this provision was not rigidly enforced. Those residents of the area who owned slaves at the time the United States assumed jurisdiction were allowed to retain them and some additional slaves were apparently brought into the territory in violation of the ordinance prohibition. As a result, considerable numbers of slaves were owned and kept in the southern parts of the Old Northwest, and in Michigan a few slaves were still being held as late as 1830. It must also be remembered that when a state was admitted to the Union it had all the rights of the original states, which included the right to legalize slavery. In fact, there were close contests in both Indiana and Illinois between anti-slavery and pro-slavery forces, although neither state actually legalized the slave system. However, the Northwest Ordinance did establish the precedent, so important in the later conflict between the sections, that Congress had the authority to legislate on the question of slavery in the territories.

One of the most famous statements in the Northwest Ordinance pertains to education: "Religion, morality, and knowledge being necessary to good government and the happiness of mankind, schools and the means of education shall forever be encouraged." This much-quoted sentence, which reinforced the federal government's support for educational developments that had been expressed in the Land Ordinance of 1785, was adopted as the first section of the article on education in the constitution framed by the Michigan Constitutional Convention in 1961–62. Oddly enough, there were strong objections voiced by some convention delegates that the statement could be interpreted as conflicting with the separation of church and state.

*   *   *   *   *

Under the Articles of Confederation, Congress had successfully dealt with two important problems, land disposal and government, in the territory between the Alleghenies and the Mississippi that had been ceded to the United States in 1783. But it was not able to cope with two other problems that were more immediately in need of resolution: how to deal with the Indians who resided in these lands and how to meet the challenge presented by the continued occupation of the northwest posts by the British. The lack of a strong executive, the difficulties encountered by a weak central government in dealing with foreign nations, and particularly the fact that the government did not have the power to levy taxes or to maintain an army, account in large part for the failure of Congress to deal with these problems. The framing of the Constitution of the United States, its ratification, and the inauguration of the national government under its provisions in 1789 were, therefore, of major importance in meeting the unsolved problems of the West.

An effort had been made to cope with the Indian problem prior to 1789. Commissioners appointed by Congress persuaded the Iroquois in 1784 at Fort Stanwix to cede all their claims to the Old Northwest to the United States in return for a few presents. Early the following year several tribes, including the Chippewa and Ottawa of Michigan, and the Wyandot or Huron, signed a treaty at Fort McIntosh agreeing to give up all their lands in the present state of Ohio except for a reservation. But Ohio tribesmen resented the treaty their chiefs had signed, and the important Shawnee refused to agree to it at all. On threat of war the Shawnee did consent to the terms of the agreement in the Treaty of Fort Finney, at the mouth of the Miami River, early in 1786, but as soon as they returned to their villages they repudiated it. Meanwhile, settlers were pouring across the Ohio River and settling on lands that had not been surveyed or ceded by the Indians. The attitude of the Indians now became extremely threatening. Since Congress was unable to supply troops to keep the rebellious natives in order, militiamen were assembled— one detachment under George Rogers Clark and another led by Benjamin Logan. Clark's force mutinied before a single Indian was sighted; Logan's men destroyed some Indian villages and 15,000 bushels of corn belonging to the Indians, but did not engage the natives in any battles. Both the Iroquois and Algonquian tribes now openly repudiated the treaties they had signed and declared that they would concede nothing to the whites west of Pennsylvania and north of the Ohio River.

At this stage the Indian problem merged with that of the continued occupation of the northwest posts by the British. General Frederick Haldimand, the British governor-general of Canada, with an eye to assuring Britain possession of these posts, encouraged the Indians to form a strong federation that could most effectively oppose any cession of land in the West to the United States. The Indians, true to their strong tribal loyalties, refused to adhere to any such federation. In fact, they were so divided that Arthur St. Clair, first governor of the Northwest Territory, was able to persuade them to sign a treaty at Fort Harmar, situated at the mouth of the Muskingum River, confirming the treaties of Fort McIntosh and Fort Finney. While the governor was talking peace, however, frontiersmen were sending raiding parties against the Indians. Naturally, the Indians retaliated and by the fall of 1789 a new Indian war had broken out.

The new federal government under the Constitution entrusted the task of disciplining the Indians to General Josiah Harmar. Starting out from Fort Washington (Cincinnati) in October of 1790, Harmar moved so slowly that the Indians easily eluded him. Then, late in October, a detachment was ambushed with the loss of 183 men. The following year a force of approximately 3,000 men under the command of Governor St. Clair set out in the late summer from Fort Washington. When his tired army finally reached the Maumee River and pitched their tents for the night without posting adequate guards, the camp was quietly surrounded, then furiously attacked. St. Clair and a part of his army slipped through the Indian cordon, but left 630 dead and 283 wounded behind. The retreating force reached a small fort that had been built on the way north—Fort Jefferson—in twenty-four hours, whereas it had taken them ten days to cover the same ground on the northward march.

On the Ohio frontier, Marietta and Cincinnati were now the only places where safety was assured. President George Washington, who throughout his life had been deeply interested in the development of the West, now called upon "Mad Anthony" Wayne, a man who had earned his famous nickname during the Revolution by his reckless courage and daring exploits, to assume command in the war. Wayne accepted the command, and an army was collected for him at

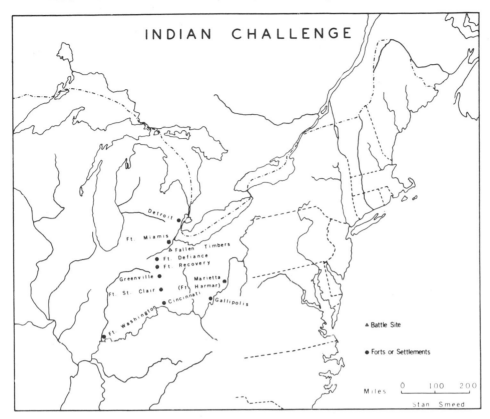

INDIAN CHALLENGE

Detroit

Ft. Miamis

Fallen Timbers

Ft. Defiance
Ft. Recovery

Greenville   Marietta

Ft. St. Clair   (Ft. Harmar)

Ft. Washington   Cincinnati   Gallipolis

▲ Battle Site

● Forts or Settlements

Miles   0   100   200

Stan Smeed

Pittsburgh. It was the same kind of army that Harmar and St. Clair had had, and numbered approximately 2,500. Wayne realized that any effective action was impossible without thorough organization and strict discipline. While the nation waited impatiently, Wayne calmly drilled his men for over a year. He enforced strict obedience to orders and even trained his men to yell like the Indians.

Wayne's advance from Fort Washington began in October, 1793. Halting at Fort Greenville, the site of the present Greenville, Ohio, he sent out spies and did some more drilling. This time supposedly friendly Indians, who had been permitted into the camps of Harmar and St. Clair, were excluded. The soldiers were not allowed to take their women friends along as they had on the St. Clair expedition. There followed an advance to the site of St. Clair's defeat where Fort Recovery was built. Meanwhile an Indian force of perhaps 2,000 had been gathered by the intrepid warrior Little Turtle. Desirous of repeating their previous success at this place, the Indians on June 30 and July 1, 1794, attacked in a determined fashion. They suffered severe casualties, were unable to carry out their objective, and had to retreat.

In his report on this engagement, Wayne wrote that he had virtual proof that there were a considerable number of British militiamen mixed with the savages in the attack on Fort Recovery. There is unmistakable evidence that the British supplied the natives with provisions and ammunition. The old French fort on the Maumee, near the present Perrysburg, Ohio, was occupied by a British force and named Fort Miamis. This was such an open violation of the peace that it was made the subject of a strong protest, communicated through John Jay, who at that time was in England attempting to negotiate a treaty between Great Britain and the United States.

After receiving reinforcements, Wayne moved forward on July 28, 1794. At the confluence of the Auglaize and Maumee rivers, Fort Defiance was built. Little Turtle, now thoroughly alarmed, urged Blue Jacket and other chiefs to make peace, but they would not listen to him. On August 20, 1794, a pitched battle between Wayne's army and the Indians took place some dozen miles south of the present Toledo, Ohio, on the Maumee. It was a place where trees had been uprooted by a violent tornado, causing the engagement to be called the Battle of Fallen Timbers. Wayne was completely victorious. Only thirty-three of his men were killed and about a hundred wounded. After burning some native villages he marched into what is now Indiana and built a fort named in his honor at the site of the present Fort Wayne. Then he retired to Greenville.[4]

The victory at Fallen Timbers broke the back of the Indian resistance. What discouraged the Indians most was the fact that the battle had been fought within two or three miles of Fort Miamis, and the British had made no move to come to their aid. Wayne now called for a conclave with all the Indian leaders. Runners were sent to remote points to summon the chiefs, including some from Michigan. In the summer of 1795 the chiefs together with a thousand or more braves assembled at Greenville. Chief spokesman for the Indians of Michigan was the Chippewa chieftain variously called Matchekewis, Mash-ipi-nash-i-wish, or Bad Bird. He had led the attack on Michilimackinac during the Indian uprising of 1763, had fought for the British cause during the Revolution, and was dignified with the title of general prefixed to his Indian name. At Greenville, Matchekewis spoke for the Ottawa, Chippewa, and Potawatomi of Michigan and pledged that they would make war no more on the Americans. After a considerable amount of oratory and palaver the Indians signed the Treaty of Greenville on August 3, 1795, in which they ceded to the United States all of Ohio except a strip along Lake Erie. They also ceded a triangle of land in Indiana and sixteen small areas for trading posts on strategic waterways. These included the first land in Michigan ceded to the United States by the Indians: a strip six miles wide along the Detroit River between the River Raisin and Lake St. Clair, all of Mackinac Island, that part of the mainland along the Straits of Mackinac to which Indians had given the French or English title, and a six-mile strip on the mainland north of the island extending three miles inland.[5]

It is noteworthy that the cessions made by the Indians at Greenville were not simply the spoils of war. They received payment in goods to the value of $20,000 and a promise that they would receive goods in the amount of $9,500 every year forever from the United States. It is a common misconception that the Americans simply confiscated the Indian lands and gave nothing in return. Actually, in the Treaty of Greenville and in the many treaties by which later purchases were made, very considerable amounts by the standards of that time were paid for the lands.[6]

Had the British garrison in Fort Miamis come to the aid of the Indians at the Battle of Fallen Timbers, it probably would have meant war between the United States and Great Britain. The British might have been willing to risk war a few years before, but by 1794 the situation in Europe had so changed as to cause the British government to avoid any chance of a conflict in America. The French Revolution entered its radical phase in 1792, and early the next year the frenzied revolutionaries executed Louis XVI. European monarchs saw in the French excesses a menace to their security. A wave of anti-French sentiment swept England. Sensing this hostility and confident of its ability to contend with the armies of its enemies, the French Republic declared war on Great Britain and Holland. The other European powers soon were involved, but, by the end of 1793, against the combined armies of their enemies, the French began to win startling victories.

In 1794, as French successes continued, the United States sent John Jay as its special envoy to London in an attempt to persuade the British to end discrimination against American commerce and to evacuate the northwest posts. Jay was cordially received and prospects seemed good for a favorable outcome, but the British subsequently adopted a hard-line attitude in the negotiations. They even balked at agreeing to evacuate the northwest posts until news arrived of Wayne's successes. The treaty Jay eventually signed included an agreement that the posts would be turned over to the United States no later than June 1, 1796, but the United States had to allow Canadian traders to continue to operate in American territory, agree not to tax the furs they carried back to Montreal, and promise not to levy any higher tax on the trading goods of the Canadians than on those of United States' nationals.

The commercial provisions of Jay's Treaty were so unsatisfactory that there was a danger that it might not be ratified by the United States Senate, but by a narrow margin the treaty was approved on June 22, 1795, with the exception of an article relating to trade with the British West Indies. The British were ready to surrender Detroit and Michilimackinac on the agreed-upon date of June 1, 1796, but the American forces were not yet ready to move in. Wayne ultimately assigned the task of occupying Detroit to a regiment commanded by Lieutenant Colonel John Francis Hamtramck. An advance unit of Hamtramck's regiment, under Captain Moses Porter, arrived at Detroit on July 11, 1796, at which time the British flag that had flown over that site since November 29, 1760, was lowered and the Stars and Stripes was raised in its place. Hamtramck and the rest of his force arrived a couple of days later. Anthony Wayne himself came to Detroit on August 13 and remained there until November, when he set out for his home in Pennsylvania. En route he was taken ill and died at Erie, Pennsylvania, at the age of fifty-one. It is appropriate that Michigan's most populous county and one of its largest universities, among many other places, institutions, and business firms, should bear his name. It was largely through his efforts that the United States won possession of the Old Northwest.

The remaining British garrison in Michigan was withdrawn when Major Henry Burbeck, with 110 American soldiers, occupied the fort on Mackinac Island on September 1, 1796. But events were to prove that Michigan was not yet free from foreign influences. Jay's Treaty provided that the residents of Michigan could obtain American citizenship rights simply by taking the oath of allegiance to the United States. The sincerity of some of those who took this oath was questionable, however, while those who chose not to take the oath were free to carry on their business activities in Michigan, along with their colleagues from across the border in Canada, thus leaving British dominance of the economy little affected by the political change. In addition, British soldiers remained close at hand. In the north, the British garrison was removed from Michilimackinac to St. Joseph Island at the mouth of the St. Mary's River, where ground had been cleared to build a new British post. Across the Detroit River, the British built Fort Malden for the troops that were withdrawn from Detroit. From these two bases the British were able to maintain the same close ties with the Indians of Michigan that they had maintained earlier when their military forces were actually located on Michigan soil.

*   *   *   *   *

By 1796, a sizable group of settlements had sprung up in the Old Northwest. At Marietta, founded in 1788, the entire process of settlement was supervised by the Ohio Company, which had purchased the land. Downstream from Marietta was Gallipolis, settled by Frenchmen who had purchased lands from an agent of the Scioto Company. Still further downriver was a settlement first called Losantville and later Cincinnati, established on land purchased by John Cleves Symmes of New Jersey. Inland the Virginia Military Reserve had been settled by a considerable number of Virginia veterans. Manchester was founded in 1791, but Chillicothe, established after Wayne's victory, soon became the chief center. Though from Virginia, the people in the Military Reserve were not strongly in favor of slavery. Shortly after Wayne's victory settlers from Connecticut began pouring into the Western Reserve along Lake Erie. Some 500,000 acres of this tract were reserved for Connecticut veterans. The surname of Moses Cleaveland, one of the leaders, was given to the principal town (though the spelling was changed). In the extreme eastern part of present-day Ohio a considerable number of settlers had drifted across the Pennsylvania line and had come up from Virginia. Fort Steuben (now Steubenville) was the center of this settlement.

In addition to these new American settlements the Northwest Territory contained forts and trading posts whose population consisted largely of French-speaking people. In the Illinois country there were Kaskaskia, Cahokia, and Vincennes. In Wisconsin there was a settlement at Green Bay. In Michigan, Detroit and Michilimackinac were the chief centers of population. A few whites were scattered among remote trading posts on the St. Joseph, Kalamazoo, and Grand rivers. South of Detroit a number of French farmers made their homes along the River Raisin.

At Detroit in 1796 there were approximately five hundred inhabitants. Most of them were of French ancestry, spoke the French language, and observed the rites of the Roman Catholic Church. The merchants and Indian traders were mainly English and Scotch. There were a few Americans already in the town while it was in British hands. Both Indian and Negro slaves are noted in the records, and there were some free Negroes. The Indians who were slaves had been taken captive in inter-tribal wars and sold to the whites.

Among the principal merchants and traders in Detroit in 1796 were John Askin, William Macomb, James May, James Abbott, and a Frenchman, Joseph Campau. These men provided the Indians with arms, blankets, and other supplies in the fall, and were paid with furs, which the Indians brought in the following spring. These merchants did business with dealers in Montreal, who forwarded the furs to London and advanced to the traders in Detroit the goods required for the Indian trade. Ste. Anne's Church, where most of the people worshipped, was a community center. Some leading residents had libraries of considerable size. There was no newspaper, but John McCall operated a printing press as early as 1796. There also was a Masonic lodge, called Zion Lodge Number 10, which was formed during the British period. The French lived in a world of their own. Their customs had changed very little during the imperial struggles. There was much dancing to the tune of the fiddle, and a kind of Mardi Gras was held each year just before the beginning of lent. Christmas was not observed, but New Year's Day was a joyous holiday.

The fort, called Fort Lernoult by the British and re-named Fort Detroit by the Americans, was the center of the town. Within it were wooden barracks for the garrison and shops for the carpenter, baker, and armorer. The town lay below the fort and consisted of about a hundred houses. Looking out from the fort, one could see the French farms on the opposite shores of the river and many kinds of craft, ranging from sloops and schooners to canoes, plying the river. Most of the houses were built of logs, although there were some frame dwellings. There were shops and taverns in the town and several stores.[7]

Far to the north of Detroit was Mackinac Island. It is described as it was in 1796 by a contemporary, Major Caleb Swan:

> On the south side of this Island, there is a small bason [sic], of a segment of a circle, serving as an excellent harbour for vessels of any burden, and for canoes. Around this bason the village is built, having two streets of nearly a quarter of a mile in length, a Roman chapel, and containing eighty-nine houses and stores; some of them spacious and handsome, with white lime plastering in front, which shews to great advantage from the sea. At one end, in the rear of the town, is an elegant government house, of immense size, and finished with great taste. It is one story high, the rooms fifteen feet and a half in the clear. It has a spacious garden in front, laid out with taste; and extending from the house, on a gentle declivity, to the water's edge. There are two natural limpid springs in the rear of the house, and a very lovely grove of sugartrees, called the park. Suitable out-houses, stables, and

offices are added; and it is enriched on three sides with beautiful distant prospects. Twenty rods from the rear, there is a sudden and almost perpendicular ascent of about a hundred feet of rock, upon the top of which stands the fort, built of stone and lime, with towers, bastions, etc., occupied by our troops and commanded by Major Burbeck.[8]

One of the houses that stood on the island in 1796 was acquired later by Edward Biddle, a leading trader of the area. Parts of it may have been built as early as 1780. Constructed in the typical Quebec rural style, this old house was restored in 1959 by the Michigan Society of Architects and is probably the oldest surviving residential building in Michigan.

Among the white inhabitants of Michigan outside Detroit and Mackinac in 1796 mention must be made of William Burnett. Precisely where he came from is not clear, nor can the date of his arrival in the St. Joseph Valley be established. Apparently he was trading there during the American Revolution, for in 1782 he was married to the daughter of a Potawatomi chief. He continued his business through all the vicissitudes of strife between the United States and Britain until his death in 1814. He was strongly pro-American, a fact that created for him no end of difficulties with the British who dominated Mackinac Island where he sold his furs. His house and trading

Biddle House, Mackinac Island

post were situated on the west bank of the St. Joseph River, about one and a half miles upstream from its mouth.[9] Upriver, beyond old Fort St. Joseph at Niles, another trader, John Kinzie, had his head-quarters before moving back to Chicago in 1804. Kinzie's post was taken over by Joseph Bertrand, whose name has been given to a Berrien County town near the site of his old trading post. On the Kalamazoo River a trader named Pepan had his headquarters near the modern city of Kalamazoo. On the Grand River near the present site of Ada, Joseph La Framboise and his bride, an Ottawa Indian maiden, established a trading post in 1796.[10]

All of present-day Michigan, after the departure of the British officials in 1796, was officially under the control of Governor Arthur St. Clair and the other officials of the Northwest Territory until 1800. Governor St. Clair was a man of considerable ability, a Federalist in politics and quite undemocratic in his views. When news arrived at Cincinnati, the territorial capital, that the British were about to evacuate the northwest posts, St. Clair was outside the territory. Hence it fell to the lot of Winthrop Sargent, the territorial secretary, to accompany Wayne's army to Detroit and to install civil government. Upon his arrival he proceeded to establish the County of Wayne, and included within its boundaries practically all of the present state of Michigan, as well as portions of northern Ohio and Indiana, and those parts of Illinois and Wisconsin bordering on Lake Michigan. The claims of Michigan's present Wayne County to date from Sargent's action of 1796 are, as the historian Milo Quaife has pointed out, erroneous since the county had its actual origins in an act of the Michigan Territory in 1815.[11] In casting about for local officials, Sargent found that the French were inclined to be more loyal to the United States than the people of British ancestry. The trouble was that few of the French could read or write. He com-promised by appointing some of each. Seven justices of the peace were designated. Sitting together, they were to constitute a "Court of General Quarter Sessions." A "Court of Common Pleas" was also established. George McDougall was appointed as sheriff. Peter Aud-rain, the only American civilian and one of the few residents who had a knowledge of both French and English, was appointed to four offices. Sargent found that land titles were in a state of terrible confusion. What records there were had been carried off by the British, and Sargent had to send word requesting the officials of Upper Canada to return them.

Having done what he could at Detroit, Sargent sailed to Mack-inac Island, arriving there after a voyage of more than a month. So illiterate and uneducated were the inhabitants that Sargent could find only two "proper persons" outside the military garrison to appoint as justices of the peace. The commandant was also made a justice of the peace to serve the needs of the many fur traders who periodically visited the post. After trying in vain to settle the troublesome problem of land titles, Sargent returned to Cincinnati by way of Detroit.

The laws to be enforced by the justices at Detroit and Mackinac were those enacted by the governor, secretary, and three judges at Cincinnati. These defined crimes and punishments, commanded the strict observance of Sunday as a day of rest, prohibited swearing and drunkenness, and regulated marriages. Murder and treason were the only capital crimes; flogging, fines, and standing in the stocks were prescribed as punishments for lesser infractions. A court house and a jail were to be provided by each county, with separate compartments for debtors and for women prisoners. Fees charged by probate judges and justices of the peace were regulated. It was stipulated that a minister or judge who performed a marriage ceremony was entitled to a fee of $1.10. Another law followed New England precedent by providing for the organization of townships within the counties. Wayne County officials in December, 1796, divided the county into four townships: St. Clair to the east, Hamtramck on the north, and Detroit and Sargent to the south. Constables, overseers of the poor, and highway inspectors were appointed for each township.[12]

Settlers poured into Ohio and increased the population of the Northwest Territory by 1798 to well over 5,000 free adult males, the number required under the Northwest Ordinance for the second stage of territorial development. Accordingly, Governor St. Clair ordered elections held for a house of representatives. At Detroit this first American election was held in John Dodemead's tavern. The voting extended over three days: December 17, 18, and 19, 1798. Since each voter announced the candidate of his choice, it was known throughout the three days of balloting how each stood. James May, a former British subject, who was supported by the British residents, and Solomon Sibley, who was favored by the Americans and many of the French, were the two rival candidates. According to May, the defeated candidate, Sibley won because he passed out liquor to the voters and had soldiers armed with clubs who threatened to beat anyone who cast his vote for May. Early in January Sibley set out on horseback for Cincinnati to take his seat in the legislative body. Then word arrived in Detroit that the census returns entitled Wayne County to two additional representatives. At an election held on January 14 and 15, 1799, James May ran again and once more was defeated. The successful candidates were Jacob Visger and François Joncaire de Chabert. Neither the December nor the January election centered around partisan lines, since the new political party that was forming around Thomas Jefferson in opposition to the Federalists was still unorganized in Detroit. The isolation of Mackinac Island during the winter months made it impossible for the eligible voters there to participate in these elections.

Division of the Northwest Territory was now being debated. Governor St. Clair at first opposed this move, but when he recognized it was inevitable, proposed a division that would have placed the Western Reserve and Marietta, both solidly Federalist, into a single territory, and would have divided the remainder of the Old Northwest into two separate territories so as to delay statehood in the area that favored the Jeffersonian Democrats and to speed up statehood in an area that might be expected to vote Federalist. But Congress rejected St. Clair's proposal, and in 1800 decreed that the Northwest Territory should be divided by a line that closely approximated the present Ohio-Indiana line extended north to the Canadian border. This brought a large proportion of the settled areas within the eastern portion, with the result that Federalist strength in Marietta and the Western Reserve was offset by the Jeffersonian preferences of Cincinnati, the Virginia Military Reserve, and other settlements where the New England element was less strong. This new territory on the east, including the eastern half of Michigan's lower peninsula and the tip of the Upper Peninsula, continued to be called the Northwest Territory, while the area to the west became the Indiana Territory.

This first division of the Old Northwest was promoted in Congress by William Henry Harrison, who had been chosen by the general assembly of the Northwest Territory as delegate to Congress in 1798. Though he had no vote, Harrison not only was influential in getting the territory divided in a manner favorable to the Democrats, but also succeeded in obtaining a revision of the land laws that made it possible to purchase government land on the installment plan and provided for the opening of land offices in the West. When the law dividing the territory was passed Harrison was appointed governor of the Indiana Territory, with its capital at Vincennes. St. Clair remained as governor of the Northwest Territory, the capital of which was moved to Chillicothe so as to be closer to the center of population.

An important event in Michigan history occurred on January 18, 1802, when a bill for the incorporation of Detroit as a town was approved by the general assembly of the Northwest Territory. It provided for a five-member Board of Trustees, other town officers, and annual meetings of the voters. The trustees were authorized to

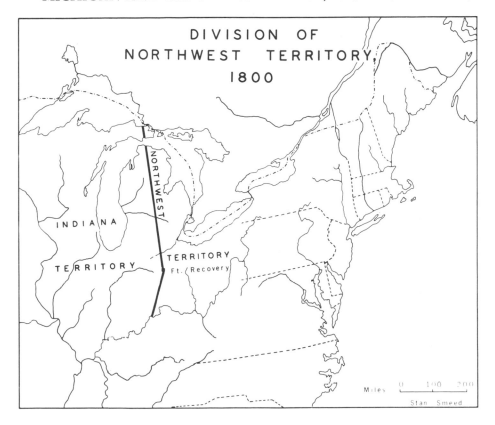

DIVISION OF
NORTHWEST TERRITORY,
1800

NORTHWEST

INDIANA

TERRITORY

TERRITORY

Ft. Recovery

Miles   0   100   200

Stan Smeed

take whatever action they deemed necessary for the health and welfare of the inhabitants. Their first act was to adopt a code of fire
regulations consisting of seventeen articles that were almost identical
with a voluntary agreement adopted four years earlier by seventy-
three householders. Regular chimney-sweeping and the provision of
barrels, buckets, and ladders were required of all those who owned
buildings. All citizens were required to turn out to fight fire. Between 1802 and 1805, the trustees levied fines on several citizens
having defective chimneys or otherwise failing to observe the fire
regulations. Ironically, despite these precautions the town would be
destroyed by fire in 1805. The second ordinance passed by the trustees regulated trade in the town. There was no holding with the
economic doctrine of *laissez-faire,* for several of the regulations were
quite exacting. Bakers, for instance, were required to sell a three-
pound loaf of bread for six pence, New York currency, and to stamp
their initials on each loaf. The town government was conducted on
lines of strict economy. During the fiscal year 1803–1804 the income

of the town government, derived chiefly from fines, amounted to $137.25. After paying fees to officers and $15.00 to repair the fire engine, the town that in recent years has been plagued by financial woes ended the year with a balance of $35.36!

Agitation for statehood now became lively in the eastern part of the divided territory. St. Clair opposed it with vehemence and finally became so obnoxious that he was removed from office. On April 30, 1802, Congress passed an act enabling the people of Ohio to write a constitution and form a state government. For the first time, the act committed the federal government to create more than three states out of the Old Northwest, for it set the northern boundary of Ohio at a line drawn due east from the southernmost extremity of Lake Michigan, as the Northwest Ordinance had provided in case Congress decided to create more than three states. Politics played a part in this decision. In Washington, it was believed that Detroit would vote Federalist. By excluding it from the new state the Jeffersonian Democrats would have a better chance to carry Ohio. The western boundary of Ohio was also in accord with the Northwest Ordinance: a line drawn due north from the mouth of the Miami River. All the Old Northwest that remained when the state of Ohio was removed was made part of the Indiana Territory. This, of course, included Michigan. The change was unpopular with Detroiters, for they had not been consulted about it. Vincennes, their new territorial capital, was farther away than Chillicothe. Because Indiana was still in the first stage of territorial development, it had no elected legislature. The dissatisfaction resulting from these changes led to the circulation of a petition asking that Wayne County be set up as a separate territory. Over three hundred signatures were obtained.

Governor Harrison visited Detroit in company with one of the territorial judges in May, 1804. His appearance did nothing to halt the movement for separate territorial status. Congress, dominated by the Jeffersonians, was at first unresponsive, but following receipt of a petition from the "Democratic-Republicans [Jefferson's party] of Michigan," a more favorable attitude was taken. The petition declared that it was the "unanimous opinion" of the people that "good order and prosperity" depended on the creation of a new territory. The petitioners argued that the proximity of the British in Canada, the general lack of "patriotic attachment" to the United States, and the lack of a safe route of communication between Detroit and Vincennes all supported the plea. Congress agreed and passed an act, approved by President Jefferson on January 11, 1805, setting off the Territory of Michigan, with the act to take effect on June 30, 1805.

This action committed Congress to carve five states out of the

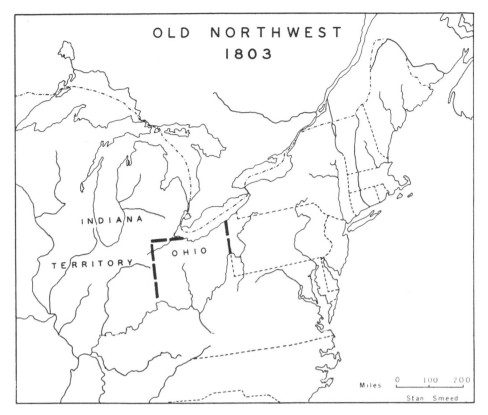

Old Northwest. The western boundary of the new territory was established at a line drawn northward from the southern extremity of Lake Michigan through the lake to its northernmost point, approximately thirty miles west of St. Ignace, and from that point due north to the international boundary. This placed the eastern tip of the Upper Peninsula, including the settlements at the Straits of Mackinac and at Sault Ste. Marie, within Michigan. The southern boundary was that specified in the Northwest Ordinance: a line drawn due east from the southernmost extremity of Lake Michigan. Because of its sparse population, the government of the Michigan territory would be that set forth in the Northwest Ordinance for the first stage of territorial development.

Once again, however, the political changes that affected Michigan during the period 1796 to 1805 did not signify fundamental changes in the way of life that had developed earlier under French and British direction. The region was remote from the Ohio River, which was the route of travel utilized by most settlers coming into the West. For New Englanders, lands were available in western New York and in the Western Reserve in Ohio, much less remote than Michigan. Furthermore, the Indian title to lands in Michigan had been extinguished only in the areas around Detroit and Mackinac Island, and no government surveys had yet taken place. Hence little land was available for settlement.

The fur trade continued to remain, for the most part, in British hands. Fort Malden, on the Canadian side of the Detroit River, rapidly replaced Detroit as the nucleus of trade in the lower lakes region. Some of the British residents in Detroit moved to the other side of the river. The fort continued to dominate the town. In 1801, John Francis Hamtramck, now a colonel who had been transferred elsewhere, came back to Detroit as the commander of the Department of the Lakes. In 1803 he was ordered by Secretary of War Henry Dearborn to establish a fort at the mouth of the Chicago River. The fort was duly built and named after Dearborn. Shortly afterward, on April 11, 1803, Hamtramck died, and his passing was deeply mourned in Detroit. He eventually was buried in the Michigan city that bears his name.

In June, 1798, Father Gabriel Richard, a Sulpician priest, arrived at Detroit to assist the resident pastor of Ste. Anne's Church, Father Michel Levadoux. Both priests were Frenchmen who had fled from France after the outbreak of the revolution and had come to America where they were assigned by the American Catholic prelate to serve in the predominately French-speaking parishes in the West. Richard would become one of the most important forces for cultural and educational advancement in the early history of Michigan. The first Protestant missionary, the Reverend David Bacon, reached Detroit in 1800, and served that town and Mackinac periodically through the fall of 1804. By 1805, Detroit had five doctors of medicine. There were a number of private schools, but no public schools. Postal service had been extended to the town but the mails were slow. Considering the distance from the East and the difficulties of transportation, it is surprising to find that people in Detroit were able to obtain almost every sort of merchandise one could have found at that time in Boston or New York. A tannery provided leather for shoes, harness, and other items, but most manufactured goods had to be imported. Coffee, tea, almonds, figs, and candy were among the many articles that could be purchased.

The fur trade continued to be the dominating motif in life on Mackinac Island. Although some Americans took part in the trade, its management was almost wholly in the hands of the British. The fort, with its small garrison flying the American flag, was the only tangible evidence of United States sovereignty in the region. There was a church, but no resident priest. Father Richard paid a visit to Mackinac Island in 1799, and in his report to his superiors lamented the fact that liquor was so prevalent and so generally used in the trade with the Indians. Many Indians, he wrote, were drunk in the streets. He found a profound indifference to religion; former converts had even forgotten the sign of the cross. He also visited the Ottawa at L'Arbre Croche, finding approximately 1300 Indians living there. Only one out of this whole number had been baptized, although he found that some of the others still remembered the teachings of the Jesuits and welcomed the appearance of a priest among them once again. Richard visited St. Joseph Island and then went on the Sault Ste. Marie, where he found a number of Frenchmen living with Indian wives.

In spite of the fact that the conditions of life had not greatly changed during Michigan's first American decade, the groundwork had been laid for the development that was to come in later years. But before any great influx of settlers would occur, Michigan was to pass through another troubled period, during which the British flag once more flew over Detroit and Mackinac.

Detroit Harbor

7

MICHIGAN'S TROUBLED DECADE, 1805–1815

During the long years of its development by the French, the British, and finally the Americans, there had been many governors who had had authority over Michigan when the area was part of the colony of New France, the provinces of Quebec and Upper Canada, and the Northwest Territory. The first person to have the distinction of being named the governor of an area called Michigan was William Hull, who was appointed to the office when the Territory of Michigan was established in 1805. A native of Massachusetts, Hull was a graduate of Yale, a lawyer, and a veteran of the American Revolution who was fifty-two years old at the time he was given this appointment by President Thomas Jefferson. Hull was nominally a member of Jefferson's party, but possessed a conservative streak that seemed to place him closer in spirit to the New England Federalists. He was a man of considerable ability, but was handicapped in his new job by his total lack of acquaintance with frontier life and problems.

Jefferson appointed as secretary of the territory Stanley Griswold, a former Connecticut minister who had been unpopular with his parishioners because of his fondness for Jefferson's ideas, which were commonly considered atheistic in New England. In Michigan, Griswold proved to be so contentious and opinionated that Jefferson finally had to remove him from office. The most prominent of the three judges appointed to office in Michigan Territory was Augustus Elias Brevoort Woodward. Born in New York, he had attended Columbia College but had not graduated. He had moved to Virginia when he was twenty-one years of age, residing in Rockbridge

County, where he "read for the law" and began practice in 1799. He met Thomas Jefferson in Virginia, and a close friendship grew up between the two men. Both were deeply read in the classics and both were disciples of the eighteenth-century Enlightenment. They shared a fondness for devising elaborate and often highly complicated plans for the betterment of mankind, although Jefferson was far more practical than his younger friend. Woodward moved to Washington when his idol became president in 1801, and there he mingled with the best society. He was an intimate of the President during these years, and it was natural that Jefferson should offer him an opportunity for public service in the new Michigan Territory. Like Hull, young Woodward was profoundly ignorant of conditions in a frontier area like Michigan. He was extremely aggressive, very sensitive, and quite domineering in his attitudes. His grandiose projects appeared utterly impractical, but in his expansive visions of the future greatness of the West, Woodward was in accord with frontier psychology.[1]

The other judges first appointed were Frederick Bates and Samuel Huntington. Bates was the only one of the territorial officials who had lived in Michigan prior to 1805. He had settled at Detroit in 1797, had established a prosperous business, and had been appointed as first postmaster of his adopted city in 1803. He had read law and was an altogether admirable choice. The other judge, Huntington, was chief justice of the Ohio supreme court, and declined the appointment. So at first there were only four territorial officials. John Griffin, a native of Virginia and one of the judges of Indiana Territory, was appointed to be the third judge in Michigan Territory in 1806. But he no sooner took office than Bates resigned to accept appointment as secretary of Louisiana Territory. So Michigan was left once more with only four territorial officials. The two New Englanders—Hull and Griswold—were usually at odds with the two Virginians—Woodward and Griffin. In 1808, James Witherell of Vermont was appointed to replace Bates, giving the New Englanders a 3 to 2 advantage on the governing board.

Just before the arrival of the new territorial officials, a fire practically levelled the town of Detroit. On June 11, 1805, John Harvey, the town's baker, had—so the story goes—harnessed his pony to go to the mill for flour. A gale of wind, which was roaring up the river, caught sparks from his pipe and the still burning tobacco was blown into a pile of hay. In a moment the hay and the barn in which it was stored were ablaze. The pony, with the cart attached, dashed from the barn while Harvey spread the alarm of fire. Soon men with buckets, poles, and other crude fire-fighting equipment were at hand, but despite all they could do the blaze spread from building to building, and soon the town was a mass of smoldering ruins. Only the fort and a few large buildings along the river belonging to the navy were left. Food was scarce and the country was scoured to supply the sufferers. Shelter was found in the fort, the naval buildings, and improvised tents and shacks. A supply of lumber was obtained from the region of present-day Port Huron, sawed by hand, and floated down the river to rebuild the town.[2]

Arriving shortly after the disaster, Hull and Woodward saw it would be wise to rebuild Detroit on a new plan, since the old town had been too compact and the streets too narrow, the broadest being no more than twenty feet wide. Before permitting the erection of permanent structures the two officials went to Washington, where they secured from the federal government a grant of 10,000 acres of land for the new town. The grant provided that each citizen over the age of seventeen was to receive a city lot of not less than 5,000 square feet, with the remainder of the land to be sold and the proceeds used to build a courthouse and a jail.

While in Washington, Woodward secured the plan for the national capital that had been made by Pierre L'Enfant. Using this plan as a guide, Woodward laid out on paper his scheme for the new Detroit. A number of circular parks ("circuses") were to form the center of municipal districts or wards. Radiating from these, as spokes from the hub of a wheel, were to be wide and spacious avenues and streets. The grand avenues were to be 200 feet wide, and at their intersections were to be located the circuses, 1,000 feet in diameter. Other main streets were to be 120 feet in width. An open "campus" would be laid out wherever the 120-foot streets intersected the grand avenues. But Woodward, who is now recognized as one of America's pioneer city planners, was far ahead of his time. Only approximately nine hundred people lived in Detroit at this time, and it seemed fantastic to most of them to have streets of as much as two hundred feet in width. Possibly to obtain Hull's support, Woodward had the governor's brother Abijah draft the plan. It was then adopted by the governing board in 1807 and forwarded to Washington for approval.

In spite of local opposition, the reconstruction of Detroit was launched in accordance with Woodward's plan. A decade later in 1817, however, while Woodward was in Washington, Judge Witherell joined with Governor Lewis Cass to undo the plan for what is now downtown Detroit. Some streets were narrowed to sixty-six feet and others were made to veer or were cut off to avoid penetrating certain farms, including one belonging to Cass. One of the streets

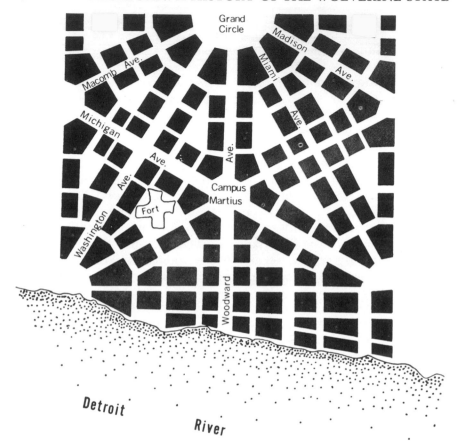

Judge Woodward's Map of Detroit

was named "Witherell Avenue," which was not unusual since nearly all these early territorial officials immortalized themselves in this fashion, including Woodward, after whom Detroit's best-known avenue is named. In a letter of protest, however, Woodward sarcastically declared: "You have well named that main avenue as Witherell, for you have withered my beautiful plan of Detroit and have spoiled the beauty and symmetry of the city of Detroit for all time."[3] Thereafter, Detroit's development increasingly followed the more conventional grid street pattern. Grand Circus Park and the streets radiating out from it are the city's most visible surviving remnant of the city as Woodward planned it. Woodward's critics were at least partly correct in attacking his ideas as impractical, but the failure of Detroit to follow the advice of men like Woodward in its subsequent expansion cost it dearly in meeting the problems that confronted the exploding metropolis of the twentieth century.[4]

In his administration of territorial affairs, Hull seems to have disregarded the fact that a majority of the inhabitants were of French extraction and understood neither the customs nor the language of the Americans. The governor established American local governmental institutions and appointed justices of the peace and militia officers in the four districts into which Wayne County was then divided: Erie, Detroit, Huron, and Michilimackinac. The code of laws adopted by the governing board was largely the work of Judge Woodward and was called the Woodward Code. The Northwest Ordinance had specified that the laws enacted by the territorial officials must be adapted from those of the original states, but much of Woodward's code was original with him. The laws were altogether too complicated and elaborate for a pioneer community. The problem of land titles was a particularly troublesome legal issue. Few French *habitants* had written deeds to their lands in the neighborhood of Detroit, and the fire of 1805 complicated and delayed the settlement of property rights inside the town. There was friction between the American newcomers and the French. The former complained of certain French habits, such as dumping dead animals in the river and racing live ones pell-mell down the streets of the town. A grand jury in 1806 complained of gambling, of "disorder and scandal" on Sunday, and of insults from the British across the river. In typical American fashion, the territorial officials responded by passing twenty-six more laws. One of these appropriated $20,000 for a new courthouse and jail. This expenditure was considered grossly extravagant by the people of Detroit, because it further complicated the already elaborate judicial system.

Included in the new laws was one that incorporated the Bank of Detroit. Hull had become interested in the plan of a group of Boston speculators to establish a fur-trading company and bank in the West. Woodward was enthusiastic when he heard of it, too. He conjectured that somehow such an institution might lure the fur trade away from Fort Malden and back to Detroit. On September 15, 1806, the territory granted a charter to the Bank of Detroit, and forwarded it to Washington for approval. Without waiting for Congressional action the bank opened for business. Woodward was elected president. Capital stock was set by the charter at $100,000, with $19,000 paid in. Woodward bought one share, on which he made a down payment of $2.00. The charter had a life of thirty years, but this was not to Woodward's liking. He persuaded the governing board to extend the charter to one hundred years and to increase the capitalization to

$1,000,000. A structure commensurate with the ambitious plan for the bank was erected at a cost of $8,000 and equipped with impressive iron doors. But it turned out that the real purpose of the eastern manipulators was not to promote the fur trade in Michigan Territory. They quickly ran off $165,000 in notes on the Bank of Detroit, which the charter stipulated it might circulate as legal tender, and sold these notes in the East at discounts varying from ten to twenty-five percent. After these were taken up $1,500,000 more in notes was printed. When these notes found their way back to Detroit and were presented for payment in gold or silver, it turned out that the bank had no means of making such payments. Congress, horrified by this skulduggery, vetoed the act of incorporation and the bank quickly passed out of existence. After careful investigation it was proved that neither Woodward nor Hull had any substantial financial interest in the bank and that they had not profited from its operation. But the episode was the first of several that would at various times give Michigan a bad reputation in financial circles.

Nothing illustrates Hull's poor judgment better than his provisions for a territorial militia. After making himself a major general of the militia he issued an order prescribing uniforms to be worn by the officers: dark blue coats, "long and faced with red, with a red cape, white buttons and lining, white under cloathes, and silver epaulettes." Their adornment was to be set off with cocked hats topped with black plumes, red tipped; red sashes, swords, pistols, and bearskin holsters. The riflemen were required to wear "short green coats, turned up with buff, buff capes, round hats, black cockades and green feathers; in the warm season white vest and pantaloons with black gaiters; in the cold season green pantaloons edged with buff."[5] Because there was no cloth in Michigan to make such uniforms, Hull had quantities shipped from the East for sale to the militiamen. It was rumored that Hull made a profit on the transactions. Most Detroiters could not afford such outfits. Some who failed to buy them were arrested and publicly flogged.

Woodward and Hull could never get along with each other. As early as 1806, the former wrote to the government in Washington condemning the acts of the territorial government. He tried to persuade officials not to reappoint Hull, whose term was to expire in 1808. When criticism of the bank scandal swirled up around him, Woodward left Detroit and retired to a farm on the River Raisin, which he named Monticello. Here he sulked for more than a year. While he was away, the governing board, now controlled by the New England faction, repealed the Woodward Code and adopted the

Witherell Code in its place. One of the new laws authorized the construction of a road between Detroit and the foot of the Maumee Rapids (where Toledo now stands)—a much needed improvement. The sum of $6,000 to finance this work was to be raised by holding a lottery, a popular revenue-raising technique at that time, and which Michigan revived in the 1970s. Some other laws in the Witherell Code were more in accord with the needs of Michigan than the Woodward Code had been. The familiar crimes of horse-stealing, as well as forgery and counterfeiting, were made punishable by severe penalties.

In spite of complaints against him, Hull was reappointed in 1808, and Woodward, swallowing his pride, returned to Detroit. Hull also secured Griswold's dismissal as secretary, for he had been a critic of both Hull and Woodward. Griswold's successor as secretary was Reuben Atwater, a Vermonter, who became a welcome ally of Hull's. Nevertheless, while Witherell was absent from the territory in 1810, Woodward persuaded his colleagues to repeal the Witherell Code and reinstate the Woodward Code. This must have created even more confusion. If Congress earlier had had doubts of the ability of frontiersmen to govern themselves, the small-minded men who were appointed to govern Michigan in these years clearly demonstrated that easterners were not necessarily any more endowed with these abilities than were the rough, untutored pioneers of the West.

While there is much to criticize in the government of Michigan from 1805 to 1812, it must be noted that those in authority worked under extreme difficulties. They were severely handicapped by the fact that American control of Michigan was still rather tenuous. The fur trade, so important in the early period of Michigan history, remained largely in British hands even after the British withdrew their troops from Detroit and Mackinac in 1796. Both the United States government and American merchants made a determined effort, however, to break that hold. In 1795 Congress enacted legislation which during the next years inaugurated the government "factory" system. Under this plan stores operated by agents of the United States government were to be opened at important trading centers in the West, where goods were to be sold at cost to the Indians in exchange for their furs. The purpose was to promote better relations with the Indians and to combat the British fur traders. Private trading was still permitted, but it was expected to slowly decline. A government "factory" was opened at Detroit in 1802 and placed in charge of Robert Munro, but it was abolished in 1805. A similar establishment was opened on Mackinac Island in 1808, and operated until the island was captured by the British in 1812. It was not reestablished after the war, and in 1822 the entire system was abandoned.

Several reasons account for the failure of this system. Private traders roaming the woods could reach the Indians before the latter could get their furs to a government factory. Furthermore, the private traders sold rum to the Indians, while this was prohibited in the government factories. American-made goods, which were sold at the government factories, were higher in price and inferior in quality to the British goods. After the war the bitter opposition of private trading interests was primarily responsible for the decline and finally the abandonment of the system.[6]

The principal threat to British control of the fur trade was John Jacob Astor's American Fur Company, chartered by the state of New York in 1808. Prior to 1806 the North West Company, owned by British and Scottish merchants operating out of Montreal, dominated the fur trade at Mackinac. In 1806, however, a new company was formed named the Michilimackinac Company (or the Mackinac Company, as it was usually called). The organizers included several of the owners of the North West Company, and they proceeded at once to divide up the trade between the two companies. Practically all of Michigan fell within the area assigned to the Mackinac Company. When Astor, an immigrant from Germany who had engaged in the fur trade in New York, formed his American Fur Company and started trading at Mackinac, there was bitter rivalry with the British firm. However, in 1811 Astor made an arrangement with the North West and Mackinac companies under which the former was to confine its trade to Canada, and the latter was to conduct its trade on a joint account with Astor's American Fur Company. Mackinac Island was the headquarters of the joint operation. Thus by the time of the War of 1812 the great fur-trading companies had made peace with each other.

For many years, however, the Americans had been irked by the prevalence of British traders on American soil. They traded not only at Mackinac, but also at several places in what is now Wisconsin, including Green Bay and Prairie du Chien. Zebulon Pike, who led an American expedition to explore the headwaters of the Mississippi River in 1805, found British traders everywhere in the northern woods who were not even aware they were on American soil. The Americans were convinced that the British were arming the Indians and constantly urging them to resist the settlement of the West. This was an important factor in building up the resentment that led to the declaration of war in 1812.

British dominance in the pre-war years could have been reduced or ended had there been a large influx of American settlers into the territory, but few came. With only a tiny area cleared of Indian title, and with no government surveys, there was no chance of the kind of vigorous growth that was being enjoyed at the time by Ohio and Indiana. To most Americans, Michigan remained a remote area, isolated from the rest of the country. Not for another twenty years, when these conditions changed, did Michigan begin to attract a substantial share of the pioneers who had been moving into the Middle West since the late 1780s.

The period of 1805–1812, however, was not barren of constructive accomplishments. Father Richard was proving to be an extremely useful citizen. He devised a plan for the education of Indian children, providing training in crafts as well as common-school education at a school he established at Springwells, below Detroit, in 1808. Richard succeeded in persuading the government in Washington to provide a modest subsidy for the school. He also brought a printing press to Michigan, the first product of which was a child's spelling book. And on August 31, 1809, Richard's press printed the first Michigan newspaper, *The Michigan Essay* or *Impartial Observer*. It is doubtful that much interest was shown in the venture, because so far as is known only one issue was published.

Woodward, though impatient and often impractical, was an able judge. One case that he tried involved slavery. Most well-to-do Detroiters owned one or more Indian or Negro slaves; William Macomb at one time owned twenty-six. The case that came before Woodward, however, involved slaves that had come into Michigan from Canada. Seeking to recover them, their owners brought suit. Woodward denied their petition on the grounds that the Northwest Ordinance had prohibited slavery and that slaves could be held in Michigan only if they had been owned before the end of the British regime, or were fugitives from another American state. His decision was acclaimed in the north and was popular in Detroit, where anti-slavery sentiment partially involved the common man's jealousy of wealthy people who owned slaves.[7]

Governor Hull's outstanding achievement as governor was a treaty he negotiated with the Ottawa, Chippewa, Wyandot, and Potawatomi Indians. In 1806 and 1807 rumors of an Indian uprising reached Hull, and he called out the militia to strengthen the fort and to repel a possible attack. Instructions were sent to Hull from Washington to negotiate a treaty with the Indians. A council of chiefs was called to meet at Brownstown, on the river below Detroit, and on November 7, 1807 a treaty was signed by Hull and the chieftains of the four Indian tribes.[8] In return for a payment of $10,000 in goods and money and an annual payment of $2,400, the Indians ceded to the United States an area that included roughly the southeastern quarter of the lower peninsula. The Indians retained the right to hunt and fish on the lands. This was the first major cession of Indian lands in Michigan.

Although there is no indication that there was any unusual difficulty in persuading the natives to make this cession, resentment against the United States government was building up, and was to constitute a major factor in bringing about war between the United States and Britain. The Indians of the Middle West found an able leader in the person of Tecumseh, a chief of the Shawnee. His name meant "shooting star," and was bestowed upon him because a meteor streaked across the sky the night of his birth. He had a handsome face, a noble bearing, and a high degree of intelligence. His oratory made him the idol of his people. He had a brother, a one-eyed mystic known as The Prophet, who proclaimed with great fervor that if the Indians would revert to their primitive way of life and cease their dependence on the white man they could drive the latter from their hunting grounds. These were the same views held by the Delaware prophet at the time of Pontiac's uprising, four decades earlier. The Shawnee prophet's influence was enormously enhanced by the performance of a miracle. Sometime earlier he had learned from a British trader that a total eclipse of the sun would take place on June 6, 1806. On that day he appeared wearing a dark robe, a crest of raven's wings in his hair, and a black scarf over his sightless eye. Pointing his finger at the sun, he ordered it to disappear, which the sun obediently did. Later he called out to the Master of Life to lift the shadow from the face of the sun, and soon the sun shone again. The combination of a skilled warrior who was highly respected and intelligent with a brother who was regarded as a miracle worker had the effect of rallying not only the Shawnee but many other Indian tribes to resist the United States.[9]

The Americans in the West were convinced that the rumblings among the Indians were the consequence of British intrigue. The extent to which this was true is difficult to estimate, but regardless of this factor there was substantial basis for Indian alarm and resistance. Year by year, through bribes, threats, doubletalk, and the covert use of liquor, the United States had gained title to more and more of the Indian lands. The most aggressive and effective United States agent in negotiating the treaties in which the natives gave up their lands was William Henry Harrison, governor of Indiana Teritory. Showing little sympathy or humaneness toward the Indians, Harrison would

Tecumseh

deal with whatever chiefs he could persuade to sign a treaty. Sometimes a parley would be called at the insistence of the Indians to protest against a cession made without the approval of all the Indians concerned; on other occasions Harrison would take the initiative to assemble the chiefs to right an alleged wrong. The result never varied: more lands were surrendered. Governor Hull was simply following the pattern set by Harrison when he secured a vast tract of land in Michigan from the Indians in 1807. The squeeze on the Indian's hunting grounds was intensified by the movement of the Sioux into Wisconsin in search of furs, forming a barrier to the expansion of the woodlands Indians in that direction.[10]

Beginning in 1806, Tecumseh bent all his effort to organize a confederation of Indians to resist the Americans. Although his attempt to enlist the Iroquois in his cause failed, he succeeded in uniting the northern Algonquian peoples. While he was in the South trying to persuade the natives of that region to rally to his cause, Governor Harrison assembled a force and moved against the Indian settlement that was the center of the resistance movement: Prophetstown, at the confluence of the Tippecanoe and Wabash rivers, near the present Lafayette, Indiana. The Prophet, who was in command, had been instructed by his brother not to begin hostilities under any circumstances, but he unwisely disregarded this advice. Early on the morning of November 7, 1811, the Indians attacked. Harrison's men, whom the Prophet had proclaimed would be rendered helpless by his magic, successfully repelled the onslaught, losing thirty-eight dead and 150 wounded. The Indian losses were about the same. Prophetstown was evacuated by the Indians and later burned by Harrison's men. Harrison's force outnumbered the Indians by almost three hundred. It was not a decisive victory by any means, but Harrison declared that the Indians had sustained the most severe defeat in the history of their relations with the whites, and this notion became enshrined in myth and legend. Twenty-nine years later, Harrison was to win a campaign for the presidency of the United States as the hero of Tippecanoe.

Even though the idea that Harrison had won a great victory became generally accepted, it was clear that he had not solved the Indian problem. Depredations against American settlers increased rather than diminished. After Tippecanoe, the common belief in the West was that the only way to eradicate the Indian menace was to drive the British out of Canada. Harrison reported that each of the Indians at Tippecanoe had received a gun, a scalping knife, a war club, and a tomahawk from the British; that some of the guns were so new that the wrappings had not been removed. On the frontier the feeling was universal that British incitement was at the base of the Indian troubles. About a month after the battle of Tippecanoe a group of young men from the West and South who zealously advocated this view took seats in Congress. Known as the War Hawks, they included Henry Clay of Kentucky, Felix Grundy of Tennessee, and John C. Calhoun of South Carolina. They were full of confidence that the United States could defeat the British; Clay declared that the Kentucky militia alone could win Canada. Their efforts won success when, on June 18, 1812, Congress declared war. The war resolution passed in the House of Representatives by a vote of 79 to 49, in the Senate by 19 to 13. Congressmen from New England, New York, and New Jersey voted against war; the heavy vote in favor of war by western and southern Congressmen was decisive.

For many years there had been a diplomatic conflict between Great Britain and the United States over the rights of neutrals on the high seas in time of war. Since 1793, the British had been engaged in a war against France, except for one brief period of truce. Although the United States had disputes with France as well as with Britain over American rights to trade with belligerents, the controversy was more heated with Britain because of the greater sea power of the British. The War of 1812, which climaxed this hostility, was called the fight for a free sea by several generations of American historians. Recent scholarly writings on the war have returned to the view that the war was caused basically by the dispute over neutral rights. Beginning in 1911, however, historians began to stress the role of the South and the West in precipitating the conflict. They pointed out that the very section of the country whose Congressmen voted against war had the largest stake in shipping and maritime commerce. They cited the irrefutable evidence that in the decisive vote in Congress, it was western and southern Congressmen who led the forces favoring war.

There is no doubt that resentment against the British, based on the conviction that they were principally responsible for Indian troubles, was a major cause of the western desire for war. But there were other components. Several writers assert that "land hunger," manifested in greed for Canadian lands, pushed the westerners to cry for war. Another element may have been the economic distress that prevailed in the West for several years prior to 1812. Westerners were disposed to blame the British blockade and British interference with American shipping for the low prices they received for their grain. Ironically, at the time Congress declared war in June of 1812, the British government had decided to remove the regulations it had imposed on neutral shipping, but the news had not yet reached Washington.[11]

Never did a nation enter a war with such supreme confidence in ultimate victory or such a lack of organized military strength to win such a victory as did the United States in 1812. It was the last of the series of wars that had been fought since the seventeenth century over the issue of who would control the North American continent. In addition to its traditional role as the staging point for war parties that attacked the enemy at other points in the Middle West and East, Michigan was for the first time the site of some of the most bitter fighting in the war. The initial engagements on Michigan soil in 1812 had disastrous consequences for the Americans, and the events of the later years of the war were only slightly more favorable from the American standpoint.

In the fall of 1811, Governor Hull had traveled to the East to visit his home in Massachussetts and to go to Washington for consultations with the government. While in Massachussetts he received the news of the battle of Tippecanoe, which caused him to offer his military services to the Secretary of War in the event that a full-scale war erupted not only with the Indians but also with the British. In February, 1812, Hull went to Washington to present his analysis of

Michigan's dangerously weak position in the event of war, and his recommendations for improving that situation. While urging the concentration of a large military force at Detroit, from which point an invasion of Upper Canada could quickly be launched, Hull warned that Detroit could not be held by the Americans if the British were allowed to have naval control of the lakes. He urged the construction, therefore, of at least one more vessel to accompany the *Adams,* the sole American armed ship on the upper lakes. At the nation's capital, however, the primary concern was the defense of the Atlantic seaboard and on various schemes for conquering Canada; thus, Hull's advice and suggestions, among the best evidence that we have that the man was not without ability and good judgment, were largely disregarded. However, after repeated urging from Secretary of War William Eustis, Hull early in April accepted the appointment of commander of the new North Western Army, with the rank of brigadier-general and the somewhat unusual provision that he would also retain his post as governor of Michigan.

By the middle of April, 1812, Hull had set off to the West to resume his old duties as governor and to assume his newly acquired military responsibilities, which included not only the forces at Detroit and Michilimackinac but those at such other military posts in the Old Northwest as Fort Wayne in Indiana and Fort Dearborn, the future city of Chicago. Hull brought with him a regiment of regular army soldiers, commanded by Lieutenant-Colonel James Miller, and three regiments of Ohio militia called into federal service, commanded by Colonels Duncan McArthur, James Findlay, and Lewis Cass, the latter making his first appearance in the history of Michigan, with which his distinguished political career would be inextricably linked during the next half century. By June 30, the force of some 1200 men had reached the mouth of the Maumee in northern Ohio. As yet, Hull had not received word that since June 18 the United States had been at war with Great Britain. Rather than notifying his commanders in the field of this development by dispatching special couriers, Secretary of War Eustis had trusted this vital message to the ordinary postal service. Hull, therefore, thought it was safe to lighten the burdens of his forces on the remaining overland journey to Detroit by loading much of their baggage onto an available schooner, including a chest containing his military papers, although this was placed on board contrary to Hull's orders. When the vessel appeared off Fort Malden, the British, aware that war had been declared, forced it to surrender and in the process secured invaluable information on the size and strength of Hull's army. Hull had advised the ship's captain to pass Bois Blanc Island on the

American side, but since the captain did not know that the war was on he chose the less difficult channel between the island and the Canadian side of the river.

Hull did not learn of the declaration of war until July 2. He received the news before his troops had reached Frenchtown (the present city of Monroe), in a letter dated June 18. Hull and his men arrived at Detroit three days later and found that Secretary Atwater had collected a small militia force, which, together with the ninety-four regulars stationed at Detroit, brought Hull's total forces to around 2,000 men, although estimates of his and other commanders' forces in the War of 1812 vary greatly.

On July 12, Hull invaded Canada, carrying out his part of the American war plan which called for a multi-pronged invasion of Canada. Hull's troops crossed the river just below the foot of Belle Isle and landed without opposition in what was then known as Sandwich. Hull established his headquarters in a newly constructed brick house which survives today in Windsor—as the community is now called—and is maintained as a local museum by the Hiram Walker Company. Hull issued a proclamation, the wording of which was probably the work of Lewis Cass, in which the Canadian people were informed that the Americans had come to free them from British tyranny and that volunteers would be accepted, but, they were warned, if "you should take part in the approaching conflict, you will be considered and treated as enemies, and the horrors and calamities of war will stalk before you." A few deserters from the British army and some civilians cast their lot with the American cause, while some Canadian militiamen returned to their homes, but on the whole this bombastic declaration seems to have had limited effect on most Canadians. Hull treated the civilians in such a manner as to win their favor, doing his best to prevent looting by his soldiers. John Askin, the old Michigan fur trader and British subject, praised Hull for protecting his property. Askin had four sons in the British service, but his wife and three sons were in Detroit, while one son-in-law was in the Michigan militia. The plight of Askin's family was typical of the divisions that this war brought to many in the Detroit River area.

The first objective of the invaders was to capture Fort Malden. Lewis Cass had gone to the fort under a flag of truce on July 6, and although he had been blindfolded when he entered the fort itself, he saw enough as he approached it to convince him that it could not withstand a determined attack. Its defenders have been variously estimated at from a few hundred to well over a thousand regulars, militiamen, and Indians. Hull, like most cautious commanders, was inclined to accept the highest estimates. In addition, however, the British had three warships based at Amherstburg that could have raked a besieging American force with their cannon, while the only American naval vessel, the *Adams,* was in drydock at River Rouge at the outbreak of the war and, as it turned out, could not be put into service in time to help Hull. At a council of war, therefore, Hull and his chief officers decided to delay the attack on Fort Malden until gun carriages for the artillery could be brought across the river which would give the Americans the firepower needed to counter the British naval supremacy. In spite of Hull's efforts to hasten this operation, it was not until August 7 that the gun carriages were ready. A week and a half earlier, however, Hull had received news that Mackinac Island had fallen to the British, and the resulting prospect of the descent upon Detroit of hostile forces from the north, particularly hordes of Indians, raised grave doubts in Hull's mind that he could hold on to Detroit, let alone continue the plans to attack Fort Malden.

The capture of Fort Mackinac less than a month after the decla-ration of war was due largely to the initiative and ability of Captain Charles Roberts, a veteran of many years' service in various outposts of the British empire who was in command of the British garrison on St. Joseph Island or St. Joseph's, as it was called at that time. By the first of July, Roberts had learned that a state of war existed. The American fur trader, John Jacob Astor, had sent an agent to safeguard trade goods that Astor's company had stored on St. Joseph's before the onset of active military operations would disrupt trade in that area. Astor's messenger was a loyal British subject who promptly relayed the news of the American declaration of war to Roberts, as he had done to other British officials on his way up to St. Joseph's. Roberts at once began preparations for an attack on Fort Mackinac. He commandeered a schooner belonging to a British fur-trading company, helped himself to guns and supplies belonging to Astor and other fur traders, and enlisted the help of John Johnston at the Soo and other traders as well as approximately 150 *voyageurs.* Roberts had less than fifty regulars, but his forces were further en-larged by hundreds of Indians, some of whom had been brought from Wisconsin by the trader Robert Dickson, who had been alerted to the possibility of war the previous winter. Other Indians were brought in from the Upper Peninsula by the British Indian agent at St. Joseph's, John Askin, Jr., who was himself half Indian.

Lieutenant Porter Hanks, the American commander at Fort Mackinac, had a force of sixty-one men. The War Department was as dilatory in notifying Hanks of the outbreak of war as it had been in the case of Hull. By mid-July, more than two weeks after Roberts had heard the news, Hanks still did not know that war had been declared. He had, however, noticed a growing sullenness among the Indians who were coming to the island. Suspecting that something was afoot, Hanks sent a resident American trader, Michael Dousman, to St. Joseph Island, to try to find out what the British were up to. Since Dousman frequently had business concerns that took him to that island, Hanks reasoned that his appearance would arouse no suspicions. However, Dousman never completed his mission, for while en route from Mackinac on the night of July 16–17, he ran into Roberts and his men on their way to attack Fort Mackinac. Dousman was taken prisoner, but was released when the British landed on Mackinac Island. Despite the fact that he was a captain in the Michigan militia, Dousman promised not to reveal the British presence on the island to Hanks, but instead warned the civilian inhabitants to seek safety in an abandoned distillery on the west side of the island where they might escape the wrath of Roberts' Indian allies.

Roberts' force landed at 3 a.m., July 17, in a cove on the northwest shore of the island, a spot that has ever since been called British Landing. Roberts had brought with him two six-pound artillery pieces, and his *voyageurs* managed to drag one of these to the high ground that rises over a hundred feet immediately behind the fort. Thirty years earlier, a British officer sent to inspect the newly-constructed fort pointed out that it would be at the mercy of artillery from this high ground. Hanks had made no attempt to safeguard the fort's rear, perhaps because he had so few men, or because he doubted that artillery could be landed on the island and hauled to that point by an enemy force. Fort Mackinac, constructed of eight-foot-thick stone walls on a high bluff, appears formidable even today, as one views it from the harbor below, and no doubt it gave the Indians in 1812 an impression of great strength. Actually, however, it was vulnerable not only because of the undefended high ground in the rear but also because the garrison was dependent for its water supply on sources outside the fort.

When Hanks was informed by Roberts of the strength of the attacking force and saw that the fort could be raked with artillery fire from above, he knew there was no chance for a successful defense. Roberts also warned him that once an attack was launched the British might not be able to restrain the Indians from killing prisoners and civilians alike. Hence, Hanks decided to surrender without firing a shot. His force was permitted to march out of the fort with the honors of war, and Hanks and most of his men were shortly shipped off to Detroit under parole, after promising not to take up arms against the British until a formal exchange of prisoners could be arranged.[12]

While control of Mackinac was falling to the British without a fight, General Hull was readying his attack on Fort Malden. Two expeditions sent into the interior of the Canadian side of the Detroit River returned with arms, provisions, and supplies. On July 16—the day that the British started for Mackinac Island—Hull learned that a British force had crossed to the north side of the Canard River, about six miles above Fort Malden. Hull sent Lewis Cass with three hundred men to investigate the report, but with orders not to engage the British. Cass disregarded the orders and drove the enemy from the bridge over the Canard. He was disgusted when Hull ordered him to withdraw because his men would be exposed to fire from a large British warship anchored in the Detroit River off the mouth of the Canard. Two British pickets were wounded and taken prisoner in the skirmish. One of the wounded men died soon after. These were the first casualties of the Detroit campaign and possibly of the entire war.

On July 28, after hearing of the fall of Fort Mackinac, Hull sent word to Captain Nathan Heald, commander at Fort Dearborn, ordering him to withdraw to Fort Wayne, Indiana. Heald began the evacuation on the morning of August 15. A small group of friendly Miami Indians escorted the fifty-four regulars, twelve militiamen, nine women, and eighteen children as they set out on their journey. Heald had been warned by one of the fur traders, John Kinzie, formerly from Michigan, not to leave the fort, but he disregarded the warning. After the Americans had proceeded about a mile, they were attacked by a band of Potawatomi Indians, most of them from southwestern Michigan. The Miami fled, and over half the whites were killed before the remainder surrendered. Two women and twelve children were tomahawked. Mrs. Heald received several bullet wounds, but she and her husband survived and were taken to Fort Mackinac where they were briefly held as prisoners.[13]

About a week after the news of the fall of Fort Mackinac was brought to Hull, and before the disaster at Fort Dearborn, the Americans in the west suffered an even more ominous setback. Hull had been requested to send a force to the River Raisin for the purpose of escorting seventy packhorses laden with flour, three hundred cattle, and reinforcements of militia to Detroit. Captain Henry Brush, in command of this supply train, refused to go on alone when he learned that he might be attacked by Tecumseh and his Indians. Hull therefore ordered Major Thomas Van Horne to lead about two hundred men by a back trail from the mouth of the Ecorse River, to avoid Tecumseh, who was reported to be farther down the Detroit River at Brownstown. Leaving Detroit on the afternoon of August 4, Van Horne camped for the night at Ecorse. The next morning, he failed to find the back trail and proceeded instead along the river trail. Although two of his men were ambushed and killed by Indians just beyond Monguagon (present-day Trenton), Van Horne pushed ahead to Brownstown Creek which he started to cross without sending scouts ahead. A sudden burst of gunfire came from the brush, and the militiamen fled in terror back to the Ecorse, although

MICHIGAN DURING THE WAR OF 1812

Tecumseh's attacking force probably numbered no more than twenty-five warriors. The Indians' fire had great effect, however, killing eighteen of the Americans and wounding twelve others. In addition, the Indians captured Hull's dispatches to Washington, which, when opened by the British at Fort Malden, informed them of how precarious Hull viewed his position to be.

After learning of the defeat at the battle of Brownstown, near the present town of Gibraltar, Hull held a council of war. It was decided to attack Fort Malden at once. A few hours later, however, Hull learned that the British General Isaac Brock was on his way from Niagara with heavy reinforcements for the garrison at Fort Malden. This caused Hull to abandon the plan to take the offensive. On August 8, the main body of his troops was moved back across the river to Detroit, leaving only a small force in a temporary fortification at Sandwich. The Ohio militia colonels again protested, but to no avail. Hull then moved to bring the supply train from the River Raisin to Detroit. He dispatched Lieutenant Colonel James Miller with 280 regulars and over 300 militiamen. A British and Indian force was encountered at Monguagon, and after a lively fight the Americans drove off the attackers. Miller lost eighteen men killed and sixty-four wounded, while British losses included twenty-one soldiers killed as well as at least forty Indians. Miller sent word to Hull asking for rations and boats to evacuate the wounded. Although these were sent, he made no move to advance to the Raisin, and on August 12, Hull ordered him to return to Detroit. The following day, Hull made one last desperate effort to move the supplies and reinforcements from the Raisin to Detroit, sending four hundred men, under McArthur and Cass, by an inland route in order to avoid contact with the British and the Indians. Late that same day, August 13, Brock and his reinforcements arrived across the river at Fort Malden.

Brock's arrival was made possible by the inactivity of General Henry Dearborn, in command of American forces in the East. Dearborn, like Hull, was an aging veteran of the American Revolution and had drawn up the plans for an American invasion of Canada. But while Hull was trying to carry out his part of this plan, Dearborn, from his headquarters in Albany, had shown no great energy in organizing the forces under his command for the planned offensives at Niagara and at one or two points farther east. Unfortunately for the Americans, the British commander in Upper Canada, General Brock, was a man of action and an experienced officer who realized that the only way he could maintain the support of the Indians and the wavering Canadian militia, who were essential to the defense of

Canada, was to win some victories. News of the fall of Fort Mackinac had raised the spirits of Brock's forces and had led him, early in August, when he saw that the Americans were not going to take any immediate action on the Niagara front, to detach approximately six hundred of his soldiers from that front and lead them across to confront Hull at Detroit. Instead of attempting any kind of diversion that might have held up Brock's departure, Dearborn, on August 9, agreed to a proposal from George Prevost, British commander-in-chief in Canada, for an armistice arrangement. Prevost believed that a negotiated settlement to the war was in the offing. The armistice at the time did not apply to the western regions, which were not under Dearborn's jurisdiction. Hull would later charge that Dearborn, by agreeing to the armistice, had made it possible for Brock to move to Fort Malden, thereby sealing Hull's fate. However, Brock had already left for the West before August 9 and knew nothing of the armistice until August 23, a week after he had captured Detroit.

Brock was a man of commanding presence, with a brilliant military record. He made a very favorable impression on Tecumseh and the other Indian chiefs when he arrived at Fort Malden. On August 15, Brock quickly called on Hull to surrender, warning the American commander, as Captain Roberts had warned Lieutenant Hanks a month earlier, of the danger of an Indian massacre if there was resistance. Hull refused, whereupon Detroit was bombarded by shore batteries on the Canadian side of the river and the guns of two ships. The American batteries returned the fire, and the artillery duel lasted until ten in the evening and was resumed the following morning. The Americans suffered several casualties, including Lieutenant Porter Hanks, who was killed on the morning of August 16 while answering to a court martial inquiry into his surrender of Mackinac Island.

Early that same morning, Brock, with some seven hundred regulars and militia, crossed the river below Detroit and joined the Indians who had already landed on the American side. During the morning, Hull decided to surrender when he learned of the massing of enemy forces down the river. In the absence of Cass and McArthur, he had only a few more than a thousand men to defend the fort. Brush had been ordered to move his supply train on the inland trail to Godfroy's trading post (the site of the present city of Ypsilanti), where it would be joined by Cass and McArthur. Brush, however, refused to move, still fearful of an Indian attack. Failing to find Brush at Godfroy's post, Cass and McArthur and their men headed back toward Detroit and camped about three miles from the town. They made no move to assist Hull, although the sound of the artillery duel must have been audible to them, nor did they let Hull know that they were so close by. It is a moot point whether Hull's decision on August 16 would have been different had he known that Cass and McArthur and their four hundred militiamen might be available to help in the defense of Detroit. It does appear, however, that Hull's fears for the safety of the civilians in the event of an attack on Detroit in which the Indians took part were the major determinant in his decision to surrender without a fight.

The terms of surrender that Hull accepted included the men under Cass and McArthur and also the detachment under Brush. The latter refused to permit the British to seize his men and supplies, withdrawing into Ohio. Cass and McArthur brought their men in, but bitterly condemned Hull for his decision. The militiamen were paroled and sent home. Hull and the regulars, several hundred in number, were sent to Quebec as prisoners of war. Leaving Colonel Henry Procter in command at Detroit, Brock returned to Niagara in time to take command of the British forces when the Americans finally invaded Canada. Unfortunately for the British cause, Brock was killed in the course of the battle of Queenston Heights on October 13. Nevertheless, his troops defeated the Americans, which left the British triumphant in the upper Great Lakes region as the winter months descended on the area.

William Hull was paroled in October, 1812, and returned to his home in Newton, Massachusetts. It was Hull himself who requested that the army convene an official inquiry into his actions at Detroit, and after long delays a court martial opened in Albany on January 3, 1814. Hull was accused of cowardice, neglect of duty, conduct unbecoming an officer, and treason. He was acquitted on the last charge, but the court found him guilty of the other charges. The court sentenced Hull to be shot, but it also suggested that the President set aside this sentence in consideration of Hull's good record during the Revolution, a suggestion that President Madison accepted.

Hull retired to his home in Massachusetts where, until his death in 1825, he fought to rehabilitate his reputation. Michigan historians have tended to give too much credence to the arguments presented by Hull in his defense. Although it is undoubtedly true that Hull's task at Detroit would have been less difficult if Dearborn, who was, ironically, the presiding officer at Hull's court martial, had been more active in the summer of 1812, and if Hull's subordinates, including Lewis Cass who testified against Hull at his trial, had been less insubordinate, Hull's own shortcomings as a military commander were an even more important factor in the loss of Detroit. The decision of the court martial may not have been entirely justified and the sentence that was originally imposed was undoubtedly unwarranted, but to contend that the entire proceedings were simply for the purpose of making Hull the scapegoat that would cause the public to overlook the failures and shortcomings of others in Washington is to ignore the fact that Hull was in command at Detroit and that he must bear the immediate responsibility for what happened there.[14]

The capture of Detroit was a stunning victory for the British, probably the most important of several that their undermanned forces in Canada achieved over the Americans in 1812. As the year closed, Napoleon—England's great foe on the European continent—was in retreat from Russia, his once great army half starved and half frozen. England prepared to move in for the kill. For most Englishmen, the war in America was only a sideshow, but even there victory seemed in sight. Fortunately for the Americans, most of Britain's might during the next year was concentrated on the defeat of France rather than on finishing off its staggering former colonies in the New World.

Following Hull's capture, his position as commander of the decimated American army in the northwest was taken by William Henry Harrison, who immediately began raising troops in Ohio to retake Detroit. In January, 1813, a detachment of Kentucky militiamen under General James Winchester had advanced as far as the rapids of the Maumee, near present-day Toledo. On January 17, Winchester sent Colonel William Lewis with nearly seven hundred men over the frozen Lake Erie to Frenchhown, from whose inhabitants he had received an urgent appeal for protection against the threat to their lives and property by the Indians. Lewis found a small force of Canadian militia and Indians in the settlement and succeeded in forcing them to retire to Fort Malden some twenty miles away. He then sent to Winchester for reinforcements. Winchester arrived on January 20 with three hundred more men, and made himself comfortable before the hearth of Colonel Francois Navarre, the principal citizen in the town. Winchester recognized the danger of an attack from the British forces but he failed to deploy his men in positions that could have enabled them to beat off an attack. Colonel Procter, meanwhile, assembled a force of from 1,200 to 1,400 British soldiers, Canadian militia, and Indians and surprised the Americans in Frenchtown in the predawn hours of January 22. The American right flank was overwhelmed, suffering heavy losses. Winchester and Colonel Lewis were among those captured. The American left, in a stronger position, had beaten off the attackers at that point, but surrendered with the rest of the American force after Procter had promised that the

Americans would be safeguarded by the British from the Indians' fury. The British commander then retired to Fort Malden with his troops and the prisoners who could walk, fearing that he might be attacked by Harrison. The wounded who were left behind were put under the care of two army surgeons. Early the next morning, two hundred Indians, angry at the losses they had sustained in the previous day's fighting, roared into the town, murdered and scalped the prisoners, and set fire to the houses in which they were lodged. How many wounded Americans were left behind in Frenchtown and how many were killed in what was immediately dubbed the River Raisin Massacre is uncertain. The numbers cited vary from as low as thirty to a high of one hundred.[15]

This frightful affair aroused bitter hatred against Procter for what was considered purposeful neglect of his captives. Throughout the West the battle cry became "Remember the River Raisin." Even in Detroit, Procter was so maligned and criticized that he declared martial law and arrested several prominent citizens, including Father Gabriel Richard. Judge Augustus B. Woodward, who had remained in the town after the British took possession, labored manfully to protect the lives and properties of American citizens from British reprisals and Indian fury. The battle of the River Raisin was the bloodiest battle ever fought on Michigan soil. Only sixty survivors of the force of about a thousand men found their way back to the Maumee.

The defeat and capture of Winchester threw Harrison on the defensive. A few miles above the present city of Toledo, Harrison built a fort on the Maumee which he named in honor of Ohio's Governor, Return J. Meigs. At this fort, artillery, ammunition, food supplies, and clothing for Harrison's army were collected. Flushed with his victory at Frenchhown, Procter, late in April, 1813, led a force of 2,500 men in an assault on Fort Meigs. Over half of his force consisted of Indians, many from Michigan, who were led by Tecumseh and another Indian leader, Roundhead. The Americans in Fort Meigs suffered very heavy losses, but Procter was forced to lift the siege on May 9, not because of the effectiveness of the American resistance but because his Indian allies were losing interest in the campaign and were drifting away. Some of the Canadian militia were also leaving in order to do their spring planting.

Attempting to salvage some prestige, Procter tried to capture a stockaded post near Lower Sandusky called Fort Stephenson. The American commander there was Major George Croghan, a twenty-one-year-old Kentuckian. His garrison was small and his artillery was limited to a single six-pound cannon, nicknamed "Old Betsy."

Nevertheless, he rejected a demand that he surrender. In reply to a warning that the Indians could not be restrained from slaughtering the entire garrison after the fort was taken, Croghan replied: "When the fort shall be taken, there will be none to massacre. It will not be given up while a man is able to resist." Harrison, who had his army in camp nearby, refused to come to Croghan's aid, believing Procter had an army larger than his own. But the heroic Kentuckian withstood the assaulting force, and lost only one man killed and seven wounded, while the British lost fifty men and two officers. Croghan was the hero of the hour, and Harrison joined in singing his praises.

The British attacks in northern Ohio in 1813 constituted the highwater mark of their efforts in the West. The whole nature of the war in that area was about to be changed by developments at what is now Erie, Pennsylvania, where the Americans in the fall of 1812 had begun the construction of a fleet to contest the British control of Lake Erie. Lieutenant Oliver Hazard Perry arrived in March, 1813, to take command of the project. Perry, whose better-known title, commodore, was an honorary title used by any naval officer who had command of a fleet, soon had two brigs and two gunboats completed. American success on the Niagara frontier enabled five additional vessels to join Perry's force. Armament had to be transported overland from Pittsburgh and Philadelphia. Still short of manpower, Perry's next problem was transporting these new vessels across a sandbar and out into Lake Erie. A British fleet under Commodore Robert H. Barclay hovered offshore, ready to pounce on Perry once the opportunity arose. Early in August, however, Barclay had taken his ships elsewhere, and Perry had his chance. By August 5 he had maneuvered his two largest vessels, as well as the smaller, shallower draft vessels, over the sandbar into Lake Erie. Perry then took his small fleet to Sandusky Bay.

Conferences with General Harrison followed. Harrison now had seven thousand men and was ready for an assault against the British in Detroit as soon as the British fleet could be defeated. Lieutenant Jesse D. Elliott arrived with 102 officers and men to help man the ships, and Harrison detailed about a hundred Kentucky riflemen—most of whom had probably never seen a ship before—to serve in place of those on Perry's sick-list. Put-in-Bay in the Bass Islands would be Perry's headquarters from which he could watch the British fleet at Amherstburg.

Commodore Barclay, meanwhile, hesitated to leave the protection of the guns of Fort Malden until construction had been completed on a large new British ship, the *Detroit*. The desperate need for food supplies at Malden, which could not be obtained so long as

Perry remained vigilant, finally prompted Barclay to sail for Long Point, chief deposit base for supplies on the Detroit River. Perry saw his opportunity and at once took his fleet out into the lake to challenge the British. Perry had nine ships to Barclay's six, and had more guns. But the British outclassed the Americans in long-range guns. For this reason, Perry instructed his officers to close in as rapidly as possible. He showed the men a blue battle flag, bearing in white letters the words "Don't give up the ship," the dying words of Captain James Lawrence, who had commanded the American ship the *Chesapeake* in a battle off Boston harbor earlier that year. At 11:45 a.m. on September 10, Perry hoisted the flag to the top of his flagship, the *Lawrence,* and the battle was on.

Well before Perry could reach the British with his guns they had started pounding his flagship with their long-range cannon. The *Lawrence* continued to approach Barclay's flagship, the *Detroit,* until the vessels were blasting at each other almost side by side. The *Detroit* was joined in the attack on the *Lawrence* by two smaller British vessels as well as by the *Queen Charlotte,* second largest of the British ships. Instead of closing with the *Queen Charlotte* as he had been instructed by Perry to do, Lieutenant Elliott, in command of the *Niagara,* Perry's second brig, stood off and fired only his two long-range guns. The British ships attacking the *Lawrence* suffered severe damage. The *Queen Charlotte* lost both her commander and her second-in-command. Captain Barclay aboard the *Detroit* was severely wounded and his second-in command was killed. The *Lawrence* was in even worse shape. Her rigging was shot to pieces, and by 2:30 p.m. every one of her guns had been knocked out of action. Of her 103-man crew, 83 had been killed or wounded. Perry, miraculously still unscathed, now made a daring move. Hauling down his flag, he embarked in a rowboat and was transported through a hail of gunfire to the *Niagara.* Taking command of this vessel, he sent Elliott to bring the smaller American ships into action, then brought the *Niagara* into the thick of the battle. This vessel, so far virtually untouched, turned the tide. Although the *Lawrence* had struck her colors she had done such damage to the British ships that the *Niagara* and the smaller American vessels quickly finished them off. On orders from Barclay the entire British fleet surrendered. The British lost forty-one killed and ninety-four wounded in the engagement; the American loss was twenty-seven killed and ninety-six wounded. Perry then penned his famous message to Harrison: "We have met the enemy and they are ours, two ships, two brigs, one schooner and one sloop."[16]

The victory won by Perry opened the road to the capture of

Detroit. Harrison transferred his main force to the Canadian side. Procter evacuated Fort Malden on September 24. Two days later the British forces were pulled out of Detroit after burning the public buildings. Procter retreated eastward toward the Thames River, hotly pursued by Harrison, whose progress was facilitated by an early frost that hardened the ground. Tecumseh, having lost faith in Procter, tried to halt Harrison's advance, but his Indian warriors were brushed aside. Forced to give battle, Procter, on October 4, chose a position on the north side of the Thames River. An impetuous charge by the Kentucky mounted regiment was completely successful. Procter fled eastward with a small number of mounted men, while his British army surrendered to Harrison. The Indians under Tecumseh put up a harder fight, but when their great leader was killed by members of the mounted Kentucky regiment commanded by Colonel Richard M. Johnson, the natives fled into a swamp, pursued by Kentuckians seeking vengeance for the massacre at River Raisin.[17] Procter, like Hull, was court-martialed after this British defeat. He was found guilty on several counts of poor leadership, was publicly reprimanded, and suspended for six months.

Meanwhile, Perry had arrived at Detroit on September 29 and found it had been evacuated by the British. The same day, General Duncan McArthur, in command of seven hundred men, occupied the town. He declared an end to British martial law, and once again placed Detroit under American civil government. The fort at Detroit, which had been called Fort Lernoult by the British and later Fort Detroit, was now renamed Fort Shelby in honor of the Kentucky governor—Isaac Shelby—who had raised a force of 3,500 Kentuckians for the war in the West.

Lacking supplies and equipment to continue his invasion of Canada, Harrison led his forces back to Detroit, and the Kentucky militiamen returned to their homes. Harrison and Perry were national heroes. Bonfires and "illuminations" lighted many a western town in their honor. Congress gave Harrison the thanks of his countrymen and a gold medal. But it had been Perry's victory that had opened the way for the British defeat at the Battle of the Thames and for the American reoccupation of Detroit. On October 19, Perry and Harrison left for Niagara, leaving Lewis Cass in command at Detroit. Ten days later, President Madison appointed Cass governor of Michigan territory, a position he would retain for eighteen years.

The American recapture of Detroit and control of Lake Erie posed a serious problem for the British on Mackinac Island. Captain Richard Bullock, who had succeeded the ailing Charles Roberts as commandant, had only a small force at his disposal. A horde of western Indians who came to Mackinac in the summer of 1813 had exhausted his scant store of provisions. Harrison had planned to send an expedition north to take Fort Mackinac in the fall of 1813, but it was so late in the season before the expedition was ready that plans to send it were postponed. However, it was also too late for the British at Mackinac to obtain supplies by an alternative route to that which they had been using by way of Lake Erie and the Detroit River. The residents of the island, therefore, were in desperate need of food that winter.

British strategists recognized the vital importance of Mackinac, and early in 1814 decisive steps were taken to hold onto it. British authorities to the east in Canada dispatched large quantities of flour, biscuits, pork, salt, rum, and armaments to Nottawasaga Bay in Georgian Bay, which bypassed the American-held Lake Erie supply route. A regiment under Lieutenant Colonel Robert McDouall, a Scotsman who was an eighteen-year veteran in the British army, accompanied the supplies, which reached Mackinac Island in May. McDouall superseded Bullock in command. Bullock had already taken steps to strengthen the island's defenses by constructing a fort on the high ground behind Fort Mackinac to prevent the Americans from using the same tactics Captain Roberts had employed in 1812 to capture the island.

In June, news reached McDouall that the Americans had captured Prairie du Chien, situated where the Wisconsin River joins the Mississippi. This was in the heart of an area long dominated by British traders. The attack had come from Missouri militiamen, under the command of Brigadier General William Clark, of Lewis and Clark Expedition fame. Clark had moved up the Mississippi from St. Louis to occupy Prairie du Chien as a means of forestalling a possible attack on Illinois and Missouri from that direction. When he heard what had happened, McDouall quickly organized a motley force of approximately one hundred fur traders, *voyageurs,* militiamen, and a Royal Artillery sergeant—James Keating—together with several hundred Indians. McDouall placed them under the command of Major William McKay, and sent them to retake Prairie du Chien. The force was almost doubled by acquisitions at Green Bay and at other points along the way. Clark had foolishly assumed that sixty men could hold the fort. After holding out three days they surrendered, largely because Sergeant Keating had effectively used a tiny cannon that he had transported all the way from Mackinac Island.[18]

News of the victory at Prairie du Chien reached Mackinac in July about the same time a report that an American expedition was approaching the island was received. This expedition had left Detroit on July 3. The naval commander was Captain Arthur Sinclair, and in his fleet were the ships that had participated in the Battle of Lake Erie the previous year, as well as the *Caledonia,* a vessel used by Captain Roberts to transport his men in the attack on Mackinac in 1812. The ship had been captured by the Americans late in 1812 and thus had the unique distinction of participating in both the British and American expeditions against Fort Mackinac. The troops aboard the vessels were under Colonel George Croghan, the hero of Fort Stephenson, with Major Andrew Hunter Holmes as second in command.

The operation was bungled and mismanaged from the outset. Sinclair and Croghan had been directed on their way north to destroy the British installations supposedly built at Matchadash Bay to supply Fort Mackinac, but when the ships arrived in Lake Huron it turned out that no one knew how to get there. After giving up on that objective, the Americans, instead of proceeding immediately to the attack on Mackinac, went to the St. Mary's River, where they burned the abandoned British fort on St. Joseph Island. After this, a force led by Holmes proceeded to Sault Ste. Marie where they burned a ship belonging to the North West Company, and seized or destroyed goods that belonged to the trader John Johnston, who was serving with the British on Mackinac.

When the expedition finally got around to its major objective of taking Fort Mackinac, there seems to have been no thought given as to how to go about it, in spite of the fact that former residents of the island and soldiers who had served at the fort were aboard. A party sent to reconnoiter Round Island at the entrance to the harbor on the south side of Mackinac Island was chased off by Indians. The next day it was discovered that the guns of the *Lawrence* and the *Niagara* could not be elevated sufficiently to hit the fort, high up on the bluff overlooking the harbor. After several days of indecision, prolonged by bad weather, a landing was made on the north side of the island near where the British had landed in 1812. But this move by the Americans, unlike that of the British two years before, was no surprise to the island's defenders. Every move of the Americans was watched. When the troops started to advance inland, the Indians ambushed them and killed Major Holmes. Croghan then withdrew his men from the island, believing the costs of a direct assault against the entrenched British and Indian positions would be too great. Instead, it was decided to force the British to surrender by cutting off their supplies.

The Americans had learned that the British were supplying Mackinac from Nottawasaga Bay, and on their way back to Detroit with the main fleet, Sinclair and Croghan attempted to destroy this base. They sailed up the river, destroyed a blockhouse, and captured a schooner laden with supplies destined for Mackinac. Meanwhile, two of the smaller American vessels had been left behind to patrol the northern Lake Huron waters and cut the British supply lines until winter. The British on Mackinac Island, however, demonstrating remarkable resourcefulness, managed to surprise, board, and capture the American ships, the *Scorpion* and the *Tigress*.[19]

The capture of these two vessels on September 3 and 5, 1814, brought an end to fighting in the Great Lakes area. It was a crowning indignity to the American cause, and left the entire northern part of the Great Lakes under British domination. A week after the capture of the *Tigress,* an American victory far to the east on Lake Champlain salvaged the American cause. Commodore Thomas Macdonough defeated a British fleet that was guarding and supplying a British invasion expedition, and thus brought about the failure of this ambitious British project. It was the turning point of the war, for when news of this defeat reached Europe, Great Britain recognized it could demand no spoils of war without making a further all-out effort. The Duke of Wellington, the British hero of the campaigns against Napoleon, turned down an offer to assume the command in Canada. Heavily in debt and tired of war, the British agreed to peace on the basis of the conditions that had prevailed before the war. Thus, Mackinac Island, Prairie du Chien, and all the northern Great Lakes area were restored to the United States. The treaty containing these provisions was signed on Christmas Eve, 1814, at the Belgian town of Ghent.

Once again, Europe's distresses had spelled American successes. Michigan was restored to the United States, not through military victory but through shrewd negotiation and war weariness in Britain. Mackinac Island was turned over to American forces on July 18, 1815, and the British garrison withdrew to Drummond Island. The exact location of the international boundary as defined in the treaty of 1783 had not been determined at that time, and the British assumed that Drummond Island lay on their side of the line. The Treaty of Ghent provided for the appointment of a joint commission that would survey the boundary. At issue were several islands in the Detroit and St. Mary's rivers. When it began its work in 1822, the commission decided not to divide any of the islands but to award them in toto either to Canada or the United States, with the channel normally used by vessels in navigating these rivers being the determining factor. The commission thus decided that Bois Blanc Island (or Bob-lo, as it has come to be called) at the mouth of the Detroit River should be part of Canada, while Drummond Island, near the entrance to the St. Mary's River, should be part of the United States.

The willingness of the British to accept the latter decision and to abandon by 1828 the fort they had constructed on Drummond Island, was one evidence of the desire of the two nations to avoid future situations that might lead again to war. The boundary commission, however, was unable to agree on the disposition of what is now called Sugar Island in the St. Mary's River, and the American ownership of this piece of Michigan territory was not conceded by the British until the Webster-Ashburton Treaty of 1842.

The Treaty of Ghent did not conclusively settle all of the issues that had precipitated the war. It made no mention, for example, of the American demand that the British guarantee freedom of the seas to neutral nations, and this issue remained a subject of contention during the years after 1815. However, although there were a number of occasions in these years when war was threatened, the two nations avoided conflict as they pioneered the practice of turning these problems over to commissions to arbitrate and settle. There was also a decision to avoid a heavy buildup of military and naval strength on either side of the American-Canadian border. The first step in this direction was an executive agreement reached in 1817, called the Rush-Bagot Agreement, which halted a naval armaments race that had begun after the war on the Great Lakes. The agreement provided that neither country would maintain armed vessels on the lakes, except a token force for the regulation of commerce. This pact was not always observed in the years that followed, and land fortifications along the border were not only maintained but increased in the period immediately after the war. But it was the first step toward disarmament along the international boundary.

The results of the War of 1812 were decisive in determining Michigan's future development. It would be many years yet before the threat of another Anglo-American war could be safely ignored, but there could be little doubt after the Treaty of Ghent that Michigan would remain an American possession. In addition, there was no doubt that the war also marked the final triumph of the farmers in their long fight to have more lands opened to them and to end the dominance of the fur-trading interests in the area. For the Indians these results had devastating consequences. Up to this time they had been regarded as a highly important element in the population because of the military role they played in time of war and the vital economic role they played in the fur trade. As the possibility of war in the area lessened after 1815, and the economy shifted away from the fur trade, the Indians soon came to be regarded as a people who could be conveniently forgotten.

Early settlers' house

8

EXIT THE FUR TRADER; ENTER THE FARMER

Although the years following the War of 1812 soon witnessed a dramatic transformation of Michigan away from the kinds of activities that had for so long dominated the area, the decade immediately after the war saw the fur trade enjoying its last great period of growth in Michigan. During this period it was dominated by John Jacob Astor and his American Fur Company, a dominance that was in effect a result of the war. Astor, as noted earlier, had entered into an agreement with the Canadian fur-trading companies in 1811 to share the trade within the United States. During the war, Astor's company was of course under a severe handicap, since Mackinac was in British hands from 1812 until 1815. Promptly upon cessation of hostilities, Astor resumed his fur-trading activities at Mackinac. The Treaty of Ghent, however, radically altered the situation with respect to the fur trade, since it did not contain a renewal of the right granted to British citizens in Jay's Treaty to trade in United States territory. Instead, in 1816, Congress forbade the licensing of anyone who was not a United States citizen to trade with the Indians or even to serve as clerks or boatmen, unless by express direction of the President. This placed Astor in a position to squeeze his Canadian associates out of the American trade, which he promptly proceeded to do. Early in 1817 he purchased the goods, buildings, and business of the South West Company, which was the name of the organization that he had formed jointly with the Canadians.

Astor then set about eliminating all his competitors. Through political influence at Washington he was able to persuade Congress in 1822 to abolish the government "factories" or trading houses. Senator Thomas Hart Benton from Missouri was retained as an attorney by the American Fur Company; it was he who led the fight against the government trading houses. While eliminating competition from this source, Astor also ruthlessly destroyed the independent traders. Through the intervention of Michigan Governor Lewis Cass, he secured exemptions from the prohibitions against the use of foreigners in the fur trade for the many traders, clerks, and boatmen in his employ who were Canadians, while making it extremely difficult for his competitors to obtain similar exemptions. It was Astor's practice to select his best traders, send them to locations where they competed with independent traders, and authorize them to sell trade goods to the Indians at extremely low prices. By such means most of the independents were squeezed out of business and forced to become vassals of the American Fur Company. Where the independents combined into strong rival companies, Astor, instead of fighting them, would buy them out. Although some of the traders who worked for Astor traded at the risk of the American Fur Company, it was Astor's aim to put them all on a share-trading basis, which allowed them to share in any profit earned in their transactions, but also required them to share any loss. Trade goods were supplied by the company at the highest market price, while the furs were bought from the traders at rates that allowed for possible declining values.[1]

In Washington, Astor wielded enormous political influence. Not only was he able to secure the passage of legislation that would benefit his company, but he also had so much influence and power that he could have the laws administered in such a manner that they would serve his ends. If the laws got in his way he seemed to be able to evade or violate them with impunity. Lewis Cass, as governor of Michigan territory during the heyday of the American Fur Company, time and time again served Astor's interests. After the passage of the law prohibiting foreigners from engaging in the fur trade but giving the President the power to grant exemptions, President Madison delegated this authority to Cass, as governor of Michigan territory, and to the Indian agents of the United States at Mackinac, Green Bay, and Chicago. Cass, in a letter to the Indian agent at Mackinac, instructed him in veiled language to provide Astor's agent there with all the licenses he asked for, while granting only a small number to other traders. Perhaps Cass should not be blamed too much for this favoritism, since the War Department had instructed him to afford Astor's agents "every facility in your power consistent with the laws and regulations."[2] But this was only one of many ways in which Cass served Astor's interests. The unusual favors granted to Astor's com-

pany by Cass as governor of Michigan territory and later as secretary
of war led many traders to assume that the American Fur Company
was actually a quasi-official institution.

It has been claimed that Cass received a bribe of $35,000 to
allow Astor's agents special privileges. This claim is based on two
newspaper accounts describing items in the account books of the
American Fur Company. Both tell that an entry in these account
books stated that Cass took about $35,000 of Astor's money from
Montreal to a place in Michigan—one says Mackinac, the other Detroit. But a careful scrutiny of these account books later by Astor's
biographer, Kenneth W. Porter, revealed no such entry, although in
one account book Porter found a page had been torn out following
the entry of May 12, 1817. In 1909, the New York *Times* gave May
13, 1817, as the date of the entry in question. Although it must be
admitted that the missing page arouses suspicions, the fact remains
there is no solid evidence that Cass took a bribe from Astor. Even
the newspaper accounts, if taken at face value, do not prove Cass
accepted a bribe, but only that he took the money from Montreal to
Michigan for Astor. To assume that Cass accepted a bribe from Astor
is not consonant with the character of this great statesman, although
one must acknowledge that ethical standards in such matters were
different in the early nineteenth century than they are today. Senator
Benton's reputation did not suffer because he accepted attorney's
fees from Astor while serving Astor's interests in Congress, nor was
Daniel Webster condemned for having accepted retainers from the
Bank of the United States while fighting that institution's battles in
Congress.[3]

Astor's principal agents at Mackinac were Robert Stuart and
Ramsay Crooks, both Scotsmen. Each received an annual salary of
around $2,500, but they profited in other ways from the enterprise.
At the lowest level of the economic scale were the boatmen, who
were paid about $83.00 per year, out of which they had to buy their
clothes and supply their personal wants, including tobacco. Astor
squeezed the traders so hard that few of them made any money, and
many incurred losses. Although the enormous Astor fortune was
ultimately derived largely from real estate investments, it is estimated that during the seventeen years he was head of the American
Fur Company, he cleared between one and two million dollars.[4]

The use of intoxicating liquor in the fur trade was the greatest
evil connected with it, as far as the Indians were concerned. Having
no conception of moderation, the Indians were debauched and de-
graded by the traders' fire-water. As early as 1802, Congress passed
an act designed to prevent the use of liquor in the fur trade. A

regulation imposed by the President in 1817, another Congressional act in 1822, and still another in 1832 failed to eradicate this curse. In one way or another the various regulations were evaded or violated. In 1832, 8,776 gallons of liquor were delivered to Mackinac. The following year, in spite of a new and stringent law passed by Congress, 5,573 gallons were imported. There is evidence that Astor actually would have preferred to bar liquor from the trade. He was convinced the Indians would be more productive trappers were they denied strong drink. But he was forced to meet the competition of independent traders who, driven to desperation by the policies of his company, used liquor to attract the Indians to their trading posts. Astor also claimed he was compelled to use liquor in trading to meet the competition of the Hudson's Bay Company.

Although Astor maintained a trading post at Detroit, Mackinac Island was the principal center of the Michigan fur trade in this era. In the fall, traders set out in all directions, their boats filled with goods for trade with the Indians, such as blankets, beads, hats, traps, spears, hooks, and firearms. Most traders had several assistants, often including one or more Indians. Each was assigned to a trading post where he would remain for the winter, exchanging his goods for the furs brought in by the Indians. In the spring the furs were put aboard craft called "Montreal barges," capable of carrying about eight tons in smooth water. They were propelled by oars or sails and when they reached the Great Lakes they clung to the shore. There were high-jinks aplenty on Mackinac Island when these traders arrived one by one, received their remuneration, and sought release from the rigors of a long winter in the woods. Dances and banquets were given, the merry-making invariably continuing until daybreak. The man or group being honored would return the courtesy the following night. As many as three thousand Indians sometimes camped along the beach, their wigwams often two or three rows deep. Woodsmen, clerks, *voyageurs,* and adventurers from many European countries met and mingled here. Their lives were rough and adventurous, punctuated by drunkenness, brawling, and frequent murders.

At the height of its success, the American Fur Company employed between two and three thousand boatmen and trappers and more than four hundred clerks on the island. Four large white-frame buildings, situated on Market Street, were utilized by the company. Two of these survive intact, a third has been reconstructed, and the fourth has been torn down. Oldest of the four was the warehouse built in 1810 with hand-hewn beams. This building is now used as a community hall. The Agency House, built in 1817, was the home of Robert Stuart and Ramsay Crooks, the principal company agents, and lodged many clerks and traders as well at the height of the season. It is now a museum. The third building was called the Clerk's Quarters and was used to house clerks and warehousemen in the summer months. Later in the century, these three structures were linked together and were operated as a hotel—the John Jacob Astor House—until 1929. In 1941, the units were separated and restored to single buildings. The Clerk's Quarters fell into decay and the structure was removed. A post office built in the same style as the other structures now stands on the site.

The fourth of the Astor buildings on Market Street, somewhat separated from the others, was the retail store. After the decline of the fur trade it was completely altered, but in 1954 it was rebuilt in what was purportedly the original style. Along the same street is the old courthouse, built in 1839, and now used as a city hall, and the Biddle House, oldest house on the island, now restored with the original structure still, in part, retained. All these buildings help make Market Street one of America's most historic thoroughfares, and the exclusion of automotive vehicles from the island helps to create the illusion, as one walks or rides in horse-drawn carriages along the street, that he is making an excursion into the past.

Some of the traders at Mackinac had remarkable careers, such as Gurdon Saltonstall Hubbard from Vermont. In 1818, when he was sixteen years old, Hubbard came to Mackinac Island to work as a clerk for the American Fur Company. He continued in the fur trade for a number of years, conducting a post on the Kalamazoo River for a time and later being assigned to a post on the site of the present city of Chicago, where, after leaving the employ of Astor, he became a meat packer and merchant. At one time he was a member of the Illinois legislature. Before his death in 1886 he was interested in plans for a huge hotel on Mackinac Island, which later materialized as the Grand Hotel.[5] Another of Astor's men was Rix Robinson, who was well educated and had completed his preparation for a career in law. During the War of 1812 he came to Detroit as a sutler in the army. He met John Jacob Astor who, much impressed by him, hired him as a trader. He was first assigned to the Illinois country. Later he conducted the fur trade for Astor on the Kalamazoo River, then transferred to the Grand, with a trading post near the present town of Ada. He lived there for the remainder of his life. He married an Indian woman to whom he was deeply devoted. He read widely and was active in political affairs as state senator for four terms and as a member of the Constitutional Convention of 1850. He came to be one of the most prominent and highly respected citizens of the state.[6]

Among the independent traders was Louis Campau, a native of Detroit and one of many French-Canadians engaged in the fur trade. He was employed soon after the close of the War of 1812 by Detroit merchants to trade with Indians in the Saginaw valley and was described as an intelligent, shrewd, and farsighted operator. He helped negotiate the Treaty of Saginaw, he befriended the first white settlers in the area, and in 1822 he platted the "Town of Sagina." In 1826, he shifted his trading operations to the present city of Grand Rapids and is regarded as that city's first settler. A square in the city is named in his honor. In 1831 he purchased a seventy-two-acre tract in the heart of Grand Rapids.

John Jacob Astor sold his American Fur Company in 1834, possibly because of advancing age and ill health. The "northern division" was acquired by Ramsay Crooks, who continued fur trading on Mackinac Island for several years under the same company name. But by 1834, the fur business was definitely shifting westward, with St. Louis, rather than Mackinac, becoming the major center of the trade. At about the same time, the substitution of silk for beaver skins in the manufacture of high hats was decreasing the demand for Michigan furs.

The fur business, however, did not completely die out in Michigan. Dealers in furs are still to be found in Detroit, where, despite all the changes that have occurred in that city, nearly fifty fur retailers, manufacturers, and wholesalers were in business in 1977. Elsewhere in Michigan in the mid-1970s, an estimated ten thousand trappers supplemented the income they received from other sources by obtaining furs and hides valued annually at approximately $9,000,000—three times the annual intake at Astor's Mackinac operations in the early 1820s. This does not include the value of the minks raised in captivity, whose pelts in 1966 were valued at nearly $6,000,000.[7]

Around the same time that Mackinac Island was a mecca for Astor's traders, a Presbyterian mission was founded on the island and a school was opened to train Indian youths to be teachers and interpreters in the mission work in the country's interior. This school, founded in 1823, was supported by eastern missionary societies, and was superintended by the Reverend William Ferry.[8] In 1825, a structure known as the "Mission House" was built for use by the school and as a boarding house. This house later became a hotel. A church, built in the New England style, was constructed in 1830, and is today one of the oldest surviving church structures in the Middle West. St. Ann's, the Catholic church, now occupies a sanctuary, surmounted by a tower and spire, that was built in 1874, and is the successor to several structures in which this church has been housed since the eighteenth century.

By the early part of the nineteenth century, Mackinac Island was well known for its healthful climate. By 1838 it was a well-established summer resort, with visitors being turned away for lack of accommodations. Several hotels and boarding houses were erected within the next few decades. That part of the island not privately owned became a national park in 1875, the second such park to be created. The Grand Hotel, with its extensive front porch, reportedly the longest in the world, was opened in 1887. Francis Stockbridge of Kalamazoo, a wealthy lumberman and United States Senator, was the leading figure in its construction, which was financed by railroad and steamship companies. The Grand became one of the nation's most fashionable summer hotels, with noted national and world figures numbered among its guests. When the army decided to abandon any further use of the fort in 1895, the national government transferred the fort and the park property to the state, which established it as Michigan's first state park, operated by the Mackinac Island State Park Commission.

During the heyday of the island's fur-trading years, an incident occurred that was to lead to one of the most famous and unusual research studies in medical history. On the morning of June 6, 1822, a young *voyageur,* Alexis St. Martin, was accidentally shot while in the Astor retail store. The young man received a shotgun charge in his chest and upper abdomen at point-blank range. Dr. William Beaumont, the fort surgeon, was summoned, and arrived twenty minutes later. Beaumont, a native of Connecticut, had studied medicine in the manner then customary: by associating himself with a practicing physician. He was thirty-six years of age in 1822, and had been surgeon at the fort for two years. When he first saw St. Martin he described the patient's condition as "an appalling and hopeless case." Membrane and muscle had been blown off, the diaphragm and left lobe of the lung had been lacerated, and the stomach had been perforated. Beaumont thought the young man could not live, but was wrong. With constant care and attention by Beaumont, who removed the patient to the fort hospital, St. Martin miraculously withstood the shock, and after fighting a violent fever for ten days he began to improve. By the fourth week his appetite became good and healing was well under way. Instead of falling back into the abdomen to its natural position, the protruded portion of the stomach adhered to the chest wall. By that means the orifice in the wounded stomach remained in contact with the external wound. By April, 1823, St. Martin was well enough to walk about and do light work. But he was not in a condition to support himself and he became a pauper. Beaumont took St. Martin into his own family, which he had to support on his meager salary of $40 a month. It was not until 1825 that the idea crystallized in his mind that he had a unique opportunity to observe the processes of digestion. For, strange as it seems, the way the wound had healed permitted free access to the interior of the stomach without impairing its functions.

Thus began a series of experiments and observations which were to extend over a period of years. St. Martin became known as "the man with a window in his stomach." He was fed different types of foods by the doctor, who then observed exactly how digestion took place. The first report on his observations was published in 1826 in a magazine called the *Medical Recorder.* In 1833, Beaumont's *Experiments and Observations on the Gastric Juice and the Physiology of Digestion* was published. This work is one of the classics of medical research, and with the passage of time it has assumed progressively greater importance. To honor Beaumont, the Michigan Medical Society in 1954 restored the Astor retail store where St. Martin was wounded, and made it a depository for artifacts related to Beaumont's discoveries.

Beaumont was transferred from Mackinac Island in 1825, but managed to take St. Martin along so that the experiments could be continued. At his own expense Dr. Beaumont maintained St. Martin until 1834. On several occasions, St. Martin unceremoniously departed for Canada, where he had found a wife, and Beaumont had to foot the bill for his return. Beaumont petitioned Congress for a grant of $1,323.75 to compensate him for the time he had spent and the expense he had incurred in treating St. Martin, since he had made the experiments "for the benefit of the public and the advancement of science," but Congress turned him down. He resigned as army surgeon in 1839 and became a medical practitioner in St. Louis, Missouri, where he died in 1853. St. Martin did not die until 1880 and was buried in Quebec. At the time of his death the way of life that he symbolized had been for a half century superseded in Michigan by that of the farmer.[9]

*　*　*　*　*

Farming on an extensive scale developed slowly in Michigan. Until 1818 it was not possible to obtain legal title to any land in Michigan except for small areas in the immediate vicinity of the two principal settlements at Detroit and Mackinac. There were "squatters," of course—pioneers who helped themselves to land in the expectation that when it was placed on the market by the government, their rights to ownership would be accepted. Pioneers repeatedly called for "pre-emption" rights that would allow a settler to buy the land on which he had settled at the minimum price when offered for sale by the government. Congress occasionally passed such special acts, but it was not until 1841 that a general pre-emption law was enacted. At best the pioneers took a risk when they invested their time and labor on the improvement of land that was not their property.

Before any land could be legally obtained by settlers, the government first had to persuade the Indian tribes to relinquish their claims to the land. To the American pioneer, the Indian was of no importance to the economy. As the fur trade declined and agriculture took its place as the mainstay of Michigan's economy, the Indian became a barrier to the exploitation of the area's land resources. Because there was no war with the Indians after the pioneers began coming to Michigan in large numbers, as there had been, for example, in Kentucky, there was no great antipathy among the settlers toward the Indians as individuals. Those Indians who engaged in petty thievery or who became bothersome when drunk were a nuisance, but no more. What the Michigan pioneer wanted was the Indian's land; what became of the Indian was of no concern to him.

The status of the Indian tribes under American law was that of nations within a nation. Each of the treaties with Indian tribes was subject to the approval of the United States Senate, just as were treaties with foreign countries. What is now Michigan was included within the territories ceded to the United States by Great Britain in 1783. But the *land* of Michigan was the property of the Indian tribes and was so recognized by law. It remained the property of those tribes until it was ceded to the United States by treaty. The first Michigan lands had been obtained from the Indians by the Treaty of Greenville in 1795, and a much larger tract had been secured by the Treaty of Detroit in 1807. The next cession in 1817 was of a small area along the Ohio border just to the west of the lands described in the treaty of 1807. Under the Treaty of Saginaw, signed in 1819, another immense tract in the northeastern sector of the lower peninsula was ceded. By the terms of the Treaty of Chicago in 1821 most of the land in the southwestern part of the lower peninsula south of the Grand River was acquired, while the northwestern section of the peninsula and the lands in the Upper Peninsula to the east of the present city of Marquette were ceded in the Treaty of Washington in 1836. By the time Michigan was admitted to the union in 1837, only the western part of the Upper Peninsula and a few tracts that had

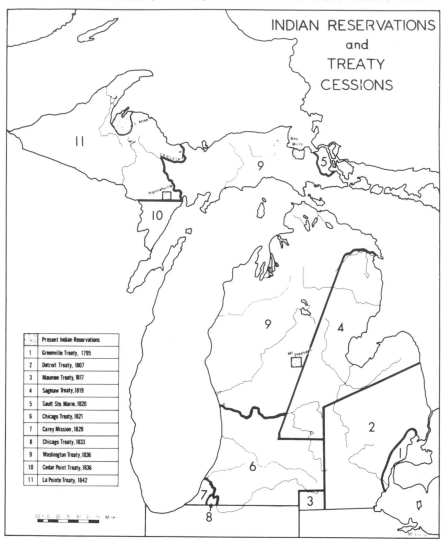

INDIAN RESERVATIONS
and
TREATY
CESSIONS

	Present Indian Reservations
1	Greenville Treaty, 1795
2	Detroit Treaty, 1807
3	Maumee Treaty, 1817
4	Saginaw Treaty, 1819
5	Sault Ste. Marie, 1820
6	Chicago Treaty, 1821
7	Carey Mission, 1828
8	Chicago Treaty, 1833
9	Washington Treaty, 1836
10	Cedar Point Treaty, 1836
11	La Pointe Treaty, 1842

been "reserved" for the Indians had not been obtained. The final major cession, involving the western Upper Peninsula, came with the Treaty of La Pointe in 1842.

The story of the Treaty of Saginaw illustrates the manner in which these Indian land cessions were generally secured. The incentive for the treaty came from individuals who had visited the Saginaw Valley, believed the area had a great future, and hence were ambitious to secure lands for settlement or speculation. They made their desires known in Washington and the government instructed Governor Cass to negotiate the desired treaty, providing him with $10,000 to defray the costs. Pursuant to these instructions, Cass sent word for the Ottawa and Chippewa to meet with him near the junction of the rivers flowing into the Saginaw. The date set was in the full of the moon in September, a time when the Indians had gathered their harvests but before they had set out on winter hunting. Two ships were loaded in Detroit with provisions and liquor for distribution at the proper time, and a company of soldiers was put aboard to protect the negotiators. Louis Campau was instructed to build a council house; this consisted of a roof of boughs supported by trees, the sides and ends left open, and in the middle a long platform with rustic benches for Cass and the other officials. Cass arrived on September 10, 1819, with a staff of assistants and interpreters. Preliminaries lasted for about two weeks, during which time anywhere from 1,500 to 4,000 Indians assembled. Cass started with a lengthy speech, with necessary pauses for translation by interpreters. In his remarks he made known the extent of the lands that he desired to purchase. Indian orators replied at length, and meanwhile the Indians pondered the question of whether they would cede their lands.

The tract Cass proposed to buy from the Indians consisted of some six million acres, nearly one-sixth of Michigan's total land area. The Indians would receive a lump sum of $3,000 in cash, and an annual payment of $1,000 plus "whatever additional sum the Government of the United States might think they ought to receive, in such manner as would be most useful to them." This flexible provision was rather unusual, and apparently was inserted by Cass. He justified it in a letter to Secretary of War John C. Calhoun as a measure of justice to the Indians, intimating that he was uncertain just how much should be paid for the lands.[10] The government also agreed to furnish the Indians with the services of a blacksmith, and to supply them with farming implements, as well as teachers to instruct them in agriculture. Calhoun had suggested to Cass that he endeavor to persuade the Indians to migrate further west, but the governor quickly perceived that they were in no mood to entertain such a proposal, so he dropped it. Reservations for the various bands were provided in the treaty, so the Indians could still live in the area. Cass sensed that even with these inducements the natives were not disposed to agree to the treaty. It was discovered by his assistants that a trapper named Jacob Smith, who had lived among the Indians for many years and had won their friendship and trust, was using his influence against the proposed treaty. They suspected that he might have his price, and this proved to be the case. Eleven sections of land (640 acres each) were set aside for Smith and his friends, after which the chiefs appeared much more favorable. The $3,000 in silver coin was stacked on the table of the council room. Louis Campau, however, claimed that the Indians owed him $1,500 of the money for goods advanced and proposed to take half the silver to fulfill that debt. This was vastly disappointing to Smith and two other traders who were present with goods to sell to the Indians when they were paid. They urged the chiefs to take all the money without deducting what they owed Campau, and this is what the chiefs demanded. Campau was furious, attacked one of the other traders, and the two had to be pulled apart. The treaty was then signed. To celebrate the occasion, Cass authorized five barrels of whiskey to be opened and the contents distributed among the natives. Campau now had his revenge. He opened ten barrels of his own whiskey and began passing it out. The Indians became roaring drunk, and their violence alarmed Cass. "Louis! Louis!" he cried, "Stop the liquor." Campau replied, "General, you commenced it; you let Smith plunder me and rob me." But after another plea, Campau restrained the Indians, saying, "I lost my money; I lost my fight; I lost my liquor; but I got good satisfaction."[11]

It is not entirely correct to assume that the United States paid the Indians little or nothing for their land. Up to 1880, the total cost to the United States government of the public domain acquired from the Indians amounted to $275,000,000, and the surveys of the land had cost another $46,000,000. Total receipts from the sale of these lands to that date were $120,000,000 less than these expenditures.[12] The Indians received for their lands cash, goods, and promises. Often the government agreed to pay annuities to a tribe over a period of years. In the Chicago treaty of 1821, negotiated by Governor Cass and Solomon Sibley, the government, in return for the cession of most of the southwest corner of Michigan, agreed to pay the Ottawa Indians an annuity of $1,000 in cash and $1,500 annually in support of a blacksmith, a teacher, and an agricultural instructor, as well as for cattle and utensils. The government also paid the Potawatomi a $5,000 annuity for twenty years, and $1,000 for fifteen years for a blacksmith and a teacher. Treaties such as this were in later years to lead to numerous suits against the government by Indian tribesmen claiming damages on the grounds that the government did not fulfill its treaty obligations, and in some cases that the Indian tribes had not been paid the fair value of their land at the time.

Until 1946, the ability of the Indians to pursue such legal action was restricted by the requirement that they first obtain Congressional permission before bringing their case to the U.S. Court of

Claims. In 1946, however, Congress created a separate Indian Claims Commission specifically to deal with these suits. This led to what amounted to a general renegotiation of the Indian land treaties, including those involving Michigan lands. By 1975, the commission, while having dismissed 187 claims, ruled in favor of 251 other Indian claims, awarding a total of $561,113,637.36 in additional compensation to the tribes, with 175 other claims still pending at that time. Among the awards that were made, one of the largest was $10,109,003.55 to the Ottawa and Chippewa of Michigan in 1972, although a sizable amount was deducted, as in other awards, for attorneys' fees and payments to expert witnesses who testified in support of the Indians' claim. Once the award was made, it was then up to the Indian organizations involved to decide who was qualified to receive this compensation, and this sometimes led to bitter disputes among the Indians that delayed actual payments.[13]

In addition to actions regarding the land cession provisions of the Indian treaties, prolonged legal actions in the 1970s, resulting in part from the emergence of a more militant attitude on the part of some Indians, revolved around other treaty provisions. In one case, Indian fishermen in northern Michigan claimed they were exempt from state fishing regulations. These claims threatened to precipitate violent reactions from non-Indian commercial and sports fishermen. Another case involved a class action suit against the University of Michigan by a Chippewa Indian student at the university. The suit contended that the treaty of 1817, in which the Chippewa, Ottawa, and Potawatomi Indians of southeastern Michigan had turned over 1,920 acres of land to the "college at Detroit," which was interpreted to mean the University of Michigania established in 1817, obligated the present University of Michigan to provide free education to members of the three tribes.[14]

Although the early land cession treaties had included provisions that permitted the Indians to remain in the area on lands reserved for their use, by the 1830s the government had adopted a policy of moving all of the Indians, including those in Michigan, to areas west of the Mississippi. This Indian removal policy was proposed by President Monroe early in 1825 and had been suggested by others, including Thomas Jefferson, in earlier years. Lewis Cass, who had become recognized as a leading authority on the Indians, at first opposed the removal because of the hardships it would impose on the Indians uprooted from their ancestral homes and forced to move to strange, new lands. In addition, the Indians already living in those lands probably would be hostile to the eastern tribes. However, by 1830, Cass supported the policy, in part because President Jackson was wholeheartedly in favor of it, and in part because Cass, like other backers of the policy, saw it as the only way of saving these Indians from the corrupting effects of contacts with the white men. Moving the tribes west would enable these tribes to preserve their culture.[15]

In a report that accompanied Monroe's proposal in 1825, Secretary of War John C. Calhoun, whose department had responsibility for Indian affairs, suggested areas in the west where the Indians in the east could move. These areas included large parts of northern Wisconsin and the western part of the Upper Peninsula. Beginning in 1825, the Indian removal policy began to be implemented.

Of the principal Indian tribes that were in or near Michigan when the French first arrived, the Miami had moved outside the present boundaries of the state shortly after the beginning of the eighteenth century and only a handful who still remain in northern Indiana escaped the nineteenth-century removal to the west. By an act of Congress in 1809, the Huron, or Wyandot, were given possession of a tract of land in southeastern Michigan. Nine years later Governor Cass negotiated a treaty under which they agreed to give up this reservation and receive instead a tract of 4,996 acres along the Huron River in Wayne County, to be held by them and their descendants as long as they should continue to occupy it. Sometime later the Wyandot left Michigan, moving down into Ohio, and by a treaty signed in 1842 they relinquished all their claims to land in Michigan to the United States. This tribe, once the largest in the upper Great Lakes area, was moved far to the West, where its tribal organization and identity was eventually lost, a victim of the unrelenting pressures the tribe had been under since the arrival of the white man in their original homeland in eastern Canada in the sixteenth century.

The Potawatomi lived in the southwestern part of the lower peninsula when the United States began the process of securing the Indian lands. The tribe ceded its last reservations in Michigan to the United States by the Treaty of Chicago in 1833, agreeing to move to the lands west of the Mississippi that had been assigned to it. The removal was delayed for several years, but between 1838 and 1840, government agents rounded up the tribesmen and their families and started them on the long trek westward. They were first located in Missouri opposite Fort Leavenworth, then after two years were moved to Iowa, near Council Bluffs. They stayed there for only a short time, after which they were moved to Kansas. Here many of the descendants of these Michigan Potawatomi continue to live to the present day, although an additional relocation of some of this group was made later in the nineteenth century to what is now Oklahoma.

A considerable number of Potawatomi, however, remained in Michigan. Some eluded the government agents. Others escaped during the trip westward and returned to Michigan. In some of the treaties, grants of land were made to individual Indians, and although the recipients in many instances sold their land to white settlers, there probably was a considerable number who retained their land. In some cases the treaty grant prohibited the Indians from selling the land for a certain period of time. Leopold Pokagon, a devout Roman Catholic, was able to get an exemption in the Treaty of 1833 that allowed him and his band to remain on the lands he had obtained in Silver Creek Township, Cass County. It is estimated that there were about 250 Potawatomi in Pokagon's group. Pokagon later obtained lands in Van Buren County, around Hartford, where a group of Potawatomi made their homes. His son, Simon Pokagon, was born there in 1830. After the death of Leopold in 1841, Simon Pokagon became the leader of the Pokagon group. In later life he was sometimes described as the best-educated full-blooded Indian in the country. There is considerable evidence, however, that indicates that he would have required a great deal of literary assistance to have written the several books that appeared under his name, the best-known of which, *Queen of the Woods,* contains much information on the Potawatomi language. Descendants of Pokagon's band still live in southwestern Michigan and northern Indiana and maintain a tribal organization.[16] Another group of Potawatomi, living near Athens in Calhoun County, refused to follow their fellow tribesmen west. In 1850, a committee of villagers in Athens managed to secure $3,000 from the government for these Potawatomi, and with the money purchased a small tract of land where descendants of these Indians still live in a settlement called "Indiantown." In addition, some Potawatomi who had lived in Wisconsin in the 1830s moved up into the Upper Peninsula where their descendants live on the Hannahville Reservation in Menominee County.

The Chippewa of the Saginaw area were also slated for removal to lands in Kansas, but as in the case of the Potawatomi, this policy was only partially implemented. A smallpox epidemic in 1837, however, decimated the ranks of these Indians, causing many who survived to flee from the Saginaw area to Canada or elsewhere. Similarly, many of the Ottawa who lived in the lower peninsula escaped the fate of their tribesmen who were removed to the west and fled to Canada where they were welcomed by the Canadian authorities and provided with annual presents. The bulk of Michigan's Chippewa and Ottawa tribesmen escaped deportation when the Treaty of Washington in 1836 reserved five tracts of land, totalling 142,000 acres, in northern Michigan for these tribes, plus several more tracts in the Upper Peninsula exclusively for the Chippewa. In 1854 and 1855 most of these reservations were given up, but by that time the removal policy had been dropped and the federal government agreed to withhold from sale certain lands that would be available to heads of Indian families or to single males over twenty-one years of age. The tribes also received more than a million dollars in payments for the lands previously reserved for them under the 1836 treaty.[17]

The total number of Michigan Indians that was removed to the west was probably considerably less than the number of those who remained in Michigan. Henry R. Schoolcraft estimated that there were 7,737 Indians in Michigan in 1837 before many had been removed, although this figure is probably too low. The federal census of 1860 enumerated 6,172 Indians in the state. The state census of 1874 placed the figure at 10,250, although in 1880 the regular federal census counted only 7,249 Indians. These figures at least would indicate that the number of Indians removed to the west had not been large. Disease, however, took a heavy toll of the state's Indian population; as late as 1921 the Indian death rate was more than double the rate for the population as a whole. By 1920, the total Indian population was down to 5,614, although it is difficult to determine how many people of Indian ancestry had passed over into the white classification.

Since 1920, Michigan's Indian population has increased steadily. By 1940 it stood at 6,282 and by 1970 it had risen to 16,012, behind only Minnesota and Wisconsin in the states of the upper Great Lakes area.[18] The federal government's policy of encouraging the breakup of tribes and the allotment of land to individuals was reversed in 1934 with the passage of the Indian Reorganization Act. An effort was made under this law to help the Indians regain sufficient land holdings for a self-sustaining economy and a self-satisfying social organization. Tribal reorganization was encouraged. Today there are four federal reservations in Michigan, comprising a total of 16,635 acres of land. The largest of these is the Keweenaw Bay Community in Baraga County. The others are the Bay Mills Community near Sault Ste. Marie, the Hannahville Community in Menominee County, and the Isabella Reservation near Mount Pleasant. These lands are held in trust by the United States government for the benefit of the Indians. There is a tribal organization for each reservation, with a written constitution. In addition, a total of four thousand acres are held by the Northern Michigan Ottawa Association, representing nearly six thousand members who live in widely scattered areas, and not necessarily in the L'Arbre Croche area where most of this land is located.

Regardless of federal policy, or perhaps because of it, only a small number of Michigan's Indians have maintained their culture by living together on the lands reserved for them. In 1972, only 2,069 Indians—an eighth of the state's Indian population—were living on the four federal reservations. Economic necessity forced many Indians to leave these reservations where income opportunities were severely limited, and to seek jobs in the urban areas, where 10,541 of Michigan's Indian population was found in 1970. Of the remaining Indians who were found in the state's rural areas, only 288 were actually living on farms. So much for the well-meaning attempts of the white man, dating back to the Jesuit missionaries at Huronia in the 1630s, to make farmers of the Great Lakes Indians.

*   *   *   *   *

As the Indian land titles were extinguished, the next step toward the settlement of Michigan's interior was the survey of these lands. None of the government lands acquired by Governor Hull in 1807 was surveyed until after the War of 1812. The government surveyors began their work in 1815. Their first task was to establish accurately the location of the base line and the prime meridian, from which they would proceed to lay off the townships. The base line was established east and west along what became the northern boundaries of the second tier of counties (Wayne, Washtenaw, Jackson, Calhoun, Kalamazoo, and Van Buren), where the road along these boundaries is still, in some places, called Base Line Road. The prime or principal meridian was established south from Sault Ste. Marie on longitude 84 degrees, 22 minutes, and 24 seconds west. Meridian Road and Meridian Township, east of East Lansing, are so named because they are on or near this surveyors' line. The two lines intersect on the Ingham County-Jackson County boundary, some distance east of US-127, the freeway linking Lansing and Jackson. All land surveyed in Michigan starts from these points of reference, with the townships numbered east or west and north or south of these lines. Thus "T2N, R3W" means the second township north of the base line and the third west of the meridian. The sections within each township are numbered from one to thirty-six, beginning with number one in the northeast corner, continuing westward to number six in the northwest corner. Directly south of section six is section seven. The numbering proceeds back and forth across the township to section thirty-six in the southeast corner.

By 1825, most of the southern third of the lower peninsula had been surveyed. Surveys to the north proceeded slowly from 1825 to

1835 as the government concentrated on road building. Between 1835 and 1840 the survey of the southern peninsula was virtually completed and a start was made on the eastern side of the Upper Peninsula. By 1851, the survey of the entire state was completed, except for some necessary resurveys of some of the inland lakes, rivers, and islands.

The surveys were conducted by individuals under contract with the United States Surveyor General. The surveyor's task was to run a line exactly straight in a given direction and to measure that line in units of one mile. He required two chainmen to measure the line and an axeman to clear the line of brush and to mark corners. A hardwood stake was driven into the ground at each section corner, with about a foot length left showing above the ground. The surveyor worked with a compass set on a tripod. William A. Burt, one of the most active of the surveyors in Michigan, invented a solar compass in 1835, but it did not come into general use until the forties. Surveyors had to mark all trees along the line and to maintain careful records of the crossing of streams, ravines, and hills, the character of the soil and timber, as well as a description of each township. For this work, they were paid from $2.00 to $6.50 per mile surveyed. Working eight months a year, the surveyor could earn as much as $3,000, out of which he had to pay his assistants.[19]

Finally, with the Indian claims settled and the land surveys completed, the sale of public land could begin. A land office had been established in Detroit in 1804, but for some years the officials had been concerned only with settling the land claims of the present residents of the area. On July 6, 1818, the sale of lands began, with an auction held in Detroit. The minimum price that could be bid was $2.00 an acre, but the average price bid at this auction was $4.00, with some of the better lands, located near Detroit, going for as much as $40.00 an acre. Land sales for the entire year totaled $71,108.88, a modest beginning to the settlement of the previously untapped lands of Michigan's interior. The minimum price was reduced by Congress in 1820 to $1.25 per acre payable in cash. At the same time the minimum amount of land that could be bought was reduced from 160 to 80 acres. Thus for a hundred dollars a settler could buy an eighty-acre farm.

A second land office was opened at Monroe in July of 1823, and a third at White Pigeon, in western Michigan, in 1831. The latter, however, was moved to Kalamazoo (or Bronson, as that town was then called) in 1834. Two additional offices were opened in 1836, one at Ionia and the other at Flint. Each office was assigned a given segment of public lands. At these offices, the prospective buyer could obtain maps which showed the lands that were still available, with the letter "S" marking those sections or parts of sections that had been sold. It also was possible to obtain the surveyor's notes as a guide to the quality of the land. Usually the buyer, or someone representing him, would proceed on foot or on horseback to examine the available lands, after which, if he liked what he saw, he returned to the land office and "entered" the lands he wished to buy. He paid in silver, gold, bank notes, or by draft, and was given a receipt. Eventually, after the sale was recorded in Washington, he received a "patent" giving him title to the land he had purchased. These patents were actually signed by the President of the United States until 1833, when the sheer volume of business forced Congress to permit the President to appoint a secretary to sign his name to the patents which were now numbering in the tens of thousands each year. (Thus Michigan land owners who proudly display their original land titles do not, as many of them think, have an authentic Andrew Jackson autograph if the patent is from the period after 1833.)[20]

Even though public lands were available for purchase in Michigan from 1818 on, the amount sold at first was small. It was necessary to clear other obstacles before the great land boom in Michigan could begin. There is some evidence that would support the thesis, quite popular with an earlier generation of Michigan historians, that adverse reports concerning the quality of Michigan land and doubts about health conditions had a discouraging impact on the settlement of the future state. In 1814, General Duncan McArthur, who was stationed at Detroit, declared:

> I have no hesitation to say that it would be to the advantage of Government to remove every inhabitant of the Territory, pay for the improvements, and reduce them to ashes, leaving nothing but the Garrison posts. From my observation, the Territory appears to be not worth defending, and merely a den for Indians and traitors. The banks of the Detroit River are handsome, but nine-tenths of the land in the Territory is unfit for cultivation.[21]

McArthur's remarks were made in a private letter, but if many American soldiers who served in Michigan during the war shared his view of the area they could have been the source of some damaging word-of-mouth publicity for the territory when they returned to their homes.

Another disparaging report on Michigan came from Edward

Tiffin, Surveyor-General of the United States. Congress had provided the veterans of the War of 1812 with two million acres of land as a reward for their service, and Tiffin sent surveyors north from Defiance, Ohio, into the southeastern part of Michigan in the fall of 1815 to see whether the land there could suitably be used for this purpose. The surveyors examined land in the Jackson County area where drainage has always been a problem, particularly in the wet fall season. Their report to Tiffin, therefore, was an unfavorable one, and Tiffin, in turn, reported to President Madison early in 1816 that Michigan apparently consisted of swamps, lakes, and poor, sandy soil not worth the cost of surveying. He declared that in his opinion not more than one acre in a hundred, or perhaps in a thousand, could be cultivated. As a result, Congress designated lands in Illinois and Missouri for the veterans.

How much damage Tiffin's report did to the reputation of Michigan is not clear. Most historians have assumed that it was largely because of the Tiffin Report that there was little interest in settling in Michigan's interior until the late twenties. Unquestionably, a reading of the report would have discouraged anyone from coming to Michigan, but the historian Madison Kuhn, after extensive research, has shown that Tiffin's report was not widely publicized at the time. It was not published in a form that would have made it available to the general public until the 1830s, by which time people were flocking to Michigan by the thousands. Furthermore, Kuhn declares, those reports about Michigan that were published and widely circulated in the post-war years presented a very favorable picture of Michigan. The Detroit *Gazette,* a newspaper that began publication on July 25, 1817, carried many favorable articles concerning the character of the territory, rebutting any derogatory opinions that might be circulating. These articles were widely copied in eastern papers. Three visitors to Detroit in 1818, one an authority on agriculture, gave glowing accounts of Michigan lands in books and articles printed in the East. Geography books of the time also generally lauded Michigan's potential for agriculture.[22]

In whatever way the prospective pioneer may have appraised the available information on the quality of Michigan lands, he may have been discouraged by rumors that the climate in the Detroit area was unhealthy. Hundreds of soldiers had died of disease at Detroit during the fall and winter of 1813. The most common ailment was malaria, which the people of the time attributed to the prevalence of swamps and bogs. In 1823, "intermittent fever" and typhoid fever forced the abandonment of Fort Saginaw. In the East the warning about unhealthful conditions in Michigan was put into rhyme:

> Don't go to Michigan, that land of ills;
> The word means ague, fever, and chills.[23]

In several ways Governor Cass helped undo Michigan's bad publicity. When he read Tiffin's report, which was circulated among government officials even though it was not released to the general public, Cass insisted that Tiffin send his surveyors back into Michigan to take a second look at the land. Later, in 1820, Cass obtained permission from Secretary of War John C. Calhoun to conduct an exploring expedition around the perimeter of the territory for the purpose of appraising the available natural resources, investigating the mood of the Indians, and promoting an interest in the area among prospective settlers. Illinois had become a state in 1818, and Congress had then added to Michigan Territory all the rest of the old Northwest Territory, including what is now Wisconsin and the northwestern segment of Minnesota. Hence, Cass's itinerary took him beyond Michigan's present boundaries. His party consisted of ten soldiers and an officer, two interpreters, nine Indians, twelve *voyageurs,* a physician, a geographer and two assistants, a geologist, a reporter, and a private secretary. Captain David B. Douglass was the geographer and Henry R. Schoolcraft was the geologist. The party left Detroit in three large canoes on May 25, 1820, and after a brief stop at Mackinac Island, where twenty-three soldiers were added to the expedition, Cass reached Sault Ste. Marie. Here he discovered a large band of Chippewa Indians, with their chiefs in a hostile mood. Still under British influence, the principal chief appeared wearing a British officer's red coat, denounced the Americans, and kicked aside the presents Cass had brought. A little later a British flag was raised over the Indian camp. This was more than Cass could tolerate. He walked into the camp, accompanied only by an interpreter, pulled down the British flag, and told the chief that no foreign flag could be flown over American territory. John Johnston, Indian agent at the Soo, was away at the time, but his wife, the daughter of a chief, intervened to warn the Indian leaders that if they harmed Cass' party it would mean a war of extermination against them. Apparently her words were effective, for the chiefs met Cass, recognized American sovereignty, and acknowledged the American right to a tract along the St. Mary's River. The experience led to the establishment of Fort Brady there two years later.

Skirting the southern shore of Lake Superior, the party gazed on the famed Pictured Rocks near present-day Munising and reached the Ontonagon River. Schoolcraft ascended the Ontonagon to see the copper boulder that had been reported by earlier travelers. Cass then proceeded westward by streams and portages to the Mississippi River, which he ascended, seeking its source. He was unable to find the source, however, and turned downstream again as the summer waned.[24] The party returned east by way of the familiar Wisconsin-Fox portage route.

Sending a contingent to follow the coast of Green Bay and the northern shore of Lake Michigan, Cass proceeded with the rest of the party by canoe down the lake to Fort Dearborn. Schoolcraft and Douglass continued along the eastern shore of Lake Michigan and returned to Detroit by way of Lake Huron, while Cass and the others travelled on horseback across lower Michigan from Fort Dearborn to Detroit by way of the Old Sauk Trail (now US-12). The report of the expedition, which was published soon after the parties returned, helped give Michigan a better reputation. Making light of the hardships and dangers involved, Cass stressed that the Indians were peaceful and the land promising. Schoolcraft reported numerous traces of iron and copper in northern Michigan. An important by-product of the expedition was the interest Schoolcraft developed in the Indians. Through Cass's influence he was appointed Indian agent at the Soo in 1822. The next year he married Jane Johnston, daughter of John Johnston and his Indian wife. For many years thereafter he studied every aspect of Indian life and became recognized as the greatest authority of his day on the American Indian. His work *Algic Researches,* published in 1839, contained the material used by Longfellow in his famous poem, *Hiawatha.*[25]

Regardless of the prevailing views of Michigan's land and climate, a more important factor in delaying any large-scale movement into Michigan in the immediate post-war years was the difficulty in reaching the territory. Transportation to Michigan by water was "dangerous, unreliable, and fraught with discomfort."[26] Navigation on Lake Erie was regarded as more dangerous than on the Atlantic. Accommodations for passengers were very poor. To reach Detroit from the south by land it was necessary to cross the Black Swamp in northwestern Ohio. During the war a military road had been constructed over it, but by 1815 this had all but disappeared. In rainy periods the swamp was virtually impassable. The horrors of the Black Swamp were widely publicized. At a time when there was still plenty of good land available in Ohio, Indiana, and Illinois, there was little incentive for the pioneer to brave the hazards involved in getting to Michigan.

Although the first steamboat in America dates back to 1809, it was not until 1818 that steam navigation came to the upper Great Lakes. In that year a 330-ton steamship, rigged with sails to supplement steam power, was launched at what is now Buffalo and was named the *Walk-in-the-Water*. Its appearance did much to improve transportation between Detroit and Buffalo. Where the progress of sailing vessels had depended on the vagaries of wind conditions, the steamship could provide the traveller with more dependable and less time-consuming service. Trips beyond Detroit to Mackinac Island were added in 1819. Cabin passage to Detroit cost $18.00, steerage fare was $7.00. The *Walk-in-the-Water* was wrecked in 1821, but her engine was salvaged and placed in a new ship, the *Superior*. Two additional steamships were launched in 1825, and soon afterward there were more. There was also, however, a marked increase in the number of sailing vessels in the 1820s and later in the century; although passenger service came to be dominated by the steamship, the cheaper rates of the sailing vessels continued to attract much of the freight business on the lakes.

The completion in 1825 of the Erie Canal, connecting Lake Erie with the Hudson River, was an event of major importance in Michigan history because it greatly facilitated the transportation of passengers and freight between the eastern seaboard and Michigan ports. The canal, built by the state of New York at a cost of $7,000,000, was such a success that within three years toll charges had paid the cost of construction plus interest charges. For the first time, New England families, anxious to leave rocky and infertile fields for richer lands in the West, had a route for reaching the "promised land." To the sons and grandsons of an earlier generation of Yankees who had settled in western New York after the American Revolution, the Erie Canal provided a way westward from a land that already was becoming too crowded. And the waterway provided not only an easier way to move to Michigan, but it also made available for the first time an inexpensive method of moving Michigan products to markets in the East. Freight rates between Buffalo and New York were reduced from $100 a ton to $25 a ton with the opening of an all-water route between the two cities, and the rates soon fell even lower.

Important as it was, the Erie Canal did not cause the great migration to Michigan; it only facilitated that movement. This is shown by the fact that public land sales at Detroit reached a high point in 1825, the year the Erie Canal opened, and then declined in the years immediately following. Whereas 92,232 acres had been sold in 1825, sales were down to 70,441 by 1830. Sales at the Monroe land office also declined.[27] There can be little doubt that this decline was due to rising prices in the East, a depression in 1828–29, and the tight money policy of the United States Bank, which made it difficult for prospective settlers to obtain the cash to buy land, to finance the journey westward, and to obtain the capital needed for successful pioneering. It was not until the improvement of economic conditions in the East and the availability of easier credit that pioneers could take advantage of the Erie Canal in moving to Michigan.

For the improvement of land transportation within the territory, Michigan relied heavily on the federal government. In 1816, troops of the Detroit garrison began building a road to the rapids of the Maumee River, near the present city of Toledo. By 1819, it was "cut through" and bridges over runs and marshes had been built, but the road was still poorly located and almost impassable for wagons. Congress appropriated $20,000 for the building of a new road between these points and it was completed after a supplementary appropriation of $12,000 in 1827. A road across the Black Swamp from the settled part of Ohio to the Maumee Rapids was completed the same year. Thus, by 1827, land transportation to Detroit from the south had been greatly improved.

Roads from Detroit into the interior were required, however, before any large-scale settlement was possible. In addition to the road southward, two roads from Detroit to the north and three to the west were projected during the territorial period. In 1816, the territorial government launched a project to build a road northward from Detroit, but the road was inadequate and by 1822 had reached only as far as Pontiac. A post-road from Pontiac through Flint to Saginaw was laid out in 1823, and an appropriation was made by Congress in 1829 to construct it. Intervening swamps made progress difficult, and by 1835 it had been extended only five miles beyond Flint. This is now route US-10. Another Congressional appropriation in 1829 provided funds to begin work on a military road between Detroit and Fort Gratiot (Port Huron). Although it was quite inadequate it was of some use to settlers.

The first road westward also was a military road, designed to connect Detroit with Fort Dearborn. An act of Congress, passed in 1825 at the behest of Father Gabriel Richard (then Michigan's delegate in Congress), provided for the laying out of such a road. Funds were provided in 1827 to extend the road to the Indiana line. It followed the path of the Old Sauk Trail and is the approximate route of the present US-12. It ran westward from Detroit to Ypsilanti, then veered to the southwest, and continued through the southernmost tier of Michigan counties. The eastern portions of this road were in use by the later 1820s, and by 1835 two stagecoaches a week were operated between Detroit and Fort Dearborn. This highway, known then, as parts of it still are today, as the Chicago Road, became "practically an extension of the Erie Canal and . . . a great axis of settlement in southern Michigan."[28] In 1829 the territorial council provided for another road, the Territorial Road, branching off the Chicago Road at Ypsilanti and running through the second tier of counties to its terminus at St. Joseph, approximately the route of today's I-94 freeway. It was laid out in 1830, and by 1834 a stage line, running over it from Detroit to St. Joseph and connecting there with steamers for Chicago, enabled the traveler to complete the entire journey in five days. Although heavily traveled, it was not kept in as good condition as the parallel route to the south. The third of the roads westward was known as the Grand River Road. Some federal aid apparently was secured for work on this road, but although it had been surveyed to Grand Rapids in 1832, it had been completed only as far as Howell by the time Michigan was admitted into the Union as a state. It generally followed the route of the present I-96 freeway.

These roads were a far cry from their modern counterparts. It can hardly be said that they were "built" at all, as we think of highway building today. Surveyors selected the route, often following Indian trails, axemen cut away the brush and felled trees low enough along the path so wagons could pass over the stumps, and workman constructed crude bridges over streams which could not easily be forded. Logs were laid crosswise of the road across bogs and swamps to prevent wagons and animals from miring. This was known as a "corduroy road." Other than this, little was done to provide a surface for the roads. They were notoriously bad. The noted British author Harriet Martineau, who made a journey over them when she visited the "Wild West" in 1836, wrote of the experience: "Juggernaut's car would have been 'broke to bits' on such a road. . . . such hopping and jumping; such slipping and sliding; such looks of despair from the middle of a pond; such shifting of logs, and carrying of planks, and handing along the fallen trunks of trees."[29] One story that went the rounds was that a person found a beaver hat on the Detroit-Pontiac road, and when, at the risk of his life, he waded out to it, he found a man under it and yelled for help. But the man under the hat protested: "Just leave me alone, stranger, I have a good horse under me, and have just found bottom."[30] Settlers along the roads took a proprietary interest in the mudholes, and the right to pull wagons out of one of them for a price was recognized as belonging to the man who lived nearest to it. It was said that these mudholes were fostered carefully in dry weather; one tavern-keeper found a buyer for his property partly, it was said, because he had nearby an especially profitable mudhole.[31] Since the roads were laid out to follow the routes having the fewest obstacles, they seldom were straight. A description of the Chicago Road stated that it "stretches itself by devious and irregular windings east and west like a huge serpent lazily pursuing its onward course utterly unconcerned as to its destination."[32]

Bad as they were, these roads were of utmost importance in the early settlement of Michigan. A major role in their construction was played by the soldiers stationed in the garrisons. Trails branched off along the routes followed by the major roads, which served to guide the traveler to a destination beyond the main roads. Along the chief roads taverns were built and towns sprang up.

Finally, by the end of the twenties, with the relinquishment of Indian claims to the lands in southern Michigan, the rapid progress of the surveys, the opening of land offices, and the improvement of transportation facilities, the way had been prepared for what shortly developed into one of the great land booms in all of American history as settlers poured into and across the lower third of Michigan's southern peninsula.

THE ERA OF THE PIONEERS

From 1830 to 1837, Michigan was the most popular destination for westward-moving pioneers. An "Emigrant's Song," first published in a Detroit paper in 1831, expressed the spirit of the time:

> Come all ye Yankee Farmers,
>   Who'd like to change your lot,
> Who've spunk enough to travel
>   Beyond your native spot,
> And leave behind the village
>   Where Pa' and Ma' do stay,
> Come follow me and settle
>   In *Michigania*.
>
> What country ever growed up
>   So great in little time,
> Just popping from the nurs'ry
>   Right into like its prime;
> When *Uncle Sam* did wean her,
>   'Twas but the other day,
> And now she's quite a Lady,
>   This *Michigania*.
>
> Then come ye Yankee Farmers,
>   Who've mettle hearts like me,
> And elbow-grease in plenty,
>   To bow the forest tree;
> Come take a "Quarter Section,"
>   And I'll be bound you'll say,
> This country takes the rag off,
>   This *Michigania*.[1]

193

Quarter sections aplenty were being taken up by the early thirties when the "Michigan Fever," as the contagious interest in the area
was called, brought on a sudden boom in Michigan's population.
Public land sales rose from 147,062 acres in 1830 to 498,423 in
1834. By 1833, sales in Michigan accounted for slightly more than a
tenth of the income received from this source in the country. By
1835, however, the $2,271,575.17 realized in Michigan on the sale
of 1,817,248 acres represented a seventh of the national totals.
Where sales at the Detroit office in 1834 had averaged a thousand
dollars a day in the first seven months of that year, by 1835 the
receipts at the Monroe office in June totaled $147,000. By the fall
the increased interest in the western part of the territory pushed
monthly sales there up to the $200,000 range.

The boom peaked in 1836, when sales of approximately one-
ninth of Michigan's total land area—4,189,823 acres—brought in
$5,241,228.70, more than a fifth of the total receipts for the entire
country. This was a record year for land sales in any state or territory,
with the 1836 figures for Michigan exceeding those for the entire
country as recently as 1833. The relatively undeveloped areas of
western Michigan received the most attention, with sales at the
Kalamazoo land office representing nearly two-fifths of the territorial totals for 1836, although the rush to purchase lands was so great
that the harassed officials at Kalamazoo (or Bronson, as it was still
called) had to close the office on several occasions for days or even
weeks at a time in order to catch up with their book work.[2]

Much of the activity by 1836 was generated by speculators, not
by those who intended to settle in the territory. In a day when there
was not such a variety of investment possibilities as there would be
for later generations, land was especially attractive to those who had
money to invest, and in the mid-1830s Michigan acreage was regarded as the hottest item on the market. John M. Gordon, a young
man of moderate wealth from Baltimore, was typical of these
speculators. After carefully investigating all the available areas in
1836, he concluded that none rivaled Michigan, where no one, he
was informed, who bought public land at $1.25 an acre "is known
ever to have lost any thing by a purchase and sale of real estate, nor
are any sales of land made at second hand under $2.50 per acre."
Gordon travelled across southern Michigan in the late summer and
fall of 1836, and on the basis of his on-the-spot examinations bought
over 6,700 acres of land, principally in Berrien and Van Buren counties, which he eventually disposed of at a good profit. The
Wadsworth family of western New York acquired large tracts of land
in the same general area of southwestern Michigan which they sub-

sequently sold off as part of a well-organized land development scheme. How much Michigan land was purchased for speculative purposes at this time can probably never be precisely determined, but that the figure constituted a very sizable percentage of all the public land sold is certain.[3]

Nevertheless, the population census figures for the twenties and thirties, which reveal an almost equally spectacular growth rate to those for land sales, demonstrate that Michigan's land resources were attracting a great number of permanent settlers as well as non-resident speculators. In 1820 the federal census had listed 8,765 persons in Michigan Territory, including a handful of residents of what is now Wisconsin and Minnesota in the western sections that had been added to Michigan in 1818. By 1830 the population had increased to 31,640. This included the persons residing in the region west of Lake Michigan, but at least 29,000 were living in what would shortly become the state of Michigan. In the next four years the population almost tripled. A total of 87,278 people were counted in a special territorial census taken in 1834, of which number 85,856 lived in the lower peninsula. Three years later, when Michigan had achieved statehood, another census indicated that the population had risen to 174,543. Although the influx of settlers slowed down after 1837, Michigan had the largest percentage increase between 1830 and 1840 of any state or territory, as indicated by the federal census of 1840, which listed 212,267 persons living in Michigan—a seven-fold increase over the figure of ten years earlier.

The majority of the newcomers came by way of the Great Lakes, making the journey from Buffalo to Michigan by steamship or sailing vessel. Detroit was the major point of entry. There the pioneer secured a wagon, if he had not brought one along, as well as necessary supplies for the subsistence of his family until he cleared and cultivated his land. Some settlers landed at Monroe and a few at smaller ports on the east, while some, seeking land in western Michigan, went by lake vessel around the lower peninsula, landed at St. Joseph or other ports on Lake Michigan, and proceeded from there into the interior. Sizable numbers came northward overland from Ohio and Indiana into the southern counties of Michigan. Some used the "Michigan Road," which the federal government built between Madison, Ohio, and the foot of Lake Michigan.

A man who proposed to settle in Michigan usually came west to look at the land, then decided where he wanted to settle and purchased the tract if it had been put on the market. Then he returned east, packed up his family and possessions, and brought them to the new home. The successful pioneers had to be keen judges of the quality of the land, and to some extent the pioneer was attracted to the kind of land he was accustomed to cultivating. They did not like stony soil, for obvious reasons. Good drainage was important, and the settler avoided swampy, marshy land in part because it was regarded as "unhealthy." Land was called "heavy" if its clay content was high, or "light" if it was sandy. To a considerable degree the soil was judged by the kind of trees that grew on it. The best soils were supposed to lie under a covering of black walnut, whitewood, ash, and sugar maple.[4] Burr oaks denoted good land, too, but land on which pine grew was generally sandy and infertile. When these pioneers from the east first encountered patches of treeless prairie lands in Ohio they assumed that the absence of trees was a sign of poor soils. They soon discovered that this was not at all the case, and although the absence of timber for building and heating purposes continued to be a deterrent to the rapid settlement of the vast prairies of Illinois, settlers in Michigan quickly gravitated to the small prairies scattered throughout southwestern Michigan where timber was readily available in the vicinity. The advantages of the prairie lands were that the pioneer did not have to engage in the back-breaking task of clearing the trees from the land, although it was very difficult to break up the soil, the task often requiring several yoke of oxen. Grass on the prairies grew waist-high, and naturally the root growth was heavy and deep. But the soil, once made cultivable, was fabulously rich.[5] The settlers were also attracted to "oak openings." Here the oak trees grew so tall and shaded the ground so completely that little or no brush or other vegetation grew underneath. It was possible to drive an ox team through oak openings for miles along an unblazed trail.[6]

Before deciding where to settle, other factors besides the quality of the soil were considered by the pioneer. Proximity to the main roads and the larger rivers was an advantage because it facilitated the bringing in of supplies and the marketing of products. Particular care was used to seek a location that was regarded as healthful. An abundant water supply was essential. And, finally, locations were naturally preferred as close as possible to the point of entry—in most cases, Detroit.

The spread of settlement in Michigan may be judged by the establishment of counties. When a considerable number of settlers had bought land in a given area, the territorial legislature generally provided them with a county government. Often the legislature would "establish" a county, specifying its boundaries and giving it a name, and then temporarily attaching it to another county for governmental purposes. When the population had reached the point where the lawmakers decided that a separate government for a county was justified, they passed an act providing for the "organization" of the county, which meant the election of county officials and the institution of a separate county government. In 1837, at the time Michigan was admitted into the Union as a state, thirty-eight counties had been established. Of these, twenty-three had been organized and five others were organized before the end of the year. The twenty-eight organized counties included all those in the four southernmost tiers with the exception of Barry. North of these Saginaw, Mackinac, and Chippewa counties had been organized, but the latter two embraced huge areas that were later divided.[7]

The largest number of inhabitants in 1837—23,400, or over thirteen percent of the state's total population—lived in Wayne County. Detroit accounted for about 9,000 of this figure. The rural parts of Wayne County were less thickly populated than those of neighboring counties. However, the changing character of Michigan's economy and of Detroit's importance as a result of those changes is seen in Detroit's sharply reduced proportion of the area's population as most settlers moved into the interior, searching for farming opportunities. Whereas in 1810, about a third of the territory's non-Indian population was located in Detroit, by 1840 only one of every twenty-three non-Indian residents of the state lived in that city. Washtenaw County, lying due west of Wayne County, with an essentially rural population, was a close second to Wayne County in 1837, with 21,817 residents. Not far behind was Oakland County, just north of Wayne County, with 20,176, while to the southwest, Lenawee County, another essentially rural, agricultural county, was fourth in population with 14,540.

The area along the shores of Lakes Erie and St. Clair and the Detroit and St. Clair rivers that fell within the borders of Monroe, Wayne, Macomb, and St. Clair counties was not as attractive to early settlers as the three inland counties of Oakland, Washtenaw, and Lenawee. The soil in the shore counties varied greatly; some of it was stiff clay, some was sandy. It was heavily timbered, unlike Oakland County in particular which received its name from the large number of "oak openings" found within its borders. On the other hand, the future prospects of the shore counties seemed bright since they were the entry point for most of the traffic coming in from the east. The founders of the town of Monroe (formerly Frenchtown of War of 1812 fame), named for President James Monroe who visited the community in 1817, predicted a great future for the town which they anticipated would become the great metropolis of the West. In addition, Mt. Clemens, the chief town in Macomb County, Port Huron,

Marine City, Algonac, and St. Clair (at first called Palmer), all located in St. Clair County, were other towns established in these early years that had some hopes, because of their location along the busy waterway that formed the shoreline of this part of southeastern Michigan, to compete with Detroit and Monroe as major ports.

Even though the Chicago Road had been opened before the Territorial Road, the counties that were laid out along the Territorial Road, except for Van Buren, contained a larger population in 1837 than those to the south along the Chicago Road. The importance of the relative distance of a county from Detroit is shown by the fact that each county in the second tier had a larger population than its neighbor immediately to the west. In Washtenaw County, which was second only to its eastern neighbor, Wayne County, in population, the towns of Ypsilanti, Ann Arbor, Saline, Dexter, and Manchester had sprung up in the 1820s along the main roads, serving the surrounding rural areas. West of Washtenaw, Jackson County was the most populous, its chief town, on the Territorial Road, being called at first "Jacksonburg." The names chosen in both cases remind us that the great advances in the settlement of Michigan's interior regions occurred during the administration of President Andrew Jackson from 1829 to 1837. A number of other southern Michigan counties, often referred to as the "cabinet counties," were named after members of Jackson's administration, beginning with Calhoun County, to the west of Jackson's namesake county, named for Jackson's vice-president, John C. Calhoun. Calhoun County and its neighbor on the west, Kalamazoo County, were attractive to settlers because of the abundance of small, fertile prairie lands. The early towns in these counties included Marshall, Battle Creek, and Kalamazoo (at first named Bronson).

In the southernmost tier of counties many settlers entered overland from the south; hence, distance from Detroit was less important in their populating. Hillsdale and Branch counties (the latter named after Jackson's Secretary of the Navy, John Branch), lying west of Lenawee, were hilly and heavily wooded, factors that tended to retard their growth. Jonesville, an important point on the Chicago Road, was the most important town in Hillsdale County, while Coldwater was the chief settlement in Branch. Lenawee County to the east was the most populous of the counties in this southern tier, with Tecumseh and Adrian its principal towns. To the west, the second most populous county was St. Joseph County, Branch County's neighbor on the west, with White Pigeon, Mottville, Constantine, Centreville, and Three Rivers being its principal towns. The St. Joseph River which wound through this county was vitally important in these early years in the promotion of commerce. St. Joseph County and its neighbor on the west, Cass County, had several small prairies which helped promote early settlement interest. Edwardsburg and Cassopolis were Cass County's chief towns, with the name of the town as well as that of the county honoring Lewis Cass, who went from his post of governor of the territory to head the War Department in Jackson's government in 1831. In Berrien County (named for Jackson's Attorney General, John M. Berrien) in the extreme southwest, the soils along Lake Michigan were sandy, and its potential for fruit-growing was not recognized until a little later. St. Joseph was an important town because of its port. Further south along Lake Michigan the name of New Buffalo is indicative of the soaring ambitions of this town's founders. Niles and Bertrand were the chief inland towns.

To the north of Berrien County along Lake Michigan lay Van Buren (after the future president, Martin Van Buren, who initially served as Jackson's Secretary of State), Allegan, and Ottawa counties. They were remote and their lands were less fertile, particularly near Lake Michigan where the sand drifted in for some distance. All three were thinly settled in 1837.

The counties in the third tier west of Oakland had small populations at this time. Although they contained fertile lands, they were distant from the main routes of travel and lacked ready access to rivers for transportation. Livingston County was the most thickly settled, with Howell and Brighton being its chief towns. Ingham, Eaton, and Barry counties (named respectively after Jackson's Secretary of the Treasury, Samuel D. Ingham, Secretary of War, John H. Eaton, and Postmaster General, William T. Barry) had only a few hundred inhabitants each. The fourth tier of counties was even more sparsely settled, but towns of some size had grown up at Grand Rapids in Kent County, Ionia in Ionia County, and Grand Haven in Ottawa County. Lapeer and Shiawassee counties on the eastern portion of the fourth tier were in the Saginaw Valley and constituted a unit, along with Saginaw County to the north, distinct from Clinton, Ionia, and Kent to the west. These latter counties were settled in part by pioneers coming over the crude Grand River Trail, but mainly by those moving northward from the Territorial Road.

The Saginaw River Valley contained lands that were densely forested, with occasional oak-openings. The soil was considered somewhat inferior by the early settlers. Lumbering subsequently became a major industry in this region, but the earliest settlers regarded the giant pines as a nuisance rather than a resource. Fur traders in the area in some cases frowned on settlers and because of the many marshes the Saginaw country was regarded as unhealthful. Its chief advantage lay in its easy access by water.[8]

*   *   *   *   *

What sort of people were these early Michigan settlers? In many respects they shared the characteristics of the American frontiersman wherever he was found. They were eager to better their lot in life and sought more abundant opportunity for themselves and their children. Those who were well-to-do and comfortable in the East were less likely to become pioneers in the raw western country. But it is not true that the westward-moving pioneers were the scum of the eastern states. Many men, no matter how poor their condition, preferred to accept things as they were, lacking the energy and ambition to better their lot. Such persons did not go west. Those who left for the hardships of frontier life were those with abundant vitality, the will to get ahead in life, and enough resources to obtain the essential supplies for the journey. They were neither the very rich nor the very poor. They were usually young and were looking ahead to the future, not so much living in the present as in their dreams of what the years ahead might bring.

They abounded in self-confidence and in many cases were rugged individualists. Individualism frequently went to the point of eccentricity. But it was blended with neighborliness, hospitality, and a large measure of tolerance. The pioneer had to be versatile enough to subsist with little dependence on the outside world. Mainly, these people were farmers in the East. A factory worker did not possess, as a rule, the financial means to move west; furthermore, he lacked the skills and experience demanded of the farmer.

The pioneers were democratic, although they did not necessarily believe that all men were created equal. The hardships of frontier life emphasized the weakness of the weak and the strength of the strong. These pioneers did believe passionately in equal opportunity and they were scornful of certain marks of distinction in the East such as superior cultural and social attainments.

In all these traits the Michigan pioneers resembled their counterparts elsewhere in the American West. But in some respects they were distinctive. First and foremost was the fact that they were predominantly New Englanders or sprang from New England stock. The largest numbers came from western New York, but were largely the descendants of Yankees who had settled in this region after the American Revolution. Nowhere in the West did the Yankee stock predominate to the degree that it did in Michigan. The influence of this dominant New England element on the history of Michigan has been profound. That Michigan was in the forefront of the anti-slavery crusade and other reforms of the 1840s and 1850s was due in large measure to this fact. It also accounts in part for the extraordinary strength of the Republican party in Michigan from 1854 to 1932. Michigan's leadership in public education is directly attributable to the Puritan zeal for schools, which was part of the New England heritage. The names of such towns as Vermontville, Bangor, Hartford, Rochester, Utica, and Palmyra, the strength of the Congregational Church in Michigan, and the leadership of New Englanders in the early legislatures, schools, and churches attest to the influence of the New England-New York element. As late as 1860, about a quarter of Michigan's population were native "York staters," while a sizable number had been born in the New England states proper.

An important segment of Michigan's 1837 population came from the neighboring states of Ohio and Indiana. These people settled mainly in the Detroit area and in St. Joseph, Cass, and Berrien counties. Many of them had been born in Virginia and North Carolina. In and around Detroit and Monroe, the French-Canadian influence was still observable in 1837; French was still spoken by many persons. Here and there throughout the territory were colonies of settlers representing distinctive nationality or religious groups. Generally such settlers clustered together in a neighborhood and a number of them came into Michigan together as a community. For instance, there were numerous German colonies in Shiawassee and Washtenaw counties, a "Pennsylvania Dutch" colony in Cass County, Irish settlements in Kent County and the Irish Hills area of Jackson and Lenawee counties, the latter also the site of one of several Quaker colonies in Michigan. Over-all, the proportion of foreign-born appears to have been slight. The number coming from below the Mason-Dixon Line also was small. The pioneers were predominantly Protestant in religion, the main exceptions being the Irish and some of the Germans.

*   *   *   *   *

The first concern of the settler after he arrived with his family on the land he had selected was to find shelter. Sometimes a neighbor would take in the family until it could secure its own quarters; otherwise, the pioneer would build a temporary shelter. Soon he would build a log house. For this job he required help; "house raisings" were among the many tasks that were performed by volun-

tary co-operation on the frontier. Ash, beech, maple, or poplar logs
of nearly uniform size were cut and dragged to the cabin site. Prior to
the day of the raising the pioneer might prepare timbers for window
and door frames, roof poles, and chimney slats. Ofttimes the earth
served as a floor for the log cabin, but the more energetic settlers
prepared "puncheon floors" by splitting and hewing logs. When the
neighbors arrived, the best axeman in the crowd fitted the notches at
the corners, as the logs were skidded up with forks and hand spikes.
Openings for doors and windows and the fireplace were sawed or
chopped out after the logs were in place. The longitudinal roof poles
were pegged on, and the job of preparing the "shakes" for the roof
(clapboards split from oak or ash three or four feet long) was left to
the settler. The energies and spirits of the workmen were stimulated
by liberal draughts of whisky, while the women prepared a bountiful
repast to satisfy mighty appetites.

The next progression from the primitive log cabin might be the
hewn log cabin, with the hewn logs replacing the rounded, bark-
covered timbers. However, sawmills appeared relatively early in
many communities, so that the log cabin stage was brief and frame
houses with clapboard siding soon predominated.[9]

Some settlers arrived with only the bare essentials: their clothing, a small amount of flour and salt, an axe, rifle, iron pot, a few
tools, some seeds, and bed clothing; however, many families arrived
better equipped. Frequently a choice piece of furniture, a fiddle, a
few dishes, or perhaps only a fancy doorknob or two were brought as
a reminder of the former home in the East. Beds were built by
driving crotched posts in the ground or holes in the floor and running rails to the cabin walls, with a deer hide to support a grass tick.
Three-legged stools, benches, sturdy chairs, and wooden pegs that
were inserted into the walls to hang things on, were all home-made.
Dishes were fashioned from wood. Gourds of many sizes and shapes
were highly prized by the pioneer, who always planted a liberal
supply. They could be used as bowls, dippers, wash pans, and even as
rattles for the baby.

Food for the pioneer family was often a problem, for stores
were generally far distant, and money scarce to buy supplies if they
chanced to be nearby. Heavy reliance was placed on wild game, fish,
honey, maple syrup, and wild fruits. Pioneer accounts tell of fabulous
numbers of fish that could be secured from lakes and streams with a
seine. Hunting in the woods for deer, bear, and smaller game—at
first a necessity—provided a welcome release from the humdrum of
hard work on the pioneer farm, so that many of the pioneers continued to hunt long after they had provided for their tables. A few of

the pioneers became so enamored of hunting that they gave up farming to become professional hunters. If possible, the settler brought along a cow to supply milk, butter, and cheese for the family as well as a few chickens to provide eggs and geese to provide feathers. Hogs, which could survive on acorns, were regarded as almost a necessity. They were butchered in the fall, provided fresh meat during the winter, and salt pork could be packed in barrels for use the next summer. Corn was almost always the first grain grown. "Hog and hominy" became the standard pioneer diet.

Clearing the land of trees was the most arduous task that confronted the settler. First the brush was cleared away and the large trees were "girdled" by stripping the bark from around the trunk, causing the tree to die. Later the dead trees would be felled in windrows and burned. The colossal waste of such a process, destroying primarily hardwood trees whose potential value ranged into the millions of dollars, is appalling to later generations, but the supply of timber in these early days seemed inexhaustible and to the pioneer it was the land, not its trees, that was valuable. The pioneer's faithful axe was his most useful tool. The crosscut saw was unknown to early Michigan pioneers. With his axe the settler felled the trees, chopped firewood, and split rails to build fences. Fences around cultivated fields were a necessity to keep out roving livestock, both wild and domesticated. During the growing season, women and children were required to keep constant watch to guard against squirrels, birds, raccoon, bear, deer, and other marauders from ruining the growing crops.

There were a few necessities that had to be obtained from the world beyond the pioneer homestead. One of these was salt. Some of this vital commodity came from salt springs, or salines, where a hundred gallons of water had to be boiled down to produce a bushel of salt. Much of the salt used by Michigan pioneers, however, was imported from New York. Prices frequently were high.

Wheat did not grow well in the virgin soil of cleared forest lands, but the small prairies of southern Michigan proved to be ideally adapted to this grain. Unlike the corn harvest, which could be carried on in a leisurely manner, wheat had to be cut and threshed within a rather short period. The wheat was cut with a "cradle"; this consisted of a scythe with a sort of basket attached. Two men, one cradling and the other binding the bundles, could harvest about two acres a day. Cyrus Hall McCormick invented a reaper in 1831, but it was not perfected and produced in quantity until after 1850. Obed Hussey of Ohio invented a reaper about the same time as McCormick, and a long war over patent rights began. In Kalamazoo County,

Michigan, John Hascall and Hiram Moore developed a combine, an immense contraption pulled by twelve to twenty horses. Developed in 1836, this machine was demonstrated on Climax Prairie. It cut and threshed the grain in a single operation. But it was far too large, unwieldy, and expensive to be of practical use.[10]

Clothing brought from the East was not well suited to the rigors of pioneer life. The pioneer quickly learned that deerskin was a valuable material in his environment. Moccasins of tanned buckskin, breeches and skirts made of dressed skin worked soft and thin by hand and sewed with sinews, and coonskin caps provided a dress that could withstand the wear and tear of briars and brush, repel cold winds, and ward off snake bite. Flax seed was sown in the spring, and the plants produced fibers that, with an immense amount of labor and skill, could be used to make women's clothes. Wool obtained from sheep raised on the farm provided another fiber. The spinning wheel and the hand loom kept everyone in the family busy throughout the long winters. Other tasks included candle-making, the manufacture of soft soap with wood ashes and lye, and tapping maple trees and boiling down the sap to make maple syrup.

Of primary importance to the pioneer was the construction of mills for the grinding of grain. These usually appeared within a few years after the first settlements, but often it was a long journey to the mill and back. Another trade that was important to the early settlers was that of the blacksmith. His forge was a center of social as well as industrial activity. He produced nails, chains, bullet molds, yoke rings, axles, traps, hoes, augers, bells, shears, locks, adzes, plowshares, and metal parts for just about anything. The tanning of hides was a difficult process requiring much skill, and the pioneer welcomed the establishment of a tannery to take over this job for him.

The pioneer is often thought of as a strong, healthy specimen, but accounts of pioneer life in Michigan give the impression that there was a great deal of sickness. What the settlers called fever and ague was so prevalent that it was rather unusual to escape it. "He ain't sick, he's just got the ager" was a common remark. This ailment was actually malaria and was spread by the mosquitoes that bred in the marshes and swamps that were so prevalent before the land was drained. Quinine, commonly used today in the treatment of this disease, was then known as "Peruvian bark." It was expensive and many doctors refused to prescribe it. Most victims just endured the ailment, which was debilitating but seldom fatal. The victim first yawned and stretched a great deal, felt tired, and then began to have fierce chills. After an hour or so of this a raging fever would come with racking headache and back pains. Then after copious sweating the sufferer would feel as well as ever. These attacks usually occurred at a certain time each day, or on alternate days, or even every third day. Work schedules were arranged to accommodate a person's "shakes."

Late summer usually was the most sickly time for the pioneers. Various types of "billious fevers," typhoid epidemics, "milk sick," and digestive upsets were common, caused in the main, no doubt, by lack of refrigeration, unpasteurized milk, and contaminated water. Epidemics of erysipelas (called St. Anthony's Fire) occurred in Michigan in early times. Contagious diseases such as scarlet fever, diphtheria, measles, mumps, and smallpox took a heavy toll. Infant mortality was high. Pneumonia, or "lung fever," was most prevalent in winter. Rheumatism was common, and probably was caused in part by exposure in all kinds of weather, the practice of drying wet clothing on the body, and decaying, unrepaired teeth.

The pioneers treated many ailments with roots and herbs. The lore that contained prescriptions of these remedies was brought from the East or learned from the Indians. Hideous concoctions of foul materials were resorted to; the worse the illness the more repulsive the remedy.

> For fevers, they recommended sweating and snake root with a purge of white walnut bark peeled upward, sassafras, dogwood, willow, or a glass of pearl ash and water. The breaking out in eruptive fevers, such as measles, was hastened by the use of sheep-dung tea, popularly known as "nanny tea." For pleurisy, if no bleeder was at hand, catnip or penny-royal, or butterfly tea, applications of boiled hot nettles, or brimstone, sulphur, and eggs....[11]

There were a considerable number of doctors in pioneer Michigan, but often a long journey was necessary to summon a physician, and when he came his remedies might be no better than those devised by the pioneer and his wife. Copious bleedings and the use of calomel were favorite procedures of these early doctors, and the effect was frequently little more than to sap the strength of the patient. The doctor could be of use in setting bones and, of course, the psychological effect of having the advice of a doctor was helpful. Few of the doctors had studied at a medical school; most of them had learned the secrets of their profession through an apprenticeship with an established doctor. The physicians of this early period in some cases did not devote their full time to the practice of medicine. Some operated farms or engaged in business. The first postmaster of Kalamazoo was a doctor. As early as 1819 the governor and judges had passed a law authorizing the formation of county medical societies to pass on the qualifications of persons aspiring to practice medicine. But little was accomplished; few doctors apparently bothered to secure a license to practice and quackery abounded. There were several different "schools" of medicine, one of which was called the "botanical." The first medical journal and perhaps the first magazine produced in Michigan was the *Vegetable Herald,* published in Kalamazoo and devoted to the advocacy of "botanical medicine."[12] In spite of his shortcomings the pioneer country doctor had a more intimate relationship with his people than the lawyer or the minister:

> Though frequently short of learning, intolerant of rivals and given to petty quarrels, he was abundantly possessed of those qualities which made his humanity triumph over both nature and human self-ishness, and himself usually a figure feared, loved, and venerated.[13]

When sickness and death afflicted the family there were always neighbors ready to lend a helping hand. On happier occasions when there were social gatherings such as a barn- or house-raising, husking bee, or "town meeting," strenuous sports were the order of the day. Running and jumping contests, wrestling, tug-of-war, and pitching quoits were popular. Horse racing appeared early, and betting on the nags was a common accompaniment. After a husking bee the floor was cleared for a "barn dance," unless the neighborhood was dominated by ultra-religious folk who considered it wicked. In almost every neighborhood there were fiddlers who knew not a note of music, but could rip off such tunes as "Money Musk," "Zip Coon," or "The Devil's Dream" with great gusto. For those who frowned on dancing there were always the popular marching and singing games. Social occasions, of course, found young people engaged in the age-old quest for a mate. Although the girls frequently sang a little ditty that announced,

> I am too young, I am not fit,
> I cannot leave my mamma yit,

they often said "yes" at the age of fourteen or fifteen if the right young man popped the question. Weddings were big events on the frontier, occasions for visiting, feasting, drinking, and making merry. Following the ceremony the young couple was serenaded with all sorts of noisemaking paraphernalia a night or two after the wedding. This was called a "shiver-ee."[14] The settlers were fond of spelling schools, Fourth-of-July celebrations, camp meetings, and singing schools.[15]

Sexual irregularity was harshly condemned in pioneer days. There were taboos on sex applied to conversation: male animals were euphemistically named in the presence of women, but it was respectable enough to talk about mares, sows, ewes, and cows. Pregnancy was not mentionable in mixed company. Any departure from the moral code met stern rebuke and social isolation by one's neighbors. Nevertheless, individuality to the point of eccentricity in speech, manner, and dress was tolerated and even admired. Whisky was in universal use, being obtainable at general stores at 15 to 20 cents a gallon. But in the 1830s the temperance movement was gaining momentum, and many families frowned on spirituous liquors, advocating instead the use of beer, cider, and wine.

Most of the writings on pioneer life deal with the experiences of pioneer farmers in rural neighborhoods. Less has been written about the beginnings and growth of towns, and the common problems they had to solve. No account of pioneer Michigan, however, would be complete without some reference to life in the new towns.

Detroit was not a new town when the rush of settlers to Michigan began. In fact it was a century and a quarter old. But it was hardly more than a frontier outpost until the population of Michigan began to grow at a rapid pace in the late twenties and early thirties. In 1816 it had only 850 people, and a dozen years later the number had increased only to 1,517. But by 1834 the city could boast of 4,968 inhabitants, and by 1840 it had grown to 9,192. The people were principally engaged in wholesale and retail trade; there was very little manufacturing except for local use. The city's port had become a busy place by 1836; ninety steamboats and an even larger number of sailing vessels used its facilities; an estimated 200,000 people entered and left the town that year. Hotels and boarding houses sprang up for their accommodation, while stores did a lively business in supplying settlers venturing westward. The Bank of Michigan was established in 1817, and by 1837 the city had a second bank. The most important center of activity was the government land office, where thousands of settlers and speculators came to examine records and to purchase a tract either for a homestead or with the purpose of reselling at a profit.

The city's growth created problems with which other urban communities had to wrestle as they developed. One of these was fire protection. Laws were passed after the fire of 1805, requiring each property owner to make certain preparations for the fighting of fire, but they were not well observed. Before the end of the territorial period three active voluntary fire companies had been formed. There was a great deal of rivalry among them to see which could reach a fire first and not infrequently they obstructed each other. The members wore red flannel shirts and blue pants tucked inside high boots, and girded their waists with ornamental belts. The city government provided them with fire engines, hoses, and other equipment, and grateful citizens whose property was saved from destruction by their efforts often provided them with a feast in return. A reward of $5 was voted by the common council in 1836 to the first person who gave the alarm of a fire. To sound an alarm the bell in the steeple of the Presbyterian Church at the northeast corner of Woodward and Larned streets was rung by pulling a rope that dangled down into the open porch under the spire.

Water to quench the flames was pumped from the river or nearby cisterns. For domestic use, water was obtained from the river or from open wells, which were often a hazard when left without protection. As early as 1823, Peter Berthelet was authorized to build a wharf from the shore out to deep water and to install a pump to supply water that would be "free from contamination" by the debris commonly dumped into the river. Two years later Bethuel Farrand was given the right to install water mains. These were made from bored-out tamarack logs, mortised together and connected to an elevated tank at the wharf. A reservoir was erected at the corner of Jefferson Avenue and Randolph Street to provide pressure, and the citizen obtained water from "penstocks" attached to the mains by withdrawing a wooden plug and allowing the water to pour into a bucket. Before the end of the territorial period other reservoirs were erected and service pipes were run into a number of homes.

In a growing urban community, especially in one so close to the frontier, there was certain to be a sizable number of miscreants. A public whipping post was erected near the intersection of Jefferson and Woodward avenues where evildoers were flogged. Several public executions, mostly of Indians, took place in Detroit during the territorial period. On September 24, 1830, one Stephen G. Simmons was publicly hanged for killing his wife while drunk. A grandstand was erected in front of the gallows for the accommodation of a huge throng of spectators who came from miles around to witness the event. There was some revulsion of feeling as a result of Simmons' eloquent confession of his faults and his rendition of a hymn just before he was executed. One result was the abolition of the public whipping post. A jail had been built before the War of 1812, a new one was constructed in 1819, and a larger one in 1830. No professional police force was maintained until later; however, there was a voluntary night watch.[16]

Detroit had been incorporated as a town by the legislature of the Northwest Territory in 1802, and its government had been entrusted to a board of trustees. In 1805, however, this board was abolished and the new governor, secretary, and judges of Michigan Territory took control of the government of the town. On October 24, 1815, the governing board of the territory adopted an act which incorporated Detroit as a city, with an elected board of trustees. In 1824, the governing body came to be known as the common council. The city government provided a public market and a weighmaster to see that people got honest weight. Some of the streets were paved with cobblestones. One of the persistent problems with which the city fathers had to deal was the roaming of livestock through the streets; under an act of 1817 hogs were allowed to run at large so long as rings were kept in their snouts to prevent them from rooting up lawns and gardens. The days of big government were still a long way off, however, for the total city tax collections in 1817 amounted to only $1,787.37.

There were many exciting events in Detroit during territorial times. President James Monroe visited the city in 1817, and the event was a gala occasion. The arrival of the first steamboat, the *Walk-in-the-Water,* the following year was greeted by a large crowd. The building of a territorial capitol building at the head of Griswold Street began in 1823, but the structure was not completed until 1828. Fort Shelby was abandoned by the army garrison in 1825, and the towering embankments that had dominated the town for many years were removed.

The year 1832 brought Detroit both excitement and tragedy. The excitement was induced by the so-called Black Hawk War, which could hardly be called a war. The threat to the settlers of Michigan was greatly exaggerated, and there were wild stories that Black Hawk and his warriors might ravage western Michigan in a desperate attempt to reach Fort Malden. A call for three hundred volunteers from Michigan was sent out and in Detroit two amateur military groups responded—the Detroit City Guards and the Light Dragoons. On May 24 they started westward across the territory, but the infantry was recalled after it had advanced as far as Saline. The dragoons went on to Chicago. Black Hawk was easily crushed. The fighting took place in what is now part of Wisconsin, but it was at that time attached to Michigan Territory. Black Hawk surrendered on August 2, and along with nine other chiefs was kept hostage to guarantee the good behavior of the Indians. As prisoners in Virginia, they were taken on a tour of the larger cities in the East to demonstrate the futility of any further resistance. Black Hawk met and conferred with President Andrew Jackson, and while returning west in 1833, he visited Detroit on July 4. The curious townspeople saw a man who was striking in appearance, eloquent in speech, and noble in bearing.

Just one year before, on July 4, 1832, the steamer *Henry Clay* had arrived at Detroit with several companies of soldiers under the command of General Winfield Scott, en route to meet the threat of Black Hawk's warriors. Several cases of Asiatic cholera had broken out, and when the ship stopped at Detroit, the extremely contagious disease was spread to the townspeople. It had appeared in Russia in 1831, had spread to western Europe, and was brought to America by a passenger on an emigrant ship. It soon made its appearance in cities on the eastern seaboard, where many deaths were reported. At Detroit there were fifty-eight cases, and twenty-eight deaths took place within two weeks. The territorial capitol was utilized as a hospital for the victims, and the townspeople were in a state of panic.[17] Outstate towns set up guards to prevent travelers from Detroit from using the public roads. A stage coach with passengers, attempting to elude the road block east of Ypsilanti, was fired upon and one of the horses was killed. In spite of all these precautions the disease spread beyond Detroit; eleven died at Marshall. The disease took its victims quickly; persons in excellent health were suddenly stricken with a feeling of uneasiness, shortly were consumed with burning fever and a craving for cold drinks, after which came vomiting, intestinal spasms, general debility, and death. The disease runs its course in three to five days. The modern treatment is to support the patient over this period by intravenously injecting fluids and minerals into the blood stream, and applying medications to keep him comfortable. But the treatment of the disease by the physicians of 1832 was to use counter-irritants and astringents, which only made the patient worse. Among those who died at Detroit in 1832 was Father Gabriel Richard; he did not succumb to cholera but to exhaustion caused by nursing and comforting the sick. A second epidemic of cholera broke out in Detroit in 1834; it was of relatively short duration but more deaths occurred than in 1832. Seven percent of the city's population died in August. Many widows and orphans were left without means of support, and were sent to a poorhouse that had been opened the preceding year, largely through the efforts of the Reverend Father Martin Kundig. Still another, although less severe, cholera epidemic struck Michigan in 1849.[18]

Much of the business done in Detroit came as a result of the flow of immigrants through the city. The demand for ships for the transportation of passengers and freight to Michigan from the East greatly stimulated the shipbuilding industry. A small steamship was built at Detroit in 1827, and in 1833 the steamer *Michigan,* pronounced the largest and finest on the lakes, was built at the foot of Wayne Street. Her construction was financed by Oliver Newberry, who owned the largest warehouse on the lakes. Newberry was a pioneer in lake transportation and a prominent and successful Detroit businessman for many years. He was a bachelor, let his hair grow long, always had his tall hat stuffed with business papers of all sorts, and was regarded as a shrewd operator. The arrival of settlers, speculators, businessmen, and others created a demand for lodging and meals. A total of nine hotels were meeting this need by 1835. Several physicians practiced in the city. More than a dozen lawyers handled the many legal problems connected with the sale and exchange of property as well as other civil and criminal cases.[19]

No other town in Michigan approached Detroit in size or importance. In fact, it was the only incorporated city in Michigan when the state was admitted to the Union in 1837. Fifteen villages had been incorporated by 1837: Monroe (1827), Ypsilanti (1832), Ann Arbor (1833), Niles, Adrian, Pontiac, St. Joseph, Tecumseh, Centreville, Constantine, White Pigeon, New Buffalo, Marshall, Mount Clemens, and Coldwater. The state census of 1837 lists the population of the townships in the various counties, but not the towns proper. Estimating the size of the towns from the number of inhabitants of the townships in which they were located, we may conclude that the ten largest towns in Michigan in 1837, in decreasing order of their size, were Detroit, Ann Arbor, Monroe, Tecumseh, Ypsilanti, Adrian, Marshall, Pontiac, Grand Rapids, and Niles.

The location of towns was due to a variety of factors. Many grew up along the Chicago Road (Ypsilanti, Coldwater, Jonesville, White Pigeon) and the Territorial Road (Jackson, Marshall, Battle Creek, Kalamazoo). A town sometimes developed around a tavern on one of these highways (Clinton) or where a stream could be most easily forded (Kalamazoo). Marshall was located at the head of navigation on the Kalamazoo River. Towns often grew up around early forts (Saginaw, Niles) or trading posts (Ypsilanti). Some towns were the result of the work of promoters who hoped to profit from the sale of town lots (Ann Arbor, New Buffalo, Albion). A town was apt to grow up at a promising mill site (Galesburg), or at a favorable point on an important river. Constantine was situated on the St. Joseph River and became an important shipping point for grain; Grand Rapids, as its name indicates, grew up at a point on the Grand where rapids made it necessary to interrupt travel. The growth of some towns was promoted by the location of a land office (Monroe, White Pigeon, Kalamazoo, Ionia, Flint).

By the close of the territorial period, those towns that had been incorporated as villages had local governing bodies to meet the needs of citizens for regulations to control the running at large of livestock, to provide for the fighting of fires, and to maintain law and order. In the unincorporated towns, local government was in charge of township officials. Most of the towns had one or more churches, a school, several general stores, a sawmill, and a gristmill. Streets were deep in mud during the spring season and dusty in summertime. Lawyers and doctors maintained offices, often serving the people of an extensive area. In some towns promoters set aside squares for public parks, and since the people who built the towns were largely Yankees, they tended to use the New England village as a model.

The names of the towns were selected from many different sources. Indian names, such as Kalamazoo, Pontiac, Tecumseh, and Saginaw, were common. Some took their names from geographical features, as was the case, for example, with Grand Rapids, Saline, and Coldwater. The founder's name was often utilized, as was the case with Kalamazoo, originally named Bronson after its founder, Titus Bronson. The present Bronson in Branch County, on the other hand, was named for its founder, Jobez Bronson. Dexter took its name from Samuel Dexter. New England names, such as Quincy, Vermontville, and Lawrence, were popular, and the New York influence was reflected in towns such as Utica and Rochester. Monroe and Jackson followed the practice of honoring presidents, while Marshall was named for Chief Justice John Marshall. Adrian, Constantine, and Homer derived their names from classical antiquity. Niles was named for the publisher of the popular eastern news publication, *Nile's Weekly*. Ammng the more unusual name selections are those of the neighboring communities of Ann Arbor and Ypsilanti. The former derived its name, apparently, from the name of the wives of two founders, both named Ann, while the latter was named after Demetrius Ypsilanti, a hero of the Greek War of Independence which had excited much interest in the United States at the time this town was laid out in 1823–24.

These towns growing up in the interior of Michivan were of great importance to the early settler. The story of their development is as significant as that of the pioneer farmers. In 1837, the majority of Michiganians lived on farms, but before the century ended, the number of city dwellers was rapidly approaching that of those living in rural surroundings.

Wherever Michigan's pioneers settled, whether on the farm or in a new town, life was fraught with danger. If one escaped the prevalent types of sickness, he might suffer from rattlesnake bite or die as the result of being struck by a falling tree. Pioneers had little time or disposition to admire the wild beauty of the primeval forest or the prairies covered with wildflowers in the springtime. But the life of the pioneer, though hard, had rewards. The chief reward was the feeling that he was getting ahead in the world, that he could look forward to better days for himself and his family as his land began to produce or his village grew from the trade and services it provided to the surrounding farms. The settler was exhilarated by the feeling that he was part of a growing community, that he was sharing in the creation of a new society.

Walker Inn

10

POLITICAL DEVELOPMENT AND
CULTURAL BEGINNINGS

Life in Michigan during the two decades following the War of 1812 was intensely dynamic. Nothing was fixed or static, not even the territorial boundaries. When first organized in 1805, Michigan had included the eastern tip of the present Upper Peninsula. The western boundary, as specified by Congress when Michigan Territory was created, was a line drawn through the middle of Lake Michigan from its southerly bend to "its northern extremity, and thence due north to the northern boundary of the United States." Thirteen years later, when Congress admitted Illinois into the Union as a state it attached to Michigan Territory all the region north of Illinois and east of the Mississippi, subject to the future disposition of Congress. In 1834, the western boundary of Michigan was extended west of the Mississippi as far as the Missouri River. This vast expansion placed all of what is now Iowa, the remainder of Minnesota, and portions of the Dakotas under the jurisdiction of Michigan. Two years later in 1836, however, Wisconsin Territory was set off and organized to include all this western country. What was to become the Upper Peninsula of Michigan was not included. Wisconsin's northern boundary was left so indefinite that its precise location remained a matter of dispute down into the twentieth century. It is difficult to say exactly what Michigan included after Wisconsin was demarcated. The act organizing the Wisconsin Territory clearly carried the intent to give it an outlet on Lake Superior. The following year Michigan was admitted to the Union with its present boundaries including the entire Upper Peninsula.

215

The southern as well as the western boundaries of Michigan also underwent modifications. The Northwest Ordinance had specified a line drawn due east and west through the southernmost tip of Lake Michigan. The framers of the Ohio constitution, fearing that such a line, as yet unsurveyed, might leave the mouth of the Maumee River outside Ohio's boundaries, inserted a proviso that if, when the boundary was surveyed, this proved to be the case, then the northern boundary of Ohio, with the assent of Congress, should be along a line drawn from the southern end of Lake Michigan to the northernmost cape of Maumee Bay. Congress admitted Ohio into the Union under this constitution and then two years later, in 1805, created Michigan Territory with its southern boundary as that which was set forth in the Northwest Ordinance, and without any proviso for changing the line in accordance with the Ohio constitution. Surveys of the Ordinance line were eventually made, and it was discovered that it would indeed place the mouth of the Maumee River in Michigan. The grounds were thus established for a bitter boundary

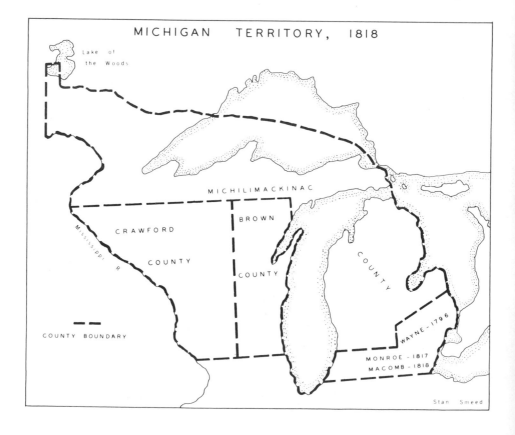

MICHIGAN   TERRITORY,   1818

Lake of the Woods

MICHILIMACKINAC

CRAWFORD

BROWN

COUNTY

COUNTY

Mississippi R.

COUNTY

COUNTY BOUNDARY

WAYNE - 1796

MONROE - 1817
MACOMB - 1818

Stan   Smeed

dispute between Michigan and Ohio that would not be completely settled until the 1970s.

In 1816, when Indiana was ready for admission to the Union, its citizens asked Congress to move the northern boundary of the new state ten miles north, so that Indiana would have as its northern boundary a line running parallel with the original line—due east and west—but ten miles north of that original line. Congress admitted Indiana with that provision, and Michigan lost the region between the original line and the new one. This gave Indiana, instead of Michigan, the area where such cities as Michigan City, Elkhart, and South Bend, with its famous University of Notre Dame, would develop in later years. Governor Cass protested this action, but to no avail. Illinoians were even more ambitious two years later, when they prevailed on Congress, when it admitted Illinois as a state, to advance its northern border sixty miles north of the Ordinance line, which resulted in the development of Chicago as the metropolis of the Prairie State and not of the Badger State to the north.

Changes also were made in the form of the territorial government, in this case somewhat more in keeping with the governmental provisions of the Northwest Ordinance rather than in violation of them, as was the case with some of the boundary changes. As early as 1809 there was agitation for an elective legislature, due largely to the quarreling and bickering between Governor Hull and Judge Woodward. Two years after the war the demand was heard again, when "Cincinnatus," writing in the Detroit *Gazette* in November of 1817, maintained that such a development would encourage immigration to the territory.

In responding to these demands in 1819, Congress did not strictly adhere to the provisions of the Northwest Ordinance which stipulated that when a territory had a population of at least five thousand free adult males its people should have the right to elect a territorial house of representatives. The right to vote for representatives was to be confined to men who had been citizens of one of the states, owned at least fifty acres of land, and had lived in the district for at least two years. The elected representatives in turn were to nominate ten men as members of the territorial council, or upper house of the legislature, and Congress was to select five of the nominees to serve on the council. The representatives and the council sitting together were then authorized to elect by joint ballot a delegate to Congress who was to have the right to participate in debates but not to vote. Michigan did not have 5,000 free adult males in 1819 (its total population in 1820 was only 8,765), nor did Congress authorize the election of a territorial house of representatives and a territorial council. Rather, it authorized the selection of a non-voting delegate to Congress by a direct vote of the residents of the territory. Requirements for voting were that one was a white male, resident of the territory for one year, and a taxpayer.

Congress was discouraged from going the full distance in giving Michigan the powers of a territory of the second grade, first, because the territory did not as yet have 5,000 free adult males, and second, because a vote taken the preceding year at the behest of Governor Cass, who believed wholeheartedly in democratic processes, had shown a majority of the voters in the territory to be unfavorable to a change from the existing system. Most of the inhabitants of Michigan were still of French origin; they were satisfied with Cass's administration and were uninterested in elections and "democratic processes." The action taken by Congress was, therefore, in the nature of a compromise: Michigan would have a non-voting delegate in the Congress of the United States, but its laws would continue to be made and administered by the governor and judges.

In 1823, however, Congress definitely raised Michigan to a territory of the second grade when it authorized the voters to nominate eighteen persons for a territorial council, from which number the President of the United States, with the advice and consent of the Senate, was to select nine to serve on the council. The lawmaking power in the territory was then to be transferred from the governor and judges to the territorial council. The governor was still to enjoy the power of veto and Congress might disapprove any act passed by the council. It is notable that Congress made no provision in this law for the election of a territorial house of representatives or "general assembly," as provided in the Northwest Ordinance. The act did contain, however, a provision that the territorial council might at any time submit to the people of the territory the question of whether a "general assembly" should be chosen in accordance with the provisions of the Northwest Ordinance. This provision is evidence that Congress still regarded itself as bound by the provisions of that Ordinance, at least in a general way. Four years later, in 1827, Congress passed another act, this one increasing the size of the territorial council from nine to thirteen members and making it wholly elective by the people of the territory.

As a result of these acts Michigan had a non-voting delegate to Congress in Washington after 1819, and after 1823 Michigan's laws were made by a Territorial Council consisting of nine men until 1827, when the number was increased to thirteen. No action was taken during the territorial period, however, to provide a general assembly or house of representatives for Michigan, as stipulated in the Northwest Ordinance. Hence Michigan had a unicameral, or one-house, legislature until it became a state.

The settlers who trickled into Michigan in the fifteen years after the War of 1812, and who then came in a torrent during the early 1830s, had none of the apathy toward democratic institutions that was characteristic of the French who constituted the large part of the population prior to their coming. These newcomers not only demanded a voice in the government of the territory, but also clamored for local self-government. They were fully supported by Governor Cass not only at the territorial level, but also at the county and township level. In 1825, Congress provided that the qualified voters in each county should choose all the county officials except the judges. The governor and council also were permitted to divide the counties into townships. In the townships the town meeting, in which all adult males had the right to take part, became the governing body. The inauguration of township government in Michigan followed the pattern set in Ohio and Indiana. The township was modeled after the New England "town," which is not really a town in the sense the word is used in the Middle West, but an area that may or may not include some sort of municipality. New York also had "towns" but in the Old Northwest the term "township" supplanted "town" as the connotation for a local governmental unit. Outside of New England, where it originated, this governmental system has been adopted by New York, Pennsylvania, New Jersey, eleven north-central states, and to a limited extent by South Carolina and Washington.

Political rivalry in territorial Michigan was of the knock-down-and-drag-out variety. A fierce spirit of liberty and individualism is evident in the political contests of the day. Newspapers were rabidly partisan, asking and giving no quarter. The pioneers were intensely interested in politics. Religion and political partisanship provided emotional outlets that were important as a release from toil and loneliness.

Michigan was represented in Congress by some able men during the territorial period. The first delegate chosen was William Woodbridge, a native of Connecticut who had come to Michigan as Indian agent of the United States, and was serving as secretary of the territory at the time of his election. He took his seat in Congress on December 10, 1819, and served for one year. He then resumed his position as territorial secretary, later was appointed to one of the judgeships, and after statehood was achieved was elected governor (1839) and then United States Senator. Solomon Sibley, a lawyer, native of Massachusetts, and the first Michiganian to be elected to the legislature of the Northwest Territory in 1798, was chosen to replace Woodbridge when the latter resigned as a result of a clamor against him for retaining his position as territorial secretary while serving in Congress. Sibley also served later as a territorial judge. There were six candidates for the office of delegate to Congress in 1823. The leading ones were Colonel John Biddle, clerk of the Detroit land office and brother of Nicholas Biddle (head of the Bank of the United States); Father Gabriel Richard, the pastor of Ste. Anne's Church, who had been born in France; and Austin Wing, sheriff of Monroe County and native of Massachusetts. Richard had the solid support of the French element and was declared the winner in the election. An attempt was made by an agent of Biddle to contest his election on the ground that he was not a citizen, but a congressional committee decided in favor of Richard. He thus became the only Catholic priest to serve as a member of the Congress of the United States until the election of Father Robert Drinan from a Massachusetts district in 1970.

Richard was at first quite a curiosity in the national capital: his French accent and his personal appearance attracted considerable attention. He wore knee breeches, silk stockings, a long black coat very short in the waist and voluminous in the collar, and a huge skirt extending almost to his ankles. Both President Monroe and Secretary of War Calhoun were fascinated by the stories he told of the Indians. When he came back to Detroit after Congress adjourned in the spring of 1824, he was put in jail. Somewhat earlier, in the pulpit of Ste. Anne's he had condemned as an adulterer and excommunicated a man named Labadie, who had divorced one wife and married another. Labadie brought suit for damages against Richard, and in 1821 the court awarded the former a judgement of $1,116. Richard refused to pay the amount, because to have done so would have acknowledged, as he saw it, the power of civil authorities over purely ecclesiastical concerns. Hence he was jailed. After spending approximately three weeks behind bars he was released when some of his friends gave bond to insure his remaining in Wayne County. He was informed, however, by Henry Clay, Speaker of the House, that he could claim immunity from arrest as a member of Congress, so he was allowed to return to Washington in the late fall. The judgment plagued him for the rest of his life. Richard spoke in Congress only on rare occasions but he did a great deal of lobbying for measures beneficial to Michigan, sought to get more lands put on the market, and was active in promoting the measure by which Congress authorized the construction of the Chicago Road.[1]

In the election of 1825, Richard was once more opposed by

Biddle and Wing. The votes were so evenly divided that the outcome was long in doubt. There were claims and counterclaims of rascality, coercion, and fraud. The board of canvassers, in its report, gave the election to Wing. The latter was given 728 votes to 724 for Richard and 689 for Biddle. A congressional committee reopened the investigation and after lengthy consideration decided Wing had 725 legal votes, Richard 722, and Biddle 714. The same contestants had it out again in 1827, 1829, and 1831. Wing retained his seat until 1831 when Biddle was the winner. Lucius Lyon was elected in 1833. He declared his residence to be Bronson (later named Kalamazoo), but his activities as a surveyor and land speculator kept him on the move a great deal. He was the first delegate to come from the western part of the territory. After statehood was attained, he was chosen as one of Michigan's first two United States senators.[2] The last territorial delegate elected was George W. Jones, who came from that part of Michigan Territory which is now the State of Wisconsin.

The contests for the election of members of the Territorial Council appear to have been somewhat less exciting than those for delegate to Congress. There were six elections between 1823 and 1833. Members were chosen to serve two-year terms and the Council met annually.[3] Among those who served on the Territorial Council were the scientist and Indian authority Henry R. Schoolcraft; noted surveyor William A. Burt; Major Abraham Edwards, a physician, who was president of the first four Councils, won his military rank during the War of 1812 and later served as register of the land office at White Pigeon and Kalamazoo; Calvin Britain, a prominent figure in the early history of Berrien County; and John McDonnell of Detroit, president of the last two councils.[4]

The people of the Territory had no voice in the selection of the governor, secretary, and judges. These were chosen by the President of the United States. Augustus B. Woodward, the most prominent of the territorial judges, served from 1805 to 1824. President Monroe refused to reappoint him in 1824 because of charges of intemperance, but upon receiving a letter from Governor Cass stating that he had never known Woodward to be intoxicated the president appointed Woodward as one of the judges in the Territory of Florida. He died there in 1827 and was buried in an unmarked grave. Judge James Witherell, Woodward's archfoe, outlasted the latter, serving from 1806 to 1828. Later appointees to the court included William Woodbridge and Solomon Sibley, each of whom had been delegate to Congress for a single term. Woodbridge was secretary of the Territory from 1818 to 1830. He was succeeded by John T. Mason of Virginia, who resigned the following year to go abroad. His successor, appointed by President Andrew Jackson, was his son, then only nineteen years of age, Stevens Thomson Mason. Whenever the governor was out of the territory, as happened quite frequently, the secretary became the acting governor. Upon the resignation and departure of Governor Cass young Mason became acting governor of the territory, and he served in this capacity later on several occasions. He was destined to become the first governor of the state of Michigan and to hold that position for two terms.

Governor Cass resigned in 1831 to accept appointment as Secretary of War in President Jackson's cabinet. His career as governor of Michigan Territory had been eminently successful. Later he was to be elected as United States Senator from Michigan, to contend unsuccessfully for the Presidency of the United States in 1848, and to serve as Secretary of State in President Buchanan's cabinet. President Jackson appointed George B. Porter to be Cass's successor as governor of Michigan Territory. Porter reached Detroit on September 17, 1831, taking over the reins of government from Acting Governor Stevens T. Mason. He was absent frequently from the territory during the next three years, during which interims Mason again assumed the duties of governor. In 1834 he fell victim to cholera and Mason once more became acting governor on July 6. In November, President Jackson nominated Henry D. Gilpin of Pennsylvania to the office of governor of the territory, but the Senate, on January 20, 1835, rejected the nomination by a 23–22 vote. Jackson made no further effort to fill the office during the remainder of the territorial period, but in 1835, as a result of the squabbles connected with Michigan's battle for statehood, the President made an attempt to oust Mason from office. He appointed Judge Charles Shaler as secretary and acting governor on August 29, but Shaler had the good sense to decline. On September 15, Jackson appointed John S. Horner to the same position. By the time Horner arrived in Detroit a state constitution had been framed, and a conflict with Ohio over the southern boundary was in progress. Horner was snubbed socially and officially. At a public meeting a resolution inviting him to "return to the land of his nativity" was endorsed, and on November 2 and 3 the new state government was inaugurated. The following May Horner was appointed secretary of the newly formed Wisconsin Territory and left Detroit.[5]

*   *   *   *   *

Michigan long has been recognized as a leader in the field of public education. The groundwork for this position of leadership was laid during territorial times.

Schools had been maintained during the British regime for children of the troops garrisoned in the fort and others. From 1790 private schools were conducted by itinerant ministers and schoolmasters. The Reverend David Bacon, a New England Protestant missionary, opened a school at Detroit in 1801, but it was short-lived, partly because of the prevalent prejudice at that time against Yankees. Other private schools were conducted in 1806 by John Guff, in 1810 by Daniel Curtis, in 1812 by "Mr. Payne," and in 1813 by "Mr. Rowe." There was little continuity in these efforts, each schoolmaster accommodating all who paid the fee he asked, regardless of age. Father Gabriel Richard was deeply concerned about education and fostered several schools in and around Detroit. His school at Spring Hill was primarily for the vocational training of Indian children. As early as 1806 he petitioned the governor and judges for a parcel of land on which to build a "college." Judge Woodward and Governor Hull both expressed interest in providing schools, and on February 26, 1809, the governor and judges passed an act authorizing the overseers of the poor to establish school districts, to act as trustees of the same, and to lay an annual tax of two to four dollars per school child. But it does not appear that any schools were established under this law.

The first serious effort to promote public education in Michigan came on August 26, 1817, with a territorial act providing for "a Catholepistemiad or University of Michigania." This act was the brain child of Judge Woodward and, as might be expected, was grandiose in conception as well as name. It was not a university in the usual sense of that term, but rather a complete system of education for the territory, under centralized control. Control was vested in thirteen "didactors," each representing a field of knowledge that was given an outlandish name invented by Woodward and based on Latin or Greek derivatives. The year before, Woodward had published a book entitled *A System of Universal Science,* in which he had organized all human knowledge into thirteen divisions. The "didactors," also called "professors," were to be appointed by the governor and were empowered to establish "colleges, academies, schools, libraries, museums, atheneums, botanical gardens, laboratories, and other useful literary and scientific institutions throughout the territory." They were authorized to employ as many "instructors and instructorixes" as were necessary to staff these institutions. Modest tuition fees were stipulated, but those unable to pay them were to be educated at public expense. The principle of tax support was established, and lotteries were authorized to provide funds.

The Catholepistemiad was greeted by hoots of derision at the time and frequently has been the butt of ridicule since. Like most

Michiganians, Governor Cass could not even pronounce its name, referring to it as the "Cathole-what's its name."[6] But the fact remains that the plan set forth a number of principles that later became basic in the Michigan system of education: (1) public education extending from the lowest grade through the college and university level; (2) tax support; (3) non-sectarian control; (4) low tuition in public institutions. The system, however, contemplated one principle that has proved impractical: centralized control.[7] Although the authorship of the act must be credited to Judge Woodward, historians have pointed out that both Father Richard and Governor Cass were equally desirous of taking steps to promote education.

All the "didactorships" or "professorships" were conferred by Cass on two men. The Reverend John Monteith, a graduate of Princeton and pastor of the First Protestant Society of Detroit, organized in 1816, was assigned seven didactorships and the presidency, while six didactorships and the vice-presidency went to Father Richard. About a month after the passage of the law a treaty was made with the Indians—the Treaty of Fort Meigs—in which the Indians deeded six sections of their lands in equal shares to Ste. Anne's Church in Detroit and the "college at Detroit." There was no such college, but Monteith and Richard, acting as didactors of the Catholepistemiad, moved to remedy this deficiency by decreeing that "there be established in the City of Detroit, a College, to be denominated the First College of Michigania."[8] The college did not materialize, but a primary school and academy were established in 1817 at the behest of the two didactors, and these schools operated more or less continuously until about 1827. Monteith and Richard also took steps to establish schools at Monroe and on Mackinac Island, but the inhabitants of these places showed little interest in the proposal.

The governor and judges amended the act of 1817 in 1821. The strange verbiage of the Catholepistemiad was abandoned, but the feature of the original act that placed the responsibility for schools in the hands of a central body rather than in local communities was retained. Within a few years this plan proved impractical, partly, at least, because the central body lacked the funds to make any program of education effective.

In 1827, the Territorial Council, which had succeeded the governor and judges as the lawmaking body, abandoned the centralized policy in favor of a measure enabling townships to maintain schools. Townships containing at least fifty families were to employ one or more schoolmasters of sound moral character who would teach children to read and write, as well as arithmetic, orthography, and good behavior. Instruction could be given either in the English or French language, a bi-lingual approach that is an indication that Michigan's French population was not yet completely resigned to being swallowed up and assimilated by the English-speaking majority. Schools were to operate at least six months a year, taxes were to be levied for their support, and the poor were to be instructed without cost. The more populous townships were also expected to provide facilities for advanced instruction beyond the elementary level required of all townships. A board of not more than five commissioners was to have charge of schools in each township. The law contained an odd provision that townships not complying with the requirements might be fined, but that any township might be exempt from these requirements if two-thirds of its electors so voted! Except for this "escape clause" the law closely resembled the famous Massachusetts Law of 1647. Obviously it was a compromise between those who wished to require townships to establish schools and those who preferred to make it optional. But it was a definite departure from the laws of 1817 and 1821 in that it placed the responsibility for starting and maintaining schools squarely on local communities rather than on a central body.

Two years later, in 1829, another law passed by the Territorial Council provided for the laying off of school districts within a township. Five school inspectors were to be elected whose duty would be to examine teachers and to grant certificates to those whose good moral character and preparation indicated they were fit to teach. This act provided that the costs of maintaining schools were to be borne by those whose children were taught, but poor children were to be taught at the expense of the district. There were no schools in Michigan in which children were taught entirely at public expense until 1842; then only in Detroit. Parents of school children paid what were called "rate bills," based on the number of children they had in school and the number of days that each attended. The schoolmaster was lodged and fed by the parents in turn.

The laws of 1827 and 1829, as well as another passed in 1833, were not rigidly enforced, and most of the actual teaching during the territorial period was done in private schools opened for various lengths of time and then abandoned. Most of these were elementary schools. Above this level there were numerous "academies" that gave advanced instruction, mainly in Greek, Latin, and mathematics. The Territorial Council passed laws authorizing groups of citizens to form corporations for the purpose of founding and operating academies. Thirteen such acts were passed prior to the admission of Michigan into the Union. One of these corporations is still in existence. The Michigan and Huron Institute, which received a charter in 1833 and opened its doors in 1836, later became Kalamazoo College. It was founded by Baptists. Spring Arbor Seminary, incorporated in 1835 under a charter granted to a group of Methodists, was the forerunner of Albion College. The other eleven academies were community projects, most of which were later absorbed into the public school system.[9]

In the pioneer schools the subjects usually taught were reading, spelling, writing, and arithmetic, with some attention to grammar and geography. Writing was done with quill pens. One of the requirements of a schoolmaster was the ability to make these quill pens; more important was his capacity for keeping order and maintaining strict discipline. The birch rod was an indispensable part of his equipment, and no pupil who strayed from the straight and narrow path of good conduct could long escape its sting. The democracy of frontier life was not reflected in the school room, for there the master was an autocrat of autocrats. In the summer term, when boys old and strong enough to work on the farm were busy in the fields, women teachers might be employed; but during the winter term, when these boys attended, men were usually employed as teachers. Only women with strength and courage could manage a school in those times.[10]

The pioneer schoolhouse was apt to be located at an intersection of roads or on the brow of a hill. It was made of logs, sometimes roughly hewn, and was generally about eighteen feet wide and twenty-four feet long. The openings between the logs were chinked with pieces of wood, stones, or any convenient material, and plastered with mortar made from soil in the area. The door was made of rough boards, hung on wooden hinges, and fastened with a wooden latch. Windows were made by cutting out spaces and fastening oiled paper over the opening, thereby admitting some light and keeping out some cold. An ample fireplace provided heat, in its immediate vicinity at least. Slabs mounted on legs were used for seats, and desks were constructed by placing boards upon pins driven into the walls of the building. The teacher's agreement usually stipulated that he would teach the school for a specified number of weeks, from six to eight hours a day, six days a week, for which parents agreed to pay him a stipulated sum for each pupil sent.[11]

Although such schools were crude and the teachers, in many instances, inadequately prepared to teach, it is remarkable that the pioneers devoted as much time and money for schools as they did when one recalls that sheer survival was often a problem. The New England element, which formed such a large proportion of the settlers who came in during the early 1830s, was especially devoted to education. It was a Yankee habit to equate learning with godliness, and ignorance with deviltry.

*   *   *   *   *

As long as the French element formed the dominant part of the population, the Roman Catholic Church continued to be the most important religious organization in Michigan Territory. Ste. Ann's Church on Mackinac Island today represents the continuation of the work of the Jesuit missionaries in the Straits area in the latter part of the seventeenth century. Some of the church's records date back to the late seventeenth century, although the parish's development in later years was interrupted on a number of occasions. On the other hand, Ste. Anne's Church in Detroit has had a continuous development from Detroit's earliest days to the present. There is a tradition that Cadillac, after landing at Detroit on July 24, 1701, immediately began the construction of a chapel, which was completed two days later on the feast of Ste. Anne and was dedicated in her honor, but George Paré, the foremost historian of the Catholic Church in Detroit, doubts the accuracy of this tradition. The two priests who accompanied Cadillac did not remain long, but one of them appears to have returned in 1702, and the history of Ste. Anne's parish may be regarded as beginning in that year. The earliest baptismal records were lost, and the first entry in those that still exist is dated 1703. This register is the oldest continuous Catholic parish register in the country with the single exception of a church in St. Augustine, Florida. The present Ste. Anne's Church is the seventh edifice bearing that name. In 1786 a Potawatomi chief granted land for a "house of prayer" near Monroe. Two years later Father Pierre Frechette of Detroit organized a parish there. The church edifice was built nearly two and a half miles west of Monroe and was called St. Anthony's. Some years later the center of the parish was moved to Monroe and a new church, called Ste. Mary's, was erected.[12]

The history of the Catholic Church in Michigan in the early nineteenth century centers around Father Gabriel Richard. Though he is remembered for his work in education, his printing press, and his brief career in Congress, his passion was his church. His residence was Detroit but his charge included not only all of Michigan but also what is now Wisconsin. Ste. Anne's Church, destroyed by the fire of 1805, was not rebuilt until 1818, services in the interim being held in farm houses and rented buildings. In 1822, Richard reported that his parish included 926 families, averaging six to a

Old Mission Lighthouse, built in 1870

family, and mostly French-Canadian. There were about 150 Irish Catholic families, widely scattered, and by this time there were six Catholic churches in the territory. Four years later, Richard reported 7,000 Catholics and nine churches. In 1831, Irish Catholics around Ann Arbor worshipped in the first English-speaking Catholic church in the territory. Many of the Germans who started arriving about 1830 were also Catholic. In that year Assumption, the first German Catholic parish, was formed. By the end of the territorial period Detroit had a second Catholic parish called Holy Trinity, which was largely for Irish Catholics.

One of the tragedies of Father Richard's life was that, in spite of his manifold services and the growth of Catholicism in Michigan, he never was consecrated as a bishop. After the American flag was raised over Detroit, Michigan was attached to the Catholic diocese of Baltimore. Then in 1808 it became part of the diocese of Bardstown, Kentucky , and in 1821 it was made a part of the diocese of Cincinnati. As early as 1827 the erection of a Michigan diocese was considered. Perhaps Father Richard's involvements in a number of controversial matters, such as the Labadie case, caused the hierarchy to hesitate in ordaining him a bishop. Within a year after his death, the diocese of Michigan and the Northwest was erected, the first bishop being Frederick Rese, a native of Hannover, Germany.

The first Protestants in Michigan were probably members of the British garrison that occupied Detroit in 1760, but no Anglican church was founded until much later. The next Protestants were the Moravians, who lived briefly in Michigan during the Revolution at Mount Clemens. Their little meeting house on the Clinton River was the first Protestant church, though it was only a temporary place of worship. The Reverend David Bacon made his way to Michigan as an agent of the Congregational churches of Connecticut as early as 1800, conducted religious services in Detroit, but found that all but a few of the people were firmly attached to the Catholic faith, so he shortly returned to the East.[13] Three years later the first Methodist preacher, Nathan Bangs, visited Michigan. He had been appointed to the Circuit of Upper Canada including Detroit by the New York Conference of the Methodist Episcopal Church. In Michigan, as elsewhere on the frontier, the Methodist circuit-rider was one of the most useful and tireless figures in the new country. Tramping or riding miles through the wilderness, he brought to lonely cabins not only spiritual consolation but also news of the outside world, books, and guidance in manners and morals. He held religious meetings wherever the opportunity presented itself, performed marriage ceremonies, buried the dead, and baptized the young.

The first Methodist society in Michigan was formed in 1810 by Methodists living on the River Rouge. Until 1818 services were held in homes, but in that year a hewn-log chapel was constructed on a site covered in later years by the vast Ford Motor Company plant. Except for the Moravian chapel on the Clinton River, this chapel was the first Protestant house of worship in Michigan. The great influx of settlers in the 1830s brought many Methodists to Michigan, and Methodist churches had sprung up by 1837 in Ypsilanti, Adrian, Port Huron, Niles, Jackson, Coldwater, Kalamazoo, Flint, Ann Arbor, Marshall, and Detroit. Almost 5,000 members were reported by 1835 and the next year the Methodist Conference of Michigan was established.[14]

The arrival of the Rev. John Monteith in 1816 was an important event in the history of Protestantism in Michigan. A graduate of Princeton, Monteith was sent into the West by a home missionary organization that represented the joint efforts of the Presbyterians and Congregationalists. Since 1801 these two denominations had been under a "Plan of Union" in their work on the frontier. The plan envisioned that Presbyterians and Congregationalists in pioneer communities would establish a single church and that the membership would decide whether to adopt the Presbyterian or the Congregational mode of worship and organization. A public meeting of Protestants was held soon after Monteith came to Detroit, and he was engaged to remain one year, the sum of $800 being subscribed to supplement the amount he received from missionary sources in the East. At the close of the first year, the First Protestant Society of Detroit was organized. It consisted of Congregationalists, Presbyterians, Methodists, and Episcopalians, as well as people of no particular denomination. Monteith remained as pastor, and a church edifice, started in 1818 and dedicated in 1820, was erected at a cost of $7,000. Monteith and Father Richard were warm personal friends, both interested in education, active in the establishment of the Catholepistemiad, and appointed as president and vice-president respectively of that institution.

Methodists in Detroit became sufficiently numerous in 1821 to form their own society and build their own church. The Episcopalians organized separately in 1824 and also built a church, which was finished in 1828. The First Protestant Society was reorganized as the First Presbyterian Church in 1825. Monteith was instrumental in organizing a Presbyterian church at Monroe in 1820, and other churches of this denomination were founded at Pontiac in 1824, Farmington in 1825, and Ann Arbor in 1826. These churches formed the Detroit Presbytery, which was organized in 1827. The Presbyterian Church grew rapidly in the early 1830s, and by 1834 the St. Joseph and Monroe Presbyteries had been formed. These and the Detroit Presbytery constituted the Presbyterian Synod of Michigan, organized in 1834.

The Congregational Church regards the Rev. Isaac Ruggles, who came from Connecticut and established himself near Pontiac, as the pioneer Congregationalist in Michigan. Next to "Father Ruggles," the Rev. John D. Pierce of Marshall was perhaps the first Congregational minister in Michigan. There were eight churches in Michigan formed under the Plan of Union prior to 1835 that adopted the Congregational polity and never relinquished it. The path of co-operation between the Congregationalists and the Presbyterians was not a smooth one, and in 1837 a split occurred in the latter denomination over whether the Plan of Union should be continued. Most Michigan Presbyterians adhered to the "New School," which favored the Plan of Union, and this helped to maintain the co-operative program. As a result there was either a Presbyterian or a Congregational church in most pioneer Michigan towns, but seldom both. Fewer churches chose the Congregational affiliation than the Presbyterian, and it was not until 1842 that the Congregationalists formed a state association.

The first Baptist church in Michigan was organized by a group of New York immigrants who settled near Pontiac in 1819. The pastor of the church was paid $100 a year, one-third in cash and the remainder in produce. The Rev. Elon Galusha was probably the first Baptist minister in Michigan; he came as a missionary to the new church at Pontiac. By 1826 there were three other Baptist churches: Stony Creek (Oakland County), Troy, and Farmington. A Baptist church was founded in Detroit in 1827, and Ypsilanti and Ann Arbor Baptists organized churches the following year. In 1836, the Michigan Baptist Convention was formed by fifty-five delegates from twenty-seven churches in Michigan. Close relations were maintained with the New York Baptist Convention. The Baptist Church was especially strong in western New York, and since so many Michigan pioneers came from that area, this denomination enjoyed rapid growth.[15]

Of major importance in promoting the growth of Protestant churches in Michigan was the home-missionary movement. New England leaders for some years opposed the expansion of the nation westward, but when they realized that the westward movement was irresistible they determined to do what they could to civilize and Christianize the new states by encouraging the founding of churches and schools. To this end they organized home-missionary societies in several of the New England states. This led to the formation of the American Home Missionary Society in 1826 as a co-operative venture of the Congregational, Presbyterian, and Reformed churches. In 1832, the American Baptist Home Missionary Society was organized. The Methodists had no comparable society, but they were very effective along the same lines through the work of the circuit riders.[16] Among the leading home missionaries who came to Michigan were the Rev. John D. Pierce, who became the first state superintendent of public instruction, and Thomas W. Merrill, a Baptist, who was instrumental in founding the institution that became Kalamazoo College. There can be no doubt that churches were established in pioneer Michigan communities earlier than would otherwise have been possible as a result of the work of the home missionaries, who received their meager stipends in whole or in part from eastern missionary agencies.[17] The reports to the American Home Missionary Society contained in letters written by the scores of home missionaries who came to Michigan provide an intimate glimpse of pioneer times, although they no doubt overstressed the prevalence of drunkenness, gambling, swearing, sabbath-breaking, and other sins as a means of encouraging continued support from the East.[18]

The home missionaries, unlike the earlier Catholic missionaries, did not work among the Indians. However, several Protestants established Indian missions in the 1820s and 1830s. Notable among these were Isaac McCoy, who conducted the Carey Mission at Niles, and Leonard Slater, whose Indian mission on the Grand River was later moved to a location near Hastings. Both these men were Baptists. The Methodist Church had missionaries working among the Indians of the Upper Peninsula. The Presbyterian mission on Mackinac Island has been mentioned earlier.

The Episcopal Church was represented in Michigan by a sizable membership during the territorial period. St. Paul's Church in Detroit, formed in 1824, was the first Episcopal church in Michigan. The first pastor received $150 from his parishioners and $150 from the church mission board as his annual salary. Services were first held in the Council House, but a new church edifice was dedicated in 1828. Other Episcopal churches were established at Ann Arbor in 1827, Troy in 1829, Tecumseh and Monroe in 1831. The edifice built by the members of St. Peter's Church at Tecumseh and dedicated in 1833 was a fine example of church architecture. It was demolished in 1963 to make way for a new structure. In 1832, the Episcopal Diocese of Michigan was established, although it had no bishop until 1836.[19]

Thus by the end of the territorial period, the Roman Catholic Church and four Protestant denominations—the Methodist, Baptist, Presbyterian, and Episcopal—had established ecclesiastical bodies which embraced all of Michigan. A number of other denominations were represented. The Congregationalists have already been mentioned. German settlers around Ann Arbor formed a Lutheran church in that town in 1833, and by 1850 there were twelve Lutheran houses of worship in Michigan. A number of "Friends" (Quakers) settled near Adrian, and there the first "monthly meeting" of Quakers in Michigan was held in 1831. Shortly thereafter, "preparative meetings" of Quakers were held at Farmington and Palmyra. The Quakers were strongly opposed to slavery and the first antislavery society in Michigan was organized by the Quakeress Elizabeth Chandler in 1832. One of the most noted leaders of this faith was Laura Smith Haviland, affectionately known as "Aunt Laura," who was an ardent worker in the Underground Railroad. The Universalist Church was represented in Michigan during territorial times by a society organized at Ann Arbor in 1828, and by 1850 seven Universalist churches were open in the state.

The religious life of early Detroit found expression not only in the formation of church bodies and the building of churches but also in inter-church efforts of several kinds. A Bible Society was formed in 1816 and was supported by such notables as Governor Lewis Cass. A religious society for seamen was started in 1830, and a tract society was formed the following year. Detroit also had a German Evangelical church, organized in 1833. Thirteen ex-slaves voluntarily withdrew from the First Baptist Church to organize the Second Baptist Church in 1836.

A smaller percentage of the population belonged to churches than is true today, but there were stricter rules for members. It was not uncommon for Protestant as well as Catholic churches to excommunicate members for not living up to the code of conduct demanded by church rules and practice. Although there were many pioneers who were unchurched, partly from preference and partly from the lack of any accessible church, there was a universal acceptance of the church as a cornerstone of society.

*   *   *   *   *

The first newspaper in Michigan came from Father Richard's press in 1809, but it is doubtful whether more than one issue was published. However, since the appearance of the first issue of the Detroit *Gazette* on July 25, 1817, newspaper publishing in Michigan has been continuous. The *Gazette* was established by John P. Sheldon and Ebenezer Reed. Although it was an English-language newspaper, most of the important articles were also printed in French on the last page. The paper measured 16½ × 9½ inches, and each page was comprised of four columns. The subscription price was $4.00 per year to city subscribers and $3.50 by mail. It was issued weekly. The primitive character of the paper is implied by this description in Farmer's *History of Detroit and Michigan:*

> Occasionally the type-cases were overtaxed, and the number for October 18, 1822, gives the names of signers to a call for a public meeting in so many kinds and sizes of type that one might imagine that the compositor had just returned from a wake.[20]

That the editorial policy was quite different from modern standards is shown by a statement in the September 11, 1818 issue. After denouncing a person who had defrauded him, the editor announced that:

> Citizens who have been wronged by scoundrels have only to send a notice of their wrongs and the name of the scoundrel to this office in order to put the public on guard. Such notices will be published gratis.

In 1829, Editor Sheldon published an editorial bitterly assailing the territorial supreme court, by which he was convicted of contempt and fined $100. Upon his refusal to pay the amount he was put in jail. Townspeople were aroused by this and held a mass meeting which adopted a resolution upholding the editor. He continued to write for the paper while in jail, and a public banquet was given for him in the jail. He was eventually released when citizens insisted on paying his fine. He was then promptly taken to a hotel and given a gala luncheon.[21]

The Detroit *Gazette* printed its last issue in 1830. Other Detroit papers that came and went during the territorial period were the *Michigan Herald* (1825–29), the *Gazette Francaise* (1825), the Detroit *Telegraph* (1829), the Detroit *Courier* (1830), the *Herald of Literature and Science* (1831), the Detroit *Journal* (1835), and the *Michigan State Register* (1836–37). Two newspapers were being published at the end of the territorial period: the Detroit *Daily Advertiser,* which was founded in 1829 under a different name and became a daily in 1836, and the *Democratic Free Press and Michigan Intelligencer,* founded in 1831. The latter became a daily in 1835, and thus became Michigan's first daily newspaper. It is the lineal ancestor of the present Detroit *Free Press.* The first editor of the paper was John P. Sheldon, who had been editor of the *Gazette.* He had gone to Pontiac in 1830, where he started publication of the *Oakland Chronicle.* He returned to Detroit the following year to launch his new venture. The *Free Press* thus has the further distinction of being the oldest existing newspaper in the state. It also had the first power press used in the West. The *Free Press* was for many years a staunchly Democratic newspaper, while the *Advertiser* took the Whig, and later the Republican side.

Detroit was the only town in Michigan with daily newspapers. Several weeklies had been started outside Detroit, however, by the close of the territorial period. The first of these was the Monroe *Sentinel,* which started publication in 1825. Second was the *Western Emigrant,* published at Ann Arbor beginning in 1829. The *Oakland Chronicle* of Pontiac, which was launched in 1830 and moved to Detroit the next year to become the *Free Press,* was the third newspaper outside Detroit. In November, 1833, the *Michigan Statesman and St. Joseph Chronicle* was established at White Pigeon by Henry Gilbert. It was the fourth outstate newspaper to be published. Gilbert was attracted to White Pigeon, it may be assumed, by the printing business that the local government land office would provide. When the land office was moved to Kalamazoo in 1835 the printer went along and started publication of the *Michigan Statesman* in Kalamazoo. He changed its name to the Kalamazoo *Gazette* in 1837, and this newspaper is still being published. Since there is no news-paper in existence today that can trace its beginning back to the Monroe *Sentinel* and the *Western Emigrant,* and since the *Oakland Chronicle* was moved to Detroit, the Kalamazoo *Gazette* has the dis-tinction of being the oldest existing newspaper in Michigan outside Detroit.

Monroe had a second newspaper in 1834—the Monroe *Advocate*—and the present Monroe *Evening News* is the descendant of that paper. Ann Arbor also had a second newspaper, the *State Journal,* which started publication in 1835. St. Clair, Niles, and Ad-rian had their first newspapers in 1835; Tecumseh, Constantine, Marshall, and Saginaw in 1836; Jackson, Mount Clemens, and Grand Rapids in 1837.

St. Clair had a second newspaper by the end of 1837, and before the close of the 1830s, rival newspapers had also been estab-lished in Kalamazoo, Jackson, Marshall, Mount Clemens, and Pon-tiac. In the latter town the short-lived *Oakland Chronicle* was fol-lowed by the Pontiac *Courier* (1836) and the Pontiac *Jacksonian* (1838). The intense partisanship of the late 1830s, with friends and foes of President Jackson and his successor in office, Martin Van Buren, contending against each other, encouraged partisan jour-nalism. Many newspapers were started purely as partisan organs, and some were published only for a few months during a campaign.[22]

Newspaper publishing in Michigan began in earnest at a time when American journalism was at a low ebb. One authority on the subject writes: "Indeed the whole period of 1801–1833 was in many respects disgraceful—a kind of 'Dark Ages' in American journalism. Few papers were ably edited; they reflected the crassness of the American society of the times. Scurrility, assaults, corruption, bla-tancy were commonplace."[23] Hezekiah Niles, one of the most reli-able observers of the time, wrote: "The press is now so conditioned in the United States, that nearly every publisher is compelled to take a side in personal electioneering."[24] In many cases newspapers de-pended for their support mainly on subsidies from political parties.

In spite of their shortcomings these early newspapers kept the people of Michigan in touch with the outside world. In addition to biting editorials and usually some bad fiction and worse poetry, they brought news from Europe (usually two or three months old) and information on happenings in the East. The advertisements advised readers on merchandise available in the stores. The papers contained some territorial news, but relatively little on local events. The reader was expected to know as well as the editor what had gone on in the community where the newspaper was published. This lack of a record of local happenings, though understandable, often is vexatious to the researcher who expects or hopes to find in old newspaper files full accounts of an important event of territorial times.

*   *   *   *   *

        Although frontier conditions obviously slowed the growth of strictly cultural activities during the territorial period, the cultural life of Michigan's largest city found expression in a variety of interests and activities. The citizens of Detroit formed a library society in 1817, and in 1831 the Detroit Athenaeum was established to maintain a club reading room. Governor Cass and John Biddle were chosen president and vice-president respectively. The Detroit Young Men's Society was formed in 1833 to "devise means for greater intellectual improvement"; meetings were held each Friday evening during the winter, at which time debates were conducted and "elocutionary exercises" were presented. A library was also maintained. Incorporated in 1836, the Society continued to exist for almost half a century. A lyceum was organized in 1818 under the leadership of Judge Woodward and Secretary Woodbridge. As usual with anything in which Woodward had a hand, this club was too grandiose in design for practical purposes. Dr. Douglass Houghton announced a series of twenty-six lectures on chemistry in 1830; admission was $2.00 for the series, or $4.00 for a family of three. A local newspaper offered a prize of $25 to the apprentice who submitted in writing the best summary of the series. The Historical Society of Michigan was incorporated in 1828, with Lewis Cass as president. At the meetings of the Society, which was, despite the name, almost entirely confined in membership to Detroiters, Cass, Henry R. Schoolcraft, and others lectured. The Society soon ceased to be active, but was revived in 1874 as the Michigan Pioneer Society. Later the name was changed to Michigan Pioneer and Historical Society; the original name, Historical Society of Michigan, was adopted in 1949.
        There was scant time for the cultivation of the arts in pioneer Michigan, but interest in music, the visual arts, and the theater were not lacking. Music was an adjunct to the worship of God at Ste. Anne's Church in Detroit, and there is evidence that the church had a chorister as early as 1755. To celebrate the end of the siege of Detroit during the Pontiac uprising of 1763 an "instrumental concert" was given. Shortly after 1800 a small pipe organ was installed in

the church; the instrument so amazed and fascinated the Indians that they stole the pipes.[25] The organ must have been repaired, or else Father Richard obtained a new one. In 1832, the organ that had been used by Ste. Anne's was given to Trinity Church. St. Paul's Episcopal Church acquired a new organ in 1831, on which a "concert" was performed by "Mr. Newell" on September 30 of that year.

There was at least one harpsichord in Detroit prior to the nineteenth century. The first piano arrived in 1803. It was an instrument that had been played by Mrs. Solomon Sibley prior to her marriage while attending a school in Pennsylvania. It was transported on horseback to Marietta, Ohio; just how it was carried from Marietta to Detroit the records do not tell. Another piano was brought to Ann Arbor from Detroit by ox team in 1827. The teamster was somewhat fearful of the contents of the box in which it was packed because "it thundered so." This was the first piano taken west of Detroit. It had only five octaves and was manufactured in New York. The Indians were also greatly attracted to this instrument, so the story goes, and the chief is said to have offered half a dozen ponies for the instrument and the young lady who played it.[26]

Singing was popular among the pioneers. Many of them sang at their work. Some were noted for their good voices or their extensive repertoire of songs, and these were called upon to perform at social gatherings. Mothers sang their children to sleep with songs they had heard their mothers sing. Mostly the words and tunes were just remembered. There were books containing the words of songs, but since only a very few people could read music the names of the tunes but not the notes were included. Singing schools were popular with the young people and were not frowned upon by the pious, as were dancing and some other kinds of amusement. More often than not the songs and ballads were sung unaccompanied; occasionally the performer would provide his own accompaniment with the dulcimer or guitar. The singer and the audience were more enraptured by the story told by a ballad than by the tune. In these stories the tragic element predominated, although happier themes were not entirely lacking. Some told of disasters and tragedies, others dealt with unrequited love. A number were in a humorous vein, and some of the love ballads had a happy ending.

The history of the theater in Michigan begins with the amateur theatricals performed by the soldiers in the Detroit garrison. Life in the western military posts was dull and monotonous for the lively young men who manned them, and to while away the hours they rehearsed and presented plays, taking both male and female roles and using improvised scenery. The plays were designed mainly for the amusement of the participants, their families, and friends. The officers of the Detroit garrison formed an amateur troupe in 1798, and produced such favorites as *The Rivals* and *The Mock Duke.* These plays continued to be presented for many years. Traveling players may have visited Detroit as early as 1810. In 1816, a theater was fitted up on the second floor of a large brick warehouse at the foot of Wayne Street. There were several other buildings used for theatricals during the next two decades, indicating that there must have been quite a lively interest in dramatics. A company of players arrived from Buffalo in 1827, was granted a license to perform, and apparently presented an entire season of plays. In 1833, another company came for the summer season, and the next year two more arrived.[27] The *Free Press,* in 1837, told of a rapid succession of "sterling comedy, showy melodrama, gorgeous spectacle, broad farce, and delightful vaudeville and drama."[28]

Without any pretense of artistic expression, the pioneers, in many of the tools and utensils they made by hand, demonstrated sound ideas of design. Simple but beautiful geometric and representational designs are found in the carved and turned wood fashioned by early craftsmen. Simple furniture made by pioneers in many instances reflects skill of workmanship and an eye for beauty. In the homes and public buildings they constructed, after sawmills made lumber available, the pioneer carpenters produced structures of lasting beauty, aesthetically far superior to the ornate monstrosities that were built later in the nineteenth century by a wealthier and more sophisticated generation. The style of pioneer houses, after the log-cabin stage was passed, was determined to a large degree by the New England and New York origins of most of the Michigan settlers. New England colonial architecture was widely copied. The houses were rectangular in plan and placed parallel with the street; they usually had a low gabled roof, molded cornice, small-paned sash, and doors framed with slender pilasters. The Snow house in Paw Paw, the Medor Tromble house in Bay City, and the Agent's house on Mackinac Island are surviving examples of the use of the New England colonial style by Michigan builders.[29] The style was also copied in some of the early churches.

Before the end of the territorial period the Greek Revival style had been introduced into Michigan and it continued to be popular throughout the 1830s and 1840s. Numerous examples of it may still be seen in the surviving homes constructed during that period. The central portion of these houses was built on the order of a Greek temple, but they vary greatly in form and composition. Builders apparently used standard designs, in the absence of architects, then added their own ideas. Heavy cornices and columns, generally of wood, were distinctive features of the Greek Revival houses. The southeastern part of Michigan, which was most thickly settled in this period, is particularly rich in examples of this type of house, though many are found in towns as far west as Kalamazoo. More have survived in rural areas and small towns than in the cities, for with urban growth old houses are often sacrificed in the name of progress. At Cambridge Junction along US-12 stands the Walker Tavern, erected by Ezra Blood in 1832 and now owned by the state of Michigan. It is basically a New York farmhouse, but the narrow veranda around two sides, with heavy, square columns supporting the roof, is a crude but typically Greek Revival characteristic. The Elijah Anderson house and the Yawger house in Tecumseh, built in the 1830s, the Charles M. Croswell house in Adrian, and the Wilson-Wahr house in Ann Arbor are excellent examples of various aspects of the Greek Revival style.[30] Perhaps the finest Greek Revival house in Michigan was built

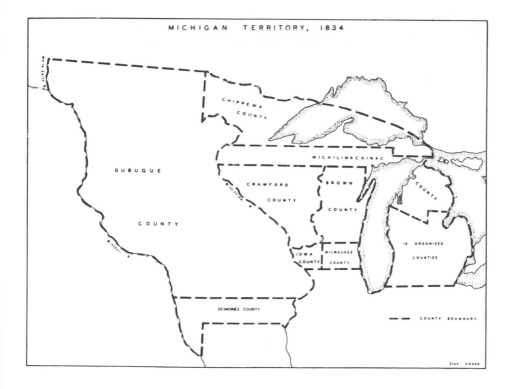

near Dexter by Samuel Dexter; this house has been pictured and described in many architectural journals.

The first professional artist in Michigan was probably James O. Lewis, who arrived at Detroit in 1824. A steel engraver and painter, he employed both these media in his portraits of Father Gabriel Richard and Governor Lewis Cass. He submitted designs for the seal of the City of Detroit, and the first seal of the state of Michigan in 1835 was probably designed by him in collaboration with Lewis Cass. He went with the Cass expedition in 1820 and made many drawings of Indian chiefs. His work went to the Smithsonian Institution in Washington, but the drawings were destroyed by fire in 1865. Two portfolios of lithographs of his Indian subjects were sold by subscription, and copies of these have been preserved.

Shortly after Lewis came to Detroit he was followed by another painter, Gildersleeve Hurd. Hurd came to visit his brother, who had married a daughter of Judge James Witherell. His portraits of the judge and members of the Witherell family have survived and show considerable skill. He opened a decorator's studio in Detroit and specialized in decorating the plastered walls of houses with paneled landscapes, surrounded by ornamentation.

Several itinerant artists turned up in Detroit in the 1830s. One was J. M. Stanley, who came to Detroit after being employed at Buffalo painting medallions and landscapes on farm wagons. He produced many landscapes which were purchased by Detroiters to hang in their homes, and, like Lewis, he painted many Indian chiefs. His "Indian Telegraph" is in the permanent collection of the Detroit Institute of Arts. T. H. O. P. Burnham, nicknamed "Alphabet Burnham," is best known for his "State election scene" of 1837. It depicts Campus Martius in Detroit on election day, and includes portraits of Governor Mason and other notables. Critics have compared this painting to the work of Hogarth and feel that it reveals an artist of keen perception and artistic understanding. Alvah Bradish, a portrait painter who arrived in 1837, set up a studio and for more than fifty years produced portraits of famous Detroiters. His style was that of the English portraiture of the eighteenth century. Several other artists came to Detroit prior to 1837. The popularity of portraits before the advent of photography created a lively demand for artists. It was not confined to the great or the near-great either. Itinerant "limners" roamed Michigan, equipped with an assortment of canvases, complete except for the face. The person desiring to have his portrait done would select a background, body, and dress, after which the artist would quickly finish the work for a small fee, sometimes accepting board and lodging in lieu of money.[31]

Although Detroit had a greater variety of cultural activities and civic associations than was found elsewhere, the new outstate towns manifested an early interest in such fields. Bible societies, temperance societies, and antislavery societies were established in many places. Lyceums had been organized in several towns outside Detroit by 1837.

Governor Stevens T. Mason

11

A STORMY ENTRANCE INTO THE UNION

As Michigan's population grew by leaps and bounds in the early thirties it was natural that the possibility of statehood should be broached. A vote on the expediency of forming a state government was taken in 1832. It carried, but only by a small margin. Nevertheless, in 1833 the territorial council formally requested that Congress pass an enabling act for Michigan. When a territory was ready for statehood, the usual procedure had been for Congress to pass such an "enabling act" authorizing the election of a constitutional convention. After a constitution had been written it was then submitted to Congress, which, if it approved that document, then admitted the state to the Union. The reason for this procedure lay in the fact that the United States constitution guarantees to each state a "republican" form of government, and thus Congress, before admitting the state, had to be assured it would have such a government. Tennessee, however, which was admitted to the Union in 1796, had framed a constitution without any enabling act and demanded statehood as a right that Congress could not deny. A governor, congressman, and two senators were elected. The congressman and senators proceeded to Philadelphia, then the seat of the federal government, and demanded to be seated. There was considerable debate over the propriety of this procedure, and political interests were involved. The Federalists opposed the admission of Tennessee because they were certain the state would favor the rival Democratic-Republican party. However, they were outvoted and Tennessee was granted statehood.

Although Tennessee was not part of the Northwest Territory,

its claim to statehood rested upon a census that showed it had more than the 60,000 people set forth in the Northwest Ordinance as a prerequisite for statehood. Whether this provision in an ordinance enacted for the "government of the territory of the United States, northwest of the River Ohio" applied also to Tennessee was debatable, but there could be no question of its applicability in the case of Michigan. However, the Constitution of the United States provides that "New States may be admitted by the Congress into this Union. . .," which would appear to give Congress the power to exercise discretion in the matter of admitting a state. Michigan's contention was, however, that the Northwest Ordinance represented a compact that gave the people who settled in the Old Northwest rights that could not be violated even by Congress. The ordinance itself stated that "the following articles shall be considered as articles of compact between the original states and the people and states in the said territory, and for ever unalterable, unless by common consent. . . ," and one of the articles guaranteed statehood when "any of the said states shall have sixty thousand free inhabitants therein."

The federal census of 1830 had enumerated 31,639 persons in the Territory of Michigan, but so great was the influx after 1830 that there could be little question that there were at least 60,000 by 1833. Michigan was fortunate to have as its delegate in Congress at the time an unusually capable man in the person of Lucius Lyon. He had a wide circle of friends and he ably supported the petition of the Territorial Council that an enabling act be passed. The House Committee on territories reported that it was "inexpedient" to grant the petition at the time, but a bill was introduced in the senate to authorize the people of Michigan to form a state government. This bill was debated between May 9 and 12, 1834, then laid on the table by a vote of 20 to 19. Lyon could accomplish little in the face of hard political facts.

The difficulty centered around the boundary dispute between Michigan and Ohio that had lain dormant for many years but now, for a variety of reasons, had become heated. In many respects, Michigan had a strong case, but on the other hand, Ohio had more voters than did Michigan, and from the political standpoint, if one side or the other was to be offended it should not be Ohio. The result was that Congress did nothing about statehood for Michigan.

Back in the territory the cholera epidemic of 1834 took Governor George Porter as one of its victims, and this once more made young Stevens T. Mason acting governor. He promptly called the Territorial Council into special session and called to the members' attention the inaction of Congress and proposed a course of action designed to attain statehood for Michigan. He asked the Council to authorize a census to ascertain the size of the population of Michigan, which, he wrote, "is beyond doubt, over sixty thousand," and then to proceed to call a convention to institute a state government, to elect a representative and two senators, and to send them to Washington to *demand* admission into the Union, the course that Tennessee had successfully taken some forty years before.[1] The Council readily assented to Mason's proposal. A census was ordered and the returns indicated there were 85,856 persons in the lower peninsula, with another 6,817 in the vast area north and west of Lake Michigan that was then part of the Territory of Michigan. Early in 1835 the Council reconvened, and on January 26 ordered an election to be held on April 4 to choose delegates to a constitutional convention that was to assemble at Detroit on May 11.

The ninety-one delegates that were elected assembled on the appointed date and within the surprisingly short time of forty-five days had completed their assigned task of drafting a constitution for the proposed new state. The speed with which they acted is especially remarkable because few of the delegates had had any previous parliamentary experience. Most of them were men of small or moderate means. Forty-five of the delegates were farmers. The next largest group—twenty—included merchants, mill operators, and lumbermen. Only ten lawyers were delegates, while among the remaining members were three physicians, two surveyors, one editor, an architect, a school teacher, and eight delegates whose occupations are unknown. A majority were Democrats, but there were a few Whigs.

After some floundering, a committee of nineteen was appointed to prepare a first draft. Five members of this committee formed a subcommittee which produced a draft in only four days which was then submitted to the full convention. Several standing committees studied the various sections of the draft constitution. When these committees gave their reports there was debate on some of the controversial issues, but on the whole the convention was notable for the relative lack of dissension. The articles dealing with the right to vote, the bill of rights, amendments, and education aroused the greatest amount of debate.

The first article, consisting of twenty-one sections, was actually a bill of rights, although not labeled as such. The provisions were copied largely from Connecticut's bill of rights and the first ten amendments to the federal constitution. Freedom of worship, trial by jury, the writ of *habeas corpus,* compensation for property seized for public use, freedom of speech, freedom of assembly, and the subordination of the military to the civil power were guaranteed to the people and placed beyond the reach of the state government to destroy. The necessity for a bill of rights in a state constitution rests upon the fact that most of the guarantees contained in the United States Constitution protect citizens from the violation of basic rights by the Congress of the United States, not the states.

There was little new in the form of government provided. Older state constitutions were freely used as models. The unicameral territorial legislature was replaced by the more customary bicameral legislature. The House of Representatives was to consist of not less than forty-eight nor more than one hundred members, while the state Senate would have one-third as many members as the house. Representatives were to be elected annually, but senators were to serve for two-year terms. The positions of governor and lieutenant-governor were also made elective for two-year terms, and the election of these officials, as well as of senators, was to take place in odd-numbered years, which meant that these offices would never be filled at a time when an election for president was also being held. Except for the representatives, senators, governor, and lieutenant-governor, all other state offices were to be filled through appointment, usually by the governor with the consent of the senate or the entire legislature. The judiciary would consist of appointees to a supreme court, probate courts, justices of the peace, and such other courts as the legislature might establish. An ultrademocratic feature was the power granted to the legislature to remove judges by a two-thirds vote.

The hottest debates in the convention centered around the question of who should have the right to vote. There were some delegates who wished to restrict the franchise to property holders, but in the face of a general trend throughout the country to eliminate such restrictions, this proposal was defeated. As a result, every white male over the age of twenty-one who resided in Michigan at the time the constitution was ratified was qualified to vote. A six-months' residence was required of those who came later. At a time when women were not voting at all and blacks outside of the New England states were entirely denied the franchise, Michigan's voting requirements were generally in keeping with national practices, and in allowing white aliens to vote they were more liberal than twentieth-century practices.

Of all the articles in the Michigan constitution, the one on education was perhaps the most farsighted. It stipulated that the legislature should encourage "the promotion of intellectual, scientifical, and agricultural improvement." It provided for the appointment of a state superintendent of public instruction—the first state constitution to make this a constitutionally established position—thereby eliminating the possibility of the legislature abolishing the office in the future. The article on education also contained safeguards against diverting to other uses the income from the land grants by the federal government to the state for education. In several other states proceeds from the school lands had been dissipated and not used for their intended purpose. Another unique provision of this article placed the proceeds from the sale of section sixteen in each township, which had been reserved from sale for school purposes, into a perpetual primary school fund, the interest on the fund to be divided annually among school districts conducting a school for at least three months a year. In some other states each township had received the proceeds from the sale of its sixteenth section. Since the value of section sixteen in different townships varied widely, this gave some townships a sizable amount and others virtually nothing. Michigan, by placing the proceeds from all the sections into a state fund and distributing the interest on the fund according to the number of pupils in each school, took the first step toward equalization of educational opportunity.

Among the other provisions of the Michigan Constitution of 1835 was one that authorized the state government to engage in works of "internal improvement," that is, the building of roads, canals, and railroads. Acts of incorporation were to require a two-thirds vote of the legislature. Lotteries, the popular method of raising money during the territorial period, were prohibited, and there were a few other specific provisions. One limited the compensation of legislators to $3.00 a day. This was continued in later constitutions and was not abolished until 1948.

The Constitution of 1835 has been lauded by political scientists, and it has been claimed by some that it was the best constitution Michigan has ever had. Among the provisions most often praised is the popular election of only the legislators, governor, and lieutenant governor, with other state offices filled by appointment. Advocates of the short ballot regard this as far better than choosing so many state officials by election that the voter can scarcely be expected to know the qualifications of all the candidates. The election of the governor, lieutenant governor, and senators in the odd-numbered years has been praised because it scheduled the chief state election at a time when the attention and interest of the voters are not diverted by national election contests and issues. The brevity and simplicity of Michigan's first state constitution has been especially acclaimed by political scientists. It placed few restrictions upon the legislature or the governor and left much to the discretion of these elected officials. In this respect, the highly acclaimed article on education was an exception since it was quite specific in detailing what could and could not be done in that one area of state activity. In particular, by requiring certain state funds to be used only for education, this article set a precedent for the practice of earmarking state funds for certain purposes that would greatly limit the ability of the state to deal with unforeseen emergencies in later years. Constitutions in 1850, 1908, and 1963 would tend to follow the example of this one article, thus destroying to a great degree that freedom of choice and action that was possible under most of the other provisions of the 1835 constitution. As the years passed, citizens found more and more policies that they wished to place beyond the power of the legislature and the governor to change. Far too many such restrictions were introduced. The present constitution drafted in the early 1960s dropped some of these, but retained many others and inserted some new ones. Whatever may be the conclusion as to the wisdom of such clauses, there can be no doubt that the constitution-makers of 1835 were wise in keeping them to a bare minimum and leaving many matters to the wisdom and the judgment of future elected state officials.[2]

In the summer of 1835, however, a long and difficult road remained to be traveled before the still-unborn state of Michigan could fully benefit from the excellent work of the constitutional convention. The constitution had to be ratified by the voters, and the delegates specified that the vote on this issue would be held on October 5, 1835, and, assuming that the voters would approve the constitution, that an election be held at the same time to choose the officials of the new state government. November 1 was then established as the date when this government would begin to function. This timetable gave the people of Michigan a little over three months to consider the proposed constitution, after which time the process of choosing officials and inaugurating a new government was to be compressed into less than one month's time. The reason for this haste no doubt was that the border controversy with Ohio was reaching a climax, and as a consequence neither the delegates nor most of the people were in a mood to delay asserting Michigan's right to statehood.

The Democrats chose Stevens T. Mason as their candidate for governor, but the Whigs, following their leader, William Woodbridge, who argued that the course Michigan was following was not legal since it lacked Congressional approval, made no formal nominations. However, John Biddle, long-time officer in the Detroit land office, was the candidate informally supported by most Whigs. Then on September 10, less than a month before the election, Mason received a letter from Washington signed by Secretary of State John Forsyth notifying him of his dismissal as secretary of Michigan Territory for failing to preserve the "spirit of moderation and forbearance" that President Jackson deemed "necessary for the preservation of public peace." This referred to Mason's leadership of armed resistance against Ohio's attempts to take over jurisdiction of the disputed Toledo strip. Mason, who at the time was watching a dress parade of his troops, at once called for attention and announced he was no longer their leader. On September 19, John S. Horner arrived in Detroit to assume Mason's position as secretary and acting governor of the territory.

Although Mason himself made no move to resist his dismissal by Jackson, the people made life miserable for his replacement. They regarded Horner as a puppet of Washington politicians who had rejected their appeal for statehood. Horner himself was an immensely fat, sour-faced man with a raspy voice—characteristics that only intensified the contempt in which he was held by Michiganians. Even worse, he released from jail those Ohioans who had been apprehended trespassing on what Michigan regarded as its territory, giving rise to the suspicion that he was in league with Governor Lucas of Ohio. These suspicions were well founded, for Horner kept Lucas informed on developments in Michigan, broadly hinting that affairs would be managed in such a way as to redound to the benefit of Ohio. He could find no one to carry out his orders. His appearance was greeted with boos and clods of dirt, and he was dubbed "Little Jack Horner." Finally he left Detroit in disgust and went to Ypsilanti, where the people, hearing he had freed the Ohioans, gathered beneath his window and woke him up with a barrage of stones and blobs of horse dung. Terrified, he returned to Detroit, where he was simply ignored.[3]

On the appointed day in October the voters approved the proposed state constitution by an overwhelming majority: 6,752 in favor and 1,374 against. They also elected Mason as governor and Edward Mundy of Ann Arbor as lieutenant governor. Both were Democrats. Mason received 7,508 votes, while his leading opponent, John Biddle, was given only 814. The newly elected legislature convened on November 1. In his inaugural, Governor Mason vigorously upheld Michigan's right to form a state government. But he recommended that the legislature pass few laws, and pointed out that the new constitution provided that territorial laws not in conflict with it should remain in effect until they expired or were altered and that all territorial officials except for governor and lieutenant governor should remain in office "until the legislature, giving due time for the legislation of Congress on the subject of our admission into the union, may deem it expedient to organize a State judiciary, and to authorize the election or appointment of other officers, under the constitution." The lawmakers heeded the advice of the governor, confining themselves to the passage of only seven laws, mostly dealing with fiscal matters, and the election of Lucius Lyon and John Norvell as United States senators. Mason made only one appointment, that of Kintzing Prichette as secretary of state. It is apparent that there was some reluctance to proceed in the absence of approval by Congress and in the face of a denial by President Jackson that the people of Michigan possessed the right to set up a government that would supersede the territorial government.

The legislature met only one day, then adjourned until February 1, 1836. Meanwhile it was hoped that Congress would take action to admit Michigan into the Union. The hope proved vain, because it was mid-June before any definite action would be taken. When the legislature reassembled on February 1, there were many who had grave doubts on the advisability of completing the organization of the state government. An act calling on the territorial auditor general and treasurer to hand over the books, papers, and funds in their custody to state officials was passed by the legislature and approved by the governor on February 19; but Levi Cook, treasurer of the territory who was appointed to the corresponding position in the state government, not only declined the appointment but refused to deliver the books, papers, and funds of the territory to the state. The three territorial supreme court judges were renominated by President Jackson and confirmed by the Senate late in February. The territorial courts continued to function through June. But the legislature, in spite of considerable opposition, took action in February and March to establish a state judiciary, headed by a state supreme court. It also enacted other laws that provided for a complete organization of the state government, the methods of selection, duties, and salaries of state officers, and the dates on which persons holding office under the territorial government would be removed. Opposition to the organization of a state government without prior approval by Congress continued, however. Curiously enough, the Whigs led the opposition, while the Democrats favored going ahead in defiance of the party's leader: President Jackson.[4]

The tension was somewhat relieved by the departure of John S. Horner, who had continued to stay on in Detroit in spite of the fact that no attention was paid to him. On April 20, 1836, an act passed by Congress establishing a territorial government in Wisconsin be-

came law. Horner was appointed as its secretary, and he left Detroit
soon afterward for his new post. Meanwhile Congress was wrestling
with the knotty problem of the Michigan-Ohio boundary and Michigan's application for statehood.

*   *   *   *   *

The clash between Ohioans and Michiganians that took place in
1835 has been called the Toledo War. Since the city of Toledo was
not chartered until 1837 and since the fracas was not actually a war,
"Toledo War" is a misnomer. The crucial issue, so far as Ohio was
concerned, was whether the mouth of the Maumee River (then
called the Miami of the Lake) should be in Ohio or Michigan. Numerous projects for the building of canals were being advanced, and
the outlet of one entire system of such canals would be the Maumee
River.

The origin of the dispute between Michigan and Ohio dated
back to the Ohio constitutional convention of 1802. There is a story
to the effect that a hunter who happened to be present asserted that
the southern end of Lake Michigan was actually further south than
was indicated on the maps of the time.[5] To be certain that the mouth
of the Maumee River would be included within Ohio, a proviso was
inserted in that part of the Ohio constitution dealing with boundaries. It stated

> that if the southerly bend or extreme of Lake Michigan should extend
> so far south that a line drawn due east from it should not intersect
> Lake Erie, or if it should intersect said Lake Erie east of the mouth of
> the Miami River of the Lakes [i.e., the Maumee] then and in that case,
> with the assent of the Congress of the United States, the northern
> boundary of this state shall be established by and extend to a line
> running from the southerly extreme of Lake Michigan to the most
> northerly extreme of the Miami [Maumee] Bay.

Congress admitted Ohio to the Union in 1803 under this constitution but with no specific assent to the change stipulated in the boundary proviso. As soon as the Ohio congressmen were seated they
worked to obtain such assent, but to no avail. The case of Michigan
rested strongly upon this failure by Congress to accept specifically
the altered boundary proviso in the Ohio constitution.[6] In 1805,
when the Territory of Michigan was established, Congress provided
that its southern boundary should be that set forth in the Northwest
Ordinance, completely disregarding Ohio's claims.

Ohio's Congressmen continued to agitate for acceptance of the

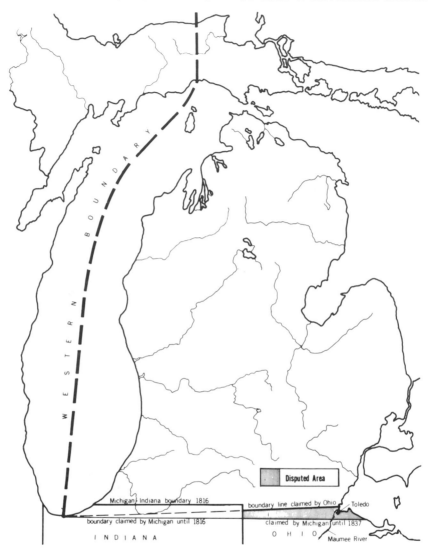

Disputed Area

Michigan-Indiana boundary 1816

boundary line claimed by Ohio

Toledo

boundary claimed by Michigan until 1816

claimed by Michigan until 1837

I N D I A N A

O H I O

Maumee River

W E S T E R N   B O U N D A R Y

MICHIGAN BOUNDARIES AND THE TOLEDO STRIP QUESTION

altered northern boundary of their state, but despite their efforts, in 1812, Congress passed a resolution providing for the survey of the Ordinance line drawn due east from the southerly extreme of Lake Michigan. The War of 1812 forced the survey to be delayed until 1817. By that time, a former Ohio governor, Edward Tiffin, was the

Surveyor-General of the United States. He employed William Harris to survey the boundary, but instructed him to run the line in accordance with the provision of the Ohio constitution. Governor Cass of Michigan immediately protested that Tiffin was not carrying out the instructions of Congress, and as a result a second survey was made in 1818 by John A. Fulton, this time in accordance with the provisions of the 1787 ordinance. This survey line intersected Lake Erie east of the mouth of the Maumee, leaving the river's outlet in Michigan. The area between the Harris line on the north and the Fulton line to the south, commonly called the "Toledo strip," was about eight miles wide on the east, five miles wide on the west, and contained 468 square miles.

Oddly enough, the dispute quieted down after 1818. The Ohio legislature declared the Harris line was the official boundary, but jurisdiction in the disputed area was assumed by Michigan. In 1825, the Territorial Council organized the township of Port Lawrence in the very heart of the area without causing any protest from Ohio. County courts were held in the strip, and residents voted in Michigan elections. A land company bought a tract that included the mouth of the Maumee and laid out two towns: Port Lawrence in 1817 and Vistula in 1832. They were united under the name of Toledo in 1833, but the place was not incorporated as a city until after the boundary question was settled. The original plat of the Toledo suburb of Sylvania is still filed with the other records of Monroe County, the Michigan county that had jurisdiction over much of the Toledo strip.

During this quiet period in the boundary dispute, Governor Cass tried to negotiate a compromise with Ohio that would permit that state to retain the mouth of the Maumee while conceding to Michigan additional territory elsewhere in northwestern Ohio, but the effort came to naught. Then on December 11, 1833, the dispute was resumed when Lucius Lyon, Michigan's delegate to Congress, presented the first formal petition for the admission of Michigan as a state. Someone discovered certain technical shortcomings in the Fulton survey, and a new one was ordered. This time the line was run by Captain Andrew Talcott, whose chief assistant in the project was the future Confederate military hero, Robert E. Lee. The Talcott line, when run, coincided with the Fulton line.[7] Meanwhile in Washington, the Senate, after a lengthy debate, passed a bill upholding Ohio and accepting the Harris line as the official boundary. In the House of Representatives, however, the bill encountered stiff opposition and was referred to a committee, where it still reposed when Congress adjourned.

In the next session of Congress, beginning in December, 1834, Ohio's senators revived the boundary bill, and this time added a section confirming the northern boundaries of Indiana and Illinois, which, when these states had been admitted in 1816 and 1818, had been pushed far beyond the ordinance line. There was no necessity to reaffirm these boundaries, but the Ohioans, by including such a provision in the bill to establish Ohio's northern boundary at the Harris line, sought support from their neighbors to the west. There was an inference that if Michigan were to make the Ordinance line stick in its dispute with Ohio, then the Indiana and Illinois lines might be of questionable legality. The Senate again passed the bill establishing the Harris line, with the additional provision confirming the northern boundaries of Indiana and Illinois, but once more the House of Representatives failed to uphold the Senate action.

While Congress was grappling with the dispute, the Michigan Territorial Council, in a conciliatory gesture, passed an act on December 26, 1834, for the appointment of three commissioners to negotiate with Ohio a settlement of the boundary dispute. Governor Robert Lucas of Ohio promptly rejected any such negotiation, ordered permanent markers to be placed along the Harris line, and proceeded to organize the area into a new Ohio county bearing his own name. The Michigan Territorial Council countered with a resolution imposing a fine of $1,000 or five years' imprisonment on anyone except Michigan or federal officers who should accept office or exercise official functions in the disputed strip. Undaunted, Lucas appointed a sheriff and judges to hold court in his newly created county, whereupon Governor Mason mobilized the territorial militia, called for volunteers, and placed himself at the head of these forces.

The danger of an armed clash between Ohioans and Michiganians now became a matter of concern to President Jackson. He sought the opinion of his attorney general, who upheld Michigan's claim. This was no comfort to Old Hickory, who had his eye fixed on the next election and worried no end about all those votes his party would lose in Ohio, Indiana, and Illinois if he came out in support of Michigan. Not knowing what else to do, Jackson appointed two commissioners to go west and try to settle the controversy. They went first to Detroit and saw Mason, who said he would refrain from using force as long as Lucas stayed out of the disputed strip. When they transmitted this proposal to Lucas, he quite naturally rejected it. Then they went back to Mason and told him Jackson would remove him from office if he started arresting Ohioans who tried to exercise authority in the disputed strip. Mason would not back down: he told the commissioners, in effect, that it would be usurpation and tyranny to remove him for enforcing the law.

Mason was not bluffing. At the head of his militia, he proceeded to the Toledo strip and arrested any Ohio officials he found who refused to leave by a specified time. He also arrested nine surveyors who were re-marking the Harris line for Ohio. The rest of the surveying party was permitted to escape, the retreat of its members being speeded by the firing of a gun high over their heads. When they got safely back within Ohio, they told a tale of hairbreadth escape from bloodthirsty Michiganians that aroused great indignation.

The story of the Michigan-Ohio fracas during the next few weeks is full of comic-opera incidents that no doubt were regarded seriously at the time but, at a distance of more than a century, appear uproariously funny. For example, when the Ohio legislature voted $300,000 to defend the Toledo strip, the Michigan Territorial Council voted $315,000. An Ohio flag, torn down by irate Michiganians, was referred to by a Michigan newspaper as "the disgraceful badge of treason," and was burned "with suitable demonstrations of contempt." There is a report that Ohio produced its own Barbara Fritchie, who unfurled the dishonored flag or one like it.[8] Then there is the story of the judges appointed by Governor Lucas who were sent to hold court in the disputed strip as a means of establishing Ohio's claim to jurisdiction. In spite of the fact that the judges were accompanied by a small armed guard, they were half scared out of their wits by fear of the Michigan militiamen. In the dead of night they crept into a schoolhouse, blacked out the windows, lit a tallow dip, went through the motions of holding court, and hastily repaired to a nearby tavern to refresh their spirits. As they were about to have a second round, a local wag dashed in and shouted that a company of Michigan militiamen was about to arrest them. They dropped their glasses, dashed to their horses, and made off at top speed. After they had gone a short distance the clerk of the court discovered his tall stovepipe hat was missing. In it he had stowed the official records of the court session. Nerving themselves to a possible clash with the Michiganians, the party retraced its route, and the lost hat was discovered under a tree, where it had been knocked off by an overhanging branch during the hasty retreat. So great was the joy in recovering the hat and its contents, that two salutes were fired to celebrate the victory. The spot was close enough to the border so that escape would be possible if the volleys were heard by the enemy.

It is surprising that no one was killed in the clashes between the two sides. Miraculously there were no casualties, with the single exception of a Michigan sheriff who was stabbed in a tavern scuffle by an Ohioan named Two Stickney. He was the son of B. F. Stickney, an ardent Buckeye who fancied himself a military genius. His two sons were named, respectively, One and Two. In spite of the fact that no one was killed, the rumors that circulated through Ohio depicted Michiganians as bloodthirsty villains of the deepest dye. One explanation for the origin of the name "Wolverines" for Michiganians is that it was invented by the Ohioans as a suitable nickname, since the wolverine has the reputation of being a particularly vicious and ornery animal.

The danger of an armed conflict evaporated in September, 1835, when Mason received word of his removal by President Jackson. Bowing to the President's authority, Mason took leave of the Michigan militia, and General Joseph W. Bown, its commander, immediately disbanded the troops. This left the decision squarely up to Congress.

Although Stevens T. Mason may appear, in retrospect, to have taken some rash and precipitate actions during this crisis, he made the most sensible and rational proposal for settling the matter. He proposed that the dispute be referred to the United States Supreme Court for a decision. Unfortunately, at that time the power of the Supreme Court to settle boundary disputes between the states had not been clearly established. Had the Michigan-Ohio dispute been referred to the Supreme Court, as Mason suggested, it is likely that the justices would have accepted jurisdiction and would have settled the dispute. Probably the reason Mason's proposal went unheeded was that a presidential-election year was in the offing. President Jackson, who was completing his second term, was grooming Martin Van Buren as his successor. He had little taste for a situation in which his party might suffer the loss of support in three western states because of Michigan's stubbornness. Hence he exercised his powerful influence to persuade Congress somehow to settle the question in such a manner that Ohio, Indiana, and Illinois would be happy.

The battle began early in the session that opened in December, 1835. Lucius Lyon and John Norvell, who had been chosen as Michigan's first two United States senators, and Isaac E. Crary, who had been elected to the House of Representatives, were on hand to take their seats, but after considerable debate they were allowed to be seated only as "spectators" and were thus compelled to listen to Ohio's congressmen set forth that state's claims in the ensuing debates without any chance to reply. In the Senate, the bill to admit Michigan was referred to a committee of which Senator Thomas Hart Benton of Missouri, a staunch backer of Jackson, was chairman.

It was from this committee that there emerged, in due course, a compromise that called for the acceptance of the Harris line to satisfy Ohio, but gave to Michigan a large area in what is now the Upper Peninsula. This compromise may have been suggested by the feeling in some quarters that the fifth state to be carved out of the Old Northwest would be too large. Acceptance of the compromise was foreshadowed in April, 1836, when the Territory of Wisconsin was established by law with its northern boundaries fixed along the lines of the Menominee and Montreal rivers. But the debate on the admission of Michigan to the Union dragged on, with southern senators resorting to delaying tactics designed to postpone the admission of Michigan until Arkansas also was ready for admission. It had long become the practice to admit a free state and a slave state at the same time so as to preserve the balance between the two sections in the Senate. During the debates an amendment to the bill was inserted requiring the assent to the compromise of delegates elected by the people of Michigan before the state could be admitted. The great debate in the Senate came to a close on April 2, 1836, when the compromise bill as amended was passed.

The battle now shifted to the House of Representatives. The result was a foregone conclusion, but the vote was delayed by a three-hour speech upholding Michigan's contention by the former president, now a Massachusetts representative, John Quincy Adams. Said Adams: "Never in the course of my life have I known a controversy of which all the right was so clear on one side and all the power so overwhelmingly on the other." The bill carried 143 to 50 and was signed by President Jackson on June 15. It meant that Michigan would be admitted into the Union *if* its people would accept the boundary compromise.

While Congress had been debating the question of how Michigan might be brought into the Union, the state government, installed in November, 1835, had been partially in operation. The state legislature met at Detroit on July 11, 1836, to consider the compromise passed by Congress, and two weeks later the legislature approved an act calling for the election of delegates to a special convention that would meet in Ann Arbor in September to decide whether or not to accept statehood on these terms.

Sentiment against the proposed compromise was almost universal at first. A resolution adopted in March had dismissed the area that Michigan was to receive as a "sterile region on the shores of Lake Superior, destined by soil and climate to remain forever a wilderness." The Detroit *Free Press* called it "a region of perpetual snows— the *Ultima Thule* of our national domain in the north." Senator Lyon said the region could furnish the people of Michigan with Indians for all time and now and then a little bear meat for a delicacy, but he was nevertheless one of the few who thought that Michigan might eventually find it got the better of the bargain.[9] There was resentment of the fact that Arkansas had been granted statehood unconditionally the same day that Michigan had been offered admission only on conditions that most Michiganians regarded as disadvantageous to the state.

If Michigan did not want the huge area in the northland that Congress offered, it is equally true that some of the residents of the Upper Peninsula did not want to be part of Michigan either. Congress had received a number of petitions from persons in this region asking that the area south of Lake Superior be organized as the Territory of Huron. Michigan Territory, as originally established in 1805, had included the eastern Upper Peninsula, including the settlements at the Straits of Mackinac and at Sault Ste. Marie. These areas had been represented in the 1835 convention that drafted Michigan's constitution and had defined the new state's boundaries so as to include these parts of the Upper Peninsula within that state. Thus the statement that Michigan received the entire Upper Peninsula in return for surrendering the Toledo strip is not correct, but nevertheless the error continues to be perpetuated by numerous writers in a variety of publications.[10] It was approximately the western three-quarters of the Upper Peninsula that was involved in the compromise. Some people in the eastern section preferred to become part of the proposed Huron Territory, pointing out that Sault Ste. Marie was cut off from Detroit for six months each year and claiming that the region was treated by the rest of Michigan as a remote and neglected colony. Congress, however, paid no attention. Politics was more important than geography, and Michigan was saddled with the problem—never satisfactorily resolved—of uniting two areas which nature, for many thousands of years, has set asunder.

The members of the convention who were to consider the Congressional compromise were elected on September 12 and assembled in the Washtenaw County Courthouse in Ann Arbor on September 26. The forty-nine delegates, representing twenty-seven counties, required four days to reach a decision, which was to reject the compromise. Those opposing the compromise had a majority of seven, but even the minority that favored acceptance did so only on the grounds that once Michigan was a state it could then go to the Supreme Court and seek to overturn the boundary settlement.

Immediately after the convention was adjourned the delegates began to have sober second thoughts. What was to be gained by rejecting Congress' offer? It was obvious that Ohio, now in complete control of the Toledo strip, could not be evicted by Michigan. Lucra-

tive federal appointments might be available to Michigan Democratic
leaders, following the victory of the Democratic party and the election of Martin Van Buren as President in November. Michigan also
stood to gain substantial federal funds if it accepted statehood on
Congress' terms. If Michigan was a state it would receive five percent
of the enormous proceeds from the sales of public lands in Michigan,
which, in the boom year of 1836, would have provided the state's
coffers with an amount in excess of $250,000. And if the state was
admitted to the Union by January 1, 1837, it would share in the
distribution of the surplus from the United States treasury which
Congress had voted to turn back to the states. Michigan's share was
estimated to be about $400,000. Governor Mason refused to call
another convention but declared that the people "in their original
capacity" had the right to reverse the decision of the so-called Convention of Assent "if found prejudicial to their interests." On October 29, 1836, therefore, Wayne County Democrats called for the
assembling of a second Convention of Assent. Washtenaw Democrats followed suit, and as a result a "Committee of the People" was
formed which called for delegates to meet at Ann Arbor on December 14. These delegates were chosen quite irregularly and only
eighteen counties sent delegates to the second convention, in part
because the Whigs boycotted the meeting, declaring that the entire
proceeding was illegal, which was probably true. Nevertheless, the
delegates took only two days to pass a resolution accepting the Congressional offer, with all but ten of the seventy-two delegates signing
the resolution. Opponents dubbed the meeting the "Frost-bitten
Convention."

When the resolution of assent reached President Jackson he
promptly sent it on to Congress with a message stating that Michigan
had "complied with the regulations of the conditional act of admission." A bill to admit Michigan into the Union was duly presented.
After a debate of several days in the Senate over the propriety of the
second convention, the bill was passed 23 to 10. The debate in the
house was brief. On January 26, 1837, President Jackson signed the
bill that made Michigan the twenty-sixth state, thereby doubling the
number of states that had comprised the original union. Lucius Lyon
and John Norvell were at once seated as members of the United
States Senate and Isaac E. Crary as the one member to which the new
state was entitled in the House of Representatives. At long last,
statehood had been achieved and Michigan was a voting participant
in the deliberations of the national government.

When Michigan actually ceased to be a territory and became a
state has been a much debated question. Clearly, from the fall of
1835 onward, the great majority of Michigan residents recognized

only the authority of the new state government. After some months, the federal government gave up any further efforts to maintain a separate territorial government in opposition to this state government, despite the latter's extralegal status so far as the federal government was concerned. However, Michigan did not enjoy the rights accorded the other states until the federal action of January, 1837. When it came time to celebrate the centennial of statehood in the 1930s, Michigan decided to observe the anniversary over a three-year period from 1935 to 1937. Because it was the period of the Depression, the celebration was fairly barebone in comparison with other state centennial observances.

The boundary dispute with Ohio that had held up Michigan's admission continued to be a subject of controversy. It was not until 1915 that the land boundary was satisfactorily surveyed and marked. At that time a ceremony was held in which the governors of the two states, standing on either side of the boundary, exchanged handshakes. However, questions still remained regarding the location of the boundary in Lake Erie as it angled off in a northeasterly direction from the north cape of Maumee Bay to the international boundary with Canada. In the 1960s, the state of Michigan went to court to try to prove its claim to a larger share of Lake Erie's waters, largely because of a belief that valuable deposits of oil and gas might be discovered beneath these waters. In 1973, however, the United States Supreme Court upheld an earlier U.S. Circuit Court of Appeals ruling that had rejected Michigan's claim and had awarded some 206 square miles of Lake Erie waters and bottomlands instead to Ohio. Presumably this marked the conclusion of what had threatened to be an interminable boundary dispute.[11]

Clinton Canal passing over the Clinton River

12

A CYCLE OF BOOM, BUST, AND RECOVERY

Speculative booms followed by economic depressions or "panics" have occurred throughout American history. It was Michigan's fortune and misfortune to be a center of one such "boom and bust" cycle at the very time it was achieving statehood. The early 1830s was a period of prosperity in the East, enabling many families to acquire the funds needed to make the move to the West and yielding to factory owners and merchants handsome profits for investment. Low tariffs and reciprocal trade treaties helped cause imports and exports to double between 1830 and 1836. Factory owners made unprecedented profits by employing women and children to work long hours at low wages. The cost of living increased seventy percent in three years, but wages failed to keep pace. These conditions gave rise to the spread of trade unionism between 1834 and 1837. Relatively few factory workers moved west, but many farm families that might have moved to the cities were repelled by the declining status of the factory worker and chose to become pioneers.

One of the major factors in the Michigan land boom in the early thirties was easy credit. Until 1833 the Bank of the United States had dominated the banks of the nation; conservatively managed by Nicholas Biddle, the bank's notes circulated as money and drove the notes of shaky state banks from circulation. But in 1832, President Jackson launched his "war on the Bank," vetoing an act passed by Congress to renew the charter of the Bank which was due to expire in 1836. Jackson's triumphant re-election in 1832 indicated that he had popular support. Prospective settlers and speculators who found it hard to borrow money clamored for easier credit, and they were

261

confident that if the Bank of the United States, dominated by the rich and well-born of the East, could be destroyed, money would become more abundant and easier to borrow. In this they were right. The amount of paper money per capita circulating in 1830 was only $6.69; by 1835 it had risen to $9.86, and two years later it went up to $13.87.

Jackson halted the deposit of government funds in the Bank of the United States even before its charter expired, and directed that the monies be deposited in selected state banks, which his enemies promptly called "pet banks." This had the effect of encouraging the establishment of state banks. Between 1829 and 1837 their number increased from 329 to 788, their note circulation rose from $48,000,000 to $149,000,000, and their loans went up from $137,000,000 to $525,000,000.[1] The result was inflationary. Prices rose, debtors paid off their loans with cheap money and borrowed more for speculative purposes. Government income from the sale of public lands and other sources increased to the point where in 1835 the entire national debt was paid off. Congress then passed an act decreeing that the surplus in the treasury should be distributed among the states.

President Jackson viewed the flood of paper money with considerable apprehension. At his suggestion Congress passed a series of acts between 1834 and 1836 to increase the supply of gold coins in circulation and to ban notes of small denomination. The states, however, refused to co-operate in curbing inflation. Banks sprang up with little capital or specie (gold or silver coin) but ready and eager to make loans in the form of notes bearing the promise of the bank to pay the bearer in specie. These notes could be used at government land offices to pay for land purchases. With prospects bright for reselling land bought at $1.25-an-acre for much more than that amount within a matter of months or even weeks, the temptation to borrow to the hilt was irresistible.

Many bona fide settlers as well as speculators obtained funds for the purchase of land in the East before coming to Michigan. In the territory itself the oldest financial institution was the Bank of Michigan, which had operated successfully since 1817. By 1834 there was another bank in Detroit and one at Monroe. In that year the Bank of Michigan established a branch in Kalamazoo (then called Bronson) to which the government land office in White Pigeon was moved. Under the constitution and laws of the new state, a special act of the legislature was required to charter any corporation. In addition to the Bank of Michigan, whose charter had been granted by the governor and judges, the Territorial Council had incorporated nine banks and the state legislature in 1836 chartered nine more. Of this total of nineteen banking corporations, at least one apparently did not establish a bank and one other was located in the Green Bay country, which was set off as the Territory of Wisconsin in 1836. Of the remaining seventeen banks, two were established by railroad companies through amendments to their charters. Three banks had also been permitted to establish branches.[2]

These banks would appear to have been sufficient to have met the needs. But there was a demand for still more banks and easier credit. As a consequence of Jackson's bitter condemnation of the Bank of the United States, it had become the fashion to regard banks as being monopolies of the monied interests and to view with suspicion the charters granted by state legislatures. It was widely believed that such charters granted special privilege to the few. These factors combined to produce Michigan's General Banking law of 1837. Enacted by the legislature and approved by Governor Mason on March 15, 1837, it empowered any twelve landowners to form a banking association by applying to a county treasurer and clerk. Capital stock to the amount of not less than $50,000 was to be subscribed and thirty percent was required to be paid in specie before the bank could start operating. These provisions and a "safety fund" system, modeled after that which New York had adopted the previous year, appeared to provide sufficient security for the soundness of the banks to be established under the new law. The General Banking law of Michigan was the first of its kind in the nation.

Under the provisions of this law forty-nine banks were organized and forty of these are believed to have started operation. It would have been quite impossible for such a large number of banks to have been established if the law concerning paid-in capital stock had been strictly enforced. But all sorts of dodges as well as wholesale fraud were resorted to by the banks' organizers in order to evade the law. Specie was sent ahead from one bank to another in advance of bank inspectors. Instead of actually paying in the specie, the organizers got by with "specie certificates," certifying that the specie had been received to be held on deposit. Sometimes specie was borrowed for the occasion, then immediately returned to its owner. These were Michigan's "wildcat banks," about which fabulous stories have been told.[3] In spite of their lack of hard cash, they issued handsome bank notes that pledged the bank to pay to the bearer on demand so many dollars in hard money. And they issued them in enormous quantities.

A contemporary reported that the notes of the different banks organized under the General Banking law were called "wild cat,"

"tom cat," "red dog," and other names according to the fancied
solvency of the different institutions.[4] Seven of these banks were
established in Washtenaw County, which had at the time a population of about 20,000. The story was told that a stranger lost his way
in the woods of Shiawassee County, and toward nightfall, while following what he thought was a trail through the woods, suddenly
came to a clearing that contained a large frame structure across the
front of which was a conspicuous sign proclaiming it was the Bank of
Shiawassee. For a brief time the demand for borrowed money was so
great that almost none of the notes was presented for redemption in
specie. One Detroiter made his way to one of these obscure banks
planning to exchange notes for specie. The president of the institution received him with cordiality, wined him and dined him, and told
him he could not redeem the notes just then, but was expecting a
shipment of gold and silver coin within a few days.

With credit so easily obtainable speculation ran riot. In 1836
every ship arriving at Detroit was packed with immigrants and
speculators, with hundreds of passengers often arriving on a single
vessel. Land offices at Detroit and Kalamazoo were swamped with
business. Long lines formed before their doors, and purchasers
sometimes paid fancy prices for a place further up in the line. In
Kalamazoo a sea of tents and makeshift shacks sheltered the men
who sought to buy land. Dozens of associations were formed to
purchase land for speculation. Many such associations would purchase land at the mouth of a river or at some other likely spot for a
town, engage a draftsman to draw up a town plan, divide the tract
into town lots, and proceed to sell them at a fancy price. Often the
purchaser was shown drawings that depicted homes, stores,
churches, schools, and factories already built, and lots were no doubt
purchased by many who labored under the impression that the town
actually existed. In some cases speculators gambled on a vast expansion of a town that really did exist. St. Joseph, for instance, had an
almost unbelievable speculative boom. Lots there sold at from
$1,800 to $5,000 each, whereas they could be had at Chicago for
$100. A plat of the town, according to a local historian, showed
streets extending for miles into what was then a wilderness. A great
university was planned—on paper.[5] The speculative fever probably
got to the point where, as in most speculative manias, sober people
realized that the whole thing was bound to blow up sooner or later,
but in the meantime they could see no reason they should not take
advantage of the opportunity to buy one week and sell the next at a
big profit.

The geologist Bela Hubbard recalled one of these speculators' dream towns, White Rock City:

> Maps executed in the highest style of the typographer's art, displayed in hotel barrooms and other places, where congregate the thousand seekers after fortune that courted the happy possessor of valuable lots and water privileges—had announced its unrivalled situation and advantages. They depicted the magnificent harbor at the mouth of the large stream into which steamboats were entering. Saw mills were converting the forests into houses; around the public square clustered a court house, churches, and other public buildings, not omitting the inevitable bank; and the air of prosperity which pervaded the place was evident at a glance. Auctioneers had sounded its praises and struck off its lots at fabulous prices to anxious buyers. None of the rising cities for which Michigan had become famous had so wide a celebrity and distributed stock so freely.
>
> And now we were to see with our own eyes this western marvel. A large white boulder in the lake marked the entrance and gave name to this modern Karnac.
>
> We found the entering river: it hardly admitted our canoe. Harbor there was none. Churches, houses, mills, people were all a myth. A thick wilderness covered the whole site. Even those marks of advancing civilization, the surveyor's marks, were wanting.[6]

Of course it must not be assumed that everyone who bought land in Michigan in the early thirties was duped by promoters. Thousands were bona fide settlers, buying land on which to settle and make homes. And there were many who regarded the purchase of public lands in Michigan as an investment rather than a speculation. Such investors carefully examined the land before they bought it and expected to hold it for several years.

Michigan's boom times in the early 1830s came in a period when the whole nation was buzzing with excitement over new methods of transportation. Hundreds of projects for the construction of canals and railroads were afoot, with state governments, rather than private enterprise, frequently taking the lead in initiating these projects. It was the state of New York that had set the pattern. Largely through the efforts of Governor DeWitt Clinton, that state had built the Erie Canal, a 363-mile stretch connecting the Hudson River at Albany with Lake Erie at Buffalo. This waterway, which was forty feet wide at the top and twenty-eight feet wide at the bottom, and four feet deep, cost the state approximately $8,000,000. Tolls collected during the first few years of operation more than paid for the cost of construction. Its success led to the building of many branches. More than any other factor, perhaps, it was responsible for making New York City the leading metropolis of the nation. Western grain, lumber, and other products now found an outlet in the East as well as at New Orleans.

Only two years after the opening of the Erie Canal the Baltimore and Ohio Railroad Company was incorporated. The idea for the railroad originated in the mines and quarries of England, where cars were let down an inclined plane by gravity and pulled back up by horses. Soon the idea of using steam to propel wheeled vehicles gave rise to experiments on both sides of the Atlantic. The Baltimore and Ohio Railroad was Baltimore's answer to the Erie Canal. That city hoped, like New York, to promote its growth by means of better transportation facilities to the West. Like many skeptics who preferred water transportation, the citizens at Baltimore were not content with their railroad venture and saw in 1828 the first shovelful of dirt thrown by President John Quincy Adams to launch construction of the Chesapeake and Ohio Canal, designed to connect Baltimore with the West by water as well as rail. Pennsylvania, not to be outdone by New York and Maryland, spent $10,000,000 between 1826 and 1834 to construct a combined canal-and-railway system to connect Philadelphia with Pittsburgh. Canal boats were hauled over the Alleghenies on a 33½-mile portage railway.

The simultaneous development of canals and railroads gave rise to the term "internal improvements" to embrace both of these new methods of transportation. Canals, having been started first and having proved their worth by the success of the Erie, were initially favored. In the Old Northwest the major canal projects were designed to connect the Great Lakes with the Ohio and Mississippi rivers. The Ohio legislature adopted a canal act in February, 1825, and the first spade of dirt was turned the following July 4. Because of local jealousies the legislators were not able to confine their plans to a single canal. Instead, provision was made for three canals connecting rivers flowing into the Ohio with those flowing into Lake Erie. By 1850, canals and rivers connected Cincinnati, Portsmouth, and Marietta on the Ohio with Toledo and Cleveland on Lake Erie. Having plunged heavily into canal construction at an early date, Ohio was content to leave railroad construction to private companies.

Indiana leaders were intrigued by the idea of building a canal to connect the Wabash River, which reached the Ohio River at Evansville, with the Maumee River, flowing into Lake Erie at Toledo. It may have been the fact that this involved both Ohio and Indiana that led to efforts to obtain federal aid. In 1827 Congress voted to donate to Indiana a strip of land consisting of alternate sections five miles on each side of the proposed canal. The portion of the grant lying in Ohio was transferred to that state. The project was completed in 1845.

A canal to connect the Great Lakes and the Mississippi River by way of the Illinois River had been suggested by the French explorer, Louis Jolliet. It was inevitable that such a canal should be proposed as a practical project during the 1820s when canal building was at the height of popularity. In 1827 Congress gave Illinois a grant similar to that made to Indiana to facilitate the building of this canal. Political and sectional bickering, however, delayed for a considerable period the start of construction.

The prospect of federal aid for internal improvements was shattered in 1830 when President Jackson vetoed a bill to provide federal funds to build a road between Lexington, Kentucky, and Maysville in the same state. In his veto message Jackson indicated his opposition to lavish expenditures for internal improvements and recommended instead that the national debt be paid. Although there were grumblings of dissent, the veto was upheld. Henceforth federal appropriations for internal improvements were curtailed sharply. Partly as a result of this the national debt was paid, a surplus was accumulated in the treasury, and Jackson approved a bill passed by Congress to distribute the surplus among the states in quarterly payments starting January 1, 1837.[7] In anticipation of these funds many states adopted extravagant plans for the building of canals and railroads. Only seven states failed to contract debts for roads, canals, and railroads. State debts that had amounted to only $12,790,728 in 1820 rose to $170,000,000 in 1837, a prodigious sum for the time.

Michigan inevitably was caught up in the mania for internal improvements. During the 1820s attention was focused on the building of roads radiating out of Detroit into the interior, and work on these roads continued into the 1830s. Improvement of the Chicago Road in 1832, completion of the Territorial Road so that stagecoaches could operate over it between St. Joseph and Detroit by 1834, and construction of the Grand River Trail were matters of more immediate interest to the pioneers than plans for future canals and railroads. Nevertheless, enterprising businessmen were manifesting an active interest in railroad development. Up to 1837 the territorial and state legislatures had granted charters to no less than twenty railroad corporations, with an authorized capital of $10,000,000.[8] The first of these, the Pontiac and Detroit Railway Company, established by an act passed on July 31, 1830, was the first railroad chartered in the Old Northwest.[9] This railroad, like the Ohio and Steubenville chartered by Ohio later the same year, never advanced beyond the charter stage. It was reincorporated as the Detroit and Pontiac Railroad in 1834, but it was not until 1838 that it began to run trains between Detroit and Birmingham. The cars were pulled by horses at first, but a locomotive was brought to Detroit in 1839 and was placed in operation on August 16.[10] Michigan's second railroad company was the Detroit and St. Joseph, which was incorporated in 1832. That the legislators were thinking about the possibility of a state-owned railroad system at this early date is indicated by a provision in the company's charter that gave Michigan the right to purchase the railroad at some later date at cost, plus fourteen percent interest. Although this company was not in operation by the time Michigan was admitted to the Union, it had secured a right of way, had graded several miles beyond Detroit, had purchased a locomotive, a passenger car, wheels and iron for six freight cars, and had bought spikes and rails for thirty miles of track.

The most noted and successful of Michigan's pioneer railroads, however, was the Erie and Kalamazoo, which was incorporated on April 22, 1833. This project was initiated by pioneers of Adrian, which was separated from Toledo (then called Port Lawrence) by thirty-three miles of forest and swamp that became impassable in wet seasons even to ox-drawn wagons. If some better way to transport goods and passengers over this route could be found, Adrian and Lenawee County would clearly enjoy great advantages. But the promoters, emulating those in other states who were planning internal improvements, did not limit their vistas to the local area. They envisioned a railroad that would connect Lake Erie at Port Lawrence with the Kalamazoo River at Marshall or some other point. The nominal capitalization of the company was set at $1,000,000, of which amount about $100,000 was paid in, principally by six investors in Adrian and Port Lawrence. Construction was started at Port Lawrence and was completed to Adrian by the fall of 1836. Rails were made of white oak, and on top of them were nailed iron "strap rails" about five-eighths of an inch thick and two and a half inches wide. Unfortunately, these rails often came loose while a train was passing over them, and sometimes plowed up through the floor of the cars, endangering the passengers, who called them "snake heads."

On November 2, 1836, to the boom of cannon, the first car to run on this railroad departed from Port Lawrence, and arrived safely in Adrian several hours later. Horses pulled the car and were driven tandem, with relays every four miles. It was the first railroad to operate not only in Michigan but anywhere in the country west of Schenectady, New York.[11] The passenger coach on the Erie and

Kalamazoo was called a "pleasure car," a top-heavy affair with ornamental openings that made it look somewhat like a traveling chapel. Later, passenger cars were provided with benches along the sides, and an entrance door on one side. Double-decker coaches were also used, with the upper deck reserved for women and furnished somewhat more lavishly than the lower deck. In 1837, the Erie and Kalamazoo received at Toledo a locomotive manufactured by the Baldwin Works in Philadelphia. This was the first locomotive to operate on a railroad west of the Alleghenies.

Although the Erie and Kalamazoo never was completed to Marshall, it did build two branch lines. Attitudes in Michigan toward the company, however, changed after the final transfer of the Toledo strip to Ohio. Now the railroad, which had been a source of pride to the residents of the southern tier of counties, and had promoted the economic growth of that area, came to be looked on as a "foreign corporation" which was causing Michigan merchants to lose business to merchants in the out-of-state port of Toledo. In 1849, the company leased its lines and right of way to the Michigan Southern Railroad, with the Erie and Kalamazoo receiving an annual rental fee of $30,000, which its directors distributed among the stockholders. The receipt of these fees ended in June, 1970, with the bankruptcy of the Penn Central system, the firm then leasing the Erie and Kalamazoo lines, and control of the company's twenty-two miles of track was transferred to Conrail on April 1, 1976. This pioneer western railroad company continues to maintain its corporate existence to the present day, for sentimental if not financial reasons.[12]

First U. S. railway locomotive

The Erie and Kalamazoo was the only one of twenty railroad companies chartered by 1837 that were actually in operation by that date. With the prospect of sharing in the distribution of the federal surplus, there were demands that the state government take action to speed up the construction of internal improvements. Much was made of the fact that settlers along the Erie and Kalamazoo were now able to buy eastern commodities, such as salt from New York, at greatly reduced prices, and also were able to sell their products more readily. The clamor for state action was irresistible. The spirit of the time was illustrated in a report of the internal improvements committee of the state house in January, 1837, which favored a state-built and state-operated rail system:

> The question for Michigan to decide is whether she will by her own enterprise sieze [sic] the present opportunities to avail herself of these vast viaducts of wealth and prosperity, and lead them laden within her own borders, or whether her timidity or apathy will allow them to pass her by to swell the power and abundance of her wiser neighbors.

On the basis of what were supposedly prudent estimates, it was asserted that an internal-improvements system would pay for itself and yield a net profit of $3,000,000 to the state in twenty years.

Governor Mason recommended that the state become a subscriber to the stock of private companies organized to build railroads and canals, borrowing money for the purpose. The legislature, however, preferred to proceed by state action alone. On March 20, 1837, the internal improvements bill became law. It authorized work to proceed on three railroads and two canals. The first of the railroads was to run from Monroe through the southernmost tier of counties to New Buffalo on Lake Michigan. The bill also called for the purchase of the Havre Branch Railroad, a line still in the planning stage that was designed to connect the terminus of the southern railroad, as the Monroe to New Buffalo line was called, with the new town of Havre which had been founded seven miles north of Toledo, within Michigan, and had ambitions of becoming a rival of the city Michigan had lost to Ohio.

The second of the three state railroads—the central—was to connect Detroit and St. Joseph by a line through the second tier of counties. The rights and properties of the Detroit and St. Joseph Railroad Company, which had been chartered to build a line between these two points, were to be acquired by purchase. The northern railroad was to be laid out from the town of St. Clair (then called Palmer) on the St. Clair River to the navigable waters of the Grand

River at Grand Rapids or to the mouth of that river at Grand Haven. Unlike the southern and central railroads, which would run through areas already settled, the northern line would run through the fourth tier of counties, which was as yet largely undeveloped.

The third tier of counties was to be served by a canal connecting the waters of the Clinton River on the east with those of the Kalamazoo on the west. Such a canal had been discussed for some time prior to 1837 and had aroused greater support among the residents of this area for this type of improvement than for a railroad. Although the project seems rather visionary today, many believed in its success, as evidenced by the founding of the town of Vermontville in western Eaton County in 1836 on a site chosen because it lay on the route of the proposed Clinton-Kalamazoo Canal.[13] A second canal in the 1837 legislation would connect the waters of the Saginaw and Grand rivers on the extreme northern fringes of settlement. In a separate act, a survey of yet a third canal, around the rapids in the St. Mary's River at Sault Ste. Marie, was also authorized.

To manage the construction and operation of the railroads and canals, a seven-man board of internal improvements was established. The financing of the program was to be taken care of by a bill that authorized the governor to negotiate a loan of $5,000,000, secured by the faith and credit of the state.

It would have been far wiser for the state to have built one railroad from Detroit to St. Joseph, through the second tier of counties, with branch lines into selected areas in the first and third tiers of counties. "Such a system," argues Robert J. Parks, author of the most recent and thorough study of this internal improvements program, "could have been economically constructed, profitably operated, and gradually extended, while the state would have been able to exist well within its means. Such a program would have clearly guaranteed profitable operation, and stimulated a high level of agricultural growth." Although the wisdom of such a limited course of action was recognized by responsible leaders, political considerations led to the adoption of the more ambitious program since it offered something for virtually every settled area of the state.[14]

Unfortunately, Michigan's internal improvements program, which, if it had any chance of success, depended on the continuance of a booming economy, was adopted on the eve of the Panic of 1837. Looking back on the boom of the mid-thirties it is difficult to understand why the people of the time failed to recognize the clear signs that they were riding for a fall. The speculation in Michigan land values in the early 1830s, for example, was fantastic. The enormous note issues of the banks were obviously out of proportion to their

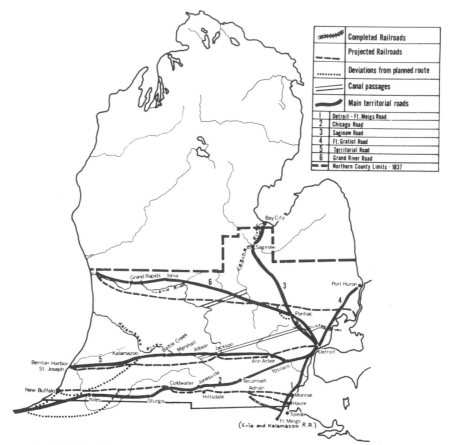

INTERNAL IMPROVEMENTS ABOUT 1837

resources. And the internal improvements programs adopted by the states were far beyond their ability to finance. The nation was importing, largely from Great Britain, much more than it was exporting, and piling up a steadily mounting debt to British merchants and manufacturers. The South was overplanting cotton. Inevitably, there would be a day of reckoning.

In July, 1836, President Jackson issued his Specie Circular which decreed that henceforth only gold and silver would be acceptable payment for public land, except for bona fide settlers, who, until December 15, were allowed to pay for no more than 320 acres in bank notes. This indicated the government's lack of faith in the soundness of the paper money that had been issued in vast amounts. It did not immediately check the buying of land. About the same time, British exporters began demanding payment of overdue debts from American buyers and refusing to extend new credits. This resulted in a drain of specie from American banks. Then on January 1, 1837, when the distribution of the government surplus began, banks were called upon to pay the states the specie that the federal government had deposited with these banks. The second quarterly payment exhausted their resources, and in May, 1837, banks throughout the country suspended specie payments. This meant that a bank note no longer could be presented for payment at full value in gold and silver. Very quickly these notes depreciated in value, and many of them became virtually worthless.

By the middle of 1837, thousands of people in the eastern part of the country were unemployed. Hundreds of firms went bankrupt and business was almost at a standstill. In the West, however, there was less distress and a measure of confidence remained. The Kalamazoo land office, which had sold 1,634,511 acres in 1836, sold only 313,885 acres in 1837, but even this was three times the amount sold in 1834 and about one-third the total sales in the entire territory of Michigan up to 1832. The state seemed to be moving ahead rapidly on the internal improvements program, despite some difficulties that Governor Mason was having in floating the $5,000,000 loan—the difficulties of which would not be apparent until later. The nation's new President, Martin Van Buren, called Congress into special session and proposed measures to strengthen the nation's finances. Movement of settlers into Michigan slowed down but by no means halted. The population, which stood at 174,543 in 1837, had increased to 212,267 by 1840, a gain for the three-year period that represented a figure more than Michigan's entire population in 1830. It was not until 1839 that the full impact of the hard times reached Michigan. At that time, several circumstances sharply reduced prices on all commodities and plunged the nation into a new economic crisis which this time hit the West harder than it did the East.

*　　*　　*　　*　　*

Following the passage of Michigan's Internal Improvements Act in 1837, surveyors and engineers set out from Detroit to blaze the way for the railroads and canals that were to transform the wilderness into prosperous farms and bring rewards to the towns along their routes. It was easier to locate the route for the northern railroad than for the others, because there were not so many towns contending that the railroad should be laid out to accommodate them. The line was surveyed to Grand Haven, a distance of 201 miles, and the cost of construction was estimated to be $1,409,015.75. The southern route was found to be 183 miles long, and the cost of building this railroad was estimated at $1,496,376.39. The cost of the central railroad was set at about $1,700,000 and the distance was 153 miles. These surveys, as well as those to be followed by the canals, were completed by January 1, 1838. The board for internal improvements by that date had bought the property of the Detroit and St. Joseph Railroad Company, had let contracts for the beginning of construction on all three of the projected state railroads, and had spent at least $415,000.

The preliminary work done by the Detroit and St. Joseph Railroad Company made it feasible to start construction on the central line first. Before the end of 1837 the railroad was in operation as far west as Dearborn, and on February 3, 1838, there was a memorable celebration when the first train made the run from Detroit to Ypsilanti. The locomotive hauled several flat cars, all loaded with passengers, and two passenger coaches having the appearance of Concord coaches with doors on each side. One of these, named the "Governor Mason," had been built in Detroit. Aboard the train was the governor, as well as many other dignitaries. A light snow had fallen that morning, and as the throng at Ypsilanti watched the train approach they witnessed two men, one sitting on each side of a crossbar in front of the engine equipped with a broom with which he brushed the snow off the track. The visitors were welcomed by a brass band, and were invited to a barbecue, at which an ox was roasted over a huge log fire. After partaking of the feast and much speechmaking the Detroiters got aboard for the return trip to Detroit. But at Dearborn the engine refused to start, and the engineer—driven to a frenzy by a storm of sarcasm, declared himself to be "clean beat." Horses were obtained to pull the engine on a siding, then were hitched to the principal car and hauled it back to Detroit.[15] The locomotive eventually was repaired, and regular operation between Detroit and Ypsilanti was provided. The fare was $1.50. Trains departed from the depot, then located at the southwest corner of Michigan Avenue and Griswold Street, at 6 a.m. and 1 p.m.

Another celebration took place at Mount Clemens in May, 1838, when ground was broken for the Clinton and Kalamazoo Canal. Visitors flocked into the town for the affair, which included a thirteen-gun salute, band music, a parade, appropriate oratory, and finally the turning of the first spade of earth by Governor Mason.[16]

Considerable progress on the entire program was made during 1838. In his report to the legislature in January of 1839, Mason maintained an optimistic note. The central railroad was completed to Ann Arbor and was under construction as far west as Jackson. The southern railroad was ready for the laying of iron on the first thirty-mile stretch from Monroe to Adrian. The two lower peninsula canals and the northern railroad were reported to be in "active progress," while the contract had been let for the canal at Sault Ste. Marie.[17]

Later that year, however, the various projects, which had begun so hopefully, began to bog down. At Sault Ste. Marie, the contractor encountered difficulty when the commandant at Fort Brady halted the digging because it interfered with a millrace of a sawmill used by the post. Although the state and the War Department agreed by August on the route of the proposed canal, the contractor refused to resume work. It is believed that he feared the state would not be able to pay him for the work, and possibly that the sum for which he had agreed to build the canal would be insufficient to pay the cost; hence, he intentionally caused the interference of the commandant by digging where the millrace would be endangered. At any rate, work was suspended and was not resumed until the fifties when a federal grant made possible the completion of the Soo Canal.

Financial problems slowed down and eventually halted the other projects. These problems arose in part from the depressed state of the nation's economy in the late thirties, but even more importantly, they arose from the manner in which Governor Mason handled the sale of Michigan's internal improvement bonds. In the past, Michigan historians, while acknowledging Mason's responsibility for helping to lead the state into the financial morass of the late thirties, tended to excuse the "Boy Governor," chalking his mistakes up to inexperience and lack of understanding of high finance. Recently, however, the historian Robert Parks has argued convincingly that Mason fully understood what he was doing and although his manipulations were attempts to continue the internal improvements program, they were also designed to enrich Mason and some of his close associates. Although the charges of misconduct against Mason were politically motivated, Parks suggests that Mason's opponents were too generous in their evaluation of the governor's actions.[18]

When Mason reached New York in the spring of 1837 and tried to sell Michigan's internal improvement bonds, financial stringency already was being felt, and he encountered several difficulties. But it was doubts about Mason's methods in negotiating the sale, not the depressed state of the economy, that were mainly responsible for Michigan losing the chance of placing its bonds with domestic and foreign investment interests that would have had the resources to provide the required money. It was not until June 1, 1838, that

Mason finally made an agreement with the Morris Canal and Banking Company. Meanwhile, the legislature had authorized an increase of the interest rate to six percent, instead of the original five and a half percent, with the stipulation that the bonds be sold at par. In order to induce the Morris Canal and Banking Company to sell the bonds, Mason agreed that it should receive a commission of two and a half percent, which reduced the proceeds from the bonds to a figure below par. For this action he was later criticized, but at the time he felt it was necessary in order to obtain the much-needed funds to advance the internal improvements program. Bonds in the amount of $1,300,000 were deposited with the company, but Mason did not receive the equivalent amount in cash. Payments were to be made to the state by the company as the bonds were sold. While traveling back to Detroit, Mason had the notes of the bank—amounting to $110,397—locked in a small trunk. After he returned to Detroit it was discovered that $4,630 in these notes had disappeared from the trunk. Subsequently a package containing all but $50 of this amount was received at the office of the company in New York, and Mason made good from his own pocket the remaining $50. The mystery of the disappearance was never solved.

When Mason returned to Detroit in the summer of 1838, he was confident that he had negotiated a fair arrangement for the sale of the bonds and that income from them would be forthcoming at regular intervals. In November, the company proposed to Mason that it would buy one-fourth of the bonds and that the remainder would be bought by the former Bank of the United States, now chartered as a Pennsylvania bank. Payments of $250,000 each quarter were promised until the bonds were paid for. Mason thereupon delivered the balance of the bonds to the company, certifying the indebtedness of Michigan of $3,700,000, or a total (including the first delivery of bonds) of $5,000,000. When the legislature met in the spring of 1839, it was informed of this arrangement and raised no objection to the delivery of all the bonds in advance of payment. The payments were made as agreed during 1839 but a dispute arose over whether the state should pay interest on the total amount of the bonds or only on that portion for which it had received payment.[19]

This was the situation in the fall of 1839 when the state election was held. By this time Van Buren's panacea for the depression—the independent treasury bill—had been buried in an avalanche of party wrangling between Whigs and Democrats. Michigan's "wildcat banks" had folded, and the paper notes they had issued, which were held by thousands of Michigan citizens, had become worthless. Little public land was being sold and immigration into the state had sharply declined. Prices for farm products had dropped disastrously. A wave of sickness, most of it malaria, swept the new state and added further misery.[20]

As is usual in such circumstances, the party in power was blamed for the woes of the people. Mason, once a popular figure, was now bitterly maligned. The political reaction was strongly in the direction of conservatism. Mason very wisely declined to run for re-election, and his party turned to Elon Farnsworth, an able but conservative Detroit lawyer, as its candidate for governor. The Whigs nominated William Woodbridge and campaigned for him on a platform of "retrenchment and reform." On election day Woodbridge received 18,195 votes while his opponent was given 17,037. The Whigs also elected a majority in both houses of the legislature.

Early in 1840 the legislature met and promptly passed an act forbidding the commissioners of internal improvement from entering into any further construction contracts. The deadline for paying 1839 taxes was extended, some offices were abolished, and the salaries of some officials were reduced. But such measures were insufficient to solve the state's problems. On April 1, 1840, the Morris Canal and Banking Company defaulted on its payments to the state, and in the following year the former Bank of the United States, which had purchased three-quarters of the Michigan bonds, went bankrupt. This precipitated a series of complicated negotiations and dealings which extended over many years. When Michigan demanded the return of the bonds for which it had received no payment, it was found that the two companies had deposited them with bankers in England as security for loans of their own. They were, of course, an obligation of the State of Michigan, but the state never received any proceeds from them. In 1842, the legislature declared that the state would contest the payment of interest and principal on those bonds for which it had received no compensation. In the end, however, the bonds for which the state had not received payment were redeemed at around one-third their face value, while interest and principal on the others were paid in full. It is possible that the state might have been able to recover a larger portion of the amount due from the bonds had it not been for the intense party rivalry of the 1840s. The five-million-dollar loan became the focus of bitter disputes between Whigs and Democrats, and between those who favored full payment and those who were willing to settle for "partial repudiation."

Michigan was by no means the only state that was unable or unwilling to pay the debts so recklessly incurred in the thirties. Mississippi, Louisiana, Maryland, Pennsylvania, and Indiana also repudiated their debts in whole or in part. One result was that the credit standing of American states in Europe, where many of these obligations were held, was seriously injured.

The internal improvements program would have been halted for lack of funds in 1841 had it not been for a grant of 500,000 acres of public land to the state by the federal government that year. Contractors and workers were frequently paid in "land scrip" rather than money. Only a small portion of the Saginaw-Grand Canal had been dug when that project was abandoned. A twelve-mile stretch of the projected Clinton-Kalamazoo Canal was completed between Mount Clemens and Rochester, and canal boats were operated briefly between Mount Clemens and Utica. But there was no further work on the canal after 1842, with the project ending in what is now Bloomer State Park No. 2 near Rochester. Some right of way was obtained and a considerable amount of grading done on a part of the northern railroad before it, too, was abandoned. The reduced resources of the state were then concentrated on the southern and central railroads.

The scandals and partisan bickering over the $5,000,000 loan, hard times, and slow progress on construction had by this time created a revulsion against the entire internal improvements program. In 1843, the legislature decided to extend the southern railroad no further than Hillsdale, which it had by that time reached, and to build the central railroad no further than Kalamazoo. Work was continued on the latter project by the state until 1846, when the first train reached Kalamazoo. Agitation for the sale of the two railroads had been growing for some time. The central railroad, under state management, had developed into a successfal operation, more than fulfilling the hopes of its promoters as to the impact it would have on the development of the area it served. But the profits earned by the central, while they would have been adequate to finance the continued operation and expansion of this line, were not great enough to carry the rest of the program. In 1846 it was estimated that the state had spent almost four and a half million dollars and had granted 305,000 acres of the 500,000 acres donated by the federal government to pay for these projects. Proceeds from the operation of the southern and central lines were being used for the repair and rehabilitation of the parts of the railroad that had been poorly constructed. To pay just the interest on the $5,000,000 loan would require an estimated one percent state property tax. For these reasons, it was agreed to sell the only two parts of the state's internal improvements system that had any market value. The southern railroad was sold to a private company for $500,000, while the longer, more profitable central railroad sold for $2,000,000. Thus ended the state's experiment in railroad and canal building and operation.

The negative consequences of this experiment have been the ones most commonly emphasized, and with good reason. In 1850, these led the state's Constitutional Convention to write into the constitution adopted that year a provision prohibiting the state from being involved in any internal improvements—a provision that would later seriously hamper the development of a more adequate road system in the state. The 1850 constitution also included provisions, such as one that placed a very low ceiling on the amount of money the state could borrow, that were clearly a response to the public criticism of the internal improvements program and which represented a regrettable tendency in the new constitution to eliminate much of the freedom that the first constitution had allowed the elected state officials in developing programs that met the needs of the time.

On the positive side, however, there can be no doubt that railroad development in Michigan progressed more rapidly as a result of the state's actions than it would have done without. Private efforts at railroad construction which had been underway for over a half a decade before the state launched its program, had scarcely any tangible results, but the demonstrated success of the state-operated central, and to a lesser extent, the southern railroads, created the interest among substantial investors that was needed to develop privately-operated lines in Michigan. The major routes that were followed in the next phase of private development were basically those that had been outlined in the state's plans.

Internal improvements were not the only area of state action to come under heavy fire during the new state's early years. Disillusionment with banks was as profound as that with state railroads and canals. By the end of 1839, only three of the older banks having special charters (one of which had a branch) and four of the "general-law" banks were still in operation. In 1838 the legislature suspended for one year the general banking law under which the "wildcats" had been organized, and the following year decreed that no more banks could be formed under its provisions. A case brought before the state supreme court in 1844 resulted in a decision that the general banking law was unconstitutional. In April, 1839, the legislature established a State Bank of Michigan with nine branches modeled after the State Bank of Indiana. But before the end of the year, it too was winding up its affairs. By 1845 only three banks remained in the entire state. A deep antipathy developed toward banks and bankers that continued until the Civil War. The only money in circulation in the 1840s consisted of United States mint coinage: gold coins with a limited number of silver dollars and smaller coins.

The Whigs who came to power in 1839 soon demonstrated that they had no cure for Michigan's ills. But Michigan voters, along with those of the rest of the country, reacted against the Van Buren administration in the hotly contested Presidential election of 1840. Martin Van Buren, running for re-election, was opposed by the Whig candidate, William Henry Harrison. Famous for the glorious victory he was reputed to have won at Tippecanoe in 1811 and credited with having saved Michigan from the British in 1813, Harrison proved to be a strong candidate. While his supporters chanted that "Van, Van, is a used-up man," the Democrats sought to cast derision on Harrison by claiming that he had retired after the Battle of the Thames to his cabin on the Ohio, where he had drunk hard cider and nailed coonskins to the logs of the cabin. Harrison men promptly adopted these symbols to prove that their candidate was one of the common people. On election day in Michigan, Harrison received 22,933 votes to 21,096 for Van Buren. Michigan's electoral votes combined with those of other states put Harrison in the White House, where the old frontiersman lasted only a month before he died of an illness contracted during his inauguration.

Even before Harrison was inaugurated, Michigan's Whig legislature elected Governor Woodbridge as United States Senator in place of Democrat John Norvell, whose term was expiring. It did not leave a good taste in the mouths of voters when Woodbridge deserted his position as governor in such hard times to go to Washington. When Woodbridge resigned as governor to accept his new position, Lieutenant Governor James W. Gordon, a native of Connecticut who had settled in Marshall in 1835, became acting governor. In the meantime the Democrats succeeded in healing the schism within their party and united upon the nomination of John S. Barry for governor in 1841. Barry, a native of New Hampshire, had become a prosperous merchant in Constantine, a town located on the St. Joseph River in St. Joseph County. He had a reputation for scrupulous honesty and stood for conservative principles. He was elected by a plurality of over 5,000 votes. Disillusioned with the Democrats, the voters had turned to the Whigs. Now, disillusioned with the Whigs, they turned back to the Democrats. For the next twelve years the Democratic candidate for governor won every election. Barry served three terms, the only nineteenth-century governor to do so. He stood for rigid economy in state government. It was even told that he had the grass on the capitol yard cut and sold, turning the proceeds into the hard-pressed state treasury.

By the middle 1840s confidence began to return. There was no repetition of the wild speculation of the early 1830s, but Michigan citizens began to take a somewhat more optimistic outlook on their future. A few men in Saginaw were proving that Michigan pine had an eastern market. A copper rush to the Upper Peninsula and the discovery of iron in another part of this area that Michigan people had scorned when they had been compelled to accept it in lieu of the Toledo strip, helped to give the state the "lift" it needed to emerge from the doldrums of the late thirties and the early forties.

Symbolic of the state's renewed effort to move forward was the decision reached in the forties to transfer the state capital from Detroit to a new interior location. The 1835 constitution had stipulated that in 1847 the legislature was to decide on a permanent site for the capital, which was in the interim to remain in Detroit—Michigan's capital since the establishment of the territory in 1805. The debate on the question began in the spring of 1846 and from the outset evidenced the rivalry between Detroit and out-state interests that has always been a major ingredient of political divisions in Michigan. In the legislative session of 1847, a furious controversy developed over the location of the capital, with Detroit supporters seeking to retain the seat of the state government, while out-state forces battled for a variety of sites, including Jackson, Ann Arbor, Marshall, Battle Creek, Albion, and even such minor locations as Dexter, Byron, and Lyons. A particularly strong bid was made by supporters of Marshall, where a site was set aside that continues to this day to be called Capitol Hill. However, for legislators to support any of these sites meant that they would antagonize supporters of the other communities.

At this juncture, James Seymour, who owned a considerable amount of land in Ingham County, offered to donate twenty acres and to erect buildings as commodious as those used in Detroit if the capital were located there. The site of Lansing was then a wilderness, with no railroads within miles, but it had the advantage of a central location in the lower peninsula. Although some regarded the proposal as a joke, it so appealed to the legislators that they passed a bill, which was signed by the governor on March 16, 1847, accepting the offer. The town to be established was to be called "Michigan," although the house had at first approved the name "Aloda." The capital city's name was changed to Lansing in 1848. On Christmas Day, 1847, a temporary building was completed and the capital was then moved to the new town on the Grand River that was to be its permanent abode. The tiny size of the state government at that time, in contrast to its subsequent development, is indicated in the story that only one wagon was needed to move the state's records from Detroit to the new capitol building.[21]

One of the major arguments used in opposition to having the capital at Detroit was that it was too vulnerable to attack from Canada if another war with Great Britain broke out. Anglo-American relations were reaching a critical stage in 1847 over the Oregon question. A decade earlier, border incidents growing out of the Canadian Rebellion of 1837 had provided Michiganians with a much closer glimpse of problems that threatened the peaceful relations of the two countries. This rebellion was caused by the desire of radical leaders of the predominantly French population of Lower Canada—as Quebec was then called—for independence from British rule, while in Upper Canada the people who were descended from the Loyalists that fled the thirteen colonies during the American Revolution sought relief from the domination of a small clique of government officials called the "Family Compact." The British put down the rebellion in Lower Canada rather promptly, but the trouble in Upper Canada was prolonged by persistent attempts made from across the border to aid the "patriots." William Lyon Mackenzie, a Toronto editor and leader of these rebels, fled to Buffalo when the attempt of the rebels to capture Toronto failed in December, 1837. In Buffalo he was given a noisy welcome, and received offers of both money and manpower to harass the Canadian authorities. Guerilla bands, consisting of both refugee Canadians and Americans, conducted frequent raids into Canada. This, of course, was something about which the federal government could not avoid being concerned, since it was a violation of British territory by American citizens and Canadians operating from the American side.

Shortly after the rebellion broke out, Governor Mason was instructed by the State Department to arrest anyone engaged in hostile acts against the British government. Mason obediently issued a proclamation reminding Michiganians of their duty under international law, even though he personally favored the rebel cause. The people of Michigan—particularly the Irish immigrants—sympathized with the patriots. In spite of the governor's warnings, a mass meeting was held in Detroit on New Year's Day, 1838, and funds were collected to aid the patriots. A few days later 450 stands of arms were stolen from the Detroit jail, where they had been placed for safekeeping. Volunteers then seized the schooner *Ann* and sailed down the Detroit River for Gibralter, opposite the Canadian shore. General Hugh Brady, United States army commander for the Great Lakes area, had his headquarters at Detroit, but he had few troops at his command. Therefore he called upon Governor Mason for militiamen to pursue the *Ann* and capture the men who had taken her. Mason obeyed, but the militiamen had to be marched to the United States arsenal at Dearborn for arms before they could start for Gibralter. By the time they secured the arms and arrived at Gibralter the raiders already had left for Canada. The force of 132 men had crossed the river, where Canadian defenders had shot down the mainsail of the *Ann,* causing the ship to drift aground, where the entire rebel force was captured.

Before the end of January, three companies of United States regulars arrived at Detroit, but they did not prevent another band of patriots from crossing the river on the ice on February 24 to Fighting Island, which belonged to Canada. When General Brady learned of the foray, he led his troops down the river to a point opposite the island with orders to arrest any armed men attempting to reach the island or to return to United States territory from it. The British attacked the invaders the next day and drove them back across the river, killing fifteen and wounding forty. Angered at this rebuff, patriot sympathizers took vengeance by collecting all the books in the city written by a noted British author, Captain Frederick Marryat, who was then visiting in Detroit, and burning them in front of his hotel.

The most serious violation of Canadian soil by Detroit raiders took place in December, 1838. A band of about 135 men seized a steamer, the *Champlain,* crossed to the Canadian side, marched on Windsor, and about two o'clock in the morning set fire to the military barracks, guardhouse, and the steamer *Thames,* which was moored at the dock. Several soldiers sleeping in the barracks were burned to death; others were shot as they escaped the burning building. When news of the marauding expedition reached Sandwich a strong Canadian militia force stationed there moved against the invaders. The raiders broke and fled; twenty-one were killed in the attack and the four taken prisoner were lined up and shot in reprisal against the alleged atrocities of the invaders. Detroiters watched this "Battle of Windsor" from across the river. The execution of the four prisoners perpetuated bad feelings for many years. In the 1840s the United States government began to build Fort Wayne on the Detroit

River to guard the border, and it was completed in 1851. But it never fired a hostile shot. Civil War volunteers were quartered within its walls, and the fort served as a troop-training center. The historic portion of the fort was transferred to the city of Detroit in 1949 and has been maintained since then as one of the city's historical attractions.[22]

American-based efforts to aid the Canadian rebels in 1837 and 1838 were not confined to Detroit. Everywhere along the border secret organizations known as "Hunters' Lodges" sprang into being to aid the patriot cause. An attempt was made to seize arms, ammunition, and artillery at Fort Gratiot in Port Huron, but the plot was foiled.[23] Not until the signing of the Webster-Ashburton Treaty between the United States and Great Britain in 1842 did the border disorders cease. During the border raids Great Britain violated its pledge in the Rush-Bagot Agreement of 1817 not to maintain armed vessels on the Great Lakes except for a limited number of small ships to enforce customs laws. And the United States launched an iron warship, the *Michigan,* at Erie, Pennsylvania, in 1844. Fortunately, however, these violations proved to be temporary and unimportant. The spirit of the Rush-Bagot Agreement was maintained and later led to the abandonment of land fortifications as well as armed ships.

The man who had been at the center of the stage during the tumultuous years of the thirties, Michigan's "Boy Governor," Stevens T. Mason, moved to New York City after the completion of his second term in 1839, his political future in Michigan ruined by the failures of the internal improvements program. He had married a New York girl, and went there to take up the practice of law but his life, which had seemed to hold great promise, was tragically short. On January 4, 1843, Mason died before reaching his thirty-first birthday. Bitter partisanship had resulted in many aspersions against him in the years that followed his retirement from office. But Michiganians could not forget this handsome young man, his winning manner, the brave and confident leadership he had provided during the exciting days of the big boom, the "Toledo War," and the struggle for statehood. There can be little doubt that his youth and lack of experience led him to make errors of judgment, but in most respects he had epitomized the strengths and weaknesses of the Michigan of his time. On June 4, 1905, his remains were brought from New York to Detroit and interred on the site of the old state capitol with appropriate ceremony. A bronze statue was erected in his honor. With the modernization of downtown Detroit in the 1950s it became necessary to move his remains once more. There was considerable agitation at the time for their removal to Lansing, but Detroiters staunchly opposed this. They had come to regard Mason as one of their own. As it turned out, one of the new state office buildings at Lansing was named in Mason's honor, just as one of Michigan's counties and a city in Ingham County had been in earlier days.

Abandoned mine shaft

13

OUT OF THE WILDERNESS, 1835–1860

During the quarter-century that elapsed between the time Michigan assumed statehood and the beginning of the American Civil War, a large portion of the southern half of the lower peninsula was cleared of forests and placed under cultivation, while the exploitation of timber and mineral resources began in the north. The building of railroads, the invention of the electric telegraph, and the extension of postal service established closer connections between the new state and the eastern seaboard. Recovery from the economic collapse that took place in the late 1830s was slow, but by the mid-forties immigration into Michigan was on the rise and a large measure of confidence had been regained.

The population of Michigan, which stood at just under 175,000 in 1837, grew to 212,267 in 1840, to 397,654 in 1850, and to 749,113 in 1860. This represents a substantial growth. But whereas Michigan had had the largest percentage increase in population of any state or territory in the decade of the thirties, it slipped to fourth in the forties and to ninth in the fifties. After settlement had reached northward in the state to approximately the Muskegon-Bay City line, heavy growth of pine was encountered under which the soils were generally sandy. Frosts came earlier in the autumn and later in the spring. The rich prairie soils of Illinois and the warmer climate of Missouri were preferred by many settlers. Another factor that probably retarded the movement into Michigan was the relative slowness of railroad construction. Railroads were becoming the principal means by which products could be moved to market. However, railroad construction that aimed at connecting southern Michigan localities with areas to the west or east were hindered by the lakes on either side while building north-south railroads into the unsettled northland was impractical. Although the export of lumber from Michigan had begun by the time of the Civil War, it was not until after 1860 that the great days of lumbering in the state's northland began, providing the economic base for the expansion of population and transportation facilities into that area.

Some indication of the origins of the people who came to Michigan during this quarter-century is found in the United States Census reports of 1860. More than one-third of the residents of the state at that time had been born in Michigan. Of the large majority that had been born elsewhere, by far the largest number were natives of New York, with over a quarter of the people in Michigan in 1860 having been born in that state. Less than five percent were natives of Ohio, while Pennsylvania natives were about half as numerous as those from Ohio. Then followed three New England states— Vermont, Massachusetts, and Connecticut. The dominance of the New England influence, however, was due not so much to those residents who had come directly from New England but to the New Yorkers, most of whom were second- or third-generation New Englanders because western New York, from which so many had come, had been settled largely by people moving west from New England.

A little less than twenty percent of Michigan's population in 1860 was foreign-born. Of these, the largest segmant consisted of people born in the British Isles: 30,049 in Ireland, 25,743 in England, and 5,705 in Scotland. The several states into which Germany was then divided contributed the second largest group—38,787. There were nearly as many who had been born in Canada: 36,482. Another significant foreign element was the Dutch, numbering 6,335, and concentrated mostly in a relatively limited area of western Michigan. There were also sizable numbers of Belgians, French, Norwegians, Swedes, and Swiss, and even four natives of the Sandwich Isles, as Hawaii was then called. A total of 6,172 Indians were enumerated, with Emmet, Isabella, Leelanau, Mackinac, and Oceana counties having the largest numbers of this element. By this time, however, another racial group—the Negroes—had surpassed Michigan's original residents in numbers. Of the 6,799 blacks in Michigan in 1860, the largest number, 1,673, lived in Wayne County, but the second largest number, 1,368, was located in rural Cass County where freed slaves had settled in Calvin Township in the 1830s and 1840s.

Although blacks would flock to Michigan's cities in the twentieth century, seeking jobs in Michigan's factories, most of those who came to Michigan in the middle decades of the nineteenth century were attracted by the same opportunities that drew most people to Michigan in those years—the lure of fertile land which was available at a relatively low price. There were also businessmen who saw in the new state a chance for profitable investments in mercantile establishments, lumbering, mining, and manufacturing. And there were professional men—lawyers, doctors, teachers, and others—who sought a more promising field for their endeavors. There were railroad builders, miners, lumbermen, and fishermen. And many were simply unskilled laborers who hoped to earn a stake to buy a farm, start a business, or in some other way improve their lot in life.

Yankees, forsaking the rocky lands of New England, and New Yorkers, finding it more and more difficult to acquire good land in the East, moved to Michigan in such numbers as to constitute the dominant element in the population of almost every county in the new state. Practically all of them used the Erie Canal and the sailing vessels or steamers of the Great Lakes to reach Detroit, from where they moved into the interior of the state either by railroad or by horse or ox team. The route of foreign immigrants into Michigan was essentially the same. Many German settlers moving into Wisconsin also landed at Detroit, traveled to Grand Haven by the Detroit and Milwaukee Railroad, and across Lake Michigan by ship. Ohioans and Pennsylvanians, as well as immigrants from the southern states, came overland from Ohio or Indiana into southern Michigan.

The influence of the predominant New England-New York element in the population of Michigan is evident in many ways. Such leaders in the early development of Michigan as Lewis Cass, the Reverend John D. Pierce, Isaac E. Crary, Lucius Lyon, and Elon Farnsworth were natives of New England. All but two of the governors of Michigan between 1835 and 1860 were born in New York or one of the New England states. The judicial system of Michigan was copied almost entirely from that of New England and New York, and the early supreme court justices were from this region.[1] One writer characterizes the New Englanders and New Yorkers in Michigan's early population as "homeseekers, a thrifty, enterprising, plucky people, with high ideals of religion, morality and education" who "brought with them the New England home, the church and the school to transplant their superior culture in the wilderness of Michigan," adding that "in spite of their venturesome spirits, they retained their hardheaded individualism, preserving that essential incentive to progress and prosperity, which would, in time, produce a better standard of living."[2]

Of the immigrants from other countries, those from England and Scotland were easily assimilated due to the absence of a language barrier and the similarity of British and American institutions. The Irish, however, tended to retain their identity longer. Most of them were Catholics, whereas a large preponderance of Michigan's residents were now Protestants. The Irish brogue and their utter poverty also tended to set them apart. Thousands had escaped to America to avoid starvation during the terrible potato famine in Ireland in the forties. They tended to settle in the cities, where the men became common laborers, frequently working for wages well below what others would accept, while the women were engaged as household servants. The labor force that built Michigan's railroads in these years was largely comprised of Irish laborers. They were anti-English in sentiment and many of them were involved in the clandestine organizations formed along the border to aid the rebels in Canada in 1837 and afterward. However, one should not make the mistake of generalizing too much about the Irish. Not all Irish immigrants were poor. Some had enough money to buy land and become successful farmers. Nor did the much larger number that settled in the cities in all cases remain for long poor laborers, ridiculed and attacked by the native Americans. By the 1850s, a substantial number of Irish residents in Detroit had established their own businesses while these and other Detroit Irishmen were already revealing the talents that would make the Irish one of the most influential forces in the political activities of this and other cities where these immigrants settled.[3]

The large migration from Canada into the United States during this period was due in part to unfavorable economic conditions in Canada. The failure of the rebellion of 1837 undoubtedly stimulated the exodus from Canada of many who had become disgusted with the ruling class. But more than anything else it was because the western and northern parts of Ontario are cold, infertile, and uninviting lands, sparsely settled even to this day, that so many Canadians migrated to Michigan. The adoption of free trade by Great Britain between 1846 and 1849 was a serious blow to Canada, and caused a severe economic depression, which also encouraged emigration. A considerable degree of prosperity returned after a trade reciprocity treaty with the United States was signed in 1854, but the loss of large numbers of their population to the United States remained a matter of grave concern to Canadian leaders until the end of the century.[4]

German immigrants to Michigan were different from most Michiganians in the language they spoke and in their religion. The majority of the Germans were Catholics while the rest were mainly Lutherans. Despite these differences, they were welcomed because of their sturdy, industrious habits as well as the cultural contributions they made to the state. Among the German states most heavily represented in Michigan in 1860 were Prussia, Württemberg, Bavaria, Baden, and Hesse. There was a sizable number of Germans in Washtenaw County by the 1830s, an area where the German influence has remained strong to the present day. A member of this group, the Reverend Frederick Schmid, a Lutheran missionary who arrived in 1833, was instrumental in settling a colony of fifteen Germans from Bavaria in Saginaw County, where they established the town of Frankenmuth. Another German colony in 1847 established the settlement of Frankentrost, to be followed the next year by still another group that helped to make the Saginaw region one of the principal centers of German settlement in the state. Other German immigrants found homes in Clinton County, where the area in and around Westphalia remains today one of the most solidly German sections in Michigan. In contrast to these Germans, who were attracted mainly by Michigan's farming opportunities, were the greater number who settled in the cities. These included German intellectuals and professional classes who fled from Germany when the revolutionary movements of 1848 collapsed. Representative of them was Dr. Herman Kiefer, a physician who became a prominent civic leader in Detroit. Other Germans were skilled workers who became the backbone of the work force in the growing number of manufacturing activities that developed in the cities of southern Michigan in the last half of the nineteenth century.

Wherever they settled, the Germans brought their love of music, organizing bands, orchestras, and singing societies. The first formal concert ever held in Detroit was one given in 1833 by a touring German singer, backed by a chorus comprised of local German talent. This encouraged Detroit's Germans to organize a brass band the following year and later in 1849 to form the Harmonie Society to promote choral music. Four years later they formed a society for physical development and political discussion, and another to produce German plays. A very active German theater movement developed in Detroit, with touring companies of German actors and actresses coming to the city and performing in several theaters in the latter part of the century. A German-language newspaper, the *Allegemeine Zeitung,* was published in Detroit as early as 1844, and the large influx of well-educated Germans to Detroit caused several other German language papers to be published by the fifties. Some of these German journalists were also active in the publication of English-language papers.[5]

Though Michigan received a large number of German immigrants during the forties and fifties, an even larger number migrated to Wisconsin. It is altogether likely that if northern Michigan had offered better farm lands most of these settlers would not have gone further west. German immigrants were eagerly sought by Michigan and other western states. Land obtained through federal grants for education and internal improvements could be sold to swell the revenues of a state, and most states needed such revenues badly. Heavily burdened with debt incurred during the 1830s, and with citizens averse to paying high taxes, the states found in land sales a welcome source of revenue as well as an added base for taxes in the future. In many instances, the federal land grants were disposed of at a low price to attract settlers, thus dissipating funds intended for education. In this respect, Michigan was less shortsighted than most of its sister states; but even so, in the early 1840s especially, school and university lands were sold cheaply to attract settlers to Michigan. In 1845, an act of the legislature empowered Governor Barry to employ an agent to reside in New York for the purpose of encouraging immigrants to come to Michigan. The agent appointed—John Almy of Grand Rapids—published a six-page pamphlet extolling the attractions of the state. In 1848, Governor Epaphroditus Ransom strongly recommended action to encourage immigration to Michigan. Ransom appointed Edward H. Thompson of Flint to represent the state in New York City, where most of the emigrants from Europe arrived, and Thompson published a 47-page pamphlet in both English and German entitled *The Emmigrant's Guide to Michigan.* Similar efforts to attract immigrants, especially Germans, continued to the Civil War and were resumed thereafter.[6]

The Michigan legislature demonstrated its interest in the first German colonies in the Saginaw country by appropriating 8,000 acres of land granted to the state by the federal government for internal improvements to construct roads to their settlements. Another 2,000 acres were set aside, the proceeds to be used to build a road to the German settlements in Clinton County. Other grants were made for the aid of the Dutch settlers who settled at Holland. To build a wharf or pier at the mouth of the Black River for their use, the proceeds from 4,000 acres were appropriated, and funds derived from the sale of 3,000 acres more were set aside to build roads to Holland from Allegan, Grandville, and Grand Haven.

The first Dutch settlers comprised a colony whose leader was the Reverend Albertus C. Van Raalte. One reason for the migration of this first group and several subsequent ones was religious. Their members objected to conforming to the state church of the Netherlands—the National Reformed Church. These seceders had been compelled to surrender their churches and to worship in barns and stables. But the economic reason for the Dutch emigration was probably more compelling than this religious factor. During 1845 the potato rot hit the Netherlands and destroyed so much of the crop upon which the poor chiefly relied for food that many faced starvation. The country was crowded and the more ambitious sought greater opportunity for themselves and their children than their small homeland afforded. The importance of the economic motive for emigration may be judged by noting that of those who came to America in 1847 nearly twice as many were members of the state church as were members of the seceding group.[7]

The leader and pastor of the first colony of Dutch settlers in Michigan, Albertus Van Raalte, was a man small in stature, possessed of an indomitable will, unflinching courage, considerable executive ability, and implicit trust in God. His group of fifty-three members arrived at New York on November 17, 1846, after a month and a half on the stormy Atlantic. Van Raalte originally intended to settle in Wisconsin, where several Dutch families had arrived in 1845 and 1846. After arriving at Detroit the men of the party found work while Van Raalte continued westward to look over the land. After considering the possibility of selecting lands in Iowa, Missouri, and Wisconsin, Van Raalte finally decided upon a location at the mouth of the Black River in Michigan, where the town of Holland was founded. The colony consisted of the members of Van Raalte's congregation, and it was governed to a large extent by the congregation's governing body, the Classis.

Unaccustomed to the use of the axe, the most important tool used by pioneers in clearing the forest, the members of the colony endured great hardships the first year. They were quickly followed by other Dutch settlers who migrated in some instances as congregations, in others as families or individuals. Zeeland was founded in 1848 by a congregation from the Dutch province of that name led by the Reverend C. Vander Meulen. Scores of these Zeelanders received financial aid from Jannes Van de Luijster. The first Dutch settlers of Kalamazoo came in 1850 under the leadership of Paulus den Bleyker. Shortly after the arrival of the party, cholera broke out among its members and spread among the townspeople of Kalamazoo. The Dutch newcomers were isolated in a pest house on the edge of the town, where several of their number died before the disease subsided.[8] Other Dutch immigrants found homes in Grand Rapids, Muskegon, and Allegan, while some formed their own communities.

The Dutch were a hard-working lot, zealously devoted to their churches, and inclined toward theological disputation. A split in the Reformed Church in America, to which most of the Dutch immigrants belonged, took place before the Civil War and resulted in the formation of the Christian Reformed Church. The Reformed Church and the Christian Reformed Church remain today the principal denominations that consist largely of people of Dutch origin, though there have been other smaller offshoots. The faith in education among these Dutch pioneers was strong, and by 1851 they had established a school in Holland that ultimately became Hope College. Many of the Dutch leaders were opposed to assimilation, and preferred that the Dutch settlers retain their identity and traditions. In Kalamazoo, the Dutch farmers were the ones who first developed bleached celery and made the city famous for this herbaceous plant. Politically, the Dutch tended toward conservatism, as did the New Englanders, although both were radical in their opposition to slavery.[9]

By the mid-forties opportunities in the mining and lumbering industries in northern Michigan attracted new peoples to those areas who had not been attracted by the predominately agricultural opportunities of southern Michigan. In the copper and iron mines in the western Upper Peninsula, Cornish miners from southwestern England were the first large immigrant group but they were soon followed by numerous other immigrants who made these mining areas among the most heavily populated by foreign-born peoples of any areas in the state. The lumber industry was largely responsible for attracting a new generation of French-speaking Canadians at a time when the descendants of the earlier wave of French-Canadians who had been drawn to Michigan by the fur-trading opportunities were rapidly losing their French ways and becoming Americanized. By the late 1840s and 1850s, Norwegian and Swedish immigrants were also beginning to come in great numbers to take jobs in the lumber camps and mill towns of central and northern Michigan. A third Scandinavian group—the Danes—who had little experience in lumbering, settled in southern Michigan, particularly in Montcalm County, where they were among the large group attracted by Michigan's farming opportunities.[10]

According to the census of 1860, Wayne County contained 75,547 inhabitants. This was approximately ten percent of the state's total population and was indicative of a growing tendency of more newcomers to find opportunity in Detroit, in contrast to the earlier emphasis on the agricultural opportunities of the interior regions which had led to Wayne County's neighbors in the 1830s having populations nearly as great as Wayne County's. By 1860, only four other counties in the state had as many as 30,000 people. Three of these, Oakland, Washtenaw, and Lenawee, were in the southeastern part of the state. The other, Kent County in western Michigan, contained Grand Rapids, which, by the 1850s, was a boom town as a result of the early development of the lumber industry.

Except for Kent County, the population in 1860 was heavily concentrated in the two southernmost tiers. Among the counties in this group, only Van Buren had fewer than 20,000 people. In the third tier, only Oakland and Macomb counties had that many inhabitants, with Barry County being the most sparsely settled. In the fourth tier, Kent was the most populous, followed by St. Clair and Genesee counties, which had over 20,000 people. Saginaw County, with a population of 12,557, was the most populous county in the areas north of the four southern tiers of counties. The total population of the Upper Peninsula was only slightly more than 20,000, with close to half that number, 8,893, found in Houghton County, in the center of the new copper-mining industry.

*   *   *   *   *

Between 1835 and 1860, the exploitation of Michigan's timber and mineral resources began, though this development was to rise far higher in the years after the Civil War. By 1860, however, the products of the state's mines and forests already were making a major contribution to its economy.

Sawmills sprang up early in the history of every Michigan community to provide sawed lumber for the building of houses, barns, stores, and shops. These mills were a profitable investment and provided jobs for many workers. By 1854, a total of 889 sawmills employing 4,579 persons were in operation in Michigan. But the lumber industry as usually conceived may be said to have begun when sawed lumber was produced beyond the quantity required to meet local demand, with the excess shipped elsewhere. The first region in which large-scale lumber production took place was the Saginaw Valley. In this valley and in valleys of the tributaries of the Saginaw, such as the Cass, the Shiawassee, and the Tittabawassee, were thousands of acres of white pine. Because of its beauty, and because it was a soft wood and easy to work, white pine was the most highly prized of all lumber. For many years lumbermen confined their cutting to the areas in proximity to rivers, down which the logs could be floated to the sawmills. The Saginaw country was threaded by rivers suitable to the needs of the lumbermen. And at the mouth of the Saginaw River access was easy to distant markets by use of Great Lakes shipping.

Harvey Williams is said to have established the first steam sawmill in the Saginaw Valley in 1834, the engine being one salvaged from the *Walk-in-the-Water,* the first steamboat on the Great Lakes. It was not until ten years later, however, that any appreciable amount of lumber was sent from this region to outside markets. In 1847, a shipment of Saginaw pine reached Albany, New York, by way of the Great Lakes and the Erie Canal, and attracted favorable notice from lumber dealers, who pronounced it the equal of pine from the Maine woods, long regarded as the best. From this time forward the export of pine lumber from the Saginaw Valley grew rapidly. There were twenty-nine mills in this valley by 1854, with a capacity of 100,000,000 board feet per year; by 1860 the number of mills had increased to seventy-two. Detroit, Cleveland, Toledo, and Buffalo provided ready markets for lumber. By 1860 a wholesale migration of lumbermen from Maine to the Saginaw Valley was taking place. Loggers, sawyers, teamsters, rivermen, and capitalists came, bringing with them their tools and techniques.

Commercial lumbering was also well under way on the western side of the lower peninsula by 1860. Huge quantities of logs were being floated down the Grand River to sawmills in Grand Rapids. From these mills, the lumber was shipped on river boats to the mouth of the Grand until the railroad arrived in 1858. Muskegon was producing the largest amount on the west coast, its mills—the first of which had started up in 1838—turning out 75,000,000 board feet in 1860, as compared with 131,000,000 board feet turned out by the Saginaw Valley mills. Sawmills had also been established by 1860 at the mouths of the Pere Marquette, Manistee, and Boardman rivers. In the Upper Peninsula lumber was being sawed by mills at Escanaba and Menominee, although the development of the lumber resources of that area lagged behind development in the lower peninsula. Large amounts of Upper Peninsula hardwoods were also being cut to feed the charcoal kilns that were springing up in the iron mining region.

Copper mining had become an important segment of Michigan's economy by the time of the Civil War. Although the existence of the Upper Peninsula's copper deposits had been known for several thousand years, the mining that started in the 1840s was a result of scientific studies of these deposits made earlier in the nineteenth century. Henry R. Schoolcraft, who had accompanied the Cass expedition in 1820, mentioned the copper deposits in the area in his account of this trip. He told of seeing the boulder of pure copper imbedded in rock on the banks of the Ontonagon River, which had inspired Alexander Henry and associates to attempt to establish a copper mine in the early 1770s. Schoolcraft visited the area again in

1831 and 1832. With him on these visits was a young Detroit physician and scientist, Dr. Douglass Houghton, who hacked off a piece of the Ontonagon boulder as a souvenir. He also found traces of copper in the rocks of the Keweenaw Peninsula. In 1837, Houghton was appointed Michigan's first state geologist, heading up one of the early state agencies, the State Geological Survey. His report to the legislature in 1841 of his first surveying activities in the Upper Peninsula indicated that there were extensive copper deposits along the Lake Superior shore. Although Houghton warned that quick riches were not to be expected from exploiting these copper deposits, news of his findings soon touched off a rush of prospectors into the Keweenaw Peninsula.

Attention was also given to the Copper Country by the determined efforts of Julius Eldred, a Detroit businessman, who wanted to transport the Ontonagon boulder from the Upper Peninsula to Detroit, where he would display it as a money-making natural wonder. He made his first trip to the site of the boulder in the summer of 1841. At that time, the entire western Upper Peninsula was still Indian land, but in 1842 title to this area was acquired by the federal government in the Treaty of La Pointe. Because the boulder lay on Indian land when he found it, Eldred paid a local chief $150 for it. He returned the next summer to haul away the six-thousand pound chunk of copper and rock but was unable to move it with the equipment at hand. The following year he was back with a small railroad car and tracks, only to find that someone else had laid claim to the boulder. After paying the claimant $1,365, Eldred succeeded in moving the boulder by loading it on his flat car with a block and tackle, pushing the car ahead a short distance, then taking up the track behind it and laying a stretch in front. In this way the expensive prize was transported to Lake Superior, where it was put aboard a ship and finally taken to Detroit. But Eldred's troubles were not over. The boulder was seized by federal officials, who declared that Eldred did not have a legal claim to the boulder. He was, however, duly compensated for his troubles and the huge specimen was then taken to Washington, where it was for many years displayed at one of the museums of the Smithsonian Institution. In recent years, however, the disappearance of the Ontonagon Boulder from public view has led some in the Upper Peninsula to ask the Smithsonian to return it to Michigan where it could receive the attention it deserves.[11]

The great copper boom, stimulated by Houghton's report and the stories of the Ontonagon Boulder, began in 1843 and reached its height in 1846—three years before the California gold rush. A few prospectors arrived at Copper Harbor in the summer of 1843, and workers from the Wisconsin lead mines began digging for copper in the vicinity of the Ontonagon River that same year. The following spring the influx began in earnest. Every ship brought parties of men from the East who were certain they would return home with vast wealth. These copper hunters had little equipment: usually a small tent, two blankets, a camp kettle, frying pan, tin plates and cup. Actually there was very little real mining during the first two years. Equipped with a pick and and some gunpowder, hundreds of men tramped through the forests, fighting off hordes of gnats and mosquitoes, picking up copper lying on the surface or easily blown free from overcropping rocks. Initially they were searching out the most promising lands for purposes of speculation. In these mining camps of the copper rush many of the same conditions existed that were later to be found in the gold mining camps of California.[12] Although American history books relate the story of the gold rush to California, they seldom mention the great Michigan copper rush. Yet the Michigan copper rush came first, and the value of the copper taken from the Lake Superior mines over the years probably was greater and contributed more to the growth of the nation than all the gold mined in California.

After Indian rights in the land had been acquired by the Treaty of La Pointe, the question arose as to how rights to mine copper could be secured. It was decided to grant leases under provisions of an act passed by Congress in 1807 for the purpose of permitting lead mining. The War Department was in charge of granting the leases, and in the summer of 1843 an agent was stationed at Copper Harbor to issue permits to prospectors. Nearly a hundred such permits had been granted by the end of 1843. At first it was possible to obtain a permit to explore nine square miles, but the area was reduced to one square mile in 1845. After a location had been made, the holder could apply for a lease, accompanied by surety bonds in the amount of $20,000. The lessee was allowed a year for exploration and three years to mine, with the privilege of two renewals of three years each. He was required to pay the government a royalty of six percent of the value of the minerals taken during the first three-year period and ten percent thereafter. In 1846, however, it was found that the issuance of these permits had been illegal, and thenceforward the lands could be acquired only by purchase. An act passed by Congress in 1847 provided for the designation of mineral lands in the Lake Superior region and stipulated that they should be sold for not less than $5.00 an acre. The price was reduced, however, in 1850 to $1.25 an acre—the same minimum price as that charged for agricultural lands.[13] The rights of those to whom permits had been granted were safeguarded. Altogether about a thousand such permits had been issued.

Prior to the sale of lands for copper mining, it was necessary that they be surveyed. Douglass Houghton conceived the idea of conducting the usual topographical surveys with the state's geological survey, and in 1844 he contracted with the United States government to take charge of this dual surveying effort. At the time of his untimely death the following year, a good start had been made, and the running of section lines and the identification of mineral resources continued according to his plans.

It soon became apparent that the individual miner could accomplish little. Accordingly, copper companies were formed, some to conduct mining operations, and others to sell stock to speculators. In 1844, capitalists from Pittsburgh and Boston organized two companies. One of these went bankrupt five years later. The other one—the Pittsburgh and Boston—also nearly expired before it hit pay dirt. Some of its workmen opened a mine near Eagle River that was given the name Cliff Mine. From it masses of pure copper and many nuggets of silver were taken, By the time the company sold the mine in 1871, after the deposits of mass copper were largely played out, the Cliff had paid its stockholders $2,327,660 in dividends on a total investment of only $110,000.[14] Many other companies, however, were less fortunate, and failures were common.

Three major copper-producing areas had been located by 1860, all of them in the western part of the Upper Peninsula. Near the tip of the Keweenaw Peninsula were the mines that centered around Copper Harbor, Eagle River, and Eagle Harbor. At the other extreme, to the southwest, were the workings in the region of the Ontonagon River. The third and richest area to be developed would be that around Portage Lake and to the north of that lake, an area lying in the middle of the Keweenaw Peninsula.

Mining in the Ontonagon area had begun in 1843, almost at the same time as in the Copper Harbor region. The Minesota Mine, opened in this area in 1847, had the largest single mass of native copper ever discovered.[15] The National Mine in the same area was paying good dividends by the time of the Civil War. The Cliff and the Minesota contained the richest mass copper deposits. A copper mass is a solid piece of native or pure copper weighing one hundred pounds or more, surrounded by a rock matrix. These mass copper deposits, which were regarded at first as the only lodes worth mining, were actually geological freaks. Much more important in the long run were the deposits of finely disseminated metal in amygdaloid and conglomerate rock. An amygdaloid rock is one that often contains pure copper in the amygdaloids, or almond-shaped cavities. Conglomerate is a rock formation held together with pure copper metal.

Another mine that was to become world-famous was the Quincy, opened in 1848. It was situated on Portage Lake in the middle of the Keweenaw Peninsula and was opened by Christopher C. Douglas, a cousin of Douglass Houghton, and his brother-in-law, Ransom Sheldon. Although the Quincy's production at first was discouraging, it was beginning to be profitable by 1860. The rich Pewabic mine was opened in the same vicinity in 1856. It was in this mine that the great amygdaloid vein was found, and this type of formation was the foundation for the amazing production record of the Quincy as well. Also in production by the time of the Civil War was the Franklin mine in the Portage Lake area. And finally, there was the Calumet and Hecla Mine, whose immense copper deposits were discovered in 1859. It would ultimately become the most famous copper mine in the world.[16]

The companies that were formed to exploit the discoveries that had been made not only supplied the necessary capital but also provided trained personnel. Dr. Charles T. Jackson was one such man, though his enthusiastic reports to the first company formed—Lake Superior Copper Company—proved unfounded. It operated at a loss until 1849 when it became bankrupt. Men with practical experience in the lead mines of Wisconsin and Illinois, James K. Paul, Nicholas Miniclier, and others, came to the Ontonagon region and were the key figures, along with a prospector, William W. Spaulding, in developing the copper resources there. Paul purchased the land on which Ontonagon was located and platted the town. The name was an adaptation of a Chippewa word. Ransom Sheldon, a key figure in the development of the Quincy Mine, opened a store on the south side of Portage Lake in 1852, and around this the town of Houghton grew up. On the opposite side, Christopher C. Douglas built a store in 1858 and the following year platted the town of Hancock, named for John Hancock, signer of the Declaration of Independence. Capital provided by eastern capitalists proved indispensable in sinking shafts and making the mines pay. Up to 1860 over $900,000 had been invested in the Quincy Mine, and although it was beginning to be productive, operations were still in the red. But in the years ahead the investors got their money back many times over. The name of the Quincy Mine, taken from a town in Massachusetts and a prominent Boston family, symbolizes the importance of eastern capital in mining Michigan copper. By 1860, no less than thirty-three companies were engaged in mining in the Copper Country. They had invested over four million dollars and were employing 3,681 workers. In these years Michigan was rich in resources but poor in the money needed to develop them. Hence, until the latter part of the century, Michigan's economic growth continued to be as dependent on outside capital investments as it had been in earlier days when the exploitation of its furs had depended on the help of investors in Montreal, Albany, New York, Paris, or London.

The federal government played an important role in laying the foundations for copper production in Michigan. It purchased the land from the Indians under treaties signed in 1842 and 1854, had it surveyed, and sold it at a low price to those who wished to engage in mining. Fearing that the Indians of the area might be resentful of the intrusion of the prospectors and miners, the War Department built Fort Wilkins at the tip of the Keweenaw Peninsula, between Lake Superior and Lake Fanny Hooe, an inland body of water. The first stockade was built in 1844. The Indians proved friendly, however, and far less dangerous than the boisterous prospectors and miners. The troops were pulled out in 1846 at the start of the Mexican War. The fort was unoccupied thereafter, except for a brief period between 1867 and 1870. In recent years the old fort, with restored stockade and barracks, has been developed as a historic park under the joint auspices of the Michigan Department of Natural Resources and the History Division of the Department of State.

A third new source of wealth to Michigan, developed during the quarter-century between statehood and the Civil War, was iron ore. Although the existence of copper in the Lake Superior region had been known for centuries, and although Houghton's 1841 report had indicated that there was iron ore in the region, it was not until 1844 that the existence of sizable deposits of this ore was confirmed. The discovery was made by a government land surveyor, William A. Burt, who was associated with Douglass Houghton in the combined linear and geological survey for which a contract had been signed with the government. Burt formed a survey team, which started its work in August. One of the assistants was Jacob Houghton, a brother of Douglass. On September 19, 1844, Burt was puzzled by the peculiar movements of the needle of his magnetic compass. While seeking the reason for this, he discovered numerous outcroppings of iron south of Teal Lake near the site of the present city of Negaunee. Though Burt is remembered by Michiganians chiefly because of this discovery, he took far more pride in his invention of a solar compass, which enabled the surveyors to run the section lines accurately in a region where iron ore deposits made the magnetic compasses unreliable.[17]

Douglass Houghton was thus directly involved in the discovery and publicizing of Michigan's best-known mineral resources. Unhappily, he was drowned in a boating accident off Eagle River on October 14, 1845, when he was only thirty-six years old. A city, a county, and Michigan's largest inland lake are named in honor of one who accomplished so much in such a brief career.

The year after Burt and his party discovered iron ore near Teal Lake, several men from Jackson, Michigan, came to the same spot. They were part of a group, headed by Philo M. Everett of that city, who had earlier organized the Jackson Mining Company. The company was apparently named not after the city but after a Boston geologist—Charles T. Jackson—whose geological reports were the indirect source of Everett's original interest in the Upper Peninsula's mineral resources. Everett had become infected by copper fever and, through the intervention of United States Senator John Norvell, had secured a permit to lease a square mile of land in northern Michigan just before the granting of such permits was discontinued. Setting out for the Upper Peninsula with four associates, he met a French-Canadian who had been a clerk in the fur trade and was thoroughly acquainted with the Lake Superior region. This man—Louis Nolan—told Everett that there was a mountain of ore near Teal Lake, and when Everett showed him some copper ore, Nolan shook his head and indicated it was not that kind of ore. Everett engaged Nolan to accompany him but Nolan was unable to locate the body of iron ore that he had heard of, probably from members of Burt's surveying team. Everett's party subsequently encountered an elderly Chippewa chief—Marji-Gesick—who knew of Burt's mountain of iron and proceeded to guide two of the Jackson men to the site.

After entering the location in the office of the United States mineral agent at Copper Harbor, Everett returned to Jackson with samples of his ore, the fine quality of which was soon confirmed. The officers of Everett's company gave Marji-Gesick a small share in the company for his services in guiding them to these rich deposits. After the death of the chieftain, his daughter, Charlotte, sought to be recognized as her father's legal heir, but the company that had by then acquired control of the Jackson mine refused to recognize the agreement made by the previous owners with Marji-Gesick or any obligations it had to make payments to his daughter. The daughter went to court and after prolonged litigation, the Michigan Supreme Court ruled in her favor. Perhaps the most significant aspect of the decision, written by Justice James V. Campbell, was its assertion of the right of Indians to be judged by the customs and practices of their own society, not by those of the white man. The mining company's attorneys had argued Charlotte's parents had not been married according to the laws of Michigan and that therefore she was illegitimate. The state court, however, declared that Marji-Gesick had been married according to accepted Indian practices, which made his daughter his legitimate offspring and entitled her to the payments outlined in the agreement between the father and the Jackson company, the validity of which the court also upheld.[18]

The original iron discovered by the Everett group was found clinging to the roots of a fallen tree. The stump of this tree, a drawing of which forms part of the seal of the city of Negaunee, was preserved until 1900 as a historical relic. A monument of native stone now marks the spot where the old stump was located.[19]

The Jackson Mining Company, which had been formed as a copper-mining business, at once took steps to produce iron instead. The company sent an expedition to Teal Lake in 1846, and it brought back enough of the ore to test. It was made into a bar of fine iron at a forge located at Hodunk, north of Coldwater, where efforts had been underway for some years to exploit the deposits of bog iron found in parts of southern Michigan. The discovery of the Lake Superior region's high-quality ores soon led to the abandonment of the mining of these low-grade southern Michigan ores. In 1847, the Jackson company proceeded to set up its own forge at its mine near Negaunce. The first iron was made from this forge in February, 1848. Fuel for the forge was charcoal made in kilns from hardwood obtained in the area. Because of the extreme difficulty of transportation, especially before the construction of the Soo Locks, the early iron companies all set up forges to smelt the iron before it was shipped, rather than shipping out the ore itself.

A second company, the Marquette Iron Company, began mining ore in 1849 at the site of the present city of Ishpeming, near Negaunee. This company also built a forge on the shore of Lake Superior. Here three officials of the firm, Robert Graveraet, Dr. Edward Clark, and Amos R. Harlow, built some cabins and started the settlement that grew into the city of Marquette. The settlement's original name was Worcester, which reflected the fact that the financing of the Marquette company came from Massachusetts, with the Michigan officials contributing claims to iron lands that they had secured. A young man named Peter White, then only nineteen years old, was a member of the first group to arrive at Marquette. In due time he became a leading citizen of the Upper Peninsula. Like so many other young men of his time, he had been caught up in the enthusiasm of the copper boom, but because he had lacked the money needed to reach the Copper Country, he had ended up as a clerk in a store on Mackinac Island. There he was found by Robert

Graveraet, who was hiring workers for the iron-mining venture. White was later put in charge of the company store at Marquette. In 1853 he opened a bank in the town, and three years later he was elected to the state legislature.[20]

White's marriage to Ellen Hewitt would link him to a wealthy Cleveland family that had been one of the first to see the importance of Michigan iron ore to the development of Ohio's iron and steel industry. The emergence of Cleveland as the investment center for Michigan iron mining had first been indicated in 1847 with the formation of the Cleveland Iron Company (shortly renamed the Cleveland Iron Mining Company), which later became the great Cleveland-Cliffs Iron Company. It was organized by a young Cleveland lawyer, Samuel L. Mather, Peter White's future father-in-law, Dr. Morgan L. Hewitt, and others. The Cleveland firm was able to establish in court its prior occupancy of the land at Ishpeming that was also claimed by the Marquette Iron Company, and in 1853 the Marquette firm was taken over by the Cleveland firm. Like the other two pioneer iron mining companies, the Cleveland Iron Mining Company built a forge and produced "bloom iron." But it was the common experience of all that this was an unprofitable business, and they turned to shipping the raw ore to be smelted in the large blast furnaces in the lower-lakes region. A blast furnace—the first in the Upper Peninsula—was built at Negaunee in 1858 by the Pioneer Iron Company. Later other blast furnaces were constructed— twenty-five in all—in various parts of the Upper Peninsula. Some of these operated for many years. But by 1860, the leading producers were shipping the ore elsewhere to be smelted.[21]

The distance between Negaunee and Marquette is only about a dozen miles and Ishpeming is about three miles further. Yet this short gap between the mines and the Lake Superior port where the ore could be shipped proved to be a difficult obstacle. The road went through a dense forest and across a high range of hills. At first ore was transported only during the winter months when sleighs could be used. A railroad was projected as early as 1851, but six years were required to complete it. In the meantime a plank road was built, over which wagons piled high with ore could be hauled.

At Marquette there were more problems. Shallow water near the shore made it necessary to transfer mining equipment and supplies from ships to barges, or else to float them ashore. The problem of loading iron ore onto ships lying offshore can readily be imagined. A dock built out into the lake in the early 1850s was shattered by the winds and waves of the lake. The first modern dock was built by the Cleveland Iron Mining Company in 1859. Resting on piles driven to solid rock, it extended four hundred feet. Railroad tracks were laid on a trestle constructed on the dock, and railroad cars could then discharge their cargoes of iron ore into chutes leading to pockets from which the ships could be loaded. The completion of the Soo Locks in 1855 removed another bottleneck in the transportation of iron ore to market. Thereafter ore carriers could proceed directly from Marquette to lower lake ports.

Until 1870 the mining of iron was a relatively simple process. After the trees, sod, and soil were scraped away, the ore could be broken off by use of the pick, hand drill, and sledge hammer. Black powder was used to break up the ore-bearing rock. It was not until the 1870s that shafts were sunk for underground mining. Thus, once the transportation problem was solved, it was relatively easy to increase production by leaps and bounds. Shipment of iron ore from the Upper Peninsula jumped from 1,449 tons in 1855 to 114,401 tons in 1860. The mines worked before the Civil War were all located in what came to be called the Marquette Iron Range. Michigan's two other iron ranges—the Menominee and the Gogebic— were not developed until later, although the presence of ore in these areas had been discovered by the beginning of the 1850s as the survey of the lands in the western Upper Peninsula was completed.

The full-scale development of the Lake Superior region's mineral resources depended on the elimination of the barrier to shipping caused by the rapids in the St. Mary's River which linked Lake Superior with the lower lakes. As early as 1797 the North West Company had built a lock to lift small vessels from the lower lakes to the level of Lake Superior, but the size of the canal limited its use to canoes and other small craft used by the fur traders. When copper and iron were discovered in the Upper Peninsula, a tramway was built around the rapids to transport ore. Lack of materials and skilled labor made shipbuilding above the rapids a difficult task. During the winter of 1839-40, the schooner *Algonquin* was moved around the rapids on rollers. In 1845 and 1846 two steam-powered vessels, the *Independence* and the *Julia Palmer,* were transferred to Lake Superior by the same laborious process. As copper and iron production increased, the movement of ore around the rapids and the transfer of supplies and equipment bound for Lake Superior called for the employment of many men. Quite clearly, a canal was needed.

Shortly after the abandonment of the canal project that had been part of Michigan's ill-fated internal improvements program of 1837, Michigan Senator John Norvell in December, 1839, introduced a bill in Congress for a donation of public lands to aid in the construction of such a canal. In 1840, the Michigan legislature offi-

PRESENT
AND
ORIGINAL
COUNTY NAMES

S	Suggested by Schoolcraft
C	Cabinet Counties
G	Named after Governors
	Original names underlined

cially requested such a grant. It required twelve years, however, to overcome opposition in Congress. Senator Henry Clay derisively commented that the canal would be "a work quite beyond the remotest settlement of the United States if not in the moon." Three times a bill passed the Senate only to be defeated in the House of Representatives. The opening of copper and iron mines in the Upper Peninsula was a factor in the eventual success of the effort. A bill was passed by both houses and approved by President Millard Fillmore on August 26, 1852.

Under the provisions of this act, a right of way through the United States military reservation at Fort Brady was granted for the canal, which was to be at least 100 feet wide and 12 feet deep, with locks at least 250 feet long and 60 feet wide. Public lands in the amount of 750,000 acres were granted to the state of Michigan to finance the waterway, but the proceeds were to be forfeited unless the construction of the canal was started within three years and completed within ten years.

At the time the bill was passed a young man named Charles T. Harvey was at Sault Ste. Marie seeking to regain his health after an attack of typhoid fever. He had visited the iron and copper mines of northern Michigan and realized how vital a canal was. Harvey was employed by the Fairbanks Scale Company. In the belief that the canal would be of great public benefit and at the same time might prove to be a profitable venture for its builders, he wrote to officials of his company suggesting that they undertake the project. Without waiting for their response, Harvey obtained the services of an engineer to make a preliminary survey, then went to Detroit where he sought the help of James F. Joy, a lawyer for the Michigan Central Railroad who was well acquainted with the members of the legislature. A bill was drawn up and passed in February, 1853. It specified a canal with locks 350 feet long and 70 feet wide. The governor was authorized to appoint five commissioners and an engineer to prepare plans and superintend the construction of the canal. And it offered to grant the 750,000 acres of land that had been donated for the purpose by the federal government to a company that would build the canal within two years.

The Fairbanks brothers, who had invested in Upper Peninsula mines, were for this reason interested in Harvey's proposal that they form a company to seek the contract. A corporation was formed under the name of the St. Mary's Falls Ship Canal Company. Among its subscribers were such prominent eastern capitalists as Erastus Corning and August Belmont. The investors' trust in Harvey was indicated by their appointment of him as their agent at the Soo to take charge of construction. An agreement between the company and the State of Michigan was signed on April 5, 1853. Harvey immediately went to Detroit where he bought tools, supplies, and horses and engaged workmen. Then he took ship for the Soo, where he rented the Indian Agency building (which is still standing) for his residence and headquarters, and contracted for the construction of shanties to lodge the workers and a mess hall to feed them. He also had a hospital built and engaged the services of a physician. Early in June, almost two months to the day from the time the contract was signed, the first excavation was made.

Formidable obstacles had to be overcome. Workers for the Chippewa Portage Company, which transported goods around the rapids, were opposed to a canal because it would cost them their jobs. Harvey pacified them by giving them work on the canal at good wages. During the long winters, of course, no progress could be made. In 1854 an epidemic of cholera hit the Soo and felled many of the workers. A constant stream of new laborers had to be brought in from the East. Enormous supplies of blasting powder—a total of 3,157 kegs—were required. And just when the work was nearing completion it was found that the rise and fall of Lake Superior would require the canal to be dug a foot deeper—through solid rock. The heavy expenditures and the difficulties encountered caused some of the investors in the St. Mary's Falls Ship Canal Company to become skeptical of the project. Although he had been the General Agent of the Chippewa Portage Company, John T. Whiting undertook a midwinter trip to the East to reassure the company members and succeeded in persuading them to continue the work. On May 31, 1855—less than two years from the time the work was started—the locks and canal were turned over to the superintendent appointed by the state. The first ship to pass through the locks, the steamer *Illinois,* was lifted to the level of Lake Superior on June 18, 1855. Later the same day or early the next, the steamer *Baltimore* made passage through the locks and the canal downward toward Lake Huron.[22]

The total cost of construction was just under one million dollars—about double the amount estimated when the project was undertaken. The company, however, realized a large return from its

First Soo lock

investment. Empowered to select from the unsold public lands the 750,000 acres to which it was entitled, the company obtained title to some of the best mineral and timber lands in northern Michigan. Charles T. Harvey chose 140,000 acres for the company in the Upper Peninsula. One of the sections he selected was the site of the fabulously rich Calumet and Hecla mine, although the company sold the quarter-section on which the mine was situated for only about $60,000.

For twenty-six years the locks were operated by the state of Michigan. A toll of four cents per registered ton was charged until 1877, when the rate was reduced to three cents. United States government ships and ships carrying troops or government supplies were exempt. The year after the locks were opened, Congress appropriated $100,000 for deepening the St. Mary's River. President Pierce vetoed the bill, but it was passed over his veto. The use of the locks increased steadily from the time they were opened. Upbound freight in the year 1857 included foodstuffs, dry goods, powder, coal, railroad iron, tools, building materials, livestock, and 6,650 passengers.[23] In 1881, the operation of the locks was taken over by the United States government and passage was made toll free. A new lock, the Weitzel Lock, was opened that same year. The Poe Lock, opened in 1896, replaced the original "State Lock." Also in 1896 a lock was opened on the Canadian side of the St. Mary's River. The Davis Lock was put into operation in 1914 and the Sabin Lock in 1919. During World War II the MacArthur Lock was built to replace the Weitzel Lock. And in 1968 the rebuilding of the Poe Lock, designed to receive freighters 1,000 feet long and 100 feet wide, was completed.

*   *   *   *   *

Although the emergence of the lumber and mining industries gave Michigan new sources of wealth in the quarter-century after statehood was achieved, agriculture remained the backbone of the state's economy. By 1850 Michigan was producing over 5,500,000 bushels of corn and a little less than 5,000,000 bushels of wheat—more than twice the production of ten years before. Nearly 3,000,000 bushels of oats were grown in 1850, over 2,000,000 pounds of wool, 2,000,000 bushels of potatoes, 8,000,000 pounds of butter and cheese, and 2,500,000 pounds of maple sugar. Rye, barley, buckwheat, tobacco, and hops were grown in smaller quantities. The somewhat primitive state of farming in 1850 is indicated by the fact that almost as many oxen (55,350) as horses (58,506) were in use on the farms of the state.

Statistics of production do not tell the whole story of agriculture. Farming in the 1840s and 1850s was a way of life. To a far greater extent than in later years, the farm family was self-sustaining. Most of the food and fiber needed for the family unit was produced and processed on the farm. Shoes and hats or caps were often secured from the general store, and also cloth for the best dresses. Salt, coffee, tea, and sugar, harnesses, tools, and wagons were also usually purchased at the nearest trading center. Perhaps a few books and other nonessentials might be bought by the families that were better off. In the southern counties the first stage of frontier life had passed. Pioneers were moving from log houses into frame houses, the lumber being supplied by a nearby sawmill. There was still plenty of wild game and fish to supplement the family diet. On the whole, the farm family was largely independent of the ups and downs of the economic cycle, although when prices for farm products fell, less profit was made. But no one needed to go cold or hungry or unhoused. Poverty existed, but it was usually due to physical or mental defects, misfortune, illness, or just plain laziness.

There were ready markets for the farm products of Michigan. Some of them were shipped to the growing urban centers of the Middle West like Chicago, Milwaukee, or Detroit. Some found their way to eastern cities. With the repeal of the English corn laws, American agricultural products were being shipped abroad in ever-increasing amounts. The vast wheatfields of the prairie states had not yet been put under the plow, and for many years Michigan was a major producer of the nation's wheat.

All but fourteen counties in Michigan reported lumber-sawing as the chief industry outside of agriculture in 1860. Even in Wayne County the sawing of lumber was second in size and importance only to the manufacture of machinery. In the northern counties almost the entire male population was engaged in some aspect of the lumber business, although this work force was far smaller than that in the southern agricultural counties.

Another industry promoting the growth of northern Michigan was fishing. In Mackinac County alone in 1860 there were thirty-two fishing companies employing 130 people. In Mason, Manitou,[24] Leelanau, Huron, Grand Traverse, Delta, Chippewa, Berrien, Bay, Alpena, and Alcona counties fishing appears in the census report of 1860 as the most important industry outside of agriculture and lumbering, and in some counties, fishing outstripped these occupations in the number of persons employed as well as in the value of the product. In the entire state 186 fishing companies were listed, employing nearly a thousand men and women. Fishing was already a source of profit on Lake Superior by 1833. Commercial fishing began on Lake Huron in 1835. Even earlier, fish were taken from the St. Clair and Detroit rivers for sale in Detroit. In the early period, whitefish, lake trout, and perch constituted most of the catch. Total production of fish in 1859 was estimated at eighteen million pounds, with a value of $650,000. In the waning years of the fur trade, the American Fur Company engaged in commercial fishing activities. Seines were used at first, but gill nets were introduced as early as 1835. In the days before refrigeration the fish had to be cleaned, and then packed in salt in barrels which enabled the fish to be preserved for a long period of time.[25]

Finally, by 1860 some slight indication of Michigan's future economic development was to be seen in the presence of a small amount of manufacturing. Apart from lumber the principal products were boots and shoes, flour, cooperage, staves, hoops (for barrels), shingles, sashes, doors, furniture, saddlery and harnesses, wagons and carts, agricultural implements, clothing, and metalware.

The advance of civilization by 1860 is shown by the number of persons engaged in what might be called luxury occupations. The 1860 census indicated that there were twenty-three actors, twenty-three ice dealers, 178 music teachers, seven florists, and 617 gardeners and nurserymen. But there were only five paper hangers and seven undertakers in the entire state. The census lists, however, no less than 14,193 persons as "servants." Among the professional classes there were 4,222 teachers, 1,266 physicians, six oculists, 791 lawyers, and 855 civil and mechanical engineers. The number of printers was surprisingly large (496). Blacksmiths, carpenters, masons, and brewers are reported in considerable numbers, while the presence of 198 professional hunters was an indication of the survival of an occupation that in a sense dated back to prehistoric times.

*   *   *   *   *

The improvement of transportation was one key to the progress of Michigan in the quarter-century preceding the Civil War. It is difficult for one living in an age that has such rapid and diverse methods of transportation to understand what it meant in these earlier times to be isolated from the outside world, and what a boon it was when transportation became available. The principal cities of the state grew up along the lakes where there were good ports, at important points along navigable rivers, and along the line of the chief roads and railroads. By means of improved transportation the movement of both goods and people was facilitated, and Michigan emerged from the wilderness into closer relations with the outside world.

The Erie Canal continued to constitute the principal link between the Great Lakes and the eastern seaboard throughout this period, although rail connections had been made by 1860. The amount of traffic carried by the railroads was small in comparison to that carried on the Great Lakes by both sailing vessels and steamships in the ante-bellum period. In 1850, a total of 2,341 vessels with a tonnage of 671,545 and crews numbering 31,784 entered the port of Detroit. Ten years later the number of ships had increased to 3,351, and the tonnage to 731,419. By 1860, Great Lakes vessels had crossed the ocean with cargoes for the European market. This was made possible by the construction of the Welland Canal between 1829 and 1833, which allowed ships to bypass the Niagara Falls. The Detroit and Cleveland Navigation Company, organized in 1850, had docks in various ports of the Great Lakes, and there were many other companies. At ports all along the coast of the lower peninsula ships picked up the products of Michigan farms and delivered goods from the East, as well as carrying passengers.[26] With the opening of the Soo Canal in 1855, the same service was more readily available to the developing northern areas.

The quarter-century prior to the Civil War was the heyday of river transportation in Michigan. River boats carried passengers, but

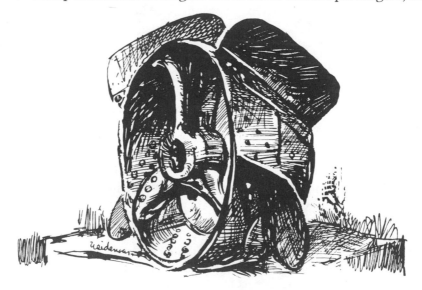

Propeller from the Independence, *an early Great Lakes steamship*

their chief usefulness was in transporting grain, salted meats, dairy and other products of the farm to the lake ports, where they could be picked up by Great Lakes vessels. On the return trips the river boats brought back to the inland towns groceries, hardware, and general merchandise. The rivers of the Saginaw country were used extensively for transportation because of bad roads. Midland, on the Tittabawassee, grew up at the head of navigation. As early as 1837 a cargo of flour was shipped by boat from Owosso to Saginaw. Boatbuilding became a sizable industry in the latter city. On the western side of the state the St. Joseph, Paw Paw, Kalamazoo, and Grand rivers were all used for transportation. David Walbridge started a line of flat boats from Kalamazoo to the mouth of the Kalamazoo River in 1841 and thereby made it possible for the farmers of the area to get a much higher return for their grain. Grain was also shipped from the village of Paw Paw down the river of that same name to its mouth at St. Joseph. Steamers carrying passengers shuttled between Grand Rapids and Grand Haven on the Grand River.

On the St. Joseph River traffic was heavy for many years. Building boats for use on the river was a lively industry in St. Joseph even before Michigan became a state. The first steamboat built for use on the St. Joseph was the *Newburyport,* built in 1832. Unfortunately, it proved to be too large for river use, and in 1833 the *Matilda Barney* was built and put into use. Within a short time several steamboats were plying up and down the river as far as Elkhart. At one time fifty keelboats were reported operating on the St. Joseph. These boats were poled upstream and floated down with the current. A captain and from eight to sixteen men constituted the crew. The operation of a keelboat has been described thus:

> The crew was divided, even numbers to a side and again divided so that half were at the bow and half at the middle of the boat. When the captain gave the word, the bow men placed their poles in the water to the river bed and pushed with all their might as they slowly walked the boat ahead. When the bow men reached the middle the stern men took up the push while the bow men raced back to the bow. The captain stood at the steering oar and repeated over and over again his commands, "Ahead, behind, ahead, behind, ahead, behind." Old residents who lived near the river tell of hearing these monotonous commands every day and often far into the night. . . . Occasionally a complacent steamer captain gave the keel boat a tow and the tired crew a rest.[27]

Canoes, flat-bottomed rowboats, and flat-bottomed scows called "arks" were other types of boats in use on the St. Joseph.

The men who operated these river boats were a rough-and-ready lot, heavy drinkers and great fighters. Some of these river men became almost legendary characters. Typical was "Stormy" Davis, six feet tall, strong as an ox, and forever singing. Later "Stormy" became religious and took up preaching. He always preached barefoot in the pulpit. Needless to say, his sermons were "sin-searing, hell-blasting, heart-stirring."

The traffic on the St. Joseph River, with shipments from as far upstream as Constantine, made the port of St. Joseph for a time a more important grain and flour shipping point than Chicago and second in Michigan only to Detroit. In 1843, St. Joseph shipped out 79,915 barrels of flour, a figure that rose to 129,333 barrels in 1844, while wheat shipments rose from 88,539 bushels in 1843 to 263,116 bushels in 1844.[28]

Although river traffic was heavy, little was done to connect rivers by canals after the breakdown of the internal improvements program. Projects for the building of canals that would connect rivers on the eastern side of the lower peninsula with those on the western side continued to be discussed down to quite recent times but none ever materialized. The great canal craze rapidly disappeared in the 1840s as railroads became more and more popular. The Illinois Canal, connecting the Great Lakes with the Mississippi, was completed in 1848, but it carried relatively little Michigan produce to market. The building of the Soo Canal in the fifties virtually marked the end of the canal era in the Middle West.

In railroad building during the two decades from 1840 to 1860, Michigan lagged behind its neighbors. In the decade of the fifties, 2,325 miles of railroad were built in Ohio, 1,897 in Indiana, 2,757 in Illinois, 902 in Wisconsin, 817 in Missouri, 679 in Iowa, and only 475 miles in Michigan. The total railroad mileage for all of Michigan in 1860 was only 799.3, less than the mileage built in any of the other states in the Middle West during the preceding decade with the exception of Iowa. The principal Michigan lines in 1860 followed the routes set forth in the internal improvements program of 1837, with some important variations. In addition there were three shorter lines connecting cities and towns on the southern and central railroads, another short line connecting Flint and Saginaw, and two short lines in the Upper Peninsula built by mining companies.

The central railroad was sold by the state in 1846 for $2,000,000 after it had been extended as far west from Detroit as Kalamazoo—a distance of 143 miles. Henceforth it was known as the Michigan Central Railroad. The purchase of the line by private investors was the work of a native of Massachusetts, John W. Brooks, who was twenty-six years old. Failing to obtain the capital he sought in

Boston, he turned to New York bankers who held some of Michigan's $5,000,000 bond issue. By facilitating the purchase of the railroad they hoped to provide Michigan with funds to pay off at least some of the bonds. After receiving favorable reactions from the New York bankers, Brooks returned to Detroit where he sought the aid of another native of New England—James F. Joy—a lawyer. The two men bargained with the legislators and finally reached an agreement. The purchase was consummated under an agreement that required the new owners to replace the wooden strap-rails with sixty-pound iron T-rails and to extend the tracks from Kalamazoo to Lake Michigan within three years. It is noteworthy that the agreement did not stipulate St. Joseph as the western terminus, which was the original state plan. Brooks was given six months to raise the necessary capital. He returned to Boston, where he received a more friendly hearing because of the promise of New York capital. His biggest catch was John Murray Forbes, a friend of Ralph Waldo Emerson and a prominent and respected New England businessman. Other Bostonians who invested in the Michigan Central were John E. Thayer, Thomas H. Perkins, Josiah Quincy, and Erastus Corning. The largest part of the capital was subscribed in Boston, Forbes was elected president, and for many years the company's chief office was in Boston.[29]

Earnings of the railroad for the first year under private ownership were $200,000, while expenses totaled only about half that amount. In 1848 receipts were almost double those of the preceding year, with about sixty percent of the revenue derived from freight. A total of 80,000 passengers were carried in 1848. The profitable operation of the line encouraged the investors to extend the tracks rapidly and to make the improvements specified in the charter, which included a relocation of the tracks entering Detroit and the erection of a new depot there. In extending the line west from Kalamazoo the company veered the route to the south from that marked out by the state. The tracks reached Niles in 1848 and New Buffalo on April 23, 1849. From there the company operated a line of steamers to Chicago, so that passengers could travel from Detroit to Chicago in a day and a half. A traveler over the railroad in 1851 wrote that trains maintained a uniform speed of eighteen miles an hour, and were punctual and safe. He described the railroad's route through primeval forests, occasional cleared fields, and "neat and thriving villages half smothered in luxuriant foliage." Wild turkeys, quail, wild pigeons, and other game could be seen from the car windows. Freight cars were fifteen feet long, had no brakes, and freight trains had no conductors. Fuel for the locomotives was wood, piled along the right of way by farmers for sale to the railroad.

Locomotives were identified by such names as Ranger, Rover, White Cloud, Trade Wind, Foxhound, Corsair, and Arab rather than by number.[30]

The coming of the railroad was generally hailed with enthusiasm by the people of the towns and villages along its route. But shortly after the Michigan Central passed into private ownership, a strong tide of opposition manifested itself in what has been called "The Great Railroad Conspiracy." The trouble arose because the trains killed livestock that strayed onto the tracks. When the old strap-rails were replaced by iron T-rails, the trains could run faster and the carnage of livestock increased. At first the Michigan Central paid the farmer the full value of his livestock killed by the trains, as the state had done, but in 1849 the management announced that henceforth only one-half the value would be paid. A storm of protest arose. East of Jackson, around Grass Lake, lawlessness broke out. Woodpiles were burned, freight cars were derailed, heavy obstructions were placed on the tracks, and engineers and firemen were targets of guns in the hands of enraged farmers. In the autumn of 1850 the interference became so serious that detectives were hired by the railroad to discover the ringleaders and bring them to justice. The lawless acts reached a climax when, on the night of November 18, 1850, the freight house of the railroad in Detroit was burned. The following April, through revelations by the detectives, two ringleaders and thirty-six others were arrested at Michigan Centre, near Jackson. A trial lasting until September followed these arrests. It was a remarkable trial, with the best legal talent available engaged by the opposing sides. Senator William H. Seward of New York was retained for the defense. Two of the chief defendants died before the trial was over. Twelve were convicted and sentenced to prison terms. This stopped the violence along the line, but for many years there was great bitterness against the railroad.[31]

The officers of the Michigan Central were much more concerned in the early fifties with the problems of eastern connections and the difficulties of extending their line into Chicago than in their troubles with Michigan farmers. As soon as Lake Erie froze over so ships could not shuttle between Detroit and Buffalo, freight traffic dropped off sharply. The Michigan Central's owners were eager to see the Great Western Railway completed across Canada to Windsor. Their corporate charter, however, prevented the company from investing in a foreign corporation. To get the railroad built, John W. Brooks, aided by a number of prominent Detroiters, succeeded in persuading New York capitalists to buy stock in the Great Western, and it was completed to Windsor in 1854. The following year the great suspension bridge over the Niagara River was completed, and railroad cars could be run from Albany to Windsor. Passengers and freight were ferried across the Detroit River to the Michigan Central line.

To reach Chicago proved an expensive feat for the Michigan Central. Entrance to Chicago was finally attained by buying the charter of a nonexistent, Indiana-chartered railroad for $500,000 and reaching an agreement with the Illinois Central for joint use of tracks into the city. It was on May 20, 1852, that the first Michigan Central train chugged into a temporary depot in Chicago, three months after the Michigan Southern had run its first trains into the future metropolis of the West. The effect on Chicago of the coming of these two railroads from the East was to greatly increase both property values and population. The effect on the Michigan Central was to increase its reputation for efficient operations, with the completed 269-mile line doing a $2,500,000 business by 1855.

The state's southern railroad, which had reached as far west as Hillsdale, was sold for $500,000 in 1846. A Detroit attorney, Elisha Litchfield, was the chief organizer of the Michigan Southern Railroad Company, which negotiated the purchase. The company was required by its charter to extend the line to Coldwater along the route mapped out by the state, but west of Coldwater it might veer from that route provided it did not build into Indiana before reaching the St. Joseph River. Its eastern terminus was Monroe, and the company planned at first to make Monroe an important port by acquiring ships to ply between that port and Buffalo. But in 1849 the Michigan Southern secured a perpetual lease of the Erie and Kalamazoo line, connecting Adrian, on the Michigan Southern, with Toledo. Henceforth the Southern began running its trains from Adrian into Toledo over the Erie and Kalamazoo tracks and using that city as the port at which connections were made to Buffalo, much to the chagrin of Monroe, which was thus bypassed. Extension of the Southern westward reached White Pigeon by 1851. Meanwhile, the officers of the Michigan Southern had acquired stock in other railroads in northern Indiana and Illinois to give their line a route into Chicago. To escape from the necessity of building to the St. Joseph River before veering southward, a four-mile line was built southward from White Pigeon across the Indiana line by a South Bend capitalist who then leased it to the Michigan Southern, and in February, 1852, the first trains were run into Chicago. The railroad now took the name of Michigan Southern and Northern Indiana.

In the 1850s the Michigan Southern and Northern Indiana acquired three lines northward between Adrian and Jackson, Jonesville and Marshall, and Toledo and Detroit. The Michigan Southern, like the Michigan Central, carried heavy traffic. A Chicago newspaper reported on June 29, 1854, that 2,000 passengers had arrived on four trains of the Michigan Southern in a single day. In addition to five steamers on Lake Erie, the Southern operated ships from Chicago to Milwaukee and Sheboygan, Wisconsin. It invested heavily in other railroads. In spite of excellent business, however, the road was in deep financial trouble just prior to the Civil War, due to over-expansion and possibly also fraud, and the value of its stock dropped precipitously.[32]

The state of Michigan never laid rails on its projected northern line. But by 1858 a railroad had been built with private capital to Grand Haven. Its eastern terminus was not on the St. Clair River as the state had planned, but at Detroit. The Detroit and Pontiac Railroad, which had been chartered in 1834, was opened from Detroit to Royal Oak—a distance of thirteen miles—in 1838, but did not reach Pontiac—thirteen miles further—until 1844. The Oakland and Ottawa Railroad Company was chartered in 1848 to build westward from Pontiac to Grand Haven, and in 1855 the two roads were consolidated as the Detroit and Milwaukee Railroad. The Great Western Railway of Canada supplied funds to complete the building of the line. In later years the Great Western became part of the Grand Trunk system, which also ultimately included the Detroit and Milwaukee. A line of steamers connected the railroad's western terminus at Grand Haven with Milwaukee. The line was sometimes called the "Emigrant route" because so many foreigners, especially German, used this railroad to reach Wisconsin.[33]

In towns and cities not located on any of the three main lines across lower Michigan, there was intense enthusiasm for railroads in the 1850s. Rallies were held and companies were formed, many of which expired without laying a mile of track. In Paw Paw, for example, a company was formed to build a railroad to connect with the Michigan Central, four miles distant. It was pointed out that whereas the people of Niles, which was on the Michigan Central, could buy flour for $5.50 a barrel, in Paw Paw the charge was $7.00.[34] In Schoolcraft about the same time "railroad fever" was rampant; a public meeting was held and subscriptions were started to form a company, without much success.[35] In spite of opposition by the Michigan Central, which had certain exclusive privileges under its charter, the legislature in 1855 passed a general incorporation law for railroad companies. Under its terms, any group of investors could secure a charter to build and operate a railroad by meeting certain minimum conditions. All new railroads organized under the act were required to install such safety devices as bells on locomotives, a steam whistle to sound before all grade crossings, "stop, look, and listen" signs at the crossings, and fences along the right of way, although no provisions were made to enforce these regulations. Maximum fares for passengers were set at three cents per mile, somewhat above the going rate.[36]

In spite of all the fervor for railroads, investors were hesitant to invest large sums in what still was regarded as a risky venture. The established railroads were making excellent profits, but many doubted that shorter lines would be paying propositions. Schemes to build rail lines into the north country, where population was relatively sparse, were hindered for want of capital. But an inducement to build such lines was provided in 1856 by an act of Congress that offered large grants of public land to the state of Michigan to award railroad companies that would undertake to construct lines into the northern part of the lower peninsula and into the Upper Peninsula. Within a year eight new railroad companies had been formed, six of which received land grants, while three existing companies also received grants. Partly because of the economic depression of 1857, however, progress in actual construction was slow. By 1860 only a portion of a line between Saginaw and Flint and another between Owosso and Lansing had been built. There were only a few miles of track laid in the Upper Peninsula.[37]

One of the factors that retarded railroad building in Michigan was the plank-road craze. The abundant timber still standing in most parts of Michigan readily provided the raw material for the building of roads out of sawed plank. Companies were formed to purchase the planks and have a road built, receiving compensation in the form of tolls charged those who used it. To do this it was necessary to obtain, in each case, a charter from the legislature until 1848 when, upon the recommendation of Governor Epaphroditus Ransom, a general plank-road law was passed, requiring companies to build "good, smooth, permanent roads," a minimum of sixteen feet wide, eight feet of which was to be built of three-inch planks. In 1855 the law was amended to permit the use of gravel instead of planks. Two cents per mile was charged for two-horse vehicles and one cent per mile for those drawn by a single horse. Scores of charters had been granted prior to the passage of this law, and more than two hundred companies were organized under its provisions, although only about one-quarter of them actually built roads. Toll houses were erected at intervals along these highways, much in the manner of twentieth-century toll roads.

The plank roads served as feeders for existing rail lines. For example, Lansing, which was without railroad service until after 1860, was connected with the railroad at Howell by means of a plank road. An important plank road connected Grand Rapids and Kalamazoo. Both passengers and freight passed over this highway. It was particularly important to Grand Rapids, which did not get a railroad until 1858—twelve years after the Michigan Central reached Kalamazoo. Large amounts of gypsum from the Grand Rapids mines were carried over the plank road for shipment at Kalamazoo. Referring to a stage trip over this road, Mark Twain wrote that it would have been enjoyable had not "some unconscionable scoundrel now and then dropped a plank across the road." This points to the fact that the plank roads when first built were fairly smooth, but soon deteriorated and became rough. Where a rail line was built along their route they quickly disappeared. Some of them, however, continued to operate until the close of the century.

Stagecoach lines already were established over the main roads by the time Michigan became a state. They continued to operate until they were superseded by the railroads. Stagecoaches over short distances between neighboring communities and as feeders to the railroads continued to function into the early years of the twentieth century. Famous foreign visitors have left records of their experiences riding Michigan stagecoaches, among them the English authoress Harriet Martineau.[38] The noted "Concord coach" was in general use in Michigan. Along the roads traversed by the stagecoaches were the taverns of pioneer days. Accommodations were crude and often inadequate, but food was abundant and friendliness the rule. Taverns were social centers and places where the latest news was discussed. In the larger towns the taverns were coming to be called "hotels" by 1860.

Improved transportation thus was a crucial factor in bringing Michigan out of the wilderness and connecting it with the outside world by 1860. Steamships, sailing vessels, river boats, railroads, and plank roads all were instrumental in breaking down the isolation of Michigan and facilitating the movement of people and products between the East and the West, as well as within the new state.

Methods of communication, meanwhile, were altered in an even more revolutionary fashion than the changes that the railroad brought to the field of transportation when telegraphic communication was introduced in the mid-forties. It was on May 24, 1844, that Samuel F. B. Morse flashed across wires strung between Baltimore and Washington the famous message: "What hath God wrought!" Even after this demonstration the public remained skeptical. To overcome this attitude, demonstrations were arranged in various parts of the country. One was held in a church in Detroit in September, 1845. At one end of the auditorium an operator clicked out a message; at the other end a recording instrument reproduced the dots and dashes on a roll of paper. Even this demonstration left many unbelieving, for they regarded it as a magic show. But businessmen soon took the electric telegraph seriously and began to invest in the stringing of wires.

The first telegraph service in Michigan was between Detroit and Ypsilanti, which were linked by telegraph wires strung along the Michigan Central tracks. The first messages were exchanged between operators in the two communities on November 30, 1847. The line was built by the Lake Erie and Michigan Telegraph Company, one of two rival companies operating under patents obtained by Morse. Building westward continued at a rapid pace, and on April 8, 1848, the first telegraph messages were sent from Detroit to Chicago. Meanwhile, Detroit had been connected with eastern lines, and on the same day that connections were made with Chicago, a message was also passed between Detroit and New York. At first the service was unreliable and subject to frequent interruptions. Improvement was slow because of the fierce competition between companies. But in 1856 fourteen of these firms were purchased by a group of Rochester capitalists who formed the Western Union Telegraph Company. Telegraph wires connected most of the larger Michigan cities by 1860, but no service was provided to the Upper Peninsula until after the Civil War.

To a generation that takes instantaneous, worldwide communications for granted it is difficult to comprehend the wonder the electric telegraph created when it was first developed. Michiganians were able to read newspaper accounts of events that had happened in the East the day before, something that must have seemed more miraculous to people of that time than did the telephone, radio, and television to those of a later age.[39] Business firms could exchange messages over thousands of miles within a few minutes. Wherever there was a telegraph station the ticking of a little instrument was a symbol of connection with the outside world.

Great improvements in the postal service also came about during the period from 1835 to 1860. Michigan had 173 post offices in 1835, and by 1837 the mails were being carried over 3,494 miles of post roads in the new state. Stagecoaches, riders, steamships, and railroads all carried the mails. A drastic reduction of postal rates was made in 1845. In 1847 further reductions were ordered, provided the postage was prepaid. Up to this time the postage was paid by the recipient rather than by the sender. Adhesive stamps were introduced the same year. By 1851 letter postage had been reduced to three cents provided the distance carried did not exceed 3,000 miles.

The post office was one of the chief centers of community life. In smaller settlements it was generally situated in a store, and here citizens gathered to talk and gossip while waiting for the arrival and distribution of the mail. The postmaster, who got his job by political appointment of the party in power in Washington, was often a leading citizen—a doctor, lawyer, newspaper publisher, or local merchant. Mail was delivered to homes and business places only in the largest cities, and there was no rural delivery. Nevertheless, the postal service was of major importance in linking the state together and providing a means of communication with associates or kinfolk far away.[40]

The improvement of postal service and the coming of the telegraph encouraged the establishment of newspapers, although the impetus provided by partisan rivalry was probably an even more potent factor. Most newspapers continued to depend heavily on party subsidies in one form or another. Every leading city had two newspapers, one representing the Democratic persuasion, the other the Whig (after 1854, the Republican) point of view. Editorial columns were filled with vitriolic prose condemning in unmeasured language the members and policies of the opposing party while praising those of the party the newspaper supported.

In Detroit the *Free Press* went all out for the Democratic cause. Its editor after 1853, Wilbur F. Storey, was an intense admirer of Lewis Cass, favored the Kansas-Nebraska Act, hated all abolitionists, and denounced the organizers of the Republican party as a "body of unmitigated abolitionists and disunionists." But he was an able newspaper man. At the *Free Press* he established the first real city department, gathered about him a brilliant staff, and published the first Sunday edition. It has been said he had a wider fame and fewer friends than any newspaper man in Michigan before or since.[41] Diametrically opposed to Storey was Joseph Warren of the *Tribune*. Described by his associates as a sedate, gentle, kind-hearted man, he could write with a pen dipped in gall. The *Tribune* was combined with the *Advertiser* in 1858 and became Detroit's leading exponent of the Republican party. James E. Scripps came to Detroit from Chicago in 1859 as business manager of the *Advertiser and Tribune*. In later years he was to become one of the nation's leading newspaper men.

Outside Detroit the rivalry of Democrats with Whigs—later Republicans—was also reflected in rival newspapers. Ann Arbor had its *State Journal* and *True Democrat,* Grand Rapids its *Enquirer* and

Eagle; Kalamazoo its *Gazette* and *Telegraph;* Hillsdale its *Gazette* and *Whig Standard;* Marshall its *Democratic Expounder* and *Marshall Statesman.* During the 1840s newspapers were established in towns that had not had them previously. The *Northern Advocate* appeared in Flint in 1840; Battle Creek's first newspaper, the *Michigan Tribune,* was launched in 1846; the Coldwater *Sentinel* dates from 1841; the *Western Chronicle* was the ambitious name of a newspaper published in Centreville, beginning in 1849. Howell's first newspaper, the Livingston *Courier,* started publication in 1843, the Paw Paw *Free Press* in 1845, the Ypsilanti *Sentinel* in 1843, and the *Eaton Democrat* in 1847. Shortly after the establishment of the state capital at Lansing, a newspaper was started there in 1848 under the name *Michigan State Journal.*[42]

Many newspapers were short-lived: the *St. Clair Whig* lasted one year; the *Western Banner* in Kalamazoo expired within a few months. Some newspapers were published only during a political campaign. The ups and downs of political fortunes and uncertain financial backing caused many casualties in the newspaper field. The average Michigan newspaper of the 1840s and 1850s, like its predecessor, contained little local news. Its columns were devoted mainly to reprints from eastern and foreign newspapers, poetry, fiction, and national news. Editorials on political subjects were long and acrimonious. The advertisements actually provide a better picture of the community than the news columns. In the larger newspapers, telegraphic dispatches were printed, but many of the small papers did not as yet have access to such material. All but a few papers were weeklies. By 1850, however, Detroit had three dailies. In 1857, the Grand Rapids *Eagle* became that city's first daily, and by 1860 eight Michigan newspapers were publishing daily editions. There were three bi-weeklies, one tri-weekly, and ninety-six weekly papers, as well as four religious periodicals and three literary magazines.

The first newspaper in the Upper Peninsula was published in the boom town of Copper Harbor. Called the *Lake Superior News and Miners' Journal,* it started publication on July 11, 1846. The owner, John N. Ingersoll, moved the paper to Sault Ste. Marie in 1847, where it folded in 1849 or 1850. It was succeeded by the *Lake Superior Journal,* first published at Sault Ste. Marie and generally regarded as the progenitor of the present Marquette *Mining Journal.* Another northern Michigan paper was the *Northern Islander,* published on Beaver Island by the Mormon leader, James Strang, from 1850 until Strang's death in 1856.

In addition to newspapers, publications appeared which were devoted to religion, reform, or other special purposes. At different times during the forties and fifties, publications advocating the cause of temperance appeared at Adrian, Jackson, Marshall, and Mount Clemens. Several were founded to cater to readers of literary taste. The Detroit *Evening Spectator and Literary Gazette,* which appeared in 1836 and 1837, and the *Michigan Literary Gem and Parlor Companion,* printed at Kalamazoo around 1841, are examples of this type. Farmers' publications included the *Farmers' Advocate,* published at Kalamazoo in 1841, and the *Michigan Farmer and Western Horticulturist,* issued at Jackson between 1843 and 1847. The *Western Farmer,* which began publication at Detroit on January 20, 1841, was subsequently renamed the *Michigan Farmer* and continues to be published to the present day. The first religious periodical was the *Michigan Christian Herald,* a Baptist journal that started at Detroit in 1842 as a monthly, had a thousand subscribers within a year, and became a weekly by 1845.

*   *   *   *   *

Detroit was not in the front rank of American cities in 1860, but it was a metropolitan center of importance in the Middle West. Trade and manufacturing flourished and the population more than doubled in the 1850s, rising from 21,019 in 1850 to 45,619 in 1860. Such an urban center developed refinements and cultural advantages not enjoyed by those who lived outside. The manufacture of illuminating gas was begun on a small scale in 1850. By 1851 gas lights illuminated the principal streets, and gradually in business places, hotels, and the homes of well-to-do citizens gas lights replaced candles. Kerosene lamps were beginning to appear by 1861, replacing whale-oil lamps and candles in the homes of persons of moderate means. The sewing machine, which was coming into use about 1860, lightened household tasks. Even before the end of the territorial period a water system was in use, the water being conveyed through wooden pipes made by hollowed-out tamarack logs. By 1839 a reservoir holding 422,000 gallons was needed to supply Detroit's needs. The open well and the pump were gradually outmoded. The use of stoves instead of fireplaces for heating was greatly expanded. The bathtub was another household accessory that many of the wealthier Detroiters were installing. Ice for refrigeration must have been used rather extensively, for there were no less than twenty-three ice dealers by 1860.

Along with these improvements in material comforts was a growing interest in cultural, religious, literary, and social affairs. Germans took the leadership in music. The Harmonie Society, a singing organization incorporated in 1852, was primarily a German group, although its membership included non-Germans. Other choral societies had been formed by 1860. The city was visited by musical artists of note, including Theresa Parodi and Adelina Patti. Many bands were formed. There was also a lively interest in the theater. Dramatic productions were presented in the City Hall in 1848, and in the following year the Metropolitan Theater was completed. Travelling players visited the city, although they came in larger numbers after 1865 than in the prewar era. The theater was frowned on by most Protestant churches, a fact that limited its patronage.[43]

Among the portrait painters in Detroit were J. M. Stanley and Alvah Bradish, both of whom were in great demand to reproduce the likenesses of such luminaries as Governor Mason, John Biddle, Senator Cass, and Henry P. Tappan. At an 1853 art exhibition, 419 paintings, 153 engravings, 42 statuaries, and many other art objects owned by artists and private citizens were shown.

For public meetings Detroit boasted at least two halls capable of seating a thousand persons and several with a smaller capacity. Here were heard debates, concerts, and political oratory. Throughout the period the hotel or tavern, with its ever present bar, was a favorite informal meeting place for the men of the population. Although fraternal orders were to attain their greatest popularity after the Civil War, Detroit had several Masonic lodges and at least one Odd Fellow lodge before 1860. In terms of public services, Detroit continued until the very end of the period to rely on volunteer fire-fighting companies. By 1837 there were four such companies; two years later a large hall was erected for them, with rooms for the city council and for public meetings.

In Detroit, as in other cities, the fire companies were social and political groups. It became the fashion to visit other cities and to receive visiting firemen in gala fashion. In 1845 the Ithaca fire laddies were treated to a torchlight procession and a banquet on the occasion of their visit to Detroit. At an annual review and parade the engines were gaily decorated and polished to the highest brilliance, the firemen decked themselves out in their stiff leather helmets, red shirts, and black trousers, and there was a contest to determine which company could throw the largest stream of water highest or furthest. Between the companies competition was fierce. When the members of a fire company reached a conflagration before their hose cart, they often threw a barrel over the hydrant to prevent a rival company from getting water, unless, that is, the rival laddies put up a scrap to attain their end. It was the custom for citizens whose property had been saved to serve refreshments after the fire. Rivalries became so intense as to become a nuisance, and something had to be done about it. In 1860 two steam fire engines were purchased by the city and a paid fire department was organized. Not for several years, however, would the city organize a paid, full-time police force. Although Detroit had had a marshal as early as 1802, merchants and other citizens had relied on privately hired night watchmen to combat any epidemic of thievery or disorder.

The life of the city was punctuated by many events of general interest during these years. At least two presidents of the United States—Martin Van Buren and Millard Fillmore—paid the city a visit and were, of course, received with much fanfare. Elaborate public funerals for prominent citizens were held. In 1845, a public funeral for Andrew Jackson was held in Detroit, even though the former president had died and was buried at his home near Nashville, Tennessee. In the early 1850s the railroad conspiracy trials were the sensation of the hour.

In the smaller cities—Grand Rapids, Jackson, Kalamazoo, Marshall, Battle Creek, Adrian, Monroe, and Saginaw—life took on a somewhat similar pattern but was affected to a greater degree by the rural environment in which they existed. The files of the Kalamazoo *Gazette* for 1854, for example, reflect the interests and concerns of the townspeople of this period. The columns of the paper indicate great interest in prohibition and the slavery issue. A new female seminary was projected. A cyclone leveled several buildings. Four circuses and an "Uncle Tom's Cabin" troupe visited the town that year. The Ladies' Library celebrated its second anniversary. The ninth annual county fair was a huge success. A plowing match, conducted by the County Agricultural Society, was an outstanding event of the year. A local artist was reported to have painted the portraits of two leading citizens. Three fire companies were supported, and Company No. 2 threw a stream of water two hundred feet over the Congregational Church steeple. A big Fourth of July celebration was held. Sunday trains on the railroad were discontinued at the request of the churches. A stage line to Three Rivers was advertised. The Kalamazoo Brass Band, en route to Allegan on its bandwagon, had an accident when the wagon ran off the plank road and overturned. Lucy Stone, champion of women's rights, the author Bayard Taylor, and the New York newspaper editor, Horace Greeley, were announced as speakers on the lyceum course. A doctor was killed when his horse ran away and threw him from his buggy. A new factory to manufacture sash, doors, and blinds was launched. Several "forty-niners" returned from California. Two new hotels were opened.

But we must not forget the people who lived in the country, for they were more numerous than those who lived in cities. Detroit, the state's largest city, contained twenty-six percent of the total population in 1950. In 1850 it accounted for only seven percent of the total. On the farm the rhythm of the seasons and the vagaries of the weather were prime determinants. Each season brought a new set of duties for the farmer and his wife, new opportunities for fun to the youngsters, a different set of diseases and ailments to combat, and a new assortment of foods for the table. Spring meant plowing and sowing to the farmer, housecleaning and fresh vegetables for the kitchen to his wife, "school's out" and fishing to the boys, unless they happened to be unfortunate enough to catch the chicken pox, mumps, measles, or whooping cough. In summer came the haying and harvesting, the hardest work of the year. Usually, however, the Fourth of July was taken off as a pleasant interruption, and the whole family climbed aboard a wagon for a trip to a nearby town where political oratory, fireworks, greased-pig and pie-eating contests, and a barbecue commemorated the late unpleasantness with John Bull. Summer had its delights as well as its hard work. Late June was strawberry time, July brought raspberries, and about the first of August that most succulent of all American delicacies, the roasted ear of corn, began to appear on the farmer's table. Watermelons and wild berries were not far behind, only sometimes these were not eaten at the table. All this was delightful if no one in the house got the "summer complaint," the fever and ague, or one of the other common summer diseases. At least one should be well enough in August to go to camp meeting and visit one's neighbors.

Then came the autumn, with its crisp morning air, the haze of eventide, and the glory of the colors on the foliage of the trees. Now the corn was to be cut, shocked, and husked, the potatoes, beans, pumpkins, squash, and cabbage harvested and stored away in the cellar, apples picked, and cider and apple butter made. All through the summer and fall the housewife made preserves, jellies, and jams, dried apples and peaches, and cared for the vegetable garden. If she had an eye for beauty she would also find time to grow some flowers. In the fall the children of the family went to school, usually walking from one to four miles morning and night and carrying lunch in a pail. Election day and Thanksgiving were holidays universally observed. Finally winter came, with bitter cold and drifting snow often isolating the farmstead for weeks. But with plenty of potatoes, meat, vegetables, and other foodstuffs on hand there was no need to worry about provender. The farmer kept busy tending his livestock and cutting wood. If he was a wise and careful man he would have at least one and usually two winters' supply of wood on hand, neatly corded near the kitchen door. When the snow came the sleighs were brought out and the family could be carried to church or to a neighbor's house in brave fashion. Your appreciation of the snow varied in direct ratio to your age, but there was no escaping it for anyone, as there is now, by running off to a warmer clime.

Except in the north country, rural areas were not so isolated as they had been in the territorial period. The railroads, plank roads, and telegraph lines connected the hinterland with the outside world. The farmer did not get a daily paper nor was his mail delivered. Still, he had close neighbors and visiting was much in vogue. The homes of the less strictly religious folk resounded to the music of the fiddle. While the young folks danced, the older ones talked endlessly of crops, politics, or neighborhood events. Revival meetings in the schoolhouse or church, spelling bees, and singing schools were occasions for community gatherings.

A tiny village with two or three stores, a church, a school, a sawmill, a gristmill, and a post office was usually found in each township. In cases where a railroad was built through the village, there were high hopes for growth. A modest hotel would be built, and certain types of specialty stores would appear. Those towns not so fortunate grew less vigorously.

Although Michigan had come a long way out of the wilderness by 1860, vast areas of the state were still covered by unbroken forests and isolated hamlets, and a large proportion of the farm houses were often out of touch with the outside world for months at a time. Rail lines, plank roads, and telegraph wire were remote from many Michigan homes. In spite of improved transportation, the world beyond still seemed strange and remote for many Michiganians. But it was coming closer.

14

MICHIGAN LEADS THE WAY IN EDUCATION

Throughout much of the nineteenth century, Michigan was a leader in the field of public education. Probably no state so successfully carried out the purpose set forth in the Northwest Ordinance that "schools and the means of education shall forever be encouraged." The Catholepistemiad, impractical though it was, had envisioned a comprehensive system of education, reaching from the primary grades to higher education. The completely centralized control of education provided under the act of 1817 was abandoned by the territory a decade later in favor of a totally decentralized approach. But then the 1835 constitution called for a return to a more comprehensive public education concept, with the state exercising a certain degree of supervision over the implementation of this concept.

In the convention that drafted that constitution, a committee headed by Isaac E. Crary of Marshall was appointed to prepare the article on education. Crary was born in Connecticut in 1804, and had graduated from Trinity College. He studied law and was admitted to practice. Apparently he had achieved an excellent reputation in his home state before he came to settle in Marshall and practice law in the early 1830s. He was often referred to by the title of "General," the office to which he was appointed in the territorial militia. His election as delegate to the constitutional convention indicates that he was highly esteemed by his fellow townsmen. One of these was a preacher, the Rev. John D. Pierce, a fellow New Englander, and, like Crary, a man well-educated for his time. The story goes that these two men, sitting under an oak tree, planned Michigan's educational system.[1]

Crary and Pierce were much impressed by a translation of Victor Cousin's report on the Prussian school system. They agreed that Michigan's school system, like Prussia's, should be centralized and controlled by a responsible official. Cousin described an educational system that was logical and complete, extending from the lowest grades through a university and co-ordinated by a central body. Curiously enough, this was almost the same system envisioned by Judge Woodward in his plan of 1817. It was also the sort of plan Thomas Jefferson advocated and sought in vain for Virginia to adopt.

Article X of the Constitution of 1835, as drafted by Crary's committee and adopted by the convention, provided for the superintendent of public instruction to be appointed by the governor. The legislature of New York had created the office of state school superintendent in that state as early as 1812, but had abolished it as a separate office in 1821, assigning the duties to the secretary of state. Several other states had also made the secretary of state responsible for schools. Maryland had provided for a state-school officer in 1826, and then had repealed the act in 1828. No other state in the union in 1837 had provided for a superintendent of public instruction in its constitution.[2]

The article included provisions designed to safeguard the lands the federal government would grant the state for education and to prevent the use of the proceeds to be derived from them for other purposes. Schools were to be conducted for at least three months out of the year. The legislature was given the duty of establishing township libraries as soon as circumstances permitted. The article foresaw the foundation of a state university "with such branches as the public convenience may hereafter demand," but it left to the legislature the decisions related to the establishment and government of such a university.

At the conclusion of the convention, the delegates, at Crary's suggestion, adopted a petition requesting that instead of turning over section sixteen in each township to the township for the support of its schools—as had been done in Ohio, Indiana, and Illinois when these states were admitted to the Union—Congress should grant these sections to the state of Michigan, the proceeds to be placed in a state school fund. The interest from this fund was to be distributed among the schools. When the constitution was ratified, Crary was elected as Michigan's first member of the national House of Representatives. He was not permitted to take his seat until the border dispute with Ohio was settled but was able to exert his influence to persuade Congress to approve the constitutional convention's petition and to grant the sixteenth sections to the state rather than to the townships in which they were located. The act became effective when Michigan was finally admitted. Partly due to this innovation Michigan realized far more income from the sale of these sections than did any other state in the Old Northwest.[3]

The total grant of land to Michigan, consisting of section sixteen in each township, amounted to over a million acres. The disposal of the lands and the management of the school fund (called the Primary School Fund) were first entrusted to the superintendent of public instruction. Then in 1842 the sale of the sections was transferred to a state land office. The legislature at first set a minimum price of $8.00 an acre on the school lands, but the depression of the late thirties impelled the lawmakers to reduce that figure repeatedly. Some of the proceeds were poorly invested and losses were suffered on this account. By 1850 it had become the practice to "loan" to the state the proceeds from the school lands in return for which the legislature each year appropriated to the Primary School Fund an amount equal to what the interest would have been if the fund had been invested. Up to the year 1886, by which time about three-quarters of the sections had been sold, the average price realized was $4.58 an acre. This was less than was originally hoped, but in contrast, the average price realized from school lands in Illinois was $3.78, in Indiana $3.69, and in Wisconsin less than $2.00.[4]

It had become the practice of Congress to grant to the states, at the time of their admission to the Union, other public lands, usually seventy-two sections, for the support of a university. As early as 1826 Congress had authorized the selection of these lands in Michigan. Accordingly, some of the finest land in the southern counties was reserved from sale. It became the property of the state at the time Michigan was admitted to the Union in 1837. The story of the disposal of these lands resembles that of the school lands: high hopes, then the coming of hard times, constant pressure on the legislature to reduce the price per acre (originally set at $20), and finally the surrender of the lawmakers to this pressure. Still, the university lands, while yielding a smaller return than had been expected, at an average of almost $12.00 an acre, brought more than twice that received for any other educational grant in the Old Northwest.

In addition to the income derived from the sales of section sixteen in each township and the university lands, Michigan's educational system benefitted from other federal land grants. At the time Michigan entered the Union, Congress granted to the state (as was customary) all salt springs and lands adjacent thereto in the state, and no less than seventy-two sections. There was a proviso that these lands could be leased but not sold; however, their sale was permitted under an act passed in 1847. The legislature, during the years that followed, appropriated the proceeds from twenty-five of these sections as an endowment for Michigan State Normal School, twenty-five sections to pay for the erection of the Michigan Asylum at Kalamazoo, and twenty-two sections to purchase a site and erect buildings for the State Agricultural College. In 1850 a large grant of swamp lands was made to Michigan and other states. In the case of Michigan it has been asserted that these were identified in the spring of the year when many lands were overflowed; at any rate, much excellent land was thus obtained. In 1858 the legislature designated fifty percent of the proceeds from these lands for the Primary School Fund. The remainder was used largely for grants to encourage the building of railroads, but 6,921 acres were given to the Agricultural College. And in 1862 Michigan received an additional 240,000 acres under the terms of the Morrill Act, passed by Congress to encourage education in agriculture and the mechanical arts. The proceeds from the sale of these lands, of course, went to the Agricultural College.

The significance of these federal land grants for education can hardly be overestimated. The development of a public school system would have been greatly retarded without them. Although the amount received each year was pitifully small, it was enough to encourage many districts to establish schools that might otherwise have neglected them for a long time. And without the federal land grants it is almost certain that neither the University of Michigan, Michigan State Normal School, nor Michigan Agricultural College would have been established until much later, if at all.

If Isaac E. Crary may be credited with being primarily responsible for laying the foundations of the Michigan system of education, John D. Pierce must receive equal credit for having been the organizer of that system. Crary was absent in Washington as a member of Congress during much of the crucial six-year period following 1835. It was upon the suggestion of Crary that Governor Mason appointed Pierce in 1836 as first superintendent of public instruction. Pierce is a neglected figure in histories of education in the United States. Historians have stressed the work of Horace Mann as secretary of the State Board of Education in Massachusetts and that of Henry Barnard, who held a similar post in Connecticut. Because Massachusetts and Connecticut were older states, Mann and Barnard undoubtedly had more national influence than Pierce did. But Pierce was, nevertheless, the real pioneer in setting up a state system of education. Not only was he the first state-school official appointed on the basis of a constitutional provision, but he also formulated his plan for Michigan's educational system two years before Mann issued his famous first annual report. Pierce started publication of his *Journal of Education* almost a year before Mann published the first issue of his *Common School Journal*.[5]

Born in New Hampshire in 1797, Pierce was taken at the age of two years, following the death of his father, to work on a Massachusetts farm. He had little formal schooling, but somehow acquired a passion for books. A meager inheritance from his grandfather gave him the opportunity to enter Brown University in 1818. Pierce financed much of his education by school teaching and graduated from Brown in 1822. He studied theology at Princeton and was licensed to preach as a Congregational minister. After serving for a time as pastor of a church in New York, Pierce was appointed as a missionary by the American Home Missionary Society, which in 1831 sent him to Michigan where he settled at Marshall, which then contained only two shanties and a partly finished log house. Using this as the center of his activities, he rode horseback to minister to many scattered pioneer communities. When Marshall was visited by the terrible cholera epidemic in 1832, his wife was one of the victims. But Pierce continued his work and saw Marshall become a boom town on the Territorial Road in the period of the great land rush. It was his association in Marshall with Isaac E. Crary that stimulated his interest in education.

The constitution provided only the framework of a system of education, and it became the responsibility of Pierce to propose to the legislature the steps that should be taken to carry out the provisions of the constitution. Before drawing up his plan Pierce made a trip to the East, where he conferred with leaders in the field of education and attended a national education meeting in Worcester, Massachusetts. He also visited Ohio, attending an annual meeting of the College of Professional Teachers, an organization founded in 1831 by teachers of the West. Pierce also carried on an extensive correspondence with educational leaders throughout the nation. He was determined to equip himself with a knowledge of the best educational practices of the day and to become acquainted with the experience of other states before drawing up his plans for Michigan. When the legislature convened in January, 1837, Pierce was ready with his proposals.[6]

On March 18 and 20, 1837, Governor Mason signed three bills that had been passed by the legislature to translate into law the recommendations made by Pierce. These acts achieved many but not all of Pierce's goals. For example, he urged a system of tax-supported public schools in which no primary-school pupil would be required to pay tuition. This was not provided in the acts of 1837, and not until 1869 did the legislature require all public primary schools to be free, although some were free prior to that date. Pierce also proposed that each teacher be required to have had a "regular course of training" and that schools be required to pay teachers a minimum wage in order to be eligible to receive aid from the Primary School Fund. He also suggested the desirability of compulsory education. In this, too, Pierce was far ahead of his time, and the laws enacted by the legislature did not make such provisions.[7]

One of the three bills signed by Governor Mason dealt with the organization of primary schools. It provided for the establishment of school districts in each township. Each district was to have a moderator, a director, and an assessor, and there were to be three school inspectors in each township. The income from the Primary School Fund was to be apportioned among the schools in proportion to the number of pupils between the ages of five and seventeen in each. School districts were authorized to pay taxes for the support of schools. Each district that voted a tax for a "suitable library case" and spent $10 a year for the purchase of books was to receive a share in the proceeds from "fines, breaches of the penal laws, and exemption from military duty." Regular reports from each district to the superintendent of public instruction were required. The law did not make it mandatory for schools to be established; the initiative was left to the people of the several townships. The superintendent of public instruction was given the responsibility for taking charge of all school and university lands that had been granted to the state, disposing of these lands according to law, and investing the monies arising from their sale. He was to apportion the proceeds from these funds and to submit an annual report.[8]

The second measure enacted dealt with the University of Michigan. Its purpose was "to provide the inhabitants of the State with the means of acquiring a thorough knowledge of the various branches of literature, science and the arts." Its government was to be under a Board of Regents consisting of twelve members to be appointed by the governor, with the lieutenant governor, supreme court judges, and the state chancellor as *ex-officio* members. The university was to include three departments: literature, science and the arts; law; and medicine. There was to be an admission fee of $10.00, but tuition was to be free to all residents of the state. The third bill signed by Governor Mason provided for the location of the University of Michigan in Ann Arbor. The incentive for this was a gift by the Ann Arbor Land Company of forty acres of land on which the university buildings were to be erected.

The most unique feature of the law establishing the state university was its provision for branches. The establishment of "such branches as the public convenience may hereafter demand" had been specified in the Constitution of 1835. The idea of branches was strongly advocated by Crary, and Pierce fully concurred. The purposes of the branches appear to have been fourfold. In the first place, each branch was to have a "female department." At that time coeducation beyond the elementary school was generally frowned on, yet it was recognized that a certain amount of advanced schooling for young women was desirable. In actual practice in the branches, young men and women attended the same classes even though a separate "female department" was maintained. Second, each branch under the original law was to have an agriculture department, though this was later changed to provide for such a department in at least one branch. The great movement for schools to teach agriculture and mechanical arts was to come about twenty years later. That Pierce should have conceived of special education in agriculture at this early date is further evidence of his farsightedness; however, so far as is known, no agriculture department was started in any of the branches. Third, each branch was to serve as a teacher-training school. Pierce placed heavy emphasis on the need for the education of teachers. Finally, the branches were designed to prepare men to enter the university. There were very few preparatory schools in the state and very few young men were qualified for studies of a college grade. Hence the branches were opened before the university proper in order to provide a student body for the latter. The plan appears to have been for students to undertake some studies at the collegiate level in the branches so that when the university was opened it might have men prepared to enter at the upper class level. The records show that when the university opened in Ann Arbor in 1841 some men already prepared in the branches were admitted as sophomores.

Pierce's plan thus embodied the establishment of elementary schools in the school districts through local initiative, the state university as the capstone of the system, and the branches as intermediary schools under the control of the University Board of Regents. When Pierce formulated his plan almost all higher education in the nation was provided in church-related colleges. Some state universities had been created, but they had tended to fall prey to sectarian and political rivalries. The predominant institution for secondary education was the private academy, which was often church-related. In Michigan a few academies had been started during the territorial period, one of these being the Michigan and Huron Institute, chartered in 1833 and opened in Kalamazoo in 1836. Its chief backers were Baptists. The Methodists had also manifested a desire to establish an academy. Pierce himself was closely associated with a project for the establishment of a Presbyterian college in Marshall. But his study of the experience of other states had convinced him by 1837 of the folly of permitting a host of colleges to be chartered, few if any with sufficient resources to provide adequate buildings, equipment, or instructional staff. He concluded that Michigan should concentrate all its resources in the building up of a great state university. He therefore counselled the legislature in his report of 1837 against granting college charters to private institutions. He was willing to permit the denominations to establish academies, but insisted it would be the best policy to confine the power of granting academic degrees to the state university.[9]

Pierce's plans for secondary schools began to be implemented when the University of Michigan regents held their first meeting in November, 1837. At that time no less than seventeen towns applied for the establishment of branches, but only eight were approved. At subsequent meetings the regents authorized eight more branches. Out of sixteen authorized, nine were opened, operated for varying lengths of time, and rendered reports at Pontiac, Monroe, Kalamazoo, Detroit, Niles, White Pigeon, Tecumseh, Ann Arbor, and Romeo. At almost all these places local interest in education had been evidenced by the establishment of an academy, and the branch simply took its place. In Kalamazoo a working arrangement was made with the trustees of the Kalamazoo Literary Institute under which the institute and the branch were merged. The course of study in the branches was prescribed by the regents. Appropriations were made for their support from university funds. The total attendance in all the branches never exceeded 315, a figure reached in 1842–43, with 243 men and 72 women enrolled. Because of decreasing revenues, the regents found they could not continue the support of the branches as well as maintain the university. Annual appropriations for the branches were reduced and in 1846 were entirely withdrawn. Several branches continued to operate thereafter at the expense of the local communities and with tuition fees collected from the students. Most of the branches became private academies chartered by the legislature.

The abandonment of state support for the branches brought considerable protest. In some quarters they were regarded as more useful than the university itself. In an act passed in 1851 which reorganized the University of Michigan, the regents were directed, as soon as the university funds would permit, to organize a branch in each judicial circuit of the state and to appropriate not more than $1,500 per year for its support. This was never done, however, presumably because the regents never thought they had sufficient funds. The attempt made through the branch system to centralize the control and management of secondary education in the hands of the university regents thus ended in failure.[10]

The severe economic depression that hit Michigan soon after the establishment of the school system devised by Pierce resulted in a retreat from the provisions of the 1837 laws. In 1839 the legislature deprived the school districts of the right to tax, and the expense of maintaining schools over and above the amount received from the Primary School Fund was placed upon the parents of the pupils. The report of the superintendent of public instruction for 1842 shows that only sixty-four percent of the districts had maintained a school for three months or more during the year, and that thirty-two percent had supported no school at all. The following year the legislature gave the school districts the power to tax at a rate of no more than one mill on each dollar of assessed valuation, beginning in 1845. In the years that followed, however, the maximum was gradually increased. By 1850 the sum of $128,189.45 was raised throughout the state by district school taxes, while a total of $32,318.75 was paid by parents in the form of "rate bills," or tuition fees.

By 1860 a total of 4,087 school districts had been formed in Michigan and the number of teachers was 7,921. Even though not all schools were free, seventy-five percent of the children between the ages of four and eighteen attended the public schools in 1860. Often, however, the school terms were much shorter than they are today.

In the cities and larger towns additional school districts were formed as the population grew. In 1843 the legislature authorized the creation of "union school districts," which made it possible for municipalities to combine their school districts into a single district. This act also authorized the classification of pupils in such districts "according to their proficiency and advancement in learning." At the time this law was passed, Michigan had only two incorporated cities: Detroit and Monroe, and twenty-three incorporated villages and towns. But the number grew rapidly. Where a union school district was formed, a large "union school" was built to replace several one-room schools. And in these union schools the students were divided into grades. Detroit organized its schools into a single district in 1842 under a special act passed in that year by the legislature especially for that city; an act which also authorized Detroit to become the first Michigan community to achieve the goal of eliminating tuition and making its schools free to all students residing in the city. Jonesville was the first town to establish a union school district under the statewide law of 1843. By 1859 about thirty union school districts had been formed. In some of these an "academic department," or high school, had developed—just how many is not known. Detroit's union school established such an "academic department" in 1848, and this may have been the first high school in Michigan. In 1859 the legislature passed an act specifically authorizing any district containing more than two hundred children to establish a high school, and to vote a tax which would support it. The constitutionality of this law was not settled, however, until 1874.[11]

Although the larger towns and cities had graded schools by 1860, the vast majority of schools were still conducted in a single room, where children ranging from five to sixteen or older recited their lessons. Pupils were usually equipped with a spelling book, a reader, an arithmetic text, and a geography book. The prevalent notion was that boys in particular were "a convincing illustration of Calvin's idea of total depravity." Various types of punishment, such as sitting with the girls, standing on one leg, or a thorough lacing with the teacher's beech or birch rod, were in common use to keep the boys in order. Spelling bees, singing schools, and quilting parties were held in the schoolhouse in the evenings, making it a kind of neighborhood center.[12] Teachers in these schools were often poorly prepared, although gifted or "natural" teachers were not uncommon. To many, teaching school was a part-time occupation. Candidates for teaching positions were examined by the inspectors of a school district with such varying standards as may be readily imagined. There was no requirement of advanced training, and most teachers had no more than a common school education. Women came more and more to dominate the teaching profession, the ratio in 1860 being about one man to two women. Men were preferred for the winter term when the older boys, freed from work on the farm, attended schools. School terms were short, often being confined entirely to the winter months.

*   *   *   *   *

The University of Michigan was opened in Ann Arbor in 1841. In that year a main building (named for Stevens T. Mason), four faculty houses, and a president's home were completed. The first faculty consisted of two men who had taught in the branches: the Rev. George P. Williams, professor of mathematics, and the Rev. Joseph Whiting, professor of languages. Six students were enrolled the first day. Only the "literary department" was operated until 1850, when a medical department was opened. The law department did not come into existence until 1859.

During its first decade, the university was torn by dissension and beset by problems that threatened its existence. The regents justified their decision to open the university proper at the cost of continuing to provide adequate support for the branches by questioning whether it was legal to use funds derived from the federal land grant to support the branches. Nevertheless, their decision was anything but popular. A bitter controversy also arose over fraternities in the university. The several religious bodies in the state were insistent on having their influence felt. Because the first Board of Regents had not included any clerical members, the university was accused by church people of being "ungodly." To meet this criticism the regents were careful to choose faculty members from different churches. The four faculty houses were designated respectively for the Presbyterian, Methodist, Baptist, and Episcopal professors, and each of the four served successively as president of the university for a one-year period. This deprived the institution of continuing leadership. Enrollment declined in the later 1840s.

When the Constitutional Convention of 1850 met, the university was clearly facing a crisis. To meet the situation the delegates made some drastic changes in the provisions for the university in the new constitution. For one thing, they made the regents an elective rather than an appointive body. They provided for the selection by the regents of a president of the university on a permanent basis, and made the president *ex officio* the presiding officer of the Board of Regents. Finally, and most important of all, they made the regents a body corporate, and gave them complete authority over the university and the expenditure of its funds. This was done, in all probability, to get the university "out of politics," and to prevent legislative interference in university affairs. During the decade of the fifties, the university enjoyed a most remarkable growth and by the end of the decade it had become probably the most successful state university in America. Because of this fact it became almost a university tradition that the success of the institution stemmed directly from the provisions in the Constitution of 1850. The extent to which such a belief may be justified is open to some question; certainly the success of the university was due in no small measure to the quality of the man selected as president. But the idea that an elected governing board, of which the university president was *ex officio* chairman, and freedom from legislative control were responsible for the growth and prosperity of the university was firmly established.

In 1852 the regents appointed to the presidency Henry Philip Tappan of New York, a Presbyterian minister, a distinguished scholar, and a man with firm ideas of how a university should be built. He was an ardent admirer of the German universities and favored modeling the University of Michigan after them. This meant heavy emphasis on high scholarship. He did not believe that progress lay along the line advocated by some American educators, that of introducing "practical" subjects into the curriculum. Rather, he stressed scholarship and science. He refused to give primary consideration to church connections in appointing faculty members, but based his choices largely on ability and scholarship. He made important additions to the library and built an observatory. Beginning in 1855, civil engineering was taught. Michigan was the first university after Harvard to inaugurate instruction in technical fields. Enrollment in both the medical department and the department of literature, science, and the arts increased rapidly as the university gained confidence and prestige. The law department was opened in 1859 with an enrollment of ninety-two students. Under Tappan's leadership the University of Michigan, which in its early years had been little more than a liberal arts college, became the leader among state universities in America.

In spite of this, Tappan aroused a great deal of opposition. Some thought his bearing was haughty and aristocratic and because he used the broad "r" of the easterner in his speech he was accused of putting on airs. There was resentment of his fondness for German universities and agitation for more "practical" studies in the curriculum. The farmers of the state were demanding an agricultural college as a separate farmer's college, while Tappan wanted it to be a part of the university. Temperance advocates criticized him for serving wine at his table. Tappan seems to have made every effort to avoid criticism from the various denominations and was so "undenominational" that opposition developed to him in his own local Presbyterian church. He was distrusted by rabid antislavery people because he was not an avowed abolitionist. Another of his policies that antagonized certain powerful ecclesiastical organizations was his opposition to the chartering of denominational colleges. Finally in 1863 he was forced to resign, "stung to death by gnats," as an able successor put it.[13]

By 1860 Michigan had established two additional state educational institutions: the State Normal School and the Michigan Agricultural College. As early as 1789 American educators had suggested the need for teacher-training courses in existing colleges or in separate schools. Normal schools had been in existence in

Europe for over a century. In 1836 Ohio sent Calvin E. Stowe to visit European, and particularly Prussian, schools. Upon his return Stowe published a report that was widely circulated throughout the nation and that contained a full description of the Prussian teachers' seminaries. Horace Mann, Henry Barnard, and John D. Pierce had all strongly emphasized the importance of thorough preparation for teaching. In 1847 Governor Alpheus Felch in his message to the legislature of Michigan proposed the establishment of a normal school. Bills were introduced for the creation of a separate department in the university for the training of teachers, and also for setting up teachers' institutes, but they failed to pass. In his 1848 report, Superintendent of Public Instruction Ira Mayhew opposed a single normal school, favoring instead teachers' institutes and the training of teachers in the union schools. Nevertheless, a bill for the establishment of a separate normal school was introduced by the House Committee on Education, and it became law on March 28, 1849. This law appropriated ten of the seventy-two sections of salt-spring lands granted to Michigan by Congress for a building fund for the normal school, and another fifteen sections for endowment, the income from which was to pay the salary of instructors in the school. The management of the institution was given to a State Board of Education and thus was entirely separated from the University of Michigan. The board was to consist of three members appointed by the governor with the approval of the senate, with the lieutenant governor and the superintendent of public instruction serving as *ex officio* members. The Constitution of 1850, however, eliminated the lieutenant governor as a member of the board and provided that the three regular members should be elected rather than appointed.

After receiving bids from several communities, the new board decided to locate the school at Ypsilanti. There is no indication that the board, in choosing the site, felt any concern about the fact that it was located less than a dozen miles from the state university. Normal schools were not regarded as being in the same category as colleges and universities. Students with only a common school education were ordinarily admitted to such schools in the East. However, in later years, as the normal school expanded its curriculum until it became Eastern Michigan University, the decision made at the time of its founding created serious identity problems for the new university when the inevitable comparisons were made between it and its close and world famous neighbor just down the road in Ann Arbor.

A three-story building was erected in Ypsilanti at a cost of $15,200, and it was dedicated on October 5, 1852. A teacher's institute lasting four weeks was held the same year, but the opening of the first regular term was delayed until March 29, 1853. When Michigan State Normal School was founded, only three states had such schools, and Michigan was the first state west of the Alleghenies to establish such a school.[14]

While the state normal school was being established, agitation grew for an agricultural college. At that time there was no such thing anywhere in America as a state agricultural college. Farmer's College at College Hill, Ohio, six miles from Cincinnati, seems to have been the first college-level agricultural school. It was founded in 1833 but soon passed out of existence. Soon, however, a national movement had emerged seeking the creation of colleges for farmers. In Michigan, the State Agricultural Society, organized in 1849, demanded that something be done for the education of farmers. The framers of Michigan's second constitution in 1850 empowered the legislature to found a school of agriculture as a branch of the university. But there is evidence that farm leaders wanted a separate college.

Both the university and the normal school arranged a series of lectures on agriculture and invited the State Agricultural Society to send a committee to inspect the teaching being done. Both schools were obviously eager to receive the twenty-two sections of salt-spring lands that the 1850 constitution had set aside for an agricultural school. The agricultural society's committee that visited both institutions reported favorably on what they had heard. But they urged that a farm be provided for experimental and demonstration work, and concluded by recommending a separate school. This became the settled policy of the society.

A large majority of the farmers in the state became adherents of the Republican party, which was organized at Jackson in 1854. When the Republicans elected their candidates for governor and the principal state offices, as well as a majority of the legislature, farm leaders redoubled their efforts to secure the establishment of a separate agricultural college. By an act approved on February 12, 1855, the Michigan Agricultural College was created, and its location was designated as a site within ten miles of Lansing. It received the twenty-two sections of salt-spring lands and a considerable grant of swamp lands located within the sections adjoining the school. A site was selected and a building was completed in 1857. In May of that year instruction began with an initial enrollment of eighty-one students. Students worked about four hours per day on the college farm. The first president was Joseph R. Williams of Constantine, and the supervision of the institution was entrusted to the State Board of Education.

For more than a decade agitation continued to have the new agricultural college attached to the university. Letters pro and con appeared in the Detroit newspapers. Farm leaders, however, persisted in favoring an independent status. This was confirmed in 1861 by a law that removed the college from the control of the State Board of Education and placed it under the supervision of a State Board of Agriculture, consisting of six members appointed by the governor.

As early as 1850 the Michigan legislature had asked Congress for a grant of an additional three townships of land for the university, probably with the intent of using the proceeds for teaching agriculture. But the time was not ripe for Congress to take such a step. The father of the movement for land grants for agricultural education was Jonathan B. Turner. A native of Massachusetts, he had been educated at Yale and had been on the faculty of Jacksonville College in Illinois from 1833 to 1848. In the latter year he became a farmer and fruit grower, a speaker at farmers' meetings, and an eloquent advocate of agricultural education. The demand for a congressional land grant grew under his leadership to nationwide proportions. A bill proposed by Congressman Justin S. Morrill of Vermont for a land grant to the states for agricultural colleges was passed by Congress in 1859, but President Buchanan vetoed it. Three years later, during the darkest days of the Civil War, a similar measure was enacted, and President Lincoln signed it into law on July 2, 1862. The states were to use the proceeds from the grant to promote education for farmers and mechanics. Under the provisions of the Morrill Act, Michigan received 240,000 acres of land, and this placed Michigan Agricultural College on a firm financial footing. Only three states—Pennsylvania, Iowa, and Michigan—had founded agricultural colleges before the Morrill Act became law, and of these Michigan was the first.[15]

Among privately supported institutions, Kalamazoo College was the first denominational college to be established in Michigan. Chartered in 1833 as the Michigan and Huron Institute, it was opened in 1836. Its name was changed soon afterward to the Kalamazoo Literary Institute, and in 1855 it became Kalamazoo College. Members of the Methodist Episcopal church had secured a charter in 1835 for a school at Spring Arbor, but it failed to materialize. Instead, they decided to accept an offer to come to Albion. Here the Wesleyan Seminary—later to become Albion College—opened its doors in 1842. John J. Shipherd, a Congregationalist and founder of Oberlin College in Ohio, came to Michigan in the lush days of the middle 1830s and planned to establish a school in the backwoods on the Grand River near the present site of Lansing. With the coming of hard times his plan went awry, but he returned in 1843 determined to found a college in Eaton County. The following year he brought a colony of settlers to the spot he selected and a school was soon started. It was called Olivet Institute. At first the legislature appears to have been reluctant to grant a charter, possibly due to the reputation Oberlin had of being a hotbed of abolitionism and other reforms. Olivet was incorporated as an academy in 1848.

In 1845 Wesleyan Methodists opened a school at Leoni, a few miles east of Jackson, and at about the same time another Methodist denomination—the Methodist Protestants—appears to have opened a "seminary" in the same place. Shortly thereafter the two denominations apparently merged their efforts under the name "Michigan Union College." In 1859 the students and faculty loaded their possessions on wagons and moved to Adrian, where the school was reopened as Adrian College. Members of another small sect, the Freewill Baptists, in 1844 opened a school at Spring Arbor, where the Methodists originally had planned to locate their educational institution. The next year a charter was granted by the legislature under the name Michigan Central College. Although it was at first denied the right to confer degrees, this power was granted in 1850. Five years later, this school was moved to Hillsdale and became Hillsdale College. Michigan Central College was the first institution in Michigan to confer a regular academic degree on a woman.

Up to 1855 none of these five schools, with the exception of Michigan Central College, was given the right to grant degrees by the legislature. Although they occasionally deviated from the policy advocated by John D. Pierce of confining the degree-granting power to the University of Michigan, the lawmakers in the main adhered to it. President Tappan of the University of Michigan strongly favored it. Leading figures in the churches that had established schools sought in vain for college powers. Most of these Protestant leaders supported the newly formed Republican party. Early in 1855, when the Republicans took over the governorship and control of the legislature, friends of the denominational schools flocked to Lansing seeking legislative approval to become colleges. President Tappan contended in vain against them. The Baptists secured an amendment to their 1833 charter, changing the name of their school to Kalamazoo College and giving it the power to grant degrees. A general college law also was enacted, providing that any school that met certain requirements might become a college. The delay in granting college status undoubtedly retarded the development of independent church-related colleges in Michigan, and gave state institutions a head start. This may be a partial explanation of the fact that Michigan in the twentieth century has a far larger proportion of its college students enrolled in tax-supported institutions than most other states.

The five church-related schools so far mentioned, Kalamazoo, Albion, Olivet, Adrian, and Hillsdale, have continued to provide education for Michigan youth to the present day. There were, however, many abortive college enterprises during the period from 1835 to 1860. In 1839 Presbyterians established Marshall College. Ironically, when he first came to Michigan, John D. Pierce, who came to actively oppose the granting of charters to denominational colleges, had been a backer of the movement for a Presbyterian college in Michigan. In spite of his subsequent opposition, a college charter was obtained, and on the same day a charter giving the right to grant degrees was approved for St. Philip's College, under Catholic auspices, to be situated near Detroit. Marshall College was given a considerable amount of land, but the decline of land values after 1837 so depleted its resources that the college failed after a few years. St. Philip's was opened and operated for a few years, but its buildings were lost in a fire in 1842 and the college expired with them. The legislature in 1850 once more departed from the policy backed by Pierce and granted two college charters. One of these was to Michigan Central College and the other was to St. Mark's College at Grand Rapids, an enterprise backed by the Episcopal Church. This institution opened the same year but never offered studies above the preparatory level, expiring after about two and a half years. The United Brethren Church opened a college at Leoni in 1859, using the buildings formerly occupied by the predecessor of Adrian College. This school continued to operate under the name Michigan Union College until 1872.

An unusual school was founded a few miles northeast of Adrian by Mrs. Laura Haviland, a Quaker woman later to achieve widespread fame as a leader of the movement to spirit slaves from the South to freedom in Canada. In 1836 she started "Raisin Institute" as a manual-labor school for dependent children. In 1839 the school was raised to the preparatory level, and was opened to students of both sexes, colored as well as white. Raisin Institute received a charter from the legislature in 1847. It operated somewhat spasmodically until 1863, when it was reincorporated as the Raisin Valley Seminary and came under the auspices of the Adrian Quarterly Meeting of the Society of Friends. It continued to operate as an academy until after 1900.

Boys and girls attended primary schools together, and coeducation was actually the rule in most of the academies, although a number of them theoretically segregated the girls into what was usually called a "female department." Michigan Central College was the only institution in Michigan to grant a regular academic degree to a woman prior to the Civil War. Among educational leaders in the state there was considerable support for coeducation, but popular prejudice against it beyond the elementary level is evident. Each of the branches had a "female department," and after the branch system ceased to receive support from the university regents there was a movement to establish a separate state educational institution for women. An effort was made in 1855 to persuade the legislature to create such a school and to allot it a portion of the swamp lands that had been granted to the state by Congress. This effort failed, probably because opinion was divided between those who favored separate schools for women and those who believed in coeducation. With little hope that women would be admitted to the university, those who were interested in education for women turned to the establishment of private seminaries and colleges.

Prior to 1855 a number of female seminaries had been established. An "Association for the promotion of female education" had been incorporated by Detroiters as early as 1830, and separate schools for girls had been chartered in at least five other places by 1855. The founders of the schools for women opened immediately after 1855 probably hoped to secure state aid in the form of a portion of the swamp lands. The Michigan Female College was founded in Lansing by Miss Abigail Rogers in September, 1855, and the following month the Marshall Female Seminary was launched. In 1856 the Michigan Female Seminary was incorporated by members of the Presbyterian church and others in Kalamazoo. In spite of the fact that state aid was not obtained, these institutions performed a useful function. Miss Rogers' college endured until 1871, the buildings originally erected for it being obtained subsequently for a State School for the Blind. The Marshall Female Seminary lasted only four years, but the Michigan Female Seminary in Kalamazoo, which was opened in 1857, continued to operate for forty years. A Catholic seminary for girls was opened at Monroe in 1847. Meanwhile, most of the denominational colleges maintained a "female department" or "female college," some of them granting the degree "Mistress of Arts."

Both men and women students attended Michigan State Normal School from its beginning in 1852. After the Civil War the cause of coeducation triumphed, and women students were admitted to Michigan Agricultural College and the University of Michigan in 1870. The denominational colleges quickly abandoned, in most cases, their separate schools for girls and became coeducational soon thereafter.

Underground railroad station, Union City, Michigan

15

POLITICS IN
MID-NINETEENTH-CENTURY
MICHIGAN

Politics! You could hear men talking politics everywhere—in taverns, in front of the meetinghouses on Sundays, after dinner at harvest time, at camp meetings in summer, around the cracker barrel in the general store in winter—in fact just about anywhere men congregated. And usually they were arguing: not discussing in the manner of polite conversation, but in all seriousness and often with rancor. Government was important, but politics was more than that—it was a sporting interest. A political party was what a major-league baseball or football team is today to many people; you followed it and supported it in the same way. Politics was a great game. Most Michiganians were ardent Jacksonians, and they firmly believed, with Old Hickory, in frequent elections and short terms of office. Every year there was at least one election and usually there were two or three. Michigan elected the members of the state house every year, while the governor, lieutenant governor, and state senators were elected in the odd-numbered years until 1850. In the even-numbered years there were congressmen to elect, and every four years came the most exciting event of all: the Presidential election.

For some years prior to Andrew Jackson's election to the presidency in 1828, party lines in the nation had been blurred. So vigorous a leader as Jackson was bound to make enemies, and he made many. They included the remaining New England Federalists, supporters of the United States Bank, anti-Masons, South Carolina nul-

349

lificationists, Clay men, Calhoun men, and Webster men. Without having anything in common except their dislike of the fiery Andrew, these groups coalesced in the early 1830s under the name of Whig, chosen because the party of that name in England had been opposed to the supporters of the king. The backbone of the early Whig party in Michigan was a group of three Detroit men who had been appointed to positions in the territorial government by Jackson's predecessor, John Quincy Adams: William Woodbridge, Henry S. Chipman, and Thomas Rowland. There was no love lost between Jackson and Adams, and so it was natural that these Adams appointees should lead the fight against "King Andrew."

The Whigs made little headway in Michigan at first. The Democratic candidate for governor in 1835, Stevens T. Mason, was elected, and was re-elected in 1837 with slight opposition. The legislature contained a large Democratic majority. The Detroit *Free Press* staunchly supported the Democratic cause, and most of the outstate newspapers were Democratic. But the situation began to change as hard times hit the state. As usual, economic distress was blamed on the party in power. This set the stage for a Whig victory in 1839, when William Woodbridge was elected governor. The next year in the famous log-cabin-and-hard-cider campaign Michigan voters gave the Whig candidate for President, William Henry Harrison, a majority. The Whig triumph, however, was short-lived. In Washington Harrison survived his inauguration by scarcely a month, and following his death and the assumption of the Presidency by John Tyler, the Whigs divided into snarling factions. Woodbridge resigned as governor to accept election by the legislature to the United States Senate, and this evoked some criticism. In 1841 the Democrats were again triumphant, electing John S. Barry of Constantine as governor on a platform of economy and retrenchment. Barry became known for his insistence on the strictest economy in state government. From 1841 to 1854 the Democrats won every state election, and every legislature had a Democratic majority. The voters also gave a majority to the Democratic candidate for President in 1844, 1848, and 1852.

Whig hopes were kept alive by factionalism in the Democratic party. At times the Democrats seemed to dislike each other about as much as they did the Whigs. The first of these groups was headed by John Norvell, the postmaster at Detroit, and consisted largely of federal appointees. The second faction, led by Lucius Lyon of Kalamazoo, Elon Farnsworth of Detroit, and Governor Barry, consisted of the conservatives: men of property who opposed the "extravagances" of the Mason administration and would have preferred to restrict the right to vote to property owners. The "radical" wing of the party was led by Kinsley S. Bingham of Livingston County. He and his followers were critical of banks, corporations, and special privilege groups of any sort. This faction included men of small means, in contrast to the more affluent conservatives. In the later 1840s and early 1850s the radicals came to include a large number of antislavery enthusiasts. Finally, there was a faction of the party that had its strength in the western part of the state and consisted of those who felt that the eastern section received too many favors from state government. Epaphroditus Ransom of Kalamazoo may be regarded as the leader of this faction.

The Whigs might have capitalized on these splits within the Democratic ranks had they not, too, been divided into factions. The conservative Whigs, led by Woodbridge, resembled in many ways the conservative faction in the Democratic party. They were monied men, large landowners, and prosperous merchants, most of whom had little time or taste for active political work. The Whig radicals, on the other hand, included a good many younger men, particularly young lawyers, and in the latter part of the period they espoused the antislavery cause.

The latter was but one of a number of causes that increasingly overshadowed such state political issues as internal improvements, education, and banking legislation, as Michigan, along with much of the country, was swept by a great wave of reforming zeal that followed a series of religious revivals in western New York led by Charles S. Finney in the 1820s.[1] Western New York was largely populated by New Englanders who had brought their Puritanism along with them. Implicit in this religious faith was the Calvinist dogma of predestination and the notion that mankind bears the taint of Adam's original sin. The effect of the Finney revivals was to destroy the attitude of resignation toward a wicked world and to substitute the view that it is the duty of the Christian to make the world a better place. Around the beginning of the nineteenth century, the churches had awakened from their lethargy and had undertaken through foreign and home missions "to spread the gospel to every creature." But the Finney revivals did something else: they imparted to religion the red-hot zeal to change society—not merely to convert the heathen or impart religion in the frontiersmen, but to eradicate evils and injustices in the older parts of the country. This spirit expressed itself in many different ways: the temperance crusade, the campaign for women's rights, anti-Catholicism, dietary reform, new religions, Utopian socialism, prison reform, new schemes for education, and, the most famous of them all, the movement for the abolition of slavery. Western New York was the fountainhead of most of these reform movements, and since so many of the people of Michigan had come from western New York, it is not surprising that almost all these manifestations were reflected in Michigan.

Concern with the evils of heavy drinking and drunkenness went back to the earliest fur-trading days in Michigan when Jesuits and others made futile efforts to prohibit the use of liquor in the trade with the Indians. The sale or gift of intoxicating liquor to Indians was prohibited by a law of the Northwest Territory passed in 1790 and by an act approved by the governor and judges of Michigan Territory in 1812. The sale of liquor to minors, servants, soldiers, prisoners, and anyone on Sundays was forbidden. Another type of restriction was the requirement that vendors of intoxicating liquors obtain a license. In 1845 the legislature empowered any township or city to refuse to issue such licenses, and the Constitution of 1850 banned licenses altogether. But the net result was only to leave the sale of liquor unregulated. "Demon rum" was also attacked by means of "moral suasion." Societies were formed to promote the cause of temperance, first local, then state-wide, and in 1826 the American Temperance Society was established on a national basis. The Michigan Temperance Society was formed in 1833, and had many branches. At first the temperance movement stressed moderation. Since this effort brought no concrete results, abstinence from "ardent spirits" was advocated. The drinking of beer and wine rather than whisky, rum, and brandy was encouraged. But this policy was condemned as undemocratic. Whisky was cheap, but beer and wine were relatively expensive at that time. The temperance forces were finally driven to the advocacy of total abstinence.

About 1840 the "Washingtonian movement" was started by a group of reformed drunkards in Baltimore, and it rapidly spread to the West. Some of these ex-tipplers developed mighty oratorical powers. They held meetings or attended them, told their experiences "before and after," and urged everyone to sign a pledge to abstain from all drinking. The Washingtonian meetings were characterized by lusty singing, excited oratory, and pledge-signing. Augustus Littlejohn of Allegan, brother of Flavius T. Littlejohn, candidate for governor in 1849, conducted a series of meetings in Kalamazoo County in 1844. Littlejohn is described as a man of medium height, well-proportioned, "straight as a Choctaw," with a face of "clear intellectual cast and a keen black eye." His voice was "strong and splendidly modulated to express feelings of pathos or to emphasize a point." In one town the meetings were held every evening and a part of each day for two weeks. Crowds came from miles around.

Littlejohn organized his work carefully, put great emphasis on the singing of temperance songs, drilling a choir an hour before each meeting, and then lectured so as to entertain as well as persuade. He practically forced the preachers of the community to attend. Sometimes in his shows he included a description of the Battle of Bunker Hill or Waterloo, climaxing the latter description by kneeling at the pulpit (his meetings always were held in churches) and imitating Wellington dramatically: "Oh that night or Blücher would come." Saloon keepers made every effort to bring disrepute on Littlejohn and his cause, but without success. Similar meetings were held in Battle Creek, Marshall, and other parts of the state, and the people came to be sold on the temperance cause even though they did not stop drinking.[2]

Soon the temperance crusade turned from "moral suasion" and pledge-signing to prohibition as the answer to the liquor problem. The movement for prohibition started in Maine, where in 1851 the legislature passed a prohibitory act that became a model for other states to the extent that prohibition acts came to be known as "Maine laws." This act prohibited the manufacture, sale, or keeping for sale of intoxicating liquors and set heavy penalties for violations. Minnesota, Rhode Island, Massachusetts, and Vermont enacted prohibition laws of this kind in 1852. In Michigan the legislature adopted a prohibition law in 1853, but provided that it should go into effect only upon approval by the voters in a popular referendum. This approval was given by a substantial majority, but in 1854 the state supreme court declared that the legislature did not have the right to make the law dependent on a popular referendum and, for that reason, declared the law to be invalid. The Republican-controlled legislature in 1855, however, passed an acceptable law. After this the temperance forces rested on their oars, thinking that the battle had been won. They soon found that it was one thing to pass a law and quite another to enforce it. Loopholes were discovered and soon liquor was being sold openly. In 1857 Detroit is reported to have had 420 saloons, fifty-six hotel and tavern bars, twenty-three breweries, and six distilleries. The prohibition law remained on the statute books until 1875, but for many years prior to that date it was in reality a dead letter.[3]

The crusade for women's rights, inaugurated at the Seneca Falls Convention in New York in 1848, was considered by many to be the most radical of the reform movements of the time. Two years before the Seneca Falls meeting one of the leaders of the movement, Ernestine L. Rose, addressed the Michigan legislature in an appeal for women's rights. The future Civil War governor, Austin Blair, then a young Whig legislator from Jackson, spoke up in favor of the vote for women, and in 1849 a Senate committee headed by Rix Robinson of Grand Haven reported a resolution in favor of a state women's suffrage amendment, but it was ridiculed by other lawmakers. At the time, women had virtually no rights before the law. The Michigan Constitution of 1850 gave women property rights but not the ballot. Another phase of the women's rights movement aimed at greater educational opportunities for women, part of the great upsurge in efforts to improve educational opportunities for all that was also high on the reformers' agenda. The conflict between those who favored coeducation and those who thought there should be separate schools and colleges for women already has been described. The opening of the University of Michigan to women in 1870, although not the first move in the state to lower the barriers to women being admitted to college, was regarded as a landmark in the women's rights struggle. The incentive for this move was largely the result of the work of Lucinda Hinsdale Stone of Kalamazoo, who had conducted a successful female college in connection with Kalamazoo College. She also had been a leader in the formation of the Ladies' Library Association in Kalamazoo in 1852, which was the first women's club in Michigan and the third oldest in the United States. In later years Mrs. Stone came to be known as the "mother of women's clubs" in Michigan.[4]

The reform crusade that began in the late twenties gave rise to several new religious denominations, among them the Spiritualists, Seventh-day Adventists, and Mormons. By 1860 Battle Creek had become the foremost center of the Seventh-day Adventists, a denomination that had originated in the East in the 1840s and whose leaders ultimately embraced the dietary changes that were another of the popular reforms of this period. An offshoot of the Mormon church also grew up in Michigan. The founder of Mormonism was Joseph Smith. Following their beginnings in western New York, the Mormons moved to Ohio, then to Missouri, then back to Illinois. Their city of Nauvoo in southern Illinois was a community of considerable size and importance. Some of Smith's followers had also settled in Michigan, where, in Pontiac, Joseph Smith preached to the members of the first Mormon church established in the territory, in October, 1834.[5] Because of claims that Joseph Smith practiced polygamy, he was generally condemned. In 1844 Joseph and his brother Hyrum were murdered in Nauvoo by an angry mob. After Smith's death, most Mormons accepted the leadership of Brigham Young, who in 1846–47 led them to Utah. But not all Mormons followed Young. One relatively small group accepted the leadership of James J. Strang and settled in Voree, Wisconsin. Sufficient lands were not available for the entire group, and Strang began to look for greener pastures for his flock. His attention was drawn to the Beaver Islands, which lie in the northern part of Lake Michigan and are a part of the state of Michigan. There are twelve of these islands, the largest and best known—Beaver Island—being twelve miles long and six miles wide. The only inhabitants at the time were a few Irish fishermen. Here was an ideal spot for his people, Strang believed, and in 1848 and 1849 they began to arrive in large numbers.

Strang, like Joseph Smith, was from western New York, and claimed to have been favored with divine revelations. In accordance with one of these revelations, Strang had himself crowned as "King James, Viceregent of God on Earth." At first he was not a polygamist, but in the early fifties, dutifully following the commands of another revelation, he took unto himself four additional wives. Although "plural marriage" was now permitted in the Strang settlement on Beaver Island, few of Strang's followers could support more than one wife, and the code of the community was very strict in regards to immoral conduct, drinking, and profanity. Strang absolutely dominated the settlement. But he made enemies, and on one occasion was taken to Detroit for trial in federal district court. He was acquitted of the charges against him and returned home in triumph. He then ordered his followers to elect him to the state legislature. In 1852 he went to Lansing where he was highly regarded by his fellow legislators. Both Whigs and Democrats courted his favor, for it was said that he could control nearly 2,500 votes.

Strang's downfall was the result of the enmities he had incurred among the earlier residents of the area, particularly the Irish fishermen, and the jealousies that had developed toward him among his own followers. On June 16, 1856, he was assassinated. Shortly thereafter, his assassins were released by the authorities. Strang's followers, left leaderless, were attacked by mobs of fishermen from the mainland and were forced to flee for their lives.[6]

Despite the plethora of biographies written about him, Strang had virtually no lasting impact as a religious leader. The last federal census of religious groups, taken in 1936, revealed only fifteen Strangite Mormons in Michigan, a figure that probably did not greatly increase in later years.

The same fascination with that which is out-of-the-ordinary that helps to account for the attention Strang has received also helps to explain the interest in utopian societies which in this period led to such experiments as the Brook Farm project in New England and the Oneida community in New York. A similar experiment called the Alphadelphia community was located near Kalamazoo and lasted but a brief time in the mid-forties. It numbered no more than three hundred members at its peak, less than one-tenth of one percent of the state's population. In 1848 the project was abandoned because of internal dissension. The property was divided and the members drifted away.[7]

These developments on the fringes of the reforms of this era were interesting but of rather questionable significance. One reform movement whose significance cannot be questioned, even though its hardcore supporters were also limited in number, was the movement against slavery. In the forefront of the antislavery forces were the Friends, or Quakers, although several other religious denominations in Michigan were almost equally opposed to slavery. Abolition societies were formed throughout the North by the thirties, with the Michigan Antislavery Society being organized in 1832, followed by county and other local societies throughout much of southern Michigan. During the 1840s, the sentiment against slavery was politically expressed in third-party movements, and coalesced in 1854 in the Republican party. But many people found other ways to aid the cause than by voting for polite resolutions or casting a ballot. There was the "Underground Railroad," an informal organization for the assistance of escaped slaves in reaching free soil. Slaves who escaped across the Ohio River found their way northward through Indiana or Ohio and were welcomed by many Michiganians. The Quakers everywhere took the lead in this work, but others assisted as well. An established route ran from Niles through Cassopolis, Schoolcraft, Climax, Battle Creek, and along the old Territorial Road to Detroit or northward to Port Huron. From these points Negroes were aided in reaching Canada, though many remained in Michigan. Erastus Hussey of Battle Creek was one of the most active "conductors." On the eastern side of the state Mrs. Laura Haviland was deeply involved in Underground Railroad activities. Some, however, who claimed to have been active in this work may have exaggerated their contributions. Aiding a fugitive was against the law, and therefore many who were involved at the time did not publicize their actions. Most of the information that is available is in the nature of reminiscences published after the Civil War, when there was no longer any danger of being arrested, fined, or imprisoned for this kind of activity. The historian Larry Gara, among others, believes that much of this evidence is suspect, and that the impact of the Underground Railroad was far less significant and widespread than many in the past have assumed.[8]

In order to escape the vigilance of slave hunters, the refugees generally were concealed in houses or barns during the day and

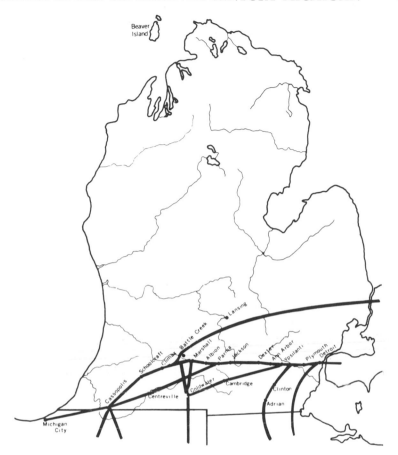

MICHIGAN'S PART IN THE UNDERGROUND RAILWAY

carried on to the next "station" in the night. There are several documented cases of slave owners, usually from Kentucky, who came to Michigan to reclaim their slave property and were subjected to delays and even violence. Most famous of all these was the Crosswhite Case. Adam Crosswhite, his wife, and four children were fugitives from Kentucky. They had escaped and settled near Marshall. It has been claimed that Crosswhite was the prototype of George Harris in the novel, *Uncle Tom's Cabin.* Fearing that he might be kidnapped by his former owner, Crosswhite had arranged to fire a signal shot should he be threatened. One morning in January, 1847, this shot was heard, and neighbors came running to find four Kentuckians and a local law officer at Crosswhite's door. The mob of nearly a hundred citizens succeeded in foiling the Kentuckians' plans and spiriting the Crosswhite family away to Canada on board a Michigan Central train. The enraged Kentuckians returned to bring suit against the leaders of the mob for having prevented them from regaining their property. The result of the first trial was a hung jury, but in the second trial the jury brought in a verdict of guilty against the Marshall citizens, after the judge had advised the members of the jury that no matter what their feelings might be in the case, the law was definitely on the side of the Kentuckians. Fines were assessed against the Marshall citizens equal to the value of the Crosswhites if they had been sold in a slave market. Local tradition in Marshall would later claim that the Crosswhite Case had national repercussions and that Senator Henry Clay, a neighbor of the owners of the Crosswhites, demanded the harsher Fugitive Slave Law of 1850 because of his outrage at the manner in which the rights of his fellow Kentuckians had been abused by the Marshall mob. In actuality, a careful search of the record has revealed no evidence that Clay's actions were in any way influenced by the Crosswhite Case. The Fugitive Slave Act of 1850, however, did lead the first Republican-controlled legislature of Michigan in 1855 to adopt a strong personal liberty law which went to the very limit of every constitutional device to prevent the recovery of fugitive slaves in Michigan by forbidding state and local officials to cooperate with federal marshals in the recovery of slave property.[9]

At the end of the 1830s many activists in the antislavery movement, discouraged at the lack of progress they had thus far achieved in their efforts to end slavery, turned to political action, and since the Democrats and Whigs tended to avoid the slavery issue in order not to alienate their supporters in either the North or the South, the abolitionists formed their own party, the Liberty party. The party's candidate for President in 1840 was James G. Birney, a former slaveholder who had been converted to the antislavery cause and had moved north to live in Bay City. Running on a platform that emphasized only the slavery issue, Birney and his party were not successful, polling only 294 votes in Michigan. Two years later, Birney was the Liberty party candidate for governor, and, although he again ran far behind the Democratic and Whig candidates, he received 2,776 votes. In the hotly contested Presidential election of 1844, Birney, again his party's candidate, polled over 62,000 votes across the country, nearly nine times as many votes as he had received in 1840, and in this instance the votes that went to Birney in a few key states, particularly New York, drew enough support away from the

Whig candidate, Henry Clay, to give the victory to the Democratic candidate, James K. Polk.

Shortly after this election, Birney fell ill and was unable to play an active role in subsequent political battles. The party that he had led also disappeared in the next few years, its members joining with certain disaffected northern Democrats to form the Free-Soil party, which, while still opposed to slavery, took a stand on other issues, in hopes of attracting more support to its candidates. In the 1848 Presidential election, the party's candidate was one of the nation's best-known political figures—former President Martin Van Buren—who received ten percent of the votes cast, including over ten thousand votes in Michigan, despite the fact that the Democratic Presidential candidate was Lewis Cass.

Cass was, until the nomination of Gerald Ford by the Republicans in 1976, the only Michigan resident to be nominated for the Presidency by one of the major parties. (Thomas E. Dewey, the Republican candidate in 1944 and 1948, was a native of Owosso, Michigan, and a graduate of the University of Michigan, but he was a resident of New York at the time of his nomination and it was his political strength in the latter state that gained him the nomination.[10]) Cass had been grooming himself for the Presidency throughout much of his long political career as he advanced from the governorship of Michigan to a post in Andrew Jackson's cabinet to minister to France and finally to a seat in the United States Senate from Michigan.

By 1844, Cass, who would be sixty-two that year, was a recognized national leader of the Democrats and came within a few votes of gaining his party's nomination for President that year. As the 1844 race for the Presidency approached, it had been assumed that Martin Van Buren, who had been defeated for re-election in 1840 but was still enormously popular, would again be the party's nominee. Van Buren, however, forfeited his chances by coming out in opposition to the annexation of Texas, a move that cost him the support of the southern Democrats that he needed to get the required two-thirds of the delegates' votes at the national convention. Shortly after Van Buren's announcement and shortly before the convention was to convene, Cass, on May 10, 1844, publicly announced his wholehearted support for Texas annexation. It was a move patently intended to gain him the nomination by courting the favor of the pro-Texas delegates from the South. At the same time, by emphasizing the need of annexing Texas in order to stave off a feared British domination of the Lone Star Republic, Cass appealed to expansionist and Anglophobic sentiments in the North as the most likely means of winning support in that area where antislavery sentiments tended to create opposition to the annexation of territory that would strengthen southern slave forces. For his stand, Cass was derided by northern critics as a doughface; that is, a northern politician who was dominated by the southern wing of the party. Later, however, when Cass came out in favor of acquiring the Oregon country, no one accused him of catering to northern interests. In point of fact, his position on both the Texas and the Oregon questions was entirely consistent with his long-time commitment to western expansion.[11]

At the Democratic convention held in Baltimore late in May of 1844, Cass's strategy appeared to be working. After several ballots, his delegate strength pushed him ahead of Van Buren, but before the Michigan Democrat could corral the needed two-thirds majority, southern support shifted to Andrew Jackson's protege and fellow Tennessean, James K. Polk, and Cass's chances evaporated, as Polk, the so-called dark-horse in the race, gained the nomination and went on to win the Presidency in the fall election. However, Cass's strong showing at the 1844 convention and Polk's pledge to serve only one term in the White House made Cass the front runner for the nomination in 1848.

The outbreak of the Mexican War in 1846 and the certainty that the United States would gain vast new areas in the Southwest as a result of the war once again, as in the earlier debate over annexing Texas, made the issue of slave expansion in the West the burning issue of the day. In response to a letter from A. O. P. Nicholson, a southern Democrat, asking Cass how he stood on the question of allowing slavery to enter the lands that Mexico would be forced to surrender to the United States, Cass on December 24, 1847, declared that the people settling in these new territories should be allowed to decide this issue for themselves, rather than allowing Congress to impose its will and decreeing that slavery should or should not be permitted to enter a territory, as Congress had done in the case of the Northwest Territory in 1787. Cass thus became the first front-rank American politician to expound the Doctrine of Squatter Sovereignty or Popular Sovereignty, as it later came to be called, although in the 1850s Senator Stephen Douglas of Illinois became so identified with this doctrine that it is often assumed that he conceived it.

The Nicholson letter was again politically motivated. Although it would not please the extremists in the North and the South who favored a policy either to exclude slavery entirely from the territories or to actively defend the rights of slaveholders to remain in those areas throughout the territorial phase of development, it would, Cass was hoping, appeal to the moderates in both sections. Cass's position, however, was consistent with his past actions as governor of Michigan when he had sought to give the people in the territory as much power as possible to govern themselves, with a minimum of federal restraints.

Squatter sovereignty gained Cass the Democratic Presidential nomination at the Baltimore convention in May, 1848, and had the Whig party, which placed the Mexican War hero, Zachary Taylor, in nomination, provided the only major opposition, Cass would have won the election. But the entry of the Free-Soil party in the race, with its candidate, Van Buren, killed Cass's chances for victory. Those Democrats in the North who felt that Cass's proposals on the issue of slavery in the territory had gone too far in appeasing the South could vote for Van Buren, and their defection from the Democratic column in New York, which Cass would normally have carried, gave that state to Taylor, which was enough to deny Cass the victory. Four years later, after Congress in the Compromise of 1850 had applied Cass's popular sovereignty ideas in organizing two new territories in the areas acquired from Mexico, Cass was again a leading contender for the Democratic nomination, but his defeat in 1848 and the fact that he would be seventy years old in October, 1852, told against his candidacy and ultimately led the party to turn to a nonentity, Franklin Pierce of New Hampshire. For Cass, this was his last chance at the office he had sought so long, and he concluded his political career as senator from Michigan and finally as Secretary of State in President James Buchanan's cabinet from 1857 to 1860. He was in these years an elder statesman who was still much respected but whose mantle of leadership had been usurped by a new generation of politicians.

After 1850 the Whig party rapidly disintegrated as the issue of slavery made it ever harder to hold together the northern and southern wings of the party. In many cases, the members of the radical faction of the Whigs in the North went over to the Free-Soil party. This party also received adherents from the radical faction of the Democratic party. In 1849 the Whigs and Free-Soilers in Michigan combined to support Flavius T. Littlejohn of Allegan for governor, but he was defeated by the Democratic candidate, John S. Barry.

There was some surcease of agitation on the slavery issue after the enactment by Congress of the Compromise of 1850, which settled the status of slavery in the areas acquired as a result of the Mexican War. But in 1854, the question was ripped wide open again when Congress passed the Kansas-Nebraska bill, repealing that part of the Missouri Compromise of 1820 that had prohibited slavery north of the southern boundary of Missouri, except in Missouri it-self. The new law applied Cass's principle of popular sovereignty to this vast western region, opening it to slavery until such time as the people who settled in the territories had had a chance to decide for themselves whether or not they wanted slavery. The prime supporter of the Kansas-Nebraska bill was Stephen A. Douglas, Democratic senator from Illinois, whose support of popular sovereignty, like Cass's support of the same policy earlier, was partly motivated by Douglas's hopes that it would advance his ambitions for the Presi-dency. But Douglas's bill brought forth violent protests throughout the North. Meetings were held at which "Free Democrats" and "Free Whigs" ultimately joined with Free-Soilers to express their outrage at this opening of the West to slavery. Out of these meetings the Republican party was born.

It is believed that the first of these meetings to form a coalition of those opposed to the Kansas-Nebraska bill was held at Ripon, Wisconsin, on February 28, 1854. In Michigan, Democrats and Whigs held separate protest meetings, and then at a meeting held in Kalamazoo late in June, leaders of both groups agreed to join in forming a new party. A call was sent out for a meeting to be held at Jackson on July 6. About fifteen hundred people appeared on that day, far too many to be accommodated at any building in Jackson. Therefore, a speaker's stand was erected "under the oaks," near the corner of Franklin and Second streets in downtown Jackson, and there the meeting was held. An organization was formed called the Republican party, the first occasion on which this name was officially attached to the newly emerging party. A platform was adopted and candidates for state office in the fall election were nominated. The question of whether the Republican party was born at Ripon or at Jackson probably never will be settled. The Ripon meeting preceded the Jackson meeting by several months, but it was hardly more than a local political gathering and only preliminary steps were taken to form a new party. The assemblage under the oaks at Jackson was the first state-wide Republican meeting; it was there that the first plat-form was adopted and the first full state ticket nominated. A marker designating Jackson as the birthplace of the Republican party was dedicated in 1910. The Republican President William Howard Taft was present on the occasion and seemed to throw his considerable weight behind the Michigan city's claim.

The Republican slate of candidates in 1854 was headed by Kinsley S. Bingham, who was nominated for governor. Bingham, a New Yorker who had come to Michigan to farm in Livingston County, was a former Democrat who had served in Congress during the Mexican War. As an antislavery Democrat his chances for political advancement had been dimmed by his opposition to the compromises that party leaders, such as Cass, had been willing to make on the slavery issue in order to avoid alienating southern support. The Whig faction of the new Republican party, however, had felt that Zachariah Chandler, a Detroit businessman who had been the Whig candidate for governor in 1852, not the former Democrat Bingham, deserved the Republican gubernatorial nomination in 1854. Chandler wished to become United States Senator, and he therefore supported Bingham's nomination after securing a promise from the former Democrats in the party that they would support his bid for the Senate two years hence when Lewis Cass's term expired.

At the November election in 1854 Bingham and the entire Republican ticket emerged victorious, and a Republican majority was elected to the legislature. It marked a complete turnaround in Michigan politics, which up to this time had been almost completely dominated by the Democratic party. From this date until 1932 Michigan was persistently Republican. The Democratic party was by no means destroyed, as was the case with the Whig party, but during the following eighty years after the formation of the Republican party in Michigan there were relatively few occasions when the Democrats were able to win national or state elections. The strength of the Republicans at the outset came from several sources. The New England element, still dominant in the state, regarded the antislavery movement, with which the Republican party was associated, as a crusade for righteousness. The temperance and women's rights advocates were impatient with the Democrats' failure to enact desired legislation. The Protestant churches, except for the Lutheran groups, were strongly Republican, with many of the leading Republicans being Protestant ministers. The farmers who were seeking the establishment of a separate agricultural college were Republicans. The Democrats relied on Detroit and, to a lesser degree, on other cities for their strength. The foreign element in the population leaned toward the Democrats, a fact that drove many Whigs who did not immediately join the Republican party into the ranks of the American or Know-Nothing party, which advocated anti-foreign policies in the mid-fifties. When that third party fizzled out, probably most of its adherents became Republicans.

Political parties, however, are built more around persons than policies. Behind the election returns are the campaigns, the human relationships, the force of personalities, and the influence of leadership. For a generation, the foremost name in Michigan politics was Lewis Cass. Age and the growing support for more extreme stands for or against slavery brought on a decline in Cass's influence in the 1850s, and when his second six-year term as senator expired at the end of 1856, there was no possibility that the state legislature, now solidly controlled by the Republicans, would fill the seat with a Democrat. Instead, Zachariah Chandler was chosen by the legislature on January 10, 1857, with 106 votes cast for him and only 16 for Cass.

Both men proceeded to go to Washington, but whereas Cass was finishing out his long and distinguished political career as secretary of state in Buchanan's administration, Chandler was launching a career that would make him one of the most powerful senators Michigan has ever had. Like Cass, Chandler was a native of New Hampshire and like him he was also the dominant force in his Michigan party for many years. Cass and Chandler are also the only nineteenth-century Michigan politicians who can be said to have risen to recognized positions of national leadership. But there the similarities end. Where Cass was a well-read, almost intellectual man, who made long, carefully thought-out, if often dull, statements of his views on issues, Chandler was a poorly educated man, given to off-the-cuff, often crudely phrased statements. Rather than being a rational debater of the merits of an issue, his reactions were more those of a street fighter, and he sometimes resorted to physical tactics in order to clarify his points. He was the boss of the Michigan Republican party during most of that party's first twenty-five years of existence and he exhibited all the characteristics associated with that term. Although he exhibited a few negative characteristics, he exhibited more positive ones, and there was no doubt that he was an effective leader who accomplished much. A wealthy Detroit wholesale merchant, Chandler's action in paying the fines of the citizens of Marshall who were convicted of aiding in the escape of the Crosswhite family was an indication of the strength of his antislavery convictions, which helped to account for much of the support he received when the Republican party was formed.

Aside from a brief period when young Stevens T. Mason was at the peak of his popularity, no other Michigan political figures from 1835 to 1860 could approach the influence that Cass and Chandler were able to wield. However, the eighteen men who served as governor or United States Senator during these years (three of these eighteen held both offices during this period) tended to share certain characteristics. All but three were born in New York or in one of the New England states. All but two studied and practiced law at some point in their careers. Measured by modern standards all of them were young when they began their public service. Although William

Woodbridge was sixty when he became governor, he had been appointed territorial secretary at the age of thirty-four. Cass became territorial governor when he was thirty-one. Lucius Lyon became a United States Senator at age thirty-five. Mason was acting governor at nineteen and became governor of the state at twenty-three. Epaphroditus Ransom, governor in 1848 and 1849, became a justice of the state supreme court at age thirty-nine, and Alpheus Felch, who was governor in 1846 and 1847 and then senator until 1853, had earlier become a supreme court justice at thirty-six. Only five of the eighteen office-holders were Detroiters, and of these, three owed their positions at first to federal appointment. Only Augustus Porter, senator from 1839 to 1845, and Chandler (both of whom had served as mayor of Detroit) attained the position of senator without the earlier prestige of federal favor. It would appear that the citizens of Detroit were handicapped in politics by their residence in that city. It is also apparent that the position of United States senator was more highly regarded than that of governor, since two governors, Woodbridge and Felch, resigned as governor to accept election to the Senate.[12] Governor Robert McClelland also resigned the office in 1853 to accept the appointment of Secretary of the Interior in Franklin Pierce's cabinet.

John Barry, the favorite of conservative Democrats, was a merchant in Constantine and was one of the organizers of the Michigan Southern Railroad. Felch, a native of Maine, was a Monroe lawyer. After his retirement from the Senate he settled in Ann Arbor, became professor of law at the University of Michigan, and served as president of the Michigan Pioneer and Historical Society. He lived to the age of ninety-two. Ransom was born in Massachusetts and came to Michigan in 1834, making Kalamazoo his home. He was the first governor to be inaugurated in the new capital of Lansing. After his term as governor he served as a regent of the University of Michigan and one term in the state house of representatives. He moved to Kansas in 1857 and died there two years later. Robert McClelland was the son of a Pennsylvania physician. He studied law and moved to Monroe in 1833. After the conclusion of his term as Secretary of the Interior he returned to Michigan. On the eve of the Civil War he counselled moderation and compromise, a policy that was in violent contrast to the views of such Republicans as Zachariah Chandler.[13] Charles E. Stuart, a Kalamazoo attorney whose term as senator expired in 1859, had the distinction of being the last Democratic senator from Michigan until the election of Woodbridge N. Ferris in 1922.[14]

Other Whig leaders besides Chandler who joined the new Republican party were Jacob M. Howard of Detroit and David Walbridge of Kalamazoo, both later to become congressmen. Kinsley Bingham, the first Republican governor, served two terms in that office and was then sent to the United States Senate, but died in 1861 before his term expired. Moses Wisner, who succeeded Bingham as governor, was a Pontiac lawyer. It was during his administration that the first law was passed requiring the registration of voters. The embezzlement of a large sum of money by the state treasurer occurred during Wisner's term, and this may have been a factor in his decision not to seek a second term. He died of typhoid fever in 1863 at the age of forty-six while serving as the commander of the Twenty-second Michigan Infantry regiment in the Civil War.

Michigan politics was greatly affected by a movement to scrap the 1835 constitution, only a decade and a half after it had been adopted. In 1849 the voters, by a lopsided margin of 33,193 to 4,095, approved the proposal. Behind this overwhelming desire for a change was the ferment of Jacksonian democracy. Michigan's first constitution had been framed before the implications of Jackson's ideas for state government had been generally understood. These included the choice of public officials by election rather than by appointment, limitations upon the powers of the legislature, and opposition to special acts of incorporation. During this time, Michigan was only one of many states that were writing new constitutions or amending old ones to incorporate these Jacksonian principles.[15]

The convention called to revise Michigan's constitution met at Lansing on June 3, 1850, and completed its work on August 15. It included one hundred delegates, only one of whom was a native of Michigan. Daniel Goodwin of Wayne County was chosen as president. The constitution framed by this body was submitted to the voters on November 5, 1850, and was ratified by a large majority.

The new constitution was more than twice as long as the state's first constitution and was much more detailed. It included many restrictions on the legislature. The lawmakers were prohibited from passing special acts of incorporation; henceforth all corporations had to be formed under a general law, thus assuring that no group would get special favors. Banking laws could take effect only after a majority vote of approval by the people. The legislature was forbidden to engage the state in building or financing internal improvements (a reflection of the antagonisms created by the act of 1837). Salaries of state officials were fixed in the constitution and thus could not be changed except by an amendment, which required the voters' approval (the governor was to receive a salary of $1,000 a year). The question of constitutional revision was to be submitted to the people automatically every sixteen years.

A major change was to make all the principal state officials elective. This included the Secretary of State, State Treasurer, Attorney General, Auditor General, Superintendent of Public Instruction, regents of the University of Michigan, state board of education, and supreme court justices, all of which had been previously appointive. This was one of several changes that served to weaken the office of governor since the governor now was forced to take whomever the voters had elected, while these elected officials, by the very fact that they owed their jobs to the voters, were more inclined to act independently of the governor than they were when they had received their jobs by appointment from the governor.

The terms of members of the state house of representatives were extended from one year to two. And henceforth, elections for the chief state officials were to be held in the even-numbered instead of the odd-numbered years, making them come at the same time as national elections and thus paving the way for long and crowded ballots. It also meant that when the state election coincided with the election of a President, which could never happen under the time schedule provided in the 1835 constitution, state issues were likely to be overshadowed by national issues, and the candidates for governor might tie their campaigns to those of their parties' Presidential candidates.

The new constitution also drastically altered the judiciary. The county courts were abolished. Instead, the state was divided into eight circuits, each of which was to have a judge elected by the people. The eight circuit judges were to constitute the supreme court, but the legislature was empowered to organize a new supreme court with a chief justice and three associate justices, to be elected by the people.

The article on education stipulated that free schools were to be maintained for at least three months each year beginning five years after the constitution was adopted, but it was not until 1869 that "rate" bills were finally abolished throughout the state. Not only were the university regents made elective, but they were also to be free of legislative interference in the operation of the university and were directed to elect a permanent president.

Aliens who had declared their intention of becoming United States citizens were given the right to vote, as were "civilized" male Indians. However, the same right was not extended to Negro males. As early as 1843, a convention of Michigan Negroes, meeting in

Detroit, had issued a manifesto demanding the right to vote, declaring "that the Declaration of Independence is the textbook of this nation and without its doctrines be maintained [*sic*], our government is insecure." The constitutional convention in 1850, however, avoided taking a direct stand on the issue. Instead of including a provision in the new constitution which would extend the vote to Negro males, it submitted the question as a separate proposal, thereby assuring its defeat by the white voters who rejected the idea of Negro suffrage by a margin of 32,000 to 12,000.[16]

The Constitution of 1850 remained the fundamental law of Michigan until January 1, 1909. During that period, seventy-one amendments were proposed, of which thirty-eight were adopted. Two attempts at a general revision, one in 1867 and a second in 1874, failed to receive the support of the voters. The constitutional conventions in 1908 and in 1961–62 attempted, with only limited success, to eliminate the defects contained in what has to rank as Michigan's worst state constitution.

16

MICHIGAN AND THE CIVIL WAR

The Civil War brought no sharp break in the continuity of Michigan history, but it was such a momentous episode in the lives of the people of the time that afterward they tended to regard it as the dividing point in all their experiences. The great wars of the twentieth century have had a similar impact on those who lived through them, but even for these later generations the Civil War still holds a special fascination and is the only war that large numbers of Americans, year after year, are interested in reading about. The reasons are not hard to discover. The war was punctuated by idealism, high adventure, trial, and tragedy. Afterward, as the veterans grew older, they tended to forget the wounds and hardships they had suffered and only remembered their service in the Union army or navy as their greatest adventure. Seen in the retrospect of a century, however, the element of tragedy predominates. It was the one major instance in American history in which the usual democratic pattern of settling controversy by compromise and accommodation failed entirely.

When Congress passed the Kansas-Nebraska Act in 1854, which opened immense regions to slavery where it previously had been prohibited, the nation started down the road to disunion. In the years that followed, the Kansas troubles, the Dred Scott decision, and John Brown's raid further heightened sectional animosity. Henry Clay, the great compromiser, was dead. So was Daniel Webster, who in 1850 had alienated his New England followers by advocating compromise. Other longtime political leaders, such as Michigan's Lewis Cass, whose devotion to the Union had led them to advocate compromises of sectional differences in order to avoid the

369

Union's destruction, were now too old to be effective in keeping the country on a middle-of-the-road course. Extremists in both sections—abolitionists in the North, secessionists in the South—were attracting more followers, although in 1860 they were probably still in the minority.

Already the leading Protestant churches had broken into northern and southern factions over the slavery issue. Many professional and business organizations had done the same. The Whig party was dead. In its place was the Republican party, a purely sectional aggregation of former Whigs, Democrats, and Free-Soilers. By 1860 only one major national organization remained that could hold together the North and the South: the Democratic party. If it could decide on a candidate for President who would be acceptable to both sections, the Union might still survive.

Delegates to the Democratic National Convention assembled in Charleston, South Carolina, in late April, 1860. It soon became apparent that they were sharply divided. The southerners not only demanded that their right to carry slaves into the territories be respected, but also that federal laws be passed to secure their possession of slave property while they resided in those territories. Northern Democrats were not willing to go that far. Stephen Douglas of Illinois, their champion, upheld the right of slaveholders to take their slaves into the territories, but he asserted at the same time that slavery could not exist without legal protection, which the territorial legislatures might provide or withhold as they saw fit. Although Douglas commanded a majority of the delegates' votes, the opposition of southern delegates prevented him from getting the two-third majority that was required for nomination. A compromise was sought but none could be found. The floor leader of Douglas's forces was Charles E. Stuart, the former senator from Kalamazoo, and according to Avery Craven, an authority on the Civil War, it was Stuart's actions that made the southern delegates decide to withdraw from the convention. The convention then adjourned to meet later in Baltimore. When it finally reconvened in June the deadlock continued. Finally the southern delegates withdrew once more and the remaining delegates then gave the nomination to Douglas. The southern Democrats proceeded to nominate John C. Breckenridge of Kentucky, thus completing the split of the party into sectional fragments.

Before the Democrats had reassembled at Baltimore, the Republicans had held their convention at Chicago, starting on May 16, in a new and immense auditorium called the Wigwam on the lake shore. The delegates demonstrated intense enthusiasm, for they scented victory. The foremost candidate for the nomination was William H. Seward of New York, who was also the choice of the Michigan delegation that was headed by Austin Blair of Jackson. There were several reasons for Seward's popularity in Michigan. He was a friend of Zachariah Chandler, and he had a firm attitude on slavery. He had become well-known in Michigan a decade earlier as the defense attorney for the men arrested and tried in Detroit in the famous "railroad conspiracy" case. He was also from New York, the state in which a quarter of Michigan's residents in 1860 had been born. Seward had carefully cultivated the support of this large expatriate New York element, and in 1860 trains carrying the New York delegation to Chicago were greeted with cheers for Seward at every stop they made in crossing Michigan. In Chicago there was great excitement and a mad scramble to secure space in the Wigwam, which was built to seat 10,000 and was decorated with evergreen boughs from Michigan. Although Seward was the leading candidate, he had his enemies, including the influential Horace Greeley, and other states had their favorite sons. Seward's opponents were able to prevent his nomination on the first or second ballots. The strongest of the other candidates was Abraham Lincoln of Illinois, and on the third ballot he was nominated. The Michigan delegates were bitterly disappointed at Seward's defeat and some must have had misgivings about the kind of leadership the winning nominee would provide. Four years before, Lincoln had made his one and only public appearance in Michigan when he addressed a Republican rally in Kalamazoo on August 27, 1856. But the views he expressed on that occasion were far too moderate for his predominantly radical audience. On the question of allowing slavery into the western territories, he advocated continuing efforts to arrive at acceptable compromises with the South, and on the fugitive slave issue he reportedly defended the highly unpopular Fugitive Slave Act of 1850. His audience vociferously expressed its displeasure with Lincoln's views on these points, and later in the day Zachariah Chandler, in a speech to the same rally, expressed ideas almost totally at variance with Lincoln's.[1] Nevertheless, in 1860, the Michigan delegation at Chicago pledged its support to the "rail splitter," with Austin Blair promising that Michigan would give Lincoln a 25,000-vote majority.

The 1860 campaign in Michigan was a lively one. Lincoln did not visit the state during the campaign, but the locally popular Seward appeared on his behalf. In October, Stephen Douglas appeared at Democratic rallies across the lower peninsula.[2] As usual, newspapers were divided between those supporting Douglas and those backing Lincoln, but both sides were strong and positive. Political clubs such as the "Wide Awakes" and the "Invincibles" whooped it up for their favorites. Although the contest in Michigan was clearly between the Republicans and the Douglas Democrats, Brecken-ridge, the southern Democratic candidate, had a few supporters, and a small number also worked on behalf of John Bell, who had been nominated by a group of former Whigs from the border states as the candidate of the Constitutional Union party. The Democrats in Michigan sought to enhance their chances by trotting out as their candidate for governor John S. Barry, who had been elected to that office three times before. But their efforts were in vain. After the ballots had been counted, the Republicans had won a clear victory. Lincoln received 88,445 votes to 64,958 votes for Douglas, not quite the 25,000-vote margin that had been promised but a convincing evidence of Republican strength in the state.[3] Breckenridge received 805 votes and Bell only 373. In the race for governor, John Barry did better than his party's Presidential candidate, picking up 67,221 votes, but this still left him far behind the Republican victor, Austin Blair, who received 87,806 votes. The Democrats won only two of the races for the state senate and gained only ten seats in the lower house, while all four of the state's Congressional victors were Repub-licans.

In the nation as a whole the Republicans were also victorious. Even though Lincoln's total popular vote count was considerably less than the combined popular vote of his three opponents, he received 180 electoral votes to only 123 for Douglas, Breckenridge, and Bell combined.

Until Lincoln was inaugurated in March of 1861, the impact that his election would have on the nation was not entirely clear. Lincoln avoided committing himself to specific actions until he assumed the full responsibilities of the Presidency. The threats of southern lead-ers during the campaign to pull their states out of the Union if Lincoln were elected were dismissed by many Michiganians, like others in the North, as mere campaign oratory.[4] Less than seven weeks after the election, however, a convention of delegates in South Carolina voted for the secession of that state from the Union, and before Lincoln was inaugurated, the other states in the Deep South had followed South Carolina and had joined together to form the Confederate States of America.

James Buchanan, whose term as President did not end until Lincoln was inaugurated, held that the southern states did not have the right to secede, but at the same time he concluded that there was nothing he could do under the Constitution to prevent them from seceding. His indecisiveness was no doubt induced by the fact that he would soon be out of office. Lewis Cass, Buchanan's Secretary of State, resigned in disgust in December and returned to Detroit, where he staunchly upheld the Union cause. He sorrowfully noted that as a boy he had witnessed the celebrations that were held at the time of the ratification of the Constitution, and now as an old man he was witnessing what threatened to be the death of the Union established under that Constitution. He now retired after nearly sixty years of public service. He lived until 1866 and thus saw his beloved Union restored at the end of the Civil War.

During the interim between his election and his inauguration, Lincoln's unwillingness to commit himself on his policy toward the South was no doubt the result of the division within his party between those who were receptive to some sort of compromise that would guarantee slavery in the states where it was already established, and those who were opposed to such a conciliatory move to appease the South. Michigan's Republican leaders were among the latter group. Retiring Governor Moses Wisner, in his farewell address on January 1, 1861, declared: "This is no time for timid and vacillating counsels when the cry of treason and rebellion is ringing in our ears." The incoming governor, Austin Blair, was equally positive in his stand for stern measures. He warned in his inaugural address that the Union "must be preserved and the laws must be enforced in all parts of it at whatever cost," adding that "secession is revolution and revolution is the overt act of treason and must be treated as such." The legislature, heeding his recommendation, passed a resolution pledging the military power and the material resources of Michigan to the support of the United States government while voting against sending a Michigan delegation to participate in the Washington Peace Conference that border-state leaders had called in a last-ditch effort to find a compromise that could preserve the Union. Senator Zachariah Chandler in Washington was in the forefront of those who opposed any compromise, making a famous statement in February that "without a little bloodletting this Union will not, in my estimation, be worth a rush."

Lincoln's inaugural address was conciliatory, but it contained a hint of how the new President planned to deal with secession. He warned that he would "hold, possess, and occupy, the property and places belonging to the Government." The Confederacy had already taken over most federal forts, navy yards, and custom houses within its borders when Lincoln spoke these words, but Fort Pickens in Florida and Fort Sumter in South Carolina still were in federal hands. It was Lincoln's announced plan to send supplies into Fort Sumter that precipitated the crisis. There can be little question that Lincoln understood this action would probably be resisted, but he could accept no alternative. Upon learning of this decision, South Carolina demanded that Major Robert Anderson, in command of the fort, evacuate the post. When his reply was not satisfactory, shore batteries at Charleston commenced the bombardment of the fort at 4:30 a.m. on April 12, forcing the surrender of the fort in a few hours. Three days after the firing on Fort Sumter, Lincoln called on the states to furnish 75,000 men for three-months' duty to suppress the rebellion in the South. The brief term of service that he stipulated helped to support a widespread belief in the North that a show of force was all that was required to bring the southern states back into the Union.

On April 15, Governor Blair was at his home in Jackson when he received a telegram from the War Department advising him that Michigan was being requested to furnish one regiment of ten companies as its share of the force that the President was asking the states to supply. The following day Blair proceeded to Detroit to confer with the state's adjutant general, John Robertson, civil officials, and others on how Michigan could meet its quota. It would be necessary not only to enlist the volunteers, but also to house, arm, clothe, and equip them during their initial training period. There were no funds in the state treasury for this purpose. The legislature had adjourned a month earlier after having authorized the governor to raise the military forces that might be needed if a war broke out, but without having appropriated any money to pay for such recruiting activities. Blair would shortly call the legislature back into special session on May 7, but in mid-April immediate action was needed that could not await formal legislative approval. Detroit businessmen suggested that the emergency be met with privately donated funds, which would later be repaid by the state. Shortly, the sum of $81,020 was supplied by individuals in Detroit and outstate communities. Once the funds had been promised, Blair issued his call for volunteers, and the adjutant general was instructed to accept the first ten militia companies that offered their services. There were at the time a total of twenty-eight such companies in the state militia. These companies were actually more local than state organizations, the state having spent less than $3,000 a year for military purposes. In addition, the militia companies, with such high-sounding names as the Detroit Light Guard, Michigan Hussars, Coldwater Cadets, and Flint Union Greys, were as much social as they were military organizations. Before the war they often took part in parades and drills, frequently visiting other cities and towns. When the call to arms came, however, they responded with enthusiasm. Within their ranks were a number of

West Point graduates and veterans of the Mexican War who formed the backbone of the state's initial war effort.[5]

In addition to the men belonging to these military organizations, hundreds of others hurried to volunteer as the state was swept by a great surge of patriotic fervor. In Detroit, a flag-raising ceremony on April 18 and a meeting two days later at which the oath of allegiance was administered to all civil and military officials, were occasions for an outpouring of public sentiment on behalf of the Union. In Ann Arbor on April 15, a large gathering in the Courthouse Square was addressed by the president of the University of Michigan, Henry P. Tappan, and other prominent citizens, and resolutions were adopted pledging support to the President and appointing a committee to prepare for Lincoln's anticipated call for troops. At a mass meeting in Kalamazoo on April 16, members of both political parties voted unanimously that the rebellion must be resisted and put down by force of arms. By the end of that day, forty-five men had enlisted, the first being a seventeen-year-old youth named William Shakespeare.[6]

The general order forming the state's requested regiment was issued on April 24. The Detroit Light Guard was to constitute Company A, while the other companies were comprised of militia units from Jackson, Coldwater, Manchester, Ann Arbor, Burr Oak, Ypsilanti, Marshall, Adrian, and a second company from Detroit. Older members of these organizations, in many cases, resigned, and their places were filled with younger volunteers. Colonel Orlando Willcox of Detroit, a graduate of West Point and a veteran of army duty in the Mexican War and the West, was appointed commander of the regiment which was designated as the First Michigan Infantry Regiment.

Nearly all of Michigan's Civil War soldiers would serve in military units that carried the Michigan name in their title. It is thus possible to determine the specific contributions of these men to the war effort by following the reports of their units' activities. In the wars of the twentieth century, the federal government, not the states, assumed the primary responsibility for assembling the nation's fighting forces, and the great bulk of Michigan's warriors served in army units whose members came from many parts of the country and which bore a United States Army designation, thereby making it nearly impossible to single out the particular contributions that Michigan's men—and women—made in these wars.

By April 29 all ten companies of the First Michigan Infantry had arrived at their rendezvous point, Fort Wayne in Detroit. Officers immediately started training the men in military discipline, use of fire arms, drill, and battle formations. Friends and relatives were allowed to visit the fort and witness the activities. On May 1, the regiment was formally inducted into federal service, and on the same day the first consignment of rifles arrived. Soon afterward uniforms were provided, and the flamboyant uniforms of the individual companies had to be shipped home. An impressive ceremony was held in the heart of Detroit on Campus Martius on May 11, with the women of Detroit presenting the regiment with the regimental colors that they had designed. Two days afterward, two steamships drew alongside the fort, and the men of the First Michigan, numbering 798, went aboard to begin their trip to the nation's capital, where they had been assigned.

At Cleveland, the regiment transferred to railroad cars. In that city and at others along the way, large crowds greeted the Michigan recruits. Delegations brought good things to eat, and women bestowed locks of their hair and an occasional kiss upon the gallant Michiganians. The regiment arrived in Washington at ten o'clock in the evening of May 16, one month and a day after Lincoln's call for troops. It was the first regiment from the western states to arrive at the national capital, which led to Lincoln reportedly exclaiming, "Thank God for Michigan!"

The First Michigan received its first marching orders on May 23 when it was sent across the Potomac to occupy the Virginia town of Alexandria. A company of New York Zouaves was sent by water to arrive at the same time as the Michigan troops. No organized resistance was encountered, but the commander of the New York force, twenty-four-year-old Elmer Ellsworth, was killed by the proprietor of a hotel, a rabid southern supporter, after Ellsworth had hauled down a Confederate flag that flew over the hotel. Back in Michigan, Commander Willcox's so-called victory was roundly cheered and was taken as further evidence supporting the view that the rebellion would be easily suppressed.

The First Michigan included only a few of the men who clamored to get into the fight. The Second Michigan Infantry Regiment was formed under an order of Adjutant General Robertson dated April 25, 1861. It consisted of uniformed militia companies except for those comprised of Kalamazoo and Niles volunteers. The regiment was called into service for three months, but on May 3 President Lincoln, in calling for 42,000 more recruits, changed the term to three years. Accordingly, the men in the Second Michigan Infantry were re-enlisted for the longer period, those not willing to do so being allowed to withdraw. Men in this regiment came from Battle Creek, Flint, Niles, Kalamazoo, Constantine, Hudson, and Detroit.

Throughout the war companies were comprised of friends and neighbors from the same community, a practice generally abandoned in later conflicts. The Third Infantry Regiment was mustered into state service May 21, and into federal service June 10. It consisted largely of men from Grand Rapids, Lansing, and Muskegon. The Fourth Infantry Regiment, largely recruited from communities in Monroe, Lenawee, Hillsdale, Washtenaw, and Branch counties, was mustered into United States service June 20. The companies of the Second Regiment, like those of the First, were assembled at Fort Wayne in Detroit before starting for the East. The Third and Fourth were transported directly to Washington from their points of rendezvous at Grand Rapids and Adrian, respectively. The period of training for the men in these regiments was very brief; all three had arrived in Washington by June 25.

And now throughout the North the cry was "On to Richmond!" With 80,000 troops in the vicinity of Washington an insistent demand for action was heard. General Winfield Scott, a hero of the War of 1812 and the Mexican War as well as the nation's highest ranking military officer, advised delay until the troops could be better trained, but his caution was attributed to his advanced age. President Lincoln, reasoning that Union troops were probably as well prepared as the Confederates, ordered General Irvin McDowell to strike a blow. The result was the Battle of Bull Run, fought on July 21. The First Michigan was in the thick of the fight. Six of its members were killed in battle, thirty-seven were wounded, and seventy were reported captured or missing. Its commanding officer, Colonel Willcox, suffered a severe wound and was taken prisoner. Although the Union forces were at first successful, the Confederates counterattacked, and the Union retreat turned into a rout. The Second and Third Michigan Infantry were not in the battle but helped cover the retreat. Members of Congress, including Michigan's Senator Zachariah Chandler, who had come out in carriages to watch the battle, scurried back to Washington. The illusion that the war was going to be brief was shattered. It was a testing time for the people of the North. There were voices of despair, but the great majority of the people simply accepted the hard fact that the task ahead was likely to be long and difficult.

For the men of the First Michigan Infantry the battle came at the end of their three-month term of enlistment. Shortly afterward, therefore, the regiment returned to Detroit where the soldiers were greeted with great enthusiasm and were hailed as heroes in speeches delivered by Lewis Cass and others. Some of the officers enlisted in the new First Michigan Infantry for three-year terms, but most of the members of the three-months regiment returned to civilian life and saw no more service in the remaining four years of the war.

These men were the first of approximately 90,000 Michigan men who served in the Union army and navy during the war.[7] This was about twenty-three percent of the male population of the state according to the census of 1860. Among the various groups in the state, a total of 181 soldiers of the Jewish faith served in Michigan units during the war, a remarkable figure when one considers that there were only about 150 Jewish families in the state at the time. The Jewish soldiers included eleven commissioned officers and thirty-eight officers and soldiers who died of disease or were killed in action.[8] The number of Negro soldiers who were credited to Michigan—1,661—was also quite large in proportion to the total Negro population in Michigan which was less than seven thousand, even though about a quarter of these black soldiers were recruits who came over from Canada. Most of the blacks were members of the First Michigan Colored Infantry Regiment, which was mustered into service early in 1864. This regiment, which was under the command of white officers, was the one Michigan unit in the war that lost its Michigan name when it was made part of the Union army, at which time it became the 102nd United States Colored Infantry Regiment. The number of Indians from Michigan who entered the army was 145, a relatively small figure in proportion to the state's total Indian population. There appears to have been some reluctance to enlist Indians because of the fear that they were not adaptable to so-called "civilized" rules of warfare. Many immigrants, some of them not yet American citizens, fought for the Union cause. The Michigan contingents included 3,929 Irishmen, 4,872 Germans, and 3,761 Englishmen. Michigan, which ranked tenth among the northern states in population, ranked eighth in the number of troops furnished. Thirty-one infantry regiments were raised, eleven cavalry regiments, one regiment of engineers and mechanics, fourteen artillery batteries, one regiment of sharpshooters, and a number of miscellaneous units. Approximately five hundred men from Michigan served in the navy and an undetermined number of Michigan men also served individually or as groups in units that were raised in other states or as members of the relatively small regular United States army. The number of Michigan-designated units was relatively small in contrast to the total number raised in other states, but this was due to Michigan's decision to keep its existing units intact by filling those whose ranks became depleted with fresh recruits rather than organizing the latter into new regiments.

Enthusiasm for the cause and a yen for adventure characterized the early volunteers. As the war advanced it became more difficult to supply the needed manpower. There was a great deal of social pressure on able-bodied men to enlist. The practice of raising companies consisting largely of men living in the same community encouraged friends to enlist together. Governor Blair also adopted the practice, common throughout the states, of appointing popular political figures in an area to be the commanders of the units that were being organized in the belief that they would be particularly good recruiters. When these techniques failed to bring a quick response in meeting the President's periodic calls for more troops, other methods were employed. The legislature authorized townships to raise taxes in order to pay $15 per month to each family whose breadwinner had gone to war. Individuals, local governmental units, the state, and Congress provided funds that were used to pay bounties to volunteers. The amounts varied, but a volunteer might pick up as much as a thousand dollars in bounties from these several sources if he enlisted in the right place at the right time. This led to the practice of bounty-jumping when unscrupulous individuals deserted as soon as they received their bounties in one place and went off to enlist somewhere else.

When the war's insatiable need for additional manpower was not met speedily enough even by these measures a draft was instituted, first by Presidential order in August, 1862, and then more formally by act of Congress on March 3, 1863. Only 4,281 Michigan men were actually inducted into the army as a result of this draft. It was possible for a draftee to be exempted not only for health reasons and other reasons common to later draft laws, but also by hiring a substitute to go in his place or by paying a commutation fee of $300. The amount of such fees that were paid in Michigan during the war totaled $594,600, indicating the number of affluent Michiganians who took advantage of this feature of the Civil War draft that was a major cause of its unpopularity, particularly among poor men who found it impossible to avoid being drafted by either of these means. Another cause of the intense dislike for the draft stemmed from the fact that it was applied only selectively in those areas that had failed to fill their assigned quotas with volunteers. The necessity of resorting to the draft seemed to reflect upon the patriotism of the residents of the affected area, thus adding to the pressures placed on young men to come forward voluntarily by the appointed deadline.

Of those who went to war nearly one out of every six did not return, as the number of Michigan men who died in service was close to 15,000.[9] Among the enlisted men more than twice as many died of disease as were killed in action or died from wounds. Most of the military hospitals were scarcely better than pesthouses; physicians and surgeons were rare, and they had no knowledge of the importance of sanitation and antiseptics. Losses among officers tell a different story with nearly three times more dying from battle action than disease. Whether this difference was due to better food, better living conditions, better care, or to the fact that the officers, in leading their men, were oftentimes more exposed to enemy fire, is hard to tell. That death from disease was a far greater threat to the lives of most soldiers than enemy bullets was best exemplified by the experience of the Sixth Michigan Infantry, which suffered the highest number of fatalities of any Michigan unit. Only seventy-eight of the 582 members of this regiment who died, died as a result of battle action. The remaining deaths were listed under the heading of disease. The latter was not a very exact term, however, since those who died from a variety of causes in prison camps or the Michigan soldiers who were among the more than fifteen hundred released prisoners killed in the explosion of the steamer *Sultana* on April 27, 1865, were included under this general heading.

Michigan men served in every section of the various theaters of war and on the sea. We hear of them in the Peninsular campaign, at Antietam, Shiloh, Fredericksburg, Chancellorsville, Gettysburg, Vicksburg, on the Mississippi, Chickamauga, Atlanta, Richmond, and Appomattox. They took part in more than eight hundred battles and skirmishes. Hundreds of examples of individual heroism can be found in the record of these engagements, with sixty-nine Michigan soldiers receiving the Medal of Honor.[10]

Michigan regiments played a crucial role in some of the war's major battles. The Twenty-fourth Michigan Infantry, part of the famed Iron Brigade, was in the thick of the first day's fighting at Gettysburg. By staving off an overwhelmingly superior Confederate force, the Iron Brigade gave the Union commander, General George Meade, time to bring up the rest of his army so they could occupy the positions that Robert E. Lee's Army of Northern Virginia assaulted in vain on the third and decisive day of the battle. The Twenty-fourth Michigan suffered eighty percent casualties in this engagement, a higher rate than any of the other four hundred Union regiments at Gettysburg. The regiment was so shattered that it saw only limited front-line duty for the remainder of the war. The First, Fifth, Sixth, and Seventh Michigan Cavalry regiments also had an important part in the Union victory at Gettysburg. They constituted the Michigan Cavalry Brigade and had been placed under the command of George Armstrong Custer only two days before the battle broke out. Custer, a dashing and flamboyant figure, was a native of Ohio, but his family had moved to Monroe, Michigan, shortly before the war, and Custer would regard that as his home town, although he spent little time there during the remaining years of his life. In 1863 he was only twenty-four years old, and a recent West Point graduate with the army rank of lieutenant when he was appointed a brigadier-general of volunteers and given the command of the Michigan cavalry regiments. At once he found himself confronting Jeb Stuart, the equally picturesque Confederate cavalry leader. Stuart had failed in his major responsibility at Gettysburg of keeping Lee informed as to the location and movements of the Union army, and hoped to retrieve his failure by assaulting the rear of Meade's army at the moment of Pickett's charge, thus assuring the South a great victory. In this design he was foiled by Custer and his Michigan cavalrymen. A cavalry charge launched by Stuart in the classic manner was turned back by the sabers of Custer's horsemen, and Meade's army was thus shielded and assured of victory in the greatest battle of the war.

The year before, on the bloody battlefield of Antietam, 350 Michigan men were killed, wounded, or missing. General Israel B. Richardson of Pontiac, who had entered the service as commander of the Second Michigan Infantry and had been promoted to the rank of major general just before Antietam, was killed while leading a charge in Bloody Lane. The Seventh Michigan Infantry was part of the brigade that crossed the Rappahannock under fire at the start of the Battle of Fredericksburg in December, 1862. Michigan regiments also took part in the western battles of 1862. The Twelfth Michigan, commanded by Colonel Francis Quinn of Niles, among other Michigan units, fought at Shiloh. The Third Cavalry and Fifteenth Infantry were commended by General William Rosecrans for their courage, efficiency, and gallantry in the Iuka-Corinth campaign. Michigan cavalry, infantry, engineers, mechanics, and artillery helped turn back the Confederate invasion of Kentucky at the Battle of Perryville. And late in December six Michigan infantry regiments and one cavalry regiment saw action in the Battle of Murfreesboro, where the casualties amounted to nearly one-third of those engaged on both sides.

In July, 1863, while Michigan soldiers were fighting at Gettysburg, others were with General Grant in the siege of Vicksburg. Seven Michigan regiments had arrived to strengthen Grant's forces prior to the start of the forty-five-day siege. Ironically, the Confederate commander at Vicksburg, John C. Pemberton, a Philadelphian who had joined the Southern ranks, had served as a young army officer at Detroit, Fort Mackinac, and Fort Brady in the 1830s and early 1840s, a few years before Grant had been stationed at Detroit immediately after the Mexican War.[11] The following September eight Michigan regiments, together with units of Michigan's First Light Artillery and First Engineers and Mechanics, took part in the fierce fighting at Chickamauga. Battery A, First Michigan Light Artillery, a unit organized at Coldwater, suffered frightful losses and its commander, George W. Van Pelt of Coldwater, was killed in a Confederate attack that overran the battery. Eight Michigan regiments helped win the Battle of Chattanooga and to retrieve the loss suffered at Chickamauga.

In retrospect, it is apparent that Gettysburg and Vicksburg were the turning points, but this was far from being apparent at the time. In many respects the darkest days of the war for the Union cause came in 1864. Heavy casualties necessitated a call for more men. General Sherman's army, which included fifteen Michigan regiments, battled it out with the Confederates in Georgia, finally capturing Atlanta and then marching across Georgia to the sea in one of the dramatic exploits of the war. The heaviest losses, however, occurred in the battles of the Wilderness in Virginia, where General Grant gradually pushed the Confederates under Lee into Richmond and Petersburg. At Spotsylvania, the Seventeenth Michigan Infantry lost 190 out of 225 men in a single attack. Once the Confederates threw up their defenses around the Confederate capital and Petersburg, the Union advance was stalled. At one juncture, a tunnel was dug underneath the Confederate works, four tons of powder were exploded, and Union soldiers rushed forward. The attack, which was poorly organized and ended in dismal failure, was made by a force that included six Michigan regiments. Enemy artillery slaughtered scores of men in the crater formed by the explosion. But in the cavalry battles around Richmond that spring, the Confederacy lost one of its most romantic figures, General Jeb Stuart. At a place called Yellow Tavern a bullet fired by a Michigan trooper named John A. Huff, who had enlisted at Pontiac on February 10, 1864, and was serving in the Fifth Michigan Cavalry, ended Stuart's life. Huff himself was mortally wounded less than a month later.

On April 3, 1865, the Confederate defenses in Virginia collapsed with the fall of Petersburg. Michigan troops were the first Union forces to enter this city, whose fall forced Lee to evacuate the capital of Richmond. All hopes that he and his men could regroup and carry on the fight were quickly ended, and on April 9 the fighting in Virginia ended with Lee's surrender to Grant at Appomattox. Even so, there were Michigan soldiers who gave their lives afterward in the fighting in the Carolinas before the Confederates surrendered to Sherman on April 26. The Fourth Michigan Cavalry, which had left Michigan in September, 1862, found itself in the Deep South at the close of the war, after having distinguished itself in the campaigns in the western theaters. Colonel Benjamin D. Pritchard of Allegan had become the regiment's commander. Shortly after occupying Macon, Georgia, Pritchard learned that the president of the Confederacy, Jefferson Davis, was somewhere in south-central Georgia attempting to flee the country. On May 10, Pritchard entered Irwinsville about one o'clock in the morning in search of Davis. He received information that the Confederate leader and his party were camped about a mile and a half away. The place was located and surrounded. Davis, attempting to escape, reached for a coat to put over his shoulders and by mistake took his wife's coat, which led to the story that he was trying to evade capture by disguising himself as a woman. Later that morning, the First Wisconsin Cavalry, also on the lookout for Davis, approached. The two Union regiments each mistook the other for a stray Confederate unit and several men were killed or wounded in the ensuing fight before the mistake was discovered. Pritchard and his staff then delivered their famous prisoner to Fortress Monroe, Virginia, on May 22. Congress had voted $100,000 in reward money to those who captured Davis, and initially it was assumed that this money would go to the Michigan cavalry regiment. However, in 1868, after a prolonged hassle, the money was finally distributed and Pritchard and his men were forced to share the money with a host of officers and other military units that had been engaged in the search for the fleeing Confederate president. In the 1960s, one of Pritchard's descendants sold to the state of Mississippi a small collection of his ancestor's papers relating to Davis's capture for a reported figure of $5,000—substantially more money than Pritchard himself gained from his famous deed.

From the hundreds of letters and diaries that have been preserved, a great deal of information is available on what life was like for a Michigan soldier during the Civil War.[12] In the early months of the war men entered the service lightheartedly, with no conception of what the life of a soldier would be like. Letters home soon reflected the disillusionment that came with endless drilling, long marches, poor food, bad weather, the tedium of life in the camps during winter, and sickness. The men were impatient to get on with the fighting, and the imminence of action, even though it entailed danger, was viewed with relief. As the going got rougher, there were desertions and "bounty jumping." Many Michigan men were captured and imprisoned at Richmond, Andersonville, or one of the other Confederate prisons where lack of good food, poor sanitation, and disease took many lives. Accounts written after the war recall attempts to escape, sometimes successful, sometimes not.

The ranks of Michigan soldiers included at least one woman. She was Sarah Emma Edmonds, who enlisted at Flint in 1861 disguised as a man under the name of Franklin Thompson. For some time she successfully carried on her masquerade and took part in several battles and skimishes as a member of the Second Michigan Infantry. Probably because of poor health she deserted in April, 1863. Her identity was finally revealed in 1882 when she applied for a pension, although there is some evidence that while she was still in the army some of her fellow soldiers knew her secret. She wrote a book describing her adventures entitled *Nurse and Spy in the Union Army*. It is a collection of tall tales that stretch the credulity of the reader. A special congressional committee examined her claim for a pension. She was granted an honorable discharge back-dated to April 19, 1863, and was given a pension. After the war she married and bore three children. She was accepted into membership in the Grand Army of the Republic—the only woman ever received into full membership by that organization. She died in Texas in 1898.[13]

A yearning for home was a common experience of men at the front. The great adventure had dimmed, and life back in Michigan that had seemed dull when the excitement of war was new now took on an aura of glamor. This is reflected not only in the letters the soldiers wrote home, but also in the songs they sang. Shortly after the Battle of Fredericksburg a Detroit woman, Winifred Lee Brent, composed words for a song to be sung to the old German tune "O Tannenbaum," which also was used for the song "Maryland, my Maryland." The verses to the song were first printed in a leaflet, then printed in the Detroit *Tribune* and later reprinted and published for the army at the front. The song became immensely popular both in Michigan and among the state's soldiers in the various sectors of the war. The first verse provided a nostalgic introduction:

> Home of my heart, I sing to thee!
> Michigan, my Michigan.
> Thy lake-bound shores I long to see,
> Michigan, my Michigan.
> From Saginaw's tall whispering pines
> To Lake Superior's farthest mines,
> Fair in the light of memory shines,
> Michigan, my Michigan.

There were ten verses in all, many of which centered around famous battles of the war.

> Dark rolled the Rappahannock's flood,
> Michigan, my Michigan.
> The tide was crimsoned with thy blood,
> Michigan, my Michigan.
> Although for us the day was lost,
> Still it shall be our proudest boast,
> At Fredericksburg the Seventh crossed,
> Michigan, my Michigan.[14]

In Michigan life went on much as usual during the war. New railroads were built, lumbering operations were continued, and manufacturing and mining developed rapidly in spite of the shortage of labor. The farmers went on about their daily tasks, working overtime and enlisting the aid of older men, boys, women, and new kinds of farm machinery. Prices rose rapidly, wages more slowly, a fact that encouraged the spread of organized labor. Capitalists dealt with sums that would have been thought fantastic a few years before. Industrialists stepped up production and made fabulous profits. Business after the war never reverted to the leisurely pace of the years before 1861.

Women were busy preparing bandages and clothing for soldiers, organizing "Soldiers' Aid Societies" to carry on this work.[15] These activities, together with recruiting, kept the war constantly before the people. Newspapers were read avidly, and the number of dailies increased. It is probable that many people first acquired the habit of reading a daily newspaper during the war.

The war proved to be a great impetus to the use of labor-saving machinery on the farm. The demand for reapers and mowers was so great that at times it could not be met. Improved harrows, wheat drills, gang plows, horse rakes, cultivators, threshing machines, and stump lifters helped alleviate the lack of male labor. It became a familiar sight to see women working in the fields. In spite of the shortage of workers, the war brought prosperity to Michigan farmers such as they had never known before. Bumper crops enabled them to send large shipments of wheat, corn, oats, and rye to feed the Union armies. The price of wheat had reached $1.84 a bushel by 1864. One of the most spectacular wartime agricultural developments in Michigan was the enormous increase in the production of hops. A heavy tax on whisky and a growing taste for lager beer heightened the demand for hops, a major ingredient in the brewing of beer. A series of crop failures in New York, the leading producer of hops, further stimulated the growth of hops in Michigan. The cutoff in supplies of southern cotton increased the demand for wool, while the loss of Louisiana cane sugar stimulated the growth of corn sorghum for molasses. The production of butter and cheese in creameries was another outgrowth of the war.[16]

One method by which the labor-shortage problem was solved was the use of immigrants. The population of the state increased by 435,169 during the decade of the sixties, and it is estimated that at least 90,000 of that number were foreign immigrants.[17] The new-comers not only found employment on the farms but also in lumbering, mining, and railroad building. During the first two years of the war the number of foreign immigrants declined. The passage of the Homestead Act of 1862, which enabled aliens who had declared their intention of becoming citizens to acquire public lands free, helped to reverse the trend, and in 1864 Congress passed a contract labor law, permitting immigrants to be brought to the United States under contract to labor for the person or persons who paid for their passage. By 1863 the number of newcomers was above the level of 1860, and it continued to increase during the next two years.

During the first year of the war the copper-mining industry in Michigan was beset by several difficult problems. The price of the metal had dropped to seventeen cents a pound; twenty cents was considered a fair price. The domestic market was disorganized and Confederate privateers threatened to cut off the foreign market. But recovery came fast. As government orders for brass buttons, copper canteens, bronze cannon, and naval equipment began to accumulate, prices rose. They were up to 46.3 cents a pound by 1864. Producing mines paid their owners fabulous profits. New discoveries were made during the war and the number of companies increased from sixteen in 1860 to thirty-six in 1865. Oddly enough, production did not keep pace with higher prices; in fact, it fell by a million and a half pounds in 1862, another half-million in 1863, and still another half-million in 1864. The reason seems to be that the scarce labor supply was being diverted to the development of new mines that had not yet come into full production. In spite of the falloff in production, seventy percent of the nation's copper during the Civil War came from Michigan.[18]

The iron-ore industry, like the copper-mining industry, had a lean year in 1861. Production at all the mines declined drastically. This may have been due partly to labor shortage, but it is also attributed to the fact that Cleveland, the main market for Michigan ore, had a large surplus on hand at the beginning of the year and buyers ceased purchasing additional supplies due to the uncertainties at the beginning of the war. Recovery in iron production, however, was even more rapid than in copper. In 1862 the leading mines—the Jackson, Cleveland, and Lake Superior mines—produced more ore than in any previous year. Stimulated by wartime demand, production increased.[19]

The lumber industry was hit even harder at the opening of the war than iron and copper mining, and in this case the lumber business did not fully recover until after the war. The market was glutted at the outbreak of hostilities. The war emergency made it difficult for the lumbermen to secure capital with which to conduct their business. The labor shortage was acute, and higher wages had to be paid to workmen. The price of lumber went up, however, almost doubling by 1865. Henry H. Crapo, a Flint lumberman, was able in 1863, for the first time, to build up a substantial and uncommitted cash balance.[20]

Railroad building slackened during the war but did not stop. In the Upper Peninsula a line from Escanaba to Negaunee was built between 1862 and 1864. A twenty-mile stretch from Marquette toward Ontonagon was completed in 1865. In the lower peninsula, towns and cities voted funds to attract railroads. In 1863 the legislature passed the first act empowering a municipality to use public credit for grants to a railroad. Twelve other such acts were passed in 1864 and eight more in 1865. So general was the belief that the growth and prosperity of a town depended on a railroad that citizens were willing to pledge thousands of dollars to induce the railroad builders to extend lines to their community. A railroad northward from Jackson to Mason was built in the lower peninsula during the Civil War. The Flint and Pere Marquette Railroad, connecting Saginaw and Flint, was completed in 1862. In 1863–64 Henry H. Crapo headed a company that built another line connecting Flint with the Detroit and Milwaukee Railroad. In spite of a delay in construction due to a strike of workmen, the line was completed by November 1, 1864.

The Civil War stimulated manufacturing in Michigan. Between 1860 and 1870 the number of manufacturing establishments increased by 174 percent and the amount of capital invested by 201 percent.[21] In Detroit the Michigan Car Company, the Detroit Bridge and Iron Works, the Detroit Safe Company, and the E. T. Barnum Wire and Iron Works were among the plants started during the war. A law passed by the legislature in 1863 permitted the manufacture of beer in spite of the 1855 prohibition law, and this legislation resulted in the launching of many breweries. Following the passage of the

National Bank Law by Congress in 1863, national banks were founded in several Michigan cities. Charter No. 22, the first to be granted to a Michigan bank, was that of the First National Bank of Ann Arbor. Also chartered in 1863 were two national banks in Detroit, and one each in Fenton, Ypsilanti, and Hillsdale.

One of the annoying features of wartime life was the scarcity of small change. When the government ceased to redeem its paper currency in gold or silver, individuals and banks hoarded the coins that had been in circulation. At first postage stamps were used for change, but the gummed backs were a nuisance and ungummed stamps were substituted. Finally came the issue of "shin plaster" paper, so called because its size was only two by three inches. It was issued in denominations of five, ten, twenty-five, and fifty cents.

Michigan remained overwhelmingly loyal to the Union cause throughout the war. There was little trouble with "copperheads." Politically, the Democrats, while making some gains during the war, were unable to score major victories. Governor Blair was re-elected in 1862, although his margin of victory over his Democratic opponent, Byron G. Stout of Pontiac, a former Repubican, was less than six thousand votes. (Blair's winning margin in 1860 was twenty thousand votes.) The Republicans also lost one of Michigan's six Congressional seats to the Democrats, who also made sizable gains in both houses of the state legislature.

Two years later, war weariness in the North caused Republican leaders to fear for the success of their tickets on the national and state levels, but late in the summer of 1864, Union victories in Georgia helped to revive support for the Lincoln administration and secured Lincoln's re-election in November. In Michigan, Lincoln's margin of victory over the Democratic candidate, General George B. McClellan, was less than half of the margin he had rolled up over Douglas in 1860. On the state level, the Republican candidate for governor, Henry Crapo, the Flint lumberman, had an easier time in defeating his opponent, even though the Michigan Democrats, following the lead of the national party, had nominated a military officer, William M. Fenton, likewise from Flint, who had commanded the Eighth Michigan Infantry from 1861 to 1863. Crapo thus became the first of the so-called lumber barons to be elected governor of Michigan. Fenton, on the other hand, represented a throwback to past days of Democratic dominance in Michigan since he had served as lieutenant governor from 1848 to 1852. The Democrats sought to recapture their bygone days of glory by also placing on their state ticket in 1864 such old favorites as John D. Pierce, Rix Robinson, and former governor Alpheus Felch. But this was to no avail as the party not only failed to win back the governorship or any other state executive office but also lost the one seat it had picked up in Congress in 1862. Its state legislative delegation was also reduced.

A highly controversial feature of the 1864 election was the soldiers' vote. At a time when there was no provision for absentee ballots, the legislature in February, 1864, had passed an act authorizing Michigan residents who were in the military service to vote, whether they were in the state on election day or not. The resulting ballots cast by Michigan soldiers in the field were overwhelmingly in favor of the Republican candidates and were the deciding factor in a number of legislative and other local contests. In response to a challenge of the legality of this act, the Michigan Supreme Court on January 28, 1865, unanimously ruled that the Soldiers' Vote Act was unconstitutional. However, the Republican majority in the state legislature chose to ignore the court and voted to seat thirteen Republican senators and representatives rather than their Democratic opponents who would have gained those seats if the votes of the soldiers had been thrown out.[22]

The war, then, saw a continuation of the Republican dominance of state politics that had begun in 1854. In 1863, Zachariah Chandler was re-elected by the legislature to the United States Senate where he emerged during the war as one of the leaders of the Radical Republican forces who were critical of Lincoln's Reconstruction plans for the Confederate states. It was Chandler, however, who was credited with helping assure Lincoln's re-election in 1864 by persuading John C. Fremont, who had been nominated by dissident Republican radicals, to withdraw from the Presidential race.

Michigan's other Senator during most of the war was Jacob M. Howard, who was, like Chandler, a Detroiter. Howard was first elected in 1862 to fill the unexpired term of the late Kinsley Bingham, and then was elected to a full six-year term in 1865. In both cases, Howard was opposed by Austin Blair, whose out-state supporters objected to having both of Michigan's Senate seats filled by Detroit residents. Howard's victories over Blair in the Republican legislative caucus were evidence of the power that Chandler had come to wield. Blair served with great distinction as the state's governor during all but the last few months of the war. He supported the Lincoln administration vigorously, and with energy and foresight did much to keep Michigan in the forefront of the loyal states. He spared no effort to provide the needed supplies and equipment for Michigan's soldiers. Because his official duties left little time to devote to his law practice, Blair left office at the end of 1864 with his personal finances shattered. He never really recovered and in 1892, toward the end of his life, friends raised four thousand dollars which they presented to the former governor at Christmas, "not as charity, but as a token of affection." Politically, too, Blair's wartime defeats in his campaigns for the Senate signalled a decline of a public career that had seemed to hold such promise at the start of the war. Although he did serve in the lower house of Congress in the immediate post-war years, the continuing opposition of Chandler's machine to Blair's higher political ambitions ultimately drove the frustrated Jackson Republican into the Democratic party ranks in the 1870s. Following his death in 1895, the state erected a bronze statue of Blair at the chief entrance to the state capitol, where it has become one of Lansing's most famous landmarks—a merited tribute to a great leader.[23]

There was much activity on the home front on behalf of the soldiers and sailors from the state. The Michigan Soldiers' Relief Association was formed in Washington, D.C., to take care of emergency needs of Michigan soldiers in the Army of the Potomac. Contributions of money, clothing, and hospital stores were made by the people back home and forwarded to the national capital. Among the services of this organization was the maintenance of a hostel in Washington called the Michigan Soup House, which provided food and lodging for soldiers on leave. A separate Michigan Soldiers' Relief Association was formed back in Michigan in April, 1862. It collected and sent to the front hundreds of boxes and barrels filled with food and clothing for Michigan soldiers, including such items as socks, underwear, handkerchiefs, canned fruit, pickles, jellies, and wines. Newspapers, books, needles, pins, thread, and other items were also included. The army maintained hospitals for sick and wounded soldiers and each regiment had a surgeon. The United States Sanitary Commission was formed to assist the government in this work. A Michigan branch of the sanitary commission was formed in Detroit in November, 1861, and was called the Michigan Soldiers' Aid Society. In various towns Ladies' Soldiers' Aid Societies were active. One in Kalamazoo in the fall of 1864 staged a big "Sanitary Fair." The regular state fair was held in Kalamazoo both in 1863 and 1864, and it was in conjunction with this agricultural fair that the women of Kalamazoo originated a plan to enlist state-wide support for the various soldiers' aid societies in 1864. Merchandise, produce, farm animals, and implements were contributed and sold for the benefit of the cause. The torn and battle-scarred flags of the Michigan regiments were displayed, and Governor Blair gave the opening address. Over $9,000 was raised. Still another wartime organization that received help from Michigan was the United States Christian Commission, which collected and sent to the front Bibles and religious literature; "delegates," usually ministers, volunteered to serve in army hospitals for a period of six weeks to comfort the sick and dying.

The firm support that the people of Michigan gave to the Lincoln administration was based primarily on a determination to restore the Union. There appears to have been little enthusiasm among most of the civilians and soldiers at the outset of the war for freeing the slaves. For example, there were highly vocal and even violent reactions on the part of some Ann Arbor residents in 1861 and 1862 to the appearance in that town of two anti-slavery lecturers, Parker Pillsbury and Wendell Phillips.[24] Lincoln's primary object in the early months of the war was to keep the border slave states in the Union, and he steadfastly refused to turn the war into a crusade against slavery. When he revoked an order by General John C. Fremont which freed the slaves in Missouri, he was subjected to a torrent of criticism, including Zachariah Chandler's. About the same time, Colonel Frederick Curtenius of Kalamazoo, commander of the Sixth Michigan Infantry, chose to resign his commission rather than obey an order to return escaped slaves in Louisiana to their owners. His action was upheld by a resolution passed by the Michigan legislature. It was not surprising, therefore, that when Lincoln issued his Emancipation Proclamation in September, 1862, the action was received with acclaim in Michigan by most Republicans. In Detroit, meetings to celebrate the event were held in Negro churches and were well attended.

Although a large majority of the people in the state were steadfast in their zeal for the Union cause, grumblers, dissenters, and defeatists were not lacking. A rally held in Detroit on July 15, 1862, following Lincoln's call for 300,000 more men, was broken up by hecklers and rowdies. The following March, when the draft was imposed, many in Detroit felt threatened and were angry at the unfair way in which it was administered. For some whites, these feelings were translated also into resentment toward blacks, who were blamed for the war. The result was a race riot on March 6, 1863. The central figure in the trouble was a Negro named William Faulkner, who was accused of raping two young girls. Faulkner's trial aroused great excitement. A howling mob attempted to drag Faulkner out of the jail. A guard fired into the crowd, killing a bystander, and the riot began. Before it was over fire had destroyed between thirty and thirty-five buildings, an estimated two hundred Negroes were homeless, and two people were dead. Soldiers from Fort Wayne and members of the Twenty-seventh Michigan Infantry in Ypsilanti had to be called in to restore order. The city quieted down quickly afterward, and there were many expressions of shame and regret over the affair. Faulkner, meanwhile, had been found guilty and sentenced to prison. Some years later, the girls who had been his accusers admitted that they had fabricated the whole story. Faulkner was then pardoned. He returned to Detroit where some businessmen helped to establish him in the produce business. The 1863 riot, while grimly foreshadowing Detroit's future racial problems, also served to convince city authorities of the need for a full-time police force.[25]

Detroit was also the center of a plot in 1864 to free Confederate prisoners who were held in a prison camp on Johnson's Island, near Sandusky, Ohio. Involved were Confederate spies and sympathizers from Canada. The ringleaders boarded the vessel *Philo Parsons* at Detroit on September 19, 1864. More men were taken on board when the ship stopped at Amherstburg on the Canadian side of the river. The conspirators seized the vessel once it left Amherstburg, locking up the officers in the cabin. The plan was to capture the *U.S.S. Michigan,* which lay off Sandusky, guarding Johnson's Island. They did not know that Lt. Col. Bennet H. Hill, acting assistant provost marshal general in charge of the Detroit district, had learned of the plot. The conspirators on the *Philo Parsons* realized that something was wrong when they failed to get the prearranged signal from the *U.S.S. Michigan,* which their fellow conspirators were to have boarded. The *Philo Parsons* thereupon returned to Canada, where she was abandoned by her thwarted mutineers. Several of the plotters were arrested, but they escaped from jail.[26]

On April 3, 1865, news came to Michigan that the Confederate capital of Richmond had fallen. The people were delirious with joy. Everywhere there were processions, bonfires, shouting, singing, and fireworks. A few days later the telegraph brought word of Lee's surrender at Appomattox, and the celebrations were resumed on April 10 with even greater enthusiasm. But then on April 15 they learned the tragic news of Lincoln's assassination, and joy was turned into profound sorrow. Memorial services were held all through the state. Detroit's observance on April 25 included a two-mile procession, and Senator Jacob M. Howard highlighted that day's activities with a funeral oration in Campus Martius. The Twenty-fourth Michigan Infantry served in the military escort at the services held when Lincoln was buried at Springfield, Illinois, on May 4.

Soon after the fighting was over, the men who had served under Grant and Sherman marched triumphantly through Washington, D.C., in a never-to-be-forgotten procession. One by one the various regiments that had fought in the campaigns in Virginia passed in review on May 23, to be followed on the next day by the parade of Sherman's veterans of the campaigns in the western theaters. Then the regiments began to return home. By June of 1865, the first of Michigan's military units had arrived in the state and were paid and disbanded at the two principal reception centers at Detroit and Jackson. It was not until June, 1866, that the last Michigan soldiers had been mustered out. A few days later, on July 4, 1866, many of the Michigan veterans reassembled in Detroit for a ceremony at which their regimental flags were formally presented to the state— flags which remain on display in the state capitol building in Lansing.

It was natural that the veterans should form an organization to promote their interests. The Grand Army of the Republic, formed in 1866, was by far the most important of these Civil War veterans' groups. A Michigan chapter was organized in 1867 but it was not until 1878 that the Michigan Department of the Grand Army of the Republic was permanently established. The state Grand Army of the Republic reached its highest point in membership in 1893 when more than 21,000 men were enrolled in the local "posts" that were found in nearly every community in the state. The organization became a powerful pressure group. It fought successfully for pensions and other benefits for veterans. Most of its members were strong Republicans, and they helped keep Michigan in the Republican column. For many years the various Michigan regiments held annual reunions, where veterans met to exchange yarns, to march once more, and to pose for photographers. The dedications of the monuments that Michigan, along with other northern states, would erect on the major battlefields, would be the occasion for some of these veterans to reassemble at the site of their most famous wartime experiences. Other monuments were erected in most Michigan cities and towns, with the most elaborate of these being the Soldiers' and Sailors' Monument in downtown Detroit, paid for with voluntary contributions of nearly $75,000, and dedicated in 1872. After a lapse of many years, state funds were appropriated during the centennial of the Civil War in the 1960s to assist in the erection of additional war-related historical markers, as well as financing other programs in commemoration of the war.

Orlando LeValley of Caro was the last Departmental Commander of the Michigan Grand Army of the Republic and the last surviving Civil War veteran of a Michigan unit. He died in 1948 at the age of 107. The state, however, continued to provide office space and to pay the salary of the secretary of the state Grand Army of the Republic until that woman's death in 1960.

17

THE HEYDAY OF THE LUMBERMAN

At about the time the Civil War was drawing to an end, an economic development occurred in Michigan with consequences for the state that were equally as important as the military and political effects of the Civil War. It was at this time that Michigan emerged as the foremost lumber-producing state in the Union, a position it would hold through most of the remaining years of the century. The economy of Michigan, and many other aspects of life in the state, was dominated in these years by the harvesting, sawing, and marketing of lumber, chiefly white pine. Thousands of men found employment in the industry, fortunes were made from it, and it made a major contribution to the establishment of farms, towns, and cities throughout mid-America.

If we search for the beginnings of the lumber industry, we might go back to the French period, for the French felled trees to construct their forts, missions, and fur-trading posts. They even built windmills to provide power for sawing the lumber they needed. When the British came they cut and sent huge oak logs down the St. Lawrence to be used for constructing the stout beams and masts of the British men-of-war and merchant ships, as well as using this wood for the ships they built at Detroit. After the War of 1812 the Americans, too, cut these timbers to build ships that would sail the Great Lakes. For these purposes hardwoods were used.

It was not the hardwood trees that predominate in the southern part of the state that built the lumber industry, however. The beech, oak, hickory, sugar maple, and ash were of only limited usefulness to the settlers in this region, who were primarily farmers desiring to clear the land in order to plant their crops. North of the forty-third parallel, however, softwoods predominated. Here were the white pine, the Norway pine, the jack pine, as well as the less valuable spruce, white cedar, tamarack, and hemlock. The pines were most highly prized. Pine was king in the heyday of the lumberman. The best of the white pines were referred to as "cork pines." These huge trees, some of them three hundred years old and measuring as much as two hundred feet in height and five feet in diameter at the base of the trunk, became the prime target of the lumberman, and only a few specimens, such as those in Hartwick Pines State Park near Gaylord, have survived.

As the northern areas of Michigan were surveyed, an awareness of the immensity of the region's pine resources began to develop. Based on the surveyors' field notes, estimates placed the amount of standing pine at 150,000,000,000 board feet,[1] enough, it was said, to build a floor that would cover Michigan's entire land area, with enough left over to cover Rhode Island. This mid-century estimate proved to be too low, however, since by 1897 some 160,000,000,000 board feet of Michigan pine had been cut, with considerable timber still to be harvested.

Information concerning Michigan pine was becoming available in the 1840s at a time when the forests in the East were beginning to be exhausted. When specimens of Michigan white pine were exhibited in these older parts of the country, lumbermen from that area, particularly Maine, began to flock to Michigan. In 1840, the leading lumber-producing states had been New York, Maine, Pennsylvania, Virginia, and South Carolina. By 1850, Michigan was beginning to edge into the picture, ranking fifth in the country behind New York, Pennsylvania, Maine, and Ohio. By 1860, Michigan was third, ahead of Maine and Ohio, and behind Pennsylvania and New York in lumber production. Somewhere in the sixties, however, Michigan moved out ahead of all others, a position the state would hold thereafter to the end of the century. During the peak years of the lumber activity (around 1880), Michigan produced about a fourth of the nation's lumber, with its production nearly equalling that of the next three states combined.

The first region in which large-scale lumber production was undertaken was in the Saginaw area. Here was an area of more than three million acres covered with white pine of unsurpassed size and quality. Since the earliest markets for lumber outside of Michigan were in the eastern states, the location of the outlet for the lumber of the Saginaw region on the east side of the lower peninsula was an advantage. But the key to the early exploitation of Saginaw's pine resources lay in the fact that they were threaded by a large number of rivers that could be utilized to float the logs to the sawmills. The Cass, Flint, Shiawassee, Bad, Tittabawassee, Chippewa, and several other rivers which converged to form the Saginaw River itself, had a total length of 864 miles for log driving. Until the development of logging railroads, the only method of transporting the logs from the forests to the sawmills was to float them down the rivers. By 1854, there were thirty-nine mills in the Saginaw Valley with a capacity of 100,000,000 board feet of lumber per year.

The methods and the tools peculiar to the logging business had been developed over a period of time in the East in Canada's Maritime provinces and in the American Northeast, particularly Maine, which had long been the source of prime lumber and the home of the lumbermen in the United States. The tools, techniques, and personnel of the eastern lumber camps, particularly those in Maine, were moved to the Wolverine State—first to Saginaw, and then in the next few years northward to the Au Sable, westward to the Grand River valley, and then northward along the west coast of the lower peninsula. In the 1880s large-scale lumbering began in the Upper Peninsula. By the turn of the century, with most of the state stripped of its virgin timber, the lumbermen left Michigan and the Great Lakes area and, repeating the process that had been followed when they first came to Michigan, moved across the country to the Pacific Northwest.

The town of Saginaw became a trading center and the site of several of the sawmills of the Saginaw Country. Located about twenty miles up the Saginaw River from Saginaw Bay, the town traced its beginning to a fur-trading post established by Louis Campau in 1816. Beginning in the 1850s and continuing for a generation, lumber was the lifeblood of Saginaw. Although the risks were great and many operators suffered losses, under the right combination of capital, management, and luck, enormous fortunes were made. The lumberjacks made it a lively place when they came in from the camps in the spring. Fabulous stories are told of their roistering. One of the colorful figures of these days was "Little Jake" Seligman—clothing merchant, banker, real-estate dealer, and operator of the horse-drawn street cars. To attract crowds, Seligman would often scatter coins in the street from the upper story of his store. He hired bands to march through the town. When the lumbermen came into town in droves, Seligman would toss them vests, promising to provide matching coats and trousers for those who caught the vests. He kept his promise, but in the process the vests were usually torn to shreds, and the captor who claimed the free coat and pants had to pay a fancy price for a matching vest. Later Seligman had workmen erect a statue of himself above a four-faced clock atop the Tower Building.[2]

On the western side of the lower peninsula the first sawmills were built at Grand Rapids in 1832 and in Muskegon in 1837. Others soon followed and by 1860 there were mills at the mouths of most of the larger rivers flowing into Lake Michigan to the north of Muskegon. The richest drives came down the Manistee, the Boardman, and particularly the Muskegon, where the town of Muskegon at the mouth of this two-hundred-mile-long river came to rival Saginaw in importance in the lumber industry. Some of the lumber towns, like Singapore at the mouth of the Kalamazoo, failed to survive the great days of lumbering and became ghost towns, but the water and port facilities that had made the major lumber towns important in the lumber era combined to make them almost equally important to the changing economic needs of later eras.

The advance of the lumberman was never on a straight line. For instance, Van Buren County, located in the second tier of counties north of Indiana, was heavily forested and contained both softwoods and hardwoods. Yet this county was scarcely touched by the lumbermen prior to 1870 because of a lack of transportation facilities. Simillaly, the first sawmill in the Upper Peninsula was built at Sault Ste. Marie in 1822, and others were built on the Lake Michigan side of the peninsula in the 1830s, but this was only to supply local needs. The great migration of lumbermen to the northern peninsula began only in the eighties, at which time lumbering in the lower peninsula was still booming. The chief rivers used by the lumbermen in the Upper Peninsula were the Tahquamenon and the Ontonagon, flowing into Lake Superior, and the Escanaba and Menominee, emptying into Lake Michigan. The original forests of the peninsula covered some ten million acres, but much of this acreage was not penetrated by navigable rivers and hence was not exploited until a much later time when railroads and eventually motor trucks were able to open up previously inaccessible areas.

The work of cutting the timber was done in the winter because then the logs could be economically transported to the banks of the rivers. This was done by the use of huge bobsleds which could be slid over the iced logging roads to the river banks. There the logs were piled twenty to thirty feet high. Each log was marked with the initial or insignia of the man or the firm to which it belonged, and which was stamped into the end of the log. These log marks were registered at the county seat of the county in which the logging operation was being conducted. The marks were designed to identify the log's owner when the log was mixed in with those of other owners in the annual river drive, just as the western cattle brand identified the ownership of the cattle that were part of the long cattle drives.[3]

As soon as the ice melted off the surface of the rivers in the spring, and while the stream was still flooded, the rivermen took over the task of getting the logs downstream. This was a difficult and perilous business. The first operation consisted of dislodging the "key" log so as to bring the whole pile rolling and plunging into the river. Then the problem was to prevent log jams from forming and if they did form, to break them up. Falls, dams, or rapids were other problems. A sluice way was built around such obstacles to get the logs through. If water was low a dam was necessary to back up the water enough to float the logs. The riverman, with his heavy spiked boots, worked night and day until the drive was over. His was a special profession, and he was generally reputed to be the toughest man in the business.[4]

The business of running logs downstream was known as "booming." On the major rivers "boom" companies were formed, and by lobbying in Lansing some of them obtained exclusive rights to handle the log drive on a certain river for an established price. The logging companies operating on a particular river would own stock in the boom company. Such companies could then afford to invest capital in making the river more usable for their purposes: removing obstacles, building dams and sluiceways, and so on. When the logs reached the mouth of the river they were sorted according to the marks on them, then fastened together into rafts to be hauled to the mills located around the river's mouth.

A new era in the lumbering business began in 1876 when the logging railroad began to achieve popularity. Winfield Scott Gerrish, a native of Maine who started logging on the Muskegon River at the age of eighteen, visited the Centennial Exposition at Philadelphia in 1876, where he saw on exhibit a small Baldwin locomotive. It occurred to him that such a locomotive could be used to pull flat cars loaded with logs from the woods to the banks of the rivers. This would enable the lumbermen to extend their operations several miles from the rivers—further than it was practical to haul logs by bobsled—while at the same time making it possible to haul logs in warm weather as well as in the cold weather which was required for sledding operations. Returning to Michigan, Gerrish organized the Lake George and Muskegon Railroad, built a six-mile rail line from his holdings to the Muskegon River, secured a locomotive and, amidst hoots of derision from fellow lumbermen, started operations. The experiment proved to be a great success. By 1882, thirty-two of

"Side-winder"; Shay logging locomotive of the 1880s

these narrow-gauge logging railroads were built in Michigan, and by 1889 a total of eighty-nine were in operation. By this means, enormous stands of pine, previously too remote to be harvested, were attacked by the lumbermen. The logging railroads not only opened immense new areas but also made year-round logging possible and practical.[5]

The logging railroad was but one of a number of inventions and improvements that greatly accelerated the pace of lumbering activity by the 1870s. Logging in the summer months, previously not practical, was facilitated not only by the widespread adoption of Gerrish's idea but also by the development by Silas Overpack from Manistee of the "big wheels." These wheels, eleven feet or so in diameter, enabled a team of horses to haul three or four logs at a time because the heavy weight of the logs was borne by the wheels' axle, from which the logs were suspended by a chain. A number of these wheels, which were manufactured by Overpack and his sons for many years, are displayed in outdoor settings in northern Michigan.

In addition to transportation improvements, the cutting and processing of the timber was greatly improved in the same period.

Until the seventies, trees had to be felled with axes, although the crosscut saw was then used to cut the logs into sixteen-foot lengths. It was only when manufacturers produced crosscut saws of improved design and with stronger steels that they were capable of sawing down standing timber. In the sawmills a major advance was achieved when the circular saw, which was reportedly first produced in the United States about 1814 by Benjamin Cummins, who is buried in a cemetery at Richland, Michigan, was introduced into mill operations around 1850. Two Michigan men, one from Kalamazoo and the other from Muskegon, improved the method of handling logs in the mills, while another productive idea was to shoot steam into the millponds to prevent the formation of ice, so that logs stored in the ponds could be used throughout the winter. By the 1880s, an average mill that had been able to cut 3,000,000 board feet annually in the fifties could now turn out from 10,000,000 to 20,000,000 board feet a year.

A logging camp in Mecosta County in the 1870s may be regarded as fairly typical. It was directed by two men and was located in the middle of a 240-acre forest area. The camp consisted of six buildings accommodating seventy men, twenty teams of horses, and seven yoke of oxen. The cook shanty, always the central building in a camp, was twenty by fifty-two feet in size, one story high, and consisted of a kitchen and a dining room. The latter contained two long tables covered with oilcloth, where forty-two men could be fed at one time. The staples consisted of potatoes, beans, pork, bread, molasses, and strong tea. These could be found on the table in some form three times a day. Five barrels of flour, five barrels of pork, and fifteen to twenty bushels of potatoes were used each week. An alarm clock set three-quarters of an hour fast went off at 4:00 a.m. The teamsters were out first, and were off to work long before daylight, making one trip to the river, a distance of two miles, before breakfast. They made five trips a day. When that was done, they unhitched and did no more, even though it might be some time before sundown. The horses were given loving care and were not overworked. The bunkhouse was a building twenty-six by thirty-six feet, and one and a half stories high. It contained eighteen bunks on the first floor and fourteen on the second, each accommodating two men. The bunks were made of boards, and were "double-deckers"; each was supplied with a straw tick and blankets. For heat there was a large box stove, and for light, kerosene lamps. In the evening there was card playing, storytelling, and tall talk. There was no drinking of intoxicating liquors in this camp or in others; that was left for the end of the season when the boys "went to town." The other buildings consisted of a barn, a granary, a blacksmith and carpentry shop, and a store where a contractor sold tobacco, clothing, and odds and ends. In a single season, this camp turned into the river 4,500,000 feet of timber. In addition to this the workers had cut another million feet that were rejected by the scaler for some defect. The chronicler states that the labor on this million feet was all lost. One is tempted to ask, "What about the trees?"[6]

Most lumber camps were intended to be merely temporary, but in the later years of the lumber era there are instances of towns being built by the operators. One such was Deward in Kalkaska County, named for a famous lumberman, David Ward. When he died in 1900 it was found that under the terms of his will his estate had to be settled within twelve years. The executors decided to clear a tract of timberland consisting of 90,000 acres within that period. They built the town of Deward in the heart of the forest, had a huge mill constructed, and started operations in September, 1901. Cottages were built for the workmen and their families. There was a company store, a schoolhouse, a church, and a community hall, but no saloons. At its height Deward had 800 inhabitants. But in 1912 the job was done, the mill was dismantled and hauled away, and gradually the people moved elsewhere. Deward, like other lumber centers, became a ghost town.[7]

The personnel of the lumber camp varied. There were always Irishmen, and large numbers of Swedes, Finns, and Norwegians. A Swede named Louis Sands brought Swedes, called "Sandies," into Michigan by the boatloads and trainloads. Hundreds of young men from southern Michigan farms spent one or more winters in the camps. Many of the lumberjacks were Yankees who had come to Michigan from the Maine woods. There were also French-Canadians, many of them also veterans of the lumber camps of Maine and Quebec. Whoever they were and wherever they came from, they were a hardy, tough lot, capable of gargantuan labors and filled to the brim with zest for living.

The lumberjacks, unlike the cowboys and the voyageurs, did not sing while working. The reason is obvious to anyone who has ever been at the business end of an axe or a crosscut saw. But in the bunkhouse in the evening they sang interminable ballads, most of them with a sad ending. Two of these, "The Jam of Garry's Rock" and "The Red-light Saloon," were sung in logging camps from coast to coast. These and others emphasized the story, not the music. Indeed, the lumberjacks rendered these ballads to almost any tune, or to no tune at all. One author states that the singers were of two principal schools—wailers and bull roarers.[8]

When the hard winter's work was over and the lumberjacks arrived at the nearest town, they let loose with unrestrained merrymaking. Fighting, with no holds barred, appears to have been their favorite sport. There were legendary battlers, such as the muscular Silver Jack, who, it was told, once felled an ox with his fist and could twist horseshoes at will with his bare hands. Then there was Joe Fournier, a French-Canadian, whose specialty was butting with his head his opponent or an oak bar or anything else in his way.[9] In the Upper Peninsula the most notorious town in the lumbering era was Seney. The accounts of the wickedness of Seney in its prime are legendary and highly exaggerated, but it was a rough place.

There is a wealth of folklore about the lumberjack. Of a somewhat different character, however, is the mythology of Paul Bunyan. Where and when it arose is not known. Some trace it back to a figure who appeared during the Canadian rebellion of 1837, a "mighty-muscled, bellicose, bearded giant" who "raged among the Queen's troops like Samson among the Philistines." But the myth is usually traced back to the Saginaw Country. Paul was the super-logger of them all, and as stories were told of his exploits, they gained by accretion. Paul Bunyan and his blue ox, which measured forty-two axe handles and a plug of chewing tobacco between the horns, became so well known that they have become the symbols of countless establishments dedicated to extracting dollars from the pockets of tourists. Paul Bunyan is not an authentic folk hero; rather he is a product of popular mythology, with a strong infusion of commercialism.[10]

Remembered through folklore and mythology, his drinking, fighting, and wenching exploited by sensation-mongers, the real lumberjack has become difficult to distinguish. There can be little doubt that the sort of lumberjacks that are the best known were far from typical. A great many and probably the majority of the lumberjacks were honest, law-abiding citizens who were as moderate in their habits as most men are. After a winter in the North, most of the men from the farms of southern Michigan returned to their homes in the spring and put away their winter's earnings to start a career or a family.[11]

Just as it is a mistake to assume that all lumberjacks resembled those about whom the tall stories were told, so is it a mistake to assume that all those who invested in timber and sawmills became fabulously rich. There were thousands of small operators; there were many who made only modest profits, and there were those who failed altogether. To make money in logging and lumber manufacture required all those qualities that success in any business enterprise demands. Another myth is that the men who made good in the industry were uniformly crooked and dishonest. One competent historian of the Saginaw area concluded that the lumbermen were as honest and straightforward as any group of businessmen. Great opportunities for wealth were available to the man who worked hard and used his head; it was not necessary to resort to shady dealing, though many unquestionably did.

The success of an investor in Michigan pinelands began with the selection of the best available tracts. Notes of government surveyors included information concerning topography, vegetation, and forests, sometimes giving hints of the quality of the timber. But more data than this was desirable. To obtain this information lumbermen engaged "timber cruisers" who were expert judges of pine and roamed the forests looking for it. They climbed tall trees to get a look at large areas, then made on-the-spot inspections. When they located a choice tract they hurried to the land office to reserve it for their employers. On occasion there were races between rival cruisers.

A considerable amount of the land obtained for logging was purchased from the United States government at $1.25 an acre, the minimum price. After the Homestead Act was passed in 1862, lumbermen hired men to enter claims to 160 acres each, which were made available without cost under the law to bona fide settlers. Settlement was maintained long enough to allow the timber to be cut. Millions of acres of land were given to railroad companies to induce them to build lines into the northern country, and lumbermen often bought or leased tracts from these companies, or from the company that received 750,000 acres for building the Soo Canal. In other cases purchases were made from the state. Millions of acres of "swamp lands" granted to the state by the federal government were sold to the lumbermen for a small amount or given outright as a reward for building roads. Operators often did not confine their cutting to the area they had purchased. There was the practice of "logging a round forty," which meant buying forty acres and then cutting the timber around it in all directions far beyond the boundaries of the area to which title had been secured.

Whether through honest or dishonest means, or both, a sizable number of men became rich through profits from lumber. By the 1890s almost every town or city in Michigan had wealthy citizens whose fortunes had been made in lumber. Such men built huge, imposing residences, replete with all the scrollwork and decoration characteristic of the "gay nineties" mansions. The first citizens to become prominent in Saginaw were Maine lumbermen who had sought and had found opportunities for money-making in the West: the Eddys, the Murphys, the Dorrs, and the Leadbetters. From elsewhere in the East came men like Henry W. Sage of New York, who perhaps best fits the lumber baron image of one who, in the 1870s and 1880s, moved into an area (in this case the Saginaw area), exploited its timber resources in a coldly efficient manner, made great profits, and then moved on to greener fields elsewhere in the country.

The experiences of two other lumbermen of the same period illustrate that Michigan's fabled timber wealth did not necessarily come easily to everyone. Henry H. Crapo, a reasonably successful businessman in Massachusetts, came out to Flint in 1855 to oversee the logging of a large tract of timber in the Flint area that he had come to control. Crapo was then in his fifties and he had had no previous experience in the lumber industry, in contrast to many of his fellow New Englanders who were coming to Michigan in that time. To make up for this lack of experience, Crapo had to devote all of his energies and the skills he had learned in previous business ventures to make a success of his Michigan business, but succeed he did. By the sixties, his lumber operation was perhaps the largest individually owned business of its type in the state, and was rather unusual for its time in the way in which Crapo had integrated in one company all aspects of the lumber business from the cutting phase in the woods right through to the retail sale of the finished lumber. To facilitate the shipment of his lumber, Crapo in 1863–64 built the Flint and Holly Railroad, which he later sold at a profit to the Pere Marquette Railroad. Because of the large stock interest he acquired from the Pere Marquette Railroad, his son—William W. Crapo—served for many years as the president of this major Michigan railroad company.

On the other hand, the experience of Gideon O. Whittemore, pioneer lumberman in the Tawas area and founder of Tawas City, demonstrated the hazards that faced the inexperienced operator who did not possess the business acumen that eventually enabled Crapo to succeed. Whittemore was a middle-aged resident of Michigan, a successful lawyer and politician in Pontiac who had served on the University of Michigan Board of Regents, on the State Board of Education, and as Secretary of State in the administration of Governor Alpheus Felch. Then in 1853, apparently caught up in the growing excitement over Michigan's timber resources, Whittemore purchased a tract of timber land at the mouth of the Tawas River, with Whittemore, his daughter, and an investor in Albany, New York, providing the initial capital to start the lumber business. Nearly every conceivable problem that could beset such an operation had to be contended with, and but for the heroic, if reluctant, efforts of Whittemore's son-in-law, A. B. Mathews, a Pontiac miller and produce broker, who, at great financial risk to his own business, carried his father-in-law's business along to the tune of thousands of dollars and did much of the leg work in lining up buyers, laborers, and supplies for the Tawas company, Whittemore could not have survived. When Gideon Whittemore died in 1863, all of the family's property was mortgaged. By 1866, however, when other lumber mills began to locate in Tawas, Whittemore's sons were finally able to profit from the position that their father's pioneering activities gave them in the booming Tawas area.[12]

Because some of them took the law into their own hands, wealthy lumbermen have been called "lumber barons." Most of them carved success out of hard work, but once they had made their fortune they were fond of living in an ostentatious style. Each tried to outdo the other in the scale and magnificence of the homes they built. One of them built a fence of brick and concrete studded with some 15,000 champagne, wine, and whisky bottles. Portions of this fence may still be seen near the town of Waters, north of Grayling. Many of these mansions, far from handsome by any standard and much too large for modern living, have been torn down.

Some of the so-called lumber barons, at least, subscribed to Andrew Carnegie's "Gospel of Wealth," which declared that the rich man had a responsibility of putting some of his wealth to work benefitting his community. Thus one lumberman, Ammi Wright, was the principal benefactor of Alma College from the time of that Presbyterian school's founding in 1887 until his death in 1912, although Wright was not himself a Presbyterian. The city of Muskegon owes its library, park, art gallery (one of the finest of its size in the country), hospital, schools, and miscellaneous other civic benefactions to the lumberman Charles H. Hackley, who came to the city in 1856 with only seven dollars in his pocket. One of a reported forty lumber millionaires living in Muskegon by 1888, Hackley's gifts to the city totaled nearly $6,000,000, with the income from his educational endowment still contributing significantly to the city's annual school budget.[13] The Sage Library in Bay City and the Hoyt Library in Saginaw are other examples of lumbermen's beneficences to the areas where they had made their fortunes.

Other lumbermen liked to mix "pine and politics." In addition to Henry Crapo—the Flint lumberman who served in the state senate and then as governor of Michigan from 1865 to 1869—David H.

Jerome, governor from 1881 to 1883, and Aaron Bliss, governor at the start of the twentieth century, were two of Saginaw's lumber millionaires who rose to the top in state politics. Russell A. Alger, a wealthy Detroiter who gained much of his fortune from lumber after winning distinction as a cavalry officer in the Civil War, served as governor in the mid-eighties. Alger then went on to serve at the cabinet level in Washington, as United States Senator from Michigan, and in 1888 was a serious contender for the Republican Presidential nomination. Francis B. Stockbridge of Kalamazoo, and Thomas W. Ferry of Grand Haven, who preceded Alger in the United States Senate in this period, also had grown wealthy in the lumber industry. Many other lumbermen served in the state legislature or as Congressmen. In addition, others such as Flint's Josiah Begole, governor in 1883 and 1884 and usually identified as a farmer, also profited from the lumber boom in the state in the late nineteenth century.

* * * * *

Waste in the harvesting and sawing of lumber was enormous. Woodsmen were paid so much per stump, and thus they often cut everything in sight, providing of course it was pine. Company inspectors, however, often rejected many of the logs that were cut because of some minor defect, and otherwise fine lumber was left to rot. No attempt was made to conserve the uncut trees or to replant. The supply of pine seemed inexhaustible.

Even more destructive than the methods employed by the industry were the fires that periodically ravaged the northland, destroying huge tracts of forest. These fires resulted from a lack of concern with fire prevention. In particular, branches that were cut off the main trunk of the trees were simply left on the ground in piles where after a dry summer any spark could ignite them. This was what happened in the fall of 1871, resulting in the most widespread of Michigan's forest fires. On Sunday, October 8, the famous Chicago fire broke out. The flames roared out of control for forty-eight hours and subsided only when most of the city had been destroyed. As the fire raged in Chicago a southwest gale of tornado-like intensity sprang up. Some contemporaries believed it carried sparks from the Chicago fire across Lake Michigan which ignited blazes in Michigan. Actually, however, the same conditions that precipitated the fire in Chicago were prevalent throughout the Great Lakes area and led to numerous fires breaking out at many points, including one that destroyed the Wisconsin town of Peshtigo on October 9 and caused the deaths of 1,182 people, nearly five times as many as died in the Chicago fire.

The summer had been extremely hot and dry. Some areas had had scarcely any rain since June. In Holland on the morning of October 9, fires broke out in the piles of sawdust, waste wood, and finished lumber in the yards of the city's several sawmills, and the winds quickly spread the flames throughout the town, forcing families to flee to open ground and to take boats out into Black Lake. Within two hours the town was almost totally destroyed. Farther north, the same fate came to Manistee, another lumber town, where homes, churches, schools, business establishments, docks, and standing piles of lumber with a total estimated value of up to $1,200,000 were destroyed. From these localities the winds spread the fires inland, or whipped up fires that farmers had lit to burn off accumulated leaves, logs, stumps, and other ground cover. In an incredibly short time the flames had cut clear across the peninsula to Saginaw Bay and beyond, to engulf large areas of the Thumb region. No count of the number of lives that were lost in this fire was ever made, but many individuals and families, particularly in the Thumb, were trapped and were unable to escape the flames. Property losses of various kinds mounted into the millions of dollars, including thousands of acres of forests whose monetary value was incalculable. The following spring, a report of Governor Henry Baldwin indicated that nearly three thousand families had been left homeless, leading Baldwin to organize relief activities to which he personally contributed a third of the $456,106 that was collected.

Exactly a decade later, another, even more terrible fire devastated the Thumb counties of St. Clair, Lapeer, Tuscola, Huron, and Sanilac. Again, the summer had been abnormally dry. In fact, no rain had fallen in the two months prior to early September. Scattered fires had broken out in August, as farmers, following the usual practice, burned brush and rubbish. But then on September 5, a southwestern gale suddenly whipped these fires out of control, and for three days nearly the entire area was engulfed in flames. This was probably the worst disaster in Michigan's history relative to loss of life. In 1882, Governor David Jerome estimated the number of fire victims at nearly three hundred, although other estimates placed the figure at less than two hundred dead. The 1881 fire is best remembered as having resulted in the first disaster-relief project of the American Red Cross, which had been organized by Clara Barton only weeks before the Michigan fire. Eight boxes of clothing and a small contribution of money were furnished by the only working chapter of the Red Cross, that in Clara Barton's home town of Dansville, New York. However, the bulk of the relief that was provided to the victims of the Thumb fire was supplied by state-organized activities, and particularly by the Port Huron Relief Committee.[14]

Lesser fires broke out frequently in the years that followed the fires of 1871 and 1881. A dense pall of smoke often was carried far to the south of these fires in late summer and autumn, further adding to the destruction of Michigan's forests due to the lumberman's efforts. The latter reached its highest point in the mid-1880s, with the output of the state's sawmills peaking at 4,292,000,000 board feet in 1888. Although the annual output declined steadily thereafter, Michigan was still ahead of other states until the late nineties, when it dropped to second place behind Wisconsin, which enjoyed a brief period as the leading lumber-producing state before that distinction was passed on to the states of the Pacific Northwest.

Ore boat

18

THE MINING BOOM

The great boom in the lumber industry in the last four decades of the nineteenth century proved to be a boon to the economy of nearly all of the regions north of the agricultural areas of southern Michigan. In the same period, a boom in the mining of Michigan's diverse mineral resources provided the stimulus needed for the development of the areas where these resources were found, many of which were likewise in the northern parts of the state. Although most of the attention came to be centered on the mining of copper and iron ore found in the extreme northwestern parts of Michigan, other mineral resources were scattered across the two peninsulas, leaving few parts of Michigan that have not been the site of some form of mining during the past century and a half.

If one excludes the relatively small-scale mining of copper by the prehistoric Indians and the abortive English copper-mining venture of the 1770s, the first significant mining activity dates from the mid-1830s when the mining of soft coal deposits found in south-central Michigan began at Jackson. In his report of 1840, state geologist Douglass Houghton reported that nearly fifteen hundred bushels of coal had been dug out in Jackson County for local use. Other outcroppings of coal were mined before the Civil War in nearby Ingham and Eaton counties, where one farmer near Grand Ledge claimed he could get six thousand tons of coal per acre on his farm and had shipped substantial amounts to Detroit, Ionia, and Grand Rapids.[1] Michigan's plentiful supply of wood, however, provided a cheap source of fuel which limited the demand for coal for many years. By 1881, only two coal mines were active, one in Jackson County, and the other near Corunna in Shiawassee County.

411

The major development came in the 1890s in the Saginaw Valley with mines at Saginaw, Bay City, and St. Charles soon accounting for the great bulk of the Michigan production. Coal output peaked in 1907, when 2,035,858 tons of coal were produced by thirty-seven mines, but the normal figures in the first two decades of the century were around a million tons annually. Higher coal prices during the era of World War I caused the value of the coal mined in the years from 1917 to 1920 to exceed that of any previous period, but beginning in the twenties production figures dropped drastically. The difficulty of mining much of Michigan's coal, combined with its generally poor quality, made it increasingly unprofitable to continue operations in the face of the competition from neighboring coal-producing states. In 1952, Saginaw County's Swan Creek Mine—the last one in production—shut down. A total of 42,248,404 tons of coal had been mined in Michigan since accurate records began to be kept in 1860.[2] After a lapse of over twenty years, a strip-mining operation near Williamston, where coal had been mined as early as 1852, initiated a modest resumption of coal mining in Michigan in the mid-1970s, with annual production of approximately ten thousand tons.

Another southern Michigan mineral is gypsum, with deposits in Kent County having been discovered as early as 1827. A mill that was built near Grand Rapids in the early 1840s to process this gypsum launched an underground mining operation that has continued to the present. By 1840, a second area of gypsum deposits had been found across the state in the Saginaw Bay region, where a surface quarrying operation began in 1861 at the newly established and appropriately named town of Alabaster, the name of one of the varieties of gypsum. Gypsum continues to be shipped from there over an unusual trestle system that carries the mineral out to vessels anchored offshore in Lake Huron. More conventional methods are used to ship gypsum obtained in other parts of Iosco County. Michigan's annual production before 1890 never exceeded 70,000 tons, but beginning in 1901, Michigan became one of the leading states in gypsum output, with the construction boom of the twenties pushing production to a peak of almost 900,000 tons in 1929. Gypsum, unlike some of Michigan's other natural resources, is one that has not been exhausted, and by the 1970s annual production levels were averaging around 1,500,000 tons. This established Michigan as the number one or two producer, with the figure in 1977 approaching the two-million-ton level, worth $10,899,000.[3]

Another resource of far greater consequence than either coal or gypsum but likewise concentrated in the more southerly parts of the state is salt. The presence of salt brine had been known to the Indians, who had discovered numerous salt springs. When Michigan became a state, Congress had granted seventy-two sections of salt spring lands to the state. In his first year as state geologist in 1837, Douglass Houghton had concentrated his efforts on locating these springs, which he found at a number of points in southern Michigan. In addition, salt is found in crystallized form in deposits in the St. Clair River-Detroit River area and at one or two locations in western Michigan. Studies have estimated that Michigan's reserves of salt are so immense that they could supply the world's needs for thousands of years.

State action was needed, however, to stimulate the first efforts to exploit these salt deposits. In 1859, Senator James Birney of Saginaw, son of the one-time Liberty party candidate for President, sponsored legislation to pay a state bounty of ten cents a barrel to producers of Michigan salt. As a joke, some lawmakers who scoffed at the idea of salt being produced commercially in Michigan amended the bill to read ten cents for each bushel, a measure one-fifth the size of a barrel. The bill was passed in this form. The East Saginaw Salt Company promptly sank a well that tapped an underground pool of brine and after evaporating the water it produced the equivalent of 58,860 bushels of salt the first year and tripled production the next year. The legislature hastily acted to stave off the threat of state bankruptcy by repealing the salt bounty, and without this state subsidy the further development of the salt industry was delayed by the high costs of extracting the salt from the brine. However, sawmill operators in the Saginaw Valley and at such West Michigan sites as Manistee soon became aware that they could supplement their income from timber production by using their scrap lumber as the fuel needed to evaporate the salt brines that were found in these areas. By the early 1870s, therefore, the production of salt was booming as a by-product of the lumber industry. By using the exhaust steam from their operations to heat the pans of brine, by 1879 the mill operators had further reduced the cost of producing a barrel of salt to forty cents. By 1880, Michigan was producing almost 2,500,000 barrels of salt a year, more than forty percent of the entire national production.

In 1882, businessman Crockett McElroy bored an experimental well at Marine City along the St. Clair River. At 1,633 feet he struck rock salt and discovered that the deposit was 115 feet thick. To extract the salt in this deposit, which it was subsequently determined extended along the southeastern fringe of the lower peninsula to the Detroit area and beyond, McElroy made an artificial brine by pumping water down into the rock salt and then pumping out the resulting solution and evaporating the water. This method became the principal one used to produce salt in Michigan, with the Michigan Chemical Corporation's operation in St. Louis, Michigan, being the only one still producing salt from natural brines.

The other method of extracting the underground rock salt deposits is to mine them. Efforts that were made in Detroit early in the twentieth century to sink a shaft down to the deposits found beneath that city were hampered by the necessity of cutting through a thousand feet of limestone which contained pockets of gas that killed or blinded a number of workers on the project. Finally, however, in 1910 a shaft was successfully sunk to the level of the rock salt near the West Fort Street crossing of the River Rouge, and a huge underground salt mine, operated by the International Salt Company, has been active ever since beneath the streets of a city better known for other products.

Between 1905 and 1958, Michigan was first in salt production in all but four years, and it ranked second on those occasions. The peak year of production came in 1956 with an output of 5,548,178 tons (by the old method of computing production, this would have been close to 39,000,000 barrels of salt). With the increasing production of salt in other states, particularly Louisiana, and declining production figures in Michigan, the state lost its dominant position after 1958, although it still ranked in the top five salt-producing states. In the 1970s, salt production averaged slightly more than 4,000,000 tons annually, with a peak of 4,818,000 in 1973 and a low of 3,859,000 in 1977. Higher salt prices, however, increased the value of Michigan salt from an annual figure of around $50,000,000 at the start of the decade to a high of $79,740,000 in 1976.[4]

Only about two percent of Michigan's salt becomes table salt. The rest is used for snow and ice removal in the winter, meat packing, and a variety of other uses, including the production of chemicals. Associated brines, known as "natural salines," have been an even greater contributor to the rise of a chemical industry in the state.

Michigan's most widely scattered mineral resources are its stones, gravel, and sand, which generally have a combined annual value that exceeds that of any of the state's other mineral products. Limestone found in Monroe County was being used as building stone in the very early days of statehood and was being burned to produce lime at an even earlier date. Similar use would be made of the limestone found elsewhere in the state, with the most important deposits being located in northern Michigan. Sandstone that was being quarried in Hillsdale and Jackson counties by the mid-nineteenth century and at various points along the south shore of Lake Superior by the later decades of the century contributed building stone of brown and red colors that made distinctive contributions to the urban landscapes of numerous towns in the Upper Peninsula and in such cities in the lower Great Lakes area as Cleveland, Detroit, Jackson, and Chicago. Grindstone City at the tip of the Thumb received its name from how the stone quarried at that location was used for many years until the development of carborundum around the time of World War I killed the market for this product, leaving the beaches littered with abandoned grindstones.

Although quarrying of northern Michigan's limestone began in the nineteenth century, its major development came in the present century with the emergence of the cement industry in Michigan, an industry which turned to limestone in the manufacturing of cement after initially relying on marl, which is also found in the state and is still produced for agricultural use. The location of much of Michigan's limestone in areas with ready access to the cheap water transportation facilities of the Great Lakes also led to its use in blast furnace operations in the lower lakes mill centers. United States Steel's Calcite Quarry at Rogers City became the world's largest limestone quarry. A final stimulus to the expansion in the use of limestone came by the 1920s with the inauguration of this century's enormous road building programs. This also was the major factor in the growth of the state's sand and gravel industry. In 1974 Michigan ranked second in the nation in the value of this product while it was third, behind Alaska and California, in terms of the volume produced.

The presence in parts of lower Michigan of oil and natural gas had been noted as early as the 1830s in the course of geological investigations and as the side result in some cases of the drillings for water or salt. At the time, however, such petroleum finds were an annoyance when no commercially useful way of exploiting this resource had been developed. The beginnings of the commercial oil industry in western Pennsylvania around the time of the Civil War, however, aroused new interest in developing petroleum deposits in other areas. The first such efforts in Michigan centered around Port Huron, beginning in 1886, and were sparked by an oil boom across the border in Sarnia. Some twenty oil wells were drilled to the west and northwest of Port Huron, but the field never developed into an important oil producer, and all the wells had been abandoned by 1920. Not until the mid-twenties did Michigan's important sources of oil and gas begin to be discovered, making the story of the development of this particular mineral resource more a part of the story of twentieth-century economic developments in the state than is the case with most of the other mining-related activities, which were firmly established in the nineteenth century.

Douglass Houghton's report in 1841 that his first geological survey of the Upper Peninsula had located traces of gold and silver helped to arouse hopes that these most recognizable sources of mineral wealth could be found in commercial quantities in Michigan, as they were soon to be found in areas farther to the west. These hopes were to be fulfilled only to a very limited extent, however. Silver City, a virtual ghost town in Ontonagon County, was the site of a flurry of attention from prospectors when silver was discovered at the site in 1872. Claims were staked out over a large area but there was only sporadic mining before all such activity ceased in 1876. Although no significant separate deposits of silver have ever been found, considerable amounts of silver have been found associated with the copper mined in the Upper Peninsula. Even though the copper miners pocketed many of the nuggets of silver that they found, the mines were reported to have produced $3,500,000 of silver by 1887. Small amounts of silver continued to be recovered in later copper-mining activity, but in recent years the White Pine mine in Ontonagon County has produced a surprising amount of silver along with the copper for which the mine is famous. In 1973, for example, over 850,000 ounces of silver added more than $2,000,000 to the mine's income, while in 1974, although silver production dropped by some 200,000 ounces, inflation increased the income from this source to over $3,000,000.

The largest gold-mining venture was the Ropes Gold Mine, near Ishpeming, which produced $647,902 worth of gold bullion between 1883 and 1897. With an increase in gold prices during the Depression, individuals working over the tailings at the abandoned mine sometimes made a day's wages from the gold they found. A company owned by the Calumet and Hecla copper-mining company sought to revive the mine, and in 1933 and 1934 state records registered a tiny amount of gold production, but the amount was not sufficient to warrant further mining operations.[5]

If gold and silver failed to make the western Upper Peninsula one of America's great mining areas, the vast copper and iron ore deposits of that area made these Michigan's most famous and, in most years, most valuable mineral resources. The mining of both copper and iron ore had begun at the same time in the mid-1840s, but the developments up to the 1860s were simply the preliminaries to the great burst of activity and production that were to follow.

The Civil War at the start of the sixties had had an unsettling effect upon both the copper and iron mining business. For six years following the war, Michigan copper companies were operating unprofitably, due mainly to the exhaustion of the older mines. In 1869, Congress imposed a protective tariff of five cents a pound on copper to help the domestic producers. In 1870 all the copper mining and smelting companies in the United States formed a "pool," the purpose of which was to export and to sell enough copper on the world market to keep up the domestic prices. The tariff and the pool enabled the companies to operate profitably and to make many technological improvements. Shafts were sunk deeper to reach the rich conglomerate lode, and air drills and high explosives were introduced. Between 1860 and 1880 the output of refined copper per worker tripled. Local railroads were built to move the copper. In 1872, the Portage Lake and Lake Superior Ship Canal, begun over a decade earlier, was completed, permitting vessels to pass through the Keweenaw Peninsula. The federal government provided a land grant of 450,000 acres to finance this project—more than half the amount granted to build the Soo Canal in the fifties. By 1884 the Copper Country was linked with Chicago by rail.[6]

From the total of 12,000,000 pounds of copper produced in 1860, Michigan copper output had risen to 25,000,000 pounds in 1872. By 1885 the Copper Country was producing 72,000,000 pounds, and it hit the 100,000,000-pound figure in 1890 and topped the 200,000,000-pound level by the turn of the century. Thereafter the advances were not so spectacular. In fact, a plateau was reached in the period from 1905 to 1912 when annual production fluctuated between 216,000,000 and 233,000,000 pounds each year, before dipping precipitously in 1913 and 1914 because of a prolonged strike. During the war years copper production reached 258,000,000 pounds in 1915, and in the record year of 1916 reached an all-time high of 266,839,000 pounds.

From 1847 to 1887, Michigan produced more copper than any other state, sometimes producing ninety percent or more of the national total. In 1884, however, Michigan's output slipped to 47.8 percent of the nation's copper production as new deposits in Montana and Arizona began to be exploited. Michigan climbed back to 51 percent in 1886 but then dropped down to 41.7 percent in 1887 and from that time on its proportion of the national total declined steadily, falling to 25.6 percent by 1904, even though overall production in the state had more than doubled since the mideighties. Although the annual production figures in the Copper Country maintained a boom atmosphere during these years, the causes of the even more spectacular rise in the output of the western mines foreshadowed problems that would ultimately prove disastrous to the Michigan mining economy in the twentieth century.

The mines near the tip of the Keweenaw Peninsula around Copper Harbor and Eagle Harbor were the first to be opened, and by 1870 they were also the first area of Michigan copper resources to be largely worked out. Copper Harbor became almost a ghost town, and Eagle Harbor's population declined. The second major copper area around Ontonagon, where mining had started nearly as soon as that at Copper Harbor, was productive somewhat longer, but by 1890 its fissure veins were almost exhausted. It was the third area—around Portage Lake in the middle of the Keweenaw Peninsula—that forged ahead to become the major center of mining in the area. It was here that the Calumet and Hecla Company originated. Edwin J. Hulbert, the prospector who in 1859 had discovered the great copper deposits that would become the basis for this most famous of Michigan's copper-mining companies' development, had formed the Calumet Mining Company in 1861. The company began mining operations in 1864, and in 1866 Hulbert had also opened the Hecla mine. Unfortunately, Hulbert was totally lacking in managerial skills, and in 1867 the Boston investors had replaced him with Alexander Agassiz, son of the noted naturalist, Louis Agassiz. In 1871, under the younger Agassiz's direction, the Calumet and Hecla mines were combined under one corporate organization, and the resulting company was immediately the giant of the industry. Its production in 1871 of 9,660 tons of copper contrasted not only with the exhausted Cliff mine's anemic production of ninety tons, but also the figures for such existing healthy mines as the Central, with 905 tons shipped, and the Phoenix with 879. It was the enormous success of the Calumet and Hecla in the following decades and the dominance of Boston investors in the company that has led to an emphasis on Boston as the investment center for the mining of Michigan copper, as symbolized by the title of William B. Gates's authoritative history, *Michigan Copper and Boston Dollars.* Actually, in the early phases of development, Pittsburgh investors were more important, but with the exhaustion of their major interests at the tip of the Keweenaw Peninsula, they were overshadowed by the Bostonians with their investments in the immensely more valuable copper deposits in the central region of the peninsula.[7]

As Michigan copper production increased, so did the profits. Dividend payments between 1885 and 1904 totalled $90,316,000. The more than $12,000,000 paid to stockholders in 1899 was four times the yearly figures of the previous decade. During the World War I era, profits made by Michigan copper companies ranged from sixteen to thirty-one percent. Even larger sums were realized from the appreciation of the price of stocks. Calumet and Hecla stock, which at one time could be bought for a dollar a share, brought a thousand dollars a share in 1907. As late as 1923, Calumet and Hecla paid a seven hundred percent stock dividend.

It was not simply a few lucky investors who profited from the sustained boom in Michigan's Copper Country. The number employed by the mining companies increased from 4,188 in 1870 to 21,014 in 1907. Besides the miners and other company employees, many thousands more earned their living as merchants, farmers, clerks, manufacturers, or in the professions. These all depended indirectly on the continued prosperity of the mining industry. Houghton County, which in 1860 had had a population of 9,234 (including 279 Indians), had grown to 66,000 by 1900, making it the fourth most populous county in the state.

Several flourishing cities grew up in the Copper Country. Oldest of these was Houghton, named after the first state geologist, whose report had attracted prospectors to the area. Through the efforts of Jay Hubbell, a resident of Houghton, the state legislature established the Michigan School of Mines in that city in 1885. Hubbell donated the land for the first building, which was named in his honor. Classes started in 1886. By 1891 the school was already the leading producer of mining engineers in the country. By 1897 the school had attained the status of a college and was renamed the Michigan College of Mines. Enrollment increased to 266 and the faculty numbered thirty members by 1909. The college provided courses in metallurgy and mining engineering, and was an important asset to the Copper Country.

Houghton's neighbor across the Portage River to the north was Hancock, which was the site of brass foundries and factories where mining machinery was manufactured. Here, too, the Finns, who came to the Copper Country in large numbers, founded Suomi College in 1899 as a cultural center and as a unique Finnish-language institution of higher education. Hancock, however, was best known as the site of the famous Quincy mine. One of the great mines of the Copper Country, the Quincy was nicknamed "Old Reliable" by its grateful stockholders. Prior to the time it was shut down in 1931, it had produced copper continuously for eighty-three years. It reopened in 1937 and continued production until 1945. By that time it had paid its stockholders more than $27,000,000 in dividends. It reached almost a mile and a quarter—6,400 feet—straight down into the earth, had ninety-one levels, and hundreds of miles of underground railroad tracks.[8]

Other sizable towns and cities grew up. If the cluster of villages, headed by Red Jacket, that had developed around the Calumet and Hecla's operations had been incorporated as one city at the end of the nineteenth century, it would have ranked as the fifth-largest city in the state. Schools and churches were built, and newspapers were established. In 1910, Houghton County had nine weekly newspapers, five dailies, one tri-weekly, three monthlies, and two quarterly publications. The number included an Italian daily, and publications in Slavonic, Finnish, and Swedish. There was an amazing amount of enthusiasm for the theater in the Copper Country. Red Jacket, Lake Linden, Laurium, Hancock, and Houghton all had their opera houses or theaters. For the opening performance in the Kerredge Theater at Hancock in 1902 box seats sold for forty dollars and seats in the orchestra section for ten dollars. First-class theatrical troupes played the theaters in the Copper Country between 1900 and 1917, with such famous names as Fritz Kreisler, Alma Gluck, Sarah Bernhardt, and Maude Adams among the performers who appeared on these stages.[9]

By 1904, in spite of consolidations, there were still nineteen producing companies in the Copper Country. The stock in nine of these, however, was controlled by the Copper Range Consolidated Company, while four others were controlled by another holding company. These, together with the Calumet and Hecla and the Quincy, produced ninety-five percent of the state's copper. Furthermore, these companies had obtained control of smelting operations. One of these was also engaged in copper manufacture, and some of them invested heavily in timber and sawmills. All of them owned short railroads, and the Calumet and Hecla had its own fleet of lake vessels. In the years immediately following the turn of the century, copper prices were high, large profits were earned, and shares of the companies skyrocketed on the stock market. Low-cost mining fields in the West, where much of the copper located close to the surface could be mined by the less expensive open-pit technique, were hurting Michigan's competitive position, but this was partially offset by speeding up technological change, and by the higher cost of living in the West, which forced the western companies to pay their miners a substantially higher wage than was paid to the Michigan miners.

The competitive problems faced by the Michigan companies, however, intensified their problems with their workers as the drive for greater efficiency caused some workers to feel they were working too hard. These workers began to object to the control that the companies had over their lives. The copper companies owned the land on which many of the miners lived and in most cases owned the houses as well. The rent was generally reasonable and the services provided by the companies, such as schools, hospitals, libraries, and health insurance, were often extraordinary for that day. But at best the companies were benevolent despots, expecting loyal obedience for the services they provided. The earliest strike of miners occurred in 1872, and labor troubles were common thereafter. The companies staunchly resisted labor organizations, but by 1911 many of the miners had joined the Western Federation of Miners, which became affiliated with the American Federation of Labor in that year. A strike began on July 22, 1913. The workers demanded an eight-hour day, improvement in working conditions, a minimum pay of $3.50 a day, and recognition of the union. A "Citizens Alliance" was formed to maintain order, but the sheriff of Houghton County appealed to Governor Woodbridge N. Ferris for help, and the state militia was sent into the Copper Country. Efforts at negotiation failed because the operators refused to recognize the union. A tragic incident occurred during the strike when someone cried "Fire" in a hall at Calumet that was filled with miners and their families attending a Christmas party. In the rush for the exits seventy-three women and children were trampled to death. The strike lasted until April 14, 1914. The miners won an eight-hour day, a minimum wage of $3.00 a day, and certain other benefits, but the operators successfully resisted the demand to recognize the union. The economic hardship resulting from the long strike and the hard feelings that it created on both sides would not soon be forgotten. World War I broke out in Europe later in 1914, and during that conflict copper production soared to new heights, but this was to be only a temporary recovery. The great strike of 1913–14 marks the real end of the Copper Country's days of glory.[10]

*   *   *   *   *

The development of iron mining in other areas of the western Upper Peninsula during these years followed much the same pattern as that of the Copper Country. During the half-century that followed the Civil War, the United States experienced its greatest period of economic expansion. Railroads spanned the continent and threaded their way to almost every town and hamlet. Iron ships were built to ply the Great Lakes and the oceans. Manufacturing grew under the wing of protective tariffs, requiring thousands of factories to be built and equipped. Skyscrapers rose in the cities. Much of this expansion in transportation and industry depended on iron and steel. Michigan was the leading producer of iron ore during much of this period, until the output of Minnesota's great Mesabi Range pushed that state ahead of Michigan in 1900. But Michigan's production of iron ore, although not keeping pace with Minnesota's, continued to rise during the early years of the twentieth century, with the peak reached in 1920.

The great increase of ore production in Michigan was made possible by the discovery and exploitation of two additional iron ranges, following the start of mining on the Marquette range in the 1840s. In 1850 and 1851, government surveyors had reported traces of iron ore in the area that later became the city of Ironwood in the extreme western part of the peninsula and in areas near the Menominee River. Lack of transportation facilities was the main factor in retarding the start of mining in these areas. With the coming of the Chicago and Northwestern Railroad to the Menominee River area, the Breen and Vulcan mines near Iron Mountain shipped their first ore in 1877, while the mines around Crystal Falls began production in 1882. During the following century, the mines on Michigan's side of the sprawling Menominee Iron Range, whose ore deposits extended across the border into Wisconsin, produced nearly 300,000,000 tons of iron ore, making it second only to the older Marquette range in total output.

In 1871, Raphael Pumpelly, a Harvard geology professor, after studying the original survey notes of William A. Burt, found traces of iron ore between the Montreal River and Lake Gogebic in the extreme western portion of the Upper Peninsula. With the financial aid of Alexander Agassiz and Quincy Shaw of the Calumet and Hecla copper-mining company, Pumpelly purchased five square miles of what came to be called the Gogebic Iron Range. The Colby Mine, first to produce ore in this area, was the result of the discovery of a lump of rock in 1873 by N. D. Moore, who was exploring for timber. This mine, located at what became the city of Bessemer, started shipping ore after the opening of a railroad into the district in 1884. Other mines were opened in rapid succession. The deposits of the Gogebic range, even more so than those of the Menominee range, extended well over into Wisconsin, and if the production of the entire range is considered as a whole, it was, in its heyday, a greater producer of iron ore than either of the other iron ranges in the Upper Peninsula. However, if only the production of the Michigan portion of the Gogebic range is considered, its output, although amounting to a quarter of a billion tons of iron ore, places it behind Michigan's two other iron ranges.[11]

The earliest iron-producing mines in the Upper Peninsula were the Jackson mine at Negaunee and the National mine at Ishpeming, three miles away. After 1865, however, many additional mines were opened in the Marquette range. Several towns take their names from these mines. The Republic mine produced ore that was eighty-eight percent pure iron oxide. Opened in 1871, it continued to produce until 1927. The Champion mine was worked from 1867 to 1910, and the Michigamme mine from 1872 to 1905. There were many other smaller mines. In the Menominee range scores of mines, large and small, were opened, worked for various periods of time, and then abandoned. Among the more famous was the Vulcan mine near Norway, opened in 1877 and worked until 1946. Iron Mountain grew up around the Chapin mine. Other heavy producers around Iron Mountain were the Pewabic, Ludington, Hewitt, Indiana, Calumet, Cornell, Garfield, and Hancock mines. Crystal Falls, so named for its location near a cascade on the Paint River, grew up around the Bristol mine, opened in 1882. Iron River and its sister city, Stambaugh, were the last of the large communities in the Menominee range to be developed. The largest producer in this area was the Caspian mine. In the Gogebic range twelve mines were opened between 1884 and 1887, and twenty others up to 1925. Ironwood is the principal city in the Gogebic range. The site of the city was platted by a railroad company in 1885. Other towns and cities that grew up around mines in the Gogebic range were Wakefield, Ramsay, and Bessemer. The Norrie-Aurora-Pabst mine at Ironwood outproduced any other mine in the Upper Peninsula. The Chapin at Iron Mountain in the Menominee range was the second largest producer.

Over twenty-five forges were built in the Upper Peninsula during the nineteenth century to process the iron ore. The early forges brought lumps of iron ore to a high degree of heat, and they were then "wrought" into iron "blooms" through a process of hammering. Vast amounts of hardwood were required to make the charcoal used in these forges. Fortunately, there were large stands of hardwood as well as pine in the Upper Peninsula. Limestone, another essential material in the process, was available in abundant quantities. It was estimated in 1903 that the furnaces of the Upper Peninsula consumed so much charcoal that thirty acres of hardwood per day had to be cut to supply the kilns.[12] By that time the supply of hardwood was beginning to be exhausted; furthermore, the process was too expensive. It was more profitable to ship the ore in the big ore carriers that were being built and to smelt it with coke in furnaces on Lake Erie and at the southern end of Lake Michigan. One by one the charcoal kilns and blast furnaces in the Upper Peninsula were abandoned until none was in use.

Some idea of this extinct industry may be gained by a visit to the ghost town of Fayette, located on the Garden Peninsula, which juts down into Lake Michigan from the Upper Peninsula. The Jackson Iron Company purchased the site of Fayette and some sixteen thousand acres of hardwood forest located nearby in 1864. Charcoal kilns and smelting furnaces were constructed. Limestone at the site provided the flux needed in the smelting process. A narrow gauge railroad brought the wood to the kilns. Docks were built. By 1869 there was a store, office building, carpenter and blacksmith shops, and over forty houses. Subsequently a hotel, post office, and even an opera house were built. The iron ore used in the furnaces was shipped by rail from Negaunee to Escanaba and from there to Fayette by scows towed by tugs. The hardwood supply of the Garden Peninsula was the key to the prosperity of this boom town, and when it was gone by the end of the century, Fayette, after a brief interlude during which it was a resort town, was abandoned.[13] Many of its buildings and the remains of its kilns and furnaces survived, however, and the site was acquired by the state in the 1960s and has been developed as a historic park by the Department of Natural Resources and the History Division of the Department of State.

During the half-century following the Civil War, improvements in the methods of mining iron matched those in copper mining. In the early years until the 1870s the production of iron ore was essentially a quarrying operation. The overburden of trees, sod, and soil was removed, and the iron ore that lay underneath was then broken up and carried away. When the surface ore had been secured, however, shafts had to be sunk through the layers of rock that lay on top of the deeper veins of ore. From these shafts, horizontal tunnels were then cut into the ore deposits. Miners descended into the shafts by wooden ladders and the ore was brought to the surface by bucket hoists. But by 1900 steam-powered machinery was employed in the mines. Elevators or "cages," as they were called, took the miners underground and later brought them back to the surface. The ore was hoisted by machinery, which also operated the pumps that were required to remove the water from the mines. Electrical power and lighting was introduced around 1895. Dynamite replaced black blasting powder; diamond drills revolutionized the methods used to search for new lodes, while power drills and electric cap lamps represented other improvements. Hard-toed boots, safety hats, and shatter-proof glasses became standard equipment for the miner.

As shafts were sunk deeper and as the tunnels or "drifts" were extended further, the iron-mining companies required large amounts of timber to support the overhang. For this reason, and also to obtain hardwood for charcoal, they acquired large tracts of timber. The Cleveland-Cliffs company became probably the largest private landowner in the Upper Peninsula as a result of such purchases. Of critical importance in mining and lumbering was transportation, and the mining companies thus built railroads and ore carriers. All this required large amounts of capital, and as a consequence, the smaller operators were gradually squeezed out. Those that survived included the three big Cleveland-based companies, Cleveland-Cliffs, Pickands, Mather, and M. A. Hanna, who sold the ores they produced to companies that in turn produced iron and steel. Increasingly, however, the latter companies acquired their own mines. The giant U. S. Steel Corporation, formed at the beginning of the twentieth century, had its Oliver Iron Mining subsidiary, controlling important ore deposits on the Gogebic Iron Range and in other areas, while the corporation's own fleet of ore boats carried the ore to ports on the lower lakes for shipment to the corporation's mills. Youngstown Sheet and Tube, Bethlehem, Republic, and other steel producers developed similar operations.

Until the early 1880s, Pennsylvania was the nation's leading source of iron ore, but Michigan's production figures, which rose from a few thousand tons a year in the 1850s to more than a half-million tons by 1867, climbed over the million-ton figure by the early seventies. The depression following the Panic of 1873 caused a sharp drop in production, but a rise to the two-million-ton level by 1880 marked the beginning of a decade of rapidly expanding production figures that hit seven million tons in 1890, as Michigan became the country's major source of iron ore in this great era in the growth of the iron and steel industry. The growth was proportionally not as spectacular in the years following the eighties, but by the end of the century, Michigan's three ranges were shipping out nine million tons of ore, an annual production rate that would eventually double during the boom war years and immediate post-war years of 1916 to 1920. Nevertheless, Michigan lost its leadership in iron ore production to Minnesota beginning in 1900 and never regained the top spot again. More important for the future of the Michigan iron-mining industry was the fact that the rich ores of Minnesota's Mesabi Iron Range, which were mainly responsible for that state's leadership, were mined by the open-pit method, a method that was only rarely used in Michigan by the beginning of the twentieth century. The higher costs of Michigan's underground iron mines would place these operations at an increasing disadvantage competitively with Minnesota's open-pit mines, exactly the same situation that Michigan's copper mines faced in the same period with the predominantly open-pit copper mining operations of the West. By the third decade of the century these effects would begin to show up in sharply reduced production, which would result in severe economic repercussions for these mining areas.

*   *   *   *   *

Mining, like farming and lumbering, became one of the major attractions that drew new settlers to the state in the nineteenth century, and in the case of iron and copper mining, it attracted a far higher percentage of foreign-born than any of the other economic opportunities that developed in that century. The proportion of foreign-born in the Copper Country and the three iron ranges at the end of the century was as high or higher than any other comparable area in the state. From the beginning, Cornishmen from southwestern England were the backbone of the mine work forces. In fact, a few Cornish miners apparently had been imported from England in the early 1770s during the unsuccessful attempt of Alexander Henry and associates to establish a mine in the Ontonagon region. In the summer of 1844, a geologist visiting the mine that had just commenced operations in the Eagle River area reported that Cornish miners were busily sinking shafts. Most of these early Cornishmen had come up from Wisconsin where several thousand immigrants from Cornwall since 1830 had been working the lead deposits of the Upper Mississippi. Some of the other Cornish miners that came to Michigan in this early period came from other parts of the United States or Canada where they had found opportunities of employing their mining skills. By 1846, however, the Boston and Lake Superior Mining Association was going directly to Cornwall to enlist the services of ten miners who were imported to work in that company's mine in the Copper Country.

Cornishmen had been mining tin and copper in their homeland for centuries, and because of their acquired skills they were in great demand by those involved in mining ventures in America. The underground mining operations that would be required to extract most of Michigan's copper and iron ore were particularly suited to the Cornishmen, who had faced similar problems in Cornwall and had become recognized as the best hard-rock miners in the world. By the nineteenth century the growth rate of the Cornish mining industry had slowed down, and although the production of both copper and tin remained at high levels through the first half of the century, foreign competition, declining prices, and the exhaustion of the most readily available Cornish deposits created serious economic problems by the fifties and brought on the near collapse of the industry in the late sixties and early seventies. This came at the very time when Michigan's mining industry was requiring more and more laborers to sustain the increasingly rapid rate of its growth, and the unemployed Cornish miners, who had been kept well informed of these American developments by letters from the pioneer Cornish miners in Michigan and by the reports that appeared in the columns of Cornish newspapers, began flocking to America and to northern Michigan to recoup their fortunes.

How many Cornish immigrants came to Michigan is impossible to say, since the census records list only the country, not the region from which the immigrants came. The Cornish historian, John Rowe, estimates that there were never more than a hundred thousand first-generation Cornishmen in the United States at any one time, but the influence of these people and of their children (born in this country) in mining areas such as the Upper Peninsula was almost as great as that of the Dutch in the Holland-Grand Rapids area or the Germans in the Saginaw area. These "Cousin Jacks" and "Cousin Jennies," as they were nicknamed (for reasons that no two people have ever been able to agree upon), were actually closer in spirit to these other immigrant groups, exhibiting the clannishness that was more typical of the continental Europeans than it was of the majority of immigrants from England. Like other immigrants, the Cornish contributed much to the diverse fabric of the developing Michigan society: a love of singing, a strong support for Methodism, and several new foods—saffron buns, scalded cream, which did not survive in America, and pasties—a mixture of beef, potatoes, turnips, and onions, enclosed in a crust, that was originally designed to provide a warm meal at work to the miner but which soon became the national food of the Upper Peninsula.[14]

Unlike some other parts of Michigan, where one immigrant group remained dominant, the Upper Peninsula's mining areas did not support only the Cornish. During the Civil War the scarcity of labor was so acute that mine owners in the Copper Country contributed to a pool of $90,000 for a young Swedish engineer named Silverspar, who promised to go to Europe and bring back workers. The workers were to be divided among the contributors, and deductions from the wages of the new miners were to reimburse the employers. Silverspar returned with more than a hundred Swedes, Norwegians, and Finns, but lost some of the men to an army recruiter en route to the Upper Peninsula. It was rumored that some of the men were long-term prisoners in Sweden whose release for immigration to America had been secured from the Swedish government. Whatever their origins, the Swedes that came were forerunners of large numbers of this nationality who would become as common in these mining towns as other Swedes were in the lumber towns.[15] The Finns, too, were among the first of a group that would arrive in far greater numbers in later years and would become perhaps the most widely distributed immigrant group in the entire Upper Peninsula.

Adding further to the ethnic diversity of the Copper Country and the iron ranges was the introduction of groups from southern and eastern Europe, beginning with some Slovenians who were brought into the Copper Country in 1866. Their arrival was perhaps aided by the fact that the first Catholic bishop in the Upper Peninsula was the Slovenian Frederic Baraga. By the end of the century, a great number of Slavic peoples and Italians were common to the populations of these mining towns.

Each immigrant group stuck close together, but the one thing that could unite them was their opposition to the continued preference that was given to the Cornishmen, who, although they no longer constituted the bulk of the mining force, held most of the supervisory jobs—those that entitled them to be called "Captain." The greatest rivals of the Cousin Jacks were other immigrants from the British Isles—the Irish—who also came to be among the most numerous in the mining work force. Between the Cornish and the Irish there was a traditional and unfriendly rivalry. Numerous stories were told of battles fought between these two groups. In one instance of a fight between Cornishmen and Irishmen in Ontonagon, the outnumbered Irish fled to the second story of a local saloon, which the Cornishmen proceeded to set on fire. In the melee the saloon owner felled a Cornishman from behind with an axe. When word reached the Portage Lake region that the Ontonagon Irish were outnumbered, several hundred Irishmen prepared to march overland to the relief of their countrymen. Wiser heads finally called a halt to the plan, but the word that the "Micks" were coming got to Ontonagon, and Cornishmen by the dozens immediately took passage on a departing steamer in order to escape the wrath of the Irish.[16]

As in the case of the workers in the lumber industry and the stories that are recounted of their hell-raising, many of the reports of rowdyism and wild living in the mining towns must be discounted as exaggerations of the real conditions that existed in the boom times of the late nineteenth century. Most miners were hard-working, law-abiding, religious, family men, and the differences between the numerous ethnic and nationality groups, although real enough, rarely led to outright violence. Nevertheless, the differences that were present, the hazardous nature of the miners' occupation, and the rugged character of the topography and climate of the iron- and copper-mining regions all combined to give the life of the western Upper Peninsula a unique and discernible quality that survives to some extent to the present day in spite of the great changes that the twentieth century brought to the area's economy.

Michigan Central Railroad engine, at Kalamazoo, 1874-88

19

AN EXPANDING TRANSPORTATION NETWORK

The economic growth of northern Michigan, even more than the earlier developments in the southern part of the state, was dependent on the construction of systems of transportation that could open the timber and mineral resources in these previously remote regions to full exploitation. For the most part, this meant the improvement of water transportation routes and the development of larger lake vessels, and on land it meant the construction of railroads as well as roads for horse-drawn traffic which had been so vital to the development of southern Michigan's farm economy. These roads were less important in northern Michigan, where the bulky products of the lumber camps, mines, and quarries could most effectively be transported via rail and water.

It was no coincidence, therefore, that the state's railroad network was being constructed at the very time when the production of pine lumber and minerals was reaching its height in Michigan in the last four decades of the nineteenth century. On the eve of the Civil War, Michigan, although it had been the first area in the west to develop railroads, had fallen far behind its neighbors, with less than eight hundred miles of railroad tracks, consisting mainly of three lines crossing the southern part of the lower peninsula. By 1900, however, the state had 7,945 miles of main-line track, 2,903 miles of other tracks and yard tracks, or a total of 10,848 miles. During the first two decades of the twentieth century additional tracks were laid both by the railroad companies and by electric interurban companies, before a combination of the over-expansion of railroad service and

431

the onset of competing forms of transportation brought about a decline in mileage figures in subsequent years.

The construction of railroads into the northern parts of the state was vastly stimulated by federal subsidies in the form of land grants. Indeed, without such grants it is doubtful if many of these lines would have been built. In the southern portion of the lower peninsula, however, railroad construction was for the most part unsubsidized by federal grants and was undertaken to serve the needs of the growing agricultural population and of the towns and cities with their commercial and manufacturing enterprises. In 1860 stage lines and wagons loaded with merchandise, traveling over plank roads where possible, served as feeders for the three principal east-west rail lines. During the Civil War the construction of railroads to supplant them as feeders was begun, and as soon as the war was over this process was greatly intensified. Additional main lines across the lower peninsula were also built, and they, too, constructed their feeder lines. By 1900 southern Michigan was crisscrossed with rail lines.

The building of railroads attracted large amounts of capital and was supported by immense popular enthusiasm. Dozens of small railroad companies were formed to build short lines with the expectation that they would ultimately be absorbed by the larger companies, which, indeed, most of them were. Every town and hamlet had ambitions to be on a railroad. The rail companies, seeking to capitalize on this feeling, sought financial assistance from cities, townships, and counties to finance construction. Some local government units voted bond issues to encourage railroad construction without waiting for state approval. Then, beginning in 1863, the state legislature, by a series of special acts, granted permission to local units for bond issues. These were approved by Governors Blair, Crapo, and Baldwin, although Crapo, in the latter part of his administration, vetoed a large number of bills passed to approve local bond issues, warning the legislature that in his opinion it was unconstitutional for public funds to be used to subsidize a privately owned company. Crapo vetoed fourteen such bills in a single day. By 1870 state-approved bonds to the amount of $1,646,300 had been sold and the proceeds handed over to the railroads. Additional bonds with a face value of more than twice this sum had been issued and deposited with the state treasurer but had not yet been delivered to the railroad companies. In April, 1870, the state supreme court declared one of the acts that had been passed by the legislature to approve such a bond issue to be unconstitutional, and this decision in effect made all the bonds so issued valueless. The railroads sought in vain to secure a constitutional amendment to validate the bonds, but it was voted down by the people. In the end, after long litigation, some of the bondholders were able to collect by turning their bonds over to non-residents of the state who then brought suit in federal courts.[1]

Each of the three rail lines that spanned lower Michigan in 1860 built branches and feeders after the Civil War and also purchased or leased lines that had been built by small companies. The Michigan Southern, with its eastern termini at Monroe and Toledo, Ohio, ran through the southernmost tier of counties, then, west of White Pigeon, veered southward into Indiana to reach Chicago. This line built or otherwise acquired lines reaching northward from Hillsdale to Lansing, from Hillsdale to Ypsilanti, from Jonesville to Marshall, from Adrian to Jackson, and from White Pigeon to Grand Rapids. The Michigan Central's main line extended westward from Detroit through Ann Arbor, Jackson, Battle Creek and Kalamazoo, then veered southward to Niles and Chicago. Fiercely competitive for many years with the Michigan Southern, the Central secured branch and feeder lines from Jackson northward to Lansing, Saginaw, and Mackinaw City (which was reached in 1881); from Detroit northward to Bay City; from Jackson northwestward to Grand Rapids; from Kalamazoo westward to South Haven; and from Battle Creek southward to Sturgis. In the 1870s, the Central also acquired an "Air Line" on a shorter and more direct route between two points on its main line, Jackson and Niles. The Detroit and Milwaukee, which had its western Michigan termini in Grand Haven and Muskegon, also built branches running northward to Bay City and the Thumb area, a parallel line running slightly to the north of the main line, and a branch southward to Jackson. This railroad subsequently merged with the Grand Trunk lines.

Other major railroad lines were being constructed across lower Michigan in the 1870s and 1880s. The Peninsular Railroad was built from Chicago, entering Michigan through Cass County and following a diagonal line northeastward to Lansing. There it was connected with another line from Port Huron, and in 1871 the two were combined and acquired by the Grand Trunk. The Ann Arbor Railroad had its origin in 1869 when building was started on a line that ultimately ran from Toledo, Ohio, northwesterly across Michigan to Frankfort far to the north. Still another east-west line was constructed from Saginaw west to Ludington on Lake Michigan. This became part of the Pere Marquette System.

The Pere Marquette was a consolidation, formed in 1900, of more than a hundred different railroad companies. These had previously been merged into three main groups. The original Flint and Pere Marquette Railroad was opened in 1863, connecting Saginaw and Flint. During the next thirty-seven years this railroad acquired many independent lines, secured connections with Detroit, Monroe, and Toledo, and built the line from Saginaw to Ludington mentioned earlier. The second main constituent of the Pere Marquette was the Chicago and West Michigan, which had built or acquired a line running northward through towns and cities in western Michigan to Grand Rapids, Traverse City, and Petoskey, with numerous branches reaching out to Muskegon, Pentwater, Allegan, and other cities. The third main division of the Pere Marquette was a line connecting Detroit and Grand Rapids through Lansing, which also owned a line connecting Grand Rapids and Saginaw.

As noted earlier, Congress had, in 1856, passed a measure that granted to the states millions of acres of public lands to be doled out to the railroads at a rate of three sections on each side of the tracks for every mile constructed, provided that at least twenty miles were built within the period of one year. So many scandals and shady transactions resulted that in 1872 further aid was withdrawn but not before more than 3,000,000 acres had been granted to Michigan railroads. In addition to these lands the state of Michigan granted to the railroads 1,659,509 acres of "swamp lands" that had been donated by the federal government to the state.

The amounts obtained by the railroads from these land grants by no means paid for the cost of construction, but they were sufficient to attract capital from domestic and foreign sources to do so. The lands were generally awarded to induce railroads to build into sparsely settled areas; thus in Michigan most of the land grants were made to railroad companies that built lines into the northern part of the lower peninsula and into the Upper Peninsula. It is a common misconception that these land grants were outright gifts.[2] Under the terms of the grants, the land-grant railroads were obligated to carry government property and personnel at approximately half-price. It has been estimated that in the period since these railroads were built the saving to the government by these reduced rates amounts to over ten times the original value of the lands granted. In the lower peninsula land grants were made to a number of railroads that built lines into the north. The companies that merged into the Pere Marquette system in 1900 received land grants for building the line from Saginaw to Ludington and the line northward from Grand Rapids. The largest single land grant in the lower peninsula was made to the Grand Rapids and Indiana Railroad for building a line northward from Sturgis to Mackinaw City, which was completed in 1882. The

Michigan Central was another major recipient, being granted over 721,000 acres to build its tracks northward from Jackson to Mackinaw City. A small amount was granted to the Grand Trunk for building its northern lines. But it should be noted that not all railroads built into the north received grants. Neither the Ann Arbor, whose line ran from Toledo to Frankfort, nor the Detroit and Mackinac, which constructed a line northward from Bay City to Cheboygan, received land grants.[3]

Not all the railroads built during this period were gobbled up by the big companies. There were dozens of short lines that were operated independently. Many such companies had grandiose ideas of becoming through lines. One such, the Toledo and South Haven, meandered through Van Buren County from South Haven to Lawton, eventually reached Kalamazoo, but never got any further.[4] The Manistee and Northeastern and the East Jordan and Southern are examples of independent lines in the north. Literally hundreds of railroad companies, formed with great expectations, never laid any track at all.

As lumbering declined after 1900 the railroads that had been built into the northern part of the lower peninsula suffered a serious decline in passenger and freight traffic. They sought to meet this challenge in a number of ways. In co-operation with lumber companies that had cut-over lands for sale and with local development associations, the railroads sought to lure farmers into the area by offering land at low prices. At first some measure of success was achieved, but it was quickly demonstrated that the sandy soils could not compete with the rich prairie lands in the states further west. Some townships in northern Michigan where almost every section had three or four farms in 1890 are completely overgrown with brush and trees. Scores of abandoned farm buildings may still be seen.[5]

Another device used by the railroads to obtain business as lumbering dwindled was the promotion of northern Michigan as a resort area. The Grand Rapids and Indiana Railroad called itself "the fishing line" and widely advertised the attractiveness of northern Michigan for the angler and hunter. This railroad, as well as the Michigan Central and the Pere Marquette, built huge resort hotels at such places as Petoskey, Harbor Springs, and Charlevoix. The largest of all, the Grand Hotel on Mackinac Island, was financed by the Grand Rapids and Indiana and the Michigan Central Railroads and the Detroit and Cleveland Navigation Company. It was opened on July 10, 1887, with Chauncey Depew presiding at the opening dinner. The Grand Hotel quickly became the most fashionable resort in the Middle West. Mackinac Island had been known for many years for its pleasant summer climate and its clear air, which was especially attractive to people suffering from hay fever. Summer visitors had been coming before 1850. Numerous northern Michigan cities and towns, once centers of the lumber industry, were in process of becoming resort towns by 1900. In 1875 the Bay View Assembly, modeled after the original Chautauqua at Lake Chautauqua, New York, was organized. This provided an educational and cultural program to supplement the health and recreation attractions of northern Michigan. Bay View Assembly was formed principally by Methodists. Other religious groups established camps and colonies for summer visitors to Michigan's north country.

The summer resorts provided increased traffic for the railroads, even though many of the visitors came by steamship. But this traffic was confined largely to the three summer months. The railroads could hardly operate profitably with heavy business only a quarter of the year, and relatively little for the remainder. There were numerous bankruptcies. The Pere Marquette was in chronic financial trouble. Some lines were abandoned. The railroads next turned to consolidation with larger systems, to which they were valuable as feeders. The merger of three different groups of railroads into the Pere Marquette system in 1900 was a first step in this direction. Ultimately the Pere Marquette itself was merged with the Chesapeake and Ohio. The Grand Rapids and Indiana was acquired by the Pennsylvania Railroad. The Ann Arbor formed an alliance with the Wabash. The Grand Trunk became part of the Canadian National Railway. And both the Michigan Southern and the Michigan Central merged with the New York Central Railroad.

The Great Lakes and their connecting rivers on three sides of the lower peninsula constituted serious barriers to through railroad traffic. This handicap was overcome to some degree by the railroad companies through the construction of tunnels and car ferries. Prior to the Civil War passengers and freight reached Detroit by steamboat or sailing vessel, from whence they were transferred to railroad trains running westward. The Michigan Central reached Chicago by running its lines around the southern tip of Lake Michigan. Goods and passengers on trains to Grand Haven and Muskegon were transferred to ships crossing Lake Michigan to Milwaukee. The first rail line across southern Canada reached Windsor, across the Detroit River from Detroit, in 1854. Ferries were put into service to transport passengers and freight across the river. In 1867 a ferry, the *Great Western,* capable of carrying twelve railroad cars, was put into service. Thenceforth passengers could remain in railroad coaches while crossing the river, and freight could be transferred without the labor and expense of handling on both sides of the river. In 1872 the Grand Trunk placed a similar but larger car ferry into service between Port Huron and Sarnia, Ontario. In 1887 railroad companies operating lines in the two peninsulas formed an association that ordered the building of a car ferry to transport cars across the Straits of Mackinac between Mackinaw City and St. Ignace. It was placed in service the following year and was so constructed as to be able to operate the year around.

Up to this time car ferries had operated only across rivers or narrow bodies of water. The first car ferry in the world to navigate open waters was placed in service by the Toledo, Ann Arbor, and North Michigan (later called simply the Ann Arbor Railroad) on November 24, 1892. It operated from the mouth of the Betsie River in western Michigan across Lake Michigan to Kewaunee, Wisconsin. Although the ferry leaves from the south side of the Betsie, in what became the town of Elberta, the railroad has always publicized Frankfort, on the north side of this waterway, as the ferry terminus, to the dismay of Elberta's boosters.[6] The Ann Arbor later operated ferries to Manitowoc, Wisconsin, and to Menominee and Manistique in the Upper Peninsula. The success of these ferries induced other railroads to use the same method of promoting through traffic by securing a connecting link with western railroads having termini on the Wisconsin side of Lake Michigan. The Pere Marquette's first car ferry between Ludington and Manitowoc crossed Lake Michigan in February, 1897. Subsequently, car ferries were put into service between Ludington and both Milwaukee and Kewaunee on the Wisconsin side. In 1903 the Grand Trunk began operating car ferries between Grand Haven and Milwaukee.[7]

The car ferries did much to promote railroad traffic. In later years they also became carriers of automobiles, although sometimes with reluctance. In 1891, the Grand Trunk completed a tunnel under the St. Clair River between Port Huron and Sarnia, replacing the car ferry. And in 1910, after several futile attempts, a railroad tunnel under the Detroit River was completed, making it possible to run through trains between Chicago and New York by way of Detroit.

Transportation improvements in the Upper Peninsula owed even more to the beneficence of the federal government than did those in the southern peninsula. A grant of 750,000 acres of public land had made possible the building of the Soo Canal. The United States government also built the new and larger Weitzel lock at the Soo. When this lock was opened to traffic in 1881, the Soo Canal was turned over by Michigan to the United States and thenceforth the locks were operated toll-free at public expense. The Poe Lock replaced the old state locks in 1896. Meanwhile, another grant of 450,000 acres of public land had been made to build the canal across the Keweenaw Peninsula. Federal land grants also made a major contribution to railroad building in the Upper Peninsula. Over sixty percent of the 5,505,336 acres of public lands granted to encourage railroad building in Michigan went to Upper Peninsula lines.

The year 1855 marked the completion of the Soo Canal, and on August 17 of that year the Brig *Columbia,* laden with ore from Marquette, was the first ore ship to pass through the locks. The same year a twenty-mile railroad connecting the iron mines at Negaunee with Marquette was completed. It was conceived and carried to completion by Herman D. Ely,[8] and was the first Upper Peninsula railroad. Cars were at first hauled by mules, but a steam locomotive was put in use in 1857. During the Civil War a company was formed to connect this railroad with a line to the Bay de Noquet on Lake Michigan. Construction was completed in 1864 from Escanaba on Bay de Noquet to Negaunee and from there by the twenty-mile line constructed earlier to Marquette. The iron from the mines around Negaunee and Ishpeming could now be shipped either east to Marquette on Lake Superior or south to Escanaba on Lake Michigan.[9]

Under the impetus of munificent land grants, railroad construction in the Upper Peninsula proceeded rapidly during the years after the Civil War. One line was built westward from Marquette and reached Michigamme in 1865. By 1883 this line had been extended to Houghton. A railroad connecting Marquette with St. Ignace was completed in 1881, and a branch linked this road with Sault Ste. Marie in 1887. Connections between this railroad and the two railroads reaching Mackinaw City from the south—the Michigan Central and the Grand Rapids and Indiana—were made by means of steamers. A car ferry placed in use in 1888 and operated jointly by the three railroads reaching the Straits made it possible to transport freight and passenger cars across the Straits and thus provided a link by rail between the two peninsulas. Passengers could entrain at Marquette or Sault Ste. Marie and travel directly to Detroit or Grand Rapids. Freight shipments could be made without loading and unloading at the Straits. On the western side of the Upper Peninsula, copper companies built short railroads, one connecting Calumet with Hancock. A land-grant railroad was built southward from Ontonagon to the Wisconsin state line, where it formed a connection with one of the railroads being built northward through Wisconsin. In 1872 the Chicago and Northwestern Railroad reached Escanaba from Chicago. By using the line already built between Escanaba and Marquette, Marquette had direct rail connections with Chicago. A branch from Escanaba was built into the Menominee Range, reaching Quinnesec in 1877 and Iron Mountain in 1880.

Through the process of consolidation the railroads of the Upper Peninsula were brought together into four main systems. The Duluth, South Shore, and Atlantic stretched across the northern edge of the peninsula, extending from St. Ignace and Sault Ste. Marie in the east, through Marquette to Houghton and westward to Duluth and Superior, Wisconsin. Paralleling it along the Lake Michigan shore, the Soo Line connected Sault Ste. Marie with Manistique and extended westward to Minneapolis and St. Paul, with a branch extending southward to Chicago. From the latter city two main lines

CHIEF RAILROADS

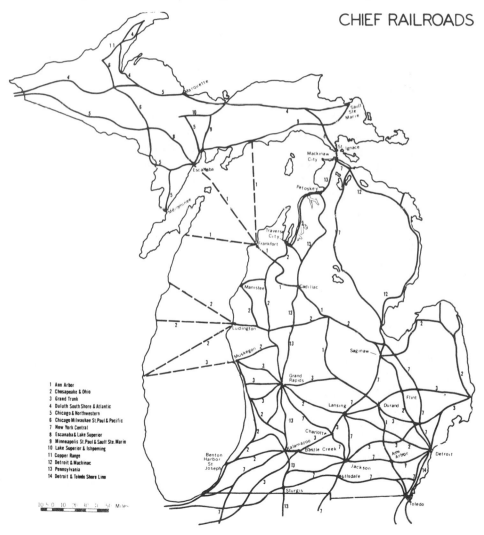

1 Ann Arbor
2 Chesapeake & Ohio
3 Grand Trunk
4 Duluth South Shore & Atlantic
5 Chicago & Northwestern
6 Chicago Milwaukee St.Paul & Pacific
7 New York Central
8 Escanaba & Lake Superior
9 Minneapolis St.Paul & Sault Ste.Marie
10 Lake Superior & Ishpeming
11 Copper Range
12 Detroit & Mackinac
13 Pennsylvania
14 Detroit & Toledo Shore Line

were built northward through Wisconsin into the copper and iron ranges of northern Michigan: the Chicago and Northwestern and the Chicago, Milwaukee, and St. Paul.

Railroads were indispensable in getting the ore from the mines to ports, and in bringing merchandise into and out of the mining and lumbering towns and cities. To a limited extent they were used for the shipment of ores directly to the smelting plants. But the most economical and practical way to ship the ores was by water. When ships first loaded iron ore most of the work had to be done by hand. Ore was loaded in barrels and put aboard the vessels. Later, wheelbarrows were used to carry the ore onto the docks, where it was dumped into the holds of vessels. When the ore reached its destination, it had to be shoveled into buckets that were hoisted and dumped on shore. In 1859 the first modern dock was built at Marquette by the Cleveland Iron Company. Other huge docks were built at Escanaba for the Menominee Range, and at Ashland, Wisconsin, for the Gogebic Range.

Schooners and other sailing vessels were first used to transport the ore, but steamships soon took their place. In 1869 the first bulk freighter, the *R. J. Hackett,* was launched. Built of wood, it was 211 feet long, had a 33-foot beam, and a capacity of 1,200 tons. In 1882, the first iron-hulled steamer was built and was called the *Onoko.* It had a gross tonnage of 2,164. The first steel ship built for service on the Great Lakes was the *Spokane,* launched in 1886. She was 249½ feet in length. Two years later Alexander McDougall of Duluth designed the famous "whaleback" for carrying ore. Built especially to withstand the storms of the Great Lakes, the "whaleback" resembled a huge floating cigar. Many ships of this design were built, and were in use for years. Later improvements in design brought the abandonment of the whaleback. The length and capacity of the ships were steadily increased. The year 1906 saw the advent of 600-foot vessels. It was not until 1952 that the first 700-footer was launched. The profitable operation of such immense ore-carriers required that they be held in port as short a time as possible. Loading could be accomplished quickly but unloading was a slower process until 1899, when Robert Aspin designed and built the first unloaders, making it possible to remove the ore from the largest carriers within a few hours.[10]

Ownership and operation of the giant ore carriers came largely into the hands of the companies that owned the mines. In the early years when small companies were the rule, owners had to pay the going price for the transportation of their ore. One of these was the Cleveland Iron Company, organized in 1847, which, in 1872, acquired a controlling interest in a fleet of steamers and schooners owned by the Cleveland Transportation Company. In 1891 a merger was effected with the Iron Cliffs Company, which had been organized in 1864 by Samuel J. Tilden of New York and William B. Ogden of Chicago. This was the origin of the great Cleveland-Cliffs company. It not only owned a fleet of ore carriers, but it also built railroads and conducted logging operations on a huge scale. In 1903, Cleveland-Cliffs purchased the Jackson Mining Company, the oldest iron-mining company in the Upper Peninsula.[11]

Another of the major iron companies came into being in 1883 when Samuel Mather, eldest son of Samuel L. Mather, one of the founders of the Cleveland Iron Company, joined forces with James Pickands, a Marquette merchant, and Jay Morse, an agent for iron companies, to form Pickands, Mather and Company. Extending its operations into the Menominee and Gogebic ranges by the time of World War I, Pickands, Mather had become the second largest producer of iron ore in the United States and operated the second largest fleet on the Great Lakes.[12] A third major company, the M. A. Hanna Company, was formed in 1885, also by Cleveland investors, and came to own a complex of iron mines, coal mines, and lake carriers. Then finally the formation of the giant U. S. Steel Corporation in 1901, which had its own iron-mining subsidiary and another division that operated the corporation's own fleet of ore carriers, helped to usher in still another phase in the development of Great Lakes shipping.

In the early days of mining in the Upper Peninsula, food in large amounts had to be brought into the mining towns. The problem of maintaining local food supplies was always a serious one. It was soon discovered that most grains except corn could be grown. Around the mining camps, as the trees were cleared away, gardens and farms began to appear. But it was years before local supplies of foodstuffs were adequate. Upbound vessels from lower-lake ports brought provisions of all kinds, and even feed for livestock. Oxen, cattle, and horses were brought in, and in the days before docks were available, they were put overboard to swim for shore.[13]

As the timber was removed, farmers moved in. But the cold climate and the thin and sandy soils in many parts of the peninsula prevented it from becoming a flourishing agricultural area. In the eastern portion there were large swamp areas. Nevertheless, the land in general was better for farming in the eastern part of the peninsula than in the western part. The better farming areas were found in Chippewa, Delta, and Menominee counties. Hay and potatoes were the best crops. Abundant pasturage encouraged the growth of livestock. A considerable amount of the population growth in the fifteen counties of the Upper Peninsula from 180,523 in 1890 to 332,556 in 1920 was due to the expansion of agriculture. The number of farms doubled between 1900 and 1920, increasing from 6,102 to 12,315. By 1920 about one-tenth of the 10,000,000 acres of the Upper Peninsula were under cultivation.

*   *   *   *   *

A traveler on a Great Lakes ship in 1855 wrote in regard to a stop at Detroit: "We have a large accession of excursionists at this point; indeed, our number is more than doubled. Among the number are some elegant-looking ladies and fine-looking men. The *North Star* has just come down from an excursion trip. And she is landing amid strains of music and shouts of excursionists." As early as 1842 a prominent Cincinnati physician was directing attention to the Great Lakes area for its beneficial effects on health. After expatiating at some length on the excellence of the climate, Dr. Daniel Drake wrote that the traveler on the Great Lakes "has then escaped from the region of miasmas, mosquitoes, congestive fevers, calomel, intermittent ague, cakes, liver diseases, jaundice, cholera morbus, dyspepsia, blue devils, and duns, on the whole of which he looks back with gay indifference, if not a feeling of good-natured contempt." The physician then contrasts the typical eastern watering place where the eye "wanders over the comingled idlers, gamblers, coquettes, and dandies," to the experience of seeing the "hourly unfolding of fresh aspects of nature." After calling attention to the historic places on the Great Lakes, he continues, "But a different inhabitant, of more interest . . . to the dyspeptic and the gourmand, is the celebrated whitefish. . . . Its flesh, which in the cold and clear waters of the lake, organized and imbued with life, is liable but to this objection—that he who tastes it once will thenceforth be unable to relish that of any other fish," but he cautions against eating too much trout, which "is said to produce drowsiness." One of those who took Dr. Drake's advice was Horace Mann, the famous eastern educator. Writing from Mackinac Island in 1857 Mann attests to the joys of a summer vacation in Michigan: "I never breathed such air before, and this must be some that was clear out of Eden, and did not get cursed. I sleep every night under sheet, blanket, and coverlet, and no day is too warm for smart walking and vigorous bowling. The children are crazy with animal spirits."[14]

Mackinac Island was Michigan's first mecca for tourists and vacationists. Among those who visited this historic spot in the 1830s and 1840s were the English writer Harriet Martineau, Prince de Joinville, son of King Louis Philippe of France, and the American writers Margaret Fuller and William Cullen Bryant. In 1871 three of the buildings constructed by the American Fur Company were linked to form a hotel, the John Jacob Astor House, to accommodate tourists. The construction of the Grand Hotel in 1887 by two railroads and a steamship company has been noted earlier.

In the Upper Peninsula Marquette was becoming noted as a tourist and resort center as early as 1857. Among the prominent personages to visit the city were Robert Dollar, Andrew Carnegie, and Mrs. Abraham Lincoln. By 1860 Marquette had a three-story frame hotel located in a grove of pines and maples with an excellent view of the harbor, built especially for vacationists. It had over a hundred family rooms and a dining hall to seat 125. There were croquet courts, arbors, swings, rustic benches, and a bandstand, as well as a dock where sailboats and rowboats could be moored. Wealthy people from Pittsburgh, New York, Chicago, and Detroit came here to spend the summers. The Northwestern Hotel, as it was called, attracted many visitors from Boston and New York who had financial interests in the iron mines and furnaces of the Marquette Range. Another four-story resort hotel, the Mesnard, was built in 1883. In 1896 an enormous hostelry called Hotel Superior was opened with a grand ball. Furnished in flamboyant willow and golden-oak furniture, it was designed to cater to the summer-cruise tourists on Great Lakes passenger steamers.[15]

Other cities in the Upper Peninsula also were summer resorts. Among them were Hancock, St. Ignace, and Sault Ste. Marie. A brochure published in 1895 mentions the "weary sameness" of eastern mountains and beach resorts and contrasts this with the natural beauties, the pure air, and the excellent fishing and hunting in the Lake Superior country.[16] Guidebooks were published to direct tourists to northern resorts.[17] At first the tourist and resort business was merely incidental to the much more important mining, lumber, and farming industries, but in 1912 the Grand Rapids *Press* proclaimed in a full-page story that "resorters bring prosperity." The story stated that railroads and steamships were among the chief benefactors, but even the small resort operator was grateful for the substantial supplement to his income from farming which he gained by courting the resort trade.[18]

As the twentieth century entered its second decade, leaders in the Upper Peninsula were becoming conscious that the great days of lumbering were about over, and that Rocky Mountain copper mines and Minnesota iron mines were outproducing Michigan mines. On February 22, 1911, some 240 delegates from the fifteen Upper Peninsula counties met to organize a co-operative organization to deal with their economic problems. The aim of the organization, as expressed in its preamble, was "to endeavor to bring about the wise use of land and water resources of the Upper Peninsula of Michigan that they might better administer to the economy of our people." Financed by contributions from transportation companies, mining firms, businessmen, and local government units, the organization issued brochures setting forth the alleged agricultural opportunities of the peninsula. It also, however, began to extol the recreational attractions of the region and to support the building of highways. Thus it was that the success of tourism, which became the economic hope of the future in the Upper Peninsula as well as much of the northern part of the lower peninsula, would be linked to improvements in the means of transportation in much the same way that the mining and lumber economies had been associated with similar developments in an earlier day.

Zachariah Chandler

20

CITADEL OF REPUBLICANISM

Closely related to the economic dominance of agriculture, lumbering, and mining in the last decades of the nineteenth century was the continued control exercised by the Republican party in the political sphere. There is no single reason for this Republican dominance. In the beginning the strong antislavery sentiment, which contributed to the strength of the Republican party, was unquestionably due to the predominance of New England stock in the state's population. But once the slavery issue was disposed of in the sixties, other factors have to be emphasized. Republican influence in Michigan was probably aided by the slow growth of cities that prevailed in the state until the early years of the twentieth century since the predominantly rural population showed a decided preference for the Republican party. Neither agrarian discontent nor industrial unrest, which frequently cut deeply into Republican vote totals elsewhere, appeared with the same serious consequences in Michigan as it did in many other parts of the Middle West. Lumber, iron, copper, and certain other industries in Michigan relied heavily on a protective tariff, which the Republicans generally favored, and the Democrats generally opposed. As a result, the Republicans so dominated Michigan politics that any young man desiring to pursue a political career had little choice but to join the ranks of the Grand Old Party, if he hoped to enjoy any lasting success.

For many years after the Civil War, wartime passions were kept alive by politicians in quest of votes who "waved the bloody shirt" to remind voters that the Republican party had saved the Union. In Coldwater, one Republican orator, Ben Butler, cried: "Show me a Democrat and I'll show you a rebel." No doubt this strategy was

445

effective, but as the war receded other issues gradually replaced the "bloody shirt." The immediate postwar period, however, saw the racial and sectional issues that had helped give birth to the party continue on, in a somewhat different form. The radical Republicans in Congress pressed for military occupation of the South and the imposition of Negro suffrage. Among the leaders of the radicals, none was more vociferous than Senator Zachariah Chandler. It is debatable whether Chandler had any sincere concern for the plight of the former slaves of the South, but he saw in Negro suffrage a means whereby the Republicans could remain in power. The southerners used poor judgment immediately after the war in passing the notorious "black codes" that many northerners believed were intended to impose slavery in another form. Fears arose that the South would snatch away the fruits of victory. Andrew Johnson, who succeeded Lincoln as President, favored a moderate and conciliatory reconstruction policy toward the ex-Confederate states, but the triumph of the radicals in the Congressional elections of 1866 spelled defeat for him. In Michigan, Governor Henry Crapo staunchly supported the radical program and his re-election in 1866 by the largest majority ever given to a gubernatorial candidate up to that time indicated that a majority of Michigan voters also approved of the radical Republicans' approach to reconstruction.

Although in 1866 Michigan's solidly Republican Congressional delegation favored forcing Negro suffrage on the South, the people of Michigan ironically made no move to enfranchise their own black citizens. Having rejected such a proposal in 1850 by an almost three to one majority, the voters had another opportunity seventeen years later when another constitutional convention included a provision in the revised 1867 state constitution that would have removed the obstacles to Negro males voting. That provision was generally regarded as being largely responsible for causing the majority of the eligible white voters to reject that constitution. Two years later, the radicals in Congress passed and sent to the states the fifteenth amendment to the federal constitution, prohibiting any state from denying the right to vote because of race, color, or previous condition of servitude. The amendment was ratified by both houses of the Michigan legislature on March 8, 1869, in what appears to have been a vote along party lines. Then the question of amending the state constitution so as to allow Negroes the same voting privileges as whites was submitted again to the voters in November, 1869. The amendment was approved by a thin margin: 54,105 for and 50,598 against. A shift of less than two thousand votes thus could have left the prohibition against Negro suffrage on the books, although the ratification of the fifteenth amendment to the federal constitution, which was completed in March, 1870, would have rendered the Michigan voting regulation invalid. As it was, black men were voting in such former slave states as Mississippi well before they were able to vote in a northern state such as Michigan.

Throughout the Reconstruction era, the leader of the Republicans in Michigan continued to be Zachariah Chandler. Although from time to time his leadership in the party was challenged, Chandler had little difficulty in beating off most of these challenges and in retaining his Senate seat for another six-year term in 1869. Until 1870, there was also no serious threat to Republican dominance in the state. Henry P. Baldwin, a Detroit merchant and banker, was elected governor in 1868 to succeed Henry Crapo by a comfortable margin of 30,851 votes. In 1870, however, although Baldwin was re-elected to a second term, his victory margin was cut to only 16,085 votes. Two years later, a split within the Republican party in the nation, principally as a result of growing opposition to the radical wing's Reconstruction policies and the scandals of the Grant administration, seemed to threaten the continued Republican control of the federal government and of such Republican strongholds as Michigan. A group known as the Liberal Republicans nominated the New York editor, Horace Greeley, for the Presidency, and the Democrats endorsed his candidacy. In Michigan, the Liberal Republicans nominated the state's Civil War governor, Austin Blair, as their gubernatorial candidate, and the Democrats also endorsed Blair. However, in the fall elections, Greeley was snowed under, and the regular Republican candidate for governor, John J. Bagley, defeated Blair by a huge plurality of 56,644

Bagley, like Crapo and Baldwin, his immediate predecessors as governor, was a wealthy businessman who had derived his fortune from a number of activities in Detroit. His principal activity had been manufacturing chewing tobacco, which had caused him to remark one day to a Detroit clergyman, "You and I thrive on the sins of the people."[1] During 1873 and 1874, however, public sentiment against the "moneyed class" grew rapidly, as the nation was plunged into one of its most severe economic depressions. The invariable habit of the electorate is to blame hard times on the party in power. Even before the Depression, there had been protests against the retirement of the "greenbacks," paper money issued by the government during the Civil War which was not backed by gold and silver. The Depression brought a demand for more paper money as an inflationary device that might help the economy. Senator Chandler strongly opposed this proposal. Congress passed an act providing for a modest expansion of the greenbacks, but it was vetoed by President Grant. The National Grange of the Patrons of Husbandry, a farmers' organization that had been founded in 1867, began to organize chapters in Michigan in 1872, and many Grangers were also Greenbackers. To complicate matters further for the Republicans, the liquor interests in the state, demanding the repeal of Michigan's prohibition law, formed an alliance with the Democratic party. All these factors resulted in sharp reverses for Michigan Republicanism in the 1874 fall elections. Bagley was re-elected governor but by a margin of less than six thousand votes. Democrats captured three of the state's nine Congressional seats, and in the state legislature, the Republican majority was reduced to ten.

Senator Chandler's third term expired in 1875. Most of the Republicans in the legislature favored returning him to the Senate for a fourth term, but six members of the party formed a coalition with the Democrats to defeat him. In his place the legislature chose Isaac P. Christiancy, a member of the state supreme court, who was a nominal Republican but had favored the Democrats on certain matters. Following his defeat, Chandler was appointed Secretary of the Interior by President Grant. In this office, Chandler served with considerable distinction. "Taking office in October, 1875," one writer declares, "Chandler overhauled the malodorous Indian and Patent bureaus and built up the morale of the entire department. He stopped one glaring fraud in the Land Office and conspicuously refused a bribe in a case on appeal which was given wide publicity at a time when charges of fraud and bribery were hanging over the Republicans in the election of 1876."[2] This give Chandler prestige as national chairman of the Republican party in the election of 1876 in which Samuel Tilden, the Democratic presidential candidate, at first appeared to have defeated the Republican candidate, Rutherford B. Hayes. Chandler, as national chairman, refused to give up. It was his dogged determination more than anything else that maintained the fight to win the electoral votes, principally in the South, that the Republicans claimed had been taken from Hayes by the Democrats through fraud and other forms of electoral irregularities. In the end, Hayes was declared elected by a single electoral vote.

In the election of 1876, Michigan gave Hayes a plurality of more than 25,000 votes. The Republican candidate for governor, Adrian lawyer Charles M. Croswell, was elected with a plurality of over 33,000 votes. The result may be attributed to the recovery of the economy and returning prosperity to the state. The Republicans scored an even more decisive victory in 1878, when Croswell was re-elected by a decisive majority, and every Congressional seat was captured by the Republicans as well as a large majority in the legislature. As a result, when Senator Christiancy resigned his seat for reasons of ill health in January, 1879, Zachariah Chandler was chosen to fill the unexpired term. Chandler resumed his old seat in the Senate on February 22, and there seemed to be no diminution in the old senator's vigor. But on the morning of November 1, 1879, he was found dead in his bed at a hotel in Chicago, where he had delivered a political address the night before. With his death, an era of Michigan politics truly had come to an end.

It was a long time before any political leader could dominate Michigan Republicanism as "Old Zach" had done for more than two decades. During the sixteen years following his death, the power in Michigan Republican circles lay with successful businessmen and lawyers. Wealthy lumbermen were especially prominent. David H. Jerome, elected governor in 1880, made his fortune in lumbering in the Saginaw valley. So did Russell A. Alger, who was the successful Republican candidate for governor in 1884. In the United States Senate, Thomas W. Ferry of Grand Haven, former Governor Henry P. Baldwin of Detroit, and Francis B. Stockbridge of Kalamazoo, who represented Michigan during this period, were all wealthy businessmen. James McMillan of Detroit, who became the most powerful Republican leader after the death of Chandler, was the head of Detroit's largest railroad car manufacturing company as well as having numerous other business interests.

In the 1880s and early 1890s, however, the Republican party did not enjoy the unbroken record of success that had been characteristic of the Chandler era. The technique of reviving Civil War issues by "waving the bloody shirt" was wearing thin, although Civil War veterans continued to be the most popular choices of the party for electoral office. In 1882, the Greenbackers and Democrats formed a Fusion ticket and nominated Josiah W. Begole of Flint for governor. Begole, although presented as a representative of the state's farmers, was, like Flint's earlier governor, Henry Crapo, a man who had benefitted substantially from the lumber industry as a founder and owner of one of that city's largest sawmills. In the election, Begole defeated the incumbent Governor Jerome by a margin of 4,572 votes. The closeness of the election was enhanced by the presence in the race of two other candidates, one of whom, the candidate of the Prohibition party, received over six thousand votes. Begole's victory was attributed to dissatisfaction among farmers due to crop failures and falling prices of farm products. Two years later, Begole was nosed out in his bid for re-election by the Republican candidate, Russell A. Alger, but by less than four thousand votes.

Fusionist candidates, however, won seven of Michigan's eleven Congressional seats, and in the spring election of 1886, the Fusionists were able to defeat Supreme Court Justice Thomas M. Cooley in his campaign for re-election, even though Cooley was the most notable jurist Michigan has ever produced.

Their defeat in the race for governor in 1882, their narrow victory in the gubernatorial race of 1884, and the mixed results in other contests in the same period convinced the Republican leaders that new tactics were required. Alger refused to accept renomination in 1886, and the Republicans turned to a Branch County farmer, Cyrus G. Luce, in an obvious attempt to win the favor of those who had become critical of the dominance of lumber barons and wealthy businessmen. Luce won by a margin of about 7,000 votes in the 1886 election and was re-elected by a slightly larger margin in 1888. A factor of considerable importance in these close elections continued to be the Prohibition party, which had been organized in 1869. In 1886 that party's candidate for governor polled 25,179 votes. In 1890, the Republican leaders, regaining their confidence following the two successful campaigns of Luce, nominated for governor James M. Turner, a wealthy Lansing railroad man. Party nominations were made in state conventions, which the lumber and railroad barons and their allies could usually control. There was strong support in the Republican ranks for the nomination of John T. Rich, a Lapeer County farmer, but the Republican convention rejected him in favor of Turner. The Democrats, sensing their opportunity, chose Edwin B. Winans, a Livingston County farmer, as their candidate. By this time the Greenback movement had faded away. Falling prices and bad seasons, however, had stirred new discontent among the farmers of the South and West, resulting in the growth of the Populist movement. This movement represented a wide range of reforms, including the expansion of the currency through the free and unlimited coinage of silver at a ratio to gold of sixteen to one. The extent of dissatisfaction in Michigan with the ruling clique in the Republican party was demonstrated in the fall election of 1890, when Winans won the governorship by a margin of 11,520 votes. Even more of an upset was scored when the Democrats elected a majority of the state house of representatives and, through a clever bit of chicanery, also got control of the state senate.

In spite of these setbacks, the Republicans could point with pride to the fact that never once since 1852 had Michigan given a single electoral vote to the Democratic candidate for President. Then, as now, the Presidential electors of each party were voted on as a group, and hence the entire electoral vote of the state went to the candidate whose electors received the largest vote, regardless of the size of the opposition. In 1891 Democrats in the Michigan legislature passed an act, however, which provided that each Congressional district should choose one elector and that two electors should be chosen by the state at large. The purpose of this was to give the Democratic candidate for President some portion of Michigan's vote. Thus in the 1892 Presidential election, for the first and only time in its history, the state's electoral vote was split. Grover Cleveland, the successful Democratic candidate, received five of Michigan's electoral votes, while Benjamin Harrison, the Republican nominee, received the remaining nine. When Republicans resumed control of the legislature in 1893 they promptly repealed this law. It is interesting to note that some critics of the electoral college system in recent times have suggested reforms that would closely resemble the system Michigan used in 1892.

Having learned their lesson, the Republican leaders gave the gubernatorial nomination in 1892 to Rich, who was elected in November and re-elected two years later. It was during Rich's term that the Panic of 1893 shattered the nation's economy, and brought widespread bankruptcies, unemployment, falling prices, and general distress. The Populists, who had polled a million votes across the country in 1892 for their Presidential candidate, were now functioning as a vigorous political party in Michigan and elsewhere. They called for "free silver" along with public ownership of the railroads, a graduated income tax, direct election of United States senators, and women's suffrage as remedies for the nation's ills. Democratic President Grover Cleveland, however, staunchly upheld the gold standard and even persuaded Congress to repeal an act passed earlier for increased silver coinage. In the state elections in Michigan in 1894 Democrats, Populists, and Prohibitionists all had candidates in the field. The fact that the Republican candidate, John T. Rich, was himself a farmer and sympathetic to the needs of the farmers, together with the division among his opposition, made possible his re-election. With a Democratic President in Washington, however, Michigan Democrats won rewards for political service. Don M. Dickinson of Detroit was chosen Postmaster General in the cabinet and four prominent Michigan Democrats received appointments to diplomatic and consular posts.[3]

The election of 1896 ended one of the most bitterly contested political campaigns in American history. The Democratic party, strongly affected by agrarian discontent in the South and West, repudiated its own President, Grover Cleveland, and adopted a platform favoring "free silver." William Jennings Bryan electrified the

Democratic National Convention with his "Cross of Gold" speech and was nominated for the Presidency. This youthful and eloquent Nebraskan so thoroughly alarmed the powerful business, corporate, and financial leaders of the nation that they exerted extraordinary efforts to bring about his defeat. The Republicans nominated William McKinley as their presidential candidate. McKinley, known as an advocate of protective tariffs, tried to soft-pedal the currency issue but was unable to do so. The fear of Bryan and "free silver" was shared by Michigan businessmen and other conservative-minded Michiganians. Their determination to defeat Bryan and elect McKinley was a primary factor in their selection of Detroit Mayor Hazen S. Pingree as the Republican candidate for governor in 1896.

Pingree, a native of Maine, was a wealthy Detroit shoe manufacturer in 1889 when he was nominated by the Republicans to run for mayor of the city. Detroit's voters had generally given the Democratic candidates a majority, in spite of Republican dominance in the state as a whole. A group of influential businessmen, hoping to break the Democratic hold on Detroit, persuaded Pingree to run. Since he was a man of wealth, they expected him to support the business interests. But following his election, he launched a reform program that quickly alienated his wealthy backers. He attacked the city's assessments, which were far higher in proportion on homes than on factories, downtown business buildings, and vacant lots owned by real-estate speculators. He attacked the gas company, proving its rates were almost twice as high as those in other cities, and he condemned the street railway company for failing to electrify its line while paying the city nothing for its franchise. Stockholders in the corporations involved violently attacked the mayor. They avoided him socially, the newspapers turned against him, and the banks even refused to do business with him. In spite of this, and perhaps in part because of it, he was immensely popular with the people. They lined up in front of the City Hall to read his statements that the newspapers refused to print. When the Panic of 1893 hit Detroit, Pingree permitted the unemployed to use vacant city land to plant gardens and grow their own food. He sold his riding horse at auction to provide seed. "Pingree's Potato Patches" were an approach to providing relief to the depression's sufferers that was continued for several years and was widely copied in other cities across the land. It also contributed to the mayor's popularity with the masses. Three times Pingree was elected mayor of Detroit, winning sixty-seven percent of the vote in the third election in spite of all the opposition to him. He succeeded in getting the gas company to lower its rates and established a municipal lighting plant. He persuaded a group to build a rival streetcar line and charge lower fares.

Pingree found that some of the changes he wished to make in Detroit were blocked by state law. This may have been one factor in arousing his interest in state politics. He was a candidate for the Republican nomination for governor in the Republican state convention of 1892, but was defeated through the influence of party leaders such as Senator James McMillan, who shared the dislike for Pingree that was so intense among the conservative business community. In 1894 Pingree withdrew his name from consideration at the last moment, but in 1896 he traveled all over the state seeking support for the nomination. Perhaps the party leaders could have blocked his nomination in 1896 as they had in 1892 and 1894, but this time there was a new factor at work. McMillan and his supporters were far more interested in defeating Bryan and electing McKinley than they were in the governorship of Michigan. To be sure, they hated Pingree, but they saw in his great popularity with the people a means whereby the end they sought could be achieved. With Pingree's name on the Republican ballot as candidate for governor, enough support might be given to the Republican party to carry McKinley to victory in the state as well. They foresaw that the state senate, which was sure to be dominated by Republican conservatives, would be able to call a halt to any dangerous reforms Pingree might try to bring about in Lansing. Furthermore, with Pingree in Lansing, he would not be able to upset conservative business interests in Detroit.

The plan worked perfectly. McKinley won Michigan's electoral vote by a majority of 56,000. Pingree's majority was over 83,000. And as the Republican bosses had anticipated, the state senate was able to block a large part of Pingree's program. For a while in the early weeks of 1897, the new governor continued to hold his position as mayor of Detroit, but when the state supreme court ruled he could not hold the two offices at the same time, he resigned as mayor. He never moved to Lansing, but retained his home and office in Detroit, regularly spending weekends there. Regarding Detroit as the business center of the state, he even suggested that the capital be moved back to that city.

As governor, Pingree enjoyed far less success in his efforts at reform than he had in Detroit. Many of the reforms he advocated were completely disregarded; others were killed at some stage in the legislative process. Pingree fought hardest, as governor, to compel the state's railroad corporations to pay a fair tax on the value of their properties. At least four governors since 1877 had urged the legisla-

ture to impose such a tax, but a conservative bloc in the senate that
came to be dubbed the "immortal nineteen" during Pingree's administration had prevented bills substantially increasing railroad taxes
from becoming law. In the first legislature during the Pingree administration a bill was introduced by a Detroit legislator, John Atkinson,
to set up a commission to assess the property of the railroads, to levy
a tax thereon, and to pay the sum so raised into the primary school
fund. The house passed the bill, but the "immortal nineteen" killed it
in the senate. In 1898 Pingree was re-elected by a large majority, and
again recommended the railroad tax measure to the legislature. This
time both houses passed the bill, but the state supreme court quickly
declared it unconstitutional. Pingree then asked the legislature to
approve a constitutional amendment that would legalize the Atkinson bill. The senate refused to approve such a resolution in both the
regular session and in a special session called by the governor, but
finally accepted it when Pingree called a second special session. The
proposed amendment was approved by a popular vote in the
November, 1900 elections. Desiring to see his favorite measure become law before his retirement from office January 1, 1901, Governor Pingree called another special legislative session to reenact the
Atkinson bill. As a final gesture of defiance the senate refused to give
the governor that much satisfaction, and deferred action until the
following May, after Pingree's successor, Governor Aaron T. Bliss,
had taken office. After that, the bill finally became law.[4]

It was during Pingree's first term that the Spanish-American
War took place. It was to be the last of the American wars in which
the states primarily furnished the nation's fighting forces. Pingree
was opposed to the war, but after it was declared he acted vigorously
to see that the five infantry regiments that the state supplied were
well cared for. He set up a military camp at Island Lake and lived
there with Michigan troops. When they left for southern camps he
made sure that the men had well-fitted shoes. He sent special trains
to return the sick and wounded from southern and eastern hospitals.
He was proud of the fact that Michigan was the only state that had
two regiments in the Cuban campaign.

Two Michigan men played major roles in the war. One was
General William R. Shafter, a native of Galesburg, who was commander of the American forces in Cuba. He had won distinction as a
volunteer during the Civil War, receiving the Congressional Medal
of Honor for his bravery. He chose the army for a career and during
the Indian wars on the western plains had won the nickname "Pecos
Bill." At the time the Spanish-American War broke out he was
sixty-three years of age, weighed nearly three hundred pounds, and

during the entire Cuban campaign suffered from illness. Nevertheless he conducted the campaign with considerable competence. Newspaper men gave the headlines to the dashing young Theodore Roosevelt and his Rough Riders rather than to Shafter, partly because Shafter refused to reveal his plans. Less than a month after Shafter and his force landed in Cuba, however, the chief Spanish stronghold, Santiago, had been captured.[5]

While one Michiganian commanded the Cuban expeditionary force, another, Russell A. Alger, served as Secretary of War. The former governor had been named to this cabinet post by President McKinley at the start of his first term in the White House in 1897. During the war, the inefficiency of Alger's department was subjected to bitter criticism. At the embarkation point in Tampa, Florida, the departing soldiers were issued wool uniforms, even though they were leaving for a campaign in the sub-tropics. Mess pans were those left over from the Civil War, and instead of being issued modern rifles the troops had to make the best of old Springfields. Food was terrible; the canned meat was so bad that it was popularly referred to as "embalmed beef." Medical supplies were totally inadequate. Secretary Alger received the blame for all of this, and he finally resigned in order to save McKinley further embarrassment. Yet it is doubtful that Alger was actually at fault so much as the spoils system—a system under which the personnel of the War Department consisted of men who obtained their positions because of political services rather than job competence. At least in Michigan, Alger's reputation survived the unfortunate experience in the war department. Governor Pingree rose to Alger's defense and joined in welcoming him when he returned to Detroit, and within a few years Alger was sent back to Washington to finish out his political career as one of Michigan's United States senators.[6]

An unexpected result of the Spanish-American War was the American acquisition of the former Spanish colony of the Philippines. One of the few Americans to have much knowledge of these Far Eastern islands was Dean Conant Worcester of the University of Michigan, who had headed a scientific expedition to the Philippines in the early nineties. This had followed an earlier trip in 1887 when he had accompanied Joseph B. Steere, zoology professor at the University of Michigan, who was making his second scientific foray to that archipelago. In 1899, McKinley named Worcester to the First Philippine Commission, thereby beginning a remarkable connection between Michigan and the Philippines that has continued to the present day. Worcester remained in the islands for over fourteen years in a variety of governmental capacities. Other Michiganians in these early years were participants in the grim war that was fought to quell the Philippine insurrection. One of these, Harry H. Bandholtz of Constantine, a West Point graduate and veteran of the Spanish-American War, continued on after the defeat of the insurrectionists to be head of the Philippine Constabulary. Others served on the Philippine Supreme Court, in teaching positions, and in other jobs. Ultimately, it would be Frank Murphy of Detroit who, as Governor-General and then High Commissioner of the Philippines in the thirties, would direct the transformation of the colony to commonwealth status, the last step before complete independence. In this job, Murphy would be assisted by University of Michigan political scientist, Joseph Ralston Hayden, who, as a result of numerous contacts with and positions in the Philippines from 1922 to his death in 1945, became recognized as the foremost American authority on those islands. The continuing relationship between Michigan and the Philippines after that colony's independence was symbolized by the service of former Michigan Senator Homer Ferguson as ambassador to the Philippines in the fifties and of former Governor G. Mennen Williams' tour of duty in the same post in the late sixties.[7]

The last year of Governor Pingree's administration was marred by a scandal involving members of his administration. The Henderson-Ames Company of Kalamazoo, through the connivance of certain state officials, was able to buy a stock of unused state military uniforms at salvage prices and after only minor alterations sold them back to the state at top prices with kickbacks to the state officials involved in the scheme. Five company officials subsequently confessed their complicity and made restitution. Several state officials, however, were tried and convicted and sentenced to prison terms. A trusted Pingree aide was accused of being part of the conspiracy but was acquitted. Pingree thought the Henderson-Ames officials had been treated more leniently than the state officials, and he proceeded to pardon two of the latter, an act for which he was sharply criticized. Pingree no doubt had these critics in mind when he lashed out at his enemies in his farewell message as governor in January, 1901: "I am satisfied," he declared, "that I could have had the praise and support of the best 'citizens' and our 'best society,' and of the press of the state generally, if I had upheld those who have for years attempted to control legislation in their own interests, to the end that they might be relieved from sharing equally with the poor and lowly the burden of taxation."[8]

Although once rather neglected by historians of the turn-of-the-century reform movements, Pingree has been more widely recognized in more recent studies as a major precursor of the Progressive reformers of the Teddy Roosevelt era. Pingree advocated many if not most of the Progressive reforms, including the direct primary, popular election of United States senators, a graduated income tax, and more stringent regulation of big business. To be sure, some of these reforms had been demanded by the Populists in the early nineties, but it was quite another thing for them to be advocated by a Republican governor who was also a successful businessman. Unfortunately, the movement in favor of the reforms he advocated had not yet gathered sufficient force to enlist the public support that was necessary for success.

Pingree did not live long after retiring from office at the end of his second term as governor on January 1, 1901. He left on a trip to Europe shortly afterward and died suddenly in a London hotel on June 18, 1901. His body was returned to Detroit, where friends and enemies joined in extolling his sterling character. Belatedly, many realized that Pingree had been one of the most dynamic, innovative political figures that Michigan has ever produced, and one of the very few to have developed a truly devoted mass following.

The Presidential election of 1900 had seen McKinley once more pitted against his opponent of 1896, William Jennings Bryan. But the issues involved were not the same. Bryan's advocacy of free silver now held little appeal, for new sources of gold had been found and silver was no longer as cheap in relation to gold as it had been in 1896. Besides, prosperity had tended to erase the demand for change. Sensing victory and longing for someone less rambunctious and more conservative than Pingree in the governor's chair at Lansing, the Michigan Republican leaders persuaded the state party convention to nominate a rich Saginaw lumberman and banker, Aaron T. Bliss. He was swept into office by a majority nearly as large as McKinley's, who picked up fifty-eight percent of Michigan's popular vote. However, Bliss in his inaugural came out in favor of Pingree's pet railroad tax measure, and the legislature proceeded to enact it. One may assume that the bill was no more palatable to the conservatives than it had been when Pingree advocated it, but conservative leaders were sensing that certain concessions to public demand needed to be made. It was this strategy of bending with the wind that enabled the conservatives to retain much of their hold on the state government and to delay for a decade the onset of another reform-minded governor of the Pingree type.

Old mill near Howell, Michigan

21

THE GROWTH OF MANUFACTURING

As governor of Michigan at the start of the twentieth century, the lumberman Aaron Bliss was something of an anomaly since he and his fellow lumber baron, Senator Russell Alger, who died in office in 1907, represented an era that was rapidly coming to an end with the cutting of most of Michigan's remaining timber resources. Although they were on opposite ends of the political spectrum, the shoe manufacturer, Hazen Pingree, and the railroad car tycoon, James McMillan, were alike in having helped to pioneer the economic wave which would in the twentieth century make Michigan one of the great manufacturing centers of the world. Although automobiles came to epitomize this development whenever the name Michigan, and particularly Detroit, was mentioned, manufacturing was assuming an increasingly important position in the state's economy long before any automobiles were produced. Even if automobile production had never taken hold, the highly diversified processing activities that had already emerged in the nineteenth century would have gone far in the twentieth century to erase the image Michigan had acquired from the earlier dominance of such extractive activities as the fur trade, farming, lumbering, mining, and fishing.

During Michigan's early development there had been little that the twentieth-century Michiganian would identify or classify as manufacturing. The existing manufacturing was, for the most part, of the domestic variety as families, particularly farm families, sought to provide, through their own labors, as much as they could for the things they needed. In the villages and towns a handful of artisans and craftsmen, such as blacksmiths and cabinetmakers, produced on demand many of the remaining items that the family was unable to make for itself or which it could afford to have made by others.

In 1850, the federal census for the first time included information about the jobs that people held and provided the first available detailed breakdown on the various occupations represented in the state. Out of a total population in 1850 of slightly less than 400,000 people, 108,978 were identified as "gainfully employed." Sixty percent of these were farmers. Of the remaining forty percent, when one subtracts the professional groups, the merchants, and the self-employed carpenters, tinsmiths, and other craftsmen, it is likely that no more than one percent of these breadwinners held what would later be thought of as a factory job. The census bureau, however, defined manufacturing in a much broader sense; for example, it included various occupations in the lumber industry under this heading which in later times would not ordinarily be associated with the manufacturing concept. Even under the census bureau's generous use of the term, however, there were only 9,344 workers in Michigan in 1850 who were identified as employed in manufacturing establishments, the number of which totalled 2,033. The total product of these establishments was worth slightly more than $11,000,000 and the wages they paid to their employees amounted to $2,700,000. By 1860, the number of plants had increased by seventy percent, while the value of manufactured products almost doubled. The largest percentage gains in this period came during the sixties, with the number of manufacturing establishments in Michigan having reached 9,455 by 1870—a gain of 174 percent over the figure of ten years earlier. The value of the product of these establishments was about $118,000,000—a gain of 262.5 percent. The employees in these establishments now totalled 64,000. Development slowed during the seventies, as the nation's economy was plunged into a lengthy depression, beginning in 1873. Development picked up again in the eighties and continued on up in the nineties, although at a reduced rate because of another severe depression in mid-decade.

According to the census bureau, by 1900 there were 16,807 manufacturing plants in the state, which employed 162,355 workers, although the highest seasonal employment during the year pushed that figure up to 232,353. The value of Michigan's manufacturing product was $356,944,000, wages amounted to $66,500,000, and the total assessed value of the manufacturing property was more than a billion dollars. Even if one were to adopt a somewhat more rigid definition of manufacturing than that used by the census bureau, it is probable that by 1900, as many as twenty-five percent of the state's working population held what most people would regard as factory jobs, an indication of the enormous strides manufacturing had made in the last half of the nineteenth century.[1]

The bulk of the manufacturing establishments were small operations, employing only a few workers, and engaged largely in custom and repair work. The lion's share of this manufacturing was concentrated in the southern part of the state, complementing and even supplanting the agricultural activities that had sparked the initial development of this area. In the northern two-thirds of the state, manufacturing activity was at best spotty, providing no major boost to an economy which was beginning to stagnate or decline as the prospects for further growth in the lumber and mining industries were disappearing. On the other hand, southern Michigan possessed the most complete transportation facilities in the state, was the site of many long-established communities who actively promoted manufacturing development, and possessed a substantial resident population that could supply the initial labor force required by most of the new manufacturing enterprises.

The emerging industries of major importance tended to be those that developed in Michigan because of the resources available or because of some of the state's earlier activities. In a state where farming had become such a major factor, it was not surprising that agriculturally-oriented industries were among the foremost of the state's manufacturers. In 1900, the value of Michigan's flouring and grist mill products was second (albeit a distant second) only to the value of the state's lumber and timber products in the census bureau's classification of the state's various categories of manufacturing activities, while leather products and slaughtering also ranked among the fifteen leading manufacturing groups.

In general, food-processing activities grew rapidly in the latter part of the nineteenth century. Early in the pioneer period, New England farmers settling in parts of southern Michigan had supplemented their income by tapping the hard maple trees to obtain maple syrup or sugar. Maple sugar would continue to be an important local product in parts of central Michigan to the present day. Around the time of the Civil War, Michigan farmers also began growing considerable quantities of sorghum, the processing of which to make sorghum molasses was an important activity for a number of years. In the nineties, the growing of beet sugar provided a far more satisfactory source of sugar. Beginning in 1898 numerous beet sugar factories were opened throughout southern Michigan before this processing activity came to be centered in the Saginaw-Bay City and Thumb areas.

The dairy industry was another food-processing activity that evolved from a strictly home industry in the middle of the nineteenth century to commercial proportions by the end of the century. Plants producing cheese began to appear in the southeastern part of the state after the Civil War and by 1899, although over 330,000 pounds were still produced on the farms of the state, more than 10,000,000 pounds were turned out by the commercial producers. Among these producers was a future governor, Fred M. Warner, who operated a dozen cheese factories in the Detroit area. Creameries, however, were slower to supplant the farm as the source of the state's butter, with creamery production in 1888 being less than 8,000,000 pounds in contrast to farm-produced butter amounting to some 60,000,000 pounds.

The food-preserving industry was still another agriculturally related activity to emerge, beginning modestly with plants that dried apples and certain other fruits, and then expanding greatly in scope with the development of canning techniques. By 1914 there were ninety-one food-preserving plants in the state, with the largest number concentrated in the western part of the lower peninsula to take care of the products of the fruit belt, with plants elsewhere involved in canning or preserving truck garden crops, such as corn and tomatoes.

One of Michigan's best-known companies by the end of the century was D. M. Ferry & Company of Detroit, one of the largest seed houses in the world. Dexter M. Ferry came to Detroit in the 1850s and became a partner with Miles Gardner in the American Seed Store. Gardner died in 1867, and Ferry took over as the sole owner of the firm. By the 1880s, Ferry was employing several hundred workers in his huge Detroit warehouse while hundreds more were serving as field hands on the seed farm he had established near Detroit. Some five hundred carloads of seeds were shipped out annually to the more than 80,000 Ferry dealers, while nearly an equal number of farmers and gardeners ordered their seeds directly after studying Ferry's seed catalogs, of which more than 325,000 were sent out each year.[2] Elsewhere in the state, S. M. Isbell and Company in Jackson, founded in 1878, was another important dealer in seeds, farm products, and fertilizers.

As farming operations became increasingly mechanized in the last half of the nineteenth century, it was only logical that producers of agricultural machinery and equipment would locate in southern Michigan, although not to the extent that such manufacturers would come to be concentrated elsewhere in the Middle West. The Moore-Hascall Combine, developed and demonstrated in the Kalamazoo area in the late 1830s, proved to be too cumbersome for farm operations in the Michigan area, but other farm equipment, of more modest proportions, was soon produced in the state. George Gale and his son began producing plows in Hillsdale in the 1840s, and then moved their operations to Albion, where the Gale Manufacturing Company made that city famous for its plows and cultivators which, by the 1890s, it was shipping out by the hundreds of thousands. Other towns, such as Birmingham, Grand Haven, Jackson, and Port Huron, were the sites of factories producing corn planters, forks, hoes, and threshing machinery. In the latter category, the claim was made that Battle Creek "made more traction engines and threshing machinery than ... any other city in America." In Battle Creek, the Advance Thresher Company, with nearly a thousand employees, was said to be second only to the J. I. Case Company in thresher production, while the smaller Nichols & Shepard Company is immortalized as the producer of steam-powered threshing machines that could move from farm to farm under their own power. The sight of one in 1876 inspired Henry Ford to work on other kinds of road vehicles in later years.[3]

Battle Creek, however, was soon to become far better known as the site of Michigan's most famous agriculturally related manufacturing activity—the making of breakfast foods. In this case, however, the location of this industry had little or nothing to do with Battle Creek's geographical location or the resources available in the area. Instead, it stemmed from the decisions made by individuals who were motivated not by economic factors but religious beliefs. A new denomination, the Seventh-day Adventists, which had had its origins in western New York in the 1840s, had established its headquarters in Battle Creek by 1860. In 1863, the denomination's spiritual head, Sister Ellen White, had a vision which inspired her to make proper diet and health care central concerns of the Seventh-day Adventists. Drawing upon some of the work of earlier dietary reformers—among them Sylvester Graham, popularizer of graham flour, who had expounded his ideas on Michigan lecture tours—Sister White and her followers now adhered to a strictly vegetarian diet. Then in 1866, again closely following the ideas of a health reformer, Dr. James Caleb Jackson of New York state, the Adventists established the Western Reform Health Institute at Battle Creek, a sanitarium where their ideas regarding health care could be put into practice.

Ten years later, the son of a leading Battle Creek Seventh-day Adventist family, Dr. John Harvey Kellogg, whose medical education had been aided financially by the Whites, took over the operation of the Battle Creek sanitarium. The sanitarium had not done well under its earlier directors, but under Dr. Kellogg's supervision it became one of the most famous medical facilities in the country. At the "San," as it was called, Dr. Kellogg began experimenting with new kinds of food that would adhere to the Adventists' dietary beliefs but would add a little variety for the patients. These patients were not required to be members of the denomination to enter the institute but were expected to be fed according to Adventist standards soon after their admission. By the early eighties, Kellogg had developed a substitute for coffee, which, along with all other stimulants, had been banned in the Adventist diet. He also developed the first of the cold cereals which came to be his main interest. Patients who had been served these new foods would shortly have the opportunity of ordering them by mail from the Sanitarium after they returned home, but aside from this small-scale business, no active effort was made to promote sales of these and other Kellogg products. Dr. Kellogg, in fact, was basically opposed to such efforts.

In 1891 one of Dr. Kellogg's new patients was Charles W. Post, a small-time businessman from Illinois. Post's wife paid for her husband's expenses while he was in the San by going door to door, selling suspenders that Post had developed. After several months Post left the Sanitarium, where he had become deeply interested in Dr. Kellogg's ideas and practices, some of which Post now sought to imitate in a modest facility of his own that he opened in Battle Creek. Most importantly, however, Post recognized the commercial possibilities possessed by Kellogg's foods, and in the mid-nineties, with a reported bankroll of only $69, he began to market a copy of Dr. Kellogg's coffee substitute, a product that Post called Postum. In 1898, Post also marketed Grape-Nuts, his version of Dr. Kellogg's first cold, prepared breakfast cereal. With a masterly advertising approach, Post was an almost overnight success with these two products, netting a million dollars a year by around 1900.

Post's success touched off a spectacular boom in Battle Creek in the early years of the twentieth century as others flocked to the city to try to steal additional Kellogg ideas and make a fortune as Post had done. The Malta Vita Pure Food Company was the first to exploit the flaked type of cereal that Dr. Kellogg and his younger brother, W. K. Kellogg, had developed some years earlier. Dr. Kellogg, who had patented the process, could not get the courts to protect his rights, since Kellogg's imitators were able to prove they had made some minor change which made their product different from Kellogg's. W. K. Kellogg (the W. stood for Willie, which he later shortened to Will) became increasingly irritated and frustrated at his brother's refusal to capitalize on the commercial value of his ideas. Finally, in 1906, the younger Kellogg, with financial backing from a St. Louis insurance man, persuaded his brother to let him form a separate company—the Battle Creek Toasted Corn Flakes Company—so he could market a cereal that the two brothers had developed some years before and which W. K. Kellogg felt had the best commercial possibilities of any of these foods. He was right. The product, which he soon renamed Kellogg's Corn Flakes, became the best-selling product of its kind on the market. Despite Kellogg's efforts to protect his cereal from imitators by placing his signature on each cereal box, close copies appeared before long, the most successful being Post Toasties. Nevertheless, W. K. Kellogg proved to be an even better advertiser and merchandiser than C. W. Post, and his company quickly emerged as the giant of the industry. Most of the thirty or forty other companies that appeared during the boom in the early years of the century soon fell by the wayside. The Post Company continued to prosper, but Charles Post, who sold his products as health foods, became increasingly despondent over his own poor health, and eventually committed suicide in 1914. In 1925 his company became part of the merger that created the General Foods Corporation. The Kellogg company, however, under W. K. Kellogg's direction remained independent, and made Battle Creek in the twentieth century one of the most famous cities of its size in the world by the constant reference to itself in its world-wide marketing and advertising as "Kellogg's of Battle Creek."[4]

Another Michigan city whose name had become synonymous with a manufactured product even before Battle Creek and breakfast food were inextricably linked in the public's mind, was Grand Rapids, which had become the best-known center of the furniture industry by the latter part of the nineteenth century. Since the furniture of this era was made largely of hardwoods, which were the kinds of trees most commonly found in the forests of southern Michigan, furniture manufacturing was one of a number of wood-related industries that could have been expected to, and did, arise in Michigan. But Grand Rapids was not well located from the standpoint of the resource required by the furniture makers, lying on the northern fringe of the hardwood forests and possessing poor transportation facilities until the 1870s. Numerous cities farther south in Michigan were better situated than Grand Rapids in these regards, but that city's economic development, like that of Battle Creek's, again demonstrates the importance of individuals in the success of a business venture.

In the pioneer period, cabinetmakers were among the first skilled craftsmen to locate in Michigan, setting up shop in the towns that were developing and making furniture for the local market, although the building of coffins is said to have been their steadiest source of income. By 1850, there were 704 cabinetmakers in the state. At that time, Boston and Cincinnati were the leading centers for large-scale furniture manufacturing which was supplying a market beyond the immediate locality of the manufacturer.

The first cabinetmaker to settle in Grand Rapids was William Haldane, who arrived in the mid-thirties and began to take orders for furniture from the residents. Some of the pieces that he built have survived to the present time and one or more of them are displayed in the Grand Rapids Public Museum. As his business grew, Haldane began to hire a few men to help him, and around 1848 he installed a circular saw in his shop, using the waters of the Grand River as the source of power. With this equipment, a lathe, and hand tools, he and his men produced tables, bedsteads, chairs, and other pieces. By 1853, Haldane's move away from the strictly hand-crafted work of the early period continued as he began using steam power in the shop.

Haldane, the pioneer Grand Rapids furniture manufacturer, was followed in the forties by a number of other cabinetmakers who settled in that city. William Powers arrived in 1847 and formed the company of Powers and Ball in 1851. The company owned its own sawmill, and was one of the first of the Grand Rapids firms to attain some size, employing thirty to forty men and turning out a variety of furniture with an annual volume of $30,000. In 1855, Enoch Winchester, who had been a partner with Haldane for a brief time, joined with his brother, S. A. Winchester, to form the Winchester Brothers Company. The company constructed a two-story factory and was the first one to seek sales outside the local area. The Winchesters were forced into bankruptcy in 1857, and the plant was acquired by Charles C. Comstock, a lumberman from New Hampshire who had come to Grand Rapids in 1852 to engage in the lumber business but who now became one of the most important figures in the city's development as a furniture center. Overcoming some initial failures by 1862, Comstock launched the city's first wholesale furniture manufacturing company. He set up branches in Peoria and St. Louis and made arrangements with dealers in Chicago and Milwaukee as he sought to market his furniture throughout the Middle West. Even though Grand Rapids was not linked by railroad to the outside world until 1858, Comstock and other local manufacturers by that time were already annually shipping out approximately $40,000 worth of furniture by wagon or steamboat to Lake Michigan and from there by boat to Chicago or Milwaukee.

A problem that all furniture manufacturers faced in the early days was the need to use dried lumber, since furniture would not hold together if any sap was left in the wood. The drying process took three to four years. The small manufacturer frequently could not afford to have his money tied up for that long a period. Various methods of speeding up the drying process proved unsatisfactory until the development of the dry kiln process, which was largely the work of two Grand Rapids men, A. D. Linn and Z. Clark Thwing.

The early Grand Rapids furniture was strictly utilitarian. For fine furniture, one had to turn to larger companies elsewhere in the country. Julius Berkey is credited with starting the trend toward quality furniture in Grand Rapids. He formed a company in 1859 which went through various changes before Berkey joined with George W. Gay to form the celebrated firm of Berkey and Gay. This firm became the largest and most famous of the Grand Rapids furniture manufacturers, shipping out $125,000 worth of furniture by 1870. Berkey and Gay engaged the very best craftsmen and emphasized the highest quality of workmanship and materials in their products. They began advertising on a national scale and opened a branch in New York. Despite various changes in ownership, the firm continued in business until after the Second World War, but the name Berkey and Gay had acquired such a high degree of public recognition that a decade after the company had gone out of business, a survey in Chicago designed to test consumer knowledge of furniture manufacturers showed Berkey and Gay was still the best-known name in the industry.

By 1870, Grand Rapids and Kent County were listed as having eight furniture companies with an annual sales volume of $348,000. The opening that year of the Grand Rapids and Indiana Railroad, which gave the city a link with the Michigan Central, the Lake Shore and Michigan Southern, and other Midwestern rail systems, helped to spur a great expansion of the furniture industry in Grand Rapids in the years that followed. Many of the companies that were formed— over eighty-five in the period from 1880 to 1900 alone—did not survive, but others had a long-lasting impact on the city's development. The Grand Rapids Chair Company, formed in 1872 by Charles C. Comstock and others, pioneered the production of matched bedroom and dining room suites in the early eighties and became one of the city's largest manufacturers. The Sligh Furniture Company, organized in 1880, pioneered in copying classic designs from the past. It turned out a great deal of solid walnut furniture, bureaus with marble tops, and the like. Such big, heavy pieces, in fact, came to be what many people thought of when the term Grand Rapids furniture was mentioned. Other companies began specializing in office and school furniture, with the Grand Rapids School Furniture Company, formed in 1886, evolving into the American Seating Company, which became the world's largest producer of public and institutional seating.

In 1876, four Grand Rapids manufacturers exhibited their furniture at the Centennial Exposition in Philadelphia and created enormous interest in the East. Buyers came to Grand Rapids from around the country, and in 1878 a semi-annual furniture market was organized for the convenience of these out-of-town buyers. In 1881, manufacturers from outside Grand Rapids began exhibiting at these markets which became the most important gathering place for the industry in the country and continued to be held twice a year until the 1960s. In 1881, the Grand Rapids Furniture Manufacturers Association was also formed, the first of a number of trade associations that were formed to represent and promote the city's furniture interests. By the end of the nineteenth century, the Grand Rapids Furniture Manufacturers Association could boast, with complete accuracy, that furniture had made Grand Rapids famous, so much so that manufacturers elsewhere sought to capitalize on the name by applying it to their products. In 1942, however, a federal court ruled in favor of several Grand Rapids manufacturers who charged a Chicago company with false and misleading advertising because it was called the Grand Rapids Furniture Company. The court declared: "The city of Grand Rapids is a large and important center of the furniture industry in the United States, which fact is generally known to the public, . . . and the words 'Grand Rapids furniture' have acquired in the trade a special significance, and furniture made in that city is held by a large part of the purchasing public to be superior in design, workmanship and value to furniture usually purchased elsewhere."[5]

Encouraged by the success of the Grand Rapids manufacturers, capital in other cities in Michigan found its way into the establishment of furniture plants. Detroit had twenty such companies by 1890, nearly half as many as were operating in Grand Rapids at that date. All told, there were 178 furniture factories in the state in 1890 which employed nearly seven thousand workers. Grand Ledge, Muskegon—where the Shaw-Walker Company, incorporated in 1899, became a leader in the office furniture and equipment field—Sturgis, Holland, and Monroe were other Michigan communities where significant furniture firms had or would develop.

In addition to the furniture industry, numerous other wood-related manufacturers developed in Michigan, obviously because wood was so abundantly available. Sashes, doors, window blinds, handles, even toothpicks and matches were among the products of these companies. At the end of the century several firms in Bay City, Saginaw, and St. Johns pioneered in the development of the precut, portable house idea which would achieve such popularity much later in the twentieth century. All the wood for a building would be cut to the exact dimensions needed, enabling the entire package to be shipped anywhere and erected in a very brief period. The Michigan companies promoted their idea particularly in times of distress, such as during World War I, when military or refugee needs required the rapid construction of many buildings.

Another industry which required large amounts of wood in its product and whose location in Michigan was certainly influenced by the abundance of this resource was the wagon and carriage industry. By the 1890s, Michigan ranked near or at the forefront in this manufacturing activity with approximately 125 companies. The bulk of these were small firms, employing only a few workers, and producing a small number of wagons and carriages for the local market. But in 1898, the forty-nine largest of the state's companies produced 371,769 horse-drawn vehicles and had long since built up a regional or national market.[6] Approximately seven thousand workers were employed in the industry, with companies located in forty or more communities. About seventy-five percent of these workers were concentrated in seven cities: Kalamazoo, Jackson, Grand Rapids, Detroit, Pontiac, Lansing, and Flint. There was considerable debate between Jackson and Pontiac as to which was more important in this manufacturing area, but by the nineties few in the state would argue with Flint's claim to being the most important center of the industry in Michigan—a claim which had led that city to call itself the "Vehicle City" long before Buick and Chevrolet production would make Flint famous for another kind of vehicle.

Flint had been a leading center of the lumber industry in the early days of the lumber boom, and a number of small manufacturers that used wood had begun to develop there at that time, including a vehicle manufacturer as early as the 1850s. With the decline in the area's timber resources by the seventies a new emphasis was placed on the development of activities that could make up for the loss of revenues from lumber production. The growth in farming in the area helped to promote the rise of agriculturally related businesses, including the wagon and carriage industry, for whose products farmers were among the biggest customers, and whose supply of lumber, although no longer so immediately available in the Flint area, could readily be brought in by rail from the booming Saginaw valley mills. Although others had preceded them into Flint, two Canadians were instrumental in pushing the industry to a leading status in the city by the seventies. In 1868, W. F. Stewart of London, Ontario, established a shop which came to specialize in making the bodies for carriages. Subsequently, during the company's sixty-seven-year existence, it made bodies for automobiles. In 1869, another Canadian, William A. Paterson, who had learned the carriage-making trade from R. D. Scott of Guelph, Ontario, established a company in Flint at the suggestion of Scott, who had meanwhile opened the first carriage factory in Pontiac. By the early 1880s, Paterson was established as the leading figure in the industry in the city.

In the 1880s two new companies emerged which soon surpassed all the other Flint carriage companies. In 1882, James H. Whiting, a forty-year-old native of Connecticut who had been in the hardware business in Flint for some years, persuaded Josiah W. Begole and Begole's associates in the Begole, Fox and Company lumber company, to organize the Flint Wagon Works. Under Whiting's able leadership, the company was soon producing wagons and other vehicles at a rate of nearly fifty thousand a year during the firm's heyday.

Before long, however, all Flint companies were cast into a secondary position with the rise of the giant Durant-Dort Carriage Company. It was the creation of William C. Durant, a grandson of Henry Crapo, the leading figure in Flint's earlier lumber era. Durant, as a young man in his twenties, demonstrated great talents as a promoter and salesman in a variety of ventures in the early eighties. Early in September, 1886, Durant happened to see a two-wheeled cart in operation on the streets of Flint, and when he was given a ride in the vehicle he recognized that the riding qualities of this cart were superior to those of other vehicles of this type. Learning that the cart was produced by a company in Coldwater, Durant proceeded to that city the following day. The proprietors of the Coldwater company had patented the design of their cart, but it was a small outfit, and they were perfectly willing to sell Durant the rights to manufacture the cart for a mere $1500.

Although he had had no experience with manufacturing or selling vehicles, Durant borrowed the money he needed to take the Coldwater carriage-makers up on their offer, took in a partner, J. Dallas Dort, and launched the Flint Road Cart Company. While Dort overlooked the company's production, Durant took on the task of selling the carts. On a swing through the Middle West he was so successful in obtaining orders that he and Dort, still novices at manufacturing vehicles, contracted W. A. Paterson to make the carts for them. Paterson soon decided to make his own cart, in competition with Durant and Dort, but he produced enough Flint Road Carts so that Durant and Dort were able to use the money from the sale of these carts to develop their own production facilities. By the time they incorporated their business in 1895 as the Durant-Dort Carriage Company, the two men had built the business into one of the giants of the carriage industry, with their production in the early years of the twentieth century probably exceeding a hundred thousand vehicles a year. (Completely accurate production figures for the industry are not available.) From the road cart, which started them on the road to success, Durant, Dort, and their able team of associates branched out to include other types of horse-drawn vehicles in their lineup of products, and also acquired control of firms making wheels, axles, harnesses, varnish, and other items essential to their business. This included several thousand acres of timber lands in the South, where they and other carriage manufacturers were now having to turn for some of their wood as Michigan's timber resources became scarce. In the process of creating this industrial empire, Durant in particular was learning skills that he would employ later in an even more spectacular way in the automobile industry.[7]

Another industry that grew rapidly in the last half of the nineteenth century which, at first glance, might also have been thought to be related to Michigan's abundant timber resources, was the paper industry. In reality, the paper mills that used large amounts of wood pulp in their product appeared long after other mills, using rags and other materials in their paper, had been well established. As early as 1834, a small amount of paper was produced near Monroe, on the River Raisin, and in later years Monroe would remain one of the leading centers of the paper industry in the state. Later, in the 1840s, a paper mill would develop along the Huron River, where, in 1867, the Peninsular Paper Company would be established in Ypsilanti. In this same period, several mills would be established along the St. Joseph River at Three Rivers and Niles. By 1850, there were ten paper makers operating in the state. By 1870, Michigan ranked twelfth in the country in number of paper mills and fifteenth among the states in tonnage of paper produced. By 1905, it had advanced to seventh and fifth respectively in these two categories.

In this period, Kalamazoo and the Kalamazoo area became the most important center of the industry in Michigan. As early as 1847, a local editor had suggested that Kalamazoo was an ideal site for a paper mill, but it was not until 1866 that the necessary local support developed, and the Kalamazoo Paper Company was organized. The company, although financed by local capital, was largely the result of the promotional efforts of an experienced paper manufacturer from Massachusetts, Benjamin F. Lyon. A mill was built and paper made from rags combined with straw from the wheat and rye fields in the area, began to be produced. After several years, Lyon left the Kalamazoo company in 1872 and started another paper mill in the nearby town of Plainwell, the first of many such companies that would expand the area of paper manufacturing from Kalamazoo out to its immediate environs.

After a shaky start that climaxed in an 1872 fire that destroyed its original mill, the Kalamazoo Paper Company prospered under the able direction of Samuel Gibson, whom Lyon had brought in from Massachusetts shortly after the company was founded. By 1879, Gibson doubled the company's output, and doubled it again by 1885. In addition, during the years that he ran the company until his death in 1899, Gibson trained many of the men who would later go on to establish paper companies in Plainwell, Otsego, and other localities in western Michigan. It was not until 1895 that two of Gibson's proteges established Kalamazoo's second paper company. In the early years of the twentieth century the paper industry in Kalamazoo enjoyed its greatest boom with the establishment of a number of new and successful paper companies as well as companies that produced materials, such as brushes and chemicals needed in paper manufacturing, and other companies that used paper, such as stationery companies, label makers, and printers of office forms.[8]

Although wood pulp was a minor factor in the early development of the paper industry in southern Michigan, around the turn of the century mills at Port Huron and Munising began drawing upon Michigan's timber resources for the kinds of paper they produced. In the same general period, several other industries that were new to the state, specifically developed because of the availability of certain resources. One of these was the chemical industry, which never would have achieved its importance had it not been for Michigan's salt deposits. Sodium carbonates, such as soda ash, which are used in the manufacture of glass, soap, paints, and in many other industrial processes, are obtained from salt. In 1890, Captain John B. Ford, the founder of the Pittsburgh Plate Glass Company, sank an experimental well at Wyandotte, seeking to tap the known vein of rock salt in that area as a source of soda ash which he required in his glassmaking operations, and which he and most other American glass producers at that time had to import from foreign sources. The experiment proved successful, and in 1894 Ford's company was incorporated as the Michigan Alkali Company under the leadership of Ford's grandsons and his son Edward. The firm prospered, and in 1943 became the Wyandotte Chemicals Corporation. This created a wealthy Ford family in Detroit that came to be referred to by society editors as the "Salt Fords" or the "Chemical Fords" to distinguish them from that other Ford family, whose wealth came from another product that began to be manufactured a decade or so after Captain Ford launched his venture.[9]

A second Detroit-area chemical company developed in 1895 when the Solvay Process Company, a New York firm that used a method developed some years before in Belgium for treating salt to produce soda ash, bicarbonate of soda, caustic soda, and other products, established a plant along the Detroit River just below Fort Wayne in Delray, a suburb annexed to Detroit in 1906. Prior to this time, Detroit had imported some 40,000,000 pounds of soda ash a year. By 1918, the Detroit area's chemical industry was shipping out 238,000,000 pounds of soda ash a year, plus large amounts of other by-products of salt.

Michigan's salt deposits are also the source of other by-products. The brines in the Midland area contain, among other things, bromine, and by 1888 Midland had become the largest producer of bromine in the world. In 1890, Herbert H. Dow, a native of Ohio and a chemist with a degree from the Case School of Applied Science in Cleveland, came to Midland and rented a well to test out a new process he had developed for extracting bromine from the Midland brines. Out of this modest beginning grew the giant Dow Chemical Company, incorporated in 1897. In addition to bromine, Dow came to be the source of over four hundred other products that it extracted from these same brines, including calcium chloride, which the company successfully promoted as an effective agent in reducing the dust that twentieth-century motor traffic created on gravel roads. In 1927, magnesium, a light metal obtained from the magnesium chloride found in these brines, began to be produced. The Dow company expanded to other Michigan communities, including Ludington, Mount Pleasant, and Marquette, where it obtained a majority interest in a chemical company established earlier by the Cleveland-Cliffs Iron Company.[10]

The "Salt" Fords' Michigan Alkali Company was also involved with the sudden emergence around the turn of the century of the cement industry, which came to be one of the largest users of Michigan's limestone—a material that the Michigan Alkali Company used in producing its chemicals. Initially, marl, which is found in over a hundred different locations in the lower peninsula, was used in the manufacturing of portland cement that began in Michigan in the 1890s, two decades after the first production of portland cement in the United States had occurred in Pennsylvania and Indiana. In 1896, one cement plant in Michigan produced 4,000 barrels of cement. By 1900, however, the number of plants had increased to six, with annual production totalling more than 60,000 barrels, a record that was quickly erased by the million-barrel production of ten plants in 1901. Production continued to rise in the years that followed, reaching nearly 14,000,000 barrels by 1927. Gradually, limestone began to replace marl in the manufacturing of cement. The impressive ruins of the Great Northern Portland Cement Company's plant at Marlborough in southern Lake County, which ceased production in 1908, testify to the decline in cement production that used marl in the face of the less costly limestone process. It was not until 1952, however, that the Consolidated Cement Corporation at Cement City in Hillsdale County abandoned the use of marl.

In 1903, Harry J. Paxton, who had been managing a small cement mill at Fenton, persuaded several Detroit-area businessmen, including Stanford T. Crapo, grandson of Governor Henry Crapo and a cousin of Flint's W. C. Durant, and John B. Ford, vice-president of the Michigan Alkali Company and grandson of the company's founder, Captain Ford, to form the Wyandotte Portland Cement Company. It took over a cement plant that the Michigan Alkali Company had operated earlier in an effort to use the leftover limestone from its chemical operations. By 1906, the Wyandotte Portland Cement Company was doing well, but in the meantime, the alkali firm had had to go outside that area to search for the large amounts of limestone that it required. It had found vast deposits on Thunder Bay, near Alpena. The first shipments from this quarry were made in 1903. By 1906, the enormous extent of its Alpena limestone holdings led officers of the Michigan Alkali Company to consider using some of this resource for cement production. Harry Paxton and Stanford Crapo of the Wyandotte Portland Cement Company did most of the work in setting up this new operation, which it was decided would be handled by a new company rather than being made part of the Wyandotte cement company's operations. In 1907, therefore, the Huron Portland Cement Company was established, and by the end of the year the first kilns had been built at the new plant in Alpena. By 1910, six kilns were in operation and 900,000 barrels of cement had been produced. In the years that followed, the Huron Portland Cement Company plant at Alpena became the world's largest cement-producing facility. There was a close link between the company and the Michigan Alkali Company, with John B. Ford, the active executive head of the alkali company, serving as president of the Huron company from its founding in 1907 to 1939, while other members of his family were also active in both firms. The same individuals were also involved with the Wyandotte Portland Cement Company, which in 1914 came under the ownership of the Huron

Portland Cement Company and which continued to operate the cement mill at Wyandotte in addition to the plant at Alpena.[11]

Besides the giant Alpena cement works, there are other major cement producers in the state. The Dundee Cement Company uses the limestone found in southeastern Michigan, and in the north, across the peninsula from Alpena, there is the Penn-Dixie Cement Company at the limestone deposits just outside of Petoskey. A short distance down the Lake Michigan shore is the Medusa Cement Company at Charlevoix. By the 1960s, Michigan's cement industry, the fourth largest in the country, had an annual production valued at close to $100,000,000. By the seventies, with production nearing the six-million-ton figure, the value of the state's portland cement in 1974 topped $140,000,000.[12]

Just as the Michigan Alkali Company was connected with both the chemical and cement industries, the Dow Chemical Company was also connected with the chemical industry and the pharmaceutical industry—an industry that rose to the forefront in Michigan in the last half of the nineteenth century, because the Dow company became one of the principal United States manufacturers of aspirin. The pioneer in establishing the pharmaceutical industry in Michigan, particularly in Detroit, was Frederick Stearns, who had studied pharmacy at the University of Buffalo and had come to Detroit in 1855 to open a retail drug store. He soon began manufacturing some of the drugs that he sold, and in the years that followed he built the business into one of the larger drug companies in the country. Stearns, who rose to be president of the American Pharmaceutical Association, enjoyed the wealth he gained by travelling extensively and acquiring a vast collection of oriental art, which he ultimately gave to the present Detroit Institute of Arts. He also donated an even more unusual collection of antique musical instruments to the University of Michigan. In a different vein, Stearns bought control of Detroit's baseball team in 1885, and in an early demonstration of buying a championship team, he bought the contracts of some of baseball's best hitters, who powered the team to the championship of the National League in 1887 and victory over St. Louis in the equivalent of the World Series later that fall.[13]

An even bigger and more long-lasting influence in the pharmaceutical industry was that of Parke, Davis, which grew out of a drug store opened in Detroit in 1862 by Dr. Samuel Duffield, who was both a physician and a pharmacist. In 1866, Duffield teamed with a businessman, Hervey C. Parke, and George Davis joined the firm the following year. Duffield retired in 1869, and two years later the firm was reorganized as Parke, Davis. With astute management, the company grew rapidly and by the 1890s was commonly referred to as the largest pharmaceutical house in the world.

Stearns and Parke, Davis both sought to distinguish their operations and their products from those of the dispensers of patent medicines. The two Detroit companies emphasized the non-secret character of their drugs, which were, for the most part, available only with a doctor's prescription, or, if sold over the counter, were simple, well-known remedies for minor ailments. On the other hand, the patent medicine industry which flourished in Michigan as elsewhere in the country in these years, made its magical cure-alls available to anyone gullible enough to pay for them. The city of Marshall, in the latter part of the century, was especially noted as a center of these fly-by-night operators.[14]

One outstanding and eminently respectable drug firm that did arise in the outstate area was the Upjohn Company of Kalamazoo. It originated in 1885, when Dr. William E. Upjohn, a physician in nearby Hastings, moved to Kalamazoo and joined with three of his brothers to begin manufacturing pills using a new process that he had developed which coated the pill in such a way that the pill could be dissolved in the human system. Many earlier pills had had an outer coating that was insoluble, causing the drug in the pill to pass through the person's system without ever taking effect. The company enjoyed a modest growth for many years before its expansion later in the twentieth century into one of the major drug firms in the nation. Another outstate drug company, L. Perrigo Company in Allegan, was established in 1887, two years after Upjohn had been started. Perrigo was for many years a relatively small packager and distributor of various patent medicines, selling the products to rural stores around the Midwest. In the 1920s, however, the management got the idea of increasing sales by imprinting the individual store's name on the product. This so-called "private label" concept caught on and led to the Perrigo company becoming the world's largest producer of health and beauty products for private-label retailing. By the 1970s, Perrigo's aspirin, mouthwash, epsom salts, toothpaste, and over three hundred other products were packaged under 125 different labels, including A & P, Cunningham, and Revco.[15]

The center of manufacturing activity in Michigan naturally developed in Detroit, if for no other reason than that it was by far the largest city in Michigan, possessing the largest pool of labor and investment capital. The chemical and pharmaceutical industries were but two areas of manufacturing that had grown to importance in Detroit by the end of the century. Diversity and variety, in fact, characterized Detroit's industry in the nineteenth century, where, in contrast, one industry would assume overriding dominance in the city's economy in the century that followed. Early in the 1800s, hides, liquor, soap, and hats had led the list of Detroit's small-scale manufactures. Later, in the thirties and forties, flour-milling and sawmills were important before these activities moved elsewhere in the state where the needed resources and swift-moving waters to power the mills were more readily available, although Detroiters continued to provide much of the capital, particularly for lumber operations to the north, and to arrange for the sale of the lumber in the East. Later, in the 1860s, the smelting of copper from the north was the leading activity, before smelters were developed at the mines in the Copper Country, reducing copper smelting in Detroit to relative insignificance by 1880.[16]

In the eighties, Detroit's manufacturing economy began to achieve more stability as a number of products boosted the city's economy. In 1880, the single most valuable group of products of Detroit's factories were, surprisingly, tobacco products. Tobacco has never been an important crop in Michigan, although it has been grown in significant amounts since prehistoric times in Ontario, some hundred miles to the east. Nevertheless, the production of chewing tobacco began in Detroit in the 1840s in the cellar of a small shop operated by Isaac S. Miller and his sons. By the 1880s, more chewing tobacco was produced in Detroit than in nearly any other location in the country. Reportedly, either Detroit's climate or the methods used by its manufacturers gave Detroit-made chewing tobacco a special flavor unmatched by that of any other area. This may account for some of the success of the industry, but another reason for the concentration of tobacco companies in Detroit at this time can probably be laid to the city's reputation as an "open shop" labor town, which enabled employers to pay a lower wage than in other areas where tobacco workers had become unionized.

Daniel Scotten and John J. Bagley, the future governor, were among those who worked for the Millers in the forties and who went on to become millionaires with their own companies. Bagley marketed his Mayflower brand chewing tobacco, and Scotten his Hiawatha brand. American Eagle, Bijah's Joy, Prairie Rose, Silk Plush, Fearless, and Honey Dew were some of the colorful names of other Detroit-made chewing and smoking tobacco. In addition, close to 40,000,000 cigars were produced annually in the city by the eighties, causing Detroit to be dubbed the "Tampa of the North." In later years, the industry would decline in importance, but in 1909 tobacco products still ranked fourth in value among Detroit's manufactures.

By the eighties, despite the fame and the value of its tobacco products, Detroit was also the site of other industries that were more in keeping with the kind of manufacturing for which the city would become world-renowned. The first of these to develop had been the shipbuilding industry, which had started as early as 1769 when the British built a merchant sailing vessel at Detroit. The British also built a number of naval vessels at Detroit. In 1827, the *Argo*, Detroit's first steamship, was built on the river near Wayne Street. In 1833, Oliver Newberry had built the *Michigan* and had gone on to be a major figure in the Great Lakes' shipping industry. In the middle of the century, shipbuilding developed in a more organized fashion. The Detroit Dry Dock Company built the first drydock at the foot of Orleans Street in 1852. A company was formed in 1863 to produce marine engines. Other companies sprang up to meet other needs of the shipbuilders, with the Berry Brothers varnish works, established in 1858, developing into one of the largest paint and varnish companies in the country.

Between 1827 and 1887, more than 175 steamboats were built at Detroit. In the early 1890s, Detroit and the neighboring Wayne County shipyards launched the largest number of ships of any shipbuilding center in the country.[17] The passing of the wooden-hulled vessel and the increasing use on the lakes of steel hulls caused problems of adjustment for the Detroit companies, but the area's shipyards continued to be busy well into the twentieth century before more and more of this business went to shipyards elsewhere in the Great Lakes area.

Detroit was not the only center of shipbuilding in Michigan. Bay City was of equal importance, with the tonnage of the ships built there exceeding that of Detroit's in the nineties, although Detroit led in total number of ships built. Another area of some importance was Marine City. There the start of the industry early in the century introduced Michigan to the state's first industrial giant. Sam Ward came to the St. Clair River in 1819 and bought land at the mouth of the Belle River. He began a brick manufacturing yard, and built a handsome brick house which still survives in Marine City. Ward started building sailing vessels early in the 1820s, later turning to steamboats and becoming part owner of Newberry's *Michigan*. In 1822, Ward's young nephew, Eber Brock Ward, began working for his uncle. In later years, the Wards moved from building ships to operating them. When the Michigan Central was built, the Wards built two steamboats to carry passengers from the Michigan Central terminal in Detroit across Lake Erie to Buffalo. Eber Brock Ward also operated two steamers in Lake Michigan, carrying rail passengers from St. Joseph to Chicago.

In 1848, the Michigan Central began operating its own steamship between Detroit and Buffalo, and in a few years through rail connections were opened to New York in the East and Chicago in the west, ending the Wards' transfer business. But Eber Ward had already turned to other interests. In 1853, he and several associates organized the Eureka Iron and Steel Company. Land was purchased downriver from Detroit and a blast furnace and rolling mill were constructed, around which the city of Wyandotte developed. The company nicely combined several of Ward's business interests. Previously, he had acquired some Upper Peninsula iron ore holdings and, to develop them, he had been one of the major promoters of the Soo Canal in the fifties. One of Ward's vessels brought the first cargo of iron ore through the newly opened locks in the summer of 1855. The ore then was unloaded at the mill in Wyandotte, where charcoal, made from timber holdings obtained by Ward, provided the fuel to convert the ore into iron.

The Eureka operation seemed to presage the rise of the Detroit area as a major iron-producing center. In addition to conventional methods of treating the ores, the Eureka works in 1864 had the distinction of being the first American firm to produce steel through what became known as the Bessemer process. Ward's staff, however, used the process as it had been developed by the American, William Kelly, whose work preceded that of the Englishman, Henry Bessemer, by several years. In the spring of 1865, the Wyandotte plant produced the nation's first Bessemer steel rails. It soon became evident, however, that the plant would have to be expanded in order to produce steel rails economically. Some of Ward's associates objected to spending money on such an expansion. Ward then turned to the Chicago area where he built the South Chicago Rolling Mills which grew into the world's largest producer of steel rails thanks to the enormous boom in railroad construction that occurred throughout the country in the last decades of the century. The Wyandotte company languished and eventually in the early 1890s shut down entirely.

Meanwhile, E. B. Ward dropped dead on a downtown Detroit street early in 1875. At the time of his death, he was worth, according to various estimates, from ten to thirty million dollars, and he was probably Michigan's richest man and certainly the first to become a millionaire through manufacturing activities.[18]

For several years, the biggest users of iron in Detroit were the stove manufacturers. Stoves had begun to be shipped into Michigan in the 1820s with the opening of the Erie Canal, and they gradually began to take the place of fireplaces in more and more homes and businesses. Troy and Albany, New York, were the centers of the industry, which meant a long wait for a Michigan stove owner who needed a new part. In the 1830s, an iron works in Detroit began to repair stoves, and an employee of the firm, Jeremiah Dwyer, became the father of Detroit's stove industry. He went to New York to learn the business, and in 1861 he and his brother James and another partner formed J. Dwyer and Company, and began to manufacture stoves in Detroit. New partners were added in 1864, and the company was renamed the Detroit Stove Works. Seven years later, Jeremiah Dwyer broke away and formed the Michigan Stove Company. Ten years later, James Dwyer formed the Peninsular Stove Company, thus completing the lineup of Detroit's big three stove manufacturers which, together with several smaller firms, made the city the largest center of this particular industrial activity in the entire world. By the early nineties, the Michigan Stove Company, which claimed to be the biggest firm of this type in the world, employed twelve hundred workers and turned out 76,000 stoves a year under the familiar "Garland" trade name. The Detroit Stove Works, which frequently contested the Michigan firm's claim to primacy, produced the equally famous "Jewel" stoves. In later years, the two companies merged and continued in business until 1957. The "Big Stove," a huge wooden replica of the Garland stove that the Michigan Stove Company built as part of its exhibit at the World's Columbian Exposition in Chicago in 1893 and then later displayed on its grounds in Detroit, was preserved by sentimentalists in Detroit after the closing of the Detroit-Michigan Stove Company as a symbol of another of the city's past industrial glories.

The stove industry was not confined to Detroit, although in 1900 eight of Michigan's twenty-one stove factories were in that city. E. Bement and Sons, a Lansing company, in the latter part of the nineteenth century made and marketed stoves, along with other products, over a wide area in the Middle West. Then in 1900, some Kalamazoo businessmen and others who had been connected with the stove industry in Detroit and Chicago, organized the Kalamazoo Stove Company, and sold directly to the customer through mail orders, using the immortal slogan "A Kalamazoo Direct to You." The company prospered and was for years one of that city's major employers with a labor force of nearly 1,100 as late as 1948. Outsiders purchased the company in the fifties, however, and further operations in the city ceased. Around the same time, a Dowagiac manufacturer who produced what some would regard as the most famous of all Michigan stoves, the Round Oak Stove, also went out of business. The Round Oak stove was the creation of Philo D. Beckwith, who established the Dowagiac stove works in 1871. The stove—a heating, not a cook stove—shortly became the most popular stove of its type. In the nineties, the company occupied fifteen acres, employed 350 men, and used forty tons of pig iron a day.[19]

By the nineties, the largest industrial employer in Detroit was not the tobacco or the stove or the pharmaceutical or the chemical industries but the "car industry," as it was familiarly called. The cars, however, were not motor cars but railroad cars. As early as the 1830s, John E. Hays had pioneered in the building of passenger coaches at Detroit for the railroads that were being opened in the state. In 1853, Dr. George B. Russel organized a company which received a contract to build twenty-five cars for the Detroit and Pontiac Railroad. Russel's company was later incorporated as the Detroit Car and Manufacturing Company, and its factory was acquired in 1871 by George M. Pullman, who began producing his new Pullman cars. Some years later his request to the Detroit city council for permission to expand his operations was denied. This decision helped to persuade Pullman to concentrate his main manufacturing activities at the new plant he built near Chicago, around which he built the model town of Pullman. He did, however, continue to use the Detroit plant as a branch operation until 1893.

Dr. Russel's three sons, Walter, George, and Henry, went on to form the Russel Wheel and Foundry Company, which specialized in railroad equipment for logging operations. Although they were the pioneers, the Russels were not to be the most important figures in this industry. In the early sixties, Edward C. Dean and George Eaton began building freight cars in Detroit. They were soon joined by John S. Newberry and the business was called Newberry, Dean and Eaton. In 1864, the firm was reorganized again as the Michigan Car Company when James McMillan, a Canadian by birth who had come to Detroit in the 1850s, invested in the organization. McMillan quickly became the dominant figure in the company, and used the influence he gained to become the most powerful force in the Detroit business world. He held this position until the time of his death in 1902, even though he spent nearly all of his time in the East after his election to the United States Senate in 1889. In 1885, the leadership of the Michigan Car Company was challenged with the organization of the Peninsular Car Company by Charles L. Freer and Frank J. Hecker. Seven years later, however, the two companies were merged with the Russel Wheel and Foundry Company, the Detroit

Car Wheel Company (another of McMillan's interests), and several other companies to become the Michigan-Peninsular Car Company. The resulting giant made Detroit the leader in railroad car production, with over nine thousand men employed in manufacturing products with an annual value in 1898 of $28,000,000 in plants that had a capacity of a hundred freight cars a day. In 1899, the combined McMillan-Hecker-Freer-Russel interests became part of an even larger merger move that created the American Car and Foundry Company, with some forty plants throughout the country. The Detroit division came to specialize in the construction of steel freight cars.

Thus, by the end of the nineteenth century a highly diversified manufacturing economy, centered in the southern part of the lower peninsula, had become well established in Michigan. As yet, however, manufacturing had not replaced in the public's mind the image that the earlier agricultural, lumbering, and mining operations had created. The 1890s witnessed an enormous increase in product advertising as publishers of mass-circulation magazines, caught up in price wars, discovered that advertising revenues enabled them to sell magazines at a price less than their cost. But on the whole, Michigan manufacturers contributed only in a small way to this advertising boom. Institutional advertising was an approach that was still in the future, and thus many of the most important industries in the Michigan economy, such as the railroad car industry and the chemical industry, as well as the lumber and mining companies, saw no point in engaging in advertising campaigns that were aimed at increasing customer sales. Few sales for the Michigan Car Company's railroad equipment or the Solvay Process Company's soda ash were likely to be generated by advertisements in the *Saturday Evening Post.* It was a different story with the stove industry, however, and even before the Kalamazoo Stove Company began its large-scale advertising campaign in the early twentieth century, Detroit's Jewel and Garland stoves were being advertised nationally.[20] At the very end of the century, Charles W. Post was regularly placing advertisements for Postum and Grape-Nuts in *Scribner's* and other magazines, an early sign of the extent to which Battle Creek's cereal manufacturers would advertise their products in the future. Surprisingly, few ads appeared for Grand Rapids furniture. Most of that city's furniture manufacturers apparently still preferred older methods of promoting sales. Some Michigan advertisers did not represent a product that was widely manufactured in the state. Such was the case with Detroit's Pingree and Smith, a frequent advertiser, which was reportedly the largest shoe manufacturing company in the Middle West but which was also the state's only significant representative of this particular industry. On the other hand, the advertisements for Wright's Dentomyrh toothpaste, produced by a Detroit pharmaceutical company, scarcely gave an indication of the true importance of that city's pharmaceutical industry. Neither did the frequent advertisements in national magazines by the Truscott Boat Manufacturing Company of St. Joseph or the Michigan Yacht and Power Company of Detroit, manufacturers of pleasure crafts, provide readers with an accurate picture of Michigan's shipbuilding industry.

An offshoot of the shipbuilding activities was the marine engine industry, and in the nineties small advertisements for such firms as the Monitor Engine Company of Grand Rapids appeared. Early in the same decade, a Lansing company, P. F. Olds and Son, began advertising its steam engines in *Scientific American.* In 1896, this company turned to the production of gasoline engines, with advertisements frequently emphasizing their marine usage. In 1900, the Olds Gasoline Engine, manufactured by the company that was now called the Olds Motor Works and was headquartered in Detroit, was advertised in such publications as *Harper's Monthly.* Early in the following year, however, these same publications began to carry advertisements for one of the company's newer products—the Oldsmobile. A new century had dawned and with it a product that would completely transform Detroit and the state of Michigan.

Ford Quadricycle, 1896

22

MICHIGAN AND THE AUTOMOBILE

The coming of the automobile affected the daily life of twentieth-century Americans to a greater degree than any of the other technological developments brought about by inventors and scientists. It was not so much the speed of the automobile as its flexibility that marks its chief significance in the history of transportation. Its impact on the nation's economy was due not only to the amount of capital and the number of workers involved in its manufacture, but also to the many service occupations it spawned: filling stations, repair garages, motels, and wayside inns, to mention a few. The success of passenger cars powered with gasoline motors prepared the way for trucks, buses, and tractors. The customs and mores of the American people were changed almost as much as their economy by the coming of the automobile. The growth of cities and suburban developments around cities was heavily influenced by the automobile. And the life of the farmer was revolutionized by motor vehicles as much as that of the city dweller or suburbanite.

All this is particularly pertinent to Michigan history, since it was Michigan that became the center of automotive manufacturing in the world. While cities like Flint, Lansing, and Pontiac grew lustily as automobile towns, it was Detroit that became the focus of the industry. Just why it happened that way is not altogether clear. No doubt Detroit's location near the source of raw materials and major markets was essential to its becoming the center of automotive manufacturing, but other cities such as Toledo, Cleveland, Chicago, or Indianapolis, where automobile manufacturing took root before it did in Detroit, were equally if not more advantageously situated. The fact that Flint, Pontiac, and to a lesser extent Detroit, had been important centers of the carriage and wagon industry might seem to have had an influence on the development in these cities of the horseless-carriage industry—until one notes that such carriage and wagon centers as Jackson, Kalamazoo, and Cincinnati did not have a similarly successful evolution into automobile production. A more important factor was the growth in the nineties of a number of firms manufacturing gasoline engines. Some of these firms helped the Michigan automotive pioneers in deciding on the source of power for their vehicles. Finally, and most important, there was a great deal of investment capital available in Detroit and several other southern Michigan cities, gained largely from lumbering and mining and some of the earlier manufacturing activities. The possessors of this wealth were willing to invest it in automobile-manufacturing facilities at a time when Michigan's older ways were no longer offering the same opportunities for economic growth as they had in the recent past.[1]

The origins of the automobile and the auto industry are not to be found in Michigan. The automobile, like the steam engine and other great discoveries, cannot be said to have been invented by any one individual. The development of the steam engine in the eighteenth century led a French engineer, Nicholas Cugnot, to the construction of a steam-carriage in 1769 that is usually credited with having been the first successful self-propelled road vehicle. Later experimenters in England, France, and the United States developed far more sophisticated steam vehicles, and by the late 1890s the manufacturing of steamers in the United States had been begun by the Stanley brothers in Massachusetts, the White brothers in Cleveland, and others. Late in the nineteenth century the electric car had also been developed, following in the footsteps of such men as Thomas A. Edison and their development of storage batteries. In the United States, William Morrison had successfully tested an electric in Des Moines in 1891, and by the end of the decade more electrics were being manufactured by the infant American auto industry than any other type of car.

Meanwhile, a third source of power had emerged with the development of the gasoline, internal combustion engine. Jean Joseph Lenoir, a Belgian, is credited with the development of the first successful engine of this type and its rather unsuccessful application to a road vehicle in the 1860s. In the seventies and eighties, three Germans—Nicholas August Otto, Gottlieb Daimler, and Karl Benz—developed more advanced gasoline engines which they applied to vehicular use in the mid-eighties. It was the French, however, who first fully capitalized on the work of these Germans, and by the early nineties France was the site of the first significant commercial production of gasoline vehicles in the world, and would lead in this product until its output was surpassed by the United States in 1904.

In the United States an Englishman living in Boston—George B. Brayton—patented a two-cycle gasoline engine in 1872. Four years later, an inventor and patent attorney from Rochester, New York—George B. Selden—saw one of Brayton's engines on display at the Philadelphia Centennial Exposition. Selden designed a smaller, lighter version of the Brayton engine which could be used in powering a vehicle, and then, although he had not built such a vehicle, Selden applied for a patent on his idea in 1879. He made frequent amendments to his application in the years that followed, and it was not until 1895 that the patent was finally granted to him. Under American law it had seventeen years to run, and before that time had elapsed, the Selden patent was the cause of the most celebrated patent infringement court case in American history, one that would have important consequences for the emerging Michigan auto industry, particularly the Ford Motor Company.

The man after whom that company was named, Henry Ford, was not, as many Michiganians assume, the first American to achieve success in the development of a gasoline car. This distinction is usually given to Charles E. Duryea and his younger brother Frank, natives of Illinois. The date was 1893, and the place where they successfully tested their vehicle was Springfield, Massachusetts. Complete success here is gauged by the ability of the developer of the machine to make the transition from the building of an experimental vehicle to the manufacturing and sale of the vehicle. Although evidence indicates that other Americans—none of them, apparently, residents of Michigan—had built gasoline-powered horseless carriages before the Duryeas, it was the Duryeas who were the first to go beyond the testing stage to organize a company, the Duryea Motor Wagon Company, and to launch the American auto industry in 1896 with the production and sale of thirteen of their motor wagons at their plant in Massachusetts.

On July 4, 1894, in Kokomo, Indiana, a gasoline-powered car designed by Elwood Haynes of that city and built in the local machine shop of Edgar and Elmer Apperson was successfully tested. After several years, Haynes and the Appersons began manufacturing a car, before splitting up and continuing on as separate auto manufacturers until the 1920s. Although they introduced the auto industry to Indiana, where the manufacturing of cars would for a time thrive to an extent greater than in any other state except Michigan, the first Haynes-Apperson carriage also represented one of the first indi-

Duryea "Gas Buggy," 1893

cations of the varied impact that Michigan would have on this emerging industry since the Kokomo vehicle was powered by an engine manufactured in Grand Rapids, Michigan. There the Sintz Company, one of several that were springing up in Michigan to capitalize on the growing market for gasoline engines, had displayed its engines at Chicago's World's Columbian Exposition in 1893. Viewing the exhibit, Elwood Haynes saw the possibility that a one-cylinder Sintz engine, designed for marine uses, could also be used to power a land vehicle.

By the mid-1890s, the number of Americans experimenting with horseless carriages (as they continued to be called until the late nineties) multiplied rapidly. Michigan had its share of these individuals, with most of them found in southern Michigan, where the existing manufacturing activities provided a ready source of many of the needed materials as well as the hoped-for facilities and financing for any manufacturing of vehicles that were successfully tested. Late in 1895, the operators of a small-carriage manufacturing company in Benton Harbor, the Baushke brothers, announced the formation of the Benton Harbor Motor Carriage Company which would manufacture the gasoline-powered vehicle that they had built in collaboration with the vehicle's designer, William Worth. It would have been Michigan's first entry into the still embryonic American auto industry, but unspecified problems with Worth's car led to the dissolution of the company in a few weeks. The Baushkes returned to building horse-drawn carriages, while Worth went to Chicago and other Mid-

west locations where he was involved in several other auto manufacturing ventures, none of which enjoyed any real success.[2] In the
same period, the experiments of others in such Michigan towns and
cities as Albion, Grand Rapids, and Charlevoix were no more successful than those at Benton Harbor in 1895-1896.

Later in 1896, however, gasoline-powered vehicles were suc-
cessfully tested by Charles B. King and Henry Ford in Detroit and by
Ransom E. Olds in Lansing. Late in the evening of March 6, 1896,
King probably became the first person to operate a gasoline car in
Michigan when he drove a wagon powered by a four-cylinder engine
along several blocks of Woodward Avenue in downtown Detroit.
King is one of the most interesting and likable of all automotive
pioneers. His mother was a Detroiter, her family having lived in
Detroit since frontier days, and the Kings settled there in the 1880s
when Charles's father retired from the army. Charles King was
briefly enrolled in an engineering program at Cornell University
before taking a job as a draftsman for the Michigan Car Company. In
1893, King served as the representative of Detroit's Russel Wheel
and Foundry Company at the Chicago World's Fair, where, in addition to winning a prize for a mechanical device he had invented, he
saw the Sintz engines on display and, like Elwood Haynes, was inspired by the sight to begin work on a gasoline-propelled horseless
carriage. Although King was eminently qualified for the task because
of his mechanical knowledge and abilities, financial problems delayed him until the successful run in 1896. After that time, financial
considerations continued to hamper King's stated desire to begin
manufacturing his vehicle. Temperamentally, however, King had so
many interests beyond the areas of engineering and mechanics that
he was not really cut out to be a manufacturer. Thus, although he
would be associated with such important names as the Duryeas,
Ford, and Olds, his role in the auto industry would be that of an
advisor or a subordinate who made significant technological contributions but who did not emerge as the head of his own auto
company.

Henry Ford's little "quadricycle," which he had built with advice and assistance from such acquaintances as Charles King in a shed
behind his home on Detroit's Bagley Avenue, passed its driving test
early in the morning of June 4, 1896, a date that the Ford Motor
Company ultimately accepted after many years of promoting Ford's
claim that he had built and driven his first car in 1893 or even
earlier—a claim that was designed to make him appear to have been
the pioneer American developer of the gasoline automobile. However, it was not until the summer of 1903 that Ford-built cars became

available to the public in any quantity. Before that happened, the importance of Detroit and Michigan in the new industry had already been firmly established by the work of the third of the gasoline automobile developers of 1896, Ransom E. Olds.

Olds had been born in Geneva, Ohio, in 1864, the decade in which most of the important pioneers of the auto industry in the United States were born. In 1880, Olds' father, Pliny F. Olds, a skilled mechanic, moved his family to Lansing, Michigan, where he started a business—P. F. Olds and Son—to repair and build engines and other metal work. In 1885, when Ransom Olds was twenty-one, he bought out the older brother who had been the son in P. F. Olds and Son. Young Olds quickly took command of the family business. He was responsible for developing a small steam engine which proved to be quite popular when the Olds company put it in production. After visiting the Chicago World's Fair in 1893 and seeing the large number of gasoline engines exhibited there, Olds turned to the development of a small, simple gasoline engine which, when it went into production early in 1896, proved even more popular than the Olds steam engine.

In 1887, Olds, who had earlier used the Olds steam engine to power boats on the Grand River in Lansing, built a three-wheeled steam carriage which he tested early one morning before anyone was likely to be out to witness its success or failure. Although this Olds steamer ran, as did a more advanced four-wheeled steamer that he built in the early 1890s and which he sold to a foreign buyer in 1893, Olds became convinced that the steam engine was not a satisfactory source of power for a horseless carriage, particularly as he became better acquainted with gasoline engines. In 1896, therefore, once he had completed the development of the Olds gasoline engine, he turned to the construction of a gasoline-powered carriage, drawing upon a Lansing carriage manufacturer to furnish the vehicle that the Olds engine would propel. On August 11, 1896, Olds successfully demonstrated the machine for the benefit of a Lansing newpaper reporter.

A few days later, Olds, who between 1891 and 1941 was granted thirty-four patents by the United States Patent Office, applied for a patent on certain features of this first Olds gasoline automobile. In his application for the patent, which was eventually granted to him in 1897, Olds declared that his objective was to build a lightweight, easily operated vehicle with just enough power to satisfy the average driver's needs. In essence, he was outlining the kind of car for the masses that would become the basis for the success of the Michigan auto industry. Companies elsewhere could concentrate on high-powered, elaborate, and expensive automobiles with a limited market, but the Michigan auto industry would control the high-volume, low-priced car market. It was not until 1901, however, that Olds succeeded in producing any significant number of cars.

Between 1896 and 1901, Olds had first to resolve the problem of where to establish these new manufacturing activities. His initial expectations of establishing them in the Olds engine plant were soon revealed to be unrealistic. The Olds engines were selling so well that no time or personnel could be diverted from the task of producing these engines to the assembling of an entire horseless carriage. By the summer of 1897, Olds realized that his new venture, which he already recognized would be the biggest opportunity of his life, required a separate factory. But that would require additional funds, which Olds did not feel that his family could handle, as they had the earlier expansions of the engine business. In August, 1897, a Lansing-based group of investors, headed by Edward W. Sparrow, who had made a fortune in real estate, including northern Michigan timber and mineral lands, joined with Olds to form the Olds Motor Vehicle Company. The investors' interest was no doubt stimulated by reports that Olds was hearing from investors in Detroit and Chicago, which might mean that Lansing would lose this promising business to one of these other cities. However, Sparrow's group provided only $10,000, too little to enable the Olds Motor Vehicle Company, Michigan's first operating auto company, to produce more than a half dozen vehicles, if that many. Thus by the fall of 1898, Olds was again looking for financial help. A promising offer from a group of New York speculators fell through, but investors in a number of other cities in the Midwest were reportedly also interested. The speculation ended in the spring of 1899 when a Detroit-based group provided the funds that were needed. This group was headed by Samuel L. Smith, whose wealth came primarily from Michigan copper, and also included Henry and George Russel of the pioneering Detroit railroad-car-manufacturing family, and Henry Ledyard, Lewis Cass's grandson and president of the Michigan Central. The Olds engine business and the anemic Olds Motor Vehicle Company were merged to form the Olds Motor Works. Engines continued to be produced in the Lansing factory, but the main emphasis of the new firm shifted to Detroit where a new factory was built on Jefferson Avenue, next to the Detroit Stove Works. Here the main product was to be the Olds cars.

The Detroit plant was completed by early in 1900 and by March a hundred men were on the job. Ransom Olds now had no more concern about the facilities, money, or manpower needed to produce his car. The continued delay in the appearance of these cars was now due to Olds' indecision regarding what kind of car to produce. Straying from the objectives he had outlined in 1896, Olds experimented with about eleven different models, ranging in price from $1200 for a two-passenger trap on up to $2,750 for a four-passenger brougham. Included among these models were two electric cars, as Olds, who had earlier accurately assessed the defects of this type that would mitigate against its long-term popularity, tried to take advantage of the short-term interest that many car buyers were then showing in the electrics. However, few, if any, of these Olds models were sold, and by the fall of 1900 the automotive division of the Olds Motor Works was $80,000 in the red. Only the continued good sales of the Olds engines kept the company afloat.

Faced with the apparent failure of his existing models to generate much interest among buyers, Olds returned to the idea he had had in 1896 of producing simple, inexpensive transportation. Since 1899, more and more American automobile companies had been putting out small, relatively cheap cars that utilized a lightweight carriage model known as the runabout. Olds, spotting a trend, came up with his own runabout, which became the first of his cars to be called an Oldsmobile. The distinctive feature of the Olds runabout, which had a one-cylinder engine attached beneath the body, weighed around six hundred pounds, and initially sold for $600, was the curved dash in front, which gave the vehicle a profile somewhat like that of a sleigh. By the early weeks of 1901, Olds and his staff began promoting their new model to the virtual exclusion of the earlier gasoline and electric models. By March, over three hundred orders for the curved-dash Oldsmobile had been received, and Olds knew that he finally had a winner.

Fire destroyed most of the Olds Detroit plant on March 9, 1901, but it caused only a temporary delay in production, for nearly all the parts for the Oldsmobile were being built by outside suppliers. By April, 1901, the Olds workers were assembling these parts in makeshift quarters. The first of the cars were being shipped out in a few weeks, and before the year ended, about 425 of the runabouts had been produced—a sizable figure when the total production in the industry amounted to only a few thousand vehicles. The importance of the March fire has been blown out of all proportions by many writers, but it did have one important consequence: It encouraged Lansing businessmen to offer the Olds Motor Works a valuable site in southwestern Lansing on which to rebuild its automobile factory. The company accepted the offer, but in addition to building a new factory at Lansing, it also rebuilt the Detroit factory. Thus, from 1902 to 1905, as production figures for the runabout rose from around 3,000 cars in the former year to 6,500 in the latter year—each year breaking the previous year's record for any company in the industry—Oldsmobiles were produced both in Detroit and in Lansing. In 1905, however, the company directors decided it would be more efficient to concentrate all work at one site and the operations were then moved entirely to Lansing, which has remained the center for Oldsmobile activities.

By the year 1905, however, Ransom Olds had been gone for a year from the company that bore his name. From the time that he had accepted the money of Samuel Smith and his associates in 1899, Olds had controlled only a minority of the stock in the Olds Motor Works. His office in the company had first been that of vice-president, with Smith as the president, but early in 1900, the two had switched positions until 1901, when Smith again became the president and Olds returned to the office of vice-president. Throughout these changes, however, Olds retained the position of general manager in charge of manufacturing. In the early period of the company's development, the other officers deferred to Olds on manufacturing policy because of his experience in dealing with such matters. But as Smith's son, Frederick, who served as secretary-treasurer, gained more knowledge of the business, a conflict began to arise between him and Olds over some of the latter's methods of carrying on the business. Although a difference of opinion on the kind of car they should continue to emphasize was part of the problem, with the younger Smith from early in 1902 pushing Olds to proceed with the development of a larger automobile while Olds was more inclined to stick with the successful runabout, the broader issue was that of who would be in charge of manufacturing. In the spring of 1903, Smith began making decisions in this area without first consulting Olds, who was supposedly the official in charge of such matters, and a blowup occurred between the two men. It was inevitable that Olds, lacking the support of the stockholders or of his fellow directors, would see his position of general manager given to Fred Smith in January of 1904. Although Olds was still a director in the company, he felt his position was untenable. He proceeded to sell his remaining stock and by August, 1904, had severed all further ties with the company which had succeeded the firm that his father had founded twenty-four years earlier.

At the age of forty, Ransom Olds was not ready to retire. He, together with several Lansing business acquaintances, formed a new automobile company in the summer of 1904 that took its name from

Olds' initials—the Reo Motor Car Company. As president, Olds was careful to make sure that he retained control of a majority of the firm's voting stock. The Reo car that he and his staff had on the market by early 1905 was a success with the public. The model that was emphasized was a touring car, the heavier, more expensive kind of car that the Smiths had been urging Olds to manufacture during his last years with the Olds Motor Works. In two years, Reo sales were surpassing those of its cross-town rival, Oldsmobile, where Fred Smith had acted too fast in moving away from the cheap one-cylinder models, which resulted in a sharp drop in sales. But this initial success of his new automobiles marked the end of Olds as a major figure in the industry. The Reo car remained on the market until 1936 and the trucks that the company began to manufacture in 1911 continued to keep this name in dealers' showrooms until 1975. After 1907, however, Ransom Olds was content to leave most of the details of the Reo company for others to handle, while he devoted himself to other business interests and investments as well as to his hobbies of travel and yachting.

Although Olds made important contributions to the technical development of the automobile during his active years in the industry, as the sales of his Oldsmobile rose to then-unheard-of levels, he had realized that he had to improve the efficiency of his manufacturing operations. Thus, he had initiated the first steps towards mass production of cars. But his most important contribution was to stimulate other Michigan manufacturers to duplicate his success with their own cars. Olds was the first one in Michigan to produce automobiles in any significant numbers, and while he was by no means the first American automaker to put a relatively inexpensive car on the market, he was one of the first to prove that great profits could be made with a car such as the little runabout. A host of men who had been associated with Olds either as employees or as suppliers of parts were inspired to follow in his tracks.

Henry M. Leland, as the head of Detroit's Leland and Faulconer machine shop, was one of that city's most respected machinists. He had been an early parts supplier for Olds, first producing transmissions and then, in June, 1901, contracting to produce 2,000 engines for the runabout. Leland had never owned a car up to this time, but he bought an Oldsmobile in order to understand the engine's function more clearly. A stickler for high quality and precision work, Leland soon had his workers turning out the engines at a rate that astonished Olds, and he and his staff also improved the engine's performance. In the summer of 1902, when Detroit businessmen who had had no luck in getting Henry Ford to develop an automobile that they could manufacture, approached Leland with their problem, Leland had his men design a car that essentially followed the lines of the Oldsmobile runabout and employed Leland's improved version of the Olds engine. He and the ex-Ford backers joined forces to form the Cadillac Automobile Company, and by 1903 the Cadillac began to compete with the Oldsmobile runabout, at a price only slightly more than the curved-dash Olds. When Leland took over the direct management of Cadillac in 1904, however, he began to upgrade the Cadillac and transform it into the prestigious and expensive automobile familiar to later generations of auto buyers.

Earlier in 1902, Will Barbour, head of the Oldsmobile factory's next-door neighbor—the Detroit Stove Works—formed the Northern Manufacturing Company to produce the Northern runabout, another copy of the successful curved-dash Olds designed by Jonathan Maxwell, a member of the Olds staff who had worked on the original development of the Oldsmobile in the fall of 1900. Charles King, who also worked for the Olds company in this same period, claimed that the Northern did not work properly until he joined Barbour's company and corrected some of Maxwell's errors. Later, in 1908, Northern was part of a merger that resulted in the formation of the E-M-F company, a Detroit company whose first initial stood for Byron F. Everitt, a Detroit carriage-maker who had gotten his start in the auto industry by supplying bodies for the early Oldsmobiles. Meanwhile, Jonathan Maxwell had left Northern and had developed a new car which retained the lightweight, relatively inexpensive pattern set by Olds. Maxwell was backed by Benjamin Briscoe, one of the owners of a Detroit sheet metal shop which had supplied radiators, fenders, and other sheet metal parts for the Oldsmobile. The Maxwell automobile which the Maxwell-Briscoe company was producing by 1904 developed into a popular car which in a later day provided the base around which Walter P. Chrysler would build the Chrysler Corporation in the mid-twenties.

In addition to Maxwell, other Olds employees also sought to establish their own companies, drawing upon the knowledge they had gained under the tutelage of Olds and his associates. Robert C. Hupp, who had started with Olds as a common laborer in 1902, had launched his own company within six years and was producing the Hupmobile. Although Hupp did not remain with the company for many years, Hupmobile production continued under the direction of another ex-Olds official, Charles D. Hastings. Not all these Olds alumni were successful, of course. Willis Grant Murray, who was the manager of the automobile department of the Olds Motor Works at the time of the fire in March, 1901, was one of the first of the Olds staffers to strike out on his own. Unfortunately, the Adrian company that he persuaded to manufacture the Murray runabout, a very close copy of the Oldsmobile, lacked the money and the experience that were needed to succeed. On the other hand, a group of young men, several of whom, including the most prominent of the group—Roy D. Chapin and Howard Coffin—had been students at the University of Michigan before going to work for Olds around 1901, left the Olds Motor Works in 1906 and after several years succeeded in establishing their own company, the Hudson Motor Car Company. Although it was financially backed by the Detroit department store magnate, J. L. Hudson, the management of the company was in the hands of Chapin, the company president, and Coffin, the engineer responsible for the design of their cars, and their fellow Olds alumni. Hudson never challenged Michigan's biggest companies in auto output, but under Chapin's able leadership the company succeeded in popularizing improvements in automotive design, particularly the closed car in the twenties. In addition, Chapin became one of the best-known spokesmen for the entire industry, especially during the difficult years of the thirties.

Another of the early suppliers for the Oldsmobile were two brothers, John and Horace Dodge. Although they were natives of Niles, they had worked in Windsor, Canada, in the nineties, developing a successful bicycle manufacturing business which they sold at the end of the decade and moved across the river to Detroit where they opened a machine shop. By 1901 they were making transmissions and engines for the new Oldsmobile. Eventually, like their fellow Detroit machine shop operator, Henry Leland, the Dodges would be in charge of their own automobile company. Although Olds may be credited with giving them the initial encouragement to move in that direction, the money and the reputation that the Dodges used to make a success of their company when they established it in 1914 had come from their association with Henry Ford, for whose company the Dodges in the summer of 1903 had begun to supply most of the vital parts for the first commercially successful Ford car, the original Ford Model A, another runabout in the Oldsmobile mold.

Unlike Ransom Olds, who, within a few years after pioneering the development of the auto industry in Michigan, was content to take a less active role in the industry and who by the time of his death in 1950 had long since ceased to have any direct managerial connection with either of the companies he had founded, Henry Ford, Olds' successor as the most famous of the Michigan auto producers, not only retained that position but went on to become the most celebrated automobile manufacturer of all time. The emphasis placed on

Ford has greatly distorted his true importance and the importance of a number of his contemporaries, but because Ford has become enshrined as one of the folk heroes of modern times it is probably impossible to convince the public that Ford is only one of many whose work must be considered when studying the development of the auto industry.

Ford was a native of Michigan, having been born on July 30, 1863, on a farm in what is now the city of Dearborn, where his father, an Irish immigrant, had settled some years before. The Fords were by no means poor. Even though Henry Ford would become one of the world's first billionaires, his career does not, as some may assume, fit the standard Horatio Alger, rags-to-riches image, because his father was for his time and in the view of the residents of that area, regarded as fairly well-to-do. As Henry Ford struck out on his own in his early adult years, he always knew that he could count on his father's help in getting a job, and if he could not succeed in the city, his father was ready, and indeed eager, to assist him in becoming a farmer. Ford, however, did not enjoy his boyhood farm experiences. "My earliest recollection," he later declared, "is that, considering the results, there was too much work on the place." His initial interest in machines, he would claim, stemmed from his dislike for the hard physical labor on the farm. Thus, he decided that he wanted "to take the work off men's back and lay it on steel and motors."[3]

In July, 1876, he and his father drove a horse and wagon into Detroit, and en route they encountered a huge self-propelled steam threshing machine, manufactured by the Nichols and Shepard company of Battle Creek. Young Ford jumped out of the wagon and talked with the operator of the machine. He had never seen anything like it, and he never forgot the incident. A photograph of one of the road machines hung in his office in later years, symbolizing what Ford came to feel was an event that had helped to shape the course of his life. However, it was twenty years from the time that Ford saw this steam-propelled machine before he had his own self-propelled vehicle on the road. In the interim, he was involved in a host of activities and occupations. In 1879, he had left the farm and gone into Detroit, where he began to apply his natural mechanical abilities in jobs with the Michigan Car Company, a machine shop, the Detroit Dry Docks Engine Works, and a jewelry store. In 1882, he became a demonstrator and repairman for a distributor of Westinghouse portable steam engines, which took him back to the rural areas of southern Michigan since farmers were major customers for these machines. In 1884, Ford's father gave him forty acres of land in the Dearborn area, and for some years Ford engaged in part-time farming, and repaired machinery part-time. In 1888 he married Clara Bryant, and three years later they moved back into Detroit, where Ford had been hired by the Edison Illuminating Company as one of its mechanics, or engineers, as the jobs were called. By 1893, Ford had advanced to the post of chief engineer.

At age thirty, therefore, Ford had a well-paying job, he was working with machines, which he loved, and was well-liked by his superiors. A promising future in the electric industry was seemingly in the offing, but during this period, Ford's interests switched to horseless carriages. A visit to the Chicago World's Fair in 1893 influenced Ford, as it had Olds, to turn from steam engines to gasoline-powered engines. After he had succeeded in building a gasoline-powered engine, probably in the winter of 1895-96, Ford proceeded to apply it to powering a lightweight vehicle which he dubbed a quadricycle and which he successfully tested on the morning of June 4, 1896.

The immediate impact of this first Ford horseless carriage was slight. Within a few months, Ford sold the vehicle to start work on what he hoped would be an improved model. To do this, however, he required financial help. He was still working for the Edison company, but although he received a good salary, it was not sufficient to cover the cost of his automotive experiments plus the ordinary family expenses. He had exhausted his savings on the first car and there were limits on the amount of materials and labor that he could get friends and acquaintances to donate. In 1897, therefore, he received help from a family acquaintance—William Maybury—a Detroit lawyer, businessman, and politician (who would succeed Hazen Pingree as mayor of the city). Maybury provided some funds and other assistance and then shortly enlisted the help of two other Detroit friends and Ellery I. Garfield, a business acquaintance from Boston. These four men agreed to furnish Ford with several thousand dollars with the understanding that when he developed a marketable automobile they, together with Ford, would form a company, with Ford receiving a one-third interest in the business. For two years, Ford worked away in his spare time, but to the disgust of Garfield, who insisted that he could raise plenty of capital in Boston to finance the manufacturing of Ford's car, Ford insisted on correcting the problems with his vehicle before he would be ready to manufacture and sell it. Finally, in the summer of 1899, Ford was sufficiently satisfied with his latest experimental model and the Detroit Automobile Company was incorporated at the end of July. In addition to Maybury and his three associates, the main investments came from an impressive group of Detroit businessmen, most of whom shared some business connections with Senator James McMillan. The latter was not himself a stockholder in the company, but his son William was, along with Frank Hecker, McMillan's associate in the railroad-car business. Other associates included representatives from the D. M. Ferry seed company, of which McMillan was an officer, as well as political associates of McMillan and others whose wealth came from the salt and lumber industry. Ford himself was given a small amount of the stock and was a member of the company's board of directors. In addition, he was hired as superintendent in charge of production, a job that enabled him to quit his job with the Edison company. The Detroit Automobile Company provided Ford with a factory, equipment, and work force, and its wealthy Detroit investors provided the funds needed to carry the business along during its initial period of production. Despite this and the optimistic predictions of its officers in the early months regarding the wide range of vehicles it would soon have on the market, the company produced little. Henry Ford, unlike Ransom Olds, had had no experience in directing a manufacturing operation, and this could have accounted for some of the company's difficulties. But the major cause of the lack of action seems to have been Ford's continued dissatisfaction with his car and his insistence that more time was needed to improve the product before it could be put into production. Aside from a gasoline-powered delivery wagon which was used on an experimental basis by the Detroit Post Office, there is little evidence that the Detroit Automobile Company produced anything. Finally, by the end of 1900, Frank Hecker and a majority of the other stockholders became totally disillusioned with Ford and voted to dissolve the company.

Some of the stockholders, especially William Murphy, whose family was from Maine and had made a fortune in Michigan lumbering activities, still had faith in Ford. They continued to supply Ford with funds to carry on his experiments after the formal dissolution of the Detroit Automobile Company in January, 1901. Although Ford worked for a time on building a passenger car, by May, 1901, he was turning his attention to a new interest—racing. Hoping both to test out some of his ideas on the track and gain valuable publicity if he succeeded in winning a race, Ford and the little group of workers he had assembled completed a lightweight racing car by the summer and entered it in a racing event held at a dirt track in Grosse Pointe on October 10, the first such event staged in Michigan. A series of short races were held that afternoon for different classes and kinds of automobiles, with the climax a race open to any car of any type. The promoters had hoped to have some of the top names in auto racing present for this final race, and although they were disappointed in the response, they did succeed in getting the most famous of all American race drivers of that day, the Cleveland automobile manufacturer Alexander Winton, to be present for the event. The only other car in the race was Ford in his vehicle. Fortunately for Ford, who had had no racing experience and whose car was far less powerful than Winton's, Alexander Winton's entry developed mechanical problems halfway through the ten-mile race, thereby securing a victory for Ford. Despite the circumstances that led to his victory, Ford received national exposure as the builder and driver of a motor vehicle that had beaten Alexander Winton.

Delighted at Ford's success, William Murphy and his associates now felt the time was right to cash in on Ford's fame and announced the formation of the Henry Ford Company. Ford was hired to be in charge of the manufacturing side of the business and was given one-sixth of the stock in the company. But Murphy and his group of investors soon discovered that Ford was no more ready to put a car into production now than he had been earlier with the Detroit Automobile Company. The reason for the delay this time, however, was not so much Ford's dissatisfaction with the cars he had thus far developed, but his new interest in auto racing. Now he spent all of his time working on the design of a bigger, more powerful machine to enhance his chances of repeating his victory at Grosse Pointe. For William Murphy and the others who had patiently waited for Henry Ford to produce something that would repay them for their investments in his experiments, this was the last straw. In March, 1902, Ford was either fired or was persuaded to leave the Henry Ford Company. In the following months, those Detroiters who had hoped to profit from the sale of Ford-built automobiles linked up with Henry Leland, who provided the production car they had been seeking. This resulted in the reorganization of the Henry Ford Company as the Cadillac Automobile Company with the successful introduction of the Cadillac in 1903.

Meanwhile, Henry Ford found new financial backing that enabled him to complete two nearly identical, powerful new racing vehicles by the summer of 1902. They were so powerful, in fact, that Ford was afraid to risk his life driving them. With races again scheduled for Grosse Pointe in October of 1902, Ford and his associates secured the services of a daring bicycle racer from Toledo, Barney Oldfield. Although he had never raced a car before, Oldfield drove Ford's "999" (the number of a record-setting railroad locomotive of the nineties) to victory at Grosse Pointe, thereby establishing Oldfield's reputation as the best known of the early American racing drivers and solidifying Ford's reputation as the builder of winning racing cars.

In the summer of 1902, while he was still working on his racing cars, Ford signed an agreement with a Detroit coal dealer, Alexander Malcomson, to work on the development of a passenger car, which they would then produce through a company in which the two men would retain a majority stock interest. Malcomson succeeded where Maybury and Murphy and their associates had failed. He got Ford to buckle down and work while Malcomson persuaded a group of relatives, business associates, and employees to invest the funds needed to form the Ford Motor Company in June, 1903. A small factory was rented in Detroit, parts were ordered from the Dodge brothers and other suppliers, and by the first part of July, the first Ford Model A runabouts were being assembled. Henry Ford was vice president and general manager of the company at a salary of $3600 a year, and he also was given a 25½ per cent share of the stock. Malcomson had a similar percentage of the stock and his uncle, John Gray, a Detroit banker, was the first president of the Ford Motor Company, while one of Malcomson's employees, James Couzens, was company treasurer. After the first Fords had been built and were ready to be shipped out, Henry Ford again doubted the quality of the vehicle and declared that the cars could not be shipped until certain defects were corrected. Nevertheless, Couzens insisted that the cars go out. The investors in the Ford Motor Company were, on the whole, not the affluent type that had backed Ford earlier. Most of them, including Couzens, had had to mortgage their homes or in other ways borrow the money they used for their investment. Even then, only about $28,000 in cash had been provided, barely enough to meet the initial costs. Unless money was forthcoming quickly from the sale of cars, the Ford Motor Company faced the early prospect of bankruptcy. Couzens, therefore, vetoed Ford's desire to delay the car shipments. The cars went out—although the company would later be generous in providing help to those unsuspecting buyers who did encounter mechanical problems with their purchases—and by the fall of 1903 the firm's financial worries were at an end.

In the early years before the introduction in 1908 of the most famous Ford car—the Model T—Henry Ford experimented with a series of new cars. The original Model A sold for $850 to $950. Next came the Model B, the first four-cylinder Ford, which sold for $2,000. There were also Models F and K. But the real progenitor of the Model T was the Model N, a good, solid, small car with a four-cylinder vertical engine that produced fifteen horsepower and could travel forty-five miles an hour. The price was $600. Models R and S were deluxe editions of Model N. Within the Ford organization there was a spirited controversy over the wisdom of concentrating on the low-priced models, which Ford favored. Alexander Malcomson favored a big car, but he was overruled and withdrew from the company in 1906. Ford purchased Malcomson's stock, thereby gaining undisputed control of the company with fifty-one per cent of the stock, control that the Ford family has continued to exercise over the company to the present day. John Gray died in 1906, and Ford was elected president in his place. By this time he had gathered together a remarkably able group of men in the organization, men who contributed much to his success. Besides Couzens, who proved to be a financial and sales genius, there were C. Harold Wills, chief engineer, Walter Flanders, who devised production methods, and Charles Sorenson, a master mechanic.

Work on the Model T began in 1907. Sorenson worked closely with Ford in designing the experimental car. Unlike most early cars, it was built with a left-hand drive. The cylinder engine block was cast in one piece instead of in separate sections, the cylinder head was removable, and the magneto was built into the flywheel.

Introduced in October, 1908, the Model T touring car initially sold for $850, but the price was increased to $950 by 1910, after which time the price began to drop until 1916, when the touring car sold for $360. This low price was made possible by economy in production. In 1913, at the new Highland Park plant, a moving assembly line was introduced—an idea originated by Ford staff members but authorized by Ford himself. The assembly line not only made it possible to turn out enormous numbers of cars at a low price, but also marked the real birth of modern mass production. Ford did not invent mass production any more than he had invented the automobile, but the results that he and his men achieved by adapting techniques previously used by others to the manufacturing of such a complicated product as an automobile were startlingly dramatic. They first applied the moving assembly approach to the assembling of the fly-wheel magneto. Where one worker had required twenty minutes to assembly one of these items, by dividing the assembling task into eighty-four separate operations and assigning these operations to a group of workers stationed along a moving assembly line, the time it took to assemble one fly-wheel magneto was reduced to five minutes and the workers assigned to this assembly line were able to turn out in one day the amount of work that would have required three times as many workmen under the old methods. These results, of course, quickly led Ford to apply the same techniques to the assembling of the entire car.[4] The advantages and economies of the

Model T Ford, 1908

moving assembly line were soon adapted to the manufacture of other products as well as by many of Ford's automotive competitors. It was made possible, of course, by the use of precision-made, interchangeable parts, an idea that Henry M. Leland had introduced into automobile manufacture. The birth of mass production methods in the Ford Highland Park plant is even more important and significant in the history of the twentieth century than the Model T itself. It would not be too much to say it was the basis of the affluent society of the mid-century.

There were other reasons for the success of the Model T. Its price was within reach of all but the poorest families; it literally, as the Ford company likes to boast, "put America on wheels." It was built with simplicity and was so easy to repair that almost anyone could fix something that went wrong with a pair of plyers and a screwdriver. Spare parts were made available to dealers everywhere. And the little car never wore out, or so it seemed. There was nothing fancy about the Model T: it was built not for faddists or for display but for practical use. In time the Model T's developed rattles, which gave rise to the popular idea that they were made from tin; hence the nickname "Tin Lizzie." The car became a national institution, and countless stories sprang up about it, usually related to its supposedly tin construction, durability, rattles, and dependability. It was once said that during a tornado in Illinois, the tin roof of a farmer's barn was blown off. As a joke, he boxed up the mangled tin and shipped it to the Ford factory. In due course he received a polite letter stating that his Ford was badly damaged but that it could be repaired, and that it would be returned in running order shortly.

The Ford Model T continued to be produced from the fall of 1908 until the end of May, 1927. During most of that time it was the only model Ford produced. Although some changes had been made over the years, these were minor, cosmetic alterations in the exterior appearance of the car. Essentially, the last of the 15,007,033 Model T's was the same car that Ford had manufactured nineteen years earlier. Not until the equally famous Volkswagen beetle of the post-World War II era would another automobile model anywhere in the world equal and surpass the production record of the Model T. Until the time of World War I, the Model T completely dominated the low-cost field. After that time it began to have important competitors. Even so, the peak year of Model T production was 1923, when 2,011,125 of these cars were manufactured—a record for one company that was not exceeded for thirty-two years. But it was in the decade after 1908 that the Model T really captured the imagination of the American people and was one of the principal developments that catapulted Henry Ford to world-wide fame.

In addition to the Model T and the association of his name with mass-production techniques, Ford and his company also received invaluable publicity as a result of a protracted legal battle over the Selden patent. After obtaining that patent in 1895, George Selden found that he lacked the resources he needed to enforce the claim that the patent applied to all gasoline-powered automobiles. In 1899, therefore, he assigned the patent rights to the Electric Vehicle Company for $10,000 and a twenty per cent share of the royalties that company collected. The Electric Vehicle Company then attempted to force gasoline car manufacturers to secure a license under this patent and pay royalties on the cars they produced. A suit was brought against the best known of these companies, the Winton Motor Carriage Company of Cleveland, in the belief that if the patent holders could secure a judgment against a firm of this stature the other companies would fall in line. In 1902, Fred Smith of the Olds Motor Works and Henry B. Joy, also of Detroit and the leading figure in the Packard Motor Car Company, took the lead in seeking a compromise with the Selden patent holders. Smith, Joy, and George H. Day, head of the Electric Vehicle Company, shared a common feeling of uneasiness concerning the outcome of the Winton suit. Smith and Joy disliked the thought of the royalties they would have to pay if the court upheld the patent claims, while Day contemplated what would happen to his company if these claims were not upheld and the patent thereby became worthless. An agreement was reached early in 1903 whereby the makers of the Oldsmobile, Packard, Cadillac, Northern, Winton, and a number of other American gasoline-automobile producers recognized the validity of the Selden patent and were granted licenses by the Electric Vehicle Company. These licensed companies formed the Association of Licensed Automobile Manufacturers (the ALAM), and in return for their cooperation with the Selden patent owners, they negotiated royalty fees that were considerably smaller than George Day had originally proposed. Even more important, the ALAM would be the sole judge of which additional companies would be granted licenses under the patent, thereby giving it the power, its advocates declared, to regulate this emerging industry and weed out the fly-by-night operators who were giving all automobile makers a bad name. The opponents of the association, on the other hand, charged that the ALAM would use its power to give its licensed members an unfair advantage in competition with those to whom it refused to grant a license.

When the Ford Motor Company was formed in 1903, Henry Ford had some preliminary talks with Fred Smith, the president of the ALAM, about securing a license to produce his gasoline car. Smith apparently told Ford that the association probably would vote not to license Ford's company at this time because Ford had not as yet demonstrated an ability to direct a successful automobile manufacturing operation. The obvious reply, of course, was that if Ford went ahead with production in order to prove that he could manage a successful automobile business, he would be violating the rights of the patent owners and inviting legal action against his company. In this situation, how could a new company break into the business? Ford and his associates decided to go ahead with production in open defiance of the ALAM. Other companies did the same thing, but by the fall of 1903, when the Ford company was publishing advertisements in which it openly attacked "The Trust," as it called the ALAM, and promised to support in court any purchaser of a Ford car who might be sued by the Selden forces for having purchased an unlicensed automobile, the licensed automobile group was almost forced to file suit against Ford. The trial dragged on for years, with over five million words of testimony, exhibits, briefs, and other materials accumulated in the proceedings. Eventually numerous other unlicensed companies, including Ransom Olds' Reo company, were added to the list of firms the Selden forces were suing, but throughout the litigation, the attention was focused on the Ford company, which gleefully took advantage of the reams of free publicity it was receiving. In September, 1909, Federal Judge Charles M. Hough of the Southern District of New York, to the very considerable surprise of all concerned, upheld the claims of the Selden patent holders. Most of the unlicensed car makers quickly fell into line and asked for and were granted licenses on whatever terms the ALAM demanded. Henry Ford, however, after some hesitation, decided to carry on the fight alone, and on January 9, 1911, the United States Circuit Court of Appeals for the Second Circuit unanimously reversed the lower court's decision. The Selden patent, the circuit court declared, covered only those automobiles which used a two-cycle gasoline engine, such as the Brayton engine which George Selden had specified as the source of power for the motorized vehicle he had designed when he originally applied for his patent in 1879. The patent, however, did not apply to cars using the Otto four-cycle engine, the kind that Ford and virtually every other American gasoline automobile producer utilized.

Since the life of the patent would expire in 1912 anyway, the ALAM decided not to appeal the circuit court's ruling. Thus Henry Ford and his company emerged as the victor in the case. Their success in standing up to "The Trust" with all its impressive Wall Street connections, during a time when Teddy Roosevelt and other politicians were campaigning noisily against trusts and monopolies, did much to create a favorable public image of both the man and his company. At the same time, the eight-year-long legal action had no detrimental effect on the Ford company's growth. If the ALAM was, as Ford charged, seeking to monopolize the auto business for its members, it failed dismally. By 1911, Ford was producing more than twenty percent of all cars in the country, far more than any other company, licensed or unlicensed. Nevertheless, Henry Ford was popularly depicted as the doughty little independent from Michigan, the David who had stood up to and had slain the ALAM Goliath.

To cap his series of publicity coups, Ford on January 5, 1914, announced that henceforth he would pay his employees at the basic rate of $5.00 a day. At a time when the going rate for American workers was half that amount, the news created a national sensation. There is much dispute over who in the Ford organization was responsible for this move, and critics would ultimately emphasize the fine print in the policy that carefully specified who could or could not receive the five-dollar wage and how Ford's own narrow moral standards entered into this determination. However, at the time, the response of the public was overwhelmingly favorable, with Ford now being hailed not only as a mechanical genius, a production wizard, and a dragon-slayer but also as the most enlightened of manufacturers in his employee relationships.

By the middle of the second decade of the twentieth century,

Henry Ford was far out in front of all other auto producers not only in the United States but in the world. Few would have thought that anyone could successfully challenge him, but within a decade he would be relegated to the secondary place that he and his company have had to be satisfied with ever since. The successful challenger was still another auto giant of Michigan origins—General Motors.

General Motors was the creation of the successful Flint carriage manufacturer, William C. "Billy" Durant.[5] By the beginning of the twentieth century, Durant's Durant-Dort Carriage Company was no longer providing him with the challenge that he liked to have in the business world. The capable staff of executives that he and Dort had hired could handle all the details of managing this successful enterprise. Durant was on the lookout for something new to do. He began spending more time in New York where his dabblings in the stock market forshadowed the activities that would eventually make him one of the most famous plungers in the stock market boom of the twenties. In 1902, he made an unsuccessful attempt to pull off a $50,000,000 merger of Durant-Dort with several other carriage manufacturers in Flint and elsewhere. Finally, in the fall of 1904, the opportunity he had been seeking came when he was asked to apply his promotional skills to making a success of the failing Buick Motor Car Company.

Buick had been started by David D. Buick, a native of Scotland who had been brought to Detroit in the late 1850s as a child of two and had been orphaned when he was five. Subsequently, young Buick went to work for a Detroit plumbing supply business which he and a partner successfully took over in the 1880s. Buick had an inventive kind of mind and he secured a dozen or so patents on various plumbing devices and improvements. By the late nineties, however, Buick's interest had shifted from plumbing fixtures to gasoline engines. Late in 1899 he sold his share of the plumbing business and used the money to establish a new company to produce the engines that were now his main interest. Although, like Ransom Olds', Buick's engines could be used in a variety of ways, by 1901 Buick was devoting more and more of his time to applying his engine to powering a vehicle. By the fall of 1902, his work on an improved engine and a vehicle was progressing well, but by then Buick had exhausted his funds. He got financial help from Benjamin and Frank Briscoe, the operators of the Detroit sheet metal shop who had been supplying some parts to Buick as well as the Olds Motor Works and other automobile manufacturers and developers. In the spring of 1903 the Briscoes loaned Buick additional funds, in return for which they were given control of the stock in the reorganized Buick business, now renamed the Buick Motor Company.

By September, 1903, the Briscoes had developed grave doubts about the future of the Buick company. By chance, they learned that James Whiting of the Flint Wagon Works was interested in acquiring control of an automobile company, perhaps as a hedge against the day when cars would become popular enough to cut into the sales of wagons and carriages. For $10,000 the Briscoes unloaded their interest in the Buick company onto Whiting and several of Whiting's associates in the Flint Wagon Works. The new Flint owners, while continuing to operate their successful wagon business, brought the Buick company to Flint as an entirely separate venture, to be managed for them by David Buick. Buick, however, seems to have lost whatever managerial skills he had demonstrated earlier in the plumbing business, and by the late summer of 1904, a year after the Whiting group had purchased the company, they had little to show for their investment and little hope that they could expect any improvement in the future under Buick's direction.

It was at this time, therefore, that the Flint businessmen approached their fellow townsman, Durant, to see if he would take over the company and save it from an early death. Until this time Durant had shown little interest in cars. However, after personally testing a Buick automobile on the roads—good and bad—of the Flint area he decided that it was a good product that could be a commercial success if he applied his organizational and promotional skills to the company's development. On November 1, 1904, with the understanding that he was to have complete control of the business, Durant took on the job of reviving Flint's faltering automobile company. He proved more than equal to the task. Using his numerous contacts in Flint, he quickly raised the additional money needed for Buick's development. Although he shortly began planning a large new factory in Flint, he temporarily provided the Buick assembly operations with the expanded facilities they required by moving them into a vacant plant that Durant-Dort had available in Jackson. Then he turned his attention to selling the car and decided to secure free publicity by entering Buicks in as many races, endurance contests, and hill climbs as possible. With such famous drivers as Louis and Arthur Chevrolet and "Bullet Bob" Burman at the wheel, Durant's strategy paid off as Buick became probably the best known and most successful car on the American racing circuit. By the summer of 1908, when Buick assembly activities were moved back to Flint in the newly completed factory which would be from thenceforward the headquarters for the company, Buick had become perhaps the most popular car in the country. Inexact production figures for these early years make it difficult to determine whether Buick or Ford was, as the supporters of these rival companies each contend, the best-selling car on the market.

Billy Durant, however, was not satisfied simply to push the sales of one automobile. While Henry Ford's decision, which he made early in 1909, to gamble his company's future success on the Model T, and to abandon all his other models, was responsible for keeping his company far ahead of the competition for many years, Durant seems to have viewed that as too risky a strategy. A safer and surer way to long-lasting success, he felt, was to offer the public not one model but a wide range of choices, just as he had done earlier in his carriage company when he had moved from the road cart, which had initially been his sole offering, to the full range of models and styles that Durant-Dort was offering by the mid-nineties. The quickest way to provide this diversity of automotive models would be by merging several existing auto companies into one corporate organization. In addition, such a corporation was more likely to attract the investment capital that would be needed to keep up with the demands of a rapidly expanding market than would the several merged firms if they continued as separate operations.

The early years of the twentieth century, despite what Teddy Roosevelt's "trust-busting" nickname might imply, were years in which mergers and consolidation became ever more widespread throughout American industry. Although Durant had shown his familiarity with this approach in his attempt in 1902 to pull off a large-scale merger in the carriage industry, he did not initiate the first steps in the move that led to the formation of General Motors in September, 1908. Instead Benjamin Briscoe approached Durant with the idea of merging the Maxwell-Briscoe company with Durant's Buick company and a miscellaneous collection of other producers. Durant liked the idea, but thought that the other companies Briscoe suggested were too dissimilar in the cars they produced. Durant suggested that Briscoe talk with Henry Ford and Ransom Olds to see if they would be interested in joining in the merger talks. At this time Buick, Ford, Reo, and Maxwell all ranked among the top five or six most popular cars on the market, with all four cars in the lower price ranges, in contrast with some of the more expensive, low-volume cars that Briscoe first had in mind.

Briscoe followed Durant's suggestion and he found both Ford and Olds receptive to the idea of a merger, although the details of how such a merger would be carried out were not clearly spelled out. On January 17, 1908, Durant, Briscoe, Olds, and Ford met in Detroit for preliminary talks on the proposed merger. A week later they traveled to New York where they met for two days in the office of Herbert L. Satterlee, an attorney and son-in-law of J. P. Morgan, whose Wall Street financial house would be handling the monetary arrangements for the merger. Durant and Briscoe differed on the form that the new corporation should take. Durant wanted a holding company that would control the stock in the several firms that would be included in the merger but would exercise a minimum of managerial control over the companies, which would continue as actual operating businesses. On the other hand, Briscoe favored a real consolidation that would result in a corporation that would set policies and centralize authority, leaving the several companies that were part of the merger as little more than manufacturing divisions of the parent firm. However, both men were in agreement that the merger would be carried off through an exchange of stock, with the stockholders in Buick, Maxwell-Briscoe, Ford, and Reo exchanging their stock for a proportionate number of shares in the consolidated company. Very little cash would change hands, but the stockholders would benefit from the high price that stock in the new company could be expected to command on the stock market. The negotiations between the four companies collapsed, however, when at one of the meetings in New York, probably one held in May, 1908, Henry Ford and Ransom Olds both announced that they wanted to be paid cash, not stock, for control of their companies. The amount of money each of them asked, whether it was $3,000,000 or $4,000,000, as different sources state, sounds like a bargain basement figure by later standards, but in 1908, when the financial world still had grave doubts as to the permanent nature of the auto industry, this was far more money than the Morgans were willing to commit themselves to obtain for this venture.

With Ford and Reo eliminated, talks continued for several weeks in the summer of 1908 seeking to merge Buick and Maxwell, but that too proved impossible. Durant, meanwhile, had obtained what amounted to options from the Buick stockholders authorizing him to vote their stock as he saw fit. He felt that he had to have some kind of merger in order to exercise this option. Thus, on September 16, 1908, Durant arranged to have the General Motors Company incorporated in New Jersey, choosing that state because of its lax corporation laws which placed virtually no limits on the amount of stock a company could issue and, more important, permitted the holding company arrangement that Durant desired by allowing a company to own stock in another company. On the other hand, Michigan's corporation laws placed strict limits on the amount of stock that a Michigan company could issue and forbade one firm from owning stock in another company.

The General Motors that Durant established in 1908 is not the same company as the present General Motors Corporation. The original corporation technically manufactured nothing. Instead, it simply controlled the stock of companies that were in the business of manufacturing automobiles. The first company that it came to control was Buick, whose stock was exchanged on October 1, 1908, for shares in General Motors with only $1500 in cash involved in the deal. The Buick Motor Company remained in existence, and was still managed by Durant. The only difference now was that Durant's holding company held nearly all the stock in the firm and thus had the voting power of putting whomever it wished on the Buick board of directors and into the top executive positions.

One acquisition hardly represented a consolidation, but Durant soon began adding company after company to those that General Motors controlled. On November 12, the Olds Motor Works was brought into the fold. The sharp decline in Oldsmobile sales since 1905 had forced Samuel Smith to advance over a million dollars to carry the business along. He and his sons, therefore, were delighted to transfer nearly all of the Olds stock to General Motors, in return for General Motors shares and the assumption by General Motors of the debt owed by the Olds company to Samuel Smith. From Durant's standpoint, the Olds company had great potential since, despite small Oldsmobile sales in 1908, the name was still one of the best known in the industry, a fact which he could use in rebuilding the car's sales. Before long, the Smiths were eased out of their positions in the Olds organization and, under new management, Oldsmobile assumed an important position in the General Motors roster of cars.

In the summer of 1909, Durant brought Cadillac into the General Motors fold. In this case, however, Henry Leland and his associates in Cadillac insisted upon a payment of over $4,500,000 in cash, in addition to stock, for control of their company, but Cadillac's financial position was so obviously sound that Durant was able to persuade the banks to advance the funds he needed to complete this acquisition. The Cadillac stockholders, of course, would have been far wiser to have accepted an equivalent amount of stock, rather than the cash, since within a few years that stock would be worth many times over the money they received in 1909.

Earlier in 1909, through the more customary stock-exchange method, General Motors had acquired control of the Oakland Motor Car Company, which Edward M. Murphy, the leading carriage manufacturer in Pontiac, had established in that city in 1907. In 1909, the

Oakland was a relatively minor car on the market, but with an application of Durant's promotional talents it quickly grew in importance and survives today as the Pontiac division of General Motors—the name resulting from the abandonment of the Oakland car at the end of the twenties and its replacement by the Pontiac. Other auto companies which Durant acquired—the Welch, Cartercar, Ewing, and Elmore, for example—did not survive. Some truck manufacturers were also acquired, as well as control of auto parts manufacturers, in order to assure the General Motors automobile manufacturers of the parts they needed. The most important of this latter group was the Weston-Mott company, makers of wheels and axles. Originally located in Utica, New York, its owners had been persuaded by Durant in 1905 to move their plant to Flint. In 1909 and 1913 Charles S. Mott, who was now the sole owner of the company, exchanged control of the firm for some cash plus stock and, from 1913 to Mott's death in 1973, a seat on the General Motors board of directors. Mott became the largest single holder of stock in General Motors, with his stock at one time estimated to be worth around $800,000,000.

Durant was not successful in getting every company he went after. Efforts to acquire the Maxwell-Briscoe company again failed in 1909, and Benjamin Briscoe then went ahead on his own and sought to duplicate Durant's success by forming the United States Motor Company, but unfortunately Briscoe's own Maxwell was the only worthwhile acquisition made by the new company, and in 1912 United States Motor went bankrupt. Durant continued to be unsuccessful in acquiring Ransom Olds' Reo company, but the major company that got away was the Ford Motor Company. In October, 1909, Henry Ford, in poor health and temporarily discouraged by the initial decision in the Selden patent case, agreed to give Durant an option to acquire his company. Again Ford insisted on cash, not stocks, and his price was now $8,000,000, in contrast with the $3,000,000 or $4,000,000 he had been asking the previous year. However, he would take the money in installments spread over several years. Despite this, and despite the sales of the Model T which were already beginning to soar, Durant was turned down by the banks in his bid to borrow the money he needed, and the chance of an outside group to gain control of Ford's company was lost— perhaps forever. By the mid-twenties, Ford could blithely ignore a more or less serious offer by a Wall Street group to purchase his company for a billion dollars.

Billy Durant's forte was promotion, not administration. Rather than establishing a centralized management in the General Motors office that could keep careful tabs on the activities of the numerous firms that the holding company controlled, Durant attempted the impossible task of personally supervising the development of the entire melange. Using the methods he had employed so successfully at Buick, he committed millions of dollars to expanding and building up the more important of the companies, such as Oakland and Oldsmobile, depending on the continued good sales of Cadillac and Buick to meet the bills until these development programs began to pay off. In the summer of 1910, however, a short recession in the country caused a sudden drop in car sales. General Motors suddenly found itself short of cash, and to save his company, Durant was forced to accept a loan from an eastern syndicate which exacted harsh terms, including an insistence that during the five-year life of the loan Durant would no longer be in charge of General Motors. Durant, who proved to be amazingly resilient throughout his business career, then proceeded to make use of the time he now had on his hands to set up the Chevrolet Motor Car Company, taking an automobile that Louis Chevrolet, the old Buick racing-car driver, had designed, changing it into a less expensive model, and by 1915 making it one of the more popular cars on the market. Durant used the profits from this to get back control of General Motors in 1916. In the meantime, however, the conservative management that the bankers installed at General Motors from 1910 to 1915 had begun to bring some order into the administration of the holding company. Even a second period of Durant-inspired mergers and expansion between 1916 and 1920 could not prevent General Motors from achieving phenomenal success.

At the end of the nineteenth century and in the early years of the twentieth, many more companies besides those already mentioned were formed in Michigan as well as in other parts of the country. It has been estimated that more than three thousand different makes of automobiles have appeared in the United States since the start of the auto industry. Few of them survived for long or were produced in any great numbers. Many of an estimated fifteen hundred automobile companies that were formed never got beyond the printing of stock certificates. A thousand or so got as far as developing one or more cars and putting them into production, limited as it might have been. But in a remarkably short time, the basic patterns that would exist in the industry from then on had begun to appear. From New England, where the initial manufacturing was centered, a movement westward was evident by 1900, with companies in Buffalo, Cleveland, Toledo, Indiana, and Wisconsin coming to the fore. But beginning in 1901, with the stimulus that Ransom Olds' success provided, Michigan began to move to the forefront. By

1904 Detroit was already the volume leader in auto production in the country. The rapid growth of several outstate auto centers after 1940 served to widen the lead that the state as a whole had over all other states, and any chance that this leadership would be lost was ended with those twin developments of the latter part of 1908: Ford's introduction of the Model T and Durant's creation of General Motors.

Within Michigan, the total value of automobile production in the early years was far less than that of other established economic activities. In 1906, for example, Detroit's automobile production was valued at about $12,000,000, double what it had been two years earlier, but still less than half the value of the production of Detroit's railroad car industry. However, by 1909, the total value of automobiles and auto parts made in Michigan, which had amounted to less than two per cent of the value of the state's manufactured goods in 1904, now accounted for about a seventh of that total, and by 1914 the Michigan automobile industry, with production valued at nearly $400,000,000—four times what it had been in 1909—contributed 36.7 percent of the value of the state's manufacturing output. Clearly, the automobile and the automaker had taken the place formerly held by such products and producers as lumber and lumber barons, and minerals and mining executives.

23

PROGRESSIVISM AND THE GROWTH OF SOCIAL CONSCIOUSNESS

The rise of the automobile industry and Michigan's assumption of leadership in the industry is clearly the most important development in American and Michigan history in the early years of the twentieth century. However, in the traditional, politically-oriented history book these are the years that are remembered as the years of the Progressive Movement, one of the major reform movements in American history. Michigan could scarcely be termed a leader in this political sphere of action as it was in the economic sphere, but significant political reforms did occur in the state in this period as well as some important early responses to the need for more government action to deal with problems created by an increasingly complex society and economy.

Cracks in the control that the Republican party's old guard had exercised for so many years began to appear both on the national and state level at the start of the new century. The assassination of President William McKinley late in the summer of 1901, a few months after the start of his second term in office, brought vice-president Theodore Roosevelt to the White House. Roosevelt soon began to speak loudly for Progressive reforms, though in practice he was far from being a radical. Beginning about 1902, articles in popular magazines, novels, and scholarly works by so-called "muckrakers" provided detailed and sometimes lurid accounts of political malfeasance, frenzied quest for wealth, and disregard of the public welfare by big business. Such articles revealed sordid conditions in city slums and graft in city and state governments. The muckrakers played a major role in bringing about an insistent public demand for reform. In different parts of the nation leaders appeared to champion one or another of dozens of different reform proposals. Thus arose what is called the Progressive Movement. It was a movement that crossed party lines, with each of the two major parties having its Progressive wing, opposed by the conservatives or "stalwarts" within the party.

In Michigan, where many of the reforms associated with the Progressives had been advocated a decade earlier by Hazen Pingree, Pingree's successor as governor—lumber baron Aaron Bliss— proved to be not quite as loyal to the party bosses as originally had been assumed. In August, 1902, Senator James McMillan, long-time leader of the state's old guard, died and efforts to keep his machine organization intact failed. William McMillan, who had looked after his father's interests in Michigan while the senator spent most of his time in the East, supported Dexter M. Ferry's candidacy for the vacancy in the senate left by McMillan's death. However, Governor Bliss surprised the McMillan forces by appointing Russell A. Alger, who had steered an independent course in Michigan Republican politics, to the senate. This early indication of Bliss' own independence, which undoubtedly helped to gain him the votes he needed to be re-elected in 1902, was followed in 1903 by a call from Bliss for the enactment of "a satisfactory primary election law." This was a somewhat belated response to the heavy criticism that had resulted from reports that $750,000 had been spent at the 1900 Republican state convention, which had nominated Bliss for governor, to buy the votes of delegates for the several wealthy candidates seeking the party's gubernatorial nomination. The direct primary, which was intended to eliminate boss control over the choice of candidates by allowing all members of the party to participate in the selection process through a special primary election, had been advocated by reformers, including Michigan's Hazen Pingree, for several years. It first had been adopted in Mississippi in 1902, although Wisconsin's primary law, passed in 1903, came to be regarded by Progressives as the model for this kind of legislation. Reform came slowly in Michigan, however. In 1903, the legislature acted to authorize primaries only for the choice of county candidates and even then only in Wayne, Kent, and Muskegon counties.

In 1904, the old McMillan machine successfully backed Fred M. Warner to succeed Bliss as governor. Warner is one of the more important, but relatively neglected Michigan political figures. He had been born in England in 1865, and he was thus Michigan's first, and until the election of the Canadian-born John B. Swainson in 1960 and the Mexican-born George W. Romney in 1962, Michigan's only foreign-born governor. As a baby, Warner was brought to this country by his parents, and he was later adopted by P. Dean Warner of Farmington, where Fred Warner late in the century began developing a highly successful cheese and dairy business. He served in the state senate in the nineties and then was elected secretary of state in 1900 and again in 1902.

In the early years of the twentieth century, the Democratic party in Michigan was so weakened by the factional disputes of the nineties that the Republican nomination for office was tantamount to election, and Warner easily won the election for governor in 1904. However, the landslide margin of the victory of Theodore Roosevelt, the symbol of Progressivism, in the Presidential election of that year gave evidence of rising popular support for Progressive reforms. These election returns obviously had an influence on Warner, whom the old guard had assumed they could control. Opinions about Warner vary greatly. Some regard him simply as an opportunist who took up a cause that he thought would assure his re-election. Others, however, feel that he was either a liberal all along or that he sincerely became convinced of the need for change. For whatever reason, Warner began pressing for the adoption of Progressive reforms, starting with a call for an effective primary law. The legislature, still controlled by the conservatives, responded in 1905 with a general primary law for the state which was so complex that it proved to be unworkable—undoubtedly the intent of the conservatives when they passed the bill. When he was re-elected in 1906, Warner became increasingly independent and worked for an improved primary law, which was finally enacted in 1909. The law made it mandatory for the major parties to nominate through the primary system their candidates for governor, lieutenant-governor, United States Senator (although the final choice of the senators still rested with the legislature), Congress, state legislators, and city offices in Grand Rapids and Detroit. Warner did not press to have candidates for other state elective offices chosen by primaries because he had learned after his nomination in the primary that he could go to the state convention following that election and dictate whom he wanted to run with him as candidates for secretary of state, state treasurer, attorney general, and other offices to be filled in the general election.

Meanwhile, the state legislature, with constant prodding from Warner, had been enacting a considerable body of Progressive legislation. In 1907 a railroad commission was established and was given power to establish railroad rates and to regulate railroads and other utilities in the state, replacing the ineffective system of regulation that had existed earlier. Taxes on telegraph and telephone companies were increased, the receipts being added to the primary-school fund. The problems resulting from industrialization began to receive greater attention. The state labor department was established. Safety measures were required in factories, and the hours of labor for employees under eighteen years of age were limited to ten hours a day or fifty-four hours a week. Pure food acts and the regulation of insurance companies were among other reforms enacted during the Warner administration—certainly one of the most active in the state's history.

Warner's second term in office also witnessed a state constitutional convention, the first one in over thirty years and the first since 1850 to succeed in securing the adoption of a new constitution. Voters in 1904 had rejected a proposal to call a convention to revise the 1850 Constitution, which had been amended numerous times. By 1906, however, supporters of a convention had succeeded in convincing a majority of the voters that a constitution drafted in the middle of the nineteenth century no longer spoke to the needs of a state that was undergoing such rapid change as was Michigan in the early years of the twentieth century. Delegates to the convention were elected in September, 1907, and the ninety-six successful candidates assembled at Lansing on October 22. All but eight of the delegates were Republicans. The conservatives who were dominant in the convention resisted much of the pressure for a wholesale change along the lines that reformers would have liked. Just enough concessions were made to the Progressives to assure popular ratification. The constitution that the convention approved at the completion of its work in February, 1908, was basically a re-writing of the 1850 Constitution, with much of that document retained word-for-word but with some reorganization of the order in which the material was presented. Woman suffrage was turned down, but women taxpayers were allowed to vote on bond issues. The popular Progressive reforms of initiative and referendum were rejected, although the legislature was allowed to refer a measure to a popular vote if it chose to do so. Cities were given the right to home rule and were authorized to own and operate public utilities. Juvenile offenders were placed under the jurisdiction of the probate court, and the legislature was given the power to pass laws limiting the hours of labor for women and children in factories and the conditions under which they worked.

The Constitution of 1850 had been noted for the restrictions it had placed upon the state officials, in contrast to the wide latitude that the 1835 Constitution had provided to permit state officials to exercise their judgment in dealing with the problems of the day. Some of these restrictions were removed in the new constitution but many more were retained. On the whole, then, the 1850 Constitution, although somewhat altered, survived in the Constitution of 1908, leaving to subsequent amendments and a new constitutional convention in 1961 the task of up-dating a pioneer-era constitution to meet the needs of a twentieth-century industrial state.

The Constitution of 1908 was approved by a nearly two-to-one margin at the general election in November, 1908. At the same time, Fred Warner was elected to a third term, becoming the first governor to serve in that office for three consecutive terms. (John S. Barry had held office for three terms but the terms had not been consecutive.) However, Warner's margin of victory in 1908 was the thinnest given to any governor since the election of 1886. Strong opposition had developed to Warner. There were allegations of poor management and corruption in his administration. In addition, even though Warner could and did boast of the impressive list of reforms that had been enacted during his administration, he failed to gain the support of the Progressives. Instead, the Progressives in the Republican party flocked to the standard of a dynamic new leader, Chase Salmon Osborn.

Osborn is one of the most interesting political figures that Michigan has produced and one of only a handful of such figures who came to have much influence outside the state. He was an independent man, unorthodox and non-conforming in his ideas. These attributes were the source of his greatest strength but in the long run were also chiefly responsible for his rapid decline in power in his party and in the state after 1912.[1]

A native of Indiana, where he had been born in 1860, Osborn had become a newspaperman, working for papers in Chicago and Milwaukee before purchasing the weekly paper in Florence, in the Wisconsin portion of the Menominee Iron Range. He sold the paper at a profit in 1887 and moved on to Sault Ste. Marie where he turned that city's *Evening News* into one of the leading papers in northern Michigan. A stint as postmaster of Sault Ste. Marie in the early nineties marked the start of an active political career. Osborn first gained state attention in 1895 when Governor John Rich appointed him state game warden. In this position Osborn first became identified as a staunch advocate of conservation measures. He supported Hazen Pingree, with whom Osborn came to share a belief in the need for reforms. In 1899, Pingree appointed him to the more important position of state railroad commissioner, which required Osborn to spend much time in Lansing, causing him to sell the *Evening*

News, although he retained his permanent residence in Sault Ste. Marie throughout the rest of his life. Osborn's four years as railroad commissioner left him convinced of the need for more effective regulatory measures.

In 1900 Osborn unsuccessfully sought the Republican nomination for governor at the party's state convention and it was his charge that the supporters of the other candidates were paying delegates as much as $3,000 to vote for their man that helped to arouse support for the abandonment of the convention in favor of a direct primary. After completing his term as state railroad commissioner, Osborn turned his attention to the development of iron ore deposits which he had located in the Lake Superior area. As a result, by 1908 he had become financially independent through the sale of these deposits to mining companies and through other investments. He then re-entered the political arena.

The campaign that Osborn now launched to achieve his ambition of becoming governor was astutely managed by Frank Knox, a Grand Rapids man who had served with Teddy Roosevelt's Rough Riders in the Spanish-American War and had then apprenticed in the newspaper business at the Grand Rapids *Herald,* which was owned by a moderate Republican politician, William Alden Smith. In 1900, Osborn had persuaded Knox to take over the Sault Ste. Marie *Evening News.* In 1908, Knox successfully urged a reluctant Osborn to support Warner for a third term, arguing that this would prevent another Republican from gaining the office and thereby give Osborn time to build up support for his own bid for the governorship two years later. Knox also furthered Osborn's career in 1908 by securing his appointment as Michigan's delegate to a White House conference on conservation and also by arranging for Osborn to be the chairman of the Michigan delegation to the Republican national convention of 1908. Warner then rewarded Osborn for his support by appointing him to fill a vacancy on the University of Michigan's board of regents, a job which Osborn tackled in his typically energetic fashion.

On October 16, 1909, Osborn formally entered the race for the Republican gubernatorial nomination in 1910, although Knox and other aides had begun planning the campaign shortly after Warner's re-election in 1908. Osborn traveled throughout the state in his campaign for the nomination, traveling about 12,000 miles in July and August, 1910, and averaging eleven speeches a day—up to a thousand during the course of his entire campaign. He used a Cutting, an automobile manufactured in Jackson during his campaign, taking advantage of the greater flexibility that this new means of transportation gave the political campaigner. He was not the first to do so in Michigan, however. Fred Warner had made extensive use of automobiles in his campaigns, but his earlier efforts in this instance, like his promotion of Progressivism, would be forgotten in face of the greater attention that Osborn's activities have received.

In his speeches, Osborn repudiated Warner, spoke of the scandals of the government in Lansing, promised to wipe out the state deficit and inaugurate an economical, efficient administration of state affairs, and committed himself to serving only one term in order that he might devote his full time to the duties of governor instead of taking time to run for a second term. He had opposition in the party. Fred Warner backed the candidacy of Lieutenant Governor Patrick H. Kelley, although Kelley, in his campaign, sought to disassociate himself from the Warner administration, so widespread had its unpopularity become. Because Kelley had already campaigned and been elected to state office, he was the best known of the candidates. Michigan Supreme Court Justice Robert Montgomery presented a more serious challenge to Osborn, since he supported the same reforms as did Osborn. His withdrawal from the race to accept a federal judicial appointment was therefore a welcome development to the Osborn forces. Grand Rapids businessman Amos Musselman was not considered a serious contender. Oddly enough, Osborn gained some backing from the remnants of the old McMillan machine who, although ideological opposites of Osborn, backed him simply to defeat the candidate backed by Warner. On the other hand, these same politicians wanted to return the conservative United States Senator Julius C. Burrows to the Senate for another term, whereas Osborn gave his backing to the moderate Charles Townsend.

In the Republican primary of September 6, Osborn received 88,270 votes to 52,337 votes for Kelley and 50,721 for Musselman. The general election in November was an anticlimax, as Osborn defeated his Democratic opponent, Lawton T. Hemans (now chiefly remembered as the author of the best biography of Stevens T. Mason) by 43,000 votes. Osborn had become the first and to date the only resident of the Upper Peninsula to be elected governor. He owed his election to the primary system, to an able organization, and to his identification with the Progressive sentiments of the day. The importance of the latter factor was emphasized by the fact that the Progressive-minded Charles Townsend defeated the incumbent Senator Burrows to gain the Republican nomination for the Senate in the 1910 primary. This led to the election of Townsend by the Republican majority in the state legislature, which still, at this time, was vested with the final say in the choice of senators.[2]

Beginning with a speech in Greenville in October, 1909, Os-

born had promised, if elected, to give the state a New Deal, employing a term that Franklin D. Roosevelt would popularize two decades
later. Osborn's New Deal called for a series of measures to be
enacted, most of which fit within the framework of Progressivism.
One of his major achievements as governor was the adoption of a
workmen's compensation law in 1912. Under the old English common law, an employer was not responsible for an injury suffered by
an employee on the job if it could be proved (as it usually could) that
he or a fellow-employee had been negligent. Under the new law
there was no escape from employer liability in such cases, and although it was not the first such law in the country, Michigan's workmen's compensation act became a model that other states would
follow. Osborn kept his promise to practice strict economy in state
government, discharging many employees in the process, and leaving
office with a large surplus in the treasury.[3] He was one of the first of
the state's governors concerned about the proliferation of state agencies, boards, and commissions. His efforts to improve the efficiency
of the state government and to restore to the governor the power as
the state's chief executive officer that he had under the Constitution
of 1835, marked the start of a fight that would enlist the support of
strong-willed governors from that time on.

Osborn, who resembled Pingree in a number of ways, had to
battle a conservative state senate over appointments and other matters. He called the legislature back for special sessions, as Pingree
had done when it failed to carry out his recommendations. Osborn
emerged from these fights with new laws giving more powers to the
state tax commission and regulating railroads, express companies,
telephone companies, banks, insurance, and saloons. In cases where
Osborn was turned down, such as on his proposals for the initiative,
referendum, and recall, he planted the seeds that were to bring a
harvest of reform after his term had ended.

While Osborn was battling for Progressive reform in Michigan,
Progressive sentiment in the Republican party was turning against
President William Howard Taft, who had been nominated for the
Presidency in 1908 upon the recommendation of retiring President
Theodore Roosevelt and subsequently had been elected over
William Jennings Bryan. Taft continued Roosevelt's program in several areas, such as prosecuting trusts, but he lacked Roosevelt's flair
for publicity. Taft's support of a high tariff act early in his administration offended Progressives. Robert M. LaFollette of Wisconsin
emerged as the leader of the Republican Progressives, and by 1911
he was mounting a campaign to seize the party's Presidential nomination away from Taft in 1912. When Teddy Roosevelt returned from

a world tour in 1910 he soon became aware of the Progressives' disenchantment with Taft, a feeling that he too began to share.

As the campaign of 1912 approached, Michigan's Governor Osborn played a key role in the efforts of the Republican Progressives to dump Taft in favor of a reform-minded candidate. Initially, Osborn seemed to be favoring LaFollette, but though he liked LaFollette's ideas he disliked the man, and in a speech in Lansing on January 2, 1912, he dealt the LaFollette campaign a crippling blow by declaring that despite the Wisconsin senator's fine reform record he did not have the qualifications to be President. Osborn called upon LaFollette to withdraw and join with the Progressives in an effort to persuade Roosevelt to enter the race.

Roosevelt was eager to run but he wished to make it appear that he was being drafted for the race. In January and February, 1912, therefore, Osborn and his faithful aide, Knox, worked with Roosevelt on the draft of a letter. Osborn then got a group of his fellow Republican Progressive governors to sign this letter which expressed the hope that because of the demands of the public, if the nomination came to Roosevelt—"unsolicited and unsought"—he would accept it. When the letter was presented to Roosevelt he acted appropriately surprised and flattered, and declared that under such circumstances he would be obliged to accept the nomination.[4]

A spirited contest now ensued between Taft and Roosevelt supporters for delegates to the June Republican National Convention that would be held in Chicago. In a few states where Presidential primaries had been adopted, the voters showed their preference for T. R. Osborn tried to induce the state legislature to approve such a primary for Michigan. A bill was passed, but Osborn was unable to get the two-thirds majority in the senate that was required to give the act immediate effect, thus delaying the implementation of the act until the 1916 Presidential campaign and killing Osborn's hopes of using it to influence the selection of delegates in 1912.

The Republican state convention was held in Bay City on April 11, 1912. It was calculated that the twelve delegates to the national convention that would be chosen by Congressional district caucuses would be evenly split between Roosevelt and Taft supporters. The fight centered around the six delegates elected at large by the convention as a whole. Frank Knox, chairman of the Republican State Central Committee which had charge of convention arrangements, was, of course, a Roosevelt man, but Paul King, the secretary, and a majority of the committee members were Taft supporters. Two delegations from both Wayne and Calhoun counties—one for Taft and the other for Roosevelt—claimed seats in the convention. The Taft majority on the state committee sought to seat the Taft delegates from these counties and exclude the Roosevelt delegates. Within the hall disorder was rampant and there were several fist fights. The keynote speaker, Senator Albert Beveridge of Indiana, was escorted out of the hall for his own protection. Police finally restored order, but in the meantime the Roosevelt delegates had entered the hall, held a meeting in one corner and had chosen six Roosevelt at-large delegates to the national convention. The remaining members chose Taft delegates. Unfortunately, the Roosevelt meeting in the corner failed to name a secretary, so there was no official record of its proceedings.

The Republican National Committee, which had charge of arrangements for the Chicago convention, was Taft-dominated. There were several contested delegations, including Michigan's, but all the Taft delegations were seated temporarily and the convention was then allowed to decide which delegation in each case should receive permanent seats. When the Michigan case came before the convention, the lack of an official record of the selection of the Roosevelt delegates proved fatal. The Taft delegation retained its seats, and Taft won renomination for a second term.

Because of a severe foot injury, Chase Osborn had been unable to attend either the state or national party conventions. Following the action of the Republicans in nominating Taft, Osborn's actions caused consternation to Roosevelt and his supporters, who had begun planning a third-party effort. Osborn urged Roosevelt to do nothing, unless the Democrats in their convention at Baltimore nominated a reactionary. On July 2, after forty-six ballots, the Democrats nominated the Progressive Governor of New Jersey, Woodrow Wilson, and Osborn announced his support for Wilson. Roosevelt, meanwhile, proceeded with the organization of a separate Progressive party which nominated him for the Presidency in August. Osborn then reversed himself and came out in support of Roosevelt although he did not actively campaign for the Rough Rider until late in October when he helped to carry on the fight for the Progressive candidate after Roosevelt had been side-lined by a would-be assassin's bullet.

On the state level, Osborn stuck with his one-term pledge and was not a candidate for re-election. The Republicans nominated Amos Musselman to succeed Osborn. Roosevelt's Progressive party put up a full state ticket headed by Lucius W. Watkins as its gubernatorial candidate while the Democrats nominated Woodbridge N. Ferris for governor. The latter, who had also been the party's candidate for governor in 1904, had become widely and favorably known in Michigan as the founder and head of Ferris Institute in Big Rapids. Ferris Institute was a school where practical subjects were emphasized and where students with small means could get an education. Ferris and his wife took a deep personal interest in each student, and over the years made many friends.

It was the split in the Republican ranks that gave the Democrats both nationally and in Michigan their best chance at victory in many years. The Michigan campaign was especially confusing, with the incumbent Republican governor openly supporting the Progressive candidate for President, but at the same time insisting that he was still a Republican and refusing to come out in support of the Progressives' slate of state candidates. Because of Osborn's backing and Roosevelt's popularity, Roosevelt received the plurality of the popular vote in Michigan and gained all of the state's electoral votes—the only time between 1852 and 1932 that the Republican Presidential candidate was shut out in Michigan.[5] Wilson, the national winner in this election, ran third in Michigan, behind Roosevelt and Taft, but in the gubernatorial contest, the Democrat, Ferris, ran ahead of his opponents, receiving 194,017 votes to 169,963 for Musselman and 152,909 for Watkins, thus becoming only the second Democrat to be elected governor of Michigan since the formation of the Republican party in 1854.[6] Ferris' victory, however, was more an indication of his personal popularity than it was of any resurgent Democratic strength, for the Republicans picked up all the other elective state executive offices, with the Progressive candidates for those offices running close seconds and the Democratic candidates trailing in third place. The Republicans also retained comfortable majorities in both houses of the legislature. The election demonstrated that the Republican party was still clearly the majority party in Michigan, but it also was the first indication of an independent streak in the Michigan electorate that sometimes would lead it to vote for the candidate and not for the party—a tendency that would become more and more evident in later years.

As governor, Ferris pushed for additional Progressive reforms and although he lacked a majority of his own party in the legislature, he was able to achieve much of what he asked for through a coalition of reform-minded legislators. In 1913, this reform coalition submitted to the voters a proposed constitutional amendment to provide for the Progressive reform known as Initiative, Referendum, and Recall. With its adoption, the voters had the power, through the petition process, to propose or reject legislation and to remove elected officials from office. Along with the institution of the direct primary, this furthered the goal of the Progressives to democratize the entire political process, and provided a mechanism that voters would employ with increasing frequency in the years ahead.

Ferris would have had little chance of winning a second term in 1914 if the Republicans had reunited their forces, but that party was still torn by dissension and was unable to mobilize its full strength against Ferris. A Detroit attorney, Alex Groesbeck, had emerged from the wreckage of the 1912 campaign as a powerful new force in the Republican party. Although he had been a Taft supporter, as the newly selected chairman of the Republican State Central Committee Groesbeck sought to persuade the Roosevelt insurgents to return to their party. In addition, Groesbeck persuaded the party regulars to accept these defectors and give them committee assignments. Groesbeck was quite successful in these efforts. In the process, he was also seeking support for his own campaign to become the party's gubernatorial nominee in 1914. When Groesbeck formally launched his campaign late in 1913 he recognized he would have opposition. Chase Osborn, after leaving the governor's office at the end of 1912, had gone on a world tour, proclaiming disinterest in seeking the governorship again. When he returned to Michigan, however, he quickly responded to the calls of his friends and entered the 1914 primary race. Groesbeck figured that Osborn would be strong in the outstate areas but that his own support in Wayne County would offset Osborn's support elsewhere in the state. Although basically a conservative, Groesbeck sought support from the Progressive wing of the party by advocating a few reforms, such as the abolition of child labor and the establishment of a labor conciliatory service. He also counted on the support of the conservative party regulars who blamed Osborn for the rift in the party ranks that had lost them the governorship in 1912. However, Frederick C. Martindale, who was serving his third term as secretary of state and was also from Detroit, entered the primary and angrily attacked Groesbeck for seeking to deny him the nomination to which he felt he was entitled because of his past record of success in state elections. The result was another badly split Republican party, with Osborn emerging as the victor in the primary with 58,405 votes to Martindale's 47,942 and Groesbeck's 43,137. Much of the Osborn vote probably came from Democrats who crossed party lines (a practice that was possible under the secret primary election system adopted in 1913) since Ferris had no opposition in the Democratic primary.

The remnants of Roosevelt's Progressive party put forth the educator, Henry R. Pattengill, as their candidate for governor, and in the November general election he received over 36,000 votes, which was approximately the margin of difference between Ferris, who got 212,000 votes, to win re-election, and Osborn, who received around 176,000 votes. The defeat marks the virtual end of Osborn's political career, which had seemed to hold such great promise only four years earlier. He would be a candidate for office on other occasions in later years but would never come close to victory. His fatal error had been in announcing that he would serve for only one term as governor. Had Osborn run for a second term in 1912 he would probably have won and could have won a third term in 1914, in which case he would have been a strong candidate for the Republican Presidential nomination in 1916.

Woodbridge Ferris' victory was again a personal, not a party, triumph. In the other contests the Democrats were swamped, with the Republicans winning twenty-nine of the thirty-two seats in the senate and ninety-five of one hundred seats in the lower house. The party also retained its hold on all the other state executive offices. Obviously, many Republicans had voted for Ferris, whom they considered less objectionable than Osborn. Ferris, in fact, had courted this anti-Osborn conservative Republican vote by repudiating some of his own party's reform platform, although after the election Ferris returned to his more normal Progressive reform position. By 1916, however, the Progressive movement had about run its course. The Republicans in Michigan finally closed ranks, giving the Republican candidate for President, Charles Evans Hughes, the state's electoral vote, while Albert E. Sleeper from Bad Axe, a candidate more in the stand-pat mold of the pre-Progressive era, won the gubernatorial race. Ferris, undoubtedly foreseeing certain defeat if he had sought a third term, was not a candidate for re-election.

*   *   *   *   *

Along with the political reforms that are the best-known accomplishments of the Progressive Period, there were other developments in these years that reflected greater consciousness of human suffering, of the plight of the poor and handicapped, and of the needs of the less fortunate members of society. During the latter part of the nineteenth century, social Darwinism had been popular, and by some this meant that progress came through social organizations that did not interfere with the natural law of the survival of the fittest. But such a concept was never generally accepted, and the Progressive Movement, with its distinctively humanitarian emphasis, gave new impetus to programs and approaches which, like the Progressives' political reforms, had their roots in the past.

One of the areas of concern was that of the treatment of criminals, with the early years of the twentieth century seeing an increasing move toward reforming criminals rather than punishing them. Back in 1837, the legislature had authorized the construction of a state prison at Jackson. The concept of a prison at that time had become one of providing a place where a person could be restrained from doing further harm to society. Although the whipping post had been used in Detroit in the early 1830s, the idea of inflicting physical suffering upon criminal offenders as a punishment for their wrongdoing was giving way to a more humane attitude. The prison at Jackson was modeled after one at Auburn, New York, which provided individual cells for prisoners but allowed them to work together in groups during the day. The first prison at Jackson was a wooden building surrounded by a palisade, but a new structure with stone walls was started in 1841. A massive, medieval-like prison was built in the 1880s, which was replaced in the 1930s by a huge new facility which earned the dubious honor of being called the world's largest walled penal institution—it housed approximately 5,500 prisoners.

Michigan was the first state in the Union to abolish capital punishment. One of the reasons for this was an incident across the river from Detroit in Canada, where, in 1838, a man named Fitzpatrick was convicted of a crime on circumstantial evidence and was hanged for the offense. A few months later another man confessed on his deathbed that he had been guilty of the crime for which Fitzpatrick had been executed. This caused a revulsion of feeling on both sides of the border. The abolition of capital punishment came about when a revised code of laws, adopted on May 18, 1846, set the maximum penalty for murder as "solitary confinement at hard labor . . . for life." There was some resistance to the change, but there was no widespread demand for the restoration of capital punishment. However, the substitution of lifetime solitary confinement for convicted murderers proved to be a less humane form of punishment than the death penalty, rendering nearly half of those so confined hopelessly insane within a few years. As a result, a legislative act in 1861 permitted prison authorities greater leeway in the handling of murderers, thus inaugurating more humane approaches.[7]

Over the years, other more lenient methods of treating criminals replaced earlier practices. The whipping post was abolished. In 1875 the legislature prohibited the "water cure" and lashes inflicted on the bare body at the state prison. In 1877 a reformatory was established at Ionia for "first offenders." By about 1887 women convicted of felonies were sent to the Detroit House of Correction. Not until 1977 was a separate state prison for women opened near Ypsilanti. The Northern State Prison was built at Marquette in 1889.

The Ionia State Hospital was opened in 1885 for mentally insane criminals. Beginning in 1896, good behavior in prisons could be rewarded by paroles under supervision—a way of reorienting the prisoner to the duties of citizenship. The principle of probation was recognized as early as 1903. Gradually it was recognized that in most cases crime arises out of broken families, poverty, and emotional imbalance rather than from the innate malevolence of the individual.[8]

The practice of treating juvenile offenders separately from adults began as early as 1855 with the establishment in Lansing of the Michigan Reform School, later the Boys' Training School. The Michigan Reform School for Girls, later the Girls' Training School, was established at Adrian in 1879. In later years these facilities were removed from the control of the Department of Corrections and placed under the control of the Department of Social Services. Beginning in 1909, a special division of the probate court in each county was given jurisdiction in juvenile cases.

Significant advances were made in the early twentieth century in the development of medical facilities in the state. In an earlier day the care of the sick had been regarded as the function of the home. Society was concerned only when a disease was communicable or contagious. The first general hospital in the state, St. Vincent's, was opened in Detroit in 1845 by the Sisters of Charity. Harper Hospital in Detroit was established during the Civil War for sick and injured soldiers. Due to a lack of knowledge concerning asepsis and its importance, disease was often spread rather than cured in hospitals. Not until the latter part of the nineteenth century, when the use of antiseptics and anesthesia became common, were many hospitals built. During the 1880s and 1890s private benefactions made possible the founding of general hospitals in many of the larger cities. Grace Hospital in Detroit was incorporated in 1888. By the turn of the century, Battle Creek, Bay City, Grand Rapids, Hancock, Ishpeming, Kalamazoo, Lansing, Manistee, Marquette, Menominee, Mt. Clemens, and Saginaw had general hospitals. The University Hospital at Ann Arbor had its beginnings as an adjunct of the Medical School soon after 1850. Facilities for this hospital were very inadequate until the end of the century when construction was begun by the state in 1899 which marked the true beginnings of the University of Michigan Medical Center.

The care of the mentally ill had been recognized as a state function as early as 1848 when the Kalamazoo Asylum for the Insane was established by legislative act. It was not until 1859, however, that the institution received its first patients. Up to this time, mentally ill

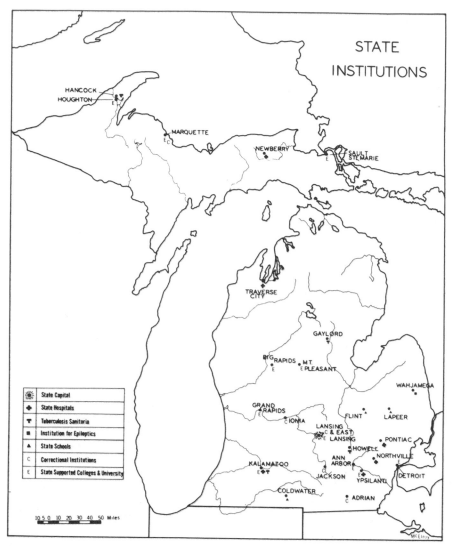

STATE
INSTITUTIONS

HANCOCK
HOUGHTON
E

MARQUETTE
E C

NEWBERRY
E

SAULT
STE MARIE
E

TRAVERSE
CITY

GAYLORD

BIG RAPIDS   M.T.
E   E PLEASANT

WAHJAMEGA

GRAND
RAPIDS
E   FLINT   LAPEER
C IONIA
LANSING
C & EAST
E LANSING   PONTIAC

HOWELL
ANN   NORTHVILLE
ARBOR   E
E

KALAMAZOO   DETROIT
E T   JACKSON YPSILANTI
C   E
COLDWATER
C ADRIAN

☀	State Capital
✚	State Hospitals
⊤	Tuberculosis Sanitoria
■	Institution for Epileptics
▲	State Schools
C	Correctional Institutions
E	State Supported Colleges & University

10 5 0 10 20 30 40 50 Miles

McElroy

persons were cared for in homes. If they were violent, they were confined in an attic, a shed, or even an iron cage in the yard. Dorothea Dix, famous for her work in calling attention to the plight of these unfortunates, spoke before the Michigan legislature to make its members more aware of the problem. For some years, however, few families would permit their loved ones to be committed to an asylum; to do so was considered a social disgrace. But in the first decade of the twentieth century, the public began to think of mental illness in the same way it thought of physical afflictions. Meanwhile other asylums had been established by the state: at Pontiac in 1873, at Traverse City in 1881, and at Newberry in 1893. In 1911 and 1912 the names of these institutions were changed to State Hospitals. A fifth such hospital was located at Ypsilanti in 1929. Tremendous advances were made in the treatment of mental cases, leading to a steady increase in demand for institutional treatment. Private mental hospitals were established to supplement the state hospitals. The Wayne County Hospital at Eloise was originally built to receive mental patients from that county, but most of its patients came to be cared for by the state.

The era of the Progressive Movement also saw the state assume the responsibility for the care of other kinds of illness and disabilities. Michigan had the first state law providing for tax-paid hospitalization for tuberculosis patients. The first state tuberculosis sanitarium was built at Howell in 1905. In subsequent decades other state sanitariums were opened at Gaylord, Kalamazoo, and Hancock, in addition to a tuberculosis unit at the University of Michigan Hospital, and fourteen approved county, city, and private tuberculosis hospitals. Free chest x-rays were provided for the early detection of tuberculosis. Several Michigan doctors, including Dr. John Alexander and Dr. Cameron Haight of the University of Michigan, and Dr. E. J. O'Brien of Detroit, were pioneers in the field of chest surgery for the treatment of the disease. Much later, the use of antibiotics was another factor in reducing the death rate from tuberculosis in Michigan from 103 per 100,000 in 1900 to 5 per 100,000 by 1958. So rapid was the decline of tuberculosis as a major killer that in 1959 all the state sanitariums except the one at Kalamazoo were turned over to the care of mental patients.

The treatment of epilepsy was also assumed as a state responsibility. In 1895 an institution was opened at Lapeer for the care and treatment of epileptics. After 1914 this became an institution for mentally retarded children, with the severe epileptic cases being treated at a new institution established at Wahjamega.

State responsibility for the handicapped was recognized in 1848 by the passage of legislation that appropriated the proceeds from the sale of twenty-four sections of salt-spring lands for the establishment of an "asylum for the deaf, dumb, blind, and insane." In addition to the institution for the insane at Kalamazoo, the state provided a school for deaf and blind children at Flint in 1854, with a separate school for the blind opened at Lansing in 1879. As the number of deaf children increased, the state, instead of building additional schools for them, provided state aid to school districts to permit them to maintain special classes for the hard of hearing. The first law giving such aid was passed in 1899. Under an act passed in 1923 similar aid was provided to districts that maintained special classes for blind and crippled children. In 1921 federal aid also became available for the vocational rehabilitation of the handicapped.

As early as 1871 a state school for dependent children was opened at Coldwater. Beginning in 1929 such children were cared for in licensed homes and attended regular schools. Private service organizations which developed early in the twentieth century, such as Rotary, Kiwanis, and Lions, made important contributions to the care of crippled children. Rotary, in particular, was instrumental in the formation of the Michigan Society for Crippled Children in 1921. Private charity, however, had been devoted to the welfare of children since the earliest years. An orphan asylum existed in Detroit as early as 1836. Among the associations that arose that were devoted to child welfare were the Michigan Children's Aid Society, founded in 1891, and the Children's Aid Society of Detroit, which developed in 1914 but was an outgrowth of two earlier societies, the Home for the Friendless, a Presbyterian women's organization formed in 1862 to care for the orphans of soldiers, and the Society for the Prevention of Cruelty to Children, established in 1893.

The Boy Scout movement, originating in England in 1908, reached Michigan about 1910. The first Boy Scout Councils, formed in 1911 and 1912, were centered at Grand Rapids, Flint, and Lansing. Troops were organized rapidly; business and professional men volunteered as troop leaders, while churches and schools cooperated fully. The movement helped to bring about a rebirth of interest in out-of-doors activities, but its cardinal purpose was to build good citizens. The Girl Scouts formed their first Michigan troop at Detroit in 1916; by 1938 there were 617 troops in the state. About 1920 the first group of Camp Fire Girls was formed at Grand Rapids, and this organization also grew rapidly. The Young Men's Christian Association (Y.M.C.A.) is somewhat older. A "young men's society" organized in Detroit prior to the Civil War was the predecessor of the Detroit Y.M.C.A. When the first state convention was held in 1868, some fifteen associations sent delegates. But the greatest growth came after 1900. Activities expanded along several lines. Athletic activities were important from the first; the Y.M.C.A. pioneered in the introduction of basketball. As early as 1903 the Jackson and Grand Rapids associations were operating boys' camps. Camp Hayo-went-ha, built on Torch Lake north of Traverse City, and opened in 1904, is reputed to be the first permanent boys' camp in the western states. The camp movement grew by leaps and bounds after World War I, with many different organizations sponsoring summer camps for boys and girls. The first Y.W.C.A. was organized in 1885 at Kalamazoo. Through a program of physical training, education, and social activities the Y.W.C.A. sought to provide a wholesome center for the use of young women employed away from home. By 1934 a total of seventeen cities had Y.W.C.A. organizations in Michigan.

These were but a few of many social agencies that grew up in cities and even in smaller communities during the first two decades of the twentieth century. Others came later. Many of them sought to obtain funds for buildings and for operations expenses by annual "drives." By the time of World War I the number of drives for funds to support social agencies had become so great that some sort of co-operative effort to raise money was clearly called for. Combined drives were held in Grand Rapids and Detroit in 1917 to support the war relief agencies as well as local agencies. The "community chest" plan was adopted by most major Michigan cities between 1917 and 1922. It soon became the accepted way to raise funds to carry on the work of such organizations as the Boy Scouts, Girl Scouts, Y.M.C.A., Y.W.C.A., Salvation Army, orphanages, homes for the aged, child-welfare clinics, and a variety of other agencies. The word "charity" disappeared as citizens began to regard the support of agencies dedicated to social betterment as a civic obligation. The proliferation of such humanitarian activities in the early years of the twentieth century, however, only suggested the enormous growth that was still to occur in later years.

Train carriers on the Great Lakes (Ludington, Michigan)

24

WORLD WAR I AND ITS AFTERMATH

On April 6, 1917, Congress voted to declare war on Germany, four days after President Woodrow Wilson had sent its members a war message. When Wilson had called Congress into special session to consider a declaration of war, the Michigan delegation had reportedly been the first to assure the President of its unanimous support. These assurances accurately reflected the sentiments in Michigan which, since the outbreak of the war in Europe in August, 1914, had sympathized more and more with the Allied cause rather than with the Germans and their allies. Hundreds of Michigan men went to Canada to enlist in Canadian military regiments. In 1916, Albert Sleeper, obviously misjudging the temper of the majority of the voters, had actively sought the support of Michigan's German-American vote. Anti-German sentiment was already so strong that Sleeper was widely criticized. Once the country was at war with Germany, the effects on those of German background in Michigan were often tragic.

At the time there were some 80,000 Michiganians of German birth and another 20,000 of Austrian birth. In addition, there were the offspring of the large number of German immigrants who had settled in the state since the mid-nineteenth century and had exerted an enormous influence on many aspects of the state's development. Although the loyalty of the vast majority of Michigan's German population could not be doubted, fantastic stories about their activities began to circulate. Housewives heard the rumor that enemy aliens were putting ground glass in the sugar supplies. One old German who had built a high tower overlooking Lake Michigan was reputed to have a wireless set that relayed messages back and forth between the Fatherland and Mexico. It became unpopular to play German music, and the teaching of German, which had ranked as one of the most popular and widely taught of foreign languages in the state, was universally abandoned by schools and colleges, with French and Spanish taking its place. Otherwise respected scholars such as William H. Hobbs, geologist and Arctic explorer from the University of Michigan, and that same university's professor of history, Claude H. Van Tyne, actively took part in or lent their names and reputations to preparedness and patriotic activities that in their anti-German phases often degenerated into shameful witch-hunting.[1] Hamburger became "liberty sausage" or "salisbury steak," while frankfurters became "hot dogs" because Hamburg and Frankfurt were German cities. The little town of Berlin near Grand Rapids changed its name to Marne, in honor of the 1914 battle where the French had blunted the initial German offensive in the west. (The annual fair in the town continued, however, to be called the "Berlin Fair.") Those who failed to buy Liberty Bonds or support war drives of other kinds frequently had their homes smeared with yellow paint.

On February 18, 1917, Governor Sleeper sent a message to Wilson, assuring him of Michigan's support in the event of war. At the request of the War Department, the state made a preliminary survey of the number of men who would be available for war service. Late in March, Sleeper asked the state's attorney general, Alex Groesbeck, to draft legislation to put Michigan on a war footing. The resulting bills, which were quickly adopted by the legislature in mid-April, called for the organization of a state militia to act as a home defense force when the Michigan National Guard was called up, and established a War Preparedness Board. The board, which was comprised of the governor, attorney general, auditor general, secretary of state, state treasurer, and superintendent of public instruction, administered a five-million-dollar fund which the state was authorized to use for various war-related expenditures. The board held its first meeting on April 6, the day war was declared, although the legislation establishing the board had not yet been enacted. When the National Guard was called into service, the board began using its funds to supply the men with shoes and blankets that the federal government was unable to supply. The board provided aid for a number of activities during the war, and administered its money so well that the fund was not exhausted by the end of the war.

All told, Michigan furnished 175,000 men to the armed forces during the war, of which number about 5,000 died in service and about 15,000 were wounded. Michigan's contribution to the armed forces included 45,917 volunteers. Governor Sleeper thought that voluntary enlistment alone should be employed to fill the ranks of the nation's fighting forces, as had generally been the case in previous wars, with each state being assigned a quota to fill. He spoke out against the draft, which the federal government relied on to meet the nation's manpower needs. The hapless Sleeper again came under heavy criticism for his views, with people again wondering aloud about the governor's loyalty. On the advice of his associates, Sleeper quickly sought to set these suspicions at rest and in June, 1917, when the first draft registration was held, he wholeheartedly participated in the proceedings.[2]

This registration on June 5 indicated that a total of 380,752 men in Michigan between the ages of twenty-one and thirty were subject to the draft. A few more were added to the list in a subsequent registration, and in 1918 when Congress lowered the minimum draft age to eighteen and set the maximum age at forty-five, the number in Michigan eligible for the draft was increased to 873,383, of whom more than 200,000 were aliens. These men were then classified into five groups, with the first group, consisting of single men, married men with no dependents, and unskilled workers, subject to immediate conscription. Thirty percent of the state's registrants fell into this first group. The state was shocked, however, when about forty percent of the 115,412 men who were called up under the draft failed to pass their physical examinations. As a result, the legislature enlarged the powers of the state health commission to make it a stronger force in promoting health and physical fitness. The draft examination figures also were a major reason for the adoption of physical education requirements in schools and colleges.

The members of Michigan's National Guard were the only ones from the state to see extensive and prolonged service on the war fronts in Europe. These units had been called up in 1916 and had taken part in the expedition led by General John J. Pershing against the Mexican revolutionary leader, Pancho Villa. Now at the start of the war the Michigan guardsmen were again called up and were combined with the Wisconsin guard to form the Thirty-second or Red Arrow Division. After training in Texas, the division began to be shipped over to France in January, 1918, with the last unit arriving there in March. By May, four battalions were in the front lines, and the division was in combat almost constantly until November 11. It took part in the battle of the Aisne, the Oise-Aisne offensive, and the Meuse-Argonne action which finally broke the back of German resistance. Casualties were high, with 2,671 men killed and 10,242 wounded out of a total complement of about 27,000.[3]

Shortly after the start of the war the federal government announced plans to construct camps in a number of places in the country where the men who were drafted would be housed and trained. Communities in Wisconsin and Michigan were invited to submit offers of land on which one such camp would be located. The Battle Creek Chamber of Commerce won the competition by locating about eight thousand acres of land west of that city which could be leased to the government, although the chamber had to track down and secure options from the owners of the more than 130 separate parcels of land that comprised this acreage. The army liked the location because of the railroad facilities that were available at the site and also because it was in a "dry" area where draftees would have a hard time getting a drink when they had a weekend pass. Construction began at the site in the summer of 1917, and in October a formal dedication took place. The camp was named in honor of General George A. Custer, and Custer's widow, still alive forty-one years after her husband's death, took part in the ceremonies. The last of the three thousand buildings in the camp was completed a few weeks after the end of the war, with the construction costs totalling nearly $10,000,000.

The first contingents of draftees from Michigan and Wisconsin began arriving at Camp Custer in September, 1917. They became part of the Eighty-fifth Division, to which Michigan ultimately contributed 30,291 men, over a third of them from Detroit. An epidemic of spinal meningitis in the bitter winter of 1917-18 caused the death of a number of men in the camp, but by March, 1918, the division was ready for duty overseas, where it arrived in July and August. Most of the members of the division served in France as replacement units for front-line forces and were demobilized at Camp Custer in the spring of 1919. However, the large complement of Michigan men in the division's 339th Infantry Regiment found themselves, much to their surprise, in Archangel, Russia, where they were a major part of America's Polar Bear expedition which aided the White Russian forces in their futile efforts to unseat Russia's new Communist regime. These Michiganians did not return home until the summer of 1919.[4]

After the departure of the Eighty-fifth Division from Camp Custer, new draftees were organized into the Fourteenth Division which had not yet completed its training when the fighting was halted by the Armistice on November 11, 1918. Although these men would never see the battlefront, many of them died as a result of an influenza epidemic in 1918-19. Almost ten thousand men were admitted to the hospital during the epidemic, with many of them developing pneumonia and 674 dying. By March, 1919, only one company remained in the camp, the rest having been demobilized, but the camp continued to be used for peacetime military training activities in the following years.

Another military facility of permanent importance established in Michigan during the war was Selfridge Field, near Mount Clemens, opened on July 8, 1917. Henry B. Joy of the Packard Motor Car Company had purchased the land at this site earlier, foreseeing the role that aviation would play in the war. He offered the land to the federal government, which proceeded to establish the country's first school of aerial gunnery. Among the many fliers who received training at Selfridge was America's most famous war ace, Eddie Rickenbacker.

The war also had a great impact on the home front. When the United States entered the war, the Allies in Europe were in urgent need of food. Herbert Hoover, the food administrator in Wilson's government, took steps to conserve food supplies in this country through such voluntary measures as proclaiming certain days "meatless days" or "wheatless days," as well as taking action to encourage greater production by the farmers. In Michigan, the War Preparedness Board dipped into its fund to furnish Michigan farmers with additional seeds and to encourage city dwellers to plant gardens. The result was a twenty-five percent increase in food production in the state in 1917. In 1918, as the shortage of labor on the farms became critical, the board purchased a thousand Ford tractors and sold them to Michigan farmers at cost. Emergency measures were also taken during harvest time when children, college students, and women were urged, as a patriotic duty, to help out the neighboring farms. In one instance in October, 1917, schools in Van Buren County were closed for three weeks to allow students to harvest the area's fruit crop.

The fuel shortage that developed in the early months of the war caused even greater problems. At this time, most homes and businesses burned coal, and Michigan needed about 15,000,000 tons of coal annually, of which amount Michigan coal mines, despite wartime efforts to increase production, could furnish no more than ten percent. Extraordinary demands for coal in war plants, the disruption of normal rail and shipping facilities, and the labor shortage all combined to produce an acute fuel shortage in the country. To top it all, the winter of 1917-18 was one of the coldest and most prolonged on record. A state fuel administrator sought to stretch existing supplies of coal as far as possible as it became more difficult to stockpile additional supplies. Factories, which had to get along with no more than two or three days' supply of coal on hand, frequently had to shut down because of a lack of fuel, and in the last weeks of 1917 more than two thousand Detroit families had no coal at all. In northern Michigan wood was used as a substitute for coal, but in other areas not so fortunately situated, local authorities occasionally confiscated coal shipments that were being hauled by rail through the area for some other destination. In January, 1918, the hours that business establishments could remain open were limited as a fuel-saving measure. Public lighting was reduced, churches could be heated only six hours a week, and theaters were closed on Mondays and Tuesdays. On January 16, the national fuel administration shut down all manufacturing plants east of the Mississippi for five days, and on Mondays for each of the following nine weeks. Restrictions remained in effect during the summer in anticipation of another crisis during the following winter but the Armistice on November 11 ended the emergency.

To help raise the money needed to finance the war effort, four Liberty Loan drives were held during the war, plus a Victory Loan drive after the Armistice. Each Federal Reserve District in the country was assigned a quota to fill. Michigan's lower peninsula fell into the Seventh District, the Upper Peninsula into the Ninth District. In each case, Michigan exceeded its assigned quota. It was estimated that one of every four persons in the state contributed to the drives by buying Liberty Bonds or Liberty Stamps. High pressure techniques were used to promote sales, with the names of those who had not contributed sometimes being published in local papers. In some instances, vigilantes took revenge on those who were branded as slackers or pro-German for not taking part in bond drives. Governor Sleeper, among others, issued a warning against those who took the law into their own hands. The example of Ontonagon County, with one of the highest percentages of foreign-born population in the state, and which exceeded its quota in one drive by 250 percent, put to shame the contentions of many of the vigilantes that there was a correlation between foreign-birth and a lack of patriotic sentiment.

Michigan's major contribution to the war effort, however, was the war materials turned out by this increasingly industrialized state. While the iron and copper mines of the Upper Peninsula broke past production records in providing vast amounts of these vital resources, the factories in southern Michigan, although not achieving the kind of spectacular results that would cause the state in the Second World War to be referred to as the "Arsenal of Democracy," demonstrated the degree to which manufacturing had replaced in importance the earlier types of economic activities for which Michi-

gan had been famous. Scores of steel ships were launched at shipyards in Saginaw, Wyandotte, Ecorse, and several other port cities to
help meet the critical shortage of ocean-going vessels required to
supply the European forces. Other manufacturing plants were remodeled for conversion from their normal peace-time output to war
production. It was natural that Michigan automobile companies received the most attention. Passenger car production was not halted
during the war, as it would be at the start of World War II, but the
war contracts that these companies received, plus the priorities given
in allocating scarce materials to war production, caused a sharp reduction in civilian car production by 1918. Much of the emphasis,
naturally, was on the production of various kinds of motorized
equipment for the army. A convoy of Packard trucks left Detroit on
December 12, 1917, and was driven to Baltimore, where the trucks
were shipped on to France, dramatically demonstrating the as-yet
untested potential of long-distance truck transport which could make
it through despite the wretched state of the roads. The Reo factory in
Lansing produced armored trucks, and the Oakland plant in Pontiac
turned out some tanks, but the true versatility of Michigan's auto
industry was demonstrated by the contribution made by Packard in
developing the Liberty airplane engine, which Packard and several
other Michigan firms then produced. No other Michigan company,
however, received as much attention for its war work as did the Ford
Motor Company, which demonstrated, with some success, that the
mass production techniques for which it had become famous could
be applied to the production of submarine chasers—vessels that were
built in the new plant that Ford had begun constructing on the River
Rouge.

The outbreak of the war in Europe in the summer of 1914 had
come at a time when Henry Ford had emerged as one of the best-
known businessmen in the country, and newsmen, ever on the lookout for a new celebrity, began to interview Ford and found him
willing to express an opinion on almost any topic. It turned out that
Ford was a pacifist. In August, 1915, he expressed a desire to spend
his fortune, if need be, to keep the country out of war and to restore
peace to the world. He repeatedly declared that he would never
produce any war materials, preferring to burn down his factory before he would take on such a task. "The word 'murderer' should be
embroidered on the breast of every soldier and every naval sailor,"
Ford asserted. Such remarks were too much for James Couzens, who
sought to kill an article in *Ford Times* that presented Henry Ford's
pacifist views. "You can't stop anything," Ford told Couzens. "It's
going to stay in." "All right," the business manager replied, "I quit."[5]

In November, 1915, the pacifist, Rosika Schwimmer, and Louis P. Lochner, secretary of the International Federation of Students, came to see Ford to ask his help in organizing an international peace conference. Ford enthusiastically agreed to the idea. He went to New York with Lochner where he and other pacifists decided to sail to Europe in an attempt to bring the warring nations to the conference table. Ford chartered an ocean liner—the *Oscar II*—and after failing to persuade President Wilson either to come along or to give his support to the mission, Ford departed, telling reporters: "We're going to try to get the boys out of the trenches before Christmas." From the outset, the project met with ridicule in the press or at best faint praise from those who said it would do little harm. With scarcely a week's time to organize the trip, the *Oscar II* left New York on December 4 and arrived in Oslo, Norway, on December 18. Ford's health was poor on the ocean-crossing and this fact, combined with his apparent recognition of how disorganized the peace mission was, led to his decision to return to the United States less than a week after the peace ship had docked. Many of those he left behind felt Ford had deserted the cause, but in succeeding months he continued to support the efforts of the group to initiate peace talks—efforts that did, to some extent, set the stage for Woodrow Wilson's subsequent idealistic approach to the negotiation of a peace settlement. In his own defense, Ford said later: "I wanted to see peace. I at least tried to bring it about. Most men did not even try."[6]

In 1916, Ford was spoken of as a candidate for President on a third-party peace ticket. He denied any interest in being a candidate, but when his name was entered in Michigan's new Presidential primary and in those of several other states, Ford did not withdraw his name until the deadline to take such action had passed. Although he did no campaigning, Ford won the Republican Presidential primary in Michigan and also picked up votes in the Democratic primary. He came in a close second in Nebraska's Republican primary and second also in Pennsylvania, where he finished well ahead of Theodore Roosevelt and Charles Evans Hughes, the eventual Republican Presidential candidate that year. In the campaign between Hughes and Wilson, Ford threw his support behind Wilson's bid for a second term, contributing nearly $60,000 for a newspaper ad campaign in several key states which may well have helped to tip the scales in favor of the Democratic candidate in this extremely close contest. Despite his well-publicized pacifist views, Ford announced his support of Wilson's subsequent actions that brought the United States into the war. Although during 1916 Ford had advocated peace, he had been privately gearing his plants for war production.

In 1918, when William Alden Smith's term in the United States Senate ended, he announced he would not run for re-election, setting the stage for a wide-open race in the party primaries in August to select candidates for Smith's seat. The Detroiter, Truman Newberry, was an early entrant in the Republican primary. Newberry had the backing of Theodore Roosevelt, under whom Newberry had served as Secretary of the Navy in the last months of Roosevelt's administration. Chase Osborn also jumped into the race, in open defiance of Roosevelt, who vigorously sought to persuade Osborn to withdraw. Osborn's old rival, Fred M. Warner, also threw his hat in the ring, while another ex-governor, Woodbridge N. Ferris, considered entering the Democratic primary.

In April, 1918, it was reported that Henry Ford would be a candidate, and petitions were circulated in May to place his name in both the Republican and Democratic primaries, which it was then possible to do. In June, Ford, who had not yet declared his intentions, conferred with President Wilson, who urged him to run for the Senate, telling him: "You are the only man in Michigan who can be elected and help to bring about the peace you so much desire." On the following day, June 14, Ford announced that he would accept the nomination for the Senate if it was offered to him. Ford unquestionably would have won the race if he had campaigned actively for the office and if he had had his name placed in only one of the party primaries. But he did neither. Democratic party leaders in the state endorsed Ford and urged all other candidates to withdraw and unite behind his candidacy. Fred Warner, who had no chance of winning in any event, withdrew from the Republican primary. Newberry and Osborn refused to do so and remained on the ballot, along with Ford, while Ford's name also appeared on the Democratic ballot, with only token opposition from a Democrat whose campaign expenses were reportedly paid by the Newberry organization. While many Democrats welcomed the prospect, which had been denied to them for many decades, of seeing their senatorial candidate win in November, some of them did not like the idea that Ford did not openly identify himself with their party by withdrawing his name from the Republican primary. Similarly, although Alex Groesbeck backed Ford, most Republican leaders and many rank-and-file party members opposed a candidate who had the backing of a Democratic President and who was running on the Democratic as well as the Republican primary ballot.[7]

The political contest that ensued was the most celebrated and controversial in Michigan's entire history. Truman Newberry's organization spent money lavishly in a furious effort to offset the initial advantage of Ford's name. Ford, meanwhile, spent virtually nothing and did no campaigning. The Detroit newspapers supported his candidacy, as did the American Federation of Labor, but the national press and such prominent individuals as Theodore Roosevelt attacked Ford, declaring that his public statements on issues revealed no evidence that he was qualified for the Senate. In the August primary, Newberry ran well ahead of Ford in the Republican race, with Osborn coming in a rather distant third, but in the Democratic primary Ford was an easy victor over his nominal opponent, James Helme. Between August and the general election in November, Ford again did no campaigning, except to issue a statement professing no interest in partisan politics but pledging, if elected, to work with the President to win the war and to achieve a lasting peace. Rumors regarding the huge amounts of money that Newberry had spent to get the Republican nomination caused some Republicans to vote for Ford out of disgust with Newberry. But if Ford was to offset the overwhelming strength of the Michigan Republican party, it was essential that he conduct an active campaign. He refused to do so, and the result in November was a victory for Newberry, who received 220,054 votes to Ford's 212,487 votes. Ford called for a recount, but the outcome was not changed, although Newberry's margin of victory was reduced to less than five thousand votes.

The critical importance of the Michigan election became evident within a few months. Newberry's election gave the Republicans control of the United States Senate by a margin of 49 to 47. Had Ford won the two parties would have been tied, in which case Wilson's vice president, as the presiding officer of the Senate, would have cast his vote with the Democrats, who would then have organized the chamber. Thus when it came time in 1919 to consider the peace treaty that Wilson brought back from Europe, the chairman of the Senate Foreign Relations Committee would have been a Democrat, as would have been a majority of the committee membership. Instead, the chairman was the Republican Senator from Massachusetts, Henry Cabot Lodge, who, with his fellow Republican committee members, is blamed by many for the Senate's defeat of Wilson's treaty and the resultant failure of the United States to be a member of the League of Nations.

After having refused to campaign for the office, Henry Ford now attempted to prevent his victorious opponent from taking the Senate seat. Federal law limited the amount that Senatorial candidates could spend in primary campaigns to $10,000. There was no doubt that Newberry had violated that law and Ford poured thousands of dollars into the legal fight that ensued. A federal grand jury indicted Newberry and 134 associates, and in the trial that followed in March, 1920, Newberry was found guilty of violating the Federal Corrupt Practices Act and was sentenced to two years in prison and a $10,000 fine. Newberry appealed, and on May 2, 1921, the Supreme Court overturned his conviction on the grounds that Congress had no power to regulate primary elections. Finally, on January 12, 1922, thirty-eight months after his election, Newberry was awarded his seat in the Senate, which had been denied to him until the resolution of the controversy surrounding his election. However, when Newberry's opponents threatened to reopen the case against him, he resigned his seat on November 18, 1922. Somewhat ironically, James Couzens, who was quite critical of his former business associate's political ambitions, was appointed to serve out the remaining months of the term in office that Ford had come close to filling.

*   *   *   *   *

The First World War, like every major war in American history, was a milestone in Michigan's history as well as in the history of the nation. As a direct consequence of the war or as an indirect result of certain impulses that were generated by the war, it was soon apparent in the post-war years that Michigan was a far different place than it had seemed to be in the years before the war.

One immediate change was the institution of Prohibition throughout the country following the ratification early in 1919 of the Eighteenth Amendment to the Constitution which Congress had passed and sent to the states during the war. This action came in part out of the idealism of the war and marked the culmination of a temperance crusade that was nearly a century old. In Michigan, the state prohibition law that was adopted in 1855 had never been completely effective, and by 1861 the legislature was already backtracking by allowing the manufacture of beer and wine that was not to be drunk on the premises. In Detroit, however, liquor of all sorts was sold openly, and in 1875 the prohibition act was repealed.

A long battle ensued between temperances forces and John Barleycorn which took different forms. The Prohibition party, formed in 1869, was made up of crusaders rather than practical politicians. It helped to spread propaganda, but accomplished little else. More effective was the Women's Christian Temperance Union, the members of which, distinguished by white ribbons, labored in season and out against the evils of the liquor traffic. The most powerful temperance organization, however, was the Anti-Saloon League, the Michigan branch of which was organized in 1896. Working largely through the churches, this group carried on a vigorous campaign against liquor through lectures, printed materials, and temperance meetings. It supported candidates for public office who favored prohibition, regardless of party. The league swung a large bloc of votes and politicians came to respect its power.

License fees levied on manufacturers and vendors of liquor came to constitute a major source of state revenue. But they did little to discourage the business. An 1877 law required saloons to close on election days and prohibited sales to Indians and minors. Any county was empowered to prohibit the sale of liquor within its boundaries, upon the approval of the voters, under a "local option" law passed by the legislature in 1887. Van Buren was the first county to "go dry"; others followed suit, then repented, and only Van Buren remained in the "dry column" by 1907. It had become apparent that there was too much seepage across county lines for local option to be effective. The Anti-Saloon League now concentrated on state-wide prohibition as its objective. In 1916 state voters endorsed a state prohibition amendment by a substantial majority. Although Detroit and some other major cities voted "wet," there were enough "dry" votes, combined with the overwhelming majorities for prohibition in the rural counties, to spell victory. Michigan became dry on May 1, 1918, over a year before the Eighteenth Amendment providing for national prohibition became effective.

The temperance forces joyfully proclaimed that John Barleycorn was dead and buried, but this proved to be a mistaken notion. Under the illusion that the battle had been won, the ill effects of alcohol were no longer taught in church and school, and a new generation of youngsters grew up unacquainted with the evils of alcoholism that had been so widely taught in earlier years. In thousands of homes, beer, wine, and assorted forms of home brew were concocted. "Blind pigs" and "speakeasies" dispensed liquor in the cities and even in the smaller towns. Detroit became a center for the smuggling of liquor from Canada into the United States across the Detroit River. Hoodlums and gangsters thrived on the business. Trucks transported cargoes of liquor from secluded boathouses along the Detroit River to various points in the Middle West. Sometimes rival gangs "hijacked" such cargoes. And this, of course, contributed to the crime wave of the 1920s. All this brought about criticism of prohibition and demands for repeal. When the Depression struck after 1929 and tax delinquencies grew, there was growing sentiment for legalizing liquor so that the state could collect taxes on it. In 1932 the voters overwhelmingly approved the repeal of the state prohibition amendment, and on April 10, 1933, a state convention chosen to pass upon the Twenty-first Amendment to the United States Constitution, which repealed the Eighteenth Amendment, voted 99-1 for approval. The era of prohibition was over.

Regulation of the liquor traffic and the power to license vendors in Michigan was entrusted to a Liquor Control Commission created in 1933. The oldtime saloon never returned in precisely the same form, and cities retained the right to prohibit the sale of liquor by the glass. More and more, addiction to liquor came to be regarded as a disease. In 1951 the legislature created the State Board of Alcoholism to promote programs and conduct studies in this field. Perhaps the most effective agency for combatting alcoholism as a disease was Alcoholics Anonymous, which established branches throughout the state to assist persons trying to break the habit of overindulgence. The Prohibition party continued to put candidates for public office on the ballot with the forlorn hope of restoring prohibition, but they received little support. One of the major concerns was the part played by drinking in automobile accidents, and many civic organizations joined to urge citizens not to drink if they had to drive a car afterward. Several Michigan cities still prohibited the sale of liquor by the glass in 1960, but the number was diminishing. For the most part, education on the evils of overindulgence was relied on to prevent addiction.

In contrast with the short-lived impact of the Eighteenth Amendment, the Nineteenth Amendment, passed by Congress on June 5, 1919, and ratified by the necessary three-fourths of the states by August, 1920, marked the end of a long fight to confer the vote on women. In a larger sense it was but one step in a fight for women's rights, the ultimate effects of which are still not completely understood. The suffragette battle for the ballot attracted the greatest amount of attention, yet the winning of political rights only symbolized a changing status that had many other ramifications.

First came the battle for legal rights. At the time of the Civil War the legal position of women in Michigan, as in most other states, was essentially in conformity with English common law. A woman lived under the tutelage of her father until she married; thereafter, under her husband's. Spinsters could not even control their own property. The New York legislature had taken the lead in removing many of these disabilities by an act passed in 1860. Other states, including Michigan, followed suit during the next few years. By 1893 the joint signature of a husband and wife were required in the sale of a homestead; a widow was given a claim to a share in her husband's property, which formerly had gone entirely to his children. But the husband could still seize any of his wife's earnings outside the home. A few years later the legislature also abolished this restriction.

Along with legal rights and educational opportunity, which women also gained in the last half of the nineteenth century, women won opportunity for economic independence. School teaching and domestic labor were the chief occupations by which women could earn a living in 1860. So long as women were dependent upon men for a livelihood true emancipation was impossible. The invention of the typewriter opened a new field for the employment of women. Typewriters came into general use about 1890. The telephone exchanges that were being established offered further opportunities. In factories and even on farms toil was lightened by new machines that could be operated by women. As American doughboys marched off to war in 1917 their places in offices, factories, and farms were taken by women. By 1920 it was possible for any woman with reasonable ambition and industry to earn her living.

On the political front the first wedge was an act of 1867 that permitted women taxpayers to vote in school elections. In 1881 women who were parents or guardians of school children were granted the same right. In 1870 the Michigan Suffrage Association was formed, but a proposal in 1874 to amend the constitution to give women the ballot was overwhelmingly defeated by the voting males. Nevertheless, two women managed to vote in 1871: Miss Mary Wilson in Battle Creek and Mrs. Nannette B. Gardner in Detroit. Mrs. Gardner, a wealthy widow, persuaded the officials to permit her to register because she had no husband to protect her interests, and thereafter she was allowed to vote.[8] The Michigan Equal Suffrage Association, organized in 1884, continued the battle for the ballot until final victory was achieved. But it was a long pull. A law enacted in 1893 enabling women to vote in municipal elections was declared unconstitutional by the supreme court. In the constitutional convention of 1907-1908 hearings were held and there were hot debates over the question of women's suffrage, but in the end the delegates defeated by a margin of 57 to 38 a proposal to incorporate in the new constitution a provision allowing women to vote. A compromise was adopted, allowing women taxpayers to vote on issues involving the expenditure of public money.

During the next decade one of the chief subjects of discussion throughout the state was women's suffrage. In 1912, the Progressive party endorsed it, as did Governor Chase Osborn. A proposed amendment permitting women to vote was turned down by a slender margin in the April, 1913, election. Though endorsed by many civic organizations, the proposal was fought by the Michigan Association

Opposed to Equal Suffrage, composed of both men and women. Active in the forces fighting against women's suffrage were the liquor interests, which feared that if women secured the right to vote, prohibition would be adopted. But many citizens opposed to the change were impelled by loftier motives. The venerable Cardinal Gibbons stated that women's suffrage "will tend to increase the searing social evil, divorce," and he opined further that it would "bring about moral looseness, discord, and dishonor in the sacred family circle."[9] But the mood of the time was favorable to reform. Furthermore, the work of women in helping to achieve victory in World War I gave the movement impetus. An amendment to the state constitution providing for women's suffrage with certain limitations was passed in 1918. Following the adoption of the Nineteenth Amendment in 1920, the state constitution was further amended to sweep away all political disabilities of women.

During the 1920s ancient taboos, restrictions, and prejudices that hampered women and denied them equal rights with men were vigorously attacked. The older generation was shocked by the "revolt of youth." Women bobbed their hair, shortened their skirts, and smoked cigarettes. Frankness in discussion of sex dealt Victorian prudery a death blow. There can be little doubt that traditional moral standards reached a low point of acceptance in the 1920s, yet the situation was never so bad as the elders imagined. The era of "whoopee" came to an abrupt end with the Great Depression, and the excesses of the 1920s were but a memory. What endured was the emancipation of women from many foolish and outmoded restraints that custom and tradition had thrust upon them.

Although the enfranchisement of women at the start of the twenties doubled the number of potential voters in the state, there was no apparent change in the traditional political patterns in Michigan as a result of this action. Instead, the political upheavals and turmoils of the first twenty years of the century were followed by a return in the twenties to the kind of dominance in state politics to which the Republican party had been accustomed in the latter years of the nineteenth century. The only significant defeat the party suffered came in 1922 when Woodbridge Ferris became the first Democrat elected to the United States Senate from Michigan since Charles Stuart left office at the beginning of 1859. But as had been the case with Ferris' election as governor in 1912 and 1914, his victory in 1922 was the result of unusual circumstances which temporarily prevented the Republican organization from operating at peak efficiency. In this case the divisions caused by the Newberry-Ford Senatorial fight enabled Ferris to win in 1922. Earlier that year, the incumbent Republican Senator Charles Townsend had been among those who voted to seat Newberry, after Newberry's conviction of violating federal law had been overturned by the Supreme Court. A feeling of loyalty to his party and state, which had been without its full Senatorial representation for three years, undoubtedly convinced Townsend that his action was the correct one to take, but anti-Newberry Republicans thought otherwise and in November voted for Ferris, rather than voting for Townsend.

The dominant figure in the Michigan Republican party during much of this period was Alex J. Groesbeck, a native of Michigan whose ancestral roots in the state went back to the French period. After his unsuccessful bid for the Republican gubernatorial nomination in 1914, Groesbeck had decided that he needed to build up his support in the state by first serving in a lesser position. Thus in 1916 he successfully gained the Republican nomination for the office of attorney general and was elected to this office in 1916 and 1918. In that position he attracted a great deal of public attention through a series of investigations which revealed the employment of prison labor by private contractors, rampant vice and lawless conditions in Hamtramck, and lamentable conditions in the State Industrial Home for Girls in Adrian. He was clearly the outstanding figure in the administration of Governor Sleeper, and in 1920 his performance record gained him the Republican nomination for governor against a large field of candidates, despite the opposition of the pro-Newberry forces in the party, who could not forgive Groesbeck for his support of Ford in 1918, his subsequent support of the legal actions instituted against Newberry, and his opposition to Governor Sleeper. In the party convention that followed the primary, the anti-Groesbeck forces succeeded in preventing Groesbeck from securing the nomination of his own men for all state offices save that of attorney general. In the general election in November, however, Groesbeck scored an impressive victory over his Democratic opponent, the ubiquitous Woodbridge Ferris, by an overwhelming margin of 703,180 votes to 310,566.

Groesbeck's greatest achievement as governor was in increasing the efficiency of the state administration so that it could better cope with the problems of a growing state. As attorney general he had become aware of the haphazard, hodge-podge administrative setup that had developed over the years. There were over one hundred departments, bureaus, commissions, and agencies, all more or less independent. The department heads never got together to discuss over-all administrative policy. Each official went his own way and sought to get as much money from the legislature as possible. The governor, although supposedly the chief executive, hardly knew what was going on in all these numerous offices, nor did he have the power to control and direct their activities in any effective manner.

In 1921, therefore, the legislature passed a bill that had been drafted by a trusted Groesbeck aide, Leland W. Carr, which set up the State Administrative Board, consisting of the governor, secretary of state, state treasurer, auditor general, attorney general, highway commissioner, and superintendent of public instruction, with the lieutenant governor added to the board at a later time. The action removed the autonomy of the individual state agencies by giving the board broad powers to set administrative policy for all agencies, and to ignore its orders was grounds for removal from office. The new board had three major functions: first, it drew up a budget to guide the legislature in making appropriations—the first state budget in Michigan's history; second, it set up a centralized purchasing system, so that the state could buy materials needed at wholesale prices; third, it devised a uniform accounting system for all state agencies. Most important, the act gave the governor veto power over board actions, thus making the governor the most powerful executive officer in the state government.

Groesbeck and the board then proceeded to deal further with the problem of decentralized administrative control by merging thirty-three previously independent or semi-independent boards and agencies into five new departments: Agriculture, Conservation, Labor, Public Safety, and Welfare. It was a major achievement, but it was only a start toward greater efficiency, since it would take years, even decades, before the old-timers in the merged agencies would forget their onetime independence and begin to think in terms of over-all policy for the departments in which they had been placed.

Groesbeck did not hesitate to use the power he now had to run the state government as he thought it should be run. A bachelor who had no family responsibilities to divert him, Groesbeck put in long hours at his job and expected his aides and associates to do likewise. He frequently employed his veto power over actions of his fellow members of the Administrative Board—actions which, together with his brusque manner and his no-nonsense attitude, all combined eventually to give weight to his critics' charges that he was an autocrat seeking to impose one-man rule on the state. However, Groesbeck's accomplishments as governor and the efficient, business-like manner in which he ran the office won him the respect of the voters, who returned him to office in 1922 and 1924, making him the third three-term governor in the state's history. In 1924 the Republican party under Groesbeck's leadership was so strong that it captured every one of the one hundred seats in the state house and all thirty-two senate seats.

In the latter years of his administration, however, Groesbeck's personal actions more and more began to play into the hands of his enemies. In 1923 and 1924 he was considered for Attorney General in the cabinet of President Calvin Coolidge, but he lost the opportunity largely through his brusque, sometimes unexplainable behavior which alienated Coolidge, who very likely also saw that Groesbeck, as Attorney General, might become as dominant in the President's cabinet as he had been in Governor Sleeper's administration. When Coolidge nominated another Detroit attorney, Charles Beecher Warren for Attorney General, another side of Groesbeck's personality was revealed when Groesbeck used his influence to block Warren's approval by the Senate.

In his third term as governor Groesbeck made the fatal error of alienating the boss of the Wayne County Republican organization, John Haggerty. The two men were both bachelors and had long been inseparable friends. Haggerty had held no state office until Groesbeck appointed him to the State Fair Board, a relatively minor position. The manager of the state fair had plans for upgrading the fair and converting the fairgrounds in Detroit to year-round use, but the methods by which he proposed to carry out these plans were opposed by Groesbeck. Groesbeck ordered the board to fire the manager, but the board members, including Haggerty, backed up the manager and refused to follow the governor's orders. He then proceeded to remove the entire board from office, ending his long-time friendship with Haggerty.

Meanwhile, a rebellion had broken out on the Administrative Board, with several members objecting to Groesbeck's handling of certain highway funds. His tactics were adding fresh fuel to the charge that he was becoming a dictator. A strong-minded executive, Groesbeck expected the other members of the board to rubber stamp his proposals, but these men had been elected to office by the voters of the state, not appointed by Groesbeck, and they felt their views deserved more consideration than the governor was giving them.

In March, 1926, Groesbeck announced he was running for a fourth term. He wanted to run in order to vindicate his reputation through the support of his constituency. Groesbeck's enemies supported Fred W. Green of Ionia in the primary. Green had been an enemy of Groesbeck since Groesbeck, as attorney general, had singled him out as one of the businessmen who had used political influence to employ prison labor in private businesses. John Haggerty joined the Green forces, as did those members of the Administrative Board who were at odds with Groesbeck. Groesbeck's support in the state now rapidly evaporated. Even James Couzens, who owed his seat in the United States Senate to Groesbeck's appointing him to replace Newberry in 1922, refused to contribute to the governor's campaign fund. In the primary in September, Green easily defeated Groesbeck—397,000 votes to 237,339—with the major difference coming in Wayne County, previously the principal source of Groesbeck's strength, which swung over into the Green column as a result of Haggerty's efforts. Green rewarded Haggerty with the nomination for secretary of state at the party convention, which also refused to renominate any remaining Groesbeck supporters.

Groesbeck's political career was now over. He sought the gubernatorial nomination again in 1930 and 1934 but without success. He remained a loner to the end, throwing his support in 1948, five years before his death, to the Democratic candidate for governor, G. Mennen Williams. Never a social reformer, Groesbeck was a brilliant administrator, and his contributions in this area were great. The fact that the state made little use of his abilities in the last quarter century of his life, however, was largely Groesbeck's own fault.[10]

In addition to Groesbeck, the 1920s saw the emergence of two other political figures whose stature would soon surpass that of Groesbeck—James Couzens and Arthur Vandenberg. Both men rose to great heights as United States Senators and both first entered that legislative body through appointment. Groesbeck's appointment of Couzens was in keeping with the governor's announced intention of appointing an "aggressive" individual who would have the courage to act as he saw fit, "regardless of personal and political considerations." Couzens, as business manager of the Ford Motor Company, had demonstrated these qualities. After leaving that company and entering the political world, he had revealed those same qualities as Detroit police commissioner and mayor, plus strong humanitarian and increasingly liberal tendencies that had not been so evident in his business career. Groesbeck appointed Couzens to the Senate even though Couzens announced that, as a Republican, he did not agree with much that his party by the twenties had come to stand for and that he would rather support Democrats than some of the Republicans he knew.

As Senator, Couzens soon attracted attention for his independence. When a Henry Ford-for-President boom began in 1923, Couzens helped derail the movement by declaring that the very idea of Ford being President was "ridiculous." Republican party leaders, who feared the Ford candidacy, praised Couzens for his sound judg-

ment, only to see Couzens in 1924 refuse to persuade anyone to vote
for Calvin Coolidge. The only reason Couzens voted for Coolidge,
he declared, was that he recognized that the third-party candidacy of
the old Wisconsin Progressive, Robert M. LaFollete, had no chance
of success. However, Couzens' most famous confrontation with a
major public figure of that period was his long fight with the Secretary of the Treasury, Andrew Mellon. Angered by Couzens' attacks on his plans to cut income tax rates in the high income brackets,
Mellon brought suit against Couzens in 1925 for $10,000,000 in
taxes which Mellon contended Couzens should have paid following
the sale of his Ford stock in 1919. After three years of one of the
most celebrated and vigorously argued court fights of the twenties,
Couzens emerged victorious. He proved conclusively that the government had repeatedly cleared him of any suspicion of tax evasion
in the years since 1919 and that he had in fact overpaid his tax by
nearly $900,000. It was a blow to Mellon's reputation, since he
appeared to be carrying on a vendetta against the Michigan Senator
with no basis for the charges he had made in the case. Couzens, on
the other hand, came out with a reputation that was greatly enhanced
not only by the outcome of the case but by his action in contributing
the $10,000,000 in question to establishing a fund that would pro-
vide for better health-care programs for children.[11]

Whereas Senator Couzens soon revealed himself to be a
maverick not only in his willingness to challenge the leaders of his
party but also in his support of policies and programs that were far to
the left of the mainstream Republican viewpoint of the Harding-
Coolidge-Hoover era, his colleague at the end of the decade, Arthur
Vandenberg, was much more orthodox in his Republican philosophy. Vandenberg had risen to prominence as the editor, since 1906,
of the Grand Rapids *Herald,* and in his early days with that paper, he,
together with the paper's owner, Senator William Alden Smith, had
supported some Progressive reforms, especially those that were designed to improve the quality of government. But by the twenties,
Vandenberg's essential conservatism had become apparent, and was
expressed in the editorials he wrote and in two books extolling the
conservative philosophy of Alexander Hamilton.[12]

Early in 1928, Senator Woodbridge Ferris died before the end
of the term to which he had been elected in 1922. Groesbeck's
successor as governor, Fred Green, appointed Vandenberg to fill out
the remaining months of Ferris' term in office, thereby choosing an
appointee who was as much in accord with Green's orthodox Republican philosophy as Couzens had been with Groesbeck's much more
irregular and independent outlook. Vandenberg then was elected to

a full six-year term in the fall of 1928, just as Couzens had won election on his own in 1924. When Vandenberg took his seat in the Senate, Couzens frankly told him that he had not favored his appointment because he felt Vandenberg was too conservative. Vandenberg's association with Couzens actually seems to have caused the Grand Rapids Republican to become somewhat more moderate on some issues in the years that followed, but both men, their party, the Democrats, and their state and nation would have much adjusting to do as fundamental changes in social problems and economic conditions demanded drastic changes in past political ideas.

Interurban railway, 1914

MICHIGAN BECOMES AN URBAN STATE

The federal census for 1920 provided one statistic that succinctly summarized what had been happening in the state for some time and now clearly separated the Michigan of an earlier day from the Michigan of the twentieth century. The division of the state's population into urban and rural categories, which in the nineteenth century had been overwhelmingly tilted toward the rural end of the scale, now had swung over in the opposite direction. Sixty-one percent of the state's population fell into what the census bureau defined as urban, while those living in a rural setting, who as late as 1910 still constituted the majority in the state, now accounted for less than two-fifths of Michigan's population.

These percentages are only rough indicators of population distribution and density. The census bureau has for many years arbitrarily used a population of 2500 as the cut-off point in deciding whether to call a community or area rural or urban. This would mean in recent years, for example, that Bad Axe, in the heart of the essentially agricultural northern Thumb area, would fall on the urban side of the line while Bloomfield Hills, in the Detroit industrial area, would be classified as rural. To correct such incongruities, the census bureau has made the urban-rural breakdown more meaningful sociologically and economically, as well as demographically. It has devised additional categories, such as metropolitan areas, in order to classify communities such as Bloomfield Hills as urban—regardless of their population—when its residents and activities are closely tied in with those of a nearby large city, in this case Detroit. Nevertheless, there are numerous isolated small communities that fall on the urban side of the census bureau's scale which, because of their strong associations with their area's agricultural activities and when the social and economic implications of the term are considered, are more rural than urban. Nevertheless, the implications of the percentage breakdowns of 1920 were quite clear. The era in which life in Michigan, because of certain economic activities (particularly farming), centered around small towns and country villages, had now given way to one in which an urban, industrialized life would more accurately reflect the average Michiganian's experience.

The movement from the farms to urban centers has been one of the most important changes that has taken place throughout much of the United States in the years following the Civil War. The trend was nation-wide, but in Michigan the movement to the cities was slower than in much of the rest of the Great Lakes region until the turn of the century. Until the 1890s, Michigan, unlike its neighbors to the south, was still partially in what could be called the frontier stage of development since it was not until that period that the last major undeveloped area in the state was settled. Until that time, Michigan's major attraction had been the potential offered by its undeveloped lands. The area south of a line from Saginaw Bay across to Muskegon had filled up first, with the agricultural opportunities being the great drawing card. This region has always contained the largest share of the state's population—99.1 percent of Michigan's entire non-Indian population resided there in 1840. This percentage declined in each successive census until it stabilized at about 75 percent of the state's population in the censuses of 1900 and 1910. A second region, containing the bulk of the state's timber resources, encompassed the remainder of the lower peninsula north of the agricultural region and that part of the Upper Peninsula east of Marquette and Dickinson counties. As the lumber boom developed, this region's share of the state's population increased steadily, reaching 11.4 percent by 1880, 16.9 percent by 1890, and peaking at 18.3 percent in 1900. The last area to be settled was the western part of the Upper Peninsula where the discovery of copper and iron ore deposits in the 1840s began to attract settlers whose numbers by 1910 constituted 7.7 percent of the state's population. As first the lumber industry and then the mining industry reached their limits of growth and then began to decline, the populations of the northern areas also began to decline, with the proportion of the state's population living in the region where the lumbermen had once been kings falling to less than nine percent of the total by the 1930s while the copper- and iron-mining districts contained only 3.8 percent of the state's population by 1940.

The declining percentages in the northern two-thirds of the state after the early years of the twentieth century indicated that the southern area's share of the population increased with each decade's census figures. However, in absolute terms, the population of this region, as well as that of the state as a whole, would have declined in the course of the twentieth century had the state still been forced to rely primarily on the older types of economic activities. What might have happened was foretold by the slow-down in the state's growth rate toward the end of the nineteenth century. Between 1890 and 1900, Michigan's population increased from 2,093,890 to 2,420,982, a percentage increase of 15.6—half the growth rate of the previous decade. More significantly the increase was due more to the natural increase of the resident population than it was to the movement into the state of new residents. Where hundreds of thousands of people from other states and foreign immigrants had poured into Michigan in the decades immediately preceding the nineties, the number of residents from other parts of the country increased by less than 120,000 during the nineties while the number of persons of foreign birth was actually less in 1900 than it had been in 1890. Michigan had lost its image of a land of opportunity and the population figures in the early years of the new century gave little indication of a return to the more positive image of the mid-nineteenth century, with the growth rate in the first decade of the century remaining well below the national average. But then came a dramatic reversal in the second and third decades. Between 1910 and 1920, Michigan's population grew by 30.5 percent, double that of the two previous decades and far above both the regional and national rates, and the figures for the twenties were even better—a growth of 32 percent. The turnaround was entirely due to the soaring population figures for the southern part of the state and within that area it was manufacturing, not farming, that was now the great magnet, particularly into the automotive centers in the southeastern part of the state.[1]

Among Michigan cities, Detroit has always been in a class by itself. As early as 1870, it had almost five times as many people as Grand Rapids, the next largest city. However, while Detroit was the Michigan metropolis from the beginning, it became one of the nation's major cities only after the coming of the automobile. Despite a steady increase in its population in the nineteenth century it had lagged behind such younger neighbors in the Great Lakes area as Cleveland and Buffalo. At the beginning of the twentieth century, nearly one of every eight Michiganians resided in Detroit, in contrast to the figure of 1840, at the height of the agricultural boom in Michigan's interior, when only one of every twenty-three people in the state lived in Michigan's largest urban center. But nationally, Detroit's population of 285,704 in 1900 placed it only thirteenth on the list of the largest cities in the country. It was a city that was noted for its beauty. Its tree-lined streets, the virtual absence of any buildings of more than three or four stories, and its comfortable residential areas helped to provide an atmosphere resembling that of a small town more than one of a big city. Geographically, the city was still concentrated along the river. Only in the latter part of the century had there been much movement inland, with the city limits reaching as far as Highland Park only in 1891. Most of the area that would come within the city by the 1920s was still farm land in 1900. Highland Park and Hamtramck, the two communities that would become entirely surrounded by Detroit's twentieth-century expansion, were small towns of about 400 and 3,000 people, respectively, in this period before the opening of the Ford assembly plant in the former and the Dodge factory in the latter would transform them into booming industrial cities after 1910.

To the west out of Detroit on Michigan Avenue, little had changed since the pioneers had taken this route into the interior. One passed through miles of farm land before reaching Dearborn, a community of less than a thousand people occupying a small portion of what is now the western section of this sprawling industrial center. Downriver from Detroit, the small communities of River Rouge, Ecorse, Wyandotte, and Trenton existed, but upriver, the Grosse Pointe area was still primarily an area of summer homes for wealthy Detroiters. It was not until 1910 that it began to change into an area of year-round occupancy. Travelling inland on Woodward Avenue and past Highland Park, one eventually reached Birmingham and Bloomfield Center (today's Bloomfield Hills). In a later time, these places, like Grosse Pointe, would become the most prestigious addresses for Detroit's industrial elite. On the other hand, such familiar present-day Detroit suburban communities as Lincoln Park, Melvindale, Livonia, Southfield, Hazel Park, and Warren did not exist at all at the start of the century.

Grand Rapids was the second largest city. There the rapid development of the furniture industry had stimulated an increase in the city's population from 32,016 in 1880 to 87,565 in 1900. By this time the Furniture City had reduced the ratio between the number of its residents and those of Detroit from the one to five figure of 1870 to a more respectable one to three margin of difference. Among other communities, only the lumber centers of Saginaw, with a population of 42,345, and Bay City, with 40,747 (counting Bay City and West Bay City as one community), would fall into what later generations would regard as cities of considerable size. Other cities, such as Lansing, Kalamazoo (which was not incorporated as a city until 1884), Jackson, Battle Creek, Ann Arbor, and Flint, would be looked upon as little more than small towns by late twentieth-century standards.

Nevertheless, typical urban problems such as supplying water for domestic use, fire fighting, police protection, sewage disposal, and public transportation had become matters of increasing concern in Michigan and were being dealt with by the end of the nineteenth century. In Grand Rapids, a private company had been incorporated in 1849 to supply water for the city. A rival concern began operations in 1854. The two were merged in 1870, but disastrous fires in that year caused citizens to clamor for a more abundant supply of water. Another conflagration in 1873 intensified the demand, and the following year the city laid eleven miles of water mains. Wooden pipes, prepared by boring out the center of logs, binding them with hoop iron, and covering them with asphalt, were installed. The private company continued to supply water until 1920, when it was purchased by the city. In Detroit, where the transition from private to public operation of the waterworks had occurred as early as 1836, approximately a fifth of the families by 1886 had running water in the home. But at the end of the century wells were still a familiar sight in the yards of Detroit homes. A similar pattern of development occurred in other cities. A series of fires in the early 1850s persuaded citizens of Kalamazoo of the need for an adequate source of water in that city, although the system was not fully developed until the late 1860s. In Flint, on the other hand, the city waterworks remained a private company until the second decade of the twentieth century, with the future auto industry giant, Billy Durant, involved in the management of the company for a time after its incorporation in 1883. As for the related development of sewage systems, the health hazards created by polluted water supplies initiated an increase in governmental expenditures as cities grew in size. East Saginaw, for example, had allocated $16,000 for sewage facilities in 1866, but by 1889 the community's expenditures in this area had reached $500,000. Of course, older methods of sewage disposal would survive for many years. In Ypsilanti, where the erection in 1890 of its distinctively designed water tower, so familiar to generations of students at the nearby college, had marked the inauguration of indoor plumbing for those residents who wished to tie into the system, an occasional septic tank was still to be found within the city in the latter part of the twentieth century. It was not until that same period that increasingly rigid public health standards, plus the infusion of federal funds, brought on a massive new sewage construction development that incorporated into these systems more and more small towns and neighboring rural areas and eliminated both septic tanks and outhouses.

In Detroit, the race riot of 1863 had led to the establishment of a city police force in 1865. By 1883 it consisted of 193 men, with an annual budget of more than $170,000. Grand Rapids abandoned the old privately financed night watchmen system in 1871 when it created its first city police force, consisting of a chief and eight patrolmen. In Kalamazoo, which was still a village, the marshal in the early seventies began employing a couple of policemen, one for daytime, the other for nighttime duty, and special police were hired when a circus or some other outside attraction came to town. The same period also saw the disappearance in Michigan's larger cities of the volunteer fire companies. Detroit, the first community to take this step, had nineteen engine houses by the eighties, staffed with professional firefighters equipped with horse-drawn steam pumpers. Although the city did experiment with self-propelled steam fire engines, they proved not to be a satisfactory substitute for the traditional horse-drawn equipment which continued to be used in the Motor City as late as 1922. After 1870, fire alarms could be turned in by means of an electric telegraph system, and by 1886 there were 188 alarm boxes at strategic points in the city. In Grand Rapids, volunteer fire companies, subsidized by the city and knee-deep in politics, carried the responsibility for fire fighting until the creation of a full-time paid force in 1895. In Kalamazoo, there was a gradual transition. Two men were hired by the village in 1870 to assist the four volunteer companies in hauling hose in case of fire, and in 1877 a full-time paid force of six men was hired to replace one of the volunteer companies. The first fire-alarm box was installed the same year, with twelve in service by 1882.

New approaches to the problem of lighting the city streets were adopted in the last half of the nineteenth century. Gas lights, using gas made from coal or some other source, were first used in Detroit in 1851 with the formation of the Detroit Gas Light Company. The formation of a rival gas company a few years later divided the city into two sections—each company having one section as its exclusive territory. The two firms were merged in 1893, forming what is now the Michigan Consolidated Gas Company, supplier of natural gas to much of the southeastern Michigan market. Naphtha lamps were experimented with in the seventies, and in 1881 a contract was made with a private company to illuminate the streets with electric lights—powerful arc lights mounted on towers as high as 160 feet.

These spectacular, though ineffective, features of the city landscape remained until 1918 when the last light tower in Detroit was taken down.

The first gas company in Grand Rapids started in 1856. The following year in Kalamazoo the first of numerous local utility firms that would later be merged to form the present Consumers Power Company began producing gas from pine resin, obtained from a local lumber mill. This proved too expensive a process, however, and the company soon switched to the more common method of making gas from coal, obtaining the latter from the nearby Jackson coal mines. During the following decade, other gas companies, which likewise eventually came into the Consumers Power organization, were established in Pontiac, East Saginaw, Saginaw, Bay City, and Flint. These outstate areas, however, did not lag behind Detroit in adopting electric street lighting, with the Grand Rapids Electric Light and Power Company, organized in 1880 by William Powers—one of the pioneers in the furniture industry—installing twelve steel light towers in 1881, some of which survived down into the 1920s. Powers used waterpower from a nearby lumber mill to power his dynamo, and his Grand Rapids operation may have been the world's first commercial hydroelectric installation. It certainly was in advance of a small installation in Appleton, Wisconsin, in 1882, and Thomas Edison's original steam station in New York City that same year, both of which are usually cited as marking the birth of commercial electricity. Electric companies were in operation later in the eighties in Saginaw, Bay City, Flint, Jackson, Kalamazoo, Battle Creek, and Pontiac. These companies, together with the gas companies in several of the same cities, would all be part of mergers that would eventually lead to the establishment of the Consumers Power Company, the major supplier of electricity and natural gas in much of the lower peninsula outside the immediate Detroit area.[2] In the nineties Kalamazoo citizens voted to establish a municipal light company, which was sold to Consumers Power in 1956, but Lansing continues to operate the city-owned electric power plant that it established in 1892. In Detroit, the present Detroit Edison Company, the principal supplier of electricity in southeastern Michigan, was formed in 1903 as an outgrowth of several earlier private power companies, mainly the Edison Illuminating Company, whose most famous employee in the nineties was its chief engineer, Henry Ford. However, in that same period, Detroit's reform-minded Mayor Hazen S. Pingree led a successful fight to establish a municipal power plant which in 1895 took over the lighting of city streets and also of public buildings. In a period when public versus private operations of such utilities was hotly debated, Detroit's municipal lighting plant, though its city service was limited, was cited by advocates of public power as an example of a successful operation of this type. Despite what may have been the hopes of its founders, however, it did not presage a move to public ownership of all electrical power service in the city. In the 1960s there were proposals to sell the city power plant to Detroit Edison as an economy measure, but the city ultimately decided to retain the facility.

In their early stages of development both gas and lighting and electric lighting were principally used for outdoor lighting or in stores, factories, and public buildings. Some private homes began to install gas lights by the sixties and seventies, but it was not until the nineties that residential use of electric lighting became widespread, and even then most homes in the state were still using either candles or kerosene lamps for lighting purposes. Similarly, telephone service, which arrived in Michigan in a surprisingly short time after Alexander Graham Bell demonstrated his invention at the Philadelphia Centennial Exposition in 1876, was not widely adopted outside of businesses and a few wealthy family residences until the very end of the nineteenth century.

One new urban development of these years that affected a broad cross-section of these cities' population was the adoption of improved systems of public transportation. Until the 1860s, the great majority of city residents got where they had to go by walking. Only wealthy families could afford the luxury of owning and operating horse-drawn carriages. In the 1840s in Detroit, horse-drawn hacks and omnibuses began to appear on the streets, but in 1863 a more adequate form of public transportation began to appear with the opening of the first street railway line on Jefferson Avenue. Later in the sixties Grand Rapids followed suit. Beginning in the 1880s cable cars were used for several years to negotiate the hilly sections of Grand Rapids.[3] In 1886, Port Huron was the first city to electrify its streetcar operations, which up to that time had been horse-drawn. Public dissatisfaction with the failure of private companies that had been franchised to operate streetcar lines in Detroit to electrify their service led to Mayor Pingree's most famous reform campaign against private traction interests. His conclusion was that the streetcars should come under municipal management, but it was not until 1922 that Detroit actually acquired ownership of the street railways, by which time the increasing use of automobiles made the acquisition far less of an asset to the city than it would have been a quarter century earlier.[4]

The streetcar was the first step toward expanding the city be-

Horse-drawn streetcar, Grand Rapids, early 1900s

cause it enabled workers to live some distance from where they were employed. The next step was to provide the same kind of cheap, frequent transportation service between neighboring communities. This was more difficult to bring about, since a company planning to develop such a line (which came to be referred to as an interurban) would have to obtain a franchise to operate within each municipality through which the line passed as well as acquiring the right of way between communities. Also, until the 1890s the problems of transmitting electric power over distances of more than twenty miles hindered the development of electric-powered transportation systems.

Michigan's first interurban, connecting Ypsilanti and Ann Arbor, was an outgrowth of Ann Arbor awarding in 1888 a franchise for the construction of a street railway system in that city. When the neighboring city of Ypsilanti sought to provide similar service to its residents, it found that it was regarded as too small to support such a system, but the New York promoter who was approached on the matter felt such a line could pay for itself if it was extended from downtown Ypsilanti to Ann Arbor, seven and a half miles away. After some negotiations, the necessary approvals were obtained from Ypsilanti and the officials of the two townships through which the line would pass, and the Ann Arbor and Ypsilanti Street Railway Company was formed in 1890. The tracks were laid and service between the two cities was inaugurated in January, 1891. Initially, the interurban cars, which were steam-driven, carried passengers to the Ann Arbor city limits, where passengers transferred to the electric cars of the Ann Arbor Street Railway Company. Shortly, however, the interurban company purchased the Ann Arbor streetcar firm and in 1896, when the interurban line was electrified, the two systems were formally combined as the Ann Arbor and Ypsilanti Electric Street Railway. From the outset, the Ypsi-Ann, as it was popularly called, was a success. The Michigan Central Railroad, which had run through the two cities since the late 1830s, charged twenty-five cents for the trip. The interurban charged only ten cents, with bargain rates for those who bought books of tickets. It soon had six hundred passengers a day, in contrast to the forty passengers that the railroad had been carrying between the two cities. The interurban passengers were attracted not only by the cheap fares but also by the greater frequency of service. It proved especially popular with the students at the University of Michigan and the Michigan State Normal since it provided the predominantly male student body at the Ann Arbor school an inexpensive way of getting together with the predominantly female student population at the Ypsilanti school.

Late in 1897, the Ypsi-Ann was purchased by a Detroit group, which reorganized the company as the Detroit, Ypsilanti and Ann Arbor. Service from Ypsilanti to Detroit was inaugurated in June, 1898, with a branch line also opened between Wayne and Northville. In 1899, another branch linked Ypsilanti with Saline, and in 1901 the decision to extend the line from Ann Arbor to Jackson led to the reorganization of the company as the Detroit, Ypsilanti, Ann Arbor and Jackson Railway. By 1902, over five thousand passengers a day rode the cars of this line between Jackson and Detroit. The company had become part of the Detroit United interurban network which by 1901 had come to control interurbans that brought Wyandotte, Orchard Lake, Pontiac, Port Huron, Flint, and Toledo, as well as Jackson, Ann Arbor, and Ypsilanti, into the system. In the outstate area, the Michigan United Traction Company, centered at Jackson, operated interurbans to Lansing, Battle Creek, and Kalamazoo, while Grand Rapids was the center of another network that linked that city with such communities as Muskegon, Holland, and Saugatuck, providing the latter town, which had never had a railroad connection, with its first adequate land transportation facility.

By 1919 there were over a thousand miles of interurban tracks in Michigan, with cars operated by eighteen companies having a total investment of approximately $140,000,000. Nearly all of this

mileage was in southern Michigan, with only scattered interurban
service in other parts of the state. The interurban was an important
transition in the development of transportation patterns. Although it
was theoretically possible to travel by interurban, with numerous
transfers, from Bay City to Cincinnati, it was a service designed for
the local market. Because of the interurban, people could commute
several miles to work each day. Once this practice had become widespread, however, the increasing availability of the automobile and its
even greater flexibility in travel, led to the rapid decline of the interurban in the twenties. On Michigan's pioneer interurban, the
Saline branch line was abandoned in 1925, the branch to Northville

INTERURBAN RAILWAYS in 1919

in 1928, and finally, on September 30, 1929, service on the main line itself was abandoned. Five years later, the last remaining interurban service in Michigan, connecting Niles and South Bend, Indiana, ceased operations.[5]

The development of the railroad and the related streetcar and interurban systems in the nineteenth century had greatly reduced the importance of roads until these avenues of travel took on mainly local significance because they enabled the farmer to get to his nearby markets. The railroads had largely assumed the function of facilitating long-distance travel that the Chicago Road and other territorial roads had performed in pioneer days. The Constitution of 1850 had given the local townships responsibility for maintaining the state's roads. In 1883 the legislature had passed a special act permitting six townships in Bay County, together with the communities of Bay City and West Bay City, to form a special road district to finance the construction of three stone roads. Ten years later, a general law permitted a county, by a vote of its residents, to establish a county road department that would build and maintain a system of arterial roads in the county, serving a larger area than the local township roads. However, by 1905, only eighteen of the state's eighty-three counties had exercised this option.

At this time, Michigan had approximately 68,000 miles of public "wagon roads," as they were called. Nearly all of these were simply dirt roads. Only 7,712 miles had gravel surfacing and only 245 miles were listed as macadam roads—the most advanced surfaced road of that day. Nearly all these roads were under township supervision. Each township elected an official to oversee its roads. He had no professional training and the need for such training was not regarded as important. The amount of money available for road work was limited. Property owners paid a road tax, but it was possible to work out this tax by putting in one or two days of work on the roads each year. No matter how diligent the local officials might be, however, the roads throughout the state generally became impassable during the rainy and wet periods in the fall and the spring. Little hope for improvement in these conditions was expected as long as a decentralized system of road control was maintained and until some new source of funds could be found to pay for the high cost of surfacing roads.

Agitation for good roads arose in the late nineteenth century as a result of the sudden popularity of the bicycle. This created a new group of road users whose interests were different from those of the farmers. Bicycle clubs sprang up, and a Michigan man, Horatio S. Earle, became president of a national association of these enthusiasts, the League of American Wheelmen. This organization became the leading promoter of road improvements because bicycle riders, desiring to take trips on their machines, were soon made acutely aware of the wretched conditions of most roads. Horatio Earle became so identified with this cause that he was nicknamed "Good-Roads" Earle. As a member of the Michigan senate in 1901, he secured the appointment of a special committee, of which he was the chairman, to investigate state road conditions. Earle brought in as a consultant to the committee Frank F. Rogers, a former Port Huron city engineer who had been active in the good-roads movement and who would later be elected to four four-year terms as state highway commissioner. At the time of Rogers' service with Earle's committee, however, the state was prohibited by the state constitution from participating in the road-building business. Earle campaigned successfully for an amendment adopted in April, 1905, that authorized the establishment of a state highway department and permitted the state to be involved in the improvement of the "leading public wagon roads."[6]

Governor Fred Warner appointed Earle to the newly established position of state highway commissioner, which was an appointive position until 1913 when it was made elective. The same legislative act of 1905 also established the state highway department and assigned Earle and his staff to the task of collecting information about the state's roads, providing instruction to county and township districts on the repair and building of roads, and the distribution of funds for the improvement of the more important wagon roads outside of cities and villages. These funds, designated as "rewards," were granted to local road districts in varying amounts according to the type of improvement that was carried out. During the twenty years that this law was in effect, about $25,000,000 in state reward money was distributed. The money came from motor vehicle license fees which were first levied in 1905.

The fact that the total amount of money collected from motor vehicle licenses through 1909 was only $20,000 illustrates the as yet limited effect of motor traffic in the state. In 1905 there were only about three thousand cars in Michigan, and as late as 1913, when the first reliable traffic counts began to be made, horse-drawn traffic on the state's roads still outnumbered automobile traffic. Nevertheless, this growing number of automobile owners began to make their voices heard in matters of road improvement. Where the farmers and merchants favored a radial system of roads, fanning out from the towns into the surrounding farm lands, the automobile tourist, like the bicyclist before him, favored the construction of a network of roads crossing the state, rather than the farm-to-market approach. Automobile enthusiasts formed groups that held annual tours in various sections of the state, both to publicize the generally miserable condition of the existing roads and to promote the desirability of constructing cross-state highways, or "pikes," as they were called. Some of these groups later evolved into organizations that promoted the benefits of tourism in their region in general. Thus the West Michigan Pike organization became the West Michigan Tourist Association.

In response to this kind of pressure, the legislature in 1913 moved to establish a three-thousand-mile state trunkline network. The construction of these through roads would still be in the hands of the local highway agencies but the state would provide double the reward money for the improvement of these roads as it would for farm-to-market roads. However, progress in the state was slow. By 1917, only thirteen percent of the state's 74,190 miles of public rural roads were listed as surfaced, that is, covered with something more than the dirt or other kinds of soil common to the area of the road. In contrast, Indiana reported that forty-two percent of its roads were surfaced.

The federal government would eventually be responsible for the development of a surfaced, all-weather network of highways that the twentieth-century motorized public demanded. The establishment of the Office of Road Inquiry in 1893 marked the return of the federal government to a more active role in encouraging road improvements, a role that it had largely abandoned in the 1830s when President Andrew Jackson decided that such matters were more appropriately dealt with by the states. For almost two decades, however, the Office of Road Inquiry was simply a gatherer of information about road conditions. In 1912 Congress appropriated half a million dollars to aid in the improvement of post roads, with the office supervising the distribution of these funds. Each state was allotted $10,000 to improve a road that was used in the rural mail delivery system. To receive this money the state had to provide matching funds of $20,000 and submit the plans that were developed for the post road project to the federal agency for approval.

Aside from the limited nature of this federal assistance, the type of road improvement that it encouraged was in the tradition of the local road. The need for national highways began to be promoted in 1910 by the Dixie Highway Association, a private group formed by Carl G. Fisher of Indianapolis. Fisher was the head of the Prest-o-lite company and promoter of the Indianapolis 500-mile auto race, who wished to create a north-south highway linking the Midwest with Florida, where he was busily developing Miami Beach. Within a year, William S. Gilbreath, field secretary of the association, had persuaded the appropriate state and local officials to make enough improvements along the chosen route so that it was possible to drive the Dixie Highway from Detroit, through southeastern Michigan, (where the road's name still survives), to Florida. In 1913, Fisher, together with the Detroit automakers Henry Joy and Roy Chapin, formed the Lincoln Highway Association, and Gilbreath, who would later head the Automobile Club of Michigan from 1916 to 1936, again blazed the way in laying out this first transcontinental highway from Indianapolis to the West Coast. In 1915, Joy drove one of his company's Packards over the Lincoln Highway, demonstrating by the incessant problems he encountered how impractical such a transcontinental tour was at that time and thereby helping to create additional pressure for action to provide motorists with surfaced highways. In Michigan, Joy and most of his fellow auto company executives supported the lobbying activities of the Michigan Good Roads Association, with the Reo company in the Lansing area, Buick in the Flint region, and Ford in Wayne County making financial contributions to the improvement of roads in their home territories.[7]

In the horse-and-buggy era, surfaced roads usually meant a macadam road or some other stone or gravel surface. The slow-moving buggy and wagon wheels gradually packed the stones at the top down into the lower layers of rocks, producing a hard surface that was usable in wet weather and dry. The fast-moving rubber tires of automobiles and the suction force of the speeding vehicle, however, tore these roads to pieces, forcing road builders in an automotive age to search for a better kind of surfacing method. In Michigan the Dow Chemical Company successfully experimented with the use of calcium chloride as an agent that helped to maintain gravel roads while the use of oil as a binding material led to the evolution of the macadam road into asphalt pavement. However, concrete pavement, first used at Bellefontaine, Ohio, in 1893-94, would come to be recognized as the most satisfactory surface on heavily traveled roads. Much of the credit for popularizing the use of this material must go to the Wayne County Road Commission, which in 1909 paved one mile of Woodward Avenue beyond Six Mile Road in the Detroit area—the first mile of concrete highway in the country. Road builders and engineers from many areas came to Wayne County to study the effects of traffic on this kind of surface, and the favorable results led to a rapid increase in the use of concrete. Whereas in 1909 there had been only 364,000 square yards of concrete pavement in the entire country, by 1914 there was an estimated 19,200,000 square yards of concrete pavement.[8]

In 1916, Congress passed the Federal Road Aid Act, which provided the first substantial infusion of federal funds in upgrading the nation's roads. Over a five-year period, $75,000,000 in matching funds would be made available to state highway departments for the improvement of rural post roads. Michigan accepted the offer in 1917 by providing the necessary matching state funds. By June, 1920, the state had received nearly a million dollars of federal money and had placed some 335 miles of federal-aid roads under construction. Only some sixty-nine miles of federal-aid roads had been completed, however, and with motor vehicle registrations in the state having risen to 326,000 by 1919, the demand for faster action could not be ignored. The state constitution that year was amended to authorize a bond issue of $50,000,000 for road building. Meanwhile, a conference of highway officials from across the country met in Detroit in 1918 and called for a half-billion-dollar federal road-building program. Senator Charles Townsend of Michigan led the fight in Congress that resulted in the passage in 1921 of the Federal Highway Act, which was specifically aimed at the creation of an interstate network of highways. Under the act, each state was to designate up to seven percent of its rural road mileage as "primary roads." Federal money to the amount of $75,000,000 a year would be available on a fifty-fifty matching basis for the improvement of these roads, which officially became part of a federal system of highways in 1924. The east-west roads, such as US-2 running through the Upper Peninsula, received even numbers, while north-south highways, such as US-31 running up through the western side of the lower peninsula, were given odd numbers.

By the close of 1924, about $81,000,000 in federal-aid money and $50,000,000 in bond money had been spent on the most massive road-building program in Michigan's history. The state trunkline system had been increased to 6,601 miles, of which only a thousand miles were not improved. Under the leadership of Governor Groesbeck, Michigan concentrated much of its efforts on building concrete roads. Old standards were now obsolete. Road widths were increased, and Michigan pioneered in building bypasses to take the heaviest motor traffic around the downtown business districts. The first steps were also made toward the construction of divided highways when Woodward Avenue between Detroit and Pontiac in the 1920s was rebuilt with forty-foot strips of concrete separated by a center section occupied by the interurban tracks. When the interurban ceased operation this was converted to a grassy mall.

By 1924, when the bond money ran out, Michigan had constructed 1,195 miles of concrete highway out of a total of 3,398 miles of surfaced roads that were built in this program. Much of the remaining mileage was gravel surface with relatively little use yet made of asphalt. Whatever the surface, however, the cost of road improvements had skyrocketed. Motor vehicle taxes were not sufficient to pay the expenses and property owners objected to paying for improvements that were designed to be of primary benefit to people who did not reside in the area and did not pay property taxes. In 1925, therefore, Michigan followed the example of other states by imposing a two-cent gas tax so that those who used the highways would pay for the cost of their improvement. Farmers backed this tax, while automobile groups opposed it on the ground that they were being penalized. The principle that the user should pay for a public facility was a new concept which had not previously been applied to such public facilities as schools or parks.[9]

The road improvements of the twenties led to an increased desire to take advantage of these roads. This, together with the generally prosperous economic conditions in much of that decade and the introduction of time-payment plans for automotive buyers, led to an enormous increase in motor vehicle registration figures, which reached 1,439,317 by 1929—nearly four and a half times the figure of ten years earlier. In addition to changes in individual family travel habits, motorbuses began to take over the city passenger trade previously handled by interurbans and railroads. A few primitive buses had begun to appear before the First World War, but in the twenties they developed rapidly. State regulations of buses were instituted in 1923. In the Upper Peninsula bus service between Marquette and Sault Ste. Marie was initiated in 1925. By 1927 regular bus schedules were maintained in the lower peninsula between Detroit and Grand Rapids, Detroit and Chicago, and Detroit and Port Huron and the Saginaw area. By 1929, there were 164 companies operating 1,500 city buses in the state. Increased regulation and higher standards imposed by the state, however, gradually drove out the small operators and forced consolidation into such major national corporations as Greyhound and a few regional bus lines, such as Shortway, serving southeastern Michigan, and the unforgettably named Blue Goose buses that served parts of northern Michigan.

The popularity of the bus, with its low fares and greater flexibility, led to the demise of the interurban by the end of the twenties, and the related development of motor trucks for freight service took a heavy toll on railroad revenues. By the end of the twenties, the Pere Marquette railroad in particular was in constant financial trouble, in part caused by this new competitition, although the major railroads were, for the most part, not seriously hurt by bus and truck competition until the Depression of the thirties.

*   *   *   *   *

Improved transportation affected all areas of Michigan, but the impact was felt most in the rural areas where it completely transformed life. The electric interurban had made it easier for those farmers who lived close to one to get to town and to cities which few would have visited prior to this development. But it was the coming of the automobile, the truck, and the bus that brought about a real revolution in transportation for the farmer. By 1920, as many as forty percent of Michigan's farms had automobiles, and by 1930, nearly twenty percent owned trucks. The automobile and the truck made it possible for the farmer to get his products to market faster. It brought him and his family closer to the cultural advantages of the cities. It made the consolidated school possible and thereby brought high school within easy reach of farm youth. In a broader sense, the automobile was a major factor in breaking down provincialism and changing a traditionally restricted and narrow point of view.

Closely related to improved transportation was faster communication. The farmer of 1865 received mail only by calling at the closest post office, which might be many miles distant. Few farmers ever read a daily or even a weekly newspaper. Rural free delivery was started in Michigan in 1896. The village of Climax in Kalamazoo County was selected as the point of departure for the first carriers. One of them used a horse and buggy, the other a bicycle. The bicycle proved impractical, and the horse and buggy was used almost exclusively up to the advent of the automobile. By 1899 some fifteen rural routes were in operation, and the service was thereafter extended to practically every part of the state. The innovation of parcel post in 1910 was of particular importance to the farmer. Now he could get the huge mail-order catalogs of Sears Roebuck, Montgomery Ward, and other firms, and he and the other members of his family were thereby introduced to a variety of merchandise undreamed of in the country store. They could order items, have them sent parcel post, and delivered by the carrier.[10]

Then came the telephone. The Bell patent expired in 1893, making possible the organization of hundreds of local companies. It

Covered bridge, Flat River, Michigan (near Smyrna)

was some time before service was extended beyond the cities, but during the first decade of the twentieth century, private companies or local co-operative concerns built many lines into rural areas. The average farm home was on a "party line," which included several neighboring farmsteads, thus promoting neighborhood visiting and gossip. By 1920 there were telephones on nearly fifty percent of the farms.

Radio brought the words and other sounds of the outside world into the rural home. Wireless telegraphy had been in use for some years and had been utilized particularly by ships at sea in distress. One of the pioneers in this field was Thomas E. Clark of Detroit, who came to be known as "Wireless Clark." Thousands of amateurs all over the land played with wireless telegraphy in the same way that their fathers had toyed with horseless carriages. As early as 1908 Clark carried on a conversation by "radiophone" from a station near Alpena with a ship eight miles out in Lake Huron. The honor of being the first broadcasting station in the world is usually given station KDKA in Pittsburgh, but station WWJ in Detroit is a close competitor for primacy in this field. Operated by the Detroit *News*, WWJ broadcast its first scheduled program on August 20, 1920. Small stations soon sprang up in different parts of Michigan, and by the later 1920s receiving sets were becoming so inexpensive that almost any family could acquire one. They brought fine music, professional players, lectures, and news as well as popular music, "soap-operas," and Hollywood chitchat into the farm home. From a more practical viewpoint, radio quickly became a necessity to keep the farmer abreast of farm prices, weather forecasts, and scientific information in the field of agriculture. Station WKAR, operated by Michigan State University, specialized in this kind of information.[11]

A third transformation in rural life has come about through the increased use of machinery in the work of the field and the home. The early combines were huge contrivances and were adaptable only to the vast stretches of the western prairies. More useful to the Michigan farmer was the binder, which came into being in 1879 to bind cut grain into sheaves, which were then placed in small "shocks" or in large stacks until the threshing machine was available. The latter, operated by a steam or gasoline engine, made its seasonal rounds of a community of farms and did away with the threshing of grain with flails on the barn floor. Threshing became a mid-summer event on the farm. The men toiled like titans in the broiling sun, while women labored in the kitchen for hours on end to provide their best cookery for the famished workers at a noon dinner and again at supper time. Then during the 1940s the more compact combines began to appear in large numbers on Michigan farms. By 1950 the threshing rig, with its puffing engine, thresher, and bailer had become almost extinct. Little shocked or stacked grain may be seen today on Michigan farms, except in St. Joseph County where Amish farmers still use the older method.

Other mechanical improvements included the Deere plow with its steel moldboard that appeared in the 1850s, and the Oliver plow, fabricated of chilled steel and put on the market about 1870. The amount of machinery required by farmers increased steadily as hay loaders, cream separators, manure spreaders, spraying equipment, cornpickers, and dozens of other contrivances became available.

The coming of the tractor effected one of the most significant revolutions in the history of American agriculture. Prior to the 1920s, when the tractor became common, the average farmer devoted a large proportion of his labor and his acres to planting, growing, and harvesting hay and grain for his work horses. As the tractor replaced the horse as a source of power on the farm, more acreage became available for the production of food and fiber. This marks the beginning of the nation's farm surplus problem. By 1930 there were 34,600 tractors on Michigan farms; the number increased to 66,500 in 1940, to 149,372 in 1949, and reached a total of 194,205 in 1959, nearly two for each farm. The number of horses and mules on Michigan farms declined from 396,000 in 1920 to 37,000 in 1959.

The farmer's wife shared with her spouse the conveniences the machine age contributed to the farmstead. To her the coming of electricity was a special blessing. This great servant not only lighted the house and the barns, but also operated the radio and television sets, cream separator, vacuum sweeper, poultry incubator, and innumerable other devices. At first, electrical current was generated by plants operated by gasoline engines in the basement or an outbuilding, but during the three decades from 1920 to 1950 lines from central power plants reached a large proportion of farmsteads. In 1920 only eight percent of Michigan farms had electricity; by 1948 the proportion had risen to 96.6 percent, a percentage exceeded only by Ohio and Rhode Island. Privately owned public utilities got the jump on the federally financed R.E.A. co-operatives in Michigan and kept ahead. The Consumers Power Company built the first rural electrical power line from Mason to Dansville in 1926. Consumers served fifty-eight percent of the Michigan farms with electricity by 1946; another twenty percent were customers of the Detroit Edison Company. The remaining twenty-two percent included customers of seven privately owned companies and forty-three municipal plants, leaving only a very small fraction of the total as members of R.E.A. cooperatives.[12]

These and other changes, as well as trial and error, brought about a transformation in the type of products that came from Michigan farms. Until almost 1900 wheat was the leading agricultural product in the state. But Michigan could not compete in wheat production with the prairie states and the prairie provinces of Canada. By 1950, Michigan had less than a third of the wheat acreage it had had in 1880. However, wheat remains the most important cash crop in the state, and Michigan is one of the largest producers in the country of winter wheat used for making pastries and breakfast foods. Almost twice as much acreage is devoted to raising corn, but two-thirds of the corn is used for feeding livestock. Wool, shorn from the backs of sheep, was another important farm product in the nineteenth century, with Michigan usually ranking third or fourth in this category each year. Again because of competition from other areas, including such foreign sources of wool as Australia, sheep raising in Michigan declined after 1900. By 1956 Michigan ranked twenty-third among wool-producing states, although its position improved slightly thereafter, so that by 1976 it had moved up to twenty-first in the nation. The place formerly held by sheep was largely taken by swine. The number of pigs and hogs on Michigan farms increased from about 301,000 in 1892 to 554,000 in 1968, and by the mid-seventies the number of market hogs alone was topping 600,000. In general, the growing of livestock and the sale of livestock products assumed much greater importance in this century. By 1960 fifty-four percent of the total farm income in Michigan came from livestock and livestock products, with dairy products alone accounting for twenty-seven percent of the farm income. Beginning in 1973, however, farm crops again exceeded the value of livestock and livestock products.

Perhaps the most marked change in Michigan farm production in the twentieth century was increased specialization. Increased specialization meant that the farmer became a producer more comparable to the manufacturer than to the farmer of a century ago. Instead of producing on the farm as much as possible of what his family needed for food and clothing, he concentrated more and more on one specialized crop or product, buying other food and supplies from the stores and markets like city people. General farming, with emphasis on maximum production of products for home consumption, has almost disappeared. Sizable areas in the Upper Peninsula and in the northern portion of the lower peninsula have farms that specialize in growing potatoes, one crop that farmers in those areas in the late nineteenth century discovered did well in conditions that rendered most other types of agricultural activities unprofitable. In the Saginaw Valley and the Thumb region, navy beans are the leading farm product. For many years Michigan has ranked far ahead of all other states in the production of field beans. After the passage of the Dingley tariff in 1897, which provided protection of domestic sugar from foreign competition, the growing of sugar beets became another major specialty of the Thumb area. Michigan generally ranked fifth among states in sugar beet production, but by the seventies it dropped to eighth place. In southwestern Michigan, notably Berrien, Van Buren, and Allegan counties, fruit is the major product. Michigan's fruit belt extends northward along the shore of Lake Michigan into Leelanau and Grand Traverse counties. In 1976, Michigan, as it generally had in the past, ranked first among the states in tart cherry production. It also was third in apple and plum production, fourth in sweet cherries and strawberries, and seventh in peach production. The Benton Harbor fruit market has long been reported to be the largest outdoor fruit market in the world.

Central and southwestern Michigan have for many years been major producers of peppermint and spearmint oil, with Michigan in 1976 still ranking fifth in the latter category. The muck lands of southern Michigan are devoted largely to the growing of vegetables. In 1976 Michigan led all states in the production of cucumber pickles, ranked second and third in seasonal production of both carrots and celery (although urban development in the Kalamazoo area has virtually wiped out the celery production there that had once been

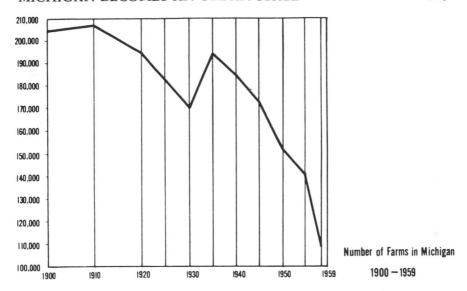

Number of Farms in Michigan
1900 – 1959

Kalamazoo's most famous product), and fifth or better in cauliflowers, onions, and sweet corn.

In addition to increased specialization, the farmer found that he could no longer farm using the pioneer methods that he had learned from his father and neighbors. He was forced by competition and perhaps by social pressure to rely increasingly on the scientist for gadgets and advice. More and more he depended on the specialists of Michigan State University (called Michigan Agricultural College until 1925 and Michigan State College from 1925 to 1955) to help him learn techniques and procedures that would increase the yield of his acres and raise his income. Michigan State was a leader in devising practical methods of serving the farmers. In 1875 extension work began. In towns all over the state "Farmers' Institutes" were held, where experts from East Lansing talked to the farmers about how scientific findings might help them better their lot. Regular bulletins describing agricultural experiments were distributed beginning in 1885. Federal aid for the establishment of experiment stations was provided in 1889. It was the agricultural college that developed new and better grains, such as American Banner wheat, Rosen rye, Markton oats, and Sparton barley. Better breeds of farm animals and new strains of fruits and vegetables have come in a steady stream from the experiment stations. Short-term courses were provided and an annual Farmers Week was set aside when farmers and their families came to East Lansing. The farmer was encouraged to keep systematic records and to use business methods. He learned how to fix his car, his truck, or his tractor if something went wrong. He continued to teach his sons what he knew about farming, but this no longer sufficed; many of these sons now spent four years at East Lansing acquiring scientific knowledge and skills to make them better farmers.

Among the faculty members at East Lansing who were leaders in the movement for scientific agriculture was Dr. Robert C. Kedzie. It was he who championed the idea of holding farmers' institutes in various parts of the state and who persuaded the legislature to reward farmers who planted roadside trees by reducing their taxes. Dr. Manly Miles demonstrated spectacular results from scientific fertilization, and William J. Beal established the first seed-testing laboratory in America, "first in a chain that led to the modern miracle of hybrid corn."[13] Most notable of all was Liberty Hyde Bailey, a native of South Haven, who after serving on the faculty of Michigan Agricultural College moved to Cornell and became one of the leading authorities and writers in America on horticulture.[14]

Farmers formed an amazing variety of organizations based on specialized aspects of farming: the Michigan State Horticultural Society (1870), the Michigan State Poultry Improvement Association (1925), the Michigan Berkshire Association (1912), and the Michigan Horse Breeders Association (1912), to mention a few. The most important farm organization in the twentieth century has been the Michigan State Farm Bureau, which came into being in 1919 as a central organization to look after such matters as transportation, taxation, and legislation for farmers. Hundreds of farm co-operatives became affiliated with the Farm Bureau. Farmers were urged to work together through the Farm Bureau on all matters of general concern. Fire and life insurance were made available after 1928 by this organization. In each county, through federal aid, a county agricultural agent and a home-demonstration agent were appointed to help the farmer and farm wife with their problems.

The various farm organizations operated as pressure groups for favorable legislation and got a great deal of it passed. The compulsory licensing and inspection of canneries, provisions for grading grapes and potatoes, milk-marketing laws, and many others found their way to the statute books. Several state agencies were created for the benefit of the farmer, these being combined in 1921 into a State Department of Agriculture. An Apple Commission was created in 1939 to promote the consumption and sale of Michigan apples, and a Cherry Commission was created in 1947 to do the same for cherries.

Agricultural associations and societies had been formed prior to the Civil War to arrange for county fairs. Some counties, Allegan for example, have held county fairs each year for more than a century. An act passed by the legislature in 1915 provided state funds to help defray the cost of premiums paid farmers on their prize-winning products exhibited at county fairs.

Farm organizations attracted rural youth as well as adults. The 4-H club program was launched in 1917. State aid to 4-H clubs to the amount of $75,000 was given in 1966. The Future Farmers of America, an organization of boys studying agriculture in the schools, also received state aid amounting to $30,000 in the same fiscal year.

The most striking development relating to Michigan agriculture in the twentieth century, however, is the drastic alteration in the size of this activity and the numbers of people it affects. In the mid-nineteenth century, nearly eighty-five percent of Michigan's population depended on agriculture for their subsistence. A century later, less than five percent of the population was still dependent on farming for the bulk of their living. The percentage of the population living in rural areas, of course, was greater than that number, but most of these people were not engaged in farming. Instead, those living in small towns depended on trade, small manufacturing, processing, or professional services for their income. Thousands who lived in rural areas had jobs in factories situated in nearby cities and could not be regarded as farmers at all. And finally, many farmers depended on work off the farm for a considerable portion of their income. In 1929, only fifteen percent of the people living on farms worked a hundred days a year or more at some other employment. By 1964, that percentage had risen to sixty-four. Other income accounted for more than the value of agricultural products on sixty-eight percent of Michigan farms by that date.[15]

The early years of the century witnessed the last period in the growth in the number of farms and the amount of farm acreage. The number of farms, which had stood at 62,422 in 1860, reached a peak of 206,906 in 1910. Thereafter, with only small exceptions, the figure has been declining, dropping to 72,000 farms by 1978. As the number of farms declined, however, the average size of those that remained has increased. Total farm acreage in the state reached a peak of 19,032,961 in 1920, more than half the entire land area of Michigan. Farm acreage has declined since that date, and by 1978 it had dropped to 11,400,000. However, the average size of the farms, which had stood at 113 acres in 1860 and had declined to only 86 acres in 1890, had risen to 158 by 1978. The value of farm land and buildings per acre rose from $33 in 1900 to $75 in 1920, but then declined to a low of $45 in 1935, before the start of another upward trend. The total value of Michigan's farm products, which was about $147,000,000 in 1900, was about $1,700,000,000 in 1976, but again the story was not one of a progressive movement upward. Surpluses after World War I caused constant problems for Michigan farmers, as they did for American farmers in general, with the result that Michigan crop receipts of nearly $400,000,000 in 1920 would not be equalled or surpassed until 1969.

Thus the agricultural statistics all tend to reinforce the evidence provided by the population census which shows a shift from a rural to an urban Michigan occurring in the early years of this century. After 1920 the declining agricultural statistics inevitably indicated that as opportunities on the farm also declined, more and more young people would be migrating from the rural areas into the cities, where the economic opportunities were now to be found.

In northern Michigan, the story was the same as in the rural areas of southern Michigan. Wartime demand for minerals and agricultural products between 1914 and 1918 brought considerable prosperity to the Upper Peninsula. But after the close of the war a long period of economic decline set in due to a combination of circumstances. Farmers all over the nation suffered from adverse conditions in the 1920s, particularly those in northern Michigan. Farmers in the Upper Peninsula, tilling soils far less fertile than those of the prairie states, could not compete successfully in such a situation. Some left to find jobs in the cities down below, but most of them hung on, hoping for better days. There was actually a small increase in the number of farms in the Upper Peninsula between 1920 and 1930, but much less than in the preceding two decades. It is probable that many workers formerly employed in logging and mining and now thrown out of work in those industries were hoping to earn a living on the land. While the population of the state as a whole increased by almost 1,200,000 between 1920 and 1930, that of the Upper Peninsula declined from 332,556 to 318,675. Iron mining reached a peak production of 18,993,000 tons in 1920, dropped to less than one-quarter of that amount in 1921, then leveled off to an average of about 15,000,000 tons annually during the remainder of the decade. But mechanization made it possible to produce the iron with less manpower, and as a result hundreds of iron miners were left without jobs.

Even more serious was the decline in copper mining. Prices of copper dropped sharply in the 1920s, and as a consequence only the richest lodes could be mined profitably. For half a century after the production of Michigan copper had begun it enjoyed a marked advantage by virtue of the fact that the rock contained copper in its

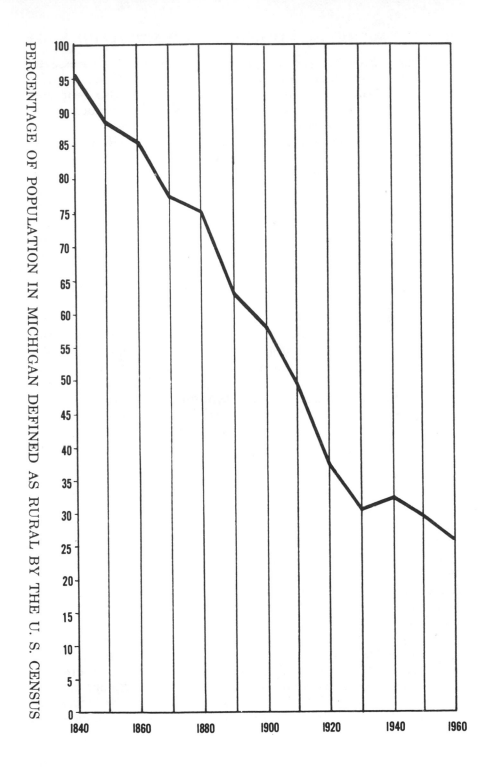

pure state. This advantage was partly overcome when the Bessemer process was adapted to convert the sulphide ores of the western mines. The Arizona and Montana mining companies also benefitted from the value of silver and gold mined as a by-product. These factors had been operative for some years before 1920. But lower labor costs in Michigan helped compensate for the difference until about the time of World War I, due to the abundance of immigrant workers who were willing to work for lower wages than western miners received. Labor costs of Michigan copper-mining companies in the 1920s increased by about fifty percent, and the passage of restrictive immigration acts cut off the supply of cheap immigrant labor. Meanwhile, copper prices in the 1920s averaged about ten percent below those of the prewar period. As a consequence, production declined from the peak of 267,000,000 pounds in 1916 to 92,000,000 pounds in 1921. There was some improvement after that, but in no year did the output reach more than eighty-three percent of the 1905-1912 average. Employment dropped faster than production, because fewer workers were required for selected mining. In 1909 copper mining had provided employment for 19,000 workers; the number was down to 12,200 in 1919 and declined still further to 7,800 in 1929.[16]

The Depression decade of the 1930s intensified the difficulties already in evidence during the preceding decade. In spite of agreements among the copper companies to control production, the price of copper declined to a low point of 5.6 cents per pound. Of the six companies that had been operating in 1929, four were completely shut down by 1933. Almost 6,000 miners lost their jobs. Between 1910 and 1940 Houghton County lost almost half its population. Two-thirds of the families in Keweenaw County and more than one-third of those in Houghton County were on relief in 1934, as compared with 12.2 percent in the state as a whole. Iron mining was also hit hard by the great Depression of the 1930s, though not so badly as copper mining. Production, which had been at an annual level of about 15,000,000 tons in the 1920s, was down to 1,000,000 tons in 1932. By 1939, however, it was back up to around 11,000,000 tons. One casualty of the depression was the fabulously rich Chapin Mine near Iron Mountain, which had produced continuously since 1880. It was closed in 1934. The distress in the mining areas had a tendency to drive people back to the land, and there was a rather significant increase in the number of Upper Peninsula farms between 1930 and 1935. Because of the effects of the Depression elsewhere, there was little opportunity to find employment by leaving the region.

But during the decade of the 1940s, while the population of the state as a whole increased by twenty percent, the population of the Upper Peninsula decreased by more than 20,000. War production and the postwar boom created a demand for labor, and encouraged an exodus from the Upper Peninsula. World War II, like World War I, stimulated both iron and copper production. But the output of Michigan mines failed to reach the high levels of World War I, and higher copper production was made possible only through the premium price set by the government on Michigan copper to compensate for the higher costs in that area. After the war, Calumet and Hecla was the only significant miner of copper in Michigan, and even its mines were closed for several months in 1949 when copper prices slumped. Iron production after the war averaged about 11,000,000 tons annually, far below the record production of thirty years before, while the reappearance of farm surpluses after the war made the marginal farming of the Upper Peninsula even less profitable.

Elsewhere in northern Michigan in areas where lumbering had prospered in an earlier day, the picture was equally dark. By the end of the nineteenth century the virgin pine forests of the lower peninsula were virtually all cutover, and the process of logging the forests of the Upper Peninsula peaked and began to decline in output within a few years after the start of the new century. Production, which had reached nearly three billion board feet annually in the eighties, dropped to less than 400,000,000 board feet and by 1932 had reached a low of 160,000,000. The lumber industry was not dead, however. Beginning around the turn of the century, the state and federal governments took steps to allow a second growth of timber to reforest the land through increased attention to forest fire prevention and other conservation measures. This new growth was then ultimately opened to selective cutting, permitting this carefully controlled logging activity to restore production to more respectable figures, such as 615,000,000 board feet in 1948. But this was still a far cry from the peak production of the boom years and this, plus the highly mechanized character of this activity, meant that the required number of workers was small compared to the late nineteenth-century figures.

One bright spot in Michigan's economy that had its impact on some areas of central Michigan in the mid-twenties and which recalled an earlier time when Michigan was famous for its raw materials was the emergence of the oil industry. In July, 1925, the central oil pool at Saginaw was discovered, and by 1927 almost two hundred wells had been drilled in and around that city. Maximum production of 1400 barrels of oil a day was reached in June, 1927, but wasteful methods reduced the pressure in the field to such a degree that probably only twenty-five percent of the available oil was produced. Then the Discovery Well at Mount Pleasant was opened in 1928 and that city quickly developed as the center of the Michigan petroleum industry. Subsequent drilling would leave few areas of the lower peninsula untouched by an oil boom, no matter how short-lived these usually were. Although Michigan never would rival Texas or Oklahoma or the other leading oil-producing states, it would remain a significant producer of both oil and natural gas. The fuel shortage of the 1970s stimulated further interest in exploration of Michigan's resources. Production, which had peaked at a little over twenty-three million barrels of oil in 1939 and had then leveled off, reached an estimated thirty-six million barrels in 1978—double the production reached only four years before—while natural gas production in 1978 was an estimated 150,000,000,000 cubic feet—more than double the production of 1974. With the sharp rise in oil and gas prices petroleum products were now the most valuable of all of the state's mineral resources.[17]

*   *   *   *   *

In contrast to northern Michigan and the rural areas of southern Michigan, where the old ways of life no longer maintained a strong, growing economy after about 1920, urban areas of southern Michigan now enjoyed their greatest periods of growth. Detroit grew from a city of 285,704 in 1900 to 993,739 in 1920 and continued on to 1,568,662 in 1930. Other cities enjoyed an even more spectacular percentage increase in their populations, with Flint growing from 9,803 in 1890 to 91,599 in 1920 and 156,492 by 1930, while Dearborn, which had had a population of less than a thousand in 1900, had topped the fifty-thousand figure by 1930 after the opening of the giant Ford Rouge plant. Urban growth, although slowed by the economic Depression of the thirties, would continue with renewed vigor in the forties and thereafter. There had been only three cities in the state with more than 50,000 inhabitants in 1910. By 1950 there were ten and by 1970 there were twenty-one. Six cities in 1910 fell in the category of having between 25,000 and 50,000 inhabitants. The number of such cities had reached ten by 1950 and twenty-three by 1970.

One notable feature of this urban growth is that it has been confined to a very large extent to the southern half of the lower peninsula. None of the cities over 25,000 in any of the censuses of the twentieth century was found north of Muskegon. Marquette, largest city in the Upper Peninsula during most of this period, had a population of 21,967 in 1970. Sault Ste. Marie, Escanaba, and Menominee were the only other Upper Peninsula cities over ten thousand in population. Several cities in the Upper Peninsula, such as Ironwood, Hancock, and Calumet, had suffered sizable losses in population.

The development of the automobile industry accounts for much of the urban growth, though not all of it. Although the automobile industry went through great changes in the period after the First World War, Michigan's dominance in the industry was not affected but instead was enhanced. Many of the smaller companies had difficulty surviving a sharp post-war depression that hit in the summer of 1920 and continued on into 1923. Two of these firms, Maxwell and Chalmers, familiar names in Detroit, were put in charge of Walter P. Chrysler, who had left the General Motors organization at the end of 1919 because of disagreements with William C. Durant. Chrysler put the two companies through bankruptcy proceedings, salvaged enough to reestablish a new Maxwell company, and abandoned the Chalmers car entirely. But Chrysler and a team of young engineers and designers were interested in a new, more advanced model, and in 1925 Chrysler was able to secure the necessary financial backing to once again reorganize the company, this time as the Chrysler Corporation. He dropped the Maxwell and began putting out the Chrysler. Realizing, however, that he could not compete effectively with only one model to offer the public, he jumped at the chance that was offered in 1928 to buy control of the Dodge company, not only because it gave him another car, and a highly respected one at that, but also because it brought the Dodge dealers, among the best in the industry, into his organization.

General Motors survived the post-war depression, but with great financial losses and the loss of its head, William C. Durant, who was forced out of the corporation in December, 1920, for complicated financial reasons. Alfred P. Sloan, Jr., who had been brought into the organization by Durant, now proceeded to establish a rational plan for managing this huge industrial complex, one that became a model for corporations. More important, perhaps, was Sloan's recognition that by the mid-twenties conditions in the industry were changing. Up to that time the automakers had had the advantage of selling their product to people who had never owned a car and were eager to buy. By the twenties, however, the market was beginning to reach a saturation point, and Sloan saw that the emphasis now, instead of being placed on the expansion of factory space to keep up with the demands of an ever expanding market, must be placed on the development of selling techniques that would persuade individuals who already owned a car to buy a new one. Although the practice of annual model changes had been present in the industry almost from the start, Sloan now placed a new emphasis on making changes in the exterior appearances of General Motors cars so that they would look distinctly different from the previous year's models. While thereby appealing to the buyer's desire to keep up with the latest styles, Sloan also encouraged people to move up the price scale by carefully differentiating between General Motors' several cars, from the least expensive Chevrolet to the most expensive and prestigious Cadillac.[18]

Under Sloan's leadership, therefore, General Motors moved to the forefront in all categories during the twenties, attaining the dominant role in American industry that it has held ever since. In the process it replaced the earlier leader, the Ford Motor Company, which continued under Henry Ford's direction. In 1919 Ford bought out all the other stockholders, placing control of the company stock entirely in the hands of the Ford family. The expense of carrying out this move—James Couzens was paid some $29,000,000 dollars for his stock holdings which he had originally acquired for a few thousand dollars sixteen years earlier—plus the financial problems brought on by the post-war depression caused Ford some anxious moments, but he carried his company through the crisis, and by 1922 and 1923 Model T sales were reaching new highs. Henry Ford, however, ignored the advice of his son and others to heed the signs that the public desired a fancier car than the trusty old Tin Lizzie. In the mid-twenties, General Motors' Chevrolet division, under William S. Knudsen's direction, moved in on Ford's previously unchallenged dominance of the low-priced automobile market. Although not as cheap as the Ford, the Chevrolet had features not available on the Model T and was more up-to-date in its appearance. By 1927, virtual parity between the two cars had been reached, and in May, Henry Ford recognized the need for change. The last Model T was turned out and the Ford operations came to a near standstill while Ford and his staff worked on the design of a new model. When that model, the Model A, was introduced early in 1928 it temporarily regained for Ford the number one spot in the low-priced field, but it was only temporary. The superior management of General Motors and the wide range of models it offered, assured that corporation of the top spot in over-all automotive production, while Ford, under the increasingly inflexible and out-moded management policies of its founder, was soon struggling to maintain the number two spot in the face of the rapidly rising challenge presented by the Chrysler Corporation.

By the end of the twenties, the Big Three auto companies, as they were now dubbed, produced about seventy-five percent of all the cars in America. Although General Motors, Ford, and Chrysler had production facilities throughout the country, their main operations were centered in Michigan. Among the smaller companies, Hudson, Packard, and Reo gave Michigan a sizable share of the remaining United States auto production, leaving the non-Michigan companies with an ever shrinking share of the market.

Of the cities that owe their growth largely to the automotive industry, none outside Detroit could match Flint. There the great Buick and Chevrolet plants, together with the AC Spark Plug factory and the Fisher Body plants, employed thousands of workers. It was a General Motors town. In 1961, for example, General Motors paid its employees and suppliers in Flint almost half a billion dollars, a figure that could hardly have been comprehended by the lumber men who had dominated that city in a much earlier day. Saginaw, which like Flint was a former lumber town, also felt the impact of the automobile age. The largest gray-iron foundry in the world and an extensive Chevrolet plant testified to that fact, while huge bean-storage elevators and sugar refineries provided the city with a link to an older economic heritage. Lansing owed more of its growth in the twentieth century to the genius and enterprise of R. E. Olds and Oldsmobile than to the fact that it is the center of the state government. Only a minority of the city's population was employed in governmental positions. The majority depended on manufacturing, business, and service trades for their living. Jackson was another southern Michigan city that grew in population. It was the home of many automobile companies whose products turned out to be failures. The Jackson, the Imperial, the Cutting, the Briscoe, and the Earl are examples. But industries supplying automotive plants proved to be more successful. Goodyear Tire and Rubber built a major plant in Jackson, as did Dow Chemical. Plants supplying automobile engines and other parts also contributed heavily to the growth of Muskegon, the one-time lumber capital of western Michigan. The production of various kinds of auto or truck parts was also carried on in cities such as Kalamazoo and Grand Rapids, better known for other manufactured products, as well as such small places as Allegan and Owosso.

But of all Michigan cities, Detroit attracted the most attention. Life in that city between 1900 and 1930 was reminiscent of the boom towns of the mining regions of an earlier era, only on a far bigger scale. As the city's population increased nearly sixfold, the city expanded geographically to the Oakland County line on the north, encircling, in the process, the towns of Highland Park and Hamtramck which also boomed but were now unable to annex any additional land to sustain increased population. Subdivisions sprang up overnight, and the city was unable to keep up with the demand to extend full city services into the new residential developments. The lovely shade trees which had once helped to justify Detroit's claim that it was America's most beautiful city were cut down to widen the streets. The old mansions, abandoned by their owners when they moved to more fashionable parts of the city or out of the city entirely to Grosse Pointe, Birmingham, or other wealthy suburbs, were transformed into rooming houses or were torn down to meet the need for more business properties. It was an age of bustle, confusion, construction, vast schemes, big financial deals, and colorful personalities. The old slogan of "Detroit the Beautiful" was replaced by "Dynamic Detroit." Even before the First World War, reporters were beginning to flock to the city to write stories about how they found an excitement in the air which made the great majority of them—both American and foreign observers—view Detroit in a favorable light as the city that best typified the new machine age of the twentieth century.[19]

In addition to reporters and observers who visited Detroit in these years, hundreds of thousands of other people flocked to the Motor City and its industrial satellites seeking jobs in the booming factories. Foreign immigration reached new peaks in the early years of the century. This was no new experience for Detroit or for Michigan, of course, but there was a decided shift in the areas from which the bulk of these immigrants came. The majority of the immigrants prior to 1900 had come from the British Isles, Germany, other parts of northwestern Europe, and Canada. Many immigrants continued to arrive in Michigan from these areas. A sizable number of Germans came in the twenties, for example, and persons of Dutch background in western Michigan continued to sponsor immigrants from the Netherlands who helped to preserve much of the original flavor of the Dutch culture in the Holland-Grand Rapids area. But the majority of the immigrants who came in the twentieth century were from southern and eastern Europe, and because they were so different in language and culture from much of the existing population in the state, they were inclined to settle together in certain areas and to retain their customs, language, and habits. Unlike the earlier peoples that had come to Michigan, these immigrants were almost entirely attracted by the possibility of jobs in the cities and not by the opportunities in agriculture, lumbering, or mining. In addition, the very movement toward mass-production techniques that was fostered by Michigan's auto industry proved a powerful incentive for much of this new wave of immigration. These immigrants came mainly from a rural peasant background and lacked the skills that were so important in earlier manufacturing activities but which now had become increasingly less important as most jobs along the assembly line could be learned by a new worker in only a few hours.[20]

The most numerous of these new European immigrants were the Poles, who in Detroit replaced the Irish and the Germans—the most prominent of Detroit's foreign-born element in the last half of the nineteenth century. Poles also settled in sizable numbers in such other industrial areas as Lansing, Saginaw, and Grand Rapids, where those of Polish background became second only to the Furniture City's Dutch population. Polish immigrants could be found in Michigan in earlier times, and in the mid-nineteenth century some of the first Polish immigrants were attracted by the state's agricultural opportunities, with Parisville in Huron County, a rural settlement founded in 1856, constituting the first Polish community in Michigan. A few years later, other Polish farmers settled at Posen in Presque Isle County in northern Michigan. In Detroit, the first Polish Catholic parish, St. Albertus, was established in 1871, and by 1882 there were as many as twelve hundred Polish families living in Detroit. The population census figures are not an accurate indication of the true size of the Polish population, since many of these immigrants were recorded as Germans, Austrians, or Russians, after the nations that then occupied the various parts of Poland. It was, however, the growth of the auto industry in the twentieth century that brought the greatest influx of Poles into Detroit. By 1930, despite restrictions on immigration that had been enforced for some time, Poles constituted the largest foreign-born group in Detroit, numbering 66,113. Despite the size of Detroit's Polish population, however, the industrial enclave of Hamtramck came to symbolize the Polish influence. As late as 1907, that town was still basically a farming community, strongly dominated by Germans, with a population of around 2,200. The opening of the Dodge plant soon changed all that. By 1915, Hamtramck's population was over 21,000, of which number eighty percent were Polish. By 1920, the population had soared to 48,615 and the last traces of the earlier non-Polish influence had disappeared. Although in later years the proportion of Hamtramck's population of Polish origins was reduced by the movement into the city of people of other backgrounds, the Polish influence still remained dominant, as indicated in a news story in 1954 which noted that some city council sessions were conducted in Polish, Polish newspapers could be bought on almost any street corner, kielbassa and parowki were sold at Polish meat markets, and young people learned to dance the "mazur" and "kujawiak."[21]

Despite the attention that has been centered on the Poles, the ethnic population of Detroit and other industrial centers in Michigan was very diverse. Among other major eastern and southern European groups to settle in the state were the Italians, of whom there were 28,581 living in Detroit by 1930. That same census for Detroit showed 21,711 of Russian birth, 11,162 of Hungarian birth, 9,014 from Yugoslavia, 7,576 native Rumanians, and 6,385 Greeks. Detroit's Macedonian settlement was the largest in the United States, as was its Belgian settlement, which was of earlier origins. In some parts of Detroit the foreign-born element in 1930 was as high as sixty percent of the population.

The eastern and southern European element, however, did not constitute the only largely new additions to Michigan's diverse population. The 1930 census indicated that there were more than 27,000 persons of Finnish birth in Michigan. The greatest number of these immigrants had come in the early years of the twentieth century and although most followed the earlier nineteenth-century Finnish immigrants into the Upper Peninsula, a sizable number were attracted by the job opportunities in the auto plants of the Detroit area. There they made the residents of southern Michigan, as they had of northern Michigan, acquainted with such distinctively Finnish institutions as the sauna. Peoples from the Near East also began appearing, most of them, again, finding jobs in the auto plants. Ransom Olds became well known for his employment of immigrants from the Holy Lands, and by the twenties the Ford Rouge plant was responsible for making Dearborn one of the few cities in the United States with an Arab settlement. Even earlier, in 1919, the first Moslem Mosque in the country was built in Highland Park to serve that town's Arabic-speaking population, although the greatest number of the Near Eastern immigrants were members of the Eastern Orthodox religion. By 1973, Detroit had the largest Arabic-speaking community in North America, while those of Armenian descent who were living in southeastern Michigan were reported to number 35,000 in 1967.

World War I and the tight restrictions that were imposed by Congress on immigration after the war curtailed the flow of peoples from outside the country on which Michigan's manufacturers had been depending to supply their never-ending need for more workers. They then turned to the South where they found a large surplus population eager to find the economic opportunities that the southern agricultural economy could not provide. By the 1940s and after, this would bring a massive movement of southern whites into southern Michigan, but earlier in the century the principal movement was of the southern blacks. Negroes had been found in Michigan since colonial times, when a few had come here voluntarily to engage in fur-trading activities and more were brought in as slaves. In the first half of the nineteenth century the pioneers who moved into the interior of the lower peninsula included some blacks, with one of the largest rural black settlements in the North developing in and around Calvin Township in Cass County.[22] After the Civil War there was a small movement of freed slaves into Michigan, but after 1880, Michigan's Negro population remained quite stable, increasing from 15,100 in 1880 to 17,115 in 1910.

At the latter date, there were 5,741 blacks living in Detroit. They resided in a small area which previously had been inhabited by Germans, Italians, and Jews. Although the professional class among this group had increased in size, most of these people were engaged in unskilled jobs and rented, rather than owned, their homes. They had gradually won a degree of acceptance from the overwhelmingly white majority in the city, probably, in most cases, because the small size of this black population appeared to present no threat to the whites. These conditions all changed after 1916, as Detroit's booming war industries actively promoted the migration to Detroit of southern blacks. By 1920, Detroit's Negro population numbered 40,838, a seven-fold increase over the figure of ten years before, and the great expansion of the auto industry in the twenties brought about a continued influx of southern blacks, with Detroit's Negro population by 1930 having reached about 120,000. The population in the entire state was up to 169,453, ten times the number found in Michigan only twenty years before. Those living in a rural area now constituted no more than five percent of Michigan's blacks, and by the twenties there were ample warnings of the racial strife that would intensify in the urban areas as the growing black populations in the industrial cities aroused increasingly hostile feelings among many of the white residents of those cities, based on age-old prejudices and the economic threat that the Negro seemed to present in the minds of many white workers. The virulence of these feelings would become evident in a few years and would be but one sign of the growing problems, along with the benefits, that the industrialized, urbanized Michigan of the twentieth century would have to cope with.[23]

26

DEPRESSION AND WAR

As the 1920s drew to a close, the country appeared to many to have reached a limitless plateau of prosperity. Despite the economic problems that had begun to beset inhabitants of rural areas of the state and northern Michigan in general, the years from 1923 on were the best that the majority of residents, especially those who lived in the cities of southern Michigan, had ever enjoyed. Auto production reached a peak of over five million vehicles by 1929, and the employment figures in the auto plants and the businesses that supplied the automakers and the automobile owner reflected this booming activity.

In the latter part of the decade, Senator James Couzens of Michigan was one of the few public figures who expressed concern about economic conditions. He became convinced that the trend toward installment buying that fueled so much of the consumer purchases of the twenties was not good for the economy and he became a crusader against the system. In 1928, Couzens headed a Senate committee that investigated the problem of unemployment, a problem that few people took very seriously at that time. Out of the committee's investigations came a remarkable report, largely the work of Couzens, which stated that in a democracy "every man is entitled to the opportunity to provide for himself and his family. That is a fundamental right and society cannot consider itself successfully organized until every man is assured of the opportunity to preserve himself and his family from suffering and want." Couzens stressed the evils of cyclical unemployment, so common to the auto industry with its annual layoffs to prepare for the next year's models, and he declared that society must find a way to eliminate this and other kinds of unemployment. In particular, Couzens recommended that the federal and local governments immediately adopt legislation to plan public works programs that would provide jobs in time of depression as well as a system of old-age pensions.[1]

Little attention was paid to Couzens' warning or to his recommendations, but a year later, in October, 1929, the stock market crash ushered in the most terrible depression in the nation's history. Michigan citizens soon realized how much more difficult it was for their highly industrialized society to deal with this kind of economic disaster than it had been in the more self-sufficient society of the nineteenth century. Automobile sales are one of the most sensitive indicators of a change in the economic climate, since, when economic prospects dim, consumers tend to delay the purchase of such expensive items until times improve. Despite the efforts of the auto companies, led by Ford, to counter this trend by cutting the prices of their cars, by 1930 motor vehicle production figures had already dropped off two million units from the peak figures of 1929. By 1932, the output of the auto plants plumbed the depths with a production of only 1,331,860—a decline of four million from the 1929 figure.

In the long run, the Depression affected the remaining non-Michigan auto producers far more than it did the Michigan firms. The thirties, in fact, saw the end of most of these out-of-state companies, including such famous names as the Pierce-Arrow, the Stutz, the Marmon, and the Peerless. The Michigan companies, in a stronger competitive position, did much better, with the Big Three by the end of the decade controlling about ninety percent of the nation's auto production, up from the seventy-five percent share they had held in the twenties. General Motors improved its position noticeably, producing forty percent of all American motor vehicles by 1937, and thirty-five percent of all such vehicles built in the entire world. Alfred P. Sloan, Jr., relinquished the post of president in 1937, stepping up to the post of board chairman, with William S. Knudsen succeeding him as president. Chrysler, under Walter P. Chrysler's direction, became the number two producer in the industry, and, despite the financial problems of the Depression, by 1936 the company had successfully retired the debt that had resulted from borrowing large amounts of money in the mid-twenties. The Ford Motor Company fared the worst of the three major firms, primarily because of the continuing decay of its leadership under Henry Ford, who, despite his age and at least one stroke in the latter part of the decade, refused to turn over the reins of the company to younger, more imaginative executives.

The smaller Michigan companies fared worse. One well-known

passenger car disappeared from dealers' showrooms in 1936 when the Reo company in Lansing ceased production of cars and concentrated on trucks, a move that enabled this manufacturer to stave off bankruptcy for nearly forty years. Ransom Olds, the company's founder who had briefly returned to a more active role in the firm during the early years of the Depression, resigned his last position with Reo at the end of 1936, and during the remaining fourteen years of his life had no further official links with the industry he had helped found. Packard, which had been the most prestigious of all Michigan cars, survived the Depression with little apparent damage, but the decision of company executives in the late thirties to boost sales by introducing a lower-priced Packard to accompany the high-priced model was probably a fatal error since owning a Packard might now no longer mean instant status for its owner. The Hudson Motor Car Company almost went under due to the heavy losses it suffered early in the Depression. Roy Chapin came back to assume the presidency in 1933 and managed to save the company from bankruptcy, but the strain probably was responsible for his death in 1936.

Finally, the Depression killed off Durant Motors, which Billy Durant had formed in 1921 when he had been forced out of General Motors for the second time. In the twenties, Durant seemed to be performing his old magic, as he built up what appeared to be an impressive company with a variety of cars, including the Durant, produced in Lansing, and the Star, a popular low-priced model produced in Flint. But the company was already in financial difficulties in the late twenties and Durant was more interested in the stock market, where he became one of the most famous speculators during the bull market of the twenties. He was astute enough to see the danger signs in the market in 1929, and he sold off most of his stocks before the market collapsed late in the year. But then he misjudged conditions and began to buy up stocks within a year, anticipating an upswing in the market. Instead, stock prices continued to plummet downward and Durant was wiped out. Durant Motors struggled along for a time, but was forced into bankruptcy in 1933, and three years later Durant himself declared personal bankruptcy. Although he was now in his seventies, he still attempted a comeback, first with an early-day supermarket operation in New Jersey, and then in 1940 with a bowling alley in his hometown of Flint which he intended to be the first of a chain of such facilities. However, a stroke in 1942 left Durant virtually incapacitated, and he died five years later in his apartment in New York, with little in the way of material possessions to show for his earlier entrepreneurial triumphs.[2]

Over-all, despite the general success of most Michigan automobile companies in pulling through the Depression, the thirties brought staggering economic problems to Michigan. Unemployment among the state's non-agricultural workers went up to twenty percent in 1930, twenty-nine percent in 1931, forty-three percent in 1932, and by 1933, nearly one of every two workers in these categories was unemployed. In addition to the areas where the auto plants were concentrated, the mining industry in the western Upper Peninsula was especially hard hit, with most mines ceasing production entirely in 1932-33. With hundreds of thousands of Michigan workers either unemployed or with greatly reduced incomes to support themselves and their families, actions had to be taken to provide relief.

The problem of providing relief for the poor was by no means a new one. Even when Michigan was on the frontier there were those who were too lazy to work or were incapacitated for work through some disability. That poverty existed is demonstrated by the passage of a law by the Territorial Council in 1827 making the township the unit for dispensing poor relief. This continued to be the pattern for more than a century. However, a law passed in 1830 authorized counties to erect poorhouses, the first of which was built by Wayne County in 1832. Eventually all but one of the state's eighty-three counties built a poorhouse. Township supervisors, cities, or neighborly help provided relief for temporary poverty cases, but those who were unable to support themselves over any extended period of time were sent to a poorhouse. Conditions in these institutions were sordid. The disgrace and the sense of tragedy attached to being sent to a poorhouse was immortalized by the lachrymose verses of Hillsdale's poet, Will Carleton, in his "Over the hills to the poorhouse."

Until the 1930s it was usually regarded as a disgrace for a person to accept any support from a public agency. Pride in self-reliance prevented most people from asking for such assistance except in cases of the direst need. The Puritan notion that poverty is due to sloth, lack of industry, indulgence, drunkenness, laziness, or some other shortcoming prevailed in an age when America provided almost unlimited opportunity for those who were willing to work. But a marked change in attitude came about during the Depression years. The unprecedented amount of unemployment compelled acknowledgment of the fact that poverty might be the consequence of the maladjustment of the economic system, that the individual might be without the means of providing for himself and his family through no fault of his own. This altered point of view led to revolutionary changes in relief and welfare administration after 1930.

In cases where want was clearly the result of circumstances beyond the control of the individual, some provision had been made even prior to 1930 for assistance short of poor relief. Before 1912 an employer was not held responsible for the care and support of an employee injured while at work if it could be proved that the employee, or even a fellow employee, had been negligent. In that year, however, the legislature passed the Workmen's Compensation Law, which held the employer fully responsible. In 1913 a mother's pension act was passed. It provided an allowance ranging from $2 to $10 a week to mothers lacking other means of support, depending on the number of children. But until after 1930 there was no provision for the aged or the unemployed save such scanty aid as the township or city or private charitable agencies might provide, or, as a last recourse, the county poorhouse.

Following 1929, as unemployment figures soared, the existing methods of providing relief proved totally inadequate. In rural communities, most families managed to get along, although even there conditions were critical in some parts of the state. But in the cities in southern Michigan, where fifty percent or more of the workers were laid off by 1932-33, and in the mining areas in the north, where one-third of the families in Houghton County were without any means of support and two-thirds of the families in Keweenaw County were dependent on some form of relief, the task facing the administrators of relief was entirely beyond their ability to control. By 1932, public relief cost more than $30,000,000. Of this amount, about $24,000,000 was paid from taxes by cities, townships, and counties. The remainder was provided by the state government. A large share of the automobile-license fees was returned to the counties for relief. The legislature also authorized the cities to borrow more money to finance their relief programs. But it was increasingly felt that the only agency that had the resources needed to meet this emergency was the federal government. In Washington, President Herbert Hoover expressed his opposition to pleas for federal relief programs. The Reconstruction Finance Corporation, a federal agency established in 1932, did begin to loan money to states for relief purposes, and by 1933 Michigan had received $21,000,000 from this source, but this still was not enough for a comprehensive relief program.

The situation caused many to advocate radical remedies. In the election of 1932, a Communist candidate for governor received 7,906 votes. In Detroit, Mayor Frank Murphy, who had gained this office in 1930 when a recall election had resulted in the removal of Mayor Charles Bowles for his handling of the city's unemployment problems, allowed critics of the social and economic system to "blow off steam" in Grand Circus Park, though many criticized him for doing so. An abandoned warehouse was used to house homeless men, and Murphy declared that no one should starve. He was among the leaders of a delegation of big-city mayors that went to Washington in 1932 in an unsuccessful effort to get the federal government to provide more relief assistance. Many of the idle in Detroit and elsewhere in Michigan listened to the radio talks of Father Charles E. Coughlin, the radio priest of Royal Oak. He violently attacked President Hoover and the businessmen of the nation, and in the Presidential campaign of 1932, he told his listeners to vote for the Democratic candidate for President, Franklin D. Roosevelt, declaring that the alternatives were Roosevelt or ruin.

However, the tirades of Father Coughlin were not needed to swing the traditionally Republican state of Michigan into the Democratic column in 1932. This election ended the one-party rule that had dominated Michigan almost since the formation of the Republican party at Jackson in 1854. Already by 1930, there were many Michigan Republicans who felt that the economic situation demanded the return of Alex Groesbeck to the governor's office. Groesbeck was an experienced administrator who had led the state through the short but severe depression of the early twenties. However, the forces of Fred Green, who was retiring from the governor's position after two terms, were successful in defeating Groesbeck in the primary and in electing their candidate, a young attorney from Detroit, Wilber M. Brucker, as well as the entire Republican slate running with Brucker, a majority in the legislature, and all of the state's Congressional delegation. But the Depression had already brought a noticeable increase in the size of the Democratic vote, and in the months that followed more and more blame was placed on the Republican administrations, both in the nation and in the state, for not having headed off the Depression and for not effectively dealing with it when it hit. By 1932 it was clear that the tide was running strongly in favor of the Democrats. In Michigan, William A. Comstock, who had been the party's unsuccessful candidate for governor in the previous three campaigns, was swept into office over the incumbent Governor Brucker, a man of considerable ability who had the misfortune to be governor at the worst possible time from the standpoint of his party and of his own political future. Not only did Comstock win, but the Democrats won a majority in the legislature (where only eight years earlier there were no Democrats) and a majority of the Congressmen from Michigan, and provided the Democratic Presidential candidate, Roosevelt, with all of the state's electoral votes, the first time this had happened since the election of

1852.[3] The only Republican candidate on the state level to survive was Frank D. Fitzgerald, the candidate for secretary of state.

Comstock had been born in Alpena, but after graduating from the University of Michigan in 1899 he had later moved to Detroit where he was a highly successful businessman. Although he had been elected to office along with Roosevelt, and, in fact, had polled considerably more votes than Roosevelt, Comstock was a conservative Democrat, a leader of the old guard that had controlled the party in Michigan since the Wilson administration. Although Comstock and his associates had never had much hope of winning elections in the state, they had kept the party alive in Michigan in the hope of a return of the Democratic party to office in Washington, thereby enabling the party to share in the distribution of federal jobs in Michigan. However, after Comstock was in the governor's office in Lansing, he discovered that he had to deal with some immediate and very critical problems in the weeks before Roosevelt was inaugurated as President in March, 1933, and could begin to dispense jobs to the faithful in Michigan.

The first problem that confronted Comstock was a bank crisis. Going into the Depression, Michigan bankers had thought they were prepared for emergencies. The Federal Reserve System, established in 1913, had been designed to provide the national pooling of resources that was needed in times of emergencies, and in 1929 the state legislature had passed a banking law that permitted the formation of holding companies which, by controlling several banks, could provide a pooling of bank resources that would further strengthen the ability of the state's banks to weather a crisis. However, during the booming twenties, banks had invested heavily in real estate mortgages, stocks, and bonds at the inflated prices that prevailed at that time. With the collapse of the economy after 1929, the value of real estate, stocks, and bonds fell far below the face value of the bank holdings in these areas, making it impossible for the banks to dispose of them except at a great loss. As bank depositors withdrew funds to meet current needs or because of growing doubts as to the soundness of these financial institutions, more and more banks found that they did not have the necessary money to meet depositors' demands and were forced to close their doors. By December, 1932, nearly two hundred Michigan banks—about a quarter of all the banks in the state—had failed.

In this crisis, the Reconstruction Finance Corporation was authorized in 1932 to loan money to hard-pressed banks. Unfortunately, Congress stipulated that when a bank borrowed from the Reconstruction Finance Corporation such loans were to be publicized. Thus, when newspapers reported that a bank had obtained a loan from this federal agency, depositors became wary and withdrew their funds faster than ever. The key to the establishment of some degree of stability in the state's banking structure lay in the ability of two large Detroit-based banking groups that had been organized under the 1929 law to remain in operation. The Guardian Detroit Union Group controlled three financial institutions in Detroit plus a number of other such institutions in suburban Detroit and across southern Michigan. The Detroit Bankers Company controlled two Detroit institutions and eight other banks in the suburbs in addition to having minority stock holdings in a number of outstate banks. In 1932, the Union Guardian Trust Company of the Guardian group had been forced to borrow about $16,000,000 from the Reconstruction Finance Corporation, although it had asked for much more than that. In January, 1933, the trust company asked for an additional loan of about $44,000,000, offering as collateral investments with a face value far in excess of the amount requested. The Reconstruction Finance Corporation examiners, however, reported that the institution's collateral did not warrant such a loan. An offer was finally made to provide part of the amount the trust company was requesting if large local depositors would loan the rest. General Motors and Chrysler agreed to the plan, but Henry Ford refused to do so, despite personal appeals from President Hoover and Hoover's Secretary of Commerce, Roy Chapin. In Washington, Senator James Couzens advised Hoover not to try to save the Michigan banks if their holdings did not warrant it, and threatened to "scream from the housetops" if a loan were given without adequate security. A crisis was reached on February 13, a banking holiday following Lincoln's birthday, which fell on a Sunday. It was decided that Union Guardian could not open for business Tuesday morning. Since this would certainly cause a run on other banks, Governor William Comstock was called into conference. He soon recognized that the closing of Union Guardian would create panic conditions in the state unless something were done. Therefore he issued a proclamation continuing the bank holiday until February 23, and word of his decision greeted citizens all over Michigan when they turned on their radios that Tuesday morning.[4]

Michigan was not the first state to close its banks. Banks already had been temporarily closed in Nevada, Iowa, and Louisiana. But the news came, nevertheless, as a shock. Many people found themselves with little or no cash on hand. But somehow they got along. Merchants extended credit. Friends and neighbors helped each other. On February 21 Governor Comstock extended the holiday, but allowed banks to pay out limited sums. Other states also were forced to close their banks, and the day after he was inaugurated, President Roosevelt declared a national bank holiday. On March 9, Congress passed an act that gave federal examiners power to decide which national banks were sound enough to reopen, and which should be liquidated. The Michigan legislature passed an act March 21 providing for a similar procedure for state banks.

The liquidation of the state banks and trust companies that had been closed during the Depression was not completed until 1949. A total of 436 state banks and trust companies had been closed. Of this number 207 were allowed to reopen and their depositors suffered no loss. Of the remainder, 170 were authorized to reorganize and 59 were placed in receivership. Reorganized banks made payments to depositors aggregating 93.8 percent of the amount of deposit at the time they were reorganized; the closed banks paid off 85.4 percent of their deposits. Of the total on deposit in all state banking institutions at the time of the crash 96.11 percent was eventually returned to depositors.[5] Although no great permanent loss was suffered, there were fears at the time of the crisis that little would be salvaged. A repetition of the 1933 experience was averted by the establishment in June, 1933, of the Federal Deposit Insurance Corporation, an action for which Senator Arthur Vandenberg of Michigan was given much of the credit.

The closing of the banks, added to increasing unemployment, created a situation in 1933 that made it impossible for local communities even with state aid to continue to meet the needs for relief. President Roosevelt, unlike Hoover, did not hesitate to involve the federal government in providing relief to people in need. The Federal Emergency Relief Administration was established under an act passed by Congress on March 22, 1933. A federal relief administrator was appointed for each county, and the costs were borne by the federal and state governments, relieving townships and cities of the burden. By the summer of 1933, 640,000 people in Michigan were on relief. After 1935, the federal government withdrew from direct relief, and in 1939 the Michigan legislature passed an act that gave each county the responsibility for establishing a department of social welfare. Costs were shared by the state and the counties, but the policies governing direct relief were determined by each county.

Meanwhile, through a wide variety of means, efforts were made to reduce the number of persons on direct relief. The federal government sought to provide work for those needing help. The Civil Works Administration in 1933 and 1934 and the Works Progress Administration after 1935, made funds available so that workers

could be employed on public projects such as building parks, installing sewers, and a variety of other activities. The W.P.A. had projects
for white-collar workers, such as artists and writers, as well as for
blue-collar laborers. All told, about a half-billion dollars was spent in
the state on W.P.A. projects, with as many as 200,000 people on this
agency's payroll in Michigan at any one time. The Public Works
Administration made federal aid available for major projects, such as
public buildings. The Civilian Conservation Corps gave unemployed
youth an opportunity to do useful work in return for food, lodging,
and a small stipend. In northern Michigan, young men at 103 C.C.C.
camps carried out a variety of conservation and reforestation projects. The National Youth Administration enabled many Michigan
young people to remain in college through payments by the federal
government to the colleges for the employment of students. These
programs reduced the number of persons on direct relief.

On July 7, 1933, a state law providing old-age assistance was
approved by Governor Comstock. Later, Congress made federal assistance available, and in 1937 the state law was amended to bring the
state program into conformity with the federal system. In each
county a Bureau of Social Aid was established to dispense regular
payments to needy citizens over the age of sixty-five who had been
residents of the state for at least five years. In addition to old-age
assistance, the Bureau of Social Aid, financed by state and federal
funds, granted aid to dependent children and to the blind.

In 1936, the legislature established an Employment Security
Commission, which was given the duty of operating a state employment service and superintending the payment of unemployment-
insurance benefits. A fund was to be built through contributions
from employers so that unemployed workers, for a limited time,
could secure unemployment compensation. This made Michigan
eligible for federal benefits under the Social Security Act passed by
Congress in 1935. This act also provided for payments from employers and employees to provide payments to retired workers.

By 1939, therefore, an entirely new concept of social welfare
had developed. The temporarily unemployed person could draw unemployment compensation benefits. He or she could use the state
employment service to find other work. If injured on the job, the
worker was covered by workmen's compensation, an obligation of
the employer. After retirement, if the worker came under the social
security law, he or she could draw regular payments for the rest of his
or her life. If the worker was not covered by social security, old-age
assistance was still available to those who were in need. The federal
and state governments also provided aid for dependent children and

the blind. And finally, there was direct relief, financed by state and county funds. Under the Social Welfare Act of 1939, the State Department of Social Welfare co-ordinated and administered a large part of this program.

These and other Depression-born programs required the expenditure of large amounts of money, and in order to meet its share, Michigan had to make some drastic changes in its tax structure. Even without a depression, the increase in governmental activities in earlier years had been placing an ever greater strain on the sources of revenue on which the state and local governments had always relied. The major source of revenue had always been the property tax, and this was still true at the start of the Depression, despite the introduction in the twenties of such additional taxes as a corporation franchise tax, an aircraft registration tax, a tax on building and loan associations, an oil and gas severance tax, additional taxes on motor vehicles, and the gasoline tax of 1925.

By 1932, as a consequence of the Depression, tax delinquency in Michigan had increased to frightening proportions, thus drastically reducing the yield from property tax assessments at the very time when additional monies were so desperately needed. By 1933, the delinquency rate was reported to be the highest in the country. The legislature yielded to public pressure by cancelling penalties on delinquent taxes, postponing tax sales, and other actions designed to ease the burden on the property owner. In November, 1932, voters approved an amendment to the constitution that limited property taxes to no more than fifteen mills (one and a half percent) of assessed valuation.[6] This virtually forced the legislature to find new sources of revenues since fifteen mills was inadequate to support state as well as county, township, and school programs. Thus in 1933, the legislature, with a Democratic majority, passed an act under which property taxes would go entirely to local units of government. To replace the $23,500,000 the state had received from property taxes in 1932, the legislature enacted a three percent sales tax. By 1937, this tax was bringing in over $55,000,000.

Although the yield from the sales tax was gratifying, the demands for state aid for welfare relief, schools, and other purposes were so great that other sources of revenue had to be tapped. Furthermore, an amendment added to the constitution in 1939 forbade the use of revenues derived from the gasoline and weight taxes for anything but highways. With the end of prohibition in 1933, a tax was levied on the manufacture and sale of beer and wine. Largely as a result of pressure from independent retail merchants, a chain-store tax was adopted in 1933. The same year a tax was levied on horse-race wagering. In 1939 a tax was laid on intangible property (stocks and bonds), but half the expected return was allocated to local governments. A use tax on goods bought outside the state was authorized in 1937 and a tax on producing oil in 1939. Employers were taxed beginning in 1937 in order to establish an unemployment-compensation fund.

Taxes are never popular, and the fact that Michigan's new Democratic administration under Governor Comstock pushed through several new taxes shortly after taking office in 1933 hardly inspired voters to support the party, even though the times clearly demanded action. In particular, Democrats in later years regretted that the sales tax, a flat rate levy that hits lower income groups much harder than it does wealthier individuals, had been adopted during Comstock's term as governor.[7] In addition, many of the Democrats who had been elected in 1932 were party hacks who had never had any expectation of winning and were unprepared for the responsibilities of the offices they had been chosen to fill. The party was also torn by a bitter fight over who should control the awarding of federal political jobs in the state. As a result of these divisions, Comstock was defeated in his bid for renomination in the Democratic primary in 1934, and in the general election the Republican party made a strong comeback. Secretary of State Frank D. Fitzgerald of Grand Ledge, the sole Republican survivor of the 1932 debacle, was elected governor and most other Republican candidates for state office were also successful. Senator Vandenberg was elected to another six-year term and the Republican party again secured a majority of Michigan's seats in the lower house of Congress, along with the control of the state legislature. Most of the outstate rural areas that had deserted the Republicans in 1932 returned to the fold but, significantly, voters in the Detroit area and the copper and mining areas of the Upper Peninsula, where the effects of the Depression had been most severe, did not return to supporting the Republicans to the extent that they had earlier in the century. The Michigan Democratic party organization, however, was unable to capitalize on the hopes that the majority of the state's voters had expressed in 1932 that the Democrats would do a better job of coping with the Depression's problems than the Republicans had done—hopes that seemed to have been fulfilled on the national level by the new programs established by the Roosevelt administration but which were frittered away in Michigan by mistakes, inexperience, and bickering within the Comstock administration.

In 1936, Franklin Roosevelt, seeking a second term as President and fearing that he might be defeated, intervened in Michigan

Democratic party politics to assure the nomination of a gubernatorial candidate who was sympathetic to Roosevelt's New Deal, was popular with the voters, and whose presence on the ticket would help Roosevelt carry the state. In addition to facing a well-financed attack from traditional conservatives, Roosevelt was also concerned with the potential strength represented by a burgeoning third-party movement that sought to unite the followers of the late Louisiana Senator Huey Long, led by the Rev. Gerald L. K. Smith, the believers in Dr. Francis Townsend's pension schemes, and the radio listeners of Royal Oak's Father Charles Coughlin, who had turned against Roosevelt after having supported his election in 1932. Roosevelt's desire to have Frank Murphy named the Democratic candidate for governor in 1936 was in part due to his hope that Murphy, a Catholic, would prevent a large number of Michigan Catholics from deserting the Democratic ticket that year in favor of Coughlin's new Union party slate.

Murphy had been born in the Thumb area in 1890, but after graduating from the University of Michigan law school he had established a law practice in Detroit.[8] After service in the army in the First World War, Murphy returned to Detroit where in 1923 he was elected to the Detroit Recorder's Court, a position he held until he was elected mayor of the city in 1930. In 1933, Roosevelt, whom Murphy had actively supported for the Presidency, named Murphy to the post of governor-general of the Philippines. When the Philippines achieved commonwealth status in 1935, Murphy was named high commissioner. It was with some reluctance that he agreed to give up this office and return to campaign for the gubernatorial nomination, and it was not without some difficulty that Roosevelt and Murphy overcame the opposition of conservative Democratic leaders. However, Murphy won the nomination, and in November defeated incumbent Governor Fitzgerald in his bid for a second term. Roosevelt campaigned in Michigan and the election returns, which showed him receiving considerably more votes than Murphy, indicated that Murphy rode into office in the wake of a Roosevelt landslide which won the President every state in the Union except Maine and Vermont.

Murphy, a handsome bachelor with a magnetic personality, announced plans to institute a "Little New Deal" in Michigan. The liberal programs of the New Deal were fully in keeping with the humanitarian concerns that Murphy had evidenced during his time on the bench in Detroit, as mayor during the worst part of the Depression, and as the top American official in the Philippines. Like William Comstock in 1933, however, as soon as Murphy took office on January 1, 1937, he found that one overriding problem required his immediate attention: A strike of Fisher Body workers in Flint which had begun on December 30, 1936, had precipitated the most important labor-management confrontation in modern American history.

The emergence of labor organizations as one of the most influential forces in Michigan is a dual result of the rise of industry in the state and the devastating effects of the Depression of the thirties. Prior to the thirties, labor unions were by no means unknown in Michigan, but their strength had been of a decidedly limited character. Michigan, in fact, was known as an "open-shop" state, and business groups in Detroit and elsewhere had fought to maintain this image and to capitalize on it as a means of inducing companies to locate in the state. To a considerable extent, however, the weakness of labor unions was not so much the result of business opposition to them as it was to the narrow outlook that had come to dominate the most important labor organizations in the country.

In Michigan some union activity can be found as far back as territorial days. The scarcity of workers during the Civil War had the effect of encouraging the formation of trade unions, but in the post-war period they did not prosper. A new labor organization, the Knights of Labor, was organized in 1869, and a Detroit branch was founded in 1878. Its leading member was Charles Joseph (Jo) Labadie, a journalist, poet, idealist, and philosophical anarchist. For a time the organization flourished; it was reputed to have had 25,000 members in Michigan in 1886. Through its efforts the legislature in 1883 established a Bureau of Labor and two years later passed a law limiting the hours of labor for children. A sawmill strike in the Saginaw Valley in 1885 was led by the Knights of Labor. About the same time a strike hit the Muskegon sawmills. The strike leaders' slogan was "Ten Hours or No Sawdust." Governor Russell A. Alger sent the militia to Saginaw, and the operators hired 150 Pinkerton men to break up the strike. The strike ended when a new state law providing for a ten-hour day became effective.

The Knights of Labor suffered from promoting strikes the membership could not sustain, and it also was hurt by being unjustly blamed for the notorious Haymarket Riot in Chicago in 1886. Furthermore, skilled workers in the different trades had a different set of interests from that of the unskilled workers, who were also included within the Knights of Labor. Consequently, in the late 1880s the movement declined. Its leadership of organized labor was taken over by the American Federation of Labor, a combination of craft unions formed in 1881. The Michigan Federation of Labor, an organization made up of craft unions within the state, was organized in 1889. Jo Labadie was its first president. The craft unions refrained from any involvement in politics and concentrated on improving wages, hours, and working conditions.[9]

Although the Michigan Federation of Labor played a relatively passive role in political campaigns, it did much to secure the passage of legislation favored by its members. Laws providing for factory inspection, the abolition of prison labor, municipal ownership of public utilities, and the suppression of child labor were backed. But the membership of labor unions until 1933 was relatively small, and the labor movement was weak. The bulk of the workers in the cities remained unorganized. Some unskilled laborers, excluded from the craft unions, were attracted about the time of World War I by an organization called the Industrial Workers of the World (I.W.W.), but it was considered too radical by the majority. A strike in the Detroit Studebaker plant in 1913 was blamed on the I.W.W., and some lumber workers around Cadillac joined the organization, but the I.W.W. failed to make much of an impression.

Several factors prevented organized labor from becoming an effective force in Michigan's automobile plants during the early decades of that industry's development. The American Federation of Labor, with its craft-union orientation, was temperamentally and organizationally unsuited to the task. Dozens of crafts were represented among the auto workers. To try to fit each of these crafts into the appropriate A.F.L. union would mean that many voices, not simply one, would be speaking for these auto workers. But since the majority of the labor force in the auto industry was comprised of unskilled or semi-skilled workers, they would not be represented by any A.F.L. union. Another factor discouraging labor organizations was the rapid turnover. Excellent wages were paid on an hourly or daily basis by the auto plants—higher than were paid in other industries—causing the A.F.L. official in Detroit who was supposedly in charge of the drive to organize the auto workers to tell an astonished reporter in 1920 that there was really not much reason why these workers should complain.[10] The fact that these workers were recruited largely from people who came from a rural environment who had had no previous experience with factories or unions further complicated the task of even the most energetic labor organizers.

The onset of the Depression completely altered these conditions. Workers who had been relatively content during the halcyon days of the late twenties were now unemployed. Those that were able to find employment found that working conditions had greatly worsened as the companies sought to get as much work out of their limited staff, at as low a wage as possible. The need for unions to represent them in these difficult times was now recognized by increasing numbers of workers. In 1933, Congress passed the National Industrial Recovery Act, containing a section recognizing the right of labor to organize and to bargain collectively. The act permitted producers in an industry to enter into agreements to limit production and eliminate price-cutting. Ford refused to enter into such an agreement in the auto industry, but the other major companies cooperated with the N.R.A., as it was called, and attempted to meet the labor provisions of the law by promoting the formation of company unions. In 1935 the United States Supreme Court declared the National Industrial Recovery Act unconstitutional, but Congress quickly re-enacted its labor provisions by passing the Wagner Act.[11]

Meanwhile, within the ranks of organized labor a movement toward industrial unions, comprising all workers, skilled and unskilled, within a particular industry, was gaining momentum. The workers in the mining and clothing industries were the first to form such unions. Between 1933 and 1935 there was a 132 percent increase in the membership of the industrial unions, while the craft unions grew by only 13 percent. Out of this movement came the United Automobile Workers of America (U.A.W.), organized in 1935. At first the industrial unions were represented within the American Federation of Labor by the Committee for Industrial Organizations (C.I.O.), but in 1936 the Executive Committee of the A.F.L. voted to exclude these unions from the organization. The industrial unions then formed the Congress of Industrial Organizations and the two federations remained separate until 1955. Shortly after the break, in September, 1936, the United Automobile Workers joined the C.I.O.

The U.A.W. lost no time in moving toward its objectives. Its leaders decided to tackle General Motors, the biggest firm in the business. Among the grievances it cited were the speed-up of assembly lines, low wages, insecurity, degrading working conditions, and denial of individual rights. In reply to these charges Alfred P. Sloan, president of General Motors, claimed that his company was paying the highest wages in history, even though the purchasing power of the dollar was greater than at any time since 1929. He stated that the corporation's policy was to bargain collectively with any group selected by the workers, but that it would not recognize any one group as the sole representative. On December 30, 1936, an unfounded rumor circulated among workers at Fisher Body Plant Number One in Flint that dies were being transported out of Flint to other cities where unions were weaker. A spontaneous sit-down strike began, and it quickly spread to other General Motors plants in the city.[12]

The sit-down strike was not unprecedented. There had been one in 1934 at the Goodyear plant in Akron, Ohio. The essential reason for the sit-down rather than the walk-out was to prevent management from bringing in strikebreakers. The Flint sit-downs set a pattern; there were many strikes in 1937 and one out of ten was a sit-down. General Motors at once declared the workers were occupying the plants illegally and asked the Genesee County Circuit Court for an injunction ordering the men to leave the premises. On January 2, 1937, Judge Edward S. Black issued a sweeping injunction directing the sheriff to eject the men from the plants. The workers ignored the injunction, and weakened the position of General Motors by proving that Judge Black held 3,665 shares of General Motors stock. At the plant gates disturbances arose and in one melee, twelve policemen and sixteen strikers were injured.

Frank Murphy was under immense pressure to call out the National Guard and carry out the orders of the court. Recognizing the tenseness of the situation in Flint and fearing that if he were to attempt to have the men forcibly ejected from the plants there would be bloodshed, which could embitter labor-management relations for years, Murphy finally decided to send the Guard to Flint to keep order but not to evacuate the plants. Meanwhile he sought to effect a truce between the parties. An agreement for a truce was worked out, but the union claimed that a statement issued by William S. Knudsen indicated bad faith on the part of the corporation, and the sit-downs continued. General Motors adamantly refused to negotiate with the U.A.W. unless the plants were evacuated first. It was only an indirect hint that President Franklin D. Roosevelt wanted the two parties to negotiate that finally brought them together. An agreement on February 11 finally brought an end to the sit-down strike. On March 12 a final agreement was reached. Both sides made concessions, and the settlement was in the nature of a compromise. On the crucial question of union recognition, General Motors agreed to recognize the U.A.W. as the bargaining agent only of those workers who belonged to it, but pledged that there would be no negotiations with any other organization for six months without the express permission of Governor Murphy. In addition, the company agreed to cease its anti-union activities, thereby freeing the U.A.W. to engage in a full-scale recruiting drive among General Motors employees.

Following the strike against General Motors, the U.A.W. turned to Chrysler, which quickly recognized the union. Ford, however, held out much longer. In an incident on May 26, 1937, several union officers were beaten and mauled outside the Rouge plant in Dearborn. Ford used a strong-arm squad under the leadership of Harry Bennett to root out union men from his factories. A decision of the Supreme Court upholding the powers of the National Labor Relations Board under the Wagner Act, however, forced Ford to capitulate. In May, 1941, an election held in the Ford plants resulted in seventy percent of the workers selecting the U.A.W. as their bargaining agent. Ford now gave the union all it asked and more. He agreed to the closed shop and the check-off, which had not been included in the other contracts.[13] This brought an end to the period of acute labor troubles and completed the process of transforming Michigan from an "open-shop" state into a state with one of the most powerful labor organizations in the country.

In addition to being credited for the ultimate resolution of the Flint sit-down strike early in his term and for pushing for legislation that would more effectively implement New Deal social reforms on the state level, Governor Murphy helped to establish a civil service system among state employees for the first time in the state's history. From time immemorial, those holding elective office in government had appointed their friends and supporters to lucrative government jobs. So long as government was simple and the duties of most public offices required no special training or skill, the so-called "spoils system" was seldom challenged. But as government became more complex, technical knowledge and skill were needed for many positions, and the practice of appointing favorites to such positions began to arouse opposition. In the federal government a beginning was made in 1883 in introducing a merit system of appointments through civil-service examinations. One objective was to give government workers more job security and to avoid a wholesale turnover whenever the Presidency passed from one party to another. In Michigan, due to the domination of the Republican party for many years prior to 1932, there was seldom such a turnover. But beginning that year, the two major parties alternated in winning the governorship each term for a decade. This intensified the need for a civil-service system in the state. The legislature in 1937 created a civil-service commission to handle appointments and dismissals of most state employees. Under the law officeholders could be "blanketed in" by passing an examination. Since the state at the time had a Democratic governor, a majority of important officeholders were Democrats. In 1939 the Republican legislature, resenting the "blanketing in" of so many Democrats, exempted some 8,000 positions from the civil service. Public protest resulted in an initiatory petition that placed before the voters in 1940 a proposal to amend the constitution by writing into it a provision establishing a civil-service commission with power to appoint, dismiss, and set the salaries of all state employees except for elected officials, employees of the courts, employees of state educational institutions, and a few others. Each agency was allowed two "unclassified" positions—positions not under civil service. The amendment was adopted. Thus the governor and the legislature ceased to control the employment, dismissal, and salary rates of most state employees.[14]

Despite his accomplishments in office, however, Frank Murphy was vulnerable in his campaign for another term as governor in 1938. The conservative, old guard element in the Michigan Democratic party that had been unhappy with Murphy in 1936 was even less happy with the liberal policies that Murphy had sought to carry out as governor. William Comstock now led a faction that was openly anti-New Deal. On the other hand, while Murphy's pro-labor attitude, particularly in the Flint sit-down strike, caused him to be denounced by conservatives in the state as a dangerous radical, left-wing factions in the state were not united in their support of Murphy's candidacy because several felt that he had not gone far enough in their direction. Finally, Murphy was in the great tradition of Pingree, Osborn, Groesbeck, and Couzens—an individualist in politics who was not really interested in the party. He had an opportunity to use his position as governor and his sincere commitment to humanitarian ideals to build a coalition of fellow liberal intellectuals and the newly emerging forces of labor to create an organization that could have mobilized the strong pro-Democratic sympathies that the Depression had created among many Michigan voters. But Murphy disdained such an effort. The result in 1938 was that, without the magic of the Roosevelt name on the ballot in this non-presidential year, Murphy lost to Frank Fitzgerald. While Murphy went on to complete one of the most distinguished political careers in Michigan's history through successive appointments as Attorney General in Roosevelt's cabinet and then associate justice of the United States Supreme Court, Fitzgerald unhappily did not long enjoy his triumph in his third run for the governorhip, for he died in office on March 16, 1939, and was succeeded by the Republican lieutenant governor, Luren D. Dickinson.

The only truly effective Democratic party organization built up in these Depression years was that of Murray D. Van Wagoner, who had been elected state highway commissioner in 1933. This was one of the choicest political plums in the state because of patronage that the holder of this office controlled and the funds he disbursed for road-building purposes. Van Wagoner effectively used these opportunities to build up the support needed to secure his re-election to the highway position in 1937 and then to advance his ambitions for higher office. With Murphy's defeat in 1938 and subsequent departure for Washington, the way was open for Van Wagoner to be his party's gubernatorial candidate in 1940. He won that election in part because he had been an excellent highway commissioner—even Republicans had praised him for his work. He was also helped by the organization he had built up during his years in the highway department. But his victory was principally due to the fact that his Republican opponent, the incumbent Governor Dickinson, was an octogenarian who was completely out of touch with the times and who had been an easy mark for ridicule when he was quoted as saying he had a "pipeline to God." The fact that many Republicans crossed party lines to vote for the Democrat Van Wagoner rather than subject Michigan to two more years of Dickinson was evident when it is observed that Franklin Roosevelt, running for an unprecedented third term as President, failed to carry Michigan after having carried the state by comfortable margins in 1932 and 1936.

*   *   *   *   *

The issues in the election of 1940 had less to do with the Depression, the effects of which were finally beginning to recede, than they did with World War II, which had begun in September, 1939. Within a year, the war had involved the United States as a whole and Michigan in particular in ways that would profoundly affect developments not only during the war but in the years and decades that followed. In the summer of 1940, after the fall of France to the forces of Nazi Germany, the United States government under Roosevelt dropped all pretense of neutrality and took extraordinary steps to back Great Britain in its efforts to stave off the expected German invasion and to turn the tide in the war against the Hitler regime. In this Presidential election year, Thomas E. Dewey, a native of Owosso but a resident of New York, and Michigan Senator Arthur Vandenberg, were leading contenders for the Republican nomination. Both men, especially Vandenberg, were spokesmen for citizens who opposed any actions that might lead to United States entry into the war. However, they lost the nomination to Wendell Willkie of Indiana, who favored many of the same policies regarding the British as did Roosevelt. Further blurring of the issue was the appointment by Roosevelt in June, 1940, of two Republican internationalists to his cabinet—Henry Stimson of New York, and Frank

Knox, Chase Osborn's old political ally who had moved on from Michigan to become the publisher of the Chicago *Daily News* and the Republican candidate for vice-president in 1936.

In September, 1940, Congress, by a narrow margin, approved the first peacetime draft and in November the first Michigan draftees were inducted, the first of the approximately 670,000 Michigan men and women who would serve in the armed forces during these war years. Earlier in the year, on May 28, 1940, William S. Knudsen, president of General Motors, was drafted by Roosevelt to be the director of the industrial production division of the National Defense Advisory Commission. In this job and later as head of the Office of Production Management and with the war department, Knudsen directed the transformation of American industry from peacetime to wartime production. It was only natural that Knudsen would turn repeatedly to that segment of American industry that he knew best—the Michigan automobile companies—and it was in this area that Michigan made its greatest contribution to the war effort, the contribution that would lead to it being called the "Arsenal of Democracy."

Shortly after the Japanese attack on Pearl Harbor on December 7, 1941, and the direct entrance of the United States into the war, the automobile industry was recruited in toto for war production. On February 10, 1942, automobile production for civilian use ceased altogether for the remainder of the war. Tires and gasoline were rationed. Once-busy highways were often nearly deserted except for huge trucks, buses, and cars on essential missions. Most people were able to keep their cars running, however, and replacement parts continued to be manufactured. Citizens hoarded their gasoline coupons to enable them to go on short trips, and somehow the army of deer hunters still managed to make the annual trek into northern Michigan each November.

From September 1, 1939, to the end of the war in August, 1945, the auto industry delivered almost $50,000,000,000 worth of war materials. Thirty-nine percent of this output consisted of aircraft and aircraft parts. About thirty percent was comprised of military vehicles and parts. Another thirteen percent went for tank production. Marine equipment, guns, artillery, and ammunition were among the other major items. Because Michigan was the hub of the auto industry, the greater share of this frenzied war production occurred in this state.[15]

One of the first individuals whom Knudsen approached in the summer of 1940 was K. T. Keller, Walter P. Chrysler's successor as head of the Chrysler Corporation. Keller was persuaded to have his company take on the task of manufacturing tanks. The Chrysler Tank Arsenal began to be constructed north of Detroit in Macomb County in November, 1940. By January, 1941, Chrysler engineers and draftsmen were laying out the plans for assembling the tanks, and by September the plant was completed and the first tanks were being shipped. During the war, Chrysler produced over 25,000 tanks at this facility. Tanks were also produced by General Motors at a huge new factory at Grand Blanc. Packard made aircraft engines, as it had done in the First World War, while Hudson operated an ordnance plant in Macomb County.

But the best known of Michigan's war production achievements was that of the Ford Motor Company at the bomber plant built at Willow Run, just east of Ypsilanti.

At the outbreak of the war in Europe in 1939, Henry Ford had voiced the same opposition to American entry into the war as he had a quarter of a century earlier in the early months of World War I. However, although he turned down at least one contract that was offered by Knudsen when he learned that the materials were to be furnished to the British, Ford expressed his willingness to use his production facilities to produce materials that would be used to strengthen America's own defense forces. On the day of Knudsen's appointment to his war production job, Ford remarked that the Ford Motor Company was capable of producing "a thousand airplanes of standard design a day"—a claim that Charles Lindbergh, a friend of Ford's, called "preposterous."[16] However, Ford's reputation as a mass-production genius had not been diminished by the managerial and labor problems that had beset his company in recent years, and in December, 1940, Ford and his chief production man, Charles Sorenson, were asked by the government if the Ford company would build 1200 Liberator B-24 bombers. Ford agreed to look into the project. In January, 1941, Edsel Ford and two of Edsel's sons, Benson Ford and Henry Ford II, flew to California with Sorenson to the plant of the Consolidated Aircraft Company, which had developed the plane. That company, in accordance with existing concepts in the aircraft industry as to how planes should be built, was proposing to build the B-24 at the rate of one plane a day. Sorenson examined the bomber, and then overnight drafted plans to apply the mass-production techniques that he had helped institute at Ford thirty years before to the assembly of one plane an hour. Sorenson's ideas were accepted, the Ford Motor Company was given the contract, and the government agreed to build a huge assembly plant, designed by Albert Kahn, the Detroit architect who, since designing the Packard company's Detroit plant in 1903, had become not only the auto industry's favorite architect but the leading designer of factories in the entire world.

Construction of the bomber plant, at a cost of $100,000,000, began in April, 1941. The site selected was at Willow Run, in the extreme western part of Wayne County, where Ford already owned some land and where additional land for this industrial development could be obtained at reasonable rates. The problem of bringing the tens of thousands of workers who would be employed in the plant to their place of work was partially dealt with by constructing a divided highway from Detroit to the plant to enable workers from that city to commute to work. But the bulk of the work force would be new to the area, coming in from all over the country, and $20,000,000 was spent on the construction of Willow Run Village to provide housing for the workers and their families.[17] Even this was not enough to meet the demand, however, and nearby Ypsilanti was flooded with people seeking accommodations. That town, previously a rather sleepy college community, was transformed overnight into a bustling factory town. The large nineteenth-century residences in the town were transformed into rooming houses or were divided into as many apartments as the owners could pack into these former single-family dwellings.

By September, 1942, the bomber plant, the largest assembly plant ever built to that time, was completed as well as the adjacent full-scale airport from which the completed bombers would be flown. But months dragged by with few bombers being produced. Sorenson and his staff encountered more difficulties than they had anticipated in mass producing the plane. The workers had to be trained for their tasks, many of which were far different from those used in assembling cars. The air corps kept making changes in the design of some features of the bomber, forcing the Ford engineers to make changes in the assembly operations. By 1943, critics in Congress and in the national press were expressing doubts that Ford could ever meet its production schedule. Suggestions were even made that the contract be taken away from Ford and given to one of its competitors. But as the year wore on, Sorenson and the much-maligned Ford staff resolved the problems and by the end of 1943 they were turning out B-24s at a rate in excess of the one-an-hour schedule that Sorenson had originally set. By the time production of the bomber ceased on June 30, 1945, the Willow Run plant had produced over 8500 Liberator bombers.

This tremendous effort, which harked back to the Model T production records in the earlier heyday of the Ford company, marked the swan song of much of the old guard at Ford. Edsel Ford, who had been serving as president of the company for many years although the elder Ford was clearly the man in charge, died in May, 1943, the strain of the war production effort certainly contributing to the physical and mental condition of this sensitive man, so different in personality from his father. Henry Ford, now eighty years old, returned to the presidency, but the normal infirmities of old age, combined with the effects of strokes that he had suffered since the late thirties, made him completely incapable of exercising true control over the company's operations. A bitter fight ensued within the company to seize the reins of command. Recognizing the gravity of the situation, President Roosevelt arranged for the release of Ford's grandson, Henry Ford II, from naval duty. After his return to Dearborn, the young Ford struggled to stave off the efforts of a group headed by the longtime head of the Ford security forces, Harry Bennett, to take over the company. In the course of the fight, Sorenson, after forty years of faithful service to Henry Ford, was forced to retire. Bennett was finally defeated in 1945 and also forced out of the company. Henry Ford II replaced his grandfather as president, and the elder Ford retired to his Fair Lane estate where he died in 1947. Henry Ford II then began the process of restoring the company to its former greatness.[18]

*   *   *   *   *

War production created booming economic conditions such as Michigan had not seen since before the Depression. Workers by the thousands once again flocked into the industrial centers of southern Michigan. Detroit's population alone increased from 1,623,000 in 1940 to an estimated 2,106,000 by 1943. Nearly fifty thousand of the new residents were Negroes, whose arrival intensified long-simmering racial tensions in that community. Much of the problem related to housing, which was in short supply in general in Detroit but which was particularly acute for the city's black population because of the attempts to confine it to certain segregated sections. After the initial surge of blacks into Detroit during World War I, the over-crowded conditions in the black ghetto had led some to try to move into previously white areas of the city. When Dr. Ossian Sweet, a Negro physician, bought a house in such an area on Detroit's east side in 1925, a mob of whites had gathered outside to protest his arrival. When they began throwing rocks at the Sweet residence, someone inside the house fired into the crowd, killing two white men. Dr. Sweet and the members of his family were arrested and charged with first-degree murder. In a celebrated case heard before Recorder's Court Judge Frank Murphy, Clarence Darrow, appearing for the defendants, secured an acquittal by convincing the white jury that the Sweets had a right to protect their property. By the even-handed manner in which he conducted the trial proceedings, Murphy's reputation as a defender of the rights of minorities was established.[19]

The Sweet case, however, did not herald any change in the attitude of the majority of whites in Detroit, and during the Depression the wretchedly inadequate and overcrowded conditions of their housing and their high unemployment only added to their misery. Public housing projects, initiated by the New Deal, helped to alleviate living conditions for a few, but in 1942, when the Sojourner Truth Housing project was opened in a white section of Detroit, whites rioted to drive Negroes out. In the months ahead, Mayor Edward Jeffries was under intense pressure from whites to resist any effort to move blacks out of the ghetto. Feelings were especially strong in the predominantly Polish area immediately adjacent to the main Negro residential area. Pressures were exerted to keep anyone from moving out or from selling or renting his house to a Negro.

The influx of huge numbers of southern whites into Detroit and southeastern Michigan in this period further complicated the situation. Both groups of southerners were competing for the same jobs and hate-mongers, such as Gerald L. K. Smith and Father Charles Coughlin, sought to stir up traditional racial prejudices among these southern whites, as well as among white workers in general. The wartime shortage of cars led to increasingly crowded conditions on buses and streetcars that further exacerbated racial feelings. Recreational facilities for blacks were inadequate and many parks were off limits to them. Blacks complained that the schools in their areas were inferior to those in white sections of the city, and the number of blacks in agencies of the city government was pitifully small, particularly in the police department, which was widely suspected of having anti-Negro sentiments. Finally, the war itself made more and more Negroes unwilling to submit tamely to these conditions. When Negro Americans were fighting a war for democracy in the South Pacific and on the battlefields of North Africa and Europe, demands for full democracy at home could not be silenced. The Detroit chapter of the National Association for the Advancement of Colored People announced that the issue of civil rights "must be raised now. We refuse to listen to the weak-kneed of both races who tell us not to raise such controversies now. We believe on the contrary that we are doing a patriotic duty in raising them."[20]

In August, 1942, *Life* magazine pointed up some of the potential for trouble in an article entitled "Detroit is Dynamite."[21] The

Detroit papers covered the Sojourner Truth riot and also the racial overtones of labor troubles at the Packard plant in 1943 and the Ford Rouge strike in 1941, but they followed a conscious policy of suppressing stories of the hundreds of incidents on buses, streetcars, and in parks which, if reported, might have made responsible citizens in the city more conscious of how deep-seated and wide-spread the racial feelings actually were.

On the evening of Sunday, June 20, fights broke out between white and black youths at Belle Isle, a city park close to the Negro residential section and one of the few that were open to blacks. Wildly inaccurate reports of what happened spread through black and white sections of the city and led to the eruption of full-scale racial violence in the early morning hours of June 21. Whites, inflamed by the reports they had heard, attacked Negro cars on the western fringe of the black ghetto just off Woodward Avenue. Blacks leaving all-night theaters along Woodward Avenue, where they had gone to enjoy the air-conditioned atmosphere as much as they had the movie, were attacked and beaten by mobs of whites. At the same time, white motorists, driving through the ghetto area on their way to work, were attacked by mobs of Negroes, who also began to loot stores in the area owned by white merchants.

In the pre-dawn hours of June 21, the Detroit police thought they had the rioting under control. However, new violence erupted along Woodward Avenue, and by nine in the morning, as the number of riot victims needing hospitalization reached a rate of about one every two minutes, Mayor Jeffries and other city officials conceded that the situation was out of control, and called Governor Harry Kelly, who was in Ohio for a governors' conference. Kelly flew into Detroit at eleven in the morning. Since the forces available to the state would not be sufficient to restore order, federal troops were requested. Precious hours were lost, however, when confusion arose between Kelly, city officials, and army officials in Chicago over the proper procedure in requesting such help. Thus it was not until 10 p.m. that night that military police finally arrived. In a short time they had restored calm, and at midnight President Roosevelt issued a proclamation calling on the rioters to return to their homes.

In the aftermath of the riot, which left thirty-four persons dead (twenty-five of them blacks), hundreds injured, and substantial amounts of property damage, controversy raged over who was responsible for the tragic delay in bringing in federal troops. More serious were the charges, aired in such national publications as *Life*, that the Detroit police had been far more severe in dealing with the Negro rioters than they had been with those who were white. Calls for a grand jury investigation of the charges were turned down, however, and the report of a special governor's committee that investigated the events principally blamed the riot on Negro leaders who allegedly incited violence by the inflammatory nature of their remarks in the weeks immediately preceding the violence.

Within two days after the riot, community leaders were coming forward with ideas on to how to avoid such racial confrontations in the future. Billy Rogell, a former Detroit Tiger shortstop who was on the Detroit Common Council (and is still presently a member), proposed that the ghetto area be turned over to the Negroes to do with as they desired—a suggestion that shocked liberals and caused them to denounce Rogell as a racist and segregationist. More in keeping with the integrationist ideas that were then the liberal answer to these racial problems were proposals advanced by R. J. Thomas, president of the United Automobile Workers, calling for an end to racial discrimination in employment practices, the construction of more housing, more parks and recreational facilities, and the establishment of a bi-racial committee that would work constantly to eliminate the sources of racial friction in the city. Thomas' approach was adopted, and in the years that followed the techniques that the city developed to maintain open lines of communication between blacks and whites made Detroit a model of how a big city could deal with such issues before tensions again reached the breaking point.[22] Until 1967, at least, there seemed good grounds for believing that Detroit had indeed learned its lesson from the terrible events of 1943.

*   *   *   *   *

World War II ended in 1945. First in May, Germany surrendered, and then on August 14, the announcement of the Japanese surrender touched off spontaneous celebrations throughout the state. Men, women, and children flocked to the downtown sections of the cities to cheer and shout. Half a million people jammed downtown Detroit and a hundred thousand converged on Campau Square in Grand Rapids. Despite the festive spirit, there was no feeling of assurance as had existed in 1918 of a lasting peace or that the war had been a triumph for democracy. The lofty idealism that had so inspired Americans in the first World War was almost totally absent in the second World War. Instead there was a hard-headed realism and a general acceptance that the war had been necessary to save the United States from the Axis aggressors. Yet even during the war, churches and other organizations urged that plans be laid for a just peace and for the creation of a world organization to maintain it. Senator Arthur Vandenberg symbolized the realism of this new attitude. He who had been a leading champion of an isolationist foreign policy for many years became convinced that the United States must continue to play a leading role in world affairs after the war was over. In a courageous speech on the floor of the United States Senate on January 10, 1945, Vandenberg declared his conversion to this new internationalist point of view.[23] President Roosevelt appointed Vandenberg to the American delegation that helped to draft the charter for the United Nations later in 1945. From this time to his death in 1951, Vandenberg was the mainstay of the bi-partisan support in Congress for the new course that the United States would follow in the world after the war.

First state capitol building, Lansing

27

THE POST-WAR YEARS

In 1945, as the war ended, Michigan looked forward to the return for the first time in sixteen years to what might be termed normal conditions. The efforts to shake off the devastating effects of the Depression, which were finally beginning to show signs of success at the end of the thirties, were then interrupted by the equally unsettling events of the war in the first half of the forties. The automobile industry in particular was anticipating a resumption of the rapid growth in sales that had been halted during the Depression and World War II. In 1945, there were still over 25,000,000 cars on the road in the country—a drop of only 4,000,000 from the 1941 figures—even though no new cars had been produced since the early weeks of 1942. But a great many of the cars were decrepit and ready for the junk pile. During the war, workers had earned high wages and because of rationing they had been unable to spend their earnings except on essentials. Accordingly, when the war ended, Detroit prepared for a post-war boom because of the increased demand for cars.

Advance planning helped to speed the reconversion of war plants to civilian production. War production was cut back after the surrender of Germany in the spring of 1945, and substantial progress was made toward reconversion during the summer. One company had turned out several hundred cars before Japan surrendered. When the Japanese surrendered in August, war contracts were cancelled and reconversion began in earnest. By the end of 1945, 75,000 cars had been built, enough to supply about two cars to each of the 33,000 dealers in the country. Since it takes months and even years to design and produce new models, these early post-war cars were simply refurbished versions of the last models that had been produced four years before. These conditions created a sellers' market, something that had not existed since the early days of the auto industry, and for several years after the war any car that was produced was immediately sold. This helped the smaller, so-called independent automobile companies to enjoy their best sales in many years, and it also encouraged the formation of new companies. Preston Tucker, originally from Ypsilanti, created a flurry of excitement among car enthusiasts with his plans to produce a car with a dramatic new design at a plant which he leased in Chicago where Dodge had built aircraft engines during the war. But only a few prototypes of the Tucker Torpedo were seen on the highways before financial and legal problems forced Tucker out of business in 1949.[1]

A more serious new entry in the competition for car sales was that made by Henry J. Kaiser, a California businessman who was hailed as a new Henry Ford for his remarkable success in applying mass-production assembly techniques to the building of ships during the war. Kaiser joined with Joseph W. Frazer, president of Graham-Paige Motor Company of Detroit, to form the Kaiser-Frazer Corporation and announced plans to produce a full line of cars. As its main manufacturing facility, Kaiser-Frazer obtained the government-owned Willow Run bomber plant, which the Ford Motor Company decided not to retain when it was offered to the company after the war. When the first low-priced Kaiser and higher-priced Frazer models began coming out of the vast, reconverted B-24 factory in 1946, it appeared for a time as though Henry Kaiser would succeed in his effort to make his company the first successful new entrant in the auto industry since the appearance of the Chrysler Corporation two decades earlier. By 1948, Kaiser-Frazer accounted for five percent of all new car sales in the country, one of the most impressive performances by one of the independents since the rise of the Big Three in the twenties. But then Kaiser's prospects began to sour. The negotiation of a $44,000,000 loan from the Reconstruction Finance Corporation in 1949 was an early sign that Kaiser-Frazer was in trouble. Production of the Frazer was abandoned in 1951, and the effort to boost sales in the low-priced field by introducing the Henry J, a small car, came in a period when the public was demanding big cars—not the compacts that would achieve popularity in later years. In 1953, Kaiser sold the Willow Run plant to General Motors, which needed an immediate replacement for its Hydra-Matic transmission plant at Livonia which had been destroyed by fire on August 12 of that year. By 1955, Kaiser had abandoned passenger car production entirely and was concentrating on the production of Jeeps (a vehicle developed during the war) and commercial vehicles at the Toledo factory of Willys-Overland, an old-time non-Michigan automobile company that Kaiser had acquired in 1953.[2]

Kaiser's problems were duplicated by other small automobile companies, including Detroit's Hudson and Packard, which also saw their best sales figures in many years followed in the fifties by sharply reduced shares of the market. Seeking to strengthen their positions, Packard and Studebaker of South Bend merged in 1954, but within two years the Packard plant in Detroit was abandoned and the Studebaker-Packard operations were consolidated at the South Bend plant, where, in 1958, all further efforts to keep the Packard on the market were abandoned, and in 1963 the Studebaker car also was dropped. Somewhat more successful was the merger, also in 1954, of the Hudson company with the Nash company of Kenosha, Wisconsin, to form the American Motors Corporation. Although Detroit remained the headquarters for the executive offices of the new corporation, the Hudson assembly plant in the Motor City was closed as all automotive assembly operations were concentrated at the Kenosha factory. In 1957, the last of the Hudson automobiles, long one of Detroit's best-known automotive products, came off the Wisconsin assembly line.

It was inevitable that the successes of the smaller companies in the immediate post-war years would be short-lived since the Big Three had vastly superior manufacturing facilities and an extensive network of experienced dealers. By 1949, when total American auto production finally surpassed the record year of 1929, the sellers' market, which had benefitted the small companies, was coming to an end, and as more normal market conditions returned, the competitive edge held by the big companies became ever more evident.

Among the Big Three, the most attention was focussed on the Ford Motor Company, as businessmen and the public both wondered what would happen to that great firm now that Henry Ford and most of the other old-timers who had run it for so many years were gone. It soon became apparent that Ford's grandson had far greater managerial skills than the grandfather had ever shown. Faced with staggering problems when he took on the presidency of the company in 1945, Henry Ford II cleared the decks, completely over-hauling the company's antiquated management structure. He hired an experienced administrator, Ernest R. Breech, president of the Bendix Aviation Corporation, as executive vice-president, and later president, with Ford becoming chairman of the board, and accepted the services of ten ex-air force officers, highly trained in financial and statistical matters, who were nicknamed the "Whiz

Kids." Under this new regime, company losses, which had been averaging $9,000,000 a month in 1945, were turned to profits, and by 1950 Ford, which had dropped to third place in car sales in 1933, moved past Chrysler into second place where it was securely entrenched with sales that usually gave it control of slightly more than a quarter of the domestic car market. Although this was only half of the share held by General Motors, Ford was comfortably ahead of Chrysler, which, from the fifties on, experienced managerial and financial difficulties.

The ability of General Motors to convert its massive manufacturing facilities in Detroit, Pontiac, Flint, Lansing, and other cities in Michigan and across the country to civilian automobile production was temporarily delayed by a strike called by the United Automobile Workers on November 21, 1945, which was not finally settled until March 13 of the following year. The strike was almost as crucial to the future of the industry as the Flint sit-down strike nine years earlier because it was regarded as a test of strength. During the war, a moratorium on strikes had generally been adhered to, and so at war's end the relationship of the auto union and the auto companies was where it had been at the end of the initial negotiations in the thirties. The question now was whether the United Automobile Workers could hold on to and add to the gains it had made at that time or whether the companies could strengthen their position in post-war labor-management relations. In addition, however, the 1945-46 General Motors strike was also a test of the strength in the union of Walter Reuther, a native of Wheeling, West Virginia (where he had been born in 1907), who had come to work in the auto plants in Detroit in 1927. In the mid-thirties, Reuther had begun to rise in the ranks of the U.A.W. when he and his brothers Victor and Roy had played leading roles in the historic strikes of that period. Walter Reuther, who was in charge of the post-war strike against General Motors, hoped to use it as stepping-stone to the presidency of the union, then held by a rival faction headed by R. J. Thomas, which Reuther charged was Communist-dominated, although Thomas denied the accusation. Reuther initially demanded that General Motors grant its workers a thirty percent wage increase. More important, he asked that the corporation open its books for the union to examine—a move which Reuther declared would settle the question of whether or not General Motors could afford such a wage increase, but which the corporation steadfastly refused to agree to on the grounds that this would be the first step in involving the union in strictly managerial decisions. Although Reuther, much to the delight of his union rivals, failed to budge General Motors on this issue, and ultimately had to settle for some fringe benefits and a wage increase of eighteen-and-a-half cents an hour (about a fifteen percent wage increase; approximately what other companies had agreed to without a strike), Reuther and his supporters regarded the strike as having been successful since the union had emerged from the fray with undiminished strength as the spokesman for the auto workers.[3]

At the convention of the United Auto Workers in March, 1946, Reuther was elected president of the union by a narrow margin, but the rival Thomas faction succeeded in maintaining control of the union's executive board. However, when Reuther was re-elected to the presidency in 1947 he quickly rooted out his opponents, thereby obtaining firm control of the union which he maintained until his death in an airplane crash in northern Michigan in 1970. In April, 1948, Reuther was severely wounded in an attempted assassination and a year later Victor Reuther lost an eye when an attempt was also made on his life. Although the persons who fired the shots were never caught, it was widely assumed the attacks had been instigated by some of Reuther's union rivals. Walter Reuther recovered from his wounds to lead his union to major new victories in bargaining in 1948 and 1950 that for the first time provided automatic wage increases when the cost of living went up and guaranteed retirement benefits for employees.[4]

Reuther went on in 1952 to become president not only of the U.A.W., but also of the Congress of Industrial Organizations, that federation of industrial unions that had split off from the American Federation of Labor back in 1936. Reuther now led the C.I.O. in a successful drive to reunite its forces with those of the A.F.L. in 1955, but he was never happy with that merger because the A.F.L. forces, under George Meany, clearly emerged as dominant. In 1969 Reuther led the U.A.W. out of the A.F.L.-C.I.O.[5] Reuther viewed George Meany as an old-time union leader whose only concern was with the so-called bread-and-butter issues that directly affected his union members. Reuther, in contrast, represented a new breed of union leaders who, because of the Depression, sought to go beyond the traditional approach and use their unions' power to influence the development of wide-ranging programs of social and other humanitarian reforms. This new approach, favored primarily by the new industrial unions, led men like Reuther to abandon the political tactics of the older craft unions which had supported whatever candidates promised to protect the union's interests. Instead they allied their forces with the Democratic party led by Roosevelt, who was pushing for the kinds of liberal reforms that the C.I.O. unions favored.

The full impact of this new approach on state politics in Michigan was not felt until 1948. The elections earlier in that decade seemed to indicate a return in Michigan to the kind of one-party dominance that had prevailed before the Depression. In 1942, Harry F. Kelly, a far stronger candidate than Luren Dickinson had been two years before, recaptured the governorship for the Republicans. Kelly defeated the re-election bid of Murray D. Van Wagoner, who found that the organization he had built up when he was highway commissioner had faded away when he no longer, as governor, dispensed highway contracts and jobs. Two years later, Kelly overwhelmed his Democratic opponent, becoming the first governor since Fred Green to succeed in winning re-election, and also the first Republican to win the office when Franklin Roosevelt was on the same ballot running for the Presidency.

During Kelly's administration rumors spread that the votes of some legislators were being purchased by lobbyists for various interest groups. Judge Leland W. Carr of Ingham County was named as a one-man grand jury to look into the rumors, and Kim Sigler, a flamboyant attorney, was appointed the special prosecutor. Charles F. Hemans, a lobbyist, turned state's evidence, and revealed that he had kept records of payments to legislators from bankers, loan companies, racetrack operators, slot-machine owners, and others. Sigler secured the conviction of twenty defendants in 1944. In the continuing investigation, Senator Warren G. Hooper of Albion, who was scheduled to testify on January 12, 1945, was found murdered on January 11. The killer was never found. The prosecution's case was further weakened by the refusal of Charles Hemans to continue in his role as the star witness. Thus the ultimate resolution of this scandal—a relatively rare occurrence in Michigan's political history—left many questions unanswered, but the careers of several legislators were ruined and the reputations of some businessmen badly tarnished.[6]

One who benefitted from the investigations was Kim Sigler. Sigler made the most of his role as the prosecutor in the case even though he had been removed from that post by Judge Louis E. Coash, who had replaced Judge Carr as the grand juror when Carr was named to the state Supreme Court in September, 1945. Like Owosso's Thomas E. Dewey, who a few years before had ridden into the governorship of New York on the strength of his record as a crusading district attorney in New York City, Sigler used his role in the grand jury investigations to win the Republican gubernatorial nomination in 1946. In November Sigler defeated former governor Murray D. Van Wagoner.

Sigler had the support in his campaign of former governor Alex Groesbeck, and as governor, Sigler resumed Groesbeck's campaign of a quarter of century before for a more efficient state government. He presented the legislature with a long list of recommendations designed to lengthen the terms of the principal state executive officers to four years and to increase the powers of the governor. Although Sigler sought to get his way by calling the legislature back into special sessions, as such strong-willed predecessors in the governor's office as Hazen Pingree and Chase Osborn had also done, he failed to get most of what he requested, even though the Republicans had a strong majority in both houses. He did, however, succeed in securing the creation of the Department of Administration, headed by a controller appointed by the governor. This department was given the responsibility for overseeing state budgetary, purchasing, and accounting matters. However, Sigler's arrogant personality, together with the changes he was advocating, made him even more vulnerable than his mentor Groesbeck had been to the charge that he was seeking to impose one-man rule on the state and made his chance for re-election in 1948 appear uncertain. Groesbeck himself turned against Sigler, who possibly could have overcome the opposition that had developed within his own party had not events in the Democratic party sealed his fate.[7]

Once Walter Reuther had consolidated his control of the United Auto Workers he sought to use the power of that union to turn the Democratic party in Michigan into an organization that would support on the state level the kind of programs that Reuther favored and with which the party on the national level had been associated under the New Deal of Franklin Roosevelt and his successor, Harry Truman. On a broader scale, August Scholle, powerful head of the Michigan C.I.O. Council, now openly abandoned all pretense of non-partisanship in political matters, throwing his support behind the Democratic party in the state and making it plain to Republican candidates that they could no longer expect any endorsements from his organization. On November 21, 1947, two young Detroit attorneys, Hicks Griffiths and G. Mennen Williams, together with Neil Staebler of Ann Arbor and several others, met at Griffiths' home and laid plans to establish a coalition of liberal intellectuals and labor leaders to take advantage of the votes of the union members that Scholle and Reuther represented. They chose Williams as their standard bearer and candidate for the Democratic gubernatorial nomination in 1948.[8]

Gerhard Mennen Williams was then thirty-six years old. A native of Detroit, Williams' mother was an heir to the great Mennen soap fortune, hence Williams' nickname of "Soapy," which he had had since boyhood. As a graduate of Princeton and the University of Michigan Law School, Williams had compiled a brilliant record. As a protégé of Frank Murphy both in the state and federal government in the late thirties, Williams had been infected with the liberal idealism of Murphy and his fellow New Dealers. After service in the navy in the Second World War, Williams had returned to Detroit where he resumed his career in law and politics. Ironically, his career was given a boost by his future gubernatorial opponent when Kim Sigler appointed him as a Democratic member of the bi-partisan Liquor Control Commission.[9]

Early in 1948, Williams entered the race for the Democratic gubernatorial nomination. He immediately revealed the talents that made him one of the most formidable and effective political campaigners in Michigan history. Physically, he was tall, powerful, and handsome. His wife Nancy, member of a wealthy Ypsilanti family, was an attractive woman, and the couple appeared together frequently on the campaign trail, another change from past practices when candidates' wives were rarely seen or heard. What Williams lacked in a speaking voice was more than compensated for by the sincerity that he projected. Most important was his amazing ability, considering his family and educational background, to establish a true rapport with the workingman and a host of minority groups through such folksy techniques as wearing his familiar green polka dot bow tie, calling square dances, and travelling across the state during the 1948 campaign in a beat-up old car because the average person was still having difficulty in getting delivery on a new car.

There was strong opposition to Williams in the primary from the old-guard Democrats who were seeking to maintain their hold on the party, but he overcame that opposition and won the nomination. In November Williams defeated Kim Sigler by more than 160,000 votes at a time when Thomas E. Dewey, the Republican Presidential candidate, came in well ahead of Harry Truman in Michigan. The fact that few other Democrats were elected with Williams in 1948, and the paper-thin margins by which Williams defeated former governor Harry Kelly and Secretary of State Fred M. Alger, Jr., in gaining second and third terms in office in 1950 and 1952, indicated that Kim Sigler's unpopularity had contributed considerably to Williams' initial victory in 1948. But then in 1954, when Williams broke with past precedent and ran for a fourth term, he not only won re-election by a large majority but Democrats running with him for other state executive positions were also elected. From this time, through the remainder of the fifties, the Democratic party clearly was the major-

ity party in the state as it carried Williams into office for fifth and
sixth terms and captured the other state administrative offices, a
majority on the Supreme Court, Michigan's two United State Senate
seats, and an increasing number of seats in the lower house of Congress.

The Democratic victories came in a decade when the Michigan
Republican organization enjoyed unusual power on the national
level following the election of the party's Presidential candidate,
Dwight D. Eisenhower, in 1952. Eisenhower carried Michigan by
more than 300,000 votes and did even better in 1956. Arthur E.
Summerfield of Flint, head of the country's largest Chevrolet
dealership, who had led a takeover of the state Republican machinery by auto industry executives in the forties, was national
chairman of the party during the 1952 campaign and was rewarded
with the office of Postmaster General in Eisenhower's cabinet from
1953 to 1961. Charles E. Wilson, president of General Motors,
served as Secretary of Defense in Eisenhower's first term, delighting
administration critics with a penchant for saying the wrong thing,
such as his remark in his confirmation hearing that he had always felt
that what was good for General Motors was good for the country.
Wilson brought a number of General Motors executives into the
defense department with him, and in 1955 former governor Wilber
M. Brucker was named Secretary of the Army, an office that he held
through the remainder of Eisenhower's administration.

The fact that the Michigan Republicans were unable to use
Eisenhower's immense popularity to recapture control of the state's
administration can be attributed in part to the tendency of more and
more Michigan voters to cross party lines and vote for the man and
not the party. The man who more than anyone else attracted these
independent voters to the Democratic column was G. Mennen
Williams. He championed the cause of the little people, advocated
more support for education, and in general was sensitive to human
needs. His appointments were excellent; there was hardly a breath of
scandal during his dozen years as governor. Though Williams was
hated by his opponents, who were fond of using the nickname
"Soapy" as ridicule, he was idolized by many more. But there were
other factors behind the Democratic victories. The chairman of the
Democratic State Central Committee was Neil Staebler, a brilliant
party organizer. Another factor was the Negro vote. Prior to the
thirties, Negroes were regarded as supporters of the Republican
party, the party of Lincoln, but they were won over in overwhelming
numbers to the Democratic party by the programs of the New Deal.
In the period after 1945, the Democratic party in the North was

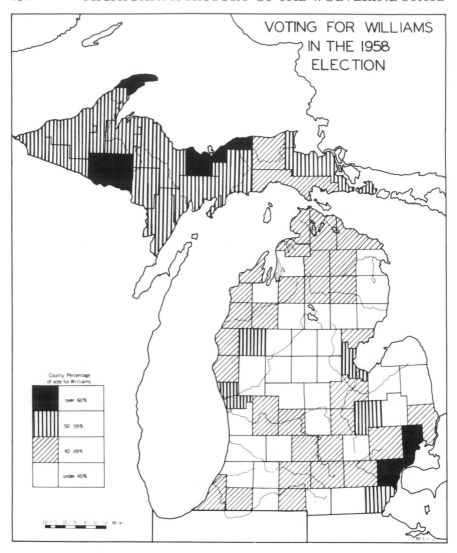

VOTING FOR WILLIAMS
IN THE 1958
ELECTION

County Percentage
of vote for Williams

over 60%

50 - 59%

40 - 49%

under 40%

perceived as being far more zealous than the Republicans in the fight
for equal rights, and beginning with the 1948 Democratic National
Convention, Williams and the liberal-labor coalition that he headed
were in the forefront of the fight to keep the party strongly committed to the civil rights cause. Finally, Democratic victories were evidence of the success of Gus Scholle and his fellow labor leaders in
recruiting union financial support and votes for the party's candidates.

But throughout the fifties, despite the success of the Democrats in gaining control of the executive and judicial branches of government, they could not achieve many of their programs because of the continued control of the Republicans in the legislature. Year after year, the recommendations that Williams sent to the legislature were rejected or approved only in a watered-down form. The consistent ability of the Republicans, with their preponderant strength in the rural, outstate regions, to elect a majority of the members of the legislature thus brought to the forefront the issue of legislative apportionment. In 1958, the Democrats came close to breaking the Republican hold on the lower house of the legislature, electing half of the members, but the illness of one of the Democratic members enabled the Republicans to retain control at the opening of the new session in 1959. In the senate, however, the Democrats still trailed the Republicans twenty-two seats to twelve. The inequality in the legislative districts was illustrated by the fact that the twelve successful Democratic candidates for the senate received 46,000 more votes than all the twenty-two winning Republican candidates combined, while the total vote received by the fifty-five winning Democratic candidates for seats in the lower house was nearly double that received by the fifty-five Republican victors.

In earlier years, the apportionment of seats in the state senate and house of representatives had been the subject of little discussion. Under the state's first and second constitutions the legislature was given the responsibility for reapportioning the legislature after each federal census; there was also to be a state census between the federal censuses, after which there also was to be a reapportionment. The legislature generally carried out this duty of reapportioning each five years. The Constitution of 1908 provided for reapportionment only every ten years after each federal census, the state census having been abandoned. The house was to be apportioned according to population, but there was some question whether the language of the constitution also obligated the legislature to apportion the senate seats on the same basis.

The phenomenal growth of Detroit and its suburban areas as well as other cities after 1900 was reflected in the 1910 census. Members of the legislature, the majority of whom represented rural areas, and small towns and cities, balked at carrying out the requirement that the legislature be reapportioned in 1913 and every tenth year thereafter. At that time Wayne County had four out of thirty-two senators and fourteen out of one hundred representatives. A weak gesture toward reapportionment was made by the 1913 legislature by giving Wayne County one more senate seat; nothing was done about reapportioning house seats. When 1923 rolled around, the legislature again failed to act at the regular session in spite of the recommendation of Governor Groesbeck. The governor called a special session and still there was no action. In the 1925 session, however, Groesbeck was able to push through reapportionment. This gave Wayne County seven more legislative seats.[10]

No action was taken in 1933 to reapportion legislative seats as required by the constitution. The senate failed to reapportion its seats in 1943, but the house passed a reapportionment that gave Wayne County twenty-seven seats. The population of that county entitled it to thirty-eight seats. There appeared to be no reason to suppose that the legislature would carry out its responsibility to provide a fair reapportionment in 1953 any more adequately than it had in the preceding decades. As the gap between the population of senatorial and house districts became wider, public demand for reapportionment became more insistent. As a result a Michigan Committee for Representative Government was formed, and proposed a plan under which four counties in southeastern Michigan which had fifty percent of the state's population, according to the 1950 census (Wayne, Oakland, Macomb, and Genesee), would have sixteen out of thirty-three senate seats and forty-nine out of ninety-nine house seats. Another plan was proposed by the Michigan Committee for a Balanced Legislature, largely made up of outstate citizens. This plan increased the senate from thirty-two to thirty-four members, and the house from one hundred to 110. The house was to be reapportioned by the legislature according to population every ten years beginning in 1953, and if the latter failed to act within 180 days of the start of its first regular session, the duty was to devolve upon the state board of canvassers. The plan for the house, however, retained the moiety provision of the 1908 constitution, which meant that any county having a population equal to one-half of the population of the state divided by one hundred was entitled to one representative. As this worked out, some larger counties had less representation in the house than the smaller counties. The plan provided fixed senatorial districts, the effect of which was to give the less populous areas of the state much more representation in the senate than they would been entitled to on a population basis.

Both proposals were placed on the ballot in November, 1952. The "balanced legislature" plan was adopted by a margin of about 300,000 votes out of over two million cast. The other proposal was defeated by nearly 500,000 votes. In 1953 the house was reapportioned according to the provisions of the new amendment, and the first legislature of thirty-four senators and 110 representatives was elected in 1954. The largest house district had a population of

67,110, according to the census of 1950, while the smallest had 32,913. Population of senatorial districts had a wider range: from 364,026 to 61,008.

Dissatisfaction with the 1952 apportionment plan became stronger as urban populations in southeastern Michigan continued to grow faster than outstate areas during the fifties. By 1960, the Thirty-second Senatorial District, comprising Ontonagon, Houghton, Baraga, and Keweenaw counties in the Copper Country, had a total population of only 55,806 people. In contrast, Oakland County, which likewise constituted a single senatorial district, had a population of 690,583, while there were three other districts in the Metropolitan Detroit area with populations in excess of 400,000, more than four times the population of four districts in the northern part of the lower peninsula which, together with the Copper Country district, had total populations of less than a hundred thousand. Such gross examples of legislative malapportionment were important factors in the increased support for complete constitutional revision, and legislative reapportionment was the hottest issue in the constitutional convention of 1961-62. Republicans, who held a large majority of the seats in the convention, favored a continuance, with some modifications, of the balanced legislature, that is, with one house apportioned according to population and the apportionment of the other determined to some degree by geographical considerations. Most Democrats, whose strength lay in populous southeastern Michigan, favored a straight population basis for both houses.[11] The outcome in the convention was a compromise. The provision written into the new constitution provided, as did the 1952 amendment, for the reapportionment of house seats every ten years on a population basis. Moiety, however, was raised from one-half to seven-tenths. This meant that a county had to have seven-tenths of the total population of the state, divided by one hundred, in order to be entitled to a single representative. The new constitution also provided for the reapportionment of the senate each ten years. In apportioning senate seats a formula was to be applied that weighted population eighty percent and area twenty percent.

Democrats might have accepted this compromise had it not been for a United States Supreme Court decision, handed down while the convention was still in session. In the case of Baker vs. Carr in 1962, the court ordered the Tennessee legislature to carry out the provisions of the Tennessee constitution, which called for reapportionment at periodic intervals according to population. This appeared to offer hope that the federal courts would order the Michigan legislature to be reapportioned on a straight population basis.

Meanwhile, a case initiated in 1959 by August Scholle was pending before the United States Supreme Court. In his suit, Scholle claimed that the 1952 amendment to the Michigan constitution violated the equal-rights provisions of the fourteenth amendment to the United States Constitution. The state supreme court had decided against him and he had appealed the case to the United States Supreme Court. After the decision in the case of Baker vs. Carr, the federal court remanded the Scholle case to the Michigan Supreme Court for reconsideration. On July 18, 1962, the state court, on a party-line 4-3 vote, found in favor of Scholle, cancelled the primary election for the nomination of senators scheduled for August 7, and ordered the legislature to reapportion the senate according to population. However, a stay order was obtained from Justice Potter Stewart of the United States Supreme Court, and the primary election was held as scheduled. With the adoption of the new constitution, the question of the constitutionality of the 1952 amendment became academic. Scholle then started over, with a suit claiming the provisions of the new constitution also were in violation of the fourteenth amendment to the federal Constitution.

In 1964 the federal courts declared that the fourteenth amendment required that state legislatures be apportioned strictly according to population. The bi-partisan apportionment commission (provided for under the new state constitution) having failed to agree on a formula, the state supreme court specified house and senatorial districts of approximately equal population, and in November, 1964, legislators were elected from these new districts.

*   *   *   *   *

The final resolution of the apportionment problem came too late to avert a bitter conflict between the Democratic state administration and the Republican-controlled legislature in the late fifties. In several ways, this conflict badly damaged the state's image and that of a good many of its leaders. The major issue, although originating with the philosophical differences between the conservative Republican legislators and the liberal Williams and his associates, came down to the amount of money needed to finance governmental activities in the state and how it was to be obtained. The sales tax that had been passed in 1933 had satisfactorily met the state's needs for more than a decade. During World War II, in fact, revenues from this and other taxes had resulted in the accumulation of a sizable surplus in the state treasury. But local governmental units found themselves caught in a squeeze. Rising costs of materials as well as wages and salaries created a serious problem for them in view of the fifteen-mill tax limitation. At every legislative session mayors and school superintendents entreated the legislature for state aid. The response was meager. As a result of this situation, a constitutional amendment providing for the diversion of a part of the state sales tax to local units was placed on the ballot by petition and adopted by the people in 1946. Under the provisions of this amendment two-thirds of the total sales-tax revenue was to be returned to local school districts and one-sixth to cities, villages, and townships. The adoption of this "sales tax diversion amendment" marked the beginning of a long period of financial problems and difficulties for the state government. At the time it was approved, it diverted some seventy-seven percent of the state's revenues to local governmental units.

The legislature in the years that followed sought to make up for the loss to state government of sales-tax revenues by levying new taxes and by striving for economy. At the same time, persistent pressures for more and better state services drove the lawmakers to adopt larger and larger budgets. Among the new taxes levied in an effort to balance income and expenditure in the state treasury were a cigarette tax (1947), a diesel-fuel tax (1947), liquor taxes (1957 and 1959), a watercraft tax (1947), and a business-activities tax (1953). But as government costs continued to rise these proved inadequate. An amendment adopted in 1954 limited the sales tax to three percent. Since the constitution limited the state debt to $250,000 it was impossible to borrow money in any substantial amount. By July 1, 1958, the state treasury showed a deficit of 21.1 million dollars. In order to meet payrolls amounts were borrowed from funds that had a balance to cover deficits in other funds. Payments of state aid to school districts were delayed, and contractors with the state had to wait beyond the usual time for the payment of their bills. The amount of the deficit increased to 95.4 million dollars by July 1, 1959.[12]

These recurring deficits and the possibility that the state might not be able to meet its payrolls got national attention. Michigan became known as the state that had gone broke. The reports were greatly exaggerated, but they gave the state a bad reputation. Michigan was by no means the only state that had financial problems in these years. But a variety of factors made the situation in Michigan more acute than elsewhere. With Michigan's increased dependence on the automobile industry, its economy, upon which its tax revenues largely depended, was subject to far more exaggerated fluctuations than was true of the nation's economy as a whole. At the beginning of the fifties, the auto industry boomed, with production

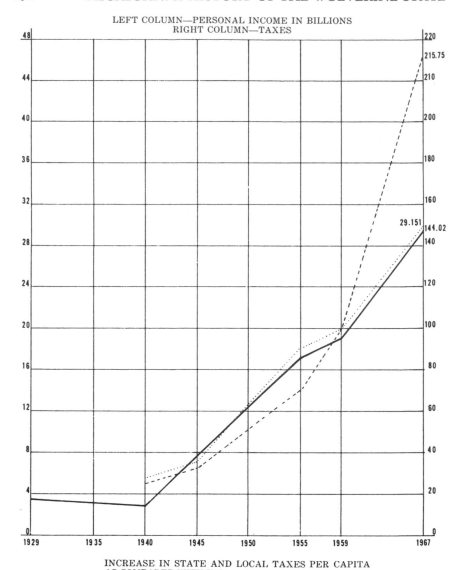

LEFT COLUMN—PERSONAL INCOME IN BILLIONS
RIGHT COLUMN—TAXES

INCREASE IN STATE AND LOCAL TAXES PER CAPITA
AS COMPARED WITH INCREASE IN PERSONAL INCOME,
1929 - 1967, IN MICHIGAN

——————PERSONAL INCOME   - - - - - LOCAL TAXES   ·············STATE TAXES

in 1950 up to 8,003,056 vehicles, nearly two million more than the
record number of cars, trucks, and buses that had been produced in
1949. World events then intervened as they had ten years before.
The fall of Czechoslovakia to the Communists in 1948, the Communist takeover in China in 1949, and finally the outbreak of war in
Korea in 1950, roused the United States to the necessity for re-

newed expenditures on armaments. Congress not only appropriated vast sums for United States rearmament but also authorized military aid to other non-Communist nations. Once more, as in 1940, the nation turned to the automobile industry for much of the needed war materials, although during the active phase of the Korean War between 1950 and 1953 civilian automobile production was not shut down. Prosperous times led to sharp increases in auto production, which surpassed 9,000,000 units by 1955. To meet the need for workers resulting from the combination of war contracts and auto production, the flow of people into Michigan in the first half of the fifties was at a rate exceeded by only two or three states in the country.

However, after 1955, employment in Michigan's auto industry declined sharply. As the emphasis in defense shifted to more sophisticated weapons, such as rockets and missiles, most prime government contracts went to other areas. For a time, Michigan received almost no defense contracts, although there was an encouraging upturn later in the early sixties. It was estimated that between 125,000 and 150,000 jobs were lost after 1953 as a consequence of awarding defense contracts to firms in other states. Related to this is the fact that Michigan lagged in the industrial research so essential to this field. The big boom, lasting from 1940 to 1955, had absorbed the energies of Michigan industrial leaders. They did not look far enough to the future.

A second factor in the loss of employment in the auto industry was decentralization. Actually this had been going on for some time. In the 1930s Michigan had accounted for over sixty percent of all automotive employment. By 1958 this state had only about forty-seven percent of the nation's employment in the industry. Assembly plants were moved elsewhere to be closer to major markets. It is a moot question whether this movement outside Michigan was induced to any appreciable extent by the relatively high taxes Michigan levied on corporate business.

Also contributing to the decline of employment in the automobile industry was automation, the installation of machinery and devices that reduced the amount of manpower needed to produce a car. Immense sums were spent by the auto companies in 1955 and 1956 for automation. It was estimated that 130,000 additional workers would have been needed in 1958 if productivity had been at the 1948 level. Other factors that also caused unemployment in the industry were the 1958 recession and the competition of the foreign car. Employment in Michigan auto plants, which stood at 503,000 in 1953, had dropped to 293,000 in 1958.

The result of this on the state as a whole was catastrophic.

Michigan had come to be so heavily dependent on automobile manufacturing that it became known as a "one industry state." The sustained boom over a fifteen-year period brought a huge influx of
workers, and when employment in the auto industry was cut almost
in half, the unemployment rate in the state, and especially in the
Detroit area, far exceeded the national averages. Unemployed
people bought less and therefore the revenues from the state sales
tax, chief source of revenues for the state government and an important source for local government and schools, declined sharply. Relief costs, of course, skyrocketed. Meanwhile the children of the
people who came to Michigan in the boom years were knocking at
the doors of the schools and colleges, and soon heavier expenditures
for education were required. Thus the decline of employment in the
auto industry became a matter of deep concern to all the people in
Michigan.

In addition, important as the auto industry had become, it was
by no means the sum total of Michigan's economy. Even when the
auto industry enjoyed good times, there were large sections of
Michigan's population that did not share in that prosperity. In 1960,
when the nation's economy was coming out of the recession of the
latter part of the fifties and the auto industry was beginning to enjoy
one of its better periods, over a fifth of Michigan's families had
annual incomes of less than $3,000, which was defined as the poverty
level. The median family income in the state at this time was $6,256,
but in six counties the median was less than $4,000. The gap between
the rural areas and manufacturing centers widened, with manufacturing workers in the early sixties enjoying an increase in their income
of twenty-one percent while the average farmer's income dropped by
six percent. But in terms of geographical areas, northern Michigan,
and particularly the Upper Peninsula, remained the most persistently
troubled of all sections in the state. In 1960, when the unemployment rate for the state was 6.9 percent, the rate in parts of the Upper
Peninsula was nearly three times as great.

Numerous committees studied the problems of the Upper
Peninsula in the fifties and sixties searching for methods of reviving
the area's economy. In the mining areas in the western portions of
the peninsula, prospects seemed to brighten considerably. In the
Copper Country, annual production in the early fifties dropped
below fifty million pounds, a fifth of the production reached in the
record years of the second decade of the century. But then the White
Pine mine in the Ontonagon area, developed by the Copper Range
Company with the aid of a $57,000,000 loan from the Reconstruc-
tion Finance Corporation, began to use new techniques to produce

copper from a huge deposit of low-grade ores that could not be worked profitably under older techniques. By the end of the decade, Michigan copper production annually was above the 100,000,000-pound level, with most of this coming from the White Pine development. Additional mining jobs became available in the mid-sixties with the announcement by Calumet and Hecla of the discovery of a similar vast deposit of low-grade copper ores in the central portion of the Copper Country which this company had been mining for a century. Although the announcement indicated that it would be several years before these new deposits could be exploited, it spurred a sudden revival of interest in this company's stock and led to a take-over of the company by a California conglomerate, Universal Oil Products, which may have been more interested in acquiring Calumet and Hecla's Wolverine Tube Division than it was the mining properties. After a prolonged strike of the Calumet and Hecla miners in 1968-69, Universal Oil broke off any further talks and shut down the mine. The action left the White Pine mine as the sole remaining copper producer in Michigan and once again created a feeling of despair in what had once been one of the state's most prosperous areas.

The outlook on the area's three iron ranges also fluctuated between optimism and gloom. In 1954, efforts that had been underway for many years to discover a feasible method of working the vast quantities of low-grade iron ores that remained in this region culminated with the establishment by the Cleveland Cliffs Iron Company (with funds also supplied by the Ford Motor Company) of a plant near Ishpeming, on the Marquette Iron Range, that would remove most of the waste from these ores and produce a concentrated product with a high percentage of iron. The process, known as beneficiation, worked well and led to the construction of several additional plants which were producing nearly ten million tons of this iron concentrate by the end of the sixties. This exceeded any production ever achieved on that range. During the sixties, beneficiation began on the Menominee Iron Range, but on January 29, 1966, the last operating iron mine on the Gogebic Iron Range was closed down. This range had produced well over 300,000,000 tons of iron ore since its opening in 1884, but now the ores were either too far underground to permit profitable mining or could not be treated by the processes that were reviving iron mining on the other two ranges.

For many, the economic future of the Upper Peninsula and for much of the northern parts of the lower peninsula rested in the development of the tourist industry, and great efforts were expended by the state, through the Michigan Tourist Council, and the regional tourist associations in promoting Michigan's numerous attractions. Helping this development was the beginning in the fifties of the most massive road building program in the nation's history, particularly after the passage of the Interstate Highway Act of 1956, which called for the construction of 41,000 miles of free express highways across the country, with the federal government paying for ninety percent of the cost. Although much of the emphasis was on the construction of expressways linking the major cities—I-94 between Detroit and Chicago and I-96 from Detroit to Lansing, Grand Rapids, and the Lake Michigan shore areas—there was great interest in the impact that I-75 to northern Michigan and other highway improvements in that direction would have on enabling greater numbers of tourists to reach those areas. By the early sixties, with the completion of much of this work, trips from the southern areas of the state to the Straits of Mackinac that had been exhausting, all-day adventures a short time before could now be made in a matter of four or five hours.

The bottleneck for motorists had always come at Mackinaw City, where the motorist had been forced to ferry his car across the straits to St. Ignace. The railroad ferries that had been operating there since the late nineteenth century had had little interest in this automobile trade, and the exorbitant rates they had charged to carry the motorist's car across the straits had led the state highway department in 1923 to establish its own car ferry operation. In normal times of the year, the motorist was likely to have only a short wait for the forty-five minute trip across the straits at the low rates the state charged. But at the peak periods of the tourist and hunting seasons, the lines of cars waiting to board the ferries caused delays of many hours. This led to renewed demands for a bridge across the straits. In 1950, Governor Williams appointed the Mackinac Bridge Authority, with Prentiss M. Brown of St. Ignace, former United States Senator, as the chairman. After a long and enormously complicated struggle, Brown and his associates, with the backing of Governor Williams and the tireless work of various individuals—particularly W. Stewart Woodfill, the long-time head of Mackinac Island's Grand Hotel— were able to resolve the doubts concerning the feasibility of such a bridge. A reluctant legislature authorized the work through the is- suance by the bridge authority of revenue bonds, to be paid off by tolls from the users of the bridge.[13]

Work on the bridge, designed by David B. Steinman, began in 1954 and proceeded in the face of formidable difficulties, but the project was completed in November, 1957, with the formal dedica- tion occurring in June, 1958. The central suspension span, extending 3800 feet between the main towers that rose 552 feet above the water, was the second longest such span in the world and the total length of the bridge between the cable anchorages was 8,614 feet, leading to the claim that it was the longest suspension bridge in the world, a claim that did not go undisputed.[14] But at any event, the bridge was a spectacular achievement and became one of the state's best-known attractions. It created an enormous boom in the development of facilities of all types to serve the influx of visitors to the area. However, the long-term hopes that the bridge, by facilitating traffic between the two peninsulas, would cause the economy of northern Michigan, particularly the Upper Peninsula, to surge ahead again were not fulfilled. There was undoubtedly an impact on the tourist industry, but this was a seasonal industry, incapable of supplying the large numbers of year-round jobs for the residents that lumbering and mining had done in the old days. As for the development of other kinds of industry, the remoteness of this region from the major markets and materials still hindered the development of many large manufacturing activities, despite the best efforts of the state's economic development department, established in 1947, and various Upper Peninsula promotional groups. Thus as the fifties drew to a close, the southern third of the state, itself hard hit by the decline in auto sales, was still in the position it had been for some years of providing most of the funds needed for schools, relief, highways, and other services in the other two-thirds of the state.

These were major factors in the tax and financial crisis that climaxed in 1959. But the political aspect of the crisis received much more attention. The winning personality of Governor Williams, which had endeared him to the majority of the state's voters, had no effect on the Republican majority in the legislature. Party rivalry is normal and healthy, but in Michigan during the latter part of the fifties, the rivalry between the Democrats and the Republicans, who had been repeatedly thwarted in their attempts to oust Williams from the governor's office, became bitter and often vicious.

It was apparent by 1957 that expenditures of state government would have to be curtailed or else new tax revenues found. The Republicans blamed Governor Williams for reckless spending. The Democrats replied that every penny spent had to be appropriated by the Republican legislature. Actually, the increased need for funds for education, mental hospitals, relief, and other state programs made it quite impossible to reduce spending. Even the enemies of Williams came to recognize that the only answer was to increase tax revenues. But at this point a serious difference of opinion arose over tax philosophy. Governor Williams repeatedly urged that the state adopt a graduated personal and corporation income tax as the fairest and most equitable kind of taxation. He met with staunch opposition in the legislature and there was evidence that the majority of Michigan citizens, while demonstrating their support of Williams, did not favor an income tax. The voters had twice rejected proposals for a state income tax in the 1920s by overwhelming majorities. The federal income tax had become so high and the task of preparing annual federal income tax returns had become so complicated by the fifties that people were not supportive of a state income tax. Newspaper polls showed popular opposition to such a tax, which encouraged the Republicans in the legislature to maintain an intransigent opposition to Williams' proposals. They derided a study of the Michigan tax system which recommended an income tax as being the work of labor-union bosses.

The mounting state deficit made it obvious that the legislature that convened January 14, 1959, would have to take some kind of action. Weeks went by, however, with no decision. There were indications that conservative Republicans in the legislature were deliberately putting off a decision on tax reform in order to destroy Williams as a possible Presidential candidate in 1960 by giving him the image of a governor of a bankrupt state. Williams, on the other hand, made the mistake of thinking that the Republicans would compromise before forcing the state to suspend payment of its obligations. On May 5, 1959, the state did not pay its employees. This "payless payday," which made headlines across the country and was featured on national television news programs that evening, further deteriorated Michigan's reputation. Even though funds were juggled and employees did receive their pay the following week, the damage had been done.

The "payless payday" incident, however, did force political leaders to deal with the problem. On August 29 lawmakers passed a series of bills to increase tax revenues. The business-receipts tax was increased, and so was the intangibles tax. Main reliance was placed, however, upon a so-called "use tax" of one percent. In effect this was an addition to the three percent sales tax, although it covered certain items such as hotel bills that the sales tax did not cover. By calling it a use tax the legislature sought to evade the constitutional limit of three percent on the sales tax. But the stratagem proved unsuccessful, for on October 22 the state supreme court found the new tax unconstitutional.[15] The legislature then reconvened and on December 18 enacted a package of nuisance taxes on telephone bills, liquor, cigarettes, and beer. The corporation franchise tax was also increased. Even with the income from these new taxes (which became effective January 1, 1960), expenditures for the fiscal year

1959-60 exceeded revenues by $9,211,630. In 1960 the legislature authorized the raiding of the Veterans' Trust Fund, pledging the state to appropriate each year an amount equal to the annual interest the fund had earned. This brought 40.7 million dollars into the state treasury, reducing the accumulated deficit on July 1, 1960, to around 64 million dollars.

But this, of course, was no permanent solution to chronic deficits. Indeed, the nuisance taxes were intended only as a stopgap. The 1960 legislature drew up a proposal to amend the constitution that would permit a four percent sales tax. The question was submitted at the November 8, 1960, election, and was approved by a very narrow margin. The legislature then reconvened and enacted a measure increasing the sales tax to the amount now authorized. It was signed by the governor and took effect on February 1, 1961. John B. Swainson, who had succeeded G. Mennen Williams as governor, recommended a tax program to the legislature that called for permitting nuisance taxes to lapse, abandonment of the sales tax on food, and enactment of a personal and corporation income tax. The legislature rejected his plan, except for allowing the nuisance taxes to expire on schedule July 1, 1961. By that time the deficit was up again to almost 72 million dollars. Even with a full year's yield of the new sales tax, the following year produced another deficit, running the total to 85 million dollars on July 1, 1962. Some of the nuisance taxes were reimposed, and this, added to a sharp increase of business activity, resulted in a reduction of the deficit by July 1, 1963, to around 45 million. Nevertheless, the need for tax reform remained one of the major unresolved issues in the state.

*   *   *   *   *

The political stalemate that reached its grim climax with the financial crisis of 1959 had far-reaching consequences for Michigan political parties and for many of its political leaders. It marked a turning point in the career of G. Mennen Williams. Michigan's best-known politician of the fifties made a serious mistake in 1958 when he chose to run for another term as governor. The state party chairman, Neil Staebler, had urged Williams to run for the United States Senate that year.[16] The Democrats had captured one of Michigan's two Senate seats in 1954 when the Detroit labor official, Patrick V. McNamara, had defeated the incumbent Republican, Homer Ferguson. The other Michigan seat was held by Charles E. Potter, a Republican who had been elected in 1952 to the seat that had been held by the late Arthur Vandenberg. Potter had been a rather obscure member of the Senate who would likely be easily defeated in 1958 by a Democrat of any stature. Williams certainly would have had no trouble winning such an election, and in Staebler's view he could do far more to advance himself as a national political figure with a shot at the party's Presidential nomination if he went on to the United States Senate than if he stayed on in Lansing, where he had achieved about all he could achieve in face of the legislature's opposition to his programs. However, Williams apparently felt that his reputation and his programs were at stake and that his career would be damaged if he stepped down from the governor's position at this critical time. Thus, while Williams' lieutenant governor, Philip A. Hart, defeated Potter in 1958, and became one of Michigan's most respected United States Senators, Williams ran for and was elected to a sixth term as governor, although by a margin that was only half of what he had run up over his Republican opponent in 1956. That sixth term was a fatal one for Williams. The state's financial embarrassments, whatever their origins, effectively destroyed any hopes Williams might have held for the Presidency. He still had great influence, of course, as the titular leader of the Democrats in one of the most populous states in the country, and his early support of John F. Kennedy in 1960 gave an important boost to Kennedy's drive to gain the Democratic Presidential nomination that year. But at the 1960 Democratic National Convention Williams was visibly and vocally dismayed when he learned of Kennedy's choice of the Texan, Lyndon B. Johnson, as his vice-presidential running mate. Then following Kennedy's narrow victory, which was greatly aided by the success of the Michigan Democrats in carrying the state for Kennedy—the first Democratic Presidential candidate to do so since 1944—Michigan Democrats were bitterly disappointed when the President-elect, rather than naming Williams to a cabinet-level position, appointed him Assistant Secretary of State for African Affairs, a job which was scarcely regarded at that time as a choice assignment in the federal government and one which did little to advance Williams' career either on the national or state levels.[17]

However, if the financial problems of 1959 served to derail the Democratic governor's political plans they also had an equally serious impact on the reputations and futures of Williams' hard-line Republican conservative opponents. When a telegram from Joseph H. Creighton of the Michigan Manufacturers Association to the Republican Senators, congratulating them on having Williams "over the barrel for the first time in ten years" and urging them to "keep him there 'til he screams 'uncle'"[18] was leaked to the newspapers, there were certainly many who were outraged that such personal partisan considerations should be given precedence over the resolution of the state's pressing problems. Further damage to the conservatives' cause resulted from the antics of such Republican Senators as John P. Smeekens, whose motto "Smeekens Never Weakens" summed up his opposition to any suggestion that an income tax be adopted, while Senator Carlton H. Morris, a member of the senate's taxation committee, strapped a mock torpedo to the top of his car to indicate what he intended to do to any tax reform measures. These tactics backfired and undoubtedly strengthened the hand of moderate Republicans who argued that the party could never regain the governorship if it continued to project a negative image of being completely opposed to Williams and the Democratic party. The nomination of Paul D. Bagwell, a moderate Republican from the faculty of Michigan State University, as the Republican gubernatorial candidate in 1958 and 1960 was an indication that the extreme conservatives did not control the party, and although Bagwell did not win either race, the narrow margins by which he was defeated, particularly in 1960, suggested that moderation was the path that Republicans should follow and which they did follow with the successful gubernatorial campaigns of George Romney in the sixties and William Milliken in the seventies.

At the same time that the Republicans began to demonstrate greater strength at the state level, the coalition of liberal intellectuals, labor unions, and ethnic and minority groups that had carried the Democrats to victory from 1948 to 1960 began to disintegrate. The importance of G. Mennen Williams in holding these diverse elements together was revealed in 1960 when he did not seek another term as governor and a bitter primary fight raged between Lieutenant-governor John B. Swainson and Secretary of State James M. Hare to gain the Democratic gubernatorial nomination. Hare had been the party's best vote-getter since he was first elected Secretary of State in 1954. His temperament and his long association with Williams indicated to many Democrats that he was best able to maintain the loyal support of the party's various factions. Swainson, however, had risen rapidly in the ranks, and with his strong union support gained the nomination and went on to defeat Bagwell in November, becoming, at age thirty-five, the state's youngest governor since Stevens T. Mason. Swainson was unable, however, to handle the problems he had inherited from the Williams administration and at the same time heal the deep divisions in his party caused by the primary campaign of 1960, and in 1962 he fell victim to a resurgent Republican party and its dynamic new leader, George W. Romney.

*   *   *   *   *

One of the major issues on which Swainson and Hare had disagreed in 1960 and which Romney was to employ with considerable skill to advance his political ambitions was that of whether to call a constitutional convention. As the fifties had drawn to a close, the state's unresolved fiscal problems, the controversy over the apportionment of the legislature and the resulting impasse between the legislature and the executive had led to rapidly growing support for the view that the only solution to these and other problems was in the complete overhauling of the state's entire governmental structure. The existing constitution, adopted in 1908, had been largely a re-write of the earlier constitution of 1850 which had been drawn up when Michigan was still a young, pioneer farm state. In attempting to up-date the 1908 constitution, seventy amendments had been added, resulting in a document full of anachronisms and inconsistencies. The constitution had provided that the question of a general revision should be submitted to the people automatically every sixteen years, beginning in 1926. At other times the question might be placed on the ballot either by initiatory petition or legislative resolution. In 1926 the proposal for general revision was rejected by more than a two-to-one majority, but the vote in 1942 had been much closer. The question was put on the ballot again in 1948. This time 855,451 votes were cast in favor of revision and 799,198 against. But the constitution provided that in order to approve general revision, a majority of those voting in the election at which the question was submitted must vote in favor of revision.[19] Although a majority of those voting *on the issue* in 1948 approved of revision, many voters had not voted on the issue at all. The number of votes in favor of revision was not a majority of those voting in the election; over two million votes had been cast for governor. Again, when the question came up automatically in 1958, a majority voting on the issue approved a general constitutional revision, but not a majority of those voting in the election.

By this time, however, the financial difficulties being experienced by the state government and growing problems of local government were important factors in convincing many citizens that in order to solve its problems the state needed a new constitution. The League of Women Voters and the Junior Chamber of Commerce took the lead in supporting the campaign for a new constitution. The difficulty of securing voter approval under the provisions of the Constitution of 1908 led the two organizations to initiate an amendment that would order constitutional revision by a majority approval of those voting on the issue. This amendment was placed on the ballot in the November, 1960, election and was approved by a majority of over 300,000. The amendment also specified that the question of revision should be submitted at the April election in 1961.

The two organizations that had led the campaign for the amendment adopted in November also worked in favor of the proposal for revision at the April, 1961, election. They were aided by many other civic groups, including Citizens for Michigan, which had been organized by George Romney, president of American Motors. In opposition to revision were the Farm Bureau, local government officials and their organizations, and some other groups. In part, the opposition was due to the fear that a new constitution would make inroads on the existing system of local government, but in the main it arose from the belief that any new constitution would involve reapportionment of the legislature that would favor the Detroit area and the Democratic party. This latter consideration created favorable sentiment toward revision in the Detroit area. The proposal carried by a margin of 23,421 out of 1,169,445 votes cast. Wayne, Oakland, Macomb, and Washtenaw counties voted heavily in favor of revision, but the vote was against it in most counties outside the Detroit area. What turned the tide was probably the work by civic organizations that produced enough additional favorable votes outstate for a majority.[20]

The favorable vote also was made possible by another provision of the amendment adopted in November, 1960. Under the original provisions of the Constitution of 1908, a convention for general revision was to consist of three delegates from each senatorial district. Since the senatorial districts were arranged so as to favor the parts of the state outside the Detroit area, any revision by a convention made up of delegates chosen in this manner was staunchly opposed by Detroit leaders. They proposed that the constitution be amended so that the convention would be composed of delegates chosen from representative, rather than senatorial districts. The organizations working for revision came up with a compromise that called for one delegate from each senatorial district and one from each representative district. This was incorporated in the amendment that was approved in November, 1960.

There was considerable sentiment in favor of choosing the delegates on a nonpartisan basis, but this was overruled by the legislature, which enacted a measure providing for partisan nomination and election of delegates. The two major parties chose their nominees in a primary held on July 25, and the election was held on September 12, 1961. Of the 144 delegates elected, ninety-nine were Republicans. The failure of the Democrats to do better, when the division between the two parties in the legislature was far closer in elections held in the same districts from which the delegates had been chosen, was due in part to the traditional difficulty the Democratic party had in mobilizing its largely urban membership to vote in special elections. In addition, however, the issue of constitutional revision had badly split the party and may have created some confusion or lingering lack of enthusiasm for the entire issue at the election in the summer of 1961. In 1960 John Swainson had sided with labor leaders and certain others in the party who were opposed to any effort to reform the constitution until the apportionment issue was settled and the party would have a better chance of controlling a convention. Others, however, including James Hare, argued that the need for a new constitution was too important for such action to be delayed any longer.

During the summer of 1961 a considerable amount of preparatory work was done by a commission appointed by the governor and financed by a grant from the Kellogg Foundation, the legislature having refused to appropriate money for this work.[21] The delegates then assembled on October 3, 1961, in the Lansing Civic Center. The first order of business was the selection of a convention president. Among the aspirants for the honor were George Romney, President John Hannah of Michigan State University, and Edward Hutchinson of Fennville—Republicans of widely varying philosophical outlooks. The Republican caucus compromised by giving its support to Stephen S. Nisbet of Fremont, a former executive of Gerber Products Company and a member of the State Board of Education. Democratic delegates made the selection of Nisbet unanimous.

The convention got down to work in short order. Committees were appointed to deal with education, legislative organization, the executive branch, the judiciary, local government, and other matters that would be involved in the new constitution. During the first three months, time was largely devoted to committee hearings. From January through April, 1962, the convention hammered out the provisions of the new constitution. On May 11, the convention completed its work, but delayed final approval of the document until August 1. On that day delegates reassembled, made some minor changes, and approved the final draft of the document by a vote of 96 to 48.

The delegates to the convention were predominantly white males, with only ten women and a handful of blacks among its members, but in other respects they represented an interesting cross-section of diverse backgrounds. George Romney of American Motors was joined by such other top business figures as Dan E. Karn of Jackson, a member of the board of Consumers Power and president of that company from 1951 to 1960. Charles L. Anspach of Mount Pleasant, former president of Central Michigan University, joined John Hannah of Michigan State University and others with a background in higher education. Ink White of St. Johns was a familiar figure in Michigan journalism circles. Tom Downs of Detroit was one of a number of delegates closely associated with labor unions, while Stanley Powell of Ionia had long been a spokesman for farm groups. Although this was for many of the delegates their first experience with elective office or any governmental position, there were others who had had extensive experience. One was Alvin M. Bentley of Owosso, who, as a member of Congress in 1954, had been severely wounded by Puerto Rican extremists who earlier had tried to assassinate President Truman. On the whole, the calibre of delegates was high and they worked hard and conscientiously.

The delegates paid considerable attention to the practices of other states, and listened to the recommendations of political scientists, and the opinions of citizens as expressed at hearings. In many instances logical conclusions on what was best for Michigan were modified or rejected for the reason that delegates did not believe the voters would approve. In other cases, the clash of opinion made compromise necessary. Special-interest groups demanded that safeguards and provisions in the old constitution be continued in the new (the earmarking of funds for highways and education are examples of such provisions). Matters that the delegates might have preferred to leave to the discretion of the legislature were dealt with in the new constitution in order to satisfy the demands of various interest groups. One delegate, James K. Pollock, an internationally known political scientist from the University of Michigan, ruefully admitted that such cherished ideals of the academic political scientist as the short ballot and other features which had been found in the 1835 constitution and which had tended to establish clear and definite lines of responsibility in government, had to be abandoned or compromised in the face of political realities.[22]

Another factor that made the new constitution a bundle of compromises was partisan rivalry. At first there was a rather remarkable degree of harmony in the convention, but soon partisan bickering and rancor rose to a fever pitch. Among the Republicans there were two major factions, commonly referred to as the liberal and conservative factions. The leader of the liberals was George Romney, while former State Treasurer D. Hale Brake of Stanton was the acknowledged leader of the conservatives. Brake generally wanted the pattern of local government to be left largely as it was, favored the election rather than the appointment of state officials, and insisted on an apportionment of the legislature that would follow the existing pattern that favored outstate Michigan over the Detroit metropolitan area. Many of the conservatives had opposed constitutional revision, and as delegates were inclined to make as few changes as possible. The liberals, in contrast, wanted a new constitution that incorporated changes recommended by political scientists—changes that would enable the state and local government to operate more efficiently in meeting the needs of a state with a predominantly urban population.

Constituting only a third of the membership of the convention, Democrats were inclined to cooperate with Republican liberals. But at a critical stage in the proceedings, Romney negotiated a series of compromise agreements with D. Hale Brake. This infuriated the Democrats, who claimed that Romney already was eyeing the governorship, and that he made his peace with the conservative Republicans as a means of uniting his party for the coming election campaign. From this point forward party acrimony was bitter and all chance of unanimity in the final outcome was dissolved. In the end all but a few Democrats voted against approval of the document, while nearly all Republicans voted in favor of it.

The compromise on the apportionment question was the most widely publicized of the delegates' actions. Not far behind was the decision to authorize a flat-rate income tax. Democrats and some Republicans had favored a graduated income tax similar to the federal income tax, but a flat-rate tax which would take the same percentage of everyone's income was as much as the conservatives would agree to, despite the protests of the liberals that such a tax, like the sales tax, was unfair to those in the lower income brackets.

The delegates dealt with the problems of improving the efficiency of state governmental operations and strengthening the powers of the governor in ways that were more satisfactory to those advocating changes in these areas than were the decisions that were made regarding apportionment and finances. Since Michigan had chosen a Democratic governor at the last seven elections there was some reluctance on the part of the majority of the Republicans to increase the governor's powers. But the arguments in favor of doing so in the interest of administrative efficiency were so strong that the delegates finally agreed to provide for a considerably stronger governor in the new constitution. For one thing, the governor, beginning in 1966, was to be elected for a four-year term. This meant that the governor would not only be less concerned about the immediate political consequences of the actions he took as had been the case when he had to spend much of the time in his second year in office running for re-election, but that the gubernatorial elections from 1966 on would never occur at the same time as the election of a President. This meant a return to the practice that had existed under the first state constitution and made it less likely that national political issues would intrude into the election of the state's chief executive.

Another vital provision of the new constitution required the consolidation of all state agencies into not more than twenty departments, most of them headed by a single executive appointed by the governor with the consent of the senate. This eliminated approximately 130 agencies, bureaus, and commissions, the sheer number of which obviously made it difficult, if not impossible, for any governor to perform effectively the duties of chief executive. However, the new constitution stopped short of providing the governor with full powers to manage state administration. Two of the largest departments were removed from his control by giving the elected State Board of Education power to appoint the superintendent of public instruction and by providing for the appointment of the state highway director by a bipartisan board. The superintendent of public instruction and the head of the highway department had previously been elective offices, filled at a spring election. The elimination of these spring elections enabled political activity at the state level to be centered entirely on elections in the fall. A move was also made toward shortening the ballot by making not only the top highway and education officers appointive, but also the offices of state treasurer and auditor general—the former appointed by the governor, the latter by the legislature. But by adding a sizable number of new offices that were to be filled by election, the new constitution created a ballot that was considerably longer than the one under the old constitution. The governor's position was strengthened by requiring candidates for the offices of governor and lieutenant-governor to run as a team, making it impossible for the voters to choose a governor from one party and a lieutenant governor from an opposing party, as had happened twice during the years that G. Mennen Williams was governor. However, by continuing the practice of filling the offices of secretary of state and attorney general by election, it was still possible for these executive offices to be held by individuals of a different party than that of the governor.

Another hotly debated issue in the convention was the state's court system. During the thirties there had been considerable agitation for "taking the judges out of politics." Proposals to choose state supreme court justices by appointment rather than by popular election were rejected by the voters in 1934 and 1938. In 1939, however, a compromise proposal was adopted in the form of a constitutional amendment. Supreme court justices were to be nominated at party conventions, but were to run on a nonpartisan ballot. Justices of all other courts were to be nominated and elected on a nonpartisan ballot. There was much criticism of this plan as it pertained to the method of choosing members of the state's highest court. It bordered on the ridiculous to presume that a candidate who was nominated at a party convention could then run as a bona-fide, nonpartisan candidate. After protracted discussion, however, the convention of 1961-62 voted to retain the 1939 system with two modifications: a justice could run for re-election if he—or she—wished without being renominated by the party convention that had nominated him for the position in the first place, and a candidate might be nominated by initiatory petitions as well as by party conventions.

The first state constitution had provided a court in each county, but beginning with the constitution of 1850 these courts had been replaced by circuit courts, of which there were originally eight. By 1897, the number of circuit courts had increased to thirty-five. Growing populations in the urban areas made it necessary to have more than one circuit judge in many counties. By 1977 there were fifty circuits in the state, with thirty-three circuit judges serving the third circuit, which comprised Wayne County, alone. The number of appeals from these courts to the supreme court was so great that the new constitution provided for the creation of a court of appeals, consisting of eighteen judges elected from three districts that encompassed the entire state. These justices were placed between the circuit courts and the supreme court.

At the bottom of the judicial ladder as early as the territorial period were the township justices of the peace. Elected by the people of the township, the justice all too often lacked adequate legal training. His remuneration came from fees levied upon litigants. Despite the efforts of organizations representing the justices of the peace and other local governmental groups that favored retaining this system, the convention voted to abolish the office of justice of the peace within five years after the adoption of the constitution. In 1968, the legislature established a system of district courts to replace the justice courts. A total of ninety-eight districts were established in the state, many of them with two or more judges who were required to have legal training, and their compensation would be in the form of salaries rather than fees. The same act of 1968 gave cities the option of merging their municipal courts into the district courts or maintaining them as separate courts. Although most cities in the outstate areas chose the former course, most cities in the suburban Detroit area chose to maintain their municipal courts, as did Detroit which had the most elaborate of all such organizations.

The convention of 1961-62 also made changes affecting other

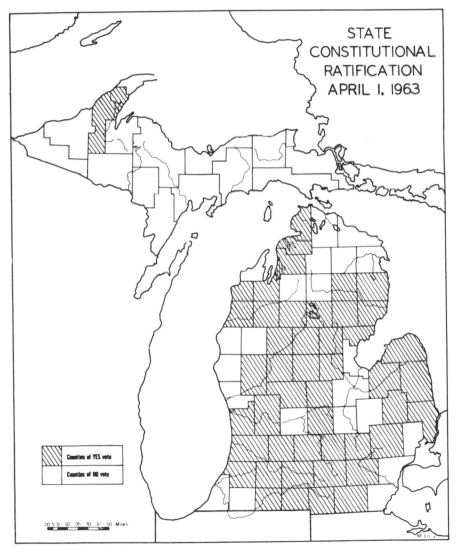

aspects of local government. There was a strong movement to give the people of each county the right to draw up and adopt forms of county government that they believed were best for their needs. Conservatives, however, opposed such a provision on the ground that it would enable cities to dominate county government. A compromise was reached which provided that the legislature would be given the power to provide for county home rule. After the adoption of the constitution, the legislature failed to take any action regarding county home rule, but a determination by the United States Supreme Court that local governing bodies must be chosen under the one-man, one-vote principle forced counties to provide for the election of members of the county board of supervisors from districts approximately equal in population, beginning in 1968. This had the effect of giving urban areas a far greater voice in county government than they had had previously.

The Article on education received high praise form both sides of the political fence. It provided for an enlarged elective State Board of Education with broad responsibility for planning and coordinating public education in the state. But its powers over the governing boards of state colleges and universities were sharply limited. Each of these institutions was to have its own governing board which would be largely independent from the control of the state board, legislature, and governor. The governing boards of the University of Michigan, Michigan State, and Wayne State would continue to be elected as in the past. The others, which, for the most part, had previously been under the control of the old State Board of Education, would be governed by boards appointed by the governor with the consent of the senate.

The new constitution guaranteed civil rights to every citizen and provided for a civil rights commission to safeguard these rights. By specifying that the commission was to be one of the twenty departments called for in the constitution, the delegates sought to prevent the weakening of the commission's role by seeing that it was not made a subordinate division of a larger department. With regard to the state legislature, more assistance was provided for legislators by the creation of a bipartisan legislative council with a full-time staff which would handle the details of drafting bills, research, and other matters relating to the legislative process. The term of senators was extended to four years, as was that of the governor. The governor and senators were to be elected in November of the even-numbered years when there was not a national Presidential election, starting in 1966.

Following adjournment of the convention, a lively campaign

was waged for and against the proposed constitution. The Democratic State Convention came out against approval, largely because Democrats hoped that the federal courts would order reapportionment of the legislature under the 1908 constitution strictly on population lines. Democratic Highway Commissioner John Mackie also opposed the new constitution because it would take the election of the highway commissioner out of the control of voters, and also because certain provisions regarding the right of eminent domain in the new constitution would make it more difficult to obtain land for highways. Considerable opposition to the new constitution was also voiced by the Republican conservatives, though the action of the Democratic party in opposing the constitution had the effect of driving many Republicans who might otherwise have opposed it to come out for it. Some Democratic leaders, notably former United States Senator Prentiss Brown, announced their support. Once more civic organizations conducted a vigorous drive in favor of approval.

The voters passed judgment on the proposed new constitution on April 1, 1963, and approved it by a margin of only about 7,000 votes. A partial recount was demanded, but the result was not changed. Detroit produced a negative majority, though not large enough to defeat the new constitution. Suburban areas around Detroit in several cases voted in favor of approval. Outstate Republican conservative strongholds in many cases produced an adverse vote, but the work of civic organizations plus the factor of Democratic opposition had the effect of turning the tide in favor of approval in populous counties such as Kalamazoo and Kent.

The constitution adopted in 1963 was somewhat more brief than that of 1908. It was more logically organized and co-ordinated. It incorporated a number of changes that were generally conceded to be desirable, notably the four-year term of governor and the educational provisions. But it did not go as far in giving Michigan a framework of government based on sound principles as many had hoped. There were provisions in it that would call for amendment in the not-too-distant future. But on the whole it was an improvement over the Constitution of 1908, more geared to the needs of a twentieth-century industrial state.

*   *   *   *   *

The constitutional convention of 1961-62 not only produced a new constitution but it also helped to launch a number of its members into prominent political positions. Glenn S. Allen, Jr., of Kalamazoo, became state controller and budget director for seven years and subsequently was elected to the new court of appeals, where he found himself serving with another ex-convention delegate, Robert J. Danhof of Muskegon. Garry Brown of Schoolcraft and Edward Hutchinson served in Congress, while a much larger number of the delegates were elected to the state legislature. Two of the black delegates from Detroit became well-known politicians. Richard H. Austin succeeded James Hare as secretary of state in 1971, while Coleman A. Young, after service in the state senate, became the first black mayor of Detroit in 1974. However, no one benefitted more from his role as delegate than did George W. Romney, who emerged from the convention as the dominant force in the Republican party.

Romney had been born in 1907 in Mexico, where his grandfather, a Mormon, had moved in the 1880s when Congress had outlawed polygamy.[23] During the Mexican Revolution, in 1912, the Romneys moved back into the United States to Idaho and then to Utah, where George Romney grew up as a devout Mormon. In the thirties, Romney went to Washington, where he eventually became a lobbyist for the Alcoa corporation. From there he moved to Detroit in 1940 to head the new office of the Automobile Manufacturers Association and became general manager of that organization two years later. After the war Romney joined the Nash automobile company and helped to engineer the merger of Nash and Hudson in 1954, becoming president of the new American Motors Corporation in the fall of 1954 after the sudden death of that corporation's first president, George Mason.

While he had been with Nash, Romney revived the Rambler name that had been used in the company's earliest days, before Charles Nash had taken it over. Romney now attached that name to a small, low-priced car, for which he was convinced there was a market in the country. For several years, however, when the attention of the American auto industry and auto owners seemed to be centered entirely on bigger and fancier cars, there did not appear to be much of a future for Romney's Rambler. He persevered, however, and in 1957 abandoned the Nash and Hudson models entirely in order to concentrate on the small Rambler. Then his gamble began paying off as the country slid into a recession in 1957-58 and consumers began to become more cost-conscious. Romney increased his attacks on the "gas-guzzling dinosaurs" his competitors were producing and pointed to the Rambler's low sticker price and low maintenance cost. Rambler sales rocketed to six figures and were reaching the half million sales figure by 1960, providing American Motors with the largest share of the American auto production it has ever enjoyed.[24]

In the process, Romney became one of the better-known business personalities in the country. In Detroit and Michigan, where cars had long since become second only to the weather as a favorite topic of conversation, there were few adults who did not know of and admire the job Romney had done with one of the smallest of the surviving automobile companies. It was only natural that some saw in Romney the potential for a winning political career. Romney, in turn, became deeply involved in civic activities in Detroit, chairing a citizens committee that sought to create support for improved educational programs in that city. In 1959 Romney founded Citizens for Michigan, a non-partisan organization that epitomized one of Romney's basic political beliefs: that the control of government was too much in the hands of organized interest groups and that this trend could only be reversed by the voluntary cooperation of responsible citizens working together for the benefit of all. Although he was labeled naive and accused of catering to business interests, Romney demonstrated the same ability to sell his political ideas as he had demonstrated in selling automobiles. Believing that constitutional revision was the best approach to the solution of Michigan's problems, Romney made his Citizens for Michigan one of the most effective organizations in overcoming the obstacles of convening a constitutional convention. He was elected to the convention in 1961, and to secure that office, Romney surrendered his non-partisan status and declared himself a Republican.

In the convention, Romney, though a relative novice in partisan political activities, was able to use his position as one of the vice-presidents of the convention and the leader of the moderate wing of the Republican delegation to gain the party's nomination for governor in 1962. On the campaign trail, Romney proved to be as formidable a campaigner as Williams in the previous decade. Although Democrats captured all the other executive offices in that fall's election, Romney defeated the incumbent Democratic governor, John Swainson. More significantly, Romney demonstrated that a moderate-to-liberal Republican candidate could make inroads into the Metropolitan Detroit area where the overwhelming size of the Democratic vote had more than offset the Republican strength in outstate areas and had been the major basis for the Democratic victories since 1948.

In 1964, the Democrats won a landslide victory in both the state and national elections. With legislative lines finally redrawn along strictly population lines, the more populous urban areas, where the Democratic strength was the greatest, now had the largest numbers of the members of the legislature. For the first time since the thirties, the Democrats elected a majority in both houses, as well as giving the state's electoral votes to the Democratic Presidential candidate, Lyndon B. Johnson, by an overwhelming two-to-one margin over the hapless Republican candidate, Barry Goldwater. In spite of this Democratic sweep, Romney easily defeated the Democratic gubernatorial candidate, Neil Staebler, by a margin nearly five times larger than that by which he had defeated Swainson two years before, and larger than that of any winning gubernatorial candidate, Republican or Democratic, since the halcyon one-party days of the twenties. Two years later, in the first election of a governor for the four-year term specified in the new constitution, Romney not only defeated the Democrat, Zoltan Ferency, by over a half million votes, but proved that the new apportionment did not automatically guarantee a Democratic legislature since a majority of the Republican candidates for the house and senate were also elected. In addition, Romney broke the hold the Democrats had held on Michigan's two United States Senate seats by helping to elect Robert P. Griffin to the seat that had become vacant with the death of Democratic Senator Patrick McNamara, even though Griffin's opponent was G. Mennen Williams, making an unsuccessful comeback bid for the elective office.

Romney's political successes made him a figure of national importance and a contender for the Republican Presidential nomination in 1968. He demonstrated considerable ability to work with the Democrats in the state's executive and judicial offices, as well as the legislature, developing a kind of informal bipartisan coalition of moderates than enabled him and his Republican successor, William Milliken, to secure the enactment of much of what they wanted, despite the fact that they were not members of the party that would generally control one or both houses of the legislature from the mid-sixties on.

Romney was governor at the time the new constitution was adopted, and as one of the principal architects of that document he took a special interest in overseeing its implementation. In one crucial area, that of resolving the state's continuing financial problems, there seemed hope that the new constitution provided the means for implementing authentic tax reforms. The new constitution's requirement that the governor must reduce expenditures when it appeared that revenues for a fiscal year would fall below the estimates on which appropriations had been based, was intended both to avoid the deficits that had resulted from the sharp decline in revenues in the fifties and to force action on new sources of revenue that would ensure the continuation of state programs.

Upon taking office at the start of 1963, Romney persuaded the legislature to hold the line on appropriations for 1963-64, and to postpone a decision on new taxes until a special session in the fall. The gratifying surplus of 1962-63, resulting in a reduction of the deficit by $40 million, might appear to indicate that no change in the tax system was necessary. But two considerations pointed in the opposite direction. First, the state was faced with a flood of students in its colleges and universities as children born in the post-war "baby boom" reached college age. Between seventy and eighty percent of Michigan's college students enrolled in its tax-supported institutions, twenty percent higher than the national average, thus requiring sharply increased appropriations for higher education. In addition, mental health needs were becoming acute. There were demands for more funds from other state departments. The second consideration was the generally conceded fact that Michigan taxed business higher than neighboring states and others with which it had to compete for new industry.[25]

More and more it became evident that an income tax was the only long-range solution to the state's need for more revenues. In 1963, therefore, Romney proposed a comprehensive tax revision plan to the legislature which embraced the flat-rate income tax authorized by the new constitution. But the lawmakers refused to act until the state again faced the prospect of a deficit. Finally, in 1967, a tax revision was enacted. It provided for a tax of 2.6 percent on personal income, 5.6 percent on corporate income, and 7 percent on the profit of financial institutions. The business-receipts tax was repealed, as was the corporation franchise tax. By 1969, greatly increased appropriations, particularly for education and social welfare, forecast the necessity of increasing the income tax rate.

The tax problem was a serious one not only for state government but for local units as well. The fifteen-mill limitation on property taxes was not written into the new constitution, but cities and school districts that sought new funds for increasing populations and demands for services found voters more and more reluctant to approve increases in property tax rates. By 1967, therefore, Detroit, Flint, Hamtramck, and Saginaw had adopted city incomes taxes, under the tax revision act of 1967, that authorized such taxes at a rate of one percent on residents and a half of one percent on nonresidents deriving an income from within the city.

Times had changed greatly from the days of Governor Barry, who had bolstered the state treasury in the 1840s by having the grass on the capitol lawn cut and sold for hay, to the late 1960s, when Michigan citizens paid state and local taxes exceeding three billion dollars, not to mention federal tax collections amounting to an additional $12.6 billion. It was a political irony that many of the programs and policies that the Democratic Governor Williams had been unable to get past the Republican legislature in the fifties were now adopted under Republican Governor Romney. In addition, the state budget, which had approached half a billion dollars a year under Williams, causing Republicans to denounce him as a spendthrift, quickly soared over the billion-dollar range in Romney's administration, and reached nearly $3,000,000,000 by 1968.

*   *   *   *   *

Romney's demonstrated success as a vote-getter in Michigan and his successes as governor, particularly in securing the adoption of his tax reform program in 1967, catapulted him into the national political limelight. Late in 1967, he announced his candidacy for the Republican Presidential nomination in 1968. But certain events derailed Romney's Presidential hopes, just as they had those of G. Mennen Williams a decade earlier. One such event which had already tarnished Romney's image as an effective leader had been the racial problems which culminated in a terrible reoccurrence of the violence that had torn Detroit in the summer of 1943. This time the impact was felt not only in that city but in several other Michigan communities.

Following the 1943 Detroit race riot, a biracial committee on human relations had been established in that city, and by 1964 similar groups had been appointed in nineteen other Michigan cities. Meanwhile, in 1949, Governor Williams had appointed an advisory committee on civil rights. He also had recommended that legislation be adopted that would prohibit discrimination in employment. Action was delayed for several years, but in 1955 a Fair Employment Practices Act was passed and a commission established to enforce its provisions. During the next eight years almost two thousand cases were handled by the commission. The constitutional convention in 1961-62 had included in the new constitution a guarantee of equal rights and had also provided for the appointment of an eight-member bipartisan civil rights commission to assure the enjoyment of equal rights by all citizens. In addition, the legislature was required to make an annual appropriation for the effective operation of the commission. This commission was the first constitutionally created civil rights agency in the United States.

Meanwhile, the Negro population of the state continued to increase at a rapid rate. The census of 1960 revealed a non-white population of 737,329, nearly 9.4 percent of Michigan's total population. Inside Detroit, the black population had risen to approximately thirty percent of the total of that city. In Detroit and in other Michigan cities, thousands of Negroes were able to get better jobs, many becoming teachers, police officers, skilled craftsmen, and professional workers. But in spite of the sizable increase in the Negro middle class, segregation in housing practices continued, and many prosperous black families were unable to obtain houses outside the ghettos. The general prosperity of the nation by the early sixties made poverty, which was especially prevalent within the black community, seem even more galling. Educated blacks became outspoken critics of continuing discrimination and became part of a vigorous new civil rights movement that had been born in the mid-fifties with the United States Supreme Court's dramatic reversal of previous court rulings that had permitted segregation. This had led to organized efforts, especially in the South, to put an end to all laws and other practices that treated blacks differently from the rest of the population. The most prominent leader of this movement, Dr. Martin Luther King, Jr., sought to use non-violent means in achieving these goals. On June 23, 1963, approximately the twentieth anniversary of the riot of 1943, Dr. King came to Detroit to lead the blacks in non-violent protest. A column of nearly 125,000 people filled Woodward Avenue for some two miles as it marched down to Cobo Hall in the city's riverfront Civic Center that had been constructed the previous decade. Leading the march, along with Walter Reuther, former governor John Swainson, Detroit Mayor Jerome P. Cavanagh, and other whites who wished to voice their support for the black's demands, was Dr. King, who declared that this was the largest such demonstration that had ever been staged in the country. At a speech in Cobo Hall climaxing the day's events, King previewed the famed speech he would give at the Lincoln Memorial in Washington two months later in which he told of his dream of Negroes and whites "walking together hand in hand, free at last, free at last, free at last."

But the non-violent approach of Dr. King, which was essentially in keeping with the gradualism and patience that earlier civil rights groups and leaders had counselled as the best way of achieving their objectives, was rejected by more militant groups that seemed to be gaining greater strength in the sixties. One militant leader was Malcolm X, who, as Malcolm Little, had lived for several years with his family in the Lansing area where he had become embittered at the manner in which blacks were treated.[26] As the leader of an offshoot of the Black Muslim movement, Malcolm X returned to Michigan on various occasions in the early sixties with a black nationalist message that was quite different from the integrationist, non-violent message of Dr. King.

The violence that seemed implicit in Malcolm X's preachings came to typify much of what happened in the sixties, beginning in 1963 with the assassination of President John F. Kennedy, whom many blacks had respected for seeking to lead them into a new age of equality. In 1965, Malcolm X himself was murdered, to be followed in 1968 by Martin Luther King and President Kennedy's brother, Robert. These incidents, combined with the active involvement of the United States in the Vietnam war beginning in 1965, no doubt influenced many blacks, particularly younger blacks, to feel that violence was the only way of venting their frustrations.

In the summer of 1965, the worst riot since the Detroit riot of 1943 ravaged the Negro area of Los Angeles. There was also rioting in Chicago in the summer of 1966, but despite these events, authorities in Detroit anticipated no such troubles there. That city, particularly under the administration of Mayor Jerome Cavanagh, who had taken office in 1962, had attracted national attention for its comprehensive anti-poverty program and its seemingly peaceful climate in race relations. But in the pre-dawn hours of Sunday, July 23, 1967, Detroit police raided an illegal after-hours liquor establishment in the predominantly Negro area of the city. As the police began hauling the patrons of the establishment away to jail, a crowd that had gathered began to riot. At first the police refrained from forceful actions, which encouraged the gathering mob to run wild and engage in wholesale looting of stores in the area. Fires broke out and the rioters refused to allow firemen to fight the blazes. Elected Negro officials who tried to calm the rioters were pelted with stones and verbal abuse.

As Sunday wore on and conditions grew worse, Governor Romney stepped in to proclaim a state of emergency and sent in the first contingents of state police and national guardsmen to assist Detroit police. Late Sunday, however, Romney and Mayor Cavanagh recognized that additional help was needed and at three in the morning of July 24, Romney phoned the United States attorney general asking for federal troops. Tragically, the same kinds of misunderstandings, misinterpretations, and mistakes that had delayed the arrival of federal troops during the riot of 1943, now delayed for twenty-four hours the arrival of federal paratroopers on the morning of July 25. This time, order was not so easily restored as it had been in 1943, and incidents continued throughout the week. When the rioting finally ceased, it left at least forty-three people dead, 1,700 stores looted, 1,383 buildings burned, and property damage amounting to probably around $50,000,000. (Initial estimates made during the riot and trumpeted across the nation and the world in the course of the massive television coverage of the riot had placed the figure as high as half a billion dollars.) In the same period, racial disturbances also broke out in Pontiac, Grand Rapids, Albion, Saginaw, and Kalamazoo.[27]

The response to the tragic summer of 1967 was twofold. On the one hand, the legislature heeded popular demands for tighter enforcement of law and order. On the other, constructive efforts were made to avoid a similar future catastrophe. Detroit's reputation as a model city in the area of race relations had been demolished, and an effort was made once again to learn from this disaster. A citizens committee, named New Detroit, was appointed to plan programs that would attack the problems of discrimination head on. It was headed by J. L. Hudson, Jr., of the department store family, and included prominent leaders from all segments of the city's population. At the state level, the civil rights commission redoubled its efforts to end discrimination. By 1968, nineteen cities had enacted housing ordinances prohibiting discrimination in the sale or rental of residential property. And in that year, the legislature enacted a state open-occupancy law. More active efforts were made to bring blacks into positions of greater prominence at governmental levels, particularly in such critical areas as the police and fire departments of cities such as Detroit. Already by 1967, Flint and Ypsilanti had chosen blacks as mayors, and Otis Smith, a black, was elected regent of the University of Michigan, following his earlier service as auditor general and member of the state supreme court.

The 1967 riot had a devastating effect on the political career of Detroit's Mayor Cavanagh, an engaging personality who during the euphoria of the Kennedy years had seemed to have a bright future as an urban politician who was able to deal effectively with the problems of a big city. In 1966, Cavanagh had run against G. Mennen Williams in the Democratic Senatorial primary. To many younger Democrats, Cavanagh represented a new breed of liberals to whom they could relate better than they could to Williams, who seemed to be a carry-over of the New Deal liberal whose programs were now seen as having failed in dealing with some of the nation's most fundamental social and economic problems. In addition, Williams, as a former member of the administrations of Presidents Kennedy and Johnson, was saddled to some degree with the policies that had led the country into the war in Vietnam. This conflict, like the earlier Korean War of the fifties, in which about 250,000 Michigan men and

women had served, was a new experience for Michiganians, as it was
for all Americans. It was a limited war with limited objectives, the
exact nature of which were difficult for the average citizen to grasp.
By 1966, a rising tide of opposition was developing toward the war,
and in Michigan, anti-war Democrats viewed Cavanagh as preferable
to Williams as the party's candidate for the Senate. In the bitter
primary campaign that resulted, Williams was able to marshal enough
of his traditional following to beat off Cavanagh's challenge, but the
wounds of the fight were not healed. Cavanagh supporters and many
anti-war Democrats withheld their support from Williams in the
general election, helping to assure his defeat by Republican Robert
Griffin. The lingering hostility of Williams Democrats towards
Cavanagh over the 1966 campaign, together with the events of the
summer of 1967, cast a shadow over any hopes the Detroit mayor
might have for state-wide elective office in the future. Cavanagh
retired from the office of mayor at the end of his term in 1970, and
efforts to revive interest in him as a candidate for public office in
following years were unsuccessful.

For Governor Romney, his handling of the Detroit riot had
been criticized by President Lyndon B. Johnson, who in a television
appearance during the riot repeatedly referred to Romney's inability
to deal with the riot with state and local forces. Romney in turn
charged Johnson with having "played politics" in his riot-related actions. But it was the Vietnam war, not the Detroit riot, that wrote an
end to Romney's Presidential hopes. Initially a supporter of the war,
he had been part of a group that had gone to that southeastern Asian
war zone in 1965, and had been given a tour and briefing by military
leaders. Later, however, Romney began to have second thoughts. In
September, 1967, while appearing on a television show hosted by a
popular Detroit television personality, Lou Gordon, Romney expressed strong reservations about the war and declared that he had
been "brainwashed" by the military into believing what they wanted
him to believe. This remark caused a furor in the nation's press and
among political leaders who supported the war, as well as those who
were opposed to the war but questioned Romney's leadership
abilities. With public opinion polls already indicating that Romney
was not developing widespread support for his candidacy, the celebrated Lou Gordon Show was simply the final blow to Romney's
hopes. In March, 1968, Romney announced his withdrawal from the
race, leaving the field open to Richard M. Nixon, who swept through
the Presidential primaries to win the party's nomination and the
Presidency in the general election in November. Nixon then named
Romney to serve as secretary of Housing and Urban Development in

his cabinet. Romney resigned as governor in January, 1969, to take up his new duties in Washington, turning over the governor's office to his lieutenant governor, William G. Milliken of Traverse City. Despite his perennially boyish appearance and his low-key style, Milliken would prove even more adept than his mentor in building and maintaining an effective coalition of moderates from both parties that could deal with the problems of the succeeding decade.

Interlochen

28

THE ENRICHMENT OF CULTURAL LIFE

From the beginnings of the fur trade to the problems of the auto industry, economic concerns have held center stage in much of Michigan's historical development. Important as the state's economic contributions have been, however, cultural developments have been just as important in making life in Michigan an enriching experience.

In the field of education, Michigan, in the century after the Civil War, continued to enjoy a position of leadership, although this leadership was less marked than in earlier years. By the Civil War era, primary school was available to children in most settled parts of the state, although they often had to travel considerable distances in order to attend school. Rate bills (tuition charges upon parents) were rapidly disappearing, but it was not until 1869 that the legislature enacted a law which made all public schools cost-free for pupils living in the district where the school was located. Michigan lagged behind its Middle Western neighbors in making all of its schools free. On the other hand, Michigan was one of the first states to pass a compulsory-education law. An act of 1871 required all children between the ages of eight and fourteen to attend school at least twelve weeks each year. In 1883, partly due to the work of the Knights of Labor, the term was extended to four months and it became illegal to employ a child until he or she had attended school the required time. But there was no adequate provision for enforcing these early compulsory-education laws, and they were evaded by many parents. It was not until 1905 that a law required all children between the ages of seven and sixteen to attend for the entire school year and provided for truant officers to enforce the law. There was resistance to the expenditure of tax revenues for the operation of schools be-

669

yond the primary grades. While conceding that a common school education for all at public expense was justifiable in a democracy, there were many who asked with regard to schools beyond the elementary level, "Why should I be taxed to educate another man's child?" It should be borne in mind that the University of Michigan, the State Agricultural College, and the State Normal School had all been founded on the basis of federal land grants, and that it was expected that they would be supported and maintained largely from the income derived from these grants. In the cities and larger towns there was a single primary school at first. As the place grew, additional districts and additional one-room schools were established. In the 1850s the legislature permitted the consolidation of the several school districts within a city to form a "Union School District." The one-room schools were abandoned and a single school was built called a "Union School." It now became possible to divide the students into grades, and those of the highest grades constituted the "high school." An act passed by the legislature in 1859 specifically empowered a district containing more than two hundred children to "grade the scholars" and to establish a high school. But in 1873, three citizens of Kalamazoo brought suit to prevent the local school board from levying taxes to support a high school. When the circuit court rejected their plea they went to the state supreme court. In 1874, Justice Thomas M. Cooley rendered the unanimous opinion of the court that the Kalamazoo board was within its rights. The "Kalamazoo Case" laid the legal foundation for the growth of high schools not only in Michigan but in other states. Cooley was a jurist of national repute and this gave the opinion weight, causing the case to be cited in every major history of education in America.[1]

Even before the decision in the Kalamazoo Case had been rendered, the legislature had begun spending tax revenues for institutions of higher learning. Modest appropriations had been made to support the Normal School at Ypsilanti from the beginning, but it was not until 1867 that a definite commitment was made for tax support to the University of Michigan. In that year the legislature passed a law levying a tax of one-twentieth of a mill on all property in the state for the support of the Ann Arbor school. As time went on the appropriations for both the University of Michigan and the other public colleges and universities increased. The number of these state-supported institutions was increased to seven by the start of the twentieth century with the establishment of the Michigan School of Mines in 1885 and three new normal schools at Mount Pleasant, Marquette, and Kalamazoo between 1895 and 1903. In the mid-twentieth century there was a great new outburst of activity along this line, part of which centered on a move to upgrade most of the existing schools to university status to reflect more clearly the ways in which their programs had expanded. In spite of intense opposition from the University of Michigan, the agricultural college in East Lansing was renamed Michigan State University on the occasion of that school's centennial in 1955. The normal schools, which had earlier been renamed colleges, now became regional universities, beginning with Western Michigan University at Kalamazoo in 1957, followed in 1959 by Central Michigan University at Mount Pleasant and Eastern Michigan University in Ypsilanti, and Northern Michigan University in Marquette in 1963.

In addition, new state schools emerged. Wayne University, founded in 1933 by the Detroit Board of Education as a consolidation of several separate colleges that had developed in Detroit since 1868, was taken over by the state and renamed Wayne State University in 1957. Ferris Institute (now Ferris State College), which had been founded by Woodbridge N. Ferris in 1884, became a state-supported institution in 1950. In 1963 a tenth state-supported, degree-granting college—Grand Valley State College—was opened near Grand Rapids, and an eleventh, Saginaw Valley State College, in 1964. Three of the older state schools established branches, with Michigan Tech's branch at Sault Ste. Marie, established in old Fort Brady in 1946, achieving separate status as Lake Superior State College in 1969. Michigan State's branch at Rochester, opened in 1957, became the separate Oakland University in 1970. Branches established by the University of Michigan at Flint in 1956 and at Dearborn in 1959 developed into full four-year operations but continued under the control of the university board of regents. Unfortunately, empire building and political considerations, rather than actual educational needs, all too often explained much of this growth and pointed up the failure of the state to maintain the kind of centralized control over the state's educational development that had been included under the plans of Augustus B. Woodward, Isaac Crary, and John D. Pierce. By the time the State Board of Education tried to assume a stronger supervisory role in the 1970s it was probably too late to turn the clock back.

The community college movement in Michigan began with the opening of Grand Rapids Junior College in 1914. At first this and other similar colleges offered only the usual college courses of the freshman and sophomore level, but beginning in the thirties they started to provide vocational and technical courses. At about the same time, the legislature authorized broader support for these colleges which had originally been financed by local school boards and tuition fees. Then, in a series of acts, the legislature permitted several school boards or even an entire county to support a community college, and finally approved multi-county support. State aid to community colleges began in 1947 and helped to foster an enormous boom in this area of higher education, particularly by the 1960s. By the 1970s there were twenty-nine such colleges in the state, several of them with more than one campus, and enrollments and facilities that rivalled or surpassed those of a number of the state's four-year public institutions of higher learning.

The wide range of vocational and technical courses offered at the community colleges represented one of the major developments in education. Until almost the turn of the century, high schools devoted their entire attention to college-preparatory subjects. One of the pioneers in vocational education in the public schools was Bay City, which taught business, sewing, cooking, carpentry, and wood turning by 1891. Muskegon and Ishpeming provided courses in shopwork, foundry, cooking, sewing, and mechanical drawing by 1896. And by 1900, Ann Arbor, Calumet, Detroit, Flint, Grand Rapids, Menominee, and Saginaw were offering vocational courses in their high schools. Thereafter, more and more schools provided classes in typing, shorthand, manual training, and domestic science. In 1908, North Adams High School in Hillsdale County introduced a full course in agriculture. The Smith-Hughes Act, passed by Congress in 1917, gave a great impetus to vocational courses, with Michigan becoming one of the first states to qualify for federal aid under this act. A State Board for Vocational Education was established to administer the program. By 1950, more than 50,000 students in 334 high schools were taking vocational courses. Beginning in 1921, the state, with federal aid, also provided a growing number of vocational rehabilitation programs for the handicapped.

Another major trend in Michigan education has been a greater equalization of educational opportunity. This objective has been the goal not only of the increased amounts of state aid to local districts that has been provided in the twentieth century, but also of the drive for district reorganization. Prior to 1903, farm youth living outside a district supporting a high school were forced to pay tuition in order to get an education beyond the eighth grade. In that year a law was passed that allowed school districts that did not have a high school to levy a tax to pay tuition and transportation of pupils to an approved high school, and in 1909 it became mandatory for a district to do so. The advantages of the graded school were obvious. Although there were many one-room country schools where able and devoted teachers gave boys and girls a good primary education, there were many in which teachers were poorly trained and ill-equipped to teach. This led to a movement for the consolidation of school districts. In 1910 there were 7,333 school districts, the great majority of them small rural districts with too few students and too limited resources to provide more than a one-room school, with the level of instruction not going beyond the eighth-grade level. With consolidation the number of districts by 1960 had been reduced to 2,145. An act in 1964 required all school districts to maintain kindergarten through high school programs, compelling those which could not do so to become incorporated into adjoining districts. By the end of 1967, the number of districts had been reduced to 740, only about ten percent of the number in 1910. By 1976, the number of districts had been further reduced to only 587. In the process of reorganization, the one-room school virtually disappeared, with only twenty-one remaining in 1979, eight of these in Huron County. This meant also that nearly all farm children now attended larger schools, where they had better educational opportunities and could become acquainted with children from towns, villages, and cities. The school bus, which made consolidated or reorganized school districts possible, also enabled thousands of rural youth to attend high school and to prepare for college. In 1947, a total of 2,000 school buses were transporting 105,733 students in 700 districts in the state. Twenty years later, the number of school buses had risen to 7,267, transporting 603,850 students in 613 districts.[2]

Still another trend in education has been toward providing better-trained teachers. In 1865, teachers were considered qualified if they could convince the local school board that they were competent to teach. The State Normal School at Ypsilanti provided training for only a small fraction of the teachers required by the schools of the state. The University of Michigan in 1879 established a professorship in the Science and Art of Teaching, the first American university to do so, and the second in the world. But this innovation helped only to provide a few more well-trained high-school teachers. It did nothing for the elementary teachers. As the demand grew for more trained teachers, the denominational schools and even the business colleges offered "normal courses." In Detroit a normal school to train teachers for the city's schools was opened. Finally, three schools founded by the state between 1895 and 1903 provided a larger number of trained teachers, especially for the elementary schools. Teachers' Institutes were held in Michigan as early as 1846, but were conducted on a voluntary basis for many years. In the 1880s, however, counties, with the help of a small allocation of state funds, provided compensation and expenses for teachers attending the institutes, which afforded a short training course lasting from one to four weeks. In spite of these efforts it was reported in 1903 that only six percent of the teachers in the rural schools had a minimum of one year's training. The new state normal schools and the county normals helped increase this percentage to thirty-six by 1921. The county normals admitted students who had graduated from the eighth grade and provided them with one year's training, graduating 10,000 between 1903 and 1921. In 1921 the legislature decreed that beginning in 1925 all teachers must have at least one year of professional training. The State Board of Education required two years of training before the life certificate would be granted, and this was raised to three years in 1928. Four years of training were specified for the life certificate in 1932, and starting in 1970 the life certificate could be earned only by completing a full course, teaching successfully for three years, and completing at least eighteen semester hours of graduate courses.

Educational theory has been in a constant state of flux during the past century. The theory developed by Friedrich Froebel in Germany that education is the guidance of the development of the child from stage to stage and that the chief agency in that development is spontaneous play activity led to the establishment of kindergartens. The demonstration kindergarten at the Philadelphia Exposition in 1876 attracted widespread attention, and kindergartens were introduced into Michigan schools about this time. By 1900 they had become common. The old injunction that to spare the rod would spoil the child was gradually abandoned, and corporal punishment slowly disappeared from the schools. About the turn of the century the study of Greek and Latin in schools and colleges suffered a sharp decline as more stress was placed on science, literature, and history. In the early years of the twentieth century the ideas of John Dewey began to affect education. Dewey held that the school is an embryonic community and that the mission of the school is to give the child a guided experience in democratic living.[3] "Progressive education," which stemmed in part from Dewey's ideas, enjoyed a great vogue in the 1920s and 1930s. In 1936 the superintendent of public instruction initiated a long-range study of the schools' curriculums. The Michigan Study of the Secondary School Curriculum was begun in 1937, financed in part by foundation funds. These studies resulted in greater emphasis on meeting the needs of individual students, in making the school a center of community life, and in stress upon democratic procedures in the classroom. After World War II, educational "progressives" made much of social adjustment as the aim of the schools, and advocated the training of the whole child, rather than purely intellectual developement. But the launching of the first Sputnik by the Russians in 1957 had the effect of re-emphasizing rigorous intellectual effort, improving scientific studies, and paying more attention to the gifted child. In the 1970s, growing dissatisfaction with the level of education provided in the schools led to a demand for a return to what was called the "basics," particularly reading and writing, and to the administration of standard tests throughout the state to determine which districts were doing a good job.

The improvement of the status of teachers and the advancement of teaching to the rank of a profession has been another notable development of the century. The Michigan Education Association has been a major factor in this change. Preliminary steps were taken to organize the association during a teachers' institute held in connection with the dedication of the first normal-school building at Ypsilanti in 1852. Semi-annual meetings were held for a number of years. At the meeting held in April, 1854, two notable figures in the history of American education, Horace Mann and Henry Barnard, were present. Some of the reforms advocated in the early days of the Michigan Education Association were abolition of rate bills, compulsory education, free textbooks, and teachers' institutes. In its early years, the M.E.A. was largely dominated by the faculty members of the colleges and the normal schools. Feeling that the organization was doing little to advance their interests, teachers lost interest in it. Only 136 out of the 13,000 teachers in the state belonged to it in 1874. A number of reforms were made in that year, but even as late as 1905, the association had only 901 members in the entire state. In that year the general meetings of the association were given official status as teachers' institutes so that members did not lose pay while attending them. This seems to have been a needed "shot in the arm," and membership soared to an unprecedented 4,488 in 1906. For many years Henry M. Pattengill published his *Moderator Topics,* which included news for Michigan teachers. This was replaced by a quarterly publication in 1919 and by the monthly *Michigan Education Journal* in 1923. By 1921, the association had grown so large that districts and regions were established, and in 1922 the first executive secretary, Ernest T. Cameron, was appointed. Growth in membership after 1922 was rapid, and the association became a potent pressure group during legislative sessions.

However, the Michigan Education Association's unwillingness to give greater emphasis to teacher welfare concerns, such as wages, retirement programs, tenure, and the like, led to dissatisfaction among many members who began to support a more aggressive, union approach. The American Federation of Teachers, affiliated with the American Federation of Labor, was formed in 1916 but its early attempts to establish locals in Michigan, in Grand Rapids and Detroit, failed. The Depression finally led to the formation of the Michigan Federation of Teachers. With the emergence of a rival teachers group, the Michigan Education Association began to be more active in promoting traditional bread-and-butter issues, but it continued to reject the labor union tactics favored by the M.F.T. With the granting by the legislature of collective bargaining rights to teachers and other public employees, however, the contest between the two rivals heated up. In 1964, the position of the M.F.T. was enormously improved when it won recognition as the sole bargaining agent for Detroit's ten thousand public teachers. Stung by this reversal, the M.E.A. now became far more militant. The Michigan Public Employment Relations Act of 1965, while permitting collective bargaining by public employees, prohibited them from striking, but by failing to prescribe any penalties for violations of the law it proved ineffective. Thus by 1967, when Detroit teachers struck and delayed the fall school opening for thirteen days and the teachers in twenty-seven other districts also went out on strike, the prospect of teachers' strikes—an unthinkable action only a few years earlier—was an ever present possibility with which every school district had to deal. The next step was the extension of union efforts into the institutions of higher education. By the end of the sixties, the faculties of the community colleges were rapidly being organized, and by the latter part of the seventies most of the four-year colleges and universities, aside from the University of Michigan and Michigan State University, had gone through a similar development. A third organization—the American Association of University Professors—successfully competed with the M.E.A. and the M.F.T. and became the bargaining agent for the faculties of a number of these institutions. A strike of the members of the American Association of University Professors at Eastern Michigan University, which virtually shut down instruction at that school for two weeks in the fall of 1978, was an indication of a practice that would be a part of the college scene from then on.[4]

Although Michigan has relied heavily on public schools and institutions of higher learning for the education of its youth, independent and church-related schools and colleges have developed alongside the tax-supported system. By 1969, the Catholics had 499 elementary schools and 144 high schools in Michigan, with a total enrollment of 266,139. The Lutherans and Seventh-day Adventists also supported parochial schools, while the members of the Christian Reformed Church maintained elementary and high schools in communities where there were sizable numbers of people of Dutch origin. In 1966-67, there were 338,450 students enrolled in non-public schools, as compared with 2,036,982 in the state's public schools. The growing expense of maintaining these private schools led to repeated efforts, generally unsuccessful, to get a measure of state aid, and also led to a large cutback by the Catholics in the number of schools they operated. At the same time, however, the seventies saw a number of other church groups, particularly fundamentalist Baptist churches, establishing their own schools because of their dislike for some of the trends they saw developing in the public schools. By 1977 the number of students enrolled in private schools stood at 212,358.

In 1865, there were only five church-related colleges in Michigan: Kalamazoo, Albion, Olivet, Adrian, and Hillsdale. By the 1970s there were more than thirty such schools along with a considerable number of other private institutions of higher education that were not church related. The Catholics had been most active along these lines. The University of Detroit, established by the Jesuit order in 1877, was the only one of Michigan's church-related schools and virtually the only one of any of the private institutions that attempted to compete in the range of its programs with the state's publicly supported universities. Except for Aquinas College, founded at Grand Rapids in 1931, the four-year Catholic colleges started as colleges for women. They included Madonna College in Livonia, founded in 1946; Marygrove in Detroit, founded in 1910; Mercy College, also in Detroit and dating from 1934; Nazareth at Kalamazoo, founded in 1924; and Siena Heights at Adrian, founded in 1919. By the 1970s, financial considerations which forced the closing of some other Catholic institutions, forced these women's colleges to become coeducational.

Protestant denominations were also active in founding colleges. Calvin College in Grand Rapids, which had its origins in 1876, was founded by the Christian Reformed Church. It followed the example of the Reformed Church in America, which had established Hope College at Holland in 1866. At Battle Creek, the Seventh-day Adventists opened a college in the 1870s which they moved to Berrien Spring in 1901 and renamed Emmanuel Missionary College. In 1960, the denomination moved Potomac University from Washington, D.C., and merged it with Emmanuel Missionary College under the name Andrews University. Suomi College at Hancock developed out of a school founded by the Finnish Evangelical Lutherans in 1896. Alma College was founded by Presbyterians in 1886. Spring Arbor College developed from a school opened by the

Free Methodists in 1873 which became a four-year college in 1963. Detroit's Michigan Lutheran College, established in 1936, did not survive the financial crunch that hit private institutions by the sixties and seventies, but Concordia College at Ann Arbor, founded by the Lutherans' Missouri Synod as a two-year junior college in 1962, advanced to full four-year status in 1976.

Independent schools and secular colleges also became part of Michigan's educational system. Several schools were established at Bloomfield Hills by the Cranbook Foundation, formed to administer the estate of George and Ellen Scripps Booth of Detroit. The most notable of these are the Cranbrook Academy of Arts, founded in 1928, which, under the direction of the famed architect Eliel Saarinen, became internationally known for the training of architects, painters, and sculptors, and the Cranbrook Science Institute, established in 1931. The Merrill-Palmer Institute in Detroit, founded in 1920, offers a number of specialized courses. General Motors Institute at Flint, Chrysler Institute of Engineering at Detroit, and Lawrence Institute of Technology in Southfield are among the state's leading technical schools. Northwood Institute in Midland, a business school founded in 1959, the Walsh College of Accounting in Troy, established in 1969, and Lansing's Thomas M. Cooley Law School, founded in 1972, are among the more important private institutions founded in recent years.

Although there was a continuing concern for the quality of education, the paramount problem faced by the state's schools for a quarter of a century after 1945 was rapidly mounting enrollments. The proportion of young men and women continuing their education through high school increased sharply during the Depression. While the state's population increased eight percent, high-school enrollments went up fifty-six percent. The birth rate began a sustained rise during World War II. During the two decades from 1940 to 1960, the population growth of Michigan was one of the largest in the nation. In the fifties the proportion of high-school graduates going to college began to rise almost as spectacularly as the proportion of primary school students attending high school had risen in the thirties. All these factors combined to bring a tidal wave of students into the schools and colleges. Colleges and universities in 1960 enrolled 160,261 students, as compared with 122,808 a decade earlier, and the "war babies" had not yet reached college age. Public-school enrollments stood at a little over a million in 1950—about what they had been in 1930—but by the next decade this enrollment figure would become double what it had been in 1950. All this led to feverish programs at all levels to expand facilities and staff to keep up with this boom. But educational leaders overreacted. By 1970, after young people born during the baby boom of the war years had attained college age, enrollments in colleges began to drop off, reflecting the declining birth rates of the fifties and thereafter. In the seventies, therefore, the problem became one of too many facilities and instructors. This was only partially offset by the growing trend among adults to return to school. This followed a trend that had been fostered early in the century when Detroit and Kalamazoo pioneered in the establishment of public evening educational programs which were aided by federal funds and followed by the famous veterans' education programs under the G.I. Bill of Rights at the end of World War II.

* * * * *

Judged by the number of their members, the growth of churches in Michigan since the Civil War has been almost as significant as that of the schools. The five major Protestant denominations had a total membership of only 60,560 out of a total population in the state of 749,113 in 1860 (approximately eight percent). In 1870, the Roman Catholic Church claimed 170,000 members in Michigan out of a total population of 1,184,509 (approximately fourteen percent). When the United States Census Bureau made its last census of religious bodies in 1936, it tabulated a total of 1,786,839 persons who were members of all churches in Michigan—nearly a third of the state's population. The most recent data, compiled by the National Council of Churches in 1971, listed the total number of "adherents" of Michigan Christian churches as 4,070,237, which was nearly forty-six percent of the state's total population.[5] These figures, however, are somewhat deceiving. There can be little doubt that many people in recent times are church members in name only, a fact that the National Council of Churches sought to take into account when it distinguished between those who were full church members and those who were merely "adherents" of a particular church. A century ago, church members were held to strict conformity to the doctrine and practices of the churches to which they belonged, and any deviation would result in expulsion or excommunication. Today's church, however, has lost its status as the center of community social life. The coming of the automobile, movies, radio, and television as well as the increased interest in sports and the emergence of the school as the center of community life have provided other means of mingling with one's fellow man. The primacy of the church in education has been taken away by publicly supported schools and colleges. Charity, once dispensed in large measure through the church, is now entrusted to a variety of public and private agencies. The theory of evolution and critical study of the Bible also has had some effect in weakening the influence of the church on its members.

The Roman Catholic church enjoyed phenomenal growth in Michigan in the century following the Civil War. The 170,000 Catholics of 1870 had increased to 844,106 by 1926, and in 1971 they increased to 2,252,827—a quarter of the state's entire population, and over fifty-five percent of all the church-goers in the state. The influx of Poles, Hungarians, Italians, and other predominantly Catholic European immigrant groups who were drawn to the state by the opportunities in the auto plants helped to explain this growth, particularly in Detroit which between 1916 and 1926 had the second largest increase in church membership of any American city.

The growth of the Catholic church contributed to the growth of educational institutions and also of other facilities. Catholic hospitals have been established in most of the state's major cities. By 1958, the church maintained thirty-one general and four special hospitals in the state. Several religious orders played an important part in the establishment of these hospitals as well as of schools and colleges. The Felician Sisters, the first of whom arrived in Michigan in 1874, were staffing thirty-three schools and two orphanages by 1937. The Sisters of St. Joseph came to Kalamazoo from New York in 1889 and around their growing community, Borgess Hospital and Nazareth Academy and College developed. The Sisters of the Immaculate Heart of Mary, who belong to an order founded at Monroe in 1845, started the school that later became Marygrove College. The Sisters of St. Dominic came to Adrian in 1878, and through their efforts Siena Heights College was established. In Grand Rapids the educational work of another group of Dominican Sisters resulted in the founding of Aquinas College.

The establishment of separate dioceses in different parts of the state reflected the growth of the Catholic church. The diocese of Upper Michigan had been carved out of the original diocese encompassing the entire state in 1853, followed by the diocese of Grand Rapids in 1882, the diocese of Lansing in 1937, and Saginaw in 1938. On August 3, 1937, the Archdiocese of Detroit was created, with its archbishop, Edward Mooney, becoming a cardinal in 1945—one of five in the United States. Cardinal Mooney died in 1958, and in 1969 John Deardon became the second archbishop of Detroit to be named a cardinal.

Among Protestant denominations, the Methodists were for many years the most numerous in the state. The Methodist circuit rider of pioneer days was an effective instrument in promoting the spread of Methodism, and the well-developed central organization of this church, with its bishops, superintendents, and assigned pulpits, was an important factor in its subsequent growth. The Methodist Episcopal Church, as the largest body of this denomination was called until 1939, grew in membership from 41,490 in 1870 to 114,326 in 1906 and 142,141 in 1936. In 1939 the Methodist Episcopal churches in the South were reunited with those in the North, along with the Methodist Protestant church, to form what is presently called the United Methodist church. In 1971 the United Methodist Church claimed 268,662 full members in the state, with an additional 60,000 who were closely affiliated with the church, making this the second largest single church group in the state. Not included in the union of 1939 were the Wesleyan Methodists, founded originally by antislavery advocates within the denomination and which in 1971 counted nearly 10,000 adherents, and the Free Methodists, which had first been organized in Michigan in the 1860s and in 1971 had a membership in the state likewise around 10,000. Also staying out of the union of Methodists in 1939 were several Negro Methodist groups, which had been organized in Michigan as early as 1841. The largest of these was the African Methodist Episcopal church, which had some 12,000 members in Michigan in 1936 and had grown to a membership of some 24,000 by 1978,[6] with several thousand others represented in two other associations.

Among the features of Methodism that had great popular appeal were the democratic character of the service, simplicity, emotional fervor, and the doctrine of "free grace." The Methodists, more than any other denomination, developed the camp meeting, which grew out of the great revivals in the early nineteenth century. One of the oldest camp-meeting sites in Michigan is Crystal Springs, near Dowagiac. Bay View Assembly, founded in 1875 along the model of the original "chautauqua" in New York, was sponsored by the Methodists, and was a sophisticated version of the summer camp meeting. In association with Albion College the Bay View Assembly took on increased educational features later in the twentieth century. Following the formation of the Methodist youth organization known as the Epworth League, this group grew rapidly in Michigan. It sponsored a recreational and educational program at Epworth Heights near Ludington. Methodists also supported a number of hospitals and social agencies, in addition to the colleges at Albion, Adrian, and Spring Arbor.

The Baptists were another Protestant group that grew in membership, although because of proliferation of Baptist organizations it is difficult to determine its over-all strength in Michigan. Baptist membership was listed as 20,051 in 1870 and this increased to 49,275 by 1936 among those churches affiliated with the Northern Baptist Convention. This organization, subsequently renamed the American Baptist Churches, USA, claimed 64,262 adherents in the state in 1971. But with the migration into Michigan, particularly southeastern Michigan, of large numbers of southerners in the twentieth century, the Southern Baptist Convention, which was not even listed in the 1936 census of religious bodies in Michigan, had established 169 churches by 1971 with a total number of adherents listed as 44,501. Most of this membership resulted from the movement into the state of southern whites, while the great influx of southern blacks which took place from 1916 onward added enormously to the membership of Negro Baptist churches that had been established in the state earlier in the nineteenth century. Although there were several distinctive Negro Baptist church organizations, the census of 1936 lumped nearly all of them under one heading and credited them with some 35,000 members. More recent figures are not available but there can be little doubt that the membership in black Baptist churches has increased greatly since 1936.[7] In addition, churches affiliated with the Baptist Missionary Association, Free Will Baptists, General Baptists, North American Baptists, several other associations, and a number of unaffiliated, independent Baptist churches, add many thousands more to the total membership of all groups that employ the Baptist name. In southeastern Michigan this has certainly been the fastest growing Protestant group in the latter part of the twentieth century.

Other Protestant denominations were also active in support of missionaries in Michigan's pioneer days and had continued to grow in numbers thereafter. By 1936 the Presbyterians included nearly 70,000 members, but by 1971 the principal Presbyterian organization—the United Presbyterian Church of the United States of America—listed a total of 188,675 adherents, while a handful of members were affiliated with several smaller Presbyterian sects. The Congregationalists, who had cooperated with the Presbyterians in the early missionary endeavors, numbered nearly 42,000 by 1936. Later in the fifties, the Congregational and Evangelical and Reformed Church—the latter having 22,000 members in the state in 1936—merged to form the United Church of Christ, which had 102,132 adherents in Michigan in 1971. About a fourth of the state's Congregational churches, however, stayed out of this union, and had an additional 18,000 adherents in 1971.

Foreign immigration was responsible not only for swelling the ranks of the Catholics but also those of a number of other religious groups. The large German immigration of the nineteenth century had been responsible for introducing the Lutheran church to Michigan, and in later years many of the Scandinavian and Finnish immigrants were also affiliated with this Protestant group. The Lutherans came to be adherents of different synods, frequently with widely varying religious viewpoints. If the members of these various Lutheran bodies were considered as one group, they had surpassed the Methodists in total numbers by 1936. The largest such Lutheran body by that time—those associated with the Missouri Synod—numbered 106,854, and it remained by far the largest in 1971, with total adherents of 283,040. The American Lutheran Conference, with 89,315 adherents, the Lutheran Church of America, with 95,925 adherents, and members of the Wisconsin Synod, numbering 48,064, rounded out the major Lutheran groups in the state in 1971. A distinctive feature of Lutheran development since the 1940s has been the large number of church structures of very contemporary design that this denomination has built, in striking contrast with their religious views which have remained relatively conservative and traditional.

Several other churches drawing their membership largely from a single nationality developed into large denominations. The Reformed Church tripled in membership between 1906 and 1936, and had more than doubled its membership again by 1971 when a total of 77,823 were listed as affiliated with this group. The Christian Reformed Church, which developed out of a split in the Reformed Church around the time of the Civil War, grew at an even faster pace, with 96,372 total adherents by 1971. Membership in Jewish congregations, established intially as an outgrowth of the German immigration in the mid-nineteenth century, grew rapidly with the arrival of immigrants from eastern Europe at the end of that century and the beginning of the twentieth century, and totalled 99,366 by 1936. By 1971, however, total membership was reported to have declined to 93,530.[8] Also adding to the diversity of church bodies was the growth of various Orthodox churches that also resulted from the immigration of peoples from eastern Europe as well as from the Near East, while the adherents of the Moslem or Islamic faiths showed a marked increase in the later years of the twentieth century with the appearance of substantial numbers of Arabs and other peoples from the Mediterranean and Near Eastern areas.

Among the smaller Christian groups, the United Brethren, the

Evangelical Church, the Society of Friends (Quakers), and the Unitarians were among those that were established well before the Civil War and which continued on to the present day. The Seventh-day Adventists, Christian Scientists, and the Salvation Army were religious organizations that developed in later years. In cities and even in many rural communities, the growth of small sects which were conservative in doctrine, preached the "old time religion," and relied heavily on emotional appeal, was a noteworthy sequel to the modernist-fundamentalist split of the 1920s. The older Protestant denominations introduced formal ritual and appealed to the head rather than the heart. Imposing church edifices were built and leadership in church organizations went to socially prominent members. All this repelled many worshipers, who sought a warmer and more personal religious faith and fellowship. Assemblies of God, the Nazarene churches, and a large number of smaller denominations rose to meet this need. Services frequently were held in vacant store buildings, garages, or tents, but in many instances more permanent church structures and regularly organized denominations evolved in due course. The first Nazarene church in Michigan was founded at Grand Rapids in 1909 by persons with various former church affiliations who organized themselves into a "Holiness Band." By 1936 the denomination had 5,560 members in the state and by 1971 it claimed a total of 38,357 adherents.

At the opposite extreme from these new evangelical churches was the Episcopal Church, with its time-honored ritual. The most tradition-oriented of all Protestant groups, its membership in the cities tended to include a large number of the wealthier, more socially elite elements of the population. Never one of the largest Protestant groups in the state, its listed membership and the total number of its churches declined between 1936 and 1971, with 80,000 confirmed members listed in 1971, and a total of 116,000 of all those who were counted as members or adherents. But even the ranks of this staid organization were rent by strife in the 1970s as many of the church leaders, concerned with its declining numbers and feeling that it must reach out to more people, carried through a revision of the church's Book of Common Prayer. Many conservatives strenuously objected to this revision as well as other departures from past practices, most striking of which was the move to ordain women priests. Coleman McGehee, bishop of the Diocese of Michigan, the largest of the state's three Episcopal dioceses, was openly sympathetic to these new moves. At the end of the seventies, some conservative Episcopalians in Michigan were participating in a nation-wide movement that threatened a permanent schism in Episcopal ranks.

*   *   *   *   *

By the twentieth century, Americans had become famous as "joiners," and some of the qualities associated with this term may have attracted some people to join churches more for the social activities than religious benefits. It may also account for the growing popularity in Michigan in later years of clubs, societies, and organizations of various types, some of which had certain religious overtones to them. This was particularly the case with the numerous fraternal orders, which became so numerous and absorbed such a large part of the interest of the people that many churches opposed them. There was a Masonic lodge in Michigan as early as 1764 and there were many Masons among the pioneers. A wave of anti-Masonic feeling that swept the west in the late twenties drove the lodges in Michigan and elsewhere underground until 1840 when a convention was held in Mount Clemens to revive the Masonic order in Michigan. Three of the old lodges surfaced again and a Grand Lodge of Michigan was instituted in 1844. Progress from this point was rapid, and by the close of the century there was a Masonic lodge in virtually every city and town in the state. The first Odd Fellow lodge was organized at Detroit in 1843; by 1865 more than a hundred lodges of this order had been founded in Michigan. The Eastern Star lodge, associated with the Masons, and the Rebekahs, associated with the Odd Fellows, were organizations for the wives of these lodge members that had been started before the Civil War. The Maccabee order was one that originated in Michigan under permission granted by the legislature in 1881. The Knights of Pythias was another order that originated in the state, its ritual written by a schoolteacher in the Upper Peninsula in 1859, with the first lodge in the state established at Detroit in 1871. These and many other lodges were designed as fraternal and social organizations, and all of them aided those of their members who were sick as well as the widows and children of those who died. Several developed life-insurance programs of considerable size and importance, with the Maccabees being the best example of this development.[9]

The noonday luncheon clubs originated during the first two decades of the twentieth century. The first of these was Rotary International, and the first club in Michigan was formed in Detroit in 1910. Two of the major luncheon or service clubs had their origin in

Michigan: the Exchange Club in 1911, and Kiwanis International, whose number one chapter was organized in Detroit in 1915. Today, although the strength of the fraternal orders is not as great as it was earlier, the luncheon clubs, comprised of business and professional men, continue to flourish. Although much of the interest in them is social, the clubs engage in various fund-raising activities to support worthy causes. The Lions' clubs, for example, support the Seeing-Eye Dog program at Rochester and the Kiwanis clubs support programs for patients at the University of Michigan Medical Center.

Important among the organizations in every Michigan community since the Civil War have been the veterans' associations. Until after 1900, the Grand Army of the Republic, the organization of Civil War veterans, wielded enormous influence on the political affairs of the state and provided a social outlet for its members and a pressure group for pensions and other benefits. The United Spanish War Veterans grew out of a number of organizations formed by the men who fought in the Spanish-American War. Although it never attained the proportions of the Grand Army of the Republic, it had about sixty-five local "camps" in Michigan as late as 1935. The Veterans of Foreign Wars originated from one of the organizations of Spanish-American War veterans which was formed in 1899. Its present name dates from 1913. A large accretion of World War I veterans to its membership led to the establishment of the Department of Michigan in 1920. A national home for widows and orphans of members was built at Eaton Rapids. Another great increase in membership came after World War II. The Disabled American Veterans and the Amvets—the latter composed exclusively of World War II veterans—were two other large veterans groups represented in Michigan. Largest of all, however, was the American Legion. Michigan was represented by forty-six delegates at the meeting in New York in 1919 at which this organization was formed. The Michigan department received its charter the next year. In addition to its work on behalf of the veterans, the American Legion promoted a program of Americanization and sponsored such projects as the Wolverine Boys State, patriotic speaking, and essay contests. Like the Veterans of Foreign Wars, it perpetuated itself by recruiting membership from veterans of subsequent wars, a feature that distinguished these twentieth-century veterans groups from the earlier ones which died out with the death of the last veteran of the war commemorated by the organizations. Despite radically different views about war and patriotism that arose among participants in the far less popular Korean and Vietnam wars, veterans' organizations succeeded in enlisting new members because of the social activities these organizations offered. For the workingman, the local American Legion or Veterans of Foreign Wars post provided some of the same kinds of outlets that the service clubs offered to businessmen in the town and which country clubs provided to an even more elite group.[10]

Women have proved no less zealous than men in forming clubs and associations. Women's clubs were formed in Kalamazoo in 1852, Battle Creek in 1864, Grand Rapids in 1869, and Detroit in 1872. The Women's Christian Temperance Union—a state-wide organization to fight the battle against the purveyors of alcohol—was formed at Grand Rapids in 1875. A State Federation of Women's Clubs originated at a meeting in Bay View in 1894. The earliest chapters of the Daughters of the American Revolution were organized in Michigan in 1893. Women's auxiliaries were attached to all the veterans' groups and there were similar groups associated with the various lodges. Women in business and the professions also had service clubs such as Zonta International, the Altrusa Club, and the Business and Professional Women's Clubs.[11]

* * * * *

The importance of libraries as repositories of our cultural heritage and as sources of information has been recognized since the earliest days in Michigan. The first three state constitutions all stipulated that monies collected from fines for penal offenses should be set aside for the support of libraries. The present State Library dates from 1828. The legislature has passed many acts to encourage the establishment and maintenance of libraries. Prior to the Civil War, however, there was relatively little done to establish public libraries. In 1861, only twelve percent of the townships were appropriating any funds for libraries. The desire of the people for libraries had to be met by private library organizations, often called "subscription libraries." A City Library was organized at Detroit in 1817 and shares of stock were sold to obtain funds. It was merged with the Detroit Young Men's Society in 1832. The Detroit Mechanics' Society, formed in 1818, also maintained a library. The Historical Society of Michigan, which came into being in 1828 with Governor Lewis Cass as its president, collected manuscripts and articles on the history of Michigan. In Kalamazoo, a Ladies' Library Association was organized in 1852 and incorporated in 1859. In 1879, this association erected a large building, reputed to be the first in the nation built exclusively for the use of a woman's club.[12] A women's library association was formed in Flint in 1853. Subsequently, similar associations were formed in other cities and even in small villages and towns.

Funds realized from the collection of fines constituted the financial basis of the Detroit Public Library, opened in 1865. The Grand Rapids Public Library originated in 1871 with the consolidation of the school district libraries. The Kalamazoo Public Library was founded about the same time, also originally as a school library. Private gifts made public library buildings possible in such cities as Battle Creek, Hillsdale, Kalamazoo, and Grand Rapids. Many cities benefitted from Andrew Carnegie's donations for library construction. Typical of these were the Carnegie libraries in Niles, St. Joseph, and Ironwood. Gradually, as the public libraries developed, private library associations disappeared or directed their attention to other objectives.

While cities of the state developed public libraries, rural areas and small towns remained for many years with no library service or only subscription libraries. The legislature passed a county library act in 1917, but little action was taken under its provisions until 1933, when federal funds were made available. The depression years of the 1930s brought a heavy demand on libraries. Unemployed workers found in libraries a means by which their idle time could be occupied profitably. Thirty county and village libraries were established through federal aid between 1934 and 1936. But there were still large areas in the state without libraries. Governor Frank Murphy in 1938 declared that nearly a quarter of the people of Michigan did not have access to a library, and that another thirty percent had only nominal service. State aid was provided on a broad scale starting in 1937. The W. K. Kellogg Foundation of Battle Creek performed a great service to rural communities of southwestern Michigan by providing thousands of new books for local libraries. Another important contributor to making books available to areas lacking libraries was the State Library in Lansing, through its "bookmobiles" and its lending services. In 1974–75, $5,998,527 was appropriated by the state legislature for libraries, while federal aid of $6,985,130 was received to strengthen state library services to local libraries.

The colleges and the universities gradually built up large collections of books, periodicals, and documents. Much more emphasis was placed on the importance of libraries after the abandonment of the classical course of study around 1900. The University of Michigan alone in 1979 had 5,000,000 volumes in its libraries. The donations of an alumnus and former regent of the University of Michigan, William L. Clements of Bay City, made possible the William L. Clements Library at the University of Michigan, one of the nation's greatest depositories of original materials on the colonial and revolutionary periods in American history. A Detroiter, Clarence M.

Burton, collected original source materials on the history of Michigan and the Northwest, which became the nucleus of the Burton Historical Collection of the Detroit Public Library. The Michigan Historical Collections at the University of Michigan, the Clarke Memorial Library at Central Michigan University, and smaller archival collections at other institutions provide the historian with the raw materials he needs for recreating the past of the state. The State Archives at Lansing is the repository for state records of historical value. Under state law no local governmental unit may destroy its records without approval of the State Administrative Board, after certification by the Michigan Historical Commission, now a division of the Department of State, that the papers proposed for destruction have no historical value. The Archives of Labor History and Urban Affairs, housed in the Walter P. Reuther Library at Wayne State University, is a recent example of the development of a new collection, which, as the major repository of labor union records in the country, has great significance not only for the student of Michigan's history but for this aspect of American history in general. On the other hand, the J. M. Longyear Research Library in Marquette, a rich depository of records relating to the Upper Peninsula, illustrates that not all of these special collections are found in the more populous parts of southern Michigan.

*   *   *   *   *

Newspapers are one of the historian's most important resources, and although many newspaper files have been lost forever, the State Library in the past quarter of a century has been performing a valuable service by ferreting out existing files and making them available on microfilm. The task is a formidable one, since no one will probably ever be able to come up with a complete inventory of all the newspapers that have appeared in the state since the one and only issue of Michigan's first paper, the *Michigan Essay or Impartial Observer,* appeared in Detroit in 1809.

In 1850 only three daily newspapers were being published in Michigan, but most cities and villages had weeklies. As the population grew many of the weeklies became dailies and new daily newspapers were established. During and after the Civil War newspapers were fiercely partisan in their particular political preference. Many were published at a loss by party leaders and their supporters as a means of influencing public opinion. Every sizable city had at least two newspapers, one supporting the Republican cause, the other championing the Democratic party.

By the turn of the century a change was evident, as publishers began to regard their newspapers more as business ventures and less as partisan outlets. In this transition James E. Scripps of Detroit became a figure of national importance. He came to Detroit in 1859 to become business manager of the *Advertiser and Tribune*. This newspaper supported the Republican party while the *Free Press* was the Democratic organ. In 1873 Scripps founded the Detroit *Evening News*, an historic event in the history of journalism in the United States. Scripps believed a newspaper should be self-supporting, not dependent on political handouts. In order to accomplish this, his first job was to increase circulation so as to attract advertisers. The paper was smaller than those being published at the time, and the news was condensed. It sold at 2¢ a copy, in contrast to the 5¢ price of other newspapers. Scripps enlisted other members of his family to secure funds to buy fast cylinder presses and to take over various responsibilities in the office. His brother, George H. Scripps, sold his Illinois farm and became business manager of the paper; his sister, Ellen B. Scripps, joined the editorial staff, and his half brother, E. W. Scripps, came to help increase circulation. New features were introduced and sensational news was featured. Circulation increased rapidly, and the venture was so profitable that E. W. Scripps established the Cleveland *Press* along similar lines. This was the beginning of the Scripps-Howard newspaper chain. James E. Scripps remained in Detroit to manage the *News*. The success of this newspaper naturally led other publishers to imitate it. Partisanship became less prominent, with more emphasis on features and the kind of news designed to attract readers and thus to win advertising contracts.[13]

Since about 1914 many daily newspapers in Michigan have been consolidated and the number of such papers greatly reduced. In 1959, the consolidation of the Grand Rapids *Herald* with the Grand Rapids *Press* made Detroit the only city in the state with more than one daily newspaper. Fifty-two dailies were still being published in Michigan in 1979. There were several reasons for these consolidations. Advertisers found it less expensive to buy space in one newspaper with general circulation, even at higher rates, than in two or more with overlapping circulation. Increasing costs of labor and the demand for more features, widespread news coverage, and attractive format were other factors.[14] The single daily newspaper that evolved from consolidations in all Michigan cities except Detroit was no longer strongly partisan, usually reflecting in its editorials prevailing public opinion in the community, although on occasion there were evidences of crusading fervor.

Another evidence of the trend toward newspapers becoming a

segment of big business in America was the development of companies owning newspapers in several cities. The largest such company in Michigan was the Booth Publishing Company. George G. Booth of Detroit, who had married a daughter of James E. Scripps, acquired the Grand Rapids *Press* in the 1890s and in due course it came to have the largest circulation of any outstate paper. Early in the twentieth century Booth's brother, Ralph, obtained control of newspapers in four other Michigan cities, and these were brought together with the *Press* under the management of the Booth Publishing Company. Three others newspapers were acquired in 1922. The Booth chain, which included the Grand Rapids *Press,* the Flint *Journal,* the Muskegon *Chronicle,* the Jackson *Citizen-Patriot,* the Kalamazoo *Gazette,* the Ann Arbor *News,* the Bay City *Times,* and the Saginaw *News,* was itself taken over by a larger national newspaper chain, Newhouse, in 1976. In 1921, the far more flamboyant Hearst newspaper chain, founded by William Randolph Hearst, had purchased the Detroit *Times,* greatly enlivening that city with Hearst's distinctively sensational and personal journalistic style. But after Hearst's death his newspaper chain began to be cut back, and in 1960 the *Times* ceased publication and its plant was taken over by the Detroit *News.* The two surviving Detroit dailies, the *Free Press* and the *News,* engaged in a fierce battle for the lead in circulation. The *Free Press,* which had itself become part of a chain of newspapers put together by John S. Knight of Akron, Ohio, maintained a large outstate following since it is the state's only major morning paper after the demise of the Grand Rapids *Herald.* The Detroit *News,* although also widely circulated outstate, gave greater emphasis to the Detroit area market and in the late seventies had built up a commanding lead in circulation over the *Free Press* and was, in fact, the largest evening newspaper in the country.

In towns and villages not large enough to support a daily paper a weekly publication invariably sprang up. In 1979 there were close to 250 such papers published in the state. The country editor traditionally had had to spend long hours to make ends meet.[15] Far more profitable than the newspaper was the job printing work done in the newspaper shop. The weeklies, like the dailies, tended to become less partisan, but editors did not hesitate to express their views on local, state, and national affairs. This type of journalism still survives among the weeklies. Bessemer's *Pick and Axe* is one of the best examples in recent times of a crusading weekly whose editor obviously had no interest in currying favor in the community in order to boost the paper's advertising revenues. In this area of newspaper publishing, as in the operation of daily papers, however, chains competed for the control of weeklies. In the Detroit suburban communities, the Panax Corporation, which also had some outstate newspapers, and Philip H. Power, heir to the fortune built up by his father—Eugene B. Power—with the University Microfilm business in Ann Arbor, were the major publishers by the late seventies.

Numerous foreign-language newspapers have been published in Michigan. As early as 1850, Holland had a Dutch-language newspaper. Between 1876 and 1930 no less than thirty-three Finnish newspapers and periodicals were published in Michigan. German, Italian, and Polish papers appeared in Detroit, which also had newspapers for Jewish and Negro readers.[16]

In addition to daily and weekly newspapers, numerous periodicals continued to be published. Monthly or in some cases weekly magazines were produced by most church groups for their members. Some of these were the *Banner,* founded at Grand Rapids in 1868 for members of the Christian Reformed Church, the *Michigan Christian Advocate,* established at Adrian in 1874 for Methodist readers, and the *Christian Herald,* founded prior to the Civil War to serve Baptists. The number of trade, professional, and business publications increased rapidly after World War I. Probably the oldest of these is the *Michigan Tradesman,* published at Grand Rapids. *Automotive News* and *Motor News* are two Detroit publications—the former an industry publication, and the latter for members of the Automobile Club of Michigan. Among magazines aimed at a more general audience, none achieved the circulation nor the popularity of the *American Boy,* a weekly published in Detroit for several decades prior to the early 1940s. In its heyday in the 1920s, *American Boy,* with its roster of authors, stories, features, and artwork, was a kind of *Saturday Evening Post* for teen-age boys. In recent years, attempts to publish a magazine about Michigan that would enjoy the same success as such state magazines as *Arizona Highways* have been short-lived, but *Michigan Natural Resources,* published by the Michigan Department of Natural Resources (and by that department's predecessor, the Department of Conservation), has come the closest to that model.

*   *   *   *   *

The arts require taste, leisure, and intelligence in order to flourish. Unquestionably, the primary necessity of providing food, clothing, and shelter in a new land left little time for the pioneer to devote to the arts. Yet it is possible to overstress this cause for lack of interest. The German people who settled in Michigan exhibited a lively interest in music from the earliest years because they had a taste for it. One of the retarding influences in the development of the fine arts in Michigan was the Puritan tradition, which regarded beauty as a snare of the devil and those who devoted themselves to music, drama, or painting as lost souls. But in the period after the Civil War, courageous people began to take interest in the arts.

Music was the first of the arts to gain converts. In pioneer times ballads, folk songs, and fiddlers' dance tunes comprised the musical fare. In the years after the Civil War every community had its brass band, usually called by some such grandiloquent name as "Silver Cornet Band," which played on patriotic occasions and for dancing. As early as 1881 the Ann Arbor High School offered a music course. In 1927 a member of the University of Michigan's School of Music, Joseph E. Maddy, founded the national high-school music camp at Interlochen, which became nationally known in the years that followed. The pianist, Van Cliburn, was the best-known graduate of the Interlochen program. In 1962 it was expanded into a year-round school for youth of high-school age gifted in the arts.[17] The chautauqua programs of the first two decades of the twentieth century introduced thousands of Michiganians to serious music. In the twenties, when the first radio stations went on the air, their programs were devoted mostly to popular music, but there was also some symphonic and operatic music broadcast, and the very surfeit of popular music turned many people to an interest in music of a more lasting character.

The growing interest in music was reflected in the organization of music clubs. A Michigan Federation of Music Clubs was formed and in 1916 it became affiliated with the National Federation. The University of Michigan has been a vital force in the musical life of the state. Concerts were sponsored by the University Choral Society, formed in 1879. The spring festival, which brought to Ann Arbor each year leading orchestras and musical artists of the world, was started in 1894. The Detroit Symphony Orchestra, founded in 1914, became one of the nation's leading orchestras under the direction of Ossip Gabrilowitsch. In later years, under other conductors and sponsors, the Detroit Symphony had only periodic success in fulfilling the hopes of its founders. It enjoyed a revival in the fifties under the French conductor, Paul Paray, and then in the late seventies another internationally known conductor, Antal Dorati, was again refurbishing the organization's reputation. Symphony orchestras were also established in Grand Rapids and Kalamazoo in 1921, and in several other cities in later years, but financial costs largely restricted their development to local talent that donated their services.

Meanwhile music was introduced into virtually all the schools of the state. Among the many interesting activities of Henry R. Pattengill, superintendent of public instruction from 1893 to 1896, was the compilation of a "knapsack" of songs for school children, known as "Pat's Pick," which remained in use for many years. By the 1920s many high schools had developed excellent bands and orchestras.

Michigan shared with the rest of the nation the craze for popular music which started about the time of World War I. After the war, dance orchestras and dance bands increased in number with great rapidity. Around Detroit and at the more populous summer-resort areas, huge pavilions or "casinos" were built to accommodate the throngs who paid to listen and dance to the rhythms of name bands.[18] However, the most distinctive impact made by Detroit in popular music came in the late fifties when a number of black artists gained national attention performing rhythm and blues music that later evolved into rock and roll. Berry Gordy, Jr., of Detroit founded the Motown Record Company, and built it into a musical empire with the talents of such groups as the Supremes, the Temptations, Stevie Wonder, and Smokey Robinson and the Miracles—Detroit blacks who became the top recording artists of the sixties by performing what became known as the "Detroit Sound." It did not remain in Detroit, however, because Gordy expanded his operations into other entertainment areas and moved the company to the West Coast by the early 1970s.[19]

Interest in painting and sculpture developed more slowly than enthusiasm for music. Painters who devoted themselves largely to portraiture were common in Michigan cities prior to the Civil War, but only the wealthy few demonstrated much awareness of the visual arts for many years after 1865. Although the Detroit Art Association was formed in 1875 to provide art exhibitions, there was no public art gallery in Michigan until 1888. In that year, the Detroit Museum of Art was made possible through private donations. Later, in 1919, this museum was taken over by the city, which established an arts commission to manage the facility. In 1927, a magnificent building designed by Paul Cret (it has been greatly expanded in recent years) was opened to house the growing collections of what was now known as the Detroit Institute of Arts. Elsewhere in Michigan, the Ann Arbor Art Association, dating from 1909, was active in providing a number of items for the permanent art collection in the Alumni Memorial Hall at the University of Michigan. The Grand Rapids Art Gallery dates from 1910, and the Hackley Art Gallery in Muskegon from 1911. The Kalamazoo Institute of Arts was organized in 1924.

It established an art center, which was housed after 1961 in a magnificent new building, the gift of Mr. and Mrs. Donald Gilmore.

Michigan produced some notable artists. Robert Hopkin, who came to Detroit from Scotland in 1832 at the age of fourteen, became a popular landscape and marine painter, surviving until 1909. The Scarab Club, an association of Detroit artists, was originally called the Hopkin Club in honor of this painter. William B. Conely was well known as a portrait painter in Kalamazoo and Detroit from 1873 to 1911. Most famous of all was Gari Melchers, son of a German wood carver who came to Detroit in 1855. His paintings won international recognition; no other Michigan artist had so many honors bestowed on him both in Europe and America. His murals for the Detroit Public Library show the landing of Cadillac's wife at Detroit, an incident in the "Conspiracy of Pontiac," and "The Spirit of the Northwest." By 1875 Detroit could boast of a sizable group of artists, some of them with a national reputation. Lewis T. Ives and his son Percy were among the most notable Detroit artists in the latter part of the nineteenth century. Many distinguished Americans and Michiganians sat for Percy Ives, among them being President Grover Cleveland, Hazen S. Pingree, Thomas W. Palmer, and Russell A. Alger. Joseph W. Gies, a native of Detroit, did figure subjects and landscapes as well as portraits. Another Detroit native, Francis Petrus Paulus, was, like Gies, closely associated with the Detroit Museum of Art. He worked abroad from 1902 to the time of World War I, when he returned to his native city and remained there the remainder of his life.

Although Detroit was the center of art life in Michigan, other cities made their contributions. Frederick Stuart Church, born in Grand Rapids in 1842, attained popularity in New York as a magazine illustrator. His "Pandora's Box," "Beauty and the Beast," and "Sorceress" won him great renown. Among the artists who were active in Grand Rapids in the 1930s was Alexander Flynn, a portrait painter, Anton Lang, the famous wood carver from Oberammergau, and Stanislav V'soske, a designer. A Saginaw native, Eanger Irving Gousem, born there in 1860, won distinction as a painter of Indian pictures. Frederick Carl Frieske, born at Owosso in 1875, won international honors for his paintings. Ezra Winters, whose murals and friezes may be seen in public buildings in Washington, D.C., New York, and Detroit, spent his early life in Manistee and Traverse City. De Jonge Smith, a muralist of distinction, and Algred Hutty, a noted etcher, came from Grand Haven.

The widespread interest in art in Michigan is evidenced by the growth of art education in the twentieth century. In Detroit the Arts and Crafts Society, formed in 1907, became established as an art school of major importance. Art instruction at the University of Michigan began as early as 1852, when a professorship of fine arts was established. Art departments and art schools were established later in almost all the state's colleges and universities. The founding of the Cranbrook Academy of Art in 1928 was an event of major significance in the history of art in Michigan. The Cranbrook Academy soon became known throughout the nation and the world. In 1910 a summer school of art was established at the summer-resort town of Saugatuck in western Michigan. Offering courses in crafts, graphic arts, and painting, this school—Ox-Bow—helped to make Saugatuck a mecca for artists. Another art center farther north along the Lake Michigan shore is located at Leland.

Starting in 1952, the Kalamazoo Institute of Arts began sponsoring an annual outdoor "clothesline" art show. Such summer shows increasingly became a familiar sight, but none was as successful as that at Ann Arbor. This art show grew from a relatively modest beginning in 1959 to an annual three-day showing of all kinds of art which filled the streets in the university area of the city as well as spilling over into the downtown area. It was the biggest and most prestigious of all such shows in Michigan, if not in the entire Midwest.[20]

In addition to art museums, many other kinds of museums are also found in Michigan: science museums, industrial museums, and historical museums. In the first building erected for the University of Michigan when it opened in 1841, a room was set aside for what was then called a "cabinet" and which would now be called a museum. By 1963, the University of Michigan had more than a dozen separate museums, containing collections in such varied fields as archaeology, musical instruments, plants, and animal life. Museums in Michigan are maintained by state agencies, cities, school districts, private associations, and individuals.

Among the museums with notable collections of natural history are the Grand Rapids Public Museum and the Kingman Museum in Battle Creek. The Grand Rapids Public Museum developed out of a collection started by the Grand Rapids Lyceum of Natural History, dating back to 1854, but it has come to include extensive treatment of historical topics relating to that city's development. Although it contains exhibits relating to the sciences, the Alfred P. Sloan, Jr., Museum in Flint is perhaps best known for its collection of transportation vehicles and other exhibits tied in with Flint's history. Among the state's distinctive exhibits are those found in the Netherlands

Museum at Holland, depicting the life and customs of the Dutch people. In recent years a fine outdoor historical attraction has been added at Holland with the erection of a windmill from the Netherlands on land reclaimed from the Black River, together with several buildings that help to explain the rich Dutch heritage of the area.

Among historical museums, the Detroit Historical Museum is one of the largest municipally supported museums of its type in the country. It started in 1928 from a collection of historical materials gathered by Clarence M. Burton. For several years it was housed in the Barlum Tower. Detroit's 250th anniversary provided the needed impetus for the establishment of a major museum. Over $400,000 was raised by popular subscription in 1943, and the city council voted an additional $500,000 to provide a spacious and beautiful new museum building at the corner of Woodward and Kirby, in the same area as the Detroit Public Library and the Detroit Institute of Arts. The building was dedicated in 1951, and a major addition was opened in 1968. A city commission was appointed in 1946 to supervise the operation of the museum. Under its long-time director, Henry Brown, the Detroit Historical Museum pioneered a new concept in its approach by seeking to display materials in such a fashion as to create a sense of living history and to illustrate a single idea, concept, or period, rather than displaying everything in ways that had tended to baffle and confuse visitors to museums of an earlier day.

There are a number of museums maintained and operated by professional staffs in other Michigan cities. The Kalamazoo Public Museum pioneered a plan of loaning exhibits for use in the schoolroom or even in the home. At Dearborn the local historical society in the 1940s secured a building that once was part of the United States arsenal and with later additions created a museum development of sizable proportions. Other historical museums were operated by local historical societies in Muskegon, Niles, and Marquette. In recent decades the numbers of these local museums have greatly increased, while Michigan State, Wayne State, and several other colleges and universities have followed the example set earlier by the University of Michigan. In Lansing, a museum operation is part of the work entrusted to the History Division of the Michigan Department of State. It is an outgrowth of the State Pioneer Museum that developed early in this century under the supervision of the Michigan Pioneer and Historical Society, and which was later transferred to the Michigan Historical Commission when that state agency was established in 1913. The problem of providing adequate housing for the museum's collections, however, has never been satisfactorily resolved.

The most extensive exhibit of Americana in Michigan is found in Greenfield Village and the Henry Ford Museum at Dearborn. Greenfield Village was built on a two-hundred-acre tract of land by Henry Ford and was one of America's first examples of an outdoor museum. Ford purchased a hundred historic buildings that were moved to the village to show how Americans lived and worked during the first three centuries of their history. The Henry Ford Museum was built to exhibit the vast collection of artifacts that Ford had begun to assemble as early as 1906. In the same area Ford established schools to carry out his "learning-by-doing" ideas in education. Greenfield Village, the museum, and the schools constituted the three divisions of the Edison Institute, which was dedicated on October 21, 1929, by President Herbert Hoover on the fiftieth anniversary of Thomas A. Edison's development of the incandescent light. Greenfield Village and the museum became one of Michigan's major tourist attractions, annually drawing over a million paying visitors by the fifties. Although the schools were abandoned after Ford's death, the non-profit private association that operates this museum complex made extensive additions to the village and museum in the seventies as well as carrying out a major renovation of existing exhibits.[21]

Another highly successful museum development in recent years has been accomplished by the Mackinac Island State Park Commission. A museum at Fort Mackinac on Mackinac Island had existed for many years, but was not given much attention and there were few visitors. Largely through the efforts of W. Stewart Woodfill, chairman of the park commission, the legislature authorized the commission to expand this museum operation through the issuance of revenue bonds, to be paid off through admission fees to the exhibits. In 1958, Fort Mackinac, with its new look, was opened, and the number of visitors who now paid to get in to view the buildings and their exhibits exceeded all expectations. The park commission, under its museum director, Eugene T. Petersen, was encouraged to expand its activities to the south side of the straits where in 1959 it began the restoration of the eighteenth-century Fort Michilimackinac. Here, in addition to the restored buildings and their exhibits, one of the most popular attractions has been the on-going archaeological excavation of the site which visitors can observe each summer and which has resulted in the accumulation of an immense number of artifacts.[22]

The success of Greenfield Village and the Mackinac Island State Park Commission's activities encouraged many others to develop similar historical attractions, which have become far too numerous to list and describe here. More and more the tourist and vacation industry came to recognize the importance of history in attracting visitors to the state. Even more important is the role that such living history plays in reminding Michigan citizens of their rich heritage and the responsibility they have to preserve and enhance that heritage.[23]

* * * * *

In spite of the antagonistic attitude toward the theater by most of the Protestant churches, travelling theatrical troupes visited Detroit and other Michigan cities even in pre-Civil War days. As early as 1830, a barn near the Steamboat Hotel in Detroit was used as a theater, and a building was constructed especially to accommodate touring players in 1848. The Athenaeum Theater was built during the Civil War but burned down in 1869. A few weeks later, however, the Detroit Opera House was opened and for forty years it remained the center of Detroit musical and theatrical life. Many other theaters were constructed in later years. The Lafayette was opened in 1925 and the Cass in 1926. The Fisher Theater, in the Fisher Building in Detroit's New Center area, opened in 1928, survives as the city's principal center for legitimate Broadway theater offerings.

In outstate cities the evolution of the theater followed a pattern similar to that in Detroit. At first theatrical productions were given in halls used for general civic purposes. About the time of the Civil War buildings especially designed for concerts and plays and usually called "opera houses" were erected in the larger cities. Grand Rapids had its first opera house in 1859, and Powers' Grand Opera House, opened there in 1873, seating 1,600 people, was the largest and best equipped for many years in western Michigan. In Kalamazoo an "Academy of Music" (actually a theater) had its grand opening in 1882. Buck's Opera House in Lansing was constructed in 1872. Between 1870 and 1900 opera houses were built in the smaller cities and even in villages. The Midland Opera House was opened about 1880. It was situated on the second floor of a store building, like most of those in the smaller cities and towns. South Haven had an opera house as early as 1879. The Beckwith Theater in Dowagiac was built as a memorial to Philo D. Beckwith, founder of the Round Oak Company, for years Dowagiac's leading and distinctive industry. Buchanan had an opera house as early as 1880. Bellevue, with a population of only a few hundred, boasted an opera house in 1876. Another example of the small-town opera house was that in Cedar Springs, built in 1880. It had a large stage and several dressing rooms. A rural scene was painted on the front curtain by a local artist; around it, as was the custom, appeared advertisements by local mer-

Typical Michigan opera house, ca. 1890

chants. The hall was lighted by acetyline lamps. Seats were removable so that the hall could be used for dances, chicken suppers, school fairs, graduation exercises, mouth organ and fiddlers' contests, political rallies, and home talent plays. The owner, a Republican, refused to rent the hall, however, to the Democrats when they wanted to hold a rally.

The theater enjoyed great popularity in the Copper Country around the turn of the century. In the 1890s Houghton had two theaters, as did Hancock, while Lake Linden, Calumet, and Laurium each had its own opera house or theater. In 1898 Laurium built an opera house to seat 1,300 people. Not to be outdone, the people of Calumet spent $70,000 for an elaborately decorated theater, which opened March 20, 1900, with a production of *The Highwayman* by a professional troupe before an audience of 1,200. The Kerredge Theater, which opened in Hancock in 1902, had a seating capacity of 1,565, a stage forty feet deep and seventy feet wide, ten dressing rooms, and a thousand incandescent electric lamps. For the opening performance, box seats sold for $40. Excellent train service to the Copper Country enabled travelling theatrical companies to appear there between engagements at Chicago and Minneapolis-St. Paul.[24]

Typical of the dozens of stock companies that toured Michigan between 1890 and 1914 was the one owned and managed by M. A. (Al) Hunt called Hunt's Stock Company. Hunt, a native of Bangor, started his career as a showman and musician in a travelling show band. Later he joined the "rube band" of Tucker's Show. Tucker, who resided in Decatur, was one of the most popular of the small-town showmen. Always genial, he received a hearty welcome when he returned to the same towns year after year. He was handsome, stockily built, and wore a conspicuous black moustache turned up at the ends. During all performances he wore overalls tucked into high boots. After several years of apprenticeship with Tucker, Hunt started his own troupe, consisting of twelve men and women. As the movies came in, the opera houses where Hunt's troupe played closed their doors, but Hunt continued, putting his show under canvas. Business was good until the Depression. The venture was discontinued in 1931 and most stock companies folded up about the same time. The Slout Players, with headquarters at Vermontville, however, continued to play the small towns after the 1950s.

A combination of factors spelled the doom of the small-town and small-city opera houses and theaters during the decade between 1910 and 1920. The prime factor was, perhaps, the coming of the movies. But the building of high-school auditoriums was important, too, because they replaced the opera house as the center of community activities. The chautauqua played its role in dooming these once pretentious and prosperous theaters.

In the larger cities the decline of the legitimate theater was slower. Touring companies playing both serious drama and musical comedy did good business up to the close of the 1920s, although the number of attractions was smaller than in the days before the movies. Vaudeville had a tremendous vogue from about 1910 to 1929. All the principal cities had their vaudeville houses, playing daily matinees and evening performances with weekly or semiweekly changes in programs. Sound pictures, radio, and the Depression killed vaudeville shortly after 1929.

Motion pictures were first demonstrated in 1894. Bertram C. Whitney brought the first moving-picture machine to Michigan in 1896 and installed it in the Detroit Grand Opera House as an oddity. It projected about a thousand feet of celluloid film. The first Detroit movie house was the Casino Theater, opened in 1905. Very quickly in Detroit and outstate cities dozens of "nickelodeons" appeared in the decade after 1905. Usually occupying vacant store buildings and charging five cents for admission, they showed short films. By the time of World War I longer films were being shown, and most Michigan towns had at least one moving-picture theater. A pianist provided "mood music," and in the larger cities orchestras were used to provide musical settings for the films. Before many years the production, distribution, and exhibition of films had developed into a big business. Enterprisers secured control of theaters in several cities and established "circuits" for the showing of movies as well as vaudeville acts. In Michigan the largest such organization was the Butterfield Circuit, formed by Walter S. Butterfield, a native of Indiana. In 1906 he acquired the Hamblin Opera House in Battle Creek and remodeled it as a popular-price vaudeville house. A few months later he opened the Bijou Theater in Kalamazoo. By 1929 he had a chain of fifty-five theaters. As vaudeville became less popular Butterfield supplemented and finally replaced the vaudeville acts with motion pictures. Expansion continued during the Depression and afterward; by 1948 the Butterfield circuit included a total of 115 theaters in thirty-three Michigan cities. Another successful operator was Claude Cady of Lansing. The Cady theaters eventually became part of the Butterfield circuit.

The coming of television in the 1950s and the construction of outdoor moving-picture theaters dealt a severe blow to the ornate movie palaces built by Butterfield and others. Many of the smaller and older moving-picture theaters were closed, and most small towns saw their once-popular movie houses discontinued. But the larger cities continued to support the moving-picture theater. The development of technicolor and wide-screen movies, which gave the viewer a greater sense of realism, helped save the movie theater. The coming of television also forced the motion-picture producers to pay more attention to artistic values in the films made for projection in moving-picture theaters.

In spite of the competition of films, radio, and television, interest in the legitimate theater did not die out. Travelling theatrical troupes still visited Detroit and other Michigan cities, though much less frequently than earlier, and Detroit still had several legitimate theaters. Of more importance, however was the development of the community theater. In Detroit Miss Jessie Bonstelle established a resident professional theater company in 1925. Three years later the company was reorganized as a non-profit group called the Civic Players, and its theater became the Detroit Civic Theater. Miss Bonstelle was known as the maker of stars. Among the great figures of the theater whose talents were recognized by her were Katherine Cornell, Ann Harding, Frank Morgan, Melvyn Douglas, and William Powell.

Jessie Bonstelle was chiefly interested in the professional theater. But amateurs played a major part in rescuing the legitimate theater from oblivion. During her career in Detroit many amateurs were forming organizations of what was at first known as the "Little Theater" movement. Fundamentally this was a response of communities to the decline of the road show. That decline was becoming apparent by 1910 as a consequence of higher rents, higher transportation costs, and dissatisfaction of theater-goers with the dramatic fare supplied by New York booking agencies. In the early stages of the "Little Theater" movement it was sometimes identified with the "Art Theater," an organization formed to provide an outlet for the creative work of play writers, actors, directors, designers, musicians, and dancers. The art theater never attained a very large popularity outside New York. Two other phases of the Little Theater movement, however, had significance throughout the nation.

One of these was the organization of community theaters. The Ypsilanti Players are regarded as being the first Little Theater group in Michigan, but the Flint Community Players have been in longest continuous operation. The Ypsilanti project started in an old carriage house, with a tiny stage and seats for two hundred people. No salaries were paid; deficits were absorbed by Daniel Quirk, a local businessman. Some excellent plays were presented. In Detroit a number of amateur theatrical groups developed, the most important being the Players' Club and the Contemporary Theater. Sheldon Cheney, who joined the latter group, became editor of a magazine called *Theatre Arts,* a publication that exerted a national influence in the Little Theater movement. Outstate other amateur theatrical groups were being formed. The earliest was founded in Allegan in the 1920s; for its use Griswold Auditorium was provided. Grand Rapids was the next to develop a community theater. In Kalamazoo the Civic Players originated in 1929, and through the generosity of Dr. W. E. Upjohn a beautiful and fully equipped theater was constructed for its productions. Community theaters were established in other Michigan cities in the 1930s and subsequently. In some cases full-time directors, managers, and technicians were employed, but in the main these theaters were for the amateur. The Community Theater Association of Michigan was formed in 1949. By 1963 there were thirty-five outstate community theaters belonging to this organization, with another twenty in Detroit.

Most Michigan high schools stage dramatic productions, and in some there is serious study of dramatic art. In the colleges, too, there has been increasing attention to the theater. As early as 1928 the institution now known as Wayne State University opened a training course in drama and the experimental theater. The University of Michigan's play-production group was formed the same year. During the summer, as the Michigan Repertory Playhouse, this group presented a play each week for a period of five weeks in the Lydia Mendelssohn Theater on campus—a splendidly equipped playhouse. In later years, a professional theater program complemented the student drama productions and provided a wide variety of plays the year round.

Another development in more recent years has been the summer theater located near vacation centers. Shortly after World War II, Jack Ragotzy started an amateur group called the Village Players at Richland, near Gull Lake and within a few miles of Kalamazoo and Battle Creek. Later he acquired an old barn near Augusta and refurbished it as a theater. Professionals replaced the amateur players, and a summer-long series of plays was presented each year. Summer theaters were opened in the fifties in Saugatuck, South Haven, Paw Paw, Grand Haven, Manistee, Petoskey, and Traverse City. In the Copper Country, the old Calumet opera house was reopened as a summer theater, an example which was subsequently followed in Coldwater and other communities where these old buildings had survived.

In 1966 an ambitious plan to establish a theater for the performance of Greek drama was carried out at Ypsilanti, which city was named for two brothers who were heroes in the Greek War for Independence. Unfortunately, although the great Bert Lahr and Judith Anderson starred in the Greek Theater's two critically-acclaimed productions, the venture was a financial disaster and had to be abandoned. More enduring was the Meadow Brook Festival, held in the Howard C. Baldwin Memorial Pavilion at Oakland University. An eight-week season each summer features the Detroit Symphony and other performers, both popular and classical. In 1967 a resident professional company was established at the Meadow Brook Theater, offering dramatic fare of the highest caliber.

*   *   *   *   *

Michigan has produced a number of writers who have achieved national recognition and a host of others whose works have varying degrees of merit. Many of these have used Michigan materials, while others show little trace of Michigan nativity or background in their work. Typical of the latter is Ring Lardner, the noted humorist who was born in Niles, but whose work, written later when he was a resident of Chicago and then in the East, showed only a very occasional reference to his native southwestern Michigan.[25] Similarly, the works of the distinguished novelist Edna Ferber, who was born in Kalamazoo, and Clarence Buddington Kelland, a popular story writer who was a native of Portland, Michigan, had little or nothing to do with Michigan. It was only in his last works in the 1970s that the prize-winning historian, Bruce Catton, who was born in Petoskey and raised in Benzonia, Michigan, returned to themes relating to his native state. On the other hand, Ernest Hemingway, although not a Michigan native, spent much time at his family's summer home near Petoskey in the period around World War I, an experience that was frequently reflected in the themes and locales he used in many of his early short stories. Numerous other writers have been similarly influenced by the environment of Michigan.

Perhaps the best-known writer in the latter part of the nineteenth century to employ Michigan settings in her work was Constance Fenimore Woolson, whose mother was a niece of James Fenimore Cooper. One of Cooper's novels, *Oak Openings,* had grown out of his own Michigan connections. Miss Woolson's novels won the praise of Henry James, and Alexander Cowie, in a monumental work on the American novel published in 1948, devotes eleven pages to her work. Probably her best-known work, *Anne, a Tale of Mackinac,* resulted from material she gathered during a summer on Mackinac Island.

The verse best liked by Michigan readers of the late nineteenth century dripped with sentimentality. Will Carleton's "Over the hill to the poorhouse" had that quality which endeared it to thousands. A bronze tablet was erected in 1925 just a little east of Hillsdale on the grounds of the old poorhouse that Carleton immortalized. He was so popular that the state legislature decreed that each year Michigan schools should honor him on his birthday—October 21—a date that

Michigan schools are still supposed to observe along with Columbus Day, Washington's birthday, and several other legally established dates. In the same category with Carleton was Rose Hartwick, whose "Curfew shall not ring tonight" was long a favorite for schoolroom recital. Another of this ilk was Julia Moore, known as the "sweet singer of Michigan," whose verse, immensely popular in the 1880s, was so incredibly bad that in the twentieth century she became a favorite of those who like to collect examples of such work. For many years in the twentieth century, however, no other poet could approach the popularity of Edgar Guest, whose verses appeared daily in the Detroit *Free Press* for over half a century, and in collected book form enjoyed enormous sales. Although William Lyon Phelps, a professor of English literature at Yale and a frequent summer visitor to Michigan, defended the literary quality of his friend Guest's work, most critics derided Guest for the sentimental nature of his poetry. Guest himself, however, never claimed to be anything but a newsman writing verses.[26]

In the early years of the twentieth century, several Michigan writers attained national recognition for their fiction. Rex Beach, a native of Atwood, Michigan, wrote more than a score of novels and many short stories, some of which used Michigan settings but the most popular of which were set in the Klondike. James Oliver Curwood, who attained an immense following, built a palatial home in his hometown of Owosso which remains that town's most famous landmark. Curwood, like Beach, wrote stories of rugged outdoor life which were classified in what was called the "he-man" school of writing. The ablest of this group was Stewart Edward White, born in Grand Rapids. His novels deal with life in the lumber camps. *The Blazed Trail* (1902), *The Forest* (1903), and *The Riverman* (1908) are his best-known novels. The days of the lumberman were romanticized by a number of writers besides White. Eugene Thwing, in his novels *The Red-Keggers* and *The Man from Red Keg,* used the Saginaw country as his setting. The legend of Paul Bunyan is well known largely through the collections of Bunyan stories published in 1925 by James Stevens and by Esther Shephard.

Farm life in Michigan was depicted with a liberal dash of nostalgia in the books written by Della T. Lutes in the 1930s and 1940s, including *The Country Kitchen, Millbrook,* and *Cousin William.* In contrast, Godfrey Dell Eaton, in *Backfurrow* (1925), describes life in a poor farm region of Michigan as one of stupidity, beastliness, and bitterness. Similarly, Curt Stadtfeld's *From the Land and Back* (1974) is an autobiographical work realistically recounting the struggles of a German family attempting to make a go of farming in the mid-twentieth century in the less than favorable conditions existing near Remus in central Michigan. Helen Rose Hull, who was born in Albion, explored the woman's place in the scheme of things in her novels, one of which, *The Islanders* (1927), depicts Michigan as it was passing out of the pioneer state into a more complex society. The transition of Michigan from an agricultural to an industrial state was the subject of Arthur Pound's *Once a Wildnerness* (1938) and *Second Growth* (1935). Edmund G. Love, with *The Situation in Flushing* (1965), turned from the subjects that had brought him considerable success on Broadway to a series of autobiographical works that effectively depicted the ways that the automobile and other modern developments had changed life in Michigan since the early years of the twentieth century.

The automobile industry has provided Michigan authors and writers elsewhere with material for dozens of works. Lawrence H. Conrad, who lived near Detroit and was the son of a father devoted to the ideals of handicraft and bitterly opposed to mass production, authored a novel entitled *Temper* (1924), giving a realistic account of the tempering of the soul of a steelworker in an automobile factory. Other novels of the auto industry include Wessel Smitter's *F. O. B. Detroit* (1938) and Gordon Webber' *What End But Love* (1959). None, however, achieved the popularity of two of the best-sellers of the seventies, Arthur Hailey's *Wheels* (1971) and Harold Robbins' *The Betsy* (1971), both of which are centered on Detroit and its auto industry and employ the sensational style associated with the works of both novelists. Of far more literary value are the writings of the prolific novelist and short story writer, Joyce Carol Oates, who used Detroit as the setting for many of her works—a setting with which she became familiar from her position on the faculty at the University of Windsor across the river in Canada.

The nationalities that comprise the people of Michigan have been the subject of many works of fiction and non-fiction. Arnold Mulder, in his *The Sand Doctor* (1921) and several other books, and David C. DeJong, in his *With a Dutch Accent* (1944), deal with the immigrants to Michigan from the Netherlands. Leonard Cline wrote in realistic fashion about a Finnish settlement in the Upper Peninsula in his *God Head* (1925), while Newton G. Thomas' *The Long Winter Ends* (1941) tells of the adjustment by Cornish immigrants to life in the Copper Country. Harriette Arnow's *The Dollmaker* (1954) describes the problems of whites migrating from rural backgrounds in the South to industrialized southeastern Michigan.

The Upper Peninsula has been a favorite subject of many writers. John F. Voelker, an Upper Peninsula lawyer who served for a time on the state supreme court and writes under the pseudonym of Robert Traver, has written several novels with northern Michigan settings. The best-known of these, *The Anatomy of a Murder* (1958), was a best-seller and was used as the subject of a successful motion picture. John B. Martin's *Call It North Country* (1944) contains a wealth of stories and tall tales of the surveyors, settlers, lumberjacks, fur traders, and miners of the Upper Peninsula. Richard Dorson, the leading authority on American folklore, collected examples of Upper Peninsula folklore while he was on the faculty at Michigan State which he published under the title *Bloodstoppers and Bearwalkers* (1952). The folkways of a Swedish family in Ironwood are recalled in a charming novel, *Latchstring Out* (1944), by Skulda Baner, whose father, Johan G. R. Baner, was a poet and writer of great talent but whose work, appearing in Swedish-language publications in Ironwood and other areas near Lake Superior, has gone relatively unrecognized because of the language in which it was written.[27]

The early history of Michigan continued to hold fascination for twentieth-century writers. *Wolves Against the Moon* (1940) by Julia Altrocchi is a dramatic story of white men and Indians, with Mackinac Island as its locale. A story of pioneering in the 1870s on Little Traverse Bay is delightfully told by U. P. Hedrick in his *Land of the Crooked Tree* (1948). The life of the circuit rider in pioneer days is the subject of Cecile Matschat's *Preacher on Horseback* (1940), while Iola Fuller won one of the coveted Avery Hopwood Prizes at the University of Michigan with *Loon Feather* (1940), a novel revolving around the supposed daughter of the Indian leader, Tecumseh.[28]

*   *   *   *   *

Twentieth-century developments have had profound effects on much of what has traditionally been considered cultural. These developments have also affected the attitudes of many people toward traditional ways and the use they make of them. Motion pictures were already cutting into the support for live drama by the 1920s, but in that decade the development of radio would have an even broader impact. Within a short time after the Detroit *News* pioneered radio broadcasts in 1920, other radio stations were opened in Detroit and a growing number of communities outstate. By 1925, some of these had become affiliates of national networks that provided a wide variety of programming material. By the thirties, the radio was the major source in more and more Michigan homes not only for dramatic presentations of all types, but comedy programs that replaced vaudeville, classical and popular music, and news. In 1947, the Detroit *News* also pioneered the introduction of television in Michigan. Within three or four years this new medium had taken away much of radio programming because of its great visual impact. Radio by no means disappeared, however. There are now hundreds of radio stations in Michigan which have gone from the variety of programming of the pre-television days to specialized programming, generally concentrating on a particular style of music. Meanwhile, the viewing of the state's twenty or so television stations' offerings assumed many of the roles that the theater, concerts, newspapers, and books had had in the lives of Michiganians of an earlier time.

Much of the programming of radio and television was devoted to sports. Aside from some interest in horse-racing, organized sporting events were virtually unknown in nineteenth-century Michigan. With the growth of urban areas, an interest in sports developed, partly as a health measure among those city-dwellers who felt the need for exercise. Sports served as a substitute for outdoor living and the hard muscular labor that men and women had known all too well on the farm. Furthermore, athletic activities constituted a psychological compensation for the tedium and monotony of assembly-line production or office routine. Whatever the cause, sports of every kind became popular.

Baseball leaped into the spotlight in the early years of the twentieth century. Thousands of boys and young men played ball on "sandlots," where old and young were equally enthusiastic as spectators or fans. Detroit had a major-league baseball team after 1900, when Frank J. Navin obtained a franchise in the American League. Since that time the Detroit Tigers have been favorites throughout the state. Beginning in the late 1920s, millions got their baseball third-handed, for they neither played the game nor attended it, but followed the radio description or later watched the play on television. A Detroit schoolboy might not be able to identify Hazen Pingree or James Couzens, but he had no trouble with such Tiger "greats" as Ty Cobb, Harry Heilmann, Mickey Cochrane, Charlie Gehringer, Willie Horton, or Al Kaline. Minor-league baseball teams appeared in other Michigan cities, but television spelled their doom. However, the number of amateur leagues continued to grow, and "little leagues" sprang up for the younger set.

As a spectator sport, football outrivals baseball for a short season. The immense stadium at Ann Arbor was built in the late 1920s not to accommodate the university student body alone, but also thousands from Detroit and elsewhere who came by train, bus, and automobile to see the games. In the early thirties, professional football became popular. Detroit's professional football team, the Lions, became a member of the National Football League in 1934. The popularity of professional football was greatly increased when the games were televised and in the seventies the Lions moved into a domed stadium at Pontiac to accommodate the increased crowds. The colleges and universities, however, had made football a major sport, and the frenzy that surrounded the annual clash between the University of Michigan and Michigan State football teams or the Michigan-Ohio State rivalry was something that professional football rarely could generate.

Hockey, like baseball and football, became a popular professional sport, with the Detroit Red Wings following the Tigers and Lions in the public eye as the seasons advanced. Basketball also had its professional teams, but in Michigan, at least, the interest remained largely centered on basketball as a high school and college sport. Boxing was another spectator sport, and in the thirties and forties the heavyweight boxing champion, Joe Louis—a product of Detroit's black ghetto—was the most celebrated sports figure in the country.

Sports of all kinds seemed to become more popular as the cities grew. Roller skating flourished intermittently, but ice skating, along with other winter sports, achieved great and lasting popularity. Lawn tennis was imported to America about 1875 and began to become popular around the turn of the century. It is only in recent years, however, that it has developed a mass following, leading not only to the building of outdoor courts but in the late seventies to the construction of elaborate indoor tennis facilities in most large cities in southern Michigan. The increase in the number of YMCAs during and after World War I provided facilities for such other indoor sporting activities as volleyball, squash, and handball. During the twenties, golf attained widespread popularity. Formerly a game played by rich men on private courses associated with exclusive country clubs, it now attracted many more players as municipal and other public courses were built that were open to everyone. By 1940, Detroit had ten public and many private courses, but by 1979, at least 120 public golf courses were readily available to the avid golfer in the metropolitan Detroit area, not to mention the numerous courses reserved for members of country clubs and their guests.

Golf and tennis, in contrast with baseball and football, which were primarily spectator sports, were examples of sports in which the individual could participate with relative ease. As the length of the workday and the workweek shortened, and as more and more businesses began giving their employees paid vacations, the amount of leisure time, a scarce commodity in earlier times, now spurred the growth in popularity of sports and recreational activities of all sorts. Cities began devoting more attention to providing parks where the residents could relax and enjoy themselves. In 1917, a system of state parks began to be established, enlarging the opportunities of enjoying Michigan's lakes and other natural attractions that had previously been out of reach of most people who could not afford the expense of resort hotels. Despite rapidly increased appropriations to expand existing parks and add new ones, crowded conditions, together with the popularity of these facilities, led voters in November, 1968, to take the rather unusual step of authorizing a $100,000,000 bond issue for recreational purposes. Additional camping facilities were developed on state and national forest grounds, as well as at private campgrounds. By the seventies, the Pictured Rocks area near Munising and the Sleeping Bear Dunes area near Traverse City had been established as part of the national parks system, which previously had been represented in Michigan only by Isle Royale National Park.

By the mid-twentieth century, traffic jams at the beginning and ending of long summer weekends were one of the prices people had to pay as they travelled to enjoy the numerous camping and vacationing opportunities throughout Michigan. Although there were doubts concerning the long-range cultural benefits of some twentieth-century developments, few questioned the belief that by bringing camping and other recreational opportunities within the reach of virtually all residents, there would be a broadened acquaintance with nature and its wonders that could provide endless and rewarding cultural experiences.

Peacetime Nuclear Plant, Big Rock Point, Charlevoix, Michigan

29

TOWARD THE TWENTY-FIRST CENTURY

As Michigan moved into the last quarter of the twentieth century, it became ever harder to realize that only three centuries—a short time as the history of mankind is measured—had elapsed since the first European settlements had been established in these peninsulas. Those three hundred years had begun when Father Marquette founded the missions at Sault Ste. Marie and St. Ignace. During the first two centuries of that period, Marquette probably would have felt fairly comfortable had he lived in the Michigan of the 1770s or even of the 1870s. But the changes that have occurred in the past century have been so great that the Michigan resident of a century or even seventy-five years ago would have been unable to understand much of what he or she would have seen or experienced in the Michigan of the 1970s.

Developments of the middle decades of the present century created a new kind of world. The capacity for the production of food and fiber as well as manufactured goods increased so rapidly that an economy of abundance replaced an economy of scarcity. International relations underwent a revolution because of the development, through science and technology, of weapons capable of destroying all life on earth. The United States, which during much of its history had enjoyed the opportunity of growing and prospering independently of the rest of the world, could no longer do so, but had to share the world's problems and responsibilities. Conditions of life made nations as well as individuals interdependent. The population explosion was unprecedented, and the number of people needing food, cloth-

713

ing, medical care, and education in the world almost outran the fantastic gains in productive capacity. What role would the American states play in this new world? What part would Michigan play?

It is not the function of historians to predict the future. They can only assess the future in terms of the past and the present. The tendency during the past half-century has been for local governmental units to lose some of their functions to state government and for the states to see more of their responsibilities shifted to the national government. There is every reason to presume this trend will continue. The trend has been consistently resisted by conservatives and others who are opposed to or fear the consequences of centralization and the loss of local control that had once been regarded as one of the basic strengths of the American political system. But rapid communication, the ease of travel, interdependence, and the growth of trade all point outward from the local community to the larger world.

The growth of population and the increasing proportion of people living in urban areas have created critical problems for local governments. These have been compounded by the move away from the central cities to the suburbs which has been underway since the 1920s, but which accelerated greatly after the Second World War. While this trend resulted in a general slowdown if not an actual decline in the rate at which Michigan cities in general had been growing earlier in the century, the most dramatic effects were seen in Detroit, whose population dropped from approximately 1,850,000 in 1950 to only slightly more than 1,500,000 by 1970. Not only people but manufacturing industries and retail stores began to move out. In 1954, Detroit's J. L. Hudson's department store pioneered in developing a huge new shopping center, Northland, in the Detroit suburb of Southfield. In the following years, Hudson's and other developers established additional centers in other suburbs of Detroit and most other major urban areas in southern Michigan. With the Westland shopping center, opened in the sixties, Hudson's introduced the enclosed shopping mall, which, in far more elaborate form, became the dominant type of shopping center built in the following years. These malls provided the shopper not only with the convenience of free and abundant parking, but also the convenience of having scores of shops, restaurants, and entertainment facilities, such as motion picture theaters and even ice-rinks, all under one roof, in attractive, well-lighted, heated, and secure surroundings. The business that these shopping centers generated and the network of highways that made them so readily accessible spurred additional growth. The Northland Shopping Center became the focus of a hotel, restaurant, and office complex that soon rivalled and surpassed that of virtually any long-established city center in the state outside of downtown Detroit. The example set by Northland was duplicated at such outstate centers as Briarwood, on the outskirts of Ann Arbor—an elaborate covered shopping mall which quickly became the center of a similar large-scale business development in the late seventies.

The evolution of fringe areas around the cities posed many problems. As suburban communities grew, the need was felt for municipal services: water supplies, storm and sanitary sewers as well as fire and police protection. In some cases, these problems were met by annexation to the central city; both Grand Rapids and Kalamazoo succeeded in consummating extensive annexations in the 1950s. But in many cases people in the fringe areas resisted annexation and under Michigan law their consent was necessary. Another solution was to purchase municipal services from the central city; for example, Detroit provided water under contract for large portions of its fringe areas. In other cases, limited agreements might be reached between a city and a suburb to share certain services. In the seventies, the city of Ypsilanti and the neighboring Ypsilanti Township formed joint authorities to operate their water and sewer systems and certain recreation facilities. Still another answer was the incorporation of new cities around the older cities. Sometimes, as in the case of Warren in Macomb County and Portage in Kalamazoo County, entire townships were incorporated as cities. Allen Park, Garden City, Hazel Park, Lincoln Park, Roseville, and Livonia are a few of the cities that were established adjacent to Detroit, which had reached its geographical limits through the annexation process in the twenties. On the fringe areas of Grand Rapids, the city of Wyoming also recently emerged to meet the needs of a suburban area.

The availability of fast transportation was the key to the development of the suburban fringe. Until after World War II mass transit was utilized to a large extent to bring workers and shoppers downtown and to return them to their homes. The trolley car began to give way to the motor bus as the backbone of mass transit about 1930. One by one the street railway systems were abandoned and buses substituted. The last streetcar in Detroit was pulled out of service in 1956. Heavy patronage had made it possible to provide transportation at a small price. But the rapid increase in the number of passenger automobiles began to hurt mass transit systems by about 1948. More and more people preferred driving their own cars downtown to taking a bus. By 1960 a number of communities, such as Benton Harbor, had no bus transportation at all. Elsewhere, mass transit was in trouble; fares were raised as patronage declined, and this in turn resulted in further declines. As auto traffic increased, downtown streets became so congested that major cities were compelled to spend millions of dollars to provide wider thoroughfares. Downtown parking became a problem of major proportions. This congestion further spurred the development of suburban areas.

By the 1950s the decay of the cities was becoming a common phenomenon. Among other results was a decline in the assessed valuation of properties, which diminished tax revenues for cities. As those people able to pay for suburban homes moved out, their homes were taken over by poorer people who were less able to maintain them in good condition. Downtown store buildings became vacant as more and more businesses left for the suburbs. In downtown Detroit, Kern's, one of the city's three major department stores, closed in 1959. Crowley's closed its downtown store in the seventies, concentrating entirely on the branches it had opened in the suburban centers. By the end of the seventies, Hudson's, which had been steadily cutting back on the size of its operation in its huge downtown store, was threatening to close that store, which had long since failed to compete with the numerous branches that Hudson's had opened in suburban Detroit and as far outstate as Grand Rapids. That same decade also saw the closing of such long-established downtown hotels as the Hilton and the Tuller and many of the theaters that had once flourished in that area. The closing of such familiar outstate businesses as Arbaugh's department store in downtown Lansing, the Pick-Durant Hotel in Flint, and the Burdick Hotel in Kalamazoo were evidence that the problems confronting downtown were not confined to Detroit.

City governing bodies began taking action to solve these problems, but this cost money and led to an increasing dependence on outside sources for the additional funds. In the late forties Ann Arbor attacked the downtown parking problem by pioneering in the construction of municipally operated parking ramps, enabling a far larger number of cars to be parked on one site than could be accommodated on the more conventional surface parking lots. In 1959 Kalamazoo transformed three blocks of its downtown streets into the first permanent pedestrian mall in the nation. By the sixties other cities, such as Lansing and Wayne, launched urban renewal projects and rebuilt huge sections of their downtowns.

As always, however, the attention was focussed on Detroit. There the main effort came to be centered on the long-neglected riverfront, where work on a huge Civic Center commenced in the fifties. In 1956, the Ford Auditorium was opened, a year after a new city-county office building had opened on the opposite side of Jefferson Avenue from the Civic Center. In 1960, Cobo Hall was opened which was, with the adjacent Convention Arena, designed to attract convention business to Detroit. These actions of the Detroit city government helped to spur a considerable construction boom of additional office buildings in the area of the Civic Center, but the city's efforts to generate new retail business developments and apartment construction in the downtown area had limited success. But then in the seventies, a group of businessmen, headed by Henry Ford II, launched a massive development, adjacent to the Civic Center, of the Renaissance Center, which included a hotel with seventy-three stories, four office buildings with thirty-nine stories, and dozens of shops, theaters, and restaurants. The estimated cost of the development was $350,000,000. This dazzling achievement attracted much attention and business to Detroit. Outstate, similar signs of returning vigor to the downtown areas were seen in Ann Arbor, Grand Rapids, Kalamazoo, and Lansing. However, in none of these cities was there much sign that retail business activity would return to earlier levels. Clearly, shoppers still preferred the more convenient, concentrated facilities of the shopping malls in the suburbs or on the outskirts of these cities. The downtowns would apparently survive and thrive as the centers of governmental, financial, and business activity.

The problems of the cities and the growth of the suburbs were forcing basic changes in antiquated governmental structures. Within a single large Michigan urban community there were many overlapping and conflicting local governmental units. Annexation of suburban areas to an existing city or the incorporation of suburbs to form a new city was part of the effort to replace township governments that were designed for governing rural, not urban, communities. But at the end of the seventies many heavily populated suburban areas still struggled under the outdated township system. Superimposed on these city and township governments was the county government, the function of which likewise was called into question in the major urban areas. The provisions of the new state constitution permitting county home rule led to changes that hopefully would refashion these county governments, enabling them to perform needed functions for a large metropolitan district. Oakland County established the office of county manager, an elected officer who would be the chief executive of county governmental operations. Political considerations, however, impeded the effort to eliminate needless duplication of governmental activities between county and large city governments in such areas as Wayne County. The development of regional agencies, such as the Southeastern Michigan Transportation Authority (SEMTA), to coordinate approaches to such problems as that of improving mass transit in urban areas, marked a beginning toward what was likely to be an ever more common approach to local problems in the future.

In at least three vital areas state government had earlier taken over functions that once had belonged to local units. By the twenties the state had assumed the responsibility of constructing and maintaining arterial highways—a responsibility which at one time had been assigned to the townships. In later years, the states assumed additional responsibility for building and maintaining county roads and even city streets. The relief of poverty, which was also a function of local government until the twentieth century, passed largely out of the control of the local areas in the Depression years because of the enormity of the problem and the desirability of equalizing the cost of welfare relief. County welfare agencies, like county highway agencies, continued to have a role in determining policies, but the funds they administered came largely from outside sources which wielded much influence over how the funds were to be spent.

Educational funding was also affected. Until the third decade of the twentieth century the functions of the state department of public instruction had been mainly informational. It was because school districts differed so widely in their financial capacity for supporting schools that state aid on a large scale began during the Depression. Property taxes continued, however, to provide the bulk of the money for local schools. By the seventies, the rapidly escalating school costs created increased resistance among property owners even in such relatively wealthy districts as Ann Arbor to requests from the school board for hikes in property taxes. In 1972, a large majority of voters in the state rejected a ballot proposal to shift the main burden of supporting the schools away from the property tax to a special state school tax. By 1978, however, voters approved the Headlee amendment, which was designed to curb property tax increases (the more radical Tisch amendment which would have drastically slashed existing property tax rates was rejected), and it became evident that the maintenance of Michigan's schools would have to be more dependent on state aid.

The demands made on local and state sources of revenue led to repeated cries for tax reform. Every governor, at least from the time of Kim Sigler in the forties, had spoken of the need for a fundamental overhauling of the state's tax structure, but political differences in the legislature stymied efforts to secure any widespread agreement on such reform. The changes that were made in the seventies generally resulted from shifting the burden of the decision to the voters, whose actions simply added to the hodge-podge character of the state's revenue-producing system. In addition to property tax changes resulting from the Headlee amendment in 1978, the voters in 1974 had approved an amendment to remove the sales tax on purchases of food and prescription drugs. With regard to the state income tax, however, which had to be hiked to make up the lost sales tax revenue, voters in 1968, 1972, and 1976 overwhelmingly rejected proposals to change the income tax from the flat rate basis authorized in the new constitution to a graduated basis which the advocates of the change argued would permit the state to shift the main burden of the tax to those who were most able to afford it. However, in 1972, in what had to be one of the most regressive political actions in Michigan's history, voters overwhelmingly approved an amendment to authorize a state lottery, a method of raising funds that had been employed in territorial days but which had been prohibited by every state constitution since 1835. New Hampshire's success with its state lottery, instituted in 1964, had demonstrated that states could raise a good deal of money by pandering to people's gambling instincts, and Michigan now followed suit. The legislature quickly took advantage of the change in the constitution to establish a Bureau of State Lottery that not only ran the lottery but also licensed and regulated bingo games, which were also now legalized. The Michigan lottery soon became one of the most successful in the country, with all revenues, minus the operating expenses, going into the state's general fund.

The seventies, however, saw an ever increasing dependence on federal funds. These had long since been the major source of money for highway and social welfare programs, and an important source for education and many other governmental activities. The cities now turned to the federal government for help. In the late seventies, Detroit's Mayor Coleman Young found a much more sympathetic response to his appeals for various work relief funds than Mayor Frank Murphy had found when he had appealed to the Hoover administration for the same kind of assistance in 1932. These funds brought with them, however, a stipulation by federal administrators that the money be used properly. Federal highway funds would be withheld if the state did not enforce federal rules regarding the use of billboards along interstate highways, and also if the state did not enforce the 55-mile-per-hour speed limit imposed in 1974 as a means of reducing gasoline consumption. In 1979, the threat of losing $600,000,000 in federal mass-transit funds forced the government agencies in Wayne, Oakland, and Macomb counties to agree on the kind of mass-transit system they wanted.

Federal actions could affect local or state governments in other respects. In 1971, educational policy and racial questions came together in the case of Bradley vs. Milliken. In this case, United States District Judge Stephen J. Roth, who had served a term as Michigan's attorney general in 1949 and 1950, ruled that Detroit's schools were racially segregated and ordered a massive program of cross-district busing between Detroit and the neighboring suburban districts in order to achieve integration of the student bodies. On appeal, the United States Supreme Court later threw out the cross-district busing aspect of the plan, and after the death of Judge Roth, a new justice made some additional modifications in the original order. The over-all effect, however, was to initiate other court actions in outstate districts such as Grand Rapids, Kalamazoo, and Benton Harbor, as well as to bring the state department of education and the Michigan Civil Rights Commission into the effort of achieving greater racial balance in the schools. Busing, a word that had once had a positive connotation as a technique of enabling rural children to enjoy educational benefits previously denied to them, now took on a new meaning with unfortunate racial overtones. To meet the cost of court-ordered programs, state funds had to be provided, not only for buses, but for construction of vocational education centers which were also part of these plans.

For a time in the seventies, the ability of Michigan to get federal aid was certainly helped by the unusually high degree of influence the state had at the national political level. This was particularly evident in Congress. In the Senate, Senator Robert Griffin from Traverse City had become minority whip of the Republicans in the upper chamber, next in line for the job of minority leader. Michigan's senior Senator, Philip Hart, had become one of the leaders of that house, respected by members of both parties. In the House of Representatives, Democrat Martha W. Griffiths of Detroit since her first election to the house in 1954 had become the best-known and most respected of the women members of Congress. Two other Detroit Congressmen, John Conyers, Jr., and Charles C. Diggs, Jr., were leaders of the Congressional Black Caucus. On the Republican side, Edward Hutchinson of Fennville was a ranking member of the conservative wing of his party while Guy Vander Jagt of Cadillac was a rising force among the more moderate Republican representatives. But the most important party position held by any of these Michigan Congressmen was that held by Gerald R. Ford, Jr., of Grand Rapids.

Ford had been born Leslie Lynch King, Jr., in Omaha, Nebraska, in 1913. After his mother's divorce and remarriage, he was given the name of his stepfather. Young Ford grew up in Grand Rapids and graduated from the University of Michigan, where he starred on the football team, and went on to obtain a law degree from Yale. After service in the navy during World War II, Ford returned to Grand Rapids, where, in 1948, he successfully unseated the incumbent Republican Congressman in the primary and then went on to win election to Congress from that traditionally Republican district, winning re-election every two years thereafter through 1972. During these years, Ford was rarely identified with initiating any significant legislation, but he gained popularity among his fellow members of Congress, and in 1965 was chosen Republican minority leader in the House of Representatives—an office that would put him in line for the house speaker's job if the Republicans regained majority control. To attain the speakership was probably the most that Ford hoped for, but in 1973, when Vice-President Spiro M. Agnew was forced to resign, President Nixon, invoking for the first time a provision of the Twenty-fifth Amendment to the United States Constitution adopted in 1967, named Ford to be Agnew's successor. Leaders of both parties in Congress quickly voiced their support of Nixon's choice and the nomination was approved with little opposition.

Ford, who became the first person to serve as Vice-President who had not been chosen by the normal electoral process, became the first appointed holder of the office of Vice-President to move on to the Presidency, when Richard Nixon resigned on August 9, 1974. Ford, who now became the first resident of Michigan to gain the nation's highest political office, enjoyed widespread bi-partisan support at the outset of his administration, but the honeymoon came to an abrupt end on September 8, 1974, when Ford granted Nixon an unconditional pardon for any crimes that he had committed or might have committed during the period that Nixon was President. This controversial action, which Ford declared he had taken in order to spare the nation any further Watergate agony, was widely criticized and plagued Ford throughout his Presidency, as did the numerous domestic and foreign problems with which he was confronted. Nevertheless, despite a lack of some leadership qualities, Ford's honesty and integrity did much to restore public confidence in the office of the Presidency.

Ford was encouraged to seek his party's nomination in 1976 for a full term as President and faced a severe challenge from Ronald Reagan of California. A decisive victory for Ford over Reagan in

Michigan's Presidential primary[1] on May 18, 1976, broke a string of Reagan victories in other state primaries, and helped Ford to nip Reagan, by a narrow margin, on the first ballot of the Republican National Convention on August 18. During the ensuing campaign, Ford narrowed the gap by which the early polls had showed him trailing his Democratic opponent, Jimmy Carter. On election day, Ford made an emotional return to Grand Rapids to cast his vote, but although he won a majority in his old district and in the state as a whole and in other states, it was not enough to prevent Carter from gaining the necessary majority in the electoral college to win the race.

Thus Gerald Ford, like Lewis Cass before him, was denied the Presidency. After surrendering the Presidency to Carter in January, 1977, Ford moved to Palm Springs, California, which he subsequently made his official place of residence. Plans soon began for a Ford Presidential museum to be located in Grand Rapids while a library, containing his papers, would be opened at his alma mater in Ann Arbor. Ford's residency in Michigan, however, would no longer be a factor in his future political plans.

Not only did Michigan lose the voice it had had in the White House in the mid-seventies, but its influence elsewhere in federal government also suffered a severe blow in 1976 when Senator Hart, dying of cancer, announced he was stepping down. Following his death later that year, his colleagues in the Senate named a new Senate office building, under construction, after him. In 1977, Senator Griffin's colleagues did not elect him to the post of minority leader. Upset by this action, Griffin announced he would not run for re-election in 1978 and for several months was absent from many Senate sessions. Early in 1978 he bowed to pressure from within his party and announced he was changing his mind and would run, but the earlier indications that he had lost interest in the job proved to be fatal to his chances and he was defeated in the general election. Democrats Donald W. Riegle, Jr., of Flint, a former Republican Congressmen who had switched to the Democrats over the Vietnam issue, and Carl Levin of Detroit were elected to replace Hart and Griffin respectively, but it would take some time before they achieved the positions of influence of the men they had succeeded. Likewise in the House, with the departure of Ford, the decisions of veteran Congressmen such as Hutchinson and Griffiths not to run for re-election, and Diggs' legal problems, the effectiveness of Michigan's Congressional delegation was further weakened at the end of the decade.

In Michigan, the political trends of the sixties continued to prevail in the seventies. In the 1968 elections, the Democrats had regained control of the state house of representatives that they had lost in the Romney sweep of 1966. In 1970, although they retained control of the lower house, the Democrats were not able to wrest control of the Senate from the Republicans. The attempts to heal the rifts in the party that had been caused by the Vietnam War failed to generate enough votes to defeat the Republican, William Milliken, who was running for the office of governor to which he had succeeded after George Romney's resignation in 1969. The burning issue of Vietnam, particularly among college-age voters, was only one of the explanations for the obvious changes in Michigan voting patterns. More and more voters considered themselves independents. The fierce party loyalties that had led most to cast votes for a straight-party ticket now had been replaced by a tendency to split the ticket. Thus in 1970, voters elected a Republican as governor and a Republican majority in the state senate while electing Democrats Richard Austin and Frank Kelley to new terms as secretary of state and attorney general. Philip Hart was also elected to a new term, even though Hart's opponent was Lenore Romney—George Romney's wife.

As Michigan voters voted for the man more than for the party, the position of the incumbent became stronger. There was a tendency to retain any elected official who had not been totally incompetent. In addition, as many labor union members grew older and more prosperous, they became more conservative. To such individuals, a moderate Republican candidate might seem preferable to a Democratic candidate. Thus in 1972, President Richard Nixon, who a few years before would have been a candidate that no Democrat of the Williams era would have dreamed of supporting, was re-elected by an overwhelming margin in Michigan and across the country, defeating his opponent, George McGovern, who came across as too liberal for the majority of voters in the seventies. That same year, Republican Senator Griffin was elected to another six-year term over his Democratic opponent, Frank Kelley, who had been a formidable vote-getter in gaining and holding the office of attorney general since 1961. Kelley, however, was unable to convince enough of those who had supported him in the past that he could do a better job in the Senate than the incumbent Griffin. The same tendency of the independent voter to support the incumbent, especially if he had had success in pursuing middle-of-the-road, moderate policies, no doubt explains Governor Milliken's success in winning re-election in 1974, when he defeated Sander M. Levin, the same candidate whom he had defeated in 1970. It also certainly explains Milliken's overwhelming defeat of state senator William B. Fitzgerald, Jr., in the election of 1978.

By the latter part of the seventies the two major parties thus found their situations exactly the reverse of what they had been two decades before. In the fifties the Democrats had controlled the executive branch of state government, but because of the manner in which the legislature was apportioned, they had been unable to overturn Republican control of that branch of the government. Now, with both houses of the legislature apportioned on the principle of "one-man, one-vote," the Democrats had firm control of the legislature, adding in 1975 control of the senate to the control of the lower house which they had held since 1969, but they still had been unable to wrest the control of the governor's office away from the Republicans. The Democratic candidates who ran against Romney and Milliken had simply failed to generate the kind of enthusiasm that Williams had been able to arouse, and the ability that Romney and particularly Milliken demonstrated in working with leaders of the Democrats in the legislature made it seem less urgent to have both branches of government controlled by the same party than it had in the fifties when the governor and legislature were at loggerheads. G. Mennen Williams, who might have been able to patch together his party's various factions if he had decided to make another run for the governorship, instead in 1970 ran for and was elected to the state supreme court, winning re-election to another term on that court in 1978. In 1970, former governor John B. Swainson was elected to the supreme court by an even larger margin than that given to Williams, and there was some speculation that Swainson might be the Democrats' best hope for regaining the governor's office. But in 1975 Swainson was convicted of perjury in a bribery case which led to his resignation from the court and the apparent end of his political career.

As always, the politics of the seventies were linked with the economic developments of that period. The high degree of dependence on a single industry—automotive manufacturing—continued to be responsible for violent fluctuations in the level of the state's economic health. In the early seventies, the industry prospered as federal economic policies served to increase substantially the price of foreign imports, which had cut deeply into domestic auto sales. Then in the mid-seventies, a sharp reduction in the amount of oil available for import into the country led to a severe gasoline shortage and a sudden doubling of gas prices, triggering the most severe economic recession in the country since the Depression. The effect on Michigan's auto industry was double-edged, since the rapid rise in gas prices greatly increased the costs of operating cars. Many people purchased the less expensive, more fuel-efficient automobiles, which were also less profitable for the industry to produce. Others could not afford to buy any car. Car sales declined rapidly, leading to massive layoffs in the auto plants. The effect on the state was by no means as bad as it had been in the thirties, since unemployment compensation and additional benefits from company funds that had been established as a result of the contracts negotiated by the United Automobile Workers, provided the idle workers with a continuing source of income. However, as the recession dragged on, company funds were exhausted, and Michigan again had a foretaste of the disastrous impact that an extended depression could still have, in spite of all the cushions built in by the social welfare programs of the New Deal. Fortunately, economic conditions began to improve by 1976, and in the last years of the decade the Michigan auto industry confounded many experts who had been predicting its imminent death by rebounding and achieving record or near-record sales once again. The industry faced many continuing problems but for the moment it could breath a little easier. Statistics released by the United States Department of Labor in the spring of 1979 indicated that aside from Anchorage, Alaska, where the extremely high cost of living forced wages to be abnormally high, the average worker's wage in the three auto centers of Flint, Detroit, and Saginaw were the highest for any cities in the country.[2]

A central concern of political and business leaders in the state was the need to diversify Michigan's economy and reduce its dependence on the auto industry. Since the economic recession of the late fifties, much more attention had been paid to the importance of research to develop new products, and large research centers, particularly around Ann Arbor, had been developed. But it seemed unlikely that much additional growth in the economy could be expected to come from new manufacturing activities. Instead, the trend in Michigan, as in the country as a whole, was away from manufacturing and toward the service and professional fields. Even in Detroit, which continued to have a heavier concentration of people employed in heavy industry jobs in its metropolitan area than any other similar area in the country, the percentage of its labor force in such blue-collar jobs declined from forty-eight percent in 1948 to thirty-two percent in 1977. The real growth was in government jobs, retail trade, and other non-manufacturing positions, many of which are usually considered white-collar jobs.[3]

The necessity of providing for the needs of about two-thirds of the state which is sparsely settled, where soils and climate are not conducive to agriculture, and which have had difficulty in attracting manufacturing plants, has been a continuing problem. Although an expansion of the vacation and recreation industry seems to hold the greatest promise for northern Michigan in the immediate future, there are long-range factors that stand to benefit the region in a variety of ways. The enormous increase in the world's population created widespread shortages of food supplies by the seventies, helping to alleviate the problem of agricultural surpluses in the United States. The soils of northern Michigan could be made productive when increased production of food and fiber is needed—a time that seems less remote than it did in the 1930s and 1940s. Much the same situation applies to the mining of iron and copper. There are vast amounts of both minerals in the Upper Peninsula and the time may not be far distant when the shortages of these minerals elsewhere will offset the high expense involved in mining this copper and iron ore. In addition, the new methods of processing these ores that made the White Pine Mine in Ontonagon County a major producer of copper and the resumption of copper mining by the Homestake Copper Company at the Calumet and Hecla's holdings which had been halted when Universal Oil had shut down its copper-mining subsidiary's operations in 1969 were hopeful signs for the resumption of more copper mining. The Cleveland-Cliffs Iron Company, the peninsula's largest employer, with more than 4,400 workers on its payroll in 1979, had upped its production of iron ore to 14,000,000 tons, and was seeking to expand its operations on the Marquette Iron Range at the end of the decade so as to increase its output to 21,000,000 tons—equal to about a quarter of the entire iron ore production in North America.[4]

However, Cleveland-Cliffs' operations now were almost all of the surface strip-mining variety and the effect that these had on the environment brought the company into conflict with a new force—those who desired to maintain what they felt was northern Michigan's greatest asset: its natural beauty. Not only were tourists visiting these areas but an ever-growing number of individuals and families, hoping to escape the city and its problems, were moving north. The Population Studies Center at the University of Michigan projected a growth in the population of the upper half of the lower peninsula of 142 percent in the last two decades of the twentieth century, while the western and eastern half of the Upper Peninsula would grow by 36 and 62 percent respectively, in contrast with an expected growth in the population of the southern half of the lower peninsula of only

34 percent.[5] Ironically, such an increase in northern Michigan's population would ultimately threaten to destroy the very wild, untamed feature of these areas that drew so many of these people to these lands.

The growing population of Michigan and the importance of its vacation industry added new emphasis to some of the traditional goals of the conservation movement and led to renewed efforts to expand park and wild-life facilities. In 1965 the first coho salmon eggs were brought from Washington, Oregon, and Alaska by Dr. Howard Tanner and Dr. Wayne Tody of the fish division of the state conservation department, and in the spring of 1966, Lake Michigan and Lake Superior were stocked with the first four-inch to six-inch smolts. The experiment was a spectacular success. As early as 1968 fishing for coho salmon had become one of the most exciting new sports, attracting thousands of fishermen. The salmon thrived and by the seventies had spread through all the waters adjacent to Michigan.

Although such activities would fit into the conservation ideas of Chase Osborn's day, they were largely outside of the concerns of the new movement of the late sixties that not only dealt with the preservation of wild life, trees, and minerals but with the environment in general. Water pollution became a matter of major concern to the people of Michigan, and in 1968, in the same election in which voters authorized a $100,000,000 bond issue for recreational purposes, they also approved, by an overwhelming majority, a bond issue of $335,000,000 to combat this problem, which was a matter of concern mainly in the heavily populated urban, industrialized areas of southern Michigan. At the same time air pollution received increased attention. Although factory pollution was an issue, most attention was given to the pollution caused by automobile exhausts. This led to federal regulations in the auto industry for more rigid standards regarding engine emissions, safety features, and, after the gas crisis in the mid-seventies, an increased emphasis on engine efficiency.

The goals of the environmentalists thus sometimes directly conflicted with those who were concerned with the expansion of Michigan's economy. The expense of cleaning operations and making changes in products because of mandatory new environmental regulations was in a few cases (such as that of the Hillsdale Foundry in Hillsdale, which shut down in 1974) too much for the company to handle. In most cases, however, as in the case of the auto companies, it was argued that the cost of the mandatory changes would have to be passed on to the consumer, which could have a serious impact on sales and the job market for Michigan workers. Thus Michigan Congressmen, particularly from southeastern Michigan, would lobby for delays in auto company deadlines, even though on other matters many of these politicians were strong advocates of environmental causes. In northern Michigan, too, the need to create new job opportunities constantly came up against the efforts of environmentalists to preserve the unique character of those areas. State Senator Joseph S. Mack, a Democrat from Ironwood, became the leading supporter of anything that would provide jobs in the Upper Peninsula, and the fact that voters in his district returned him to the senate election after election seemed to indicate that they supported his contention that it was only the city dwellers from southern Michigan who were seeking to maintain the pristine character of northern Michigan.

*   *   *   *   *

These are some of the problems faced by Michigan in the new age now dawning in the latter part of the twentieth century. Undoubtedly, there will be other problems just as difficult as those faced in earlier times. But insight and inspiration will come from the heritage of the past. The history of Michigan will help future leaders learn that answers can be found in a more diversified and stable economy without the needless waste of natural resources. Michigan's history will indicate that government can meet the needs of the state when individual effort and voluntary cooperation fail. Nevertheless, it will be the individual men and women who built Michigan that will inspire future citizens. The dedicated service of seventeenth-century Jesuit missionaries such as Father Jacques Marquette and Father Claude Allouez will give many a spirit of adventure. Douglass Houghton and William Beaumont will be emulated by young men and women entering the field of science. Laura Haviland, Lucinda Hinsdale Stone, and Martha Griffiths will inspire future leaders of worthy causes. Lewis Cass, James Couzens, G. Mennen Williams, and George Romney will be symbols of devoted public service. W. K. Kellogg, Henry Ford, and Berry Gordy, Jr., will be models for those who seek to strengthen the state's economy. Bruce Catton will inspire scholars of the future. John D. Pierce will be remembered and revered by those who devote their lives to education. Pontiac, Albertus C. Van Raalte, and John Conyers, Jr., will not be forgotten by those who fight for the rights of their people. There are many others whose lives and achievements have shaped Michigan's history and have given meaning and significance for tomorrow's Michigan.

Most of these individuals were ordinary pioneers and citizens who forsook security and comfort to accomplish their high goals. In the end, it is their achievements that provide the best inspiration for future pioneers and citizens who will seek to solve tomorrow's problems and will strive to build tomorrow's heritage.

SUGGESTIONS FOR FURTHER READING

Students used to lament the paucity of available research materials on the history of Michigan. Today there is less ground for such complaints. Numerous archives and historical collections in the state and elsewhere now house millions of letters, diaries, business records, and other kinds of unpublished papers of Michigan individuals and organizations as well as a vast quantity of published primary sources. Anyone who simply wants to read further on topics covered in the present volume will discover the shelves of any moderately large Michigan library brimming with such materials. Unfortunately, there is no comprehensive guide to these materials. Floyd B. Streeter, comp., *Michigan Bibliography*, 2 volumes (Lansing, 1921), covers only material published to July 1, 1917, thus excluding most of the best work on the state's history which has appeared in the years since 1917, particularly within the past quarter of a century. *Michigamee: Materials on Michigan,* published by the Michigan Association for Media in Education (Ann Arbor, revised edition, 1978), is a useful, but highly selective, listing of books and other materials of interest to teachers. Richard J. Hathaway, comp., *Dissertations and Theses in Michigan History* (Lansing, 1974), is a guide to unpublished graduate student papers. Other sources include the issues of *Michigan History,* a journal published since 1917, and *Michigan in Books,* a quarterly published by the State Library since 1957, where most of the materials published since Streeter's bibliography are listed. The preparation of a single publication that would compile this information in one volume is a project that most Michigan history researchers would agree deserves top priority.

The footnotes in the present history will help the reader to locate articles in the *Michigan Pioneer and Historical Collections, Michigan History,* and other publications where this type of material has appeared. Additional guidance would probably be helpful, however, in pointing out some of the

731

more valuable and useful books that relate to Michigan's history, although what follows is not a comprehensive discussion of such works.

First, of course, there are the numerous histories of Michigan that have been published prior to the latest edition of the present work. James H. Lanman, *History of Michigan* (New York, 1839, with a second edition published in 1841), represents the first attempt at a full-scale, book-length history of the then-new state. Lanman's work, although surprisingly good in view of his limited number of sources, is now little more than a curiosity, as are the other nineteenth-century general histories that followed. James V. Campbell, *Outlines of the Political History of Michigan* (Detroit, 1876), and Thomas M. Cooley, *Michigan: A History of Governments* (Boston, 1885), are of special interest because the authors were Michigan's two most distinguished jurists of the nineteenth century.

The first multi-volume history of the state, and one that still has some value because its authors recognized that there was more to the state's history than the political topics that had mainly interested the earlier Michigan historians, is Henry M. Utley and Byron M. Cutcheon (with acknowledged editorial help from Clarence M. Burton, founder of the Detroit Public Library's justifiably famous Burton Historical Collection), *Michigan as a Province, Territory and State, the Twenty-Sixth Member of the Federal Union,* 4 volumes (New York, 1906). The best of the multi-volume histories is George N. Fuller, ed., *Michigan: A Centennial History of the State and Its People,* 5 volumes (Chicago, 1939). The text in the first two volumes, which is the part of the work for which Fuller was responsible (the remaining three volumes in the set are taken up with biographies of individuals who paid to be included in the work), contains what is in many respects still the most comprehensive and satisfactory coverage of Michigan's development down to the period of its publication.

Among twentieth-century, one-volume histories, one by Milo M. Quaife and Sidney Glazer, *Michigan, From Primitive Wilderness to Industrial Commonwealth* (New York, 1948), exhibits the unfortunate tendency in much of the state's historical work of placing a disportionate emphasis on the earlier years of Michigan's history. Quaife, an authority on that era, covered those years in detailed fashion in the first half of the book, but left Glazer, one of the first academic historians to recognize the importance of such recent developments as the growth of manufacturing and labor unions, only 190 pages in which to deal with the far more complex period from statehood to the mid-twentieth century. The worst example of this unbalanced approach, however, is the brief history by the distinguished historian of the Civil War, Bruce Catton, *Michigan: A Bicentennial History* (New York, 1976). Catton, a native Michiganian who had earlier expressed the view that it was not in the heavily populated, industrialized areas of southern Michigan, but in the still unspoiled regions of northern Michigan where one can still experience the "real Michigan,"[1] devoted only sixteen of the 196 pages of his history to a discussion of twentieth-century developments. The remainder of the book, one of a series sponsored by the American Association for State and Local History, deals (not always accurately) with the Michigan that Catton loved, before factories and automobiles entered the picture.

The most evenly balanced and one of the more readable of the earlier one-volume histories is F. Clever Bald, *Michigan in Four Centuries* (New York, 1954, reprinted in an enlarged edition in 1961). This history was subsidized by the Michigan Historical Commission, with funds supplied by a bequest in the will of educator John M. Munson. The terms of this bequest were interpreted to mean that Bald was to write a book that would appeal both to high school students and a more adult audience. The result was a work that was regarded by some teachers as too advanced for their students while others regarded it as too elementary in its approach for college students and the general public.[2] To meet the need for a more detailed and scholarly one-volume treatment desired by many college teachers and adult readers, Willis F. Dunbar, who had earlier written the two historical volumes of *Michigan through the Centuries,* 4 volumes (New York, 1955), wrote the original edition of *Michigan: A History of the Wolverine State* in 1965.

Other general works include George S. May, *Pictorial History of Michigan: The Early Years* (Grand Rapids, 1967) and *Pictorial History of Michigan: The Later Years* (Grand Rapids, 1969). The two volumes were reprinted in a one-volume edition in 1978. *Michigan, A Guide to the Wolverine State,* prepared by the Michigan Writers' Project as part of the WPA's cultural program during the depression of the thirties (New York, 1941), is a unique work, a collection at one and the same time of historical minutiae and thoughtful discussions of important topics. The two-volume *Michigan Reader* (Grand Rapids, 1974), the first volume edited by George S. May and Herbert J. Brinks, the second by Robert M. Warner and C. Warren VanderHill, provides a sampling of the writings on the state's history, with an emphasis on first-hand contemporary accounts. Alan S. Brown, John T. Houdek, and John H. Yzenbaard, eds., *Michigan Perspectives: People, Events, and Issues* (Dubuque, 1974), samples recent scholarly writing on important topics relating to Michigan's development. Lawrence M. Sommers, ed., *Atlas of Michigan* (East Lansing, 1977), is not, as the title would suggest, a traditional atlas, but a highly useful and innovative work depicting a host of different kinds of information through the use of full-color maps and other graphic devices. Richard A. Santer, *Michigan: Heart of the Great Lakes* (Dubuque, 1977), fills the need for a historical geography text. John A. Dorr, Jr., and Donald F. Eschman, *Geology of Michigan* (Ann Arbor, 1970), does a superb job of discussing topics that are especially important to students of the state's history in light of the significance of mining activities in Michigan's economy, and the authors explain these in terms understandable to the non-geologist. For economic and social statistical information, *Michigan Statistical Abstract,* now published annually by the Graduate School of Business Administration at Michigan State University, is an indispensable reference tool. The familiar red-bound volumes of the *Michigan Manual,* published by the state government since the beginning of statehood and appearing biennially in essentially the same format since the 1870s, remain the principal source for election returns and other political-governmental information.

Both the quality and the quantity of general regional or local works vary greatly. Books on the Great Lakes are plentiful, with the best works of immediate interest to Michigan being four volumes in the American Lakes series: Milo M. Quaife, *Lake Michigan* (Indianapolis, 1945); Grace Lee Nute, *Lake Superior* (Indianapolis, 1944); Fred Landon, *Lake Huron* (Indianapolis, 1944); and Harlan Hatcher, *Lake Erie* (Indianapolis, 1945). Hatcher also wrote a general history, *The Great Lakes* (New York, 1944), and was co-author, with Erich A. Walters, of *A Pictorial History of the Great Lakes* (New York, 1963). Russell McKee, *Great Lakes Country* (New York, 1966), and Walter Havighurst, *The Long Ships Passing* (New York, 1943), are among other works which, like nearly all the Great Lakes histories, are anecdotal and popular in approach, with little attempt made at serious, scholarly analysis of the importance of these great waterways as avenues of transportation.

There are numerous histories of Michigan counties, communities, and regions. *Michigan County Histories: A Bibliography* (Lansing, 1978), covers these histories which first appeared largely as a result of the stimulus given to American history writing by the centennial celebration of 1876. Shortly after that date, histories of most of the counties in southern Michigan were published, with Samuel W. Durant's *History of Ingham and Eaton Counties, Michigan* (Philadelphia, 1880), and *History of Kalamazoo County, Michigan* (Philadelphia, 1880), being among the better examples of this type. Unfortunately, there have been only sporadic efforts since the 1870s to update these county histories or to prepare ones for those counties for which no such histories had been written. Those that did appear often were of the "mug book" variety, composed mainly of biographies which individuals paid to have included, with an extra charge if the subject of the biographical sketch wanted a portrait included as well. *Portrait and Biographical Album, Mecosta County, Michigan ... Also Containing a Complete History of the County from Its Earliest Settlement to the Present Time* (Chicago, 1883), is a typical example of such books that the Chicago firm of Chapman Brothers persuaded residents of several Michigan counties to subsidize. Talcott E. Wing, ed., *History of Monroe County, Michigan* (New York, 1890), and Oran W. Rowland, *A History of Van Buren County, Michigan,* 2 volumes (Chicago and New York, 1912), are examples of subsequent county works that placed a greater emphasis on history and less on biography. Milton M. Ferguson, chairman, and others, *150 Years in the Hills and Dales: A Bicentennial History of Hillsdale County, Michigan,* 2 volumes (Dallas, 1976, 1978), is one of the first indications that the bicentennial enthusiasm of the 1970s may inspire national publishers to promote a new rash of county histories of the totally unselective, unedited variety. Ford Stevens Ceasar, *The Bicentennial History of Ingham County, Michigan* (Ann Arbor, 1976), is one of the better organized and written among the newer county histories.

In many cases, the attention in local areas shifted from the county level to the preparation of histories of a city. Towering above all of the productions of this type is Silas Farmer, *History of Detroit and Wayne County and Early Michigan,* 2 volumes (Detroit, 1884), which appeared in revised editions in 1889 and 1890. This thousand-page work covers nearly every imaginable topic in truly encyclopaedic fashion, with its geographical range, as the title indicates, sometimes stretching well beyond Detroit. Numerous histories of Michigan's largest city have appeared since Farmer, but none match it for detail or replace it as the basic source for the period Farmer covers, although Clarence M. Burton, ed., *The City of Detroit, Michigan, 1701–1922,* 5 volumes (Detroit, 1922), comes the closest. (Only the first two volumes of this work deal with Detroit's history, with the remaining volumes consisting of biographies.) Among one-volume histories of more manageable scope, George B. Catlin, *The Story of Detroit* (Detroit, 1923), is the best for the period it covers; Arthur Pound, *Detroit: Dynamic City* (New York, 1940), is by far the most thoughtful, and Frank B. and Arthur M. Woodford, *All Our Yesterdays: A Brief History of Detroit* (Detroit, 1969), is the most up-to-date. Milo M. Quaife, *This is Detroit: Two Hundred and Fifty Years in Pictures* (Detroit, 1951), is a splendid pictorial treatment.

For outstate communities, Albert Baxter, *History of the City of Grand Rapids, Michigan* (New York, 1891), comes close to the high standards of comprehensiveness set by Silas Farmer. Z. Z. Lydens, ed., *The Story of Grand Rapids* (Grand Rapids, 1966), a cooperative venture of uneven quality, is one of the rare attempts made in recent decades to deal with a local community on the scale of the late nineteenth-century histories. Willis F. Dunbar, *Kalamazoo and how it grew* (Kalamazoo, 1959); Orlando W. Stephenson, *Ann Arbor: The First Hundred Years* (Ann Arbor, 1927); and Birt Darling, *City in the Forest: The Story of Lansing* (New York, 1950), are among the best of the city histories. The bicentennial enthusiasm of the seventies has stirred much activity at the community history level, with much emphasis placed on pictorial histories. Lawrence R. Gustin, ed., *Picture History of Flint* (Grand Rapids, 1976), and Lee S. Peel, *Farmington: A Pictorial History* (Dallas, 1971), are among the best of these. Dominic P. Paris, *Footpaths to Freeways: The Story of Livonia* (n. p., 1975), and Justin L. Kestenbaum, ed., *At the Campus Gate: A History of East Lansing* (East Lansing, 1976), place the main emphasis on the text.

In northern Michigan, perhaps because the sparse population makes it difficult to find support for the publication of county or city histories, the emphasis has been on histories of the entire area. John Bartlow Martin, *Call It North Country: The Story of Upper Michigan* (New York, 1944), emphasizes the colorful individuals and events in the development of the Upper Peninsula, while Richard M. Dorson, *Bloodstoppers and Bearwalkers: Folk Traditions of the Upper Peninsula* (Cambridge, Mass., 1952), examines some of the area's same colorful aspects in a more scientific vein. Alvah L. Sawyer, *A History of the Northern Peninsula of Michigan and Its People,* 3 volumes (Chicago, 1911), is the only work for that area that is comparable to the Durant-Farmer-Baxter model of county or city history for the southern part of the state. Perry F. Powers, *A History of Northern Michigan and Its People,* 3 volumes (Chicago, 1912), is the only one of this type for most of the counties of the northern half of the lower peninsula. Significant exceptions to this broad geographical approach are Joseph E. and Estelle L. Bayliss, in collaboration with Milo M. Quaife, *River of Destiny: The Saint Marys* (Detroit, 1955), dealing with the Sault Ste. Marie area, and the episodic and highly readable *Vinegar Pie and Other Tales of the Grand Traverse Region* (Detroit, 1955) by Al Barnes. However, no area in northern Michigan has received the attention that has been given to the Mackinac area, particularly Mackinac Island, where affluent summer residents and hordes of tourists provide a ready-made audience for an endless stream of books and pamphlets. Edwin O. Wood, *Historic Mackinac,* 2 volumes (New York, 1918), is a classic, while the incredibly prolific Walter Havighurst wrote of the area in his *Three Flags at the Straits: The Forts of Mackinac* (Englewood Cliffs, N. J., 1966). Eugene T. Petersen, *Mackinac Island: Its History in Pictures* (Mackinac Island, 1973), is one of the best and most attractive pictorial histories ever published in Michigan.

Turning to books that deal with particular periods, topics, or individuals, one finds that some of the best work in recent years has been on the prehistoric period and on the period of the early contact of the Indians with the European intruders. W. Vernon Kinietz, *The Indians of the Western Great Lakes, 1615–1760* (Ann Arbor, 1940), effectively uses the written records that appeared with the coming of the French to do an anthropological study of the cultures of the several tribes that lived in and around Michigan. George I. Quimby, in his *Indian Life in the Upper Great Lakes, 11,000 B.C. to A.D. 1800* (Chicago, 1960), and his *Indian Culture and European Trade Goods: The Archaeology of the Historic Period in the Western Great Lakes Region* (Madison, 1966), was the first scholar to make effective use of the archaeological evidence that has primarily accumulated in the past thirty years. James E. Fitting, *The Archaeology of Michigan: A Guide to the Prehistory of the Great Lakes Region* (Garden City, N. Y., 1970, revised edition, published at Bloomfield Hills, Mich., 1975), is the most up-to-date study.

An understanding of Canadian history is essential to anyone who wants to make sense of Michigan's development in the early phases of the historic period, when this area was simply one of the western areas of the French empire that ultimately evolved into Canada. Barry Gough, *Canada* (Englewood Cliffs, N. J., 1975), is a good, brief interpretive study, with reading suggestions for those who desire to delve more deeply into this subject area. For Michigan, the works of the Canadian historian, W. J. Eccles, particularly *The Canadian Frontier, 1534–1760* (New York, 1969), and *Canada Under Louis XIV, 1663–1701* (Toronto, 1964), are an important corrective to some of the interpretations of the great American historian, Francis Parkman, *France and England in North America,* 9 volumes (Boston, 1865–92). Parkman influenced generations of Michigan historians to treat these years in ways that are no longer always acceptable.

Louise Phelps Kellogg, *The French Regime in Wisconsin and the Northwest* (Madison, 1925), and the same author's *The British Regime in Wisconsin and the Northwest* (Madison, 1935), remain, despite their age, essential works for any serious student of Michigan's development in the seventeenth and eighteenth centuries. Samuel Eliot Morison, *Samuel de Champlain: Father of New France* (Boston, 1972), written in masterful style, is a good introduction to the man who started the French on the path to Michigan. Although written in an uncompromisingly dense and academic style, Harold A. Innis, *The Fur Trade in Canada: An Introduction to Canadian Economic History* (New Haven, 1930), is absolutely indispensable for an understanding of the ways in which the fur trade drew the French to Michigan. Grace Lee Nute, *The Voyageur* (New York, 1931), deals with what might be called Michigan's first working-class element in a scholarly, yet highly readable manner. George Paré, *The Catholic Church in Detroit, 1701-1888* (Detroit, 1951), is an outstanding work which, in spite of the title, goes back to the years before 1701 to indicate how the Jesuit missionaries influenced the French development of Michigan. No other history of any other religious group in Michigan can match Paré in his mastery of sources and subject. Raphael N. Hamilton, *Father Marquette* (Grand Rapids, 1970), is a good, brief biography of the most famous of these Jesuit missionaries, with Joseph P. Donnelly, *Jacques Marquette, S. J., 1637-1675* (Chicago, 1968), providing the most detailed account available.

Regarding the transition from French to British control, Howard H. Peckham, *Pontiac and the Indian Uprising* (Princeton, 1947), is one of the major works in Michigan historical literature. It supplants Francis Parkman's *The Conspiracy of Pontiac* (Boston, 1851), a highly readable work (still in print), which is well worth reading, if for no other reason than its insight into the prejudices that guided so much of the American writing of an earlier era because of its interpretation and treatment of the Indians and the French. Regarding Michigan during the era of the American Revolution, Howard Peckham's *The War for Independence: A Military History* (Chicago, 1958) includes the necessary background for understanding the developments in the West that affected Michigan. Not much happened in Michigan, of course, which accounts for the lack of detailed accounts of the Revolutionary War era of the state's development, but David A. Armour and Keith R. Widder, *At the Crossroads: Michilimackinac During the American Revolution* (Mackinac Island, 1978), another in the fine series of historical works produced by the Mackinac Island State Park Commission, may mark the beginning of a trend that will lead to a more comprehensive treatment of this period.

F. Clever Bald, *Detroit's First American Decade, 1796-1805* (Ann Arbor, 1948), more than adequately treats the transition to American control. Frank B. Woodford, *Mr. Jefferson's Disciple: A Life of Judge Woodward* (East Lansing, 1953), deals with one of the more important of the early territorial officials. No adequate biography of William Hull is available, but Alec R. Gilpin, *The War of 1812 in the Old Northwest* (East Lansing, 1958), is one of the best defenses of Hull's actions in that war. Harry L. Coles, *The War of 1812* (Chicago, 1965), takes a less sympathetic view toward Hull. Although only a short pamphlet, Fred C. Hamil, *Michigan in the War of 1812* (Lansing, 1960), is a most helpful interpretation of this critical period, written from the perspective of a Michigan historian who was also a native of Canada.

Floyd R. Dain, *Every House a Frontier: Detroit's Economic Progress, 1815–1825* (Detroit, 1956), treats the important changes that were occurring as Detroit—and Michigan—passed from the fur-trading era into the different kinds of development that came with the full-fledged American entry into Michigan after the war. Kenneth W. Porter, *John Jacob Astor, Businessman,* 2 volumes (Cambridge, Mass., 1931), masterfully deals with the activities of the last man to cash in on Michigan's long-time central role in the fur trade. Willis F. Dunbar, *Lewis Cass* (Grand Rapids, 1970), is the best introduction to the life of the man responsible for leading Michigan in the years of growth following the war. Frank B. Woodford, *Lewis Cass: The Last Jeffersonian* (New Brunswick, 1950), is the most detailed study, although Andrew C. McLaughlin, *Lewis Cass* (Boston, 1891), is still valuable for some of its insights. Frank B. Woodford and Albert Hyma, *Gabriel Richard: Frontier Ambassador* (Detroit, 1958), is the best biography of this Catholic priest who was important in many areas of Michigan in the first thirty years of the nineteenth century. Dolorita Mast, *Always the Priest: The Life of Gabriel Richard, S. S.* (Baltimore, 1965), looks at Richard from a somewhat different viewpoint.

George N. Fuller, *Economic and Social Beginnings of Michigan: A Study of the Settlement of the Lower Peninsula During the Territorial Period, 1805–1837* (Lansing, 1916), is the most detailed work on the opening of the interior of southern Michigan and the changes by the 1830s. Although marred in its coverage of Michigan events because of insufficient research on the state's history and geography, Malcolm J. Rohrbough, *The Land Office Business: The Settlement and Administration of American Public Lands, 1789–1837* (New York, 1968), provides the best coverage of the land boom that accompanied the settlement of these years. Lawton T. Hemans, *Life and Times of Stevens T. Mason* (Lansing, 1930), is the most detailed biography of the man that led Michigan in the difficult transition to statehood, but Kent Sagendorph, *Stevens Thomson Mason* (New York, 1947), presents what is probably a more realistic view of the "boy governor."

Robert J. Parks, *Democracy's Railroads: Public Enterprise in Jacksonian Michigan* (Port Washington, N. Y., 1972), demonstrates the new insights and life that modern scholarship can breathe into what many would have assumed was a shopworn topic—Michigan's internal improvements program. For the development of railroads in general, Willis F. Dunbar, *All Aboard: A History of Railroads in Michigan* (Grand Rapids, 1969), stands alone, although Frank N. Elliott, *When the Railroad Was King* (Lansing, 1966), a short work, is also helpful.

Educational developments, which assumed great importance in the early days of statehood, are now covered in greater depth than any other subject in the state's history, with the publication of the four-volume *History of Education in Michigan* which was sponsored by the Michigan Historical Commission through the John M. Munson Fund. Willis F. Dunbar, *The Michigan Record in Higher Education* (Detroit, 1963), reviewed the entire development of college and university education from its beginnings to the sixties. This subject had been Dunbar's major research interest since the 1930s. This volume was followed by three others which dealt chronologically with the development of education at the elementary and secondary level from colonial times to the late sixties. These were: Floyd R. Dain, *Education in the Wilderness* (Lansing, 1968); James O. Knauss and Charles Starring, *The Michigan Search for Educational Standards* (Lansing, 1969); and Donald W. Disbrow, *Schools for an Urban Society* (Lansing, 1969). One or more histories for most of the colleges and universities in the state are available, with Madison Kuhn, *Michigan State: The First Hundred Years* (East Lansing, 1955), being one of the best. Howard H. Peckham, *The Making of the University of Michigan* (Ann Arbor, 1967), is the most recent of numerous histories of the University of Michigan, while Leslie L. Hanawalt, *A Place of Light: The History of Wayne State University* (Detroit, 1968), covers its development.

Edsel K. Rintala, *Douglass Houghton, Michigan's Pioneer Geologist* (Detroit, 1954), is a relatively brief biography of this individual who was so instrumental in the development of the mining industry. William B. Gates, Jr., *Michigan Copper and Boston Dollars* (Cambridge, Mass., 1951), is one of the most complete treatments of any of the economic activities that emerged in Michigan, although Angus Murdoch, *Boom Copper: The Story of the First U. S. Mining Boom* (New York, 1943), does a better job of depicting the social conditions that developed in the Copper Country, and Donald Chaput, *The Cliff: America's First Copper Mine* (Kalamazoo, 1971), points out that Boston was not as important an investment center in the early development of Michigan's copper mines as Gates would indicate in his title. For iron mining there is no work that can match the comprehensiveness or high scholarship of Gates' study on copper mining. Stewart Holbrook, *Iron Brew* (New York, 1939); Harlan Hatcher, *A Century of Iron and Men* (Indianapolis, 1950); and Walter Havighurst, *Vein of Iron: The Pickands-Mather Story* (New York, 1958), are at best works that deal with only a portion of this activity. Herbert Brinks, *Peter White* (Grand Rapids, 1970), is an all-too-brief biographical sketch of one of the important figures in the Upper Peninsula mining industry.

For the lumber industry, Rolland H. Maybee, *Michigan's White Pine Era, 1840–1900* (Lansing, 1960), is an excellent, although lamentably brief, introduction to this subject. The popular historian, Stewart Holbrook, was at the peak of his form in the Michigan chapters of his *Holy Old Mackinaw: A Natural History of the American Lumberjack* (New York, 1938), while E. M. Beck, *Lore of the Lumber Camps* (Ann Arbor, 1948), adds additional colorful detail to an understanding of the life of the lumberjacks. William G. Rector, *Log Transportation in the Lake States Lumber Industry* (Glendale, Cal., 1953), is a scholarly treatment, which, like the work of William Gates on copper mining, stands out in the works on lumbering and mining which have tended to emphasize the colorful life of the individuals involved in these activities instead of seriously analyzing this economy. Martin D. Lewis, *Lumberman from Flint: The Michigan Career of Henry H. Crapo,*

1855–1869 (Detroit, 1958), however, is an excellent study of the problems that an individual had to overcome in order to capitalize on the potential for wealth offered by the lumber industry. On a broader scale, George W. Hotchkiss, *History of the Lumber and Forestry Industry in the Northwest* (Chicago, 1898), is, despite its age, still valuable.

For other nineteenth-century activities, the literature is less satisfactory, although Lew Allen Chase, *Rural Michigan* (New York, 1922), deals with many features of Michigan's agricultural economy. The breakfast food industry has been chronicled to the greatest extent, with Gerald Carson, *Cornflake Crusade* (New York, 1957), emphasizing the eccentricities of some of the people involved in this development, while Horace B. Powell, *The Original Has This Signature—W. K. Kellogg* (New York, 1956), and Richard M. Schwarz, *John Harvey Kellogg, M. D.* (Nashville, 1970), provide biographies of two of the most prominent individuals. Don Whitehead, *The Dow Story: The History of the Dow Chemical Company* (New York, 1968), and the earlier biography, Murray Campbell and Harrison Hatton, *Herbert H. Dow: Pioneer in Creative Chemistry* (New York, 1951), deal with Michigan's most famous chemical company, while Leonard Engel, *Medicine Makers of Kalamazoo* (New York, 1961), deals with one of the state's best-known pharmaceutical companies, Upjohn.

Regarding the new settlers that these and later activities attracted to the state, George P. Graff, *The People of Michigan* (Lansing, 1974), provides both a bibliography of important sources and a series of short articles dealing with the various groups, both those who migrated to Michigan from within the country, and those who came in from other countries. C. Warren VanderHill, *Settling the Great Lakes Frontier: Immigration to Michigan, 1837–1924* (Lansing, 1970), is both an excellent short review of this subject and a good introduction to the literature. Among important books, Lois K. Mathews, *Expansion of New England* (Boston, 1909), remains a good introduction to the Yankee migration to the west. Arnold Mulder, *Americans from Holland* (New York, 1947), is a good introduction to the literature on the Dutch, and Henry S. Lucas, *Netherlanders in America: Dutch Immigration to the United States and Canada, 1789–1950* (Ann Arbor, 1955), is the most comprehensive work. John A. Russell, *The Germanic Influence in the Making of Michigan* (Detroit, 1927), is no more than adequate. The Cornish, once one of the more neglected of Michigan's population elements, are now the subject of three books: Arthur Cecil Todd, *The Cornish Miner in America* (Glendale, Cal., 1967); A. L. Rowse, *The Cousin Jacks: The Cornish in America* (New York, 1969); and John Rowe, *The Hard-Rock Men: Cornish Immigrants and the North American Mining Frontier* (New York, 1974). Rowe's study is the best of the three. The appearance in recent years of David M. Katzman, *Before the Ghetto: Black Detroit in the Nineteenth Century* (Urbana, 1973), and Jo Ellen Vinyard, *The Irish on the Urban Frontier: Detroit, 1850–1880* (New York, 1976), marks the beginning of what one hopes is a trend among serious scholars to spend the time on the detailed studies of Michigan's numerous ethnic and racial groups which is needed for the preparation of adequate general accounts.

For political developments, Floyd B. Streeter, *Political Parties in Michigan, 1837–1860* (Lansing, 1918), was the standard work until the appearance of Ronald P. Formisano, *The Birth of Mass Political Parties: Michigan, 1827–1861* (Princeton, 1971), superseded it with the most detailed study of any political period in all of Michigan's history. Sister Mary Karl George, *Zachariah Chandler: A Political Biography* (East Lansing, 1969), deals with the politician who replaced Lewis Cass in the 1850s as the dominant force in the state. Along the same biographical line, Mildred E. Danforth, *A Quaker Pioneer: Laura Haviland, Superintendent of the Underground* (New York, 1961), and Jacqueline Bernard, *Journey Toward Freedom: The Story of Sojourner Truth* (New York, 1967), deal with two women, both of whom came to be associated with Michigan, and both of whom were involved in the ferment that precipitated the Civil War.

For the Civil War period, George S. May, ed., *Michigan Civil War History: An Annotated Bibliography* (Detroit, 1961), represents the only attempt in recent years to prepare a complete bibliography on a major topic in Michigan history. Frederick D. Williams, *Michigan Soldiers in the Civil War* (Lansing, 1960), is an excellent brief introduction to the subject. Frank B. Woodford, *Father Abraham's Children: Michigan Episodes in the Civil War* (Detroit, 1961), is, as the title indicates, not an attempt to write a history of the war but only to deal with isolated episodes and individuals. In its publications program in the 1960s, the Michigan Civil War Centennial Observance Commission encouraged studies of the non-military aspects of the war and its impact which the commission correctly felt had been neglected. Mrs. Raymond H. Millbrook, ed., *Michigan Women in the Civil War* (Lansing, 1963), and Helen H. Ellis, *Michigan in the Civil War: A Guide to the Materials in Detroit Newspapers, 1861–1865* (Lansing, 1965), were two of the best of the commission's publications. Another, George S. May, *Michigan and the Civil War Years, 1860–1866* (Lansing, 1964), attempts to provide a descriptive chronology of important events related to the war.

For the post-war period, there is a great need for a good study of political developments to replace and update Harriette Dilla, *Politics of Michigan, 1865–1878* (New York, 1912). Fortunately Arthur Millspaugh's political science treatise, *Party Organization and Machinery in Michigan Since 1890* (Baltimore, 1917), has now been superseded by the far more stimulating and historically-oriented Melvin G. Holli, *Reform in Detroit: Hazen S. Pingree and Urban Politics* (New York, 1969), and, on a much different, and far too brief scale, Stephen R. and Vera H. Sarasohn, *Political Party Patterns in Michigan* (Detroit, 1957). Robert M. Warner's pamphlet, *Chase Salmon Osborn, 1860–1949*, Michigan Historical Collections *Bulletin No. 10* (Ann Arbor, 1960), raises the hope that the author will yet find the time to complete a full-scale biography of this important figure.

Regarding the auto industry that came to tower over all other topics at the very start of the twentieth century, George S. May, *A Most Unique Machine: The Michigan Origins of the American Automobile Industry* (Grand Rapids, 1975), examines how the industry came to be centered in Michigan in the first decade of the century. The same author's *R. E. Olds: Auto Industry Pioneer* (Grand Rapids, 1977) looks at the life of the man most responsible for initiating this development. It largely replaces the earlier biography, Glenn Niemeyer, *The Automotive Career of Ransom E. Olds* (East Lansing, 1964). The three-volume study of Henry Ford and his company, written by Allan Nevins and Frank Ernest Hill (New York, 1954–63), is by far the most exhaustive treatment yet prepared of any phase of automotive history. Roger Burlingame, *Henry Ford: A Great Life in Brief* (New York, 1955), is the best introduction to the subject, while among the many other works on Ford that have appeared, David L. Lewis, *The Public Image of Henry Ford: An American Folk Hero and His Company* (Detroit, 1976), is one of the more original in its approach to an all-too-familiar subject. Lawrence R. Gustin, *Billy Durant: Creator of General Motors* (Grand Rapids, 1973), is, at this writing, the only worthwhile, available biography of this major figure. Mrs. Wilfred C. Leland, with Minnie Dubbs Millbrook, *Master of Precision: Henry M. Leland* (Detroit, 1966), is one of the few other good biographies of important individuals in the industry that have appeared, with autobiographical works by Walter P. Chrysler and Alfred P. Sloan, Jr., sufficing for those giants. Among other works, Arthur Pound, *The Turning Wheel: The Story of General Motors Through Twenty-Five Years* (Garden City, N. Y., 1934), is still well worth an examination, while for over-all coverage, John B. Rae, *The American Automobile* (Chicago, 1965), and the same author's earlier *American Automobile Manufacturers* (Philadelphia, 1959), remain the standard sources.

For other economic developments of the present century, Raymond C. Miller, *Kilowatts at Work: A History of the Detroit Edison Company* (Detroit, 1957), and, to a lesser extent, George Bush, *Future Builders: The Story of Michigan's Consumers Power Company* (New York, 1973), provide an unusual amount of detail on the histories of the two major power companies serving lower Michigan, and cannot be equalled in any studies of any of the remaining present-day business operations in the state.

Political figures of the twentieth century seem to be faring better at the hands of biographers than those of the preceding century. Frank B. Woodford, *Alex J. Groesbeck: Portrait of a Public Man* (Detroit, 1962), represents Woodford's best work and goes far to assure that Groesbeck maintains his important place in Michigan's history. Harry Barnard, *Independent Man: The Life of Senator James Couzens* (New York, 1958), does an equally good job on this businessman-turned-politician. C. David Tompkins, *Senator Arthur H. Vandenberg: The Evolution of a Modern Republican, 1884–1945* (East Lansing, 1970), takes its subject to the beginning of the most important phase of this senator's career, which is to be covered in a promised second volume. But no Michigan politician is being given the in-depth treatment that Sidney Fine is giving to the life of Frank Murphy. *Frank Murphy: The Detroit Years* (Ann Arbor, 1975), was followed by *Frank Murphy: The New Deal Years* (Chicago, 1979), with *Frank Murphy: The Washington Years* still to follow to complete the trilogy. Fine began his task after having already prepared two other major works on the decade of the thirties, a decade that lies at the heart of Murphy's activities in Michigan: *The Automobile Under the Blue Eagle* (Ann Arbor, 1963), and *Sit-Down: The General Motors Strike of 1936–1937* (Ann Arbor, 1969). With the completion of the second volume of his Murphy biography, which appeared too late to be used, except in a very cursory fashion, in preparing the present history, Fine has provided the most detailed coverage yet available on the decade of the thirties. In addition to the work of Sidney Fine, Doris B. McLaughlin, *Michigan Labor: A Brief History from 1818 to the Present* (Ann Arbor, 1970), is a useful introduction to the rise of labor, particularly of the UAW. For Michigan's most famous, and probably most important labor leader, R. L. Tyler, *Walter Reuther* (Grand Rapids, 1973), is an adequate introduction. Frank Cormier and William J. Eaton, *Reuther* (Englewood Cliffs, N. J., 1970), is more detailed but simply demonstrates the need for a more adequate, in-depth biography. Warner Pflug, *The UAW in Pictures* (Detroit, 1971), is an effective visual treatment of the union's history. The reader should refer to the footnotes of the later chapters of this book for some indication of the books that are presently available on other twentieth-century topics.

APPENDIX I

MICHIGAN'S POPULATION, 1810–1970

1810	4,762
1820	8,927
1830	31,639
1840	212,267
1850	397,654
1860	749,113
1870	1,184,059
1880	1,636,937
1890	2,093,889
1900	2,420,982
1910	2,810,172
1920	3,668,412
1930	4,482,325
1940	5,256,106
1950	6,372,009[1]
1960	7,824,018[2]
1970	8,881,783[3]

1. This is the corrected population figure, as given in *Michigan Manual, 1977–1978,* p. 474. The census bureau's original official census total for 1950 was 6,371,766.
2. This is the corrected population figure, as given in *ibid.,* p. 474. The original official announced total for 1960 was 7,823,194.
3. This is the corrected population figure, as given in *ibid.,* p. 474. The original announced total for 1970 was 8,875,083.

APPENDIX II

GOVERNORS OF MICHIGAN

Territory of Michigan

William Hull	1805–1813
Lewis Cass	1813–1831
George B. Porter	1831–1834
Henry D. Gilpin[1]	———
Stevens T. Mason[2]	1834–1835

State of Michigan

Stevens T. Mason, Democrat	1835–1839
William Woodbridge, Whig[3]	1840–1841
James Wright Gordon, Whig[4]	1841
John S. Barry, Democrat	1842–1845
Alpheus Felch, Democrat[5]	1846–1847
William L. Greenly, Democrat[6]	1847
Epaphroditus Ransom, Democrat	1848–1849
John S. Barry, Democrat	1850[7]
Robert McClelland, Democrat[8]	1851–1853
Andrew Parsons, Democrat[9]	1853–1854
Kinsley S. Bingham, Republican	1855–1858
Moses Wisner, Republican	1859–1860
Austin Blair, Republican	1861–1864
Henry H. Crapo, Republican	1865–1868
Henry P. Baldwin, Republican	1869–1872
John J. Bagley, Republican	1873–1876
Charles M. Croswell, Republican	1877–1880

David H. Jerome, Republican	1881–1882
Josiah W. Begole, Fusion	1883–1884
Russell A. Alger, Republican	1885–1886
Cyrus G. Luce, Republican	1887–1890
Edwin B. Winans, Democrat	1891–1892
John T. Rich, Republican	1893–1896
Hazen S. Pingree, Republican	1897–1900
Aaron T. Bliss, Republican	1901–1904
Fred M. Warner, Republican	1905–1910
Chase S. Osborn, Republican	1911–1912
Woodbridge N. Ferris, Democrat	1913–1916
Albert E. Sleeper, Republican	1917–1920
Alex J. Groesbeck, Republican	1921–1926
Fred W. Green, Republican	1927–1930
Wilber M. Brucker, Republican	1931–1932
William A. Comstock, Democrat	1933–1934
Frank D. Fitzgerald, Republican	1935–1936
Frank Murphy, Democrat	1937–1938
Frank D. Fitzgerald, Republican[10]	1939
Luren D. Dickinson, Republican[11]	1939–1940
Murray D. Van Wagoner, Democrat	1941–1942
Harry F. Kelly, Republican	1943–1946
Kim Sigler, Republican	1947–1948
G. Mennen Williams, Democrat	1949–1960
John B. Swainson, Democrat	1961–1962
George Romney, Republican[12]	1963–1969
William G. Milliken, Republican[13]	1969–

1. Gilpin was nominated for the office of governor by President Jackson, after George Porter, the previous governor, had died in office on July 6, 1834. The Senate, however, rejected the appointment.

2. Mason, secretary of the territory since Aug. 1, 1831, served as acting governor when that office became vacant after the death of Governor Porter in 1834. Mason was subsequently replaced as secretary on Sept. 8, 1835, by John S. Horner, who then also technically served as acting governor of the territory. However, the movement for statehood was so far advanced that few people in Michigan chose to recognize Horner as Michigan's chief executive officer.

3. Woodbridge resigned as governor on Feb. 24, 1841, to become United States Senator.

4. Gordon, the lieutenant governor, succeeded to the office of governor upon the resignation of Woodbridge.

5. Felch resigned as governor on Mar. 3, 1847, to become United States Senator.

6. Greenly, the lieutenant governor, succeeded to the office of governor upon the resignation of Felch.

7. Barry's term as governor was for one year only because, with the adoption of the 1850 Constitution, elections for governor were switched from the odd-numbered to the even-numbered years. Thus, Barry, elected in November, 1849, in the last election under the 1835 Constitution, was succeeded on January 1, 1851, by

Robert McClelland, who had been elected governor in November, 1850, in the first election under the new constitution.

8. McClelland resigned as governor on Mar. 7, 1853, to become Secretary of the Interior.

9. Parsons, the lieutenant governor, succeeded to the office of governor upon the resignation of McClelland.

10. Fitzgerald died in office on Mar. 16, 1939.

11. Dickinson, the lieutenant governor, succeeded to the office of governor upon the death of Fitzgerald.

12. Romney resigned as governor on Jan. 22, 1969, to become Secretary of Housing and Urban Development.

13. Milliken, the lieutenant governor, succeeded to the office of governor upon the resignation of Romney. Milliken subsequently became the first person to become governor of the state through this route to go on to be elected governor on his own right, winning election to four-year terms in 1970, 1974, and 1978.

NOTES

CHAPTER 1

1. John A. Dorr, Jr., and Donald F. Eschman, *Geology of Michigan* (Ann Arbor, 1970), especially pp. 164–66.

2. Lawrence M. Sommers, ed., *Atlas of Michigan* (East Lansing, 1977), p. 18.

3. David I. Verway, ed., *Michigan Statistical Abstract,* 975 (East Lansing, 1978).

4. Reference works vary widely in the land and water area they assign to Michigan due to differences in methods of measuring and maps used in measuring, as well as man-made and natural changes from year to year. The figures cited here are from the *Statistical Abstract of the United States, 1976,* pp. 180–81. No source is given for the different figures of 38,575 square miles of Great Lakes waters and 58,216 square miles of land area in Sommers, ed., *Atlas of Michigan,* p. 1.

5. The term "Michiganian" was used as early as 1813 to designate a resident of Michigan, and was used by such writers as Charles Fenno Hoffman and Harriet Martineau in the 1830s in their accounts of travels in Michigan. The term "Michigander" was made popular after Abraham Lincoln, in a speech in 1848, sarcastically referred to the Democrat, Lewis Cass, as "the great Michigander." However, although the latter term continues to be the most widely used, "Michiganian" is more sensible and consistent with the form employed in referring to residents of most other states. See Mitford M. Mathews, ed., *A Dictionary of Americanisms,* 2 (Chicago, 1951), p. 1051; Richard H. Thornton, *An American Glossary,* 2 (New York, 1962), p. 579; and an article by Don Faber in the Ann Arbor *News,* 8 April 1979.

6. Ellsworth Huntington, *Mainspring of Civilization* (New York, 1945), especially pp. 343–68.

CHAPTER 2

1. For a discussion of recent discoveries and the controversies surrounding them, see William McDonald, "How Old *Is* American Man?" *The National Observer,* 31 May 1975.

2. See Willis F. Dunbar, *Kalamazoo and how it grew* (Kalamazoo, 1959), pp. 13–14, for the meaning of Kalamazoo, and George S. May, "The Meaning and Pronunciation of Michilimackinac," *Michigan History*, 42 (Dec., 1958), pp. 385–90.

CHAPTER 3

1. Occasionally it is claimed that Norsemen and even Phoenicians reached Michigan centuries earlier than the French. There certainly is no evidence to substantiate the claim for the Phoenicians. The claim that the Norsemen, or Vikings, as they are sometimes referred to, may have seen Michigan about the year 1362 is based on the so-called "Rune Stone" found near Kensington, Minnesota, in 1898. A translation of an inscription on the stone indicated that a group of Norsemen were in the vicinity in 1362, which might mean that they also had visited the Michigan area in the same period. However, subsequent investigation has demonstrated that the Kensington Rune Stone is a fake. See Erik Wahlgren, *The Kensington Stone, a Mystery Solved* (Madison, 1958), and Russell W. Fridley, "Debate Continues over Kensington Rune Stone," *Minnesota History*, 45 (Winter, 1976), pp. 149–51.

2. Original source material on Nicolet's western exploration is very limited and the geographical references in this material are so vague that some have concluded that Nicolet, on his outward journey, went up into Lake Superior and along the northern shore of Michigan's Upper Peninsula and then overland to Green Bay, rather than following the southern shore through the Straits of Mackinac. See Milo M. Quaife and Sidney Glazer, *Michigan: From Primitive Wilderness to Industrial Commonwealth* (New York, 1948), pp. 21fn. and Harry Dever, "The Nicolet Myth," *Michigan History*, 50 (Dec., 1966), pp. 318–22. The principal narrative on Nicolet's journey is reprinted in George S. May and Herbert J. Brinks, eds., *A Michigan Reader, 11,000 B. C. to A. D. 1865* (Grand Rapids, 1974), pp. 51–52.

3. Fielding H. Yost, famous football coach of the University of Michigan Wolverines, recounts his futile efforts to find any solid evidence of wolverines in Michigan in an article, in collaboration with R. Ray Baker, "The Wolverine," *Michigan History*, 27 (Oct.–Dec., 1943), pp. 581–89. Why the name of this beast, sometimes called the "glutton," was applied to residents of Michigan and to the state is not at all certain. To the Indians, the wolverine was an animal they had traditionally disliked intensely. Some believe that when the Americans moved into Michigan in the 1830s and gobbled up the Indians' land, the Indians began calling these settlers "wolverines" because it was the worst thing they could call these people.

4. For some voyageur songs, see Grace Lee Nute, *The Voyageur* (New York, 1931), pp. 103–55.

5. Radisson's travel narrative can be found in Louise P. Kellogg, ed., *Early Narratives of the Northwest, 1634–1699* (New York, 1917), pp. 27–67.

6. Although the accuracy of this claim is arguable, it is far easier to defend than the one put forth by local enthusiasts in the Soo who push the city's founding back to 1620, the approximate date of Brule's visit to the area. No French settlement resulted from that visit, but nevertheless the advocates of this founding date blithely contend that this makes Sault Ste. Marie the third oldest city in the United States.

7. For many years historians assumed that the "Man named Jolliet" in Galinée's journal was the famous Louis Jolliet, leader of the expedition to the Mississippi in 1673. Jean Delanglez, in his *Life and Voyages of Louis Jolliet, 1645–1700* (Chicago, 1948), pp. 7–11, convincingly demonstrated that the Jolliet encountered by the Sulpicians in 1669 was Louis' older brother Adrien.

8. Raphael N. Hamilton, S. J., "Location of the Mission of St. Ignace from 1670 to 1673," *Michigan History,* 42 (Sept., 1958), pp. 260–66.

9. There are three contemporary accounts of the pageant at the Sault. One is an official state paper, translated and published in the *Wisconsin Historical Collections,* 11 (1899), pp. 26–28. An account by Nicholas Perrot appears in Emma H. Blair, ed., *Indian Tribes of the Upper Mississippi and Region of the Great Lakes,* 1, (Cleveland, 1911), pp. 220–25. An account from the *Jesuit Relations* is reprinted in May and Brinks, eds., *A Michigan Reader,* pp. 56–59.

10. Catherine L. Stebbins, *Here I Shall Finish My Voyage* (Omena, 1960), contends that the description of the place where Marquette was put ashore and later died, and the changes that have occurred in the shoreline since that time indicate that the missionary died, not near Ludington, but, rather, near Frankfort. She discusses this thesis at greater length in her article, "The Marquette Death Site," *Michigan History,* 48 (Dec., 1964), pp. 333–68. Miss Stebbins' arguments brought a rebuttal from Raphael N. Hamilton, in his "The Marquette Death Site: The Case for Ludington," *Michigan History,* 49 (Sept., 1965), pp. 228–48. Not only is the place where Marquette died a matter of dispute, but there is also uncertainty regarding the final resting place of his bones. See George S. May, ed., "The Discovery of Father Marquette's Grave at St. Ignace in 1877, as Related by Father Edward Jacker," *Michigan History,* 42 (Sept., 1958), pp. 267–87.

11. See W. J. Eccles, *Frontenac, the Courtier Governor* (Toronto, 1965).

12. The fate of the *Griffin* has piqued the curiosity of generations of students of Great Lakes lore. In 1957 parts of a vessel that tests indicated might well be three hundred years old were found near Tobermory at the tip of the peninsula that separates Lake Huron from Georgian Bay. A number of Canadian authorities have accepted these remains as those of the *Griffin.* Prior to this find it seemed most probable that the *Griffin* had been lost off the western tip of Manitoulin Island, not far north of Tobermory. See F. Clever Bald, *Michigan in Four Centuries* (New York, 1961), pp. 40–41; and Harrison John MacLean, *The Fate of the Griffin* (Toronto, 1974).

13. The name was that of a battle fought in Europe.

14. Francis Parkman, *La Salle and the Discovery of the Great West* (Boston, 1901), pp. 179–84. The Jesuit, Henry Nouvel, had journeyed from St. Ignace to the vicinity of Midland and conducted a mission there in 1675–76. See Harold W. Moll, ed., "A Canoe Trip to Midland in 1675," *Michigan History*, 46 (Sept., 1962), pp. 255–74.

CHAPTER 4

1. The modern city of Duluth, Minnesota, bears his name.

2. George Paré, *The Catholic Church in Detroit, 1701–1888* (Detroit, 1951), pp. 81 and 85.

3. The exact location of the fort has long been a subject of controversy. Some thought it stood on the hill above the present Marquette Park, others thought that it was situated on the waterfront, in the center of the present business district in St. Ignace. However, a map of the fort prepared in 1749 by Michel Chartier de Lotbinière, with an accompanying narrative discovered in the 1970s, indicates that the fort was actually located west of Point St. Ignace, west of the Mackinac Bridge. Eugene T. Petersen to George S. May, Dec. 11, 1974, with a copy of the map and a translation of the Lotbinière narrative.

4. W. J. Eccles, *Canada Under Louis XIV, 1663–1701* (Toronto, 1964), p.

174. For the favorable view of Cadillac, see Henry D. Brown and others, *Cadillac and the Founding of Detroit* (Detroit, 1976).

5. Donald Chaput, "The French Post at Detroit: An Unrealized Promise," *Detroit in Perspective*, 3 (Spring, 1979), pp. 167–84.

6. For a sympathetic view of the French settlers, see an account by Henry M. Utley reprinted in May and Brinks, eds., *A Michigan Reader*, pp. 123–30.

7. Howard H. Peckham, *Pontiac and the Indian Uprising* (Princeton, 1947), p. 30.

8. *Ibid.*, pp. 30–33.

9. Bald, *Michigan in Four Centuries*, pp. 58–59.

10. Milo M. Quaife, *Lake Michigan* (Indianapolis, 1944), pp. 57–58.

11. Claude T. Hamilton, "Western Michigan History," *Michigan History*, 13 (Spring, 1929), pp. 211–18.

12. Milo M. Quaife, "The Romance of the Mackinac Country," *Michigan History*, 13 (Summer, 1929), p. 392.

13. Louise P. Kellogg, *The British Regime in Wisconsin and the Northwest* (Madison, 1935), pp. 4–6.

14. Peckham, *Pontiac and the Indian Uprising*, pp. 59–63.

15. *Ibid.*, pp. 63–67.

16. *Ibid.*, pp. 82 and 84.

CHAPTER 5

1. Peckham, *Pontiac and the Indian Uprising*, pp. 122–25.

2. James Bain, ed., *Travels and Adventures in Canada and the Indian Territories* (reprint of the original 1901 edition, Rutland, Vermont, 1969), p. 80.

3. Irving I. Katz, "Ezekiel Solomon: The First Jew in Michigan," *Michigan History*, 32 (Sept., 1948), pp. 247–56.

4. Kellogg, *The British Regime in Wisconsin and the Northwest*, pp. 3, 4, 13, 35, 226, 253, 329.

5. The fullest account of how the British met their responsibilities is found in Clarence W. Alvord, *The Mississippi Valley in British Politics* (Cleveland, 1917). A more recent treatment is found in Lawrence P. Gipson, *The British Empire Before the American Revolution*, vol. X, *The Triumphant Empire* (New York, 1961).

6. For a discussion of Carver's work see John Parker, *The Great Lakes and the Great Rivers: Jonathan Carver's Dream of Empire* (Lansing, 1965).

7. The best biography of Rogers is John R. Cuneo, *Robert Rogers of the Rangers* (New York, 1959). Rogers is the central figure in the classic historical novel by Kenneth L. Roberts, *Northwest Passage* (New York, 1937).

8. John D. Barnhart, ed., *Henry Hamilton and George Rogers Clark in the American Revolution, with the Unpublished Journal of Henry Hamilton* (Crawfordsville, Ind., 1951), pp. 93–101.

9. Paré, *The Catholic Church in Detroit, 1701–1888*, pp. 99, 228–31.

10. For recent treatments of George Rogers Clark, see George M. Waller, *The American Revolution in the West* (Chicago, 1976), and *The French, the Indians, and George Rogers Clark in the Illinois Country; Proceedings of an Indiana American Revolution Bicentennial Symposium* (Indianapolis, 1977).

11. Philip P. Mason, *Detroit, Fort Lernoult, and the American Revolution* (Detroit, 1964).

12. De Peyster's verses were published by a descendant in the late nineteenth century and several examples of those relating to Michigan are reprinted in May and Brinks, eds., *A Michigan Reader*, pp. 137–41.

13. "The Haldimand Papers," *Michigan Pioneer and Historical Collections,* 10 (1888), pp. 450–51.

14. Lawrence Kinnaird, "The Spanish Expedition Against Fort St. Joseph in 1781: A New Interpretation," *Mississippi Valley Historical Review,* 19 (Sept., 1932), pp. 173–91, discusses the various theories as well as advancing one of his own. The article is reprinted in May and Brinks, eds., *A Michigan Reader,* pp. 143–55.

15. Quoted in J. E. Day, "The Moravians in Michigan," *Michigan Pioneer and Historical Collections,* 30 (1906), p. 55.

16. Dwight L. Smith, "The Old Northwest and the Peace Negotiations," *The French, the Indians, and George Rogers Clark,* pp. 92–105.

17. Samuel Flagg Bemis, *The Diplomacy of the American Revolution* (Bloomington, 1957), p. 233.

18. Louis C. Karpinski, "Early Michigan Maps: Three Outstanding Peculiarities," *Michigan History,* 29 (Oct.–Dec., 1945), pp. 506–507. Karpinski errs in stating that the treaty of 1783 awarded the mythical Phelipeaux Island to Great Britain. See also Annah May Soule, "The International Boundary of Michigan," *Michigan Pioneer and Historical Collections,* 26 (1896), pp. 597–632, and James C. Starbuck, "Ben Franklin and Isle Royale," *Michigan History,* 46 (June, 1962), pp. 157–66.

CHAPTER 6

1. Frank Woodford, *Yankees in Wonderland* (Detroit, 1951); Lois Kimball Mathews, *The Expansion of New England* (Boston, 1909).

2. Jefferson's manuscript map, depicting the states he proposed for the west, is in George S. May, *Pictorial History of Michigan: The Early Years* (Grand Rapids, 1967), p. 56. See also Frederick L. Paxson, *History of the American Frontier, 1763–1893* (Boston, 1924), pp. 61–63.

3. After the Federal Constitution went into operation these appointments were made by the President with the advice and consent of the Senate.

4. Anthony Wayne's correspondence relating to this Indian campaign is found in Richard C. Knopf, ed., *Anthony Wayne: A Name in Arms* (Pittsburgh, 1960).

5. The text of the treaty may be found in Charles J. Kappler, ed., *Indian Affairs: Laws and Treaties,* 2 (Washington, 1904), pp. 39–45.

6. The total amount of money spent on purchasing Indian lands between 1776 and 1880 is given in Thomas Donaldson, *The Public Domain: Its History,* U. S. House of Representatives, 47th Cong., Mis. Doc. 45 (Washington, 1884), p. 20.

7. F. Clever Bald, *Detroit's First American Decade, 1796 to 1805* (Ann Arbor, 1948), pp. 16–28.

8. Quoted in Edwin O. Wood, *Historic Mackinac,* 1 (New York, 1918), p. 280.

9. Wilbur M. Cunningham, *Land of Four Flags: An Early History of the St. Joseph Valley* (Grand Rapids, 1961), pp. 89–100.

10. Vivian Lyon Moore, "A Pocahontas of Michigan," *Michigan History,* 15 (Winter, 1931), pp. 71–79.

11. Quaife and Glazer, *Michigan: From Primitive Wilderness to Industrial Commonwealth,* pp. 129fn.

12. A careful distinction must be made between a "survey township," as defined under the Land Ordinance of 1785, which was six miles square, and a "government township," which might be any size.

CHAPTER 7

1. Frank B. Woodford, *Mr. Jefferson's Disciple: A Life of Justice Woodward* (East Lansing, 1953); William L. Jenks, "Augustus Elias Brevoort Woodward," *Michigan History,* 9 (Oct., 1925), pp. 515–46.

2. George B. Catlin, *The Story of Detroit* (Detroit, 1923), pp. 115–19.

3. For the complete text of Woodward's protest, see *Michigan Pioneer and Historical Collections,* 12 (1887), pp. 473–83.

4. John W. Reps, *Town Planning in Frontier America* (Princeton, 1969), pp. 367–76.

5. Beverly W. Bond, *The Civilization of the Old Northwest* (New York, 1934), pp. 234–35.

6. Ora B. Peake, *A History of the United States Indian Factory System, 1795–1822* (Denver, 1954).

7. Woodford, *Mr. Jefferson's Disciple,* pp. 84–91.

8. The treaty is sometimes called the Treaty of Brownstown or the Treaty of Detroit.

9. Glenn Tucker, *Tecumseh: Vision of Glory* (Indianapolis, 1956), pp. 35–92.

10. Freeman Cleaves, *Old Tippecanoe: William Henry Harrison and His Time* (New York, 1939).

11. For discussions of the different interpretations of the origins of the War of 1812, see Reginald Horsman, *The Causes of the War of 1812* (Philadelphia, 1962); Bradford Perkins, ed., *The Causes of the War of 1812: National Honor or National Interest?* (Hinsdale, Ill., 1962); and William Barlow, "The Coming of the War of 1812 in Michigan Territory," *Michigan History,* 53 (Summer, 1969), pp. 91–107.

12. George S. May, *War 1812!* (Mackinac Island, 1962), pp. 5–18.

13. Alec R. Gilpin, *The War of 1812 in the Old Northwest* (East Lansing, 1958), pp. 91–92, 126–28.

14. Gilpin, *The War of 1812 in the Old Northwest,* strongly supports Hull. The contrasting view can be found in Harry L. Coles, *The War of 1812* (Chicago, 1965), pp. 55–57.

15. G. Glenn Clift, *Remember the Raisin!* (Frankfort, Kentucky, 1961).

16. Charles J. Dutton, *Oliver Hazard Perry* (New York, 1935), pp. 71–170. The message was first seen by Lewis Cass, now a brigadier general, since Harrison was absent from the American camp on the Sandusky River. For an account of Perry's opponent, Robert Barclay, see Howard H. Peckham, "Commodore Perry's Captive," *Ohio History,* 72 (July, 1963), pp. 220–27.

17. The question of who killed Tecumseh was much debated, with Colonel Johnson claiming the responsibility as the principal basis for his successful campaign for the vice-presidency in 1836. For an interesting account by an Indian writer regarding the circumstances of Tecumseh's death, see Andrew J. Blackbird, *History of the Ottawa and Chippewa Indians of Michigan* (Ypsilanti, 1887), p. 23.

18. Milo M. Quaife, "An Artilleryman of Old Fort Mackinac," *Burton Historical Collection Leaflet,* 4 (Jan., 1928), pp. 33–48.

19. May, *War 1812!,* pp. 33–42.

CHAPTER 8

1. Kenneth W. Porter, *John Jacob Astor, Businessman,* 2 (Cambridge, Mass., 1931), pp. 686–852; John U. Terrell, *Furs By Astor* (New York, 1964), pp. 243–389.

2. Porter, *John Jacob Astor,* 2:702.

3. A thorough discussion of the claim that Cass took a bribe is found in *ibid.*, 2:723–25.

4. This included the profits from both the "northern division" and the "western division," with headquarters at St. Louis, which was established in 1822.

5. Hubbard to H. G. Wells, in a letter written in 1875 and quoted in Samuel W. Durant, *History of Kalamazoo County, Michigan* (Philadelphia, 1880), pp. 82–83. Hubbard's *Autobiography* (Chicago, 1911), contains an excellent description of the fur trade.

6. George H. White, "Sketch of the Life of Hon. Rix Robinson," *Michigan Pioneer and Historical Collections*, 11 (1888), pp. 186–200.

7. Yellow pages of Detroit city telephone directory, 1977; Michigan Department of Natural Resources, *Twenty-eighth Biennial Report, 1975–1976*, pp. 186–87.

8. While the Ferrys were on the island, they had a son, Thomas W. Ferry, who became a United States Senator and a prominent citizen of Grand Haven. As Senator, Thomas Ferry was responsible for the Congressional action in 1875 that made Mackinac Island a national park.

9. Henry B. Selleck, *Beaumont and "The Mackinac Island Miracle"* (East Lansing, 1961).

10. Frank B. Woodford, *Lewis Cass, the Last Jeffersonian* (New Brunswick, 1950), p. 125.

11. Ephraim S. Williams, "The Treaty of Saginaw in the Year 1819," *Michigan Pioneer and Historical Collections*, 7 (1886), pp. 262–70.

12. Donaldson, *The Public Domain*, p. 21.

13. Indian Claims Commission, *Annual Report, 1975*.

14. On May 8, 1979, Federal District Judge Noel Fox ruled in favor of the claims by Chippewa Indians that treaty rights exempted them from state regulations restricting commercial fishing in parts of Lake Superior, Lake Huron, and Lake Michigan. The state attorney general announced plans to appeal this decision which the state and sportsmen's groups claimed would ruin sport and commercial fishing in the area. On February 28, 1979, Washtenaw County Circuit Court Judge Edward D. Deake ruled against the Indian claims in the class action suit against the University of Michigan. The decision is being appealed by the attorney for the Indians, Elmer E. White of Ann Arbor. Detroit *Free Press*, 9 May 1979; Ann Arbor *News*, 27 August 1978; conversation with Elmer White, 14 May 1979.

15. Francis Paul Prucha, *Lewis Cass and American Indian Policy* (Detroit, 1967), pp. 14–16.

16. A. B. Copley, "The Pottawattomies," *Michigan Pioneer and Historical Collections*, 14 (1890), pp. 256–68; Everett Claspy, *The Potawatomi Indians of Southwest Michigan* (Dowagiac, 1966).

17. Darlene Gay Emmert, "The Indians of Shiawassee County," *Michigan History*, 47 (Sept., 1963), pp. 268–69; Robert F. Bauman, "Kansas, Canada, or Starvation," *ibid.*, 36 (Sept., 1952), pp. 287–99; Alpheus Felch, "The Indians of Michigan and the Cession of Their Lands to the United States by Treaties," *Michigan Pioneer and Historical Collections*, 16 (1894–95), pp. 274–97.

18. Claude S. Larzalere, "The Red Man in Michigan," *Michigan History*, 17 (Summer–Autumn, 1933), p. 373. The figure of 16,012 for Michigan's 1970 Indian population is found in the final report of the Census Bureau on American Indians. However, in its final report on population, it lists Michigan's Indian population as 16,854. Bureau of Census, *1970 Census of Population: Subject Reports, American Indians;* Bureau of Census, *1970 Census of Population: Characteristics of the Population*, vol. I, *United States Summary*, section 1, p. 293.

19. Alan S. Brown, "William Austin Burt: Michigan's Master Surveyor," *Papers of the Michigan Academy of Science, Arts, and Letters,* 47 (1962), pp. 263–74; Knox Jamison, "The Survey of the Public Lands in Michigan," *Michigan History,* 42 (June, 1958), pp. 197–214.

20. Malcolm J. Rohrbough, *The Land Office Business: The Settlement and Administration of American Public Lands, 1789–1837* (New York, 1968), pp. 257–58.

21. Quoted in Bald, *Michigan in Four Centuries,* p. 144.

22. Madison Kuhn, "Tiffin, Morse, and the Reluctant Pioneer," *Michigan History,* 50 (June, 1966), pp. 111–38. In recent years, the geographer, Bernard C. Peters, has presented evidence that indicates that an unfavorable image concerning conditions in Michigan may not have been an entirely negligible factor in retarding settlement. See Peters, "The Remaking of an Image: The Propaganda Campaign to Attract Settlers to Michigan, 1815–1840," *The Geographical Survey,* 3 (Jan., 1974), pp. 25–52.

23. B. Frank Emery, "Fort Saginaw," *Michigan History,* 30 (July–Sept., 1946), pp. 476–503; R. Carlyle Buley, *The Old Northwest: Pioneer Period, 1815–1840,* 1 (Indianapolis, 1950), p. 242.

24. The true source of the Mississippi, Lake Itasca, was discovered by an expedition led by Henry R. Schoolcraft in 1832. See Philip P. Mason, ed., *Expedition to Lake Itasca: The Discovery of the Source of the Mississippi* (East Lansing, 1958).

25. Schoolcraft's most extensive work was his *Historical and Statistical Information Respecting the History, Condition and Prospects of the Indian Tribes of the United States* (Philadelphia, 1851–57).

26. Floyd R. Dain, *Every House a Frontier* (Detroit, 1956), p. 9.

27. Willis F. Dunbar, "The Erie Canal and the Settlement of Michigan," *Detroit Historical Society Bulletin,* 21 (Nov., 1964), pp. 4–10.

28. George N. Fuller, *The Economic and Social Beginnings of Michigan* (Lansing, 1916), p. 76.

29. Quoted in *ibid.,* p. 77.

30. George Taylor, "First Visit to Michigan," *Michigan Pioneer and Historical Collections,* 6 (1884), p. 16.

31. Buley, *The Old Northwest,* 2:461.

32. Carl E. Pray, "An Historic Michigan Road," *Michigan History,* 11 (July, 1927), p. 338.

CHAPTER 9

1. The partial or complete text of this song has appeared in a number of publications, including Paul H. Johnstone, "Old Ideals Versus New Ideas in Farm Life," *The Yearbook of Agriculture, 1940* (Washington, 1940), pp. 129–30fn.

2. Rohrbough, *The Land Office Business,* pp. 241–48.

3. Douglas H. Gordon and George S. May, eds., "Michigan Journal, 1836, John M. Gordon," *Michigan History,* 43 (March, 1959), pp. 1–42; 43 (June, 1959), pp. 124–49; 43 (Sept., 1959), pp. 257–93; 43 (Dec., 1959), pp. 433–78.

4. James H. Lanman, *History of Michigan, From Its Earliest Colonization to the Present Time* (New York, 1841), pp. 15–24.

5. Albert F. Butler, "Rediscovering Michigan's Prairies," *Michigan History,* 31 (Sept., 1947) pp. 267–86; 32 (March, 1948), pp. 15–36; 33 (June, 1949), pp. 117–30; 33 (Sept., 1949), 220–31. Scattered remnants of prairie land that had survived as part of the Amtrack railroad's right-of-way in Cass, Berrien, and Van Buren counties were preserved in 1978 by an agreement between the railroad and con-

servation groups, headed by Margaret Kohring, a botanist in Niles, to prevent the destruction of the ecosystem in these prairies. Ann Arbor *News*, 24 September 1978.

6. James Fenimore Cooper's novel, *The Oak-Openings*, is set in Michigan. For a discussion of what constituted an oak opening, and its difference from a prairie, see Bernard C. Peters, "No Trees on the Prairie: Persistence of Error in Landscape Terminology," *Michigan History*, 54 (Spring, 1970), pp. 19–28, and Peters, "Pioneer Evaluation of the Kalamazoo County Landscape," *Michigan Academician*, 3 (Fall, 1970), pp. 15–25.

7. For the dates and circumstances of the establishment of Michigan's counties, see William L. Jenks, "History and Meaning of the County Names of Michigan," *Michigan Pioneer and Historical Collections*, 38 (1912), pp. 439–77. For dates of county organization and the census of 1837 by townships, see Fuller, *Economic and Social Beginnings of Michigan*, pp. 531–39.

8. John T. Blois, *Gazeteer of the State of Michigan* (Detroit, 1838), is a valuable source on early settlements. It has been reprinted on numerous occasions, most recently by the Arno Press of the *New York Times* in 1975.

9. The restored pioneer village at New Salem, Illinois, provides a good idea of the structure of earlier log cabins. There are also a number of restored log cabins in Michigan. For a classic discussion of this, and subsequent forms of pioneer building styles, see William Nowlin's *The Bark-Covered House, or Pioneer Life in Michigan*, originally published in 1876, reprinted in *Michigan Pioneer and Historical Collections*, 4 (1881), pp. 480–541, and reprinted in a paperback edition in recent years by Nowlin's hometown Dearborn Historical Society.

10. Dunbar, *Kalamazoo and how it grew*, pp. 71–72.

11. R. Carlyle Buley, "Pioneer Health and Medical Practices in the Old Northwest Prior to 1840," *Mississippi Valley Historical Review*, 30 (March, 1934), pp. 497–520. See also Madge E. Pickard and R. Caryle Buley, *The Midwest Pioneer: His Ills, Cures, and Doctors* (Crawfordsville, Ind., 1945).

12. Wallace J. Bonk, "The Botanic Luminary, a Michigan Incunabulum," *Michigan Alumnus Quarterly Review*, 67 (Feb. 25, 1961), pp. 77–84. See also Pickard and Buley, *The Midwest Pioneer*, and Fannie J. Anderson, *Doctors Under Three Flags* (Detroit, 1951). Medical doctors in this period also sometimes doubled as dentists. For the history of dentistry in Michigan, see Robert M. Warner, *Profile of a Profession: A History of the Michigan State Dental Association* (Detroit, 1964).

13. Buley, *The Old Northwest*, 1:271.

14. *Ibid.*, 1:332–33.

15. Emelyn E. Gardner and Geraldine J. Chickering, *Ballads and Songs of Southern Michigan* (Ann Arbor, 1939). See also Caroline M. Kirkland, writing under the pseudonym of Mrs. Mary Clavers, *A New Home—Who'll Follow? or, Glimpses of Western Life*. Originally published in 1839, this description of pioneer life in Michigan by a cultivated eastern woman is one of the finest portrayals of the new settlements when Michigan was young. An excerpt from this work is reprinted in May and Brinks, eds., *A Michigan Reader*, pp. 219–29. See also John C. McCloskey, "Jacksonian Democracy in Mrs. Kirkland's *A New Home—Who'll Follow?*" *Michigan History*, 45 (Dec., 1961), pp. 347–52.

16. Catlin, *The Story of Detroit*, pp. 261–63, 289–294.

17. Clarence M. Burton, "Detroit in the Year 1832," *Michigan Pioneer and Historical Collections*, 28 (1898), pp. 163–71.

18. Charles E. Rosenberg, *The Cholera Years: The United States in 1832, 1849, 1866* (Chicago, 1962); Robert C. Kedzie, *The Cholera in Kalamazoo*, edited by Alexis Praus (Kalamazoo, 1961).

19. For sidelights on the Detroit of the 1820s and 1830s, see "Detroit Half a Century Ago," and William Phelps, "Reminiscences of Detroit," and several short articles following this article, in *Michigan Pioneer and Historical Collections,* 4 (1881), pp. 89–96 and 459–79.

CHAPTER 10

1. Frank B. Woodford and Albert Hyma, *Gabriel Richard, Frontier Ambassador* (Detroit, 1958), pp. 101–141.

2. See the letters of Lucius Lyon in *Michigan Pioneer and Historical Collections,* 27 (1896), pp. 412–604.

3. The laws passed by the Council are included in *Laws of the Territory of Michigan,* published in four volumes between 1871 and 1884.

4. Members of the six legislative councils are listed in *Michigan Manual, 1977–1978,* pp. 105–107.

5. William Jenny, "Governors of Michigan Territory," *Michigan Pioneer and Historical Collections,* 3 (1881), pp. 119–20. Bela Hubbard, *Memorials of Half a Century* (New York, 1887), is a valuable source for this period. For official records of the territorial period, see Clarence E. Carter, ed., *Territorial Papers of the United States, Michigan Territory,* volumes 10, 11, and 12 (Washington, 1942–45), and volumes 36 and 37 of *Michigan Pioneer and Historical Collections.* See also Clifford I. Tobias, "Henry D. Gilpin: 'Governor In and Over the Territory of Michigan,'" *Michigan History,* 59 (Fall, 1975), pp. 153–70.

6. Cass was absent from the territory when the act was passed. Even today those who attempt to pronounce the word vary in their renderings: Cath-ol-eh-pist-eem-ead seems to be the most popular.

7. Egbert R. Isbell, "The Catholepistemiad, or University, of Michigania," in *University of Michigan Historical Essays* (Ann Arbor, 1937), pp. 159–82; Wilfred B. Shaw, ed., *The University of Michigan: An Encyclopedic Survey,* Part 1 (Ann Arbor, 1942), pp. 3–38.

8. Because of this action, the University of Michigan at Ann Arbor (which was the ultimate recipient of these lands) awarded five separate scholarships for Indians in 1932. Bald, *Michigan in Four Centuries,* p. 179 fn. However, in the late 1970s a lawsuit filed against the university by Indian groups demanded more expanded special treatment. See footnote 14 in Chapter 8 above.

9. Floyd R. Dain, *Education in the Wilderness* (Lansing, 1968), pp. 126–43; Willis F. Dunbar, *The Michigan Record in Higher Education* (Detroit, 1963), pp. 36–39.

10. Several vivid accounts of pioneer schools were written by A. D. P. Van-Buren. See "The Log-Schoolhouse Era," *Michigan Pioneer and Historical Collections,* 14 (1890), pp. 283–402; "The Old Academy and Seminary, the Classic Schools of our Pioneer Days," *ibid.,* 18 (1892), pp. 397–411; and "A Quarter-Century of Teaching," *ibid.,* 10 (1888), pp. 24–32.

11. The *Forty-fourth Annual Report of the Superintendent of Public Instruction for the Year 1880* (Lansing, 1881), includes a lengthy section on the history of education in Michigan, pp. 297–453.

12. Paré, *The Catholic Church in Detroit,* pp. 141–278.

13. Silas Farmer, *History of Detroit and Michigan* (Detroit, 1884), p. 715.

14. E. H. Pilcher, *History of Protestantism in Michigan* (Detroit, 1878), pp. 16, 56, 88, 109, 115, 129, 175–78. A more recent account is Margaret B. Macmillan's *The Methodist Church in Michigan: Nineteenth Century* (Grand Rapids, 1967).

15. M. E. D. Trowbridge, *History of the Baptists in Michigan* (Detroit, 1909); Coe Haynes, *Baptist Trail-makers in Michigan* (Philadelphia, 1936).

16. R. C. Crawford, "Reminiscences of Pioneer Ministers in Michigan," *Michigan Pioneer and Historical Collections,* 17 (1892), pp. 226–38.

17. Colin B. Goodykoontz, *Home Missions on the American Frontier, with Particular Reference to the American Home Missionary Society* (Caldwell, Idaho, 1939).

18. Many of these letters are reproduced in Maurice Cole, ed., *Voices in the Wilderness* (Ann Arbor, 1961).

19. C. C. Trowbridge, "History of the Episcopal Church in Michigan," *Michigan Pioneer and Historical Collections,* 3 (1881), pp. 213–21.

20. Farmer, *History of Detroit and Michigan,* p. 671.

21. Catlin, *The Story of Detroit,* pp. 286–87.

22. Douglas C. McMurtrie, *Early Printing in Michigan, with a Bibliography of the Issues of the Michigan Press, 1796–1850* (Chicago, 1931); William Stocking, "Prominent Newspaper Men in Michigan," *Michigan Pioneer and Historical Collections,* 39 (1915), pp. 155–69; Tom S. Applegate, "A History of the Press in Michigan," *Michigan Pioneer and Historical Collections,* 6 (1884), pp. 62–98.

23. Frank Luther Mott, *American Journalism: A History of Newspapers in the United States through 260 Years, 1690 to 1950* (New York, 1950), p. 169.

24. Quoted in *ibid.,* p. 168.

25. Farmer, *History of Detroit and Michigan,* p. 354.

26. Note in *Michigan History,* 24 (Spring, 1940), pp. 289–90.

27. Buley, *The Old Northwest,* 2:574.

28. Detroit *Free Press,* 9 August 1837.

29. Emil Lorch, "The Development of Architecture," *Michigan, A Guide to the Wolverine State* (New York, 1941), pp. 164–73.

30. Howell Taylor, "Michigan's Pioneer Architecture," *Michigan History,* 37 (March, 1953), pp. 19–26. See also Wayne Andrews, *Architecture in Michigan* (Detroit, 1967).

31. Clyde H. Burroughs, "Painting and Sculpture in Michigan," *Michigan History,* 20 (Autumn, 1936), pp. 395–409; 21 (Winter, 1937), pp. 39–54; and 21 (Spring, 1937), pp. 141–57.

CHAPTER 11

1. George N. Fuller, ed., *Messages of the Governors of Michigan,* 1 (Lansing, 1925) pp. 121–24.

2. The text of the 1835 constitution can be found in Floyd B. Streeter, *Political Parties in Michigan, 1837–1860* (Lansing, 1918), pp. 295–311. The proceedings of the convention of 1835 are in *Journal of the Proceedings of the Convention to form a Constitution for the State of Michigan* (Detroit, 1835). See also Harold M. Dorr, "The Michigan Constitution of 1835," *Papers of the Michigan Academy of Science, Arts, and Letters,* 19 (Ann Arbor, 1934), pp. 441–57.

3. Kent Sagendorph, *Stevens Thomson Mason, Misunderstood Patriot* (New York, 1947), pp. 207–211.

4. Clark F. Norton, "Michigan Statehood, 1835, 1836, or 1837?" *Michigan History,* 36 (Dec. 1952), pp. 321–50.

5. Several of the maps at that time, all showing the southern tip of Lake Michigan further north than it actually is, may be found in Louis C. Karpinski, *Bibliography of the Printed Maps of Michigan, 1804–1880* (Lansing, 1931), pp. 186ff. The story of the hunter is told in Claude S. Larzelere, "The Boundaries of Michigan," *Michigan Pioneer and Historical Collections,* 30 (1906), p. 13.

6. Annah May Soule, "The Southern and Western Boundaries of Michigan," *Michigan Pioneer and Historical Collections,* 27 (1897), p. 849.

7. Wade Millis, "When Michigan Was Born," *Michigan History,* 18 (Summer-Autumn, 1934), pp. 208–224.

8. Carl Wittke, "The Ohio-Michigan Boundary Dispute Re-examined," *Ohio Archaeological and Historical Society Quarterly,* 45 (Oct., 1936), pp. 299–319.

9. Buley, *The Old Northwest,* 2:201 fn.

10. See for example Bruce Catton, *Michigan: A Bicentennial History* (New York, 1976), p. 92, and Sommers, ed., *Atlas of Michigan,* pp. 115, 116. Discussions which continued for many years after Michigan became a state sought to promote the formation of a new state of Superior, composed of the Upper Peninsula, northern Wisconsin, and northeastern Minnesota. See Charles E. Twining, "The Long Lost State of Superior," *Wisconsin Magazine of History,* 61 (Winter, 1977–78), pp. 91–111. These discussions were unrelated to the semi-serious movement promoted by a few residents of the Upper Peninsula in the 1970s to make that area into the fifty-first state.

11. In 1926, the United States Supreme Court had dealt with a dispute between Michigan and Wisconsin over their boundary, although certain questions regarding the location of this boundary remained unresolved until 1936. George N. Fuller, ed., *Michigan: A Centennial History of the State and Its People,* 1 (Chicago, 1939), pp. 242–43.

CHAPTER 12

1. Harry J. Carman and Harold C. Syrett, *A History of the American People,* 1 (New York, 1952), p. 384.

2. Alpheus Felch, "Early Banks and Banking in Michigan," *Michigan Pioneer and Historical Collections,* 2 (1880), pp. 111–14.

3. Henry M. Utley, "The Wildcat Banking System in Michigan," *Michigan Pioneer and Historical Collections,* 5 (1884), pp. 209–22. See also Arthur M. Woodford, *Detroit and Its Banks: The Story of Detroit Bank & Trust* (Detroit, 1974), pp. 35–62.

4. "A Trip from Utica, New York, to Ingham County, Michigan," *Michigan Pioneer and Historical Collections,* 1 (1877), p. 190.

5. L. Benj. Reber, *History of St. Joseph* (St. Joseph, n. d.), p. 17.

6. Bela Hubbard, "A Michigan Geological Expedition in 1837," *Michigan Pioneer and Historical Collections,* 3 (1881), p. 200.

7. A provision in the bill approved January 26, 1837, permitted Michigan to receive the first quarterly payment of the distribution although its status as of January 1 was still that of a territory.

8. Lew Allen Chase, "Michigan's Share in the Establishment of Improved Transportation Between the East and the West," *Michigan Pioneer and Historical Collections,* 38 (1912), p. 596.

9. Fuller, *Economic and Social Beginnings of Michigan,* p. 79; *Laws of the Territory of Michigan,* 3:844.

10. Catlin, *The Story of Detroit,* p. 365. For more detail on these and other early railroad developments, see Willis F. Dunbar, *All Aboard: A History of Railroads in Michigan* (Grand Rapids, 1969), pp. 13–28.

11. Mrs. Frank P. Dodge, "Marking Terminus of Erie and Kalamazoo Railroad," *Michigan Pioneer and Historical Collections,* 38 (1912), pp. 491–98; and Clarence Frost, "The Early Railroads of Southern Michigan," *ibid.,* 38:498–501.

12. According to Lawrence Lambert, president of the Erie and Kalamazoo,

the company, as of August, 1978, had had no income since the bankruptcy of Penn Central. Through legal channels it was pressing its claims for compensation from Penn Central and it was also awaiting the promised payment of $188,000 from Conrail for the use of its tracks. However, Lambert, the major stockholder in the company, declared that he intended to keep the company in existence, regardless of the outcome of these proceedings. Telephone conversation with Lambert on August 18, 1978.

13. Edward W. Barber, "The Vermontville Colony: Its Genesis and History...," *Michigan Pioneer and Historical Collections,* 28 (1900), p. 198.

14. Robert J. Parks, *Democracy's Railroads: Public Enterprise in Jacksonian Michigan* (Port Washington, N. Y., 1972), p. 223.

15. Theodore E. Potter, "A Boy's Story of Pioneer Life in Michigan," *Michigan Pioneer and Historical Collections,* 35 (1907), pp. 394–95; Catlin, *The Story of Detroit,* pp. 370–71. Potter's boyhood reminiscences are part of an autobiography which was published by his family in 1913 and was reprinted in 1978 by the Historical Society of Michigan and Hardscrabble Books of Berrien Springs as the first in a series of Michigan Heritage Library Reprints.

16. J. N. Ingersoll, "The Clinton and Kalamazoo Canal Celebration," *Michigan Pioneer and Historical Collections,* 5 (1882), pp. 469–71.

17. O. C. Comstock, "Internal Improvements," *Michigan Pioneer and Historical Collections,* 1 (1877), p. 46.

18. Parks, *Democracy's Railroads,* pp. 186–87.

19. William L. Jenks, "Michigan's Five-Million Dollar Loan," *Michigan History,* 15 (Autumn, 1931), pp. 575–633.

20. Hubbard, *Memorials of Half a Century,* p. 103.

21. William W. Upton, "Locating the Capital of the State of Michigan," *Michigan History,* 23 (Summer, 1939), pp. 275–90; Frank E. Robson, "How Lansing Became the Capital," *Michigan Pioneer and Historical Collections,* 11 (1888), pp. 237–43; Ellen C. Hathaway, *Your Capitol and Mine: A Story of Michigan's Government for Young Readers* (Lansing, 1953), pp. 44–45.

22. Catlin, *The Story of Detroit,* pp. 338–42; Neil F. Morrison, "The Battle of Fighting Island and Pelee Island," *Michigan History,* 48 (Sept., 1964), pp. 227–32.

23. George C. Bates, "Reminiscences of the Brady Guards," *Michigan Pioneer and Historical Collections,* 13 (1889), pp. 530–46.

CHAPTER 13

1. W. V. Smith, "The Puritan Blood of Michigan," *Michigan Pioneer and Historical Collections,* 38 (1912), pp. 355–61.

2. J. Harold Stevens, "The Influence of New England in Michigan," *Michigan History,* 19 (Autumn, 1935), pp. 351–52. See also Stewart H. Holbrook, *The Yankee Exodus: An Account of Migration from New England* (New York, 1950), pp. 77–96; and Morris C. Taber, "New England Influence in South Central Michigan," *Michigan History,* 45 (Dec., 1961), pp. 305–36.

3. Jo Ellen Vinyard, "Inland Urban Immigrants: The Detroit Irish, 1850," *Michigan History,* 57 (Summer, 1973), pp. 121–39. See also Ms. Vinyard's expanded treatment of this entire subject in *The Irish on the Urban Frontier: Detroit, 1850–1880* (New York, 1976).

4. Carl Wittke, *History of Canada* (New York, 1928), pp. 134–49.

5. John A. Russell, *The Germanic Influence in the Making of Michigan* (Detroit, 1927); Mark O. Kistler, "The German Theater in Detroit," *Michigan History,* 47 (Dec., 1963), pp. 289–300. For a German visitor's account of German settle-

ments in Michigan in the 1830s, see "Karl Neidhard's Reise Nach Michigan," reprinted in May and Brinks, eds., *A Michigan Reader,* pp. 235–39.

6. William L. Jenks, "Michigan Immigration," *Michigan History,* 28 (Jan.–Mar., 1944), pp. 67–100.

7. Arnold Mulder, *Americans from Holland* (Philadelphia, 1947), p. 118.

8. Kedzie, *The Cholera in Kalamazoo.*

9. Martin L. D'Ooge, "The Dutch Pioneers of Michigan," *Michigan Pioneer and Historical Collections,* 38 (1912), pp. 204–12. The literature on the Dutch in Michigan is probably greater than that for any other single group of settlers. For a sampling of these materials, see the series of articles that were published in *Michigan History,* 31 (Dec., 1947), pp. 353–416, at the time of the centennial of the founding of Holland, Michigan, and two brief items in May and Brinks, eds., *A Michigan Reader,* pp. 228–34.

10. William B. Gates, Jr., *Michigan Copper and Boston Dollars* (Cambridge, Mass., 1951), pp. 95–96; Lew Allen Chase, "Michigan's Upper Peninsula," *Michigan History,* 20 (Autumn, 1936), p. 327; Peter White, "The Iron Region of Lake Superior," *Michigan Pioneer and Historical Collections,* 8 (1886), p. 152.

11. Bald, *Michigan in Four Centuries,* pp. 232–34.

12. Angus Murdoch, *Boom Copper: The Story of the First U. S. Mining Boom* (New York, 1943); Robert J. Hybels, "Lake Superior Copper Fever, 1841–47," *Michigan History,* 34 (June 1950), pp. 97–120; 34 (Sept., 1950), pp. 224–45; 34 (Dec., 1950), pp. 309–27.

13. Lew Allen Chase, "Early Days of Michigan Mining: Pioneering Land Sales and Surveys," *Michigan History,* 29 (Apr.–June, 1945), pp. 166–79.

14. Donald Chaput, *The Cliff: America's First Copper Mine* (Kalamazoo, 1971), p. 54.

15. The spelling "Minesota" is reputed to have come from a clerical error made in a charter application. Legally, however, this became the correct spelling once the charter was issued.

16. David S. Coon, "The Quincy Mine," *Michigan History,* 24 (Winter, 1940), pp. 91–103; William H. Pyne, "Quincy Mine: The Old Reliable," *Michigan History,* 41 (June, 1957), pp. 219–44; Anthony S. Wax, "The Calumet and Hecla Copper Mine," *Michigan History,* 16 (Winter, 1932), pp. 5–41.

17. Brown, "William Austin Burt: Michigan's Master Surveyor," *Papers of the Michigan Academy,* 47:263–75; Horace E. Burt, "William Austin Burt, Inventor," *Michigan History,* 6 (No. 1, 1922), pp. 175–93; Scott Cannon, "The Life and Times of William A. Burt," *Michigan Pioneer and Historical Collections,* 5 (1884), pp. 115–23.

18. Philo M. Everett, "Recollections of the Early Explorations and Discovery of Iron Ore on Lake Superior," *Michigan Pioneer and Historical Collections,* 11 (1888), pp. 161–74. In this account, Everett does not acknowledge the debt to Marji-Gesick. See Harlan Hatcher, *A Century of Iron and Men* (Indianapolis, 1950), pp. 32–34; and Ralph D. Williams, *The Honorable Peter White* (Cleveland, 1907), pp. 22–23. Robert Traver, *Laughing Whitefish* (New York, 1965), is a fictional account of Marji-Gesick and his daughter's claim. For the case on which the novel is based, see Charlotte Kobogum, et al., v. The Jackson Iron Company, *Michigan Reports,* 76 (Chicago, 1890), pp. 498–510. The spelling of the daughter's name, like that of the father's, varies greatly.

19. Ray A. Brotherton, "The Discovery of Iron Ore: Negaunee Centennial, 1844–1944," *Michigan History,* 28 (Apr.–June, 1944), pp. 199–213.

20. Herbert Brinks, *Peter White* (Grand Rapids, 1970); White, "The Iron Region of Lake Superior," *Michigan Pioneer and Historical Collections,* 8:145–61.

21. Walter Havighurst, *Vein of Iron: The Pickands-Mather Story* (New York, 1958).

22. Charles Moore, ed., *The Saint Mary's Falls Canal . . . Semi-centennial Celebration* (Detroit, 1907), pp. 91–129; F. Clever Bald, *The Sault Canal Through 100 Years, Sault Ste. Marie, Michigan* (Ann Arbor, 1954); Clark F. Norton, "Early Movement for the St. Mary's Falls Ship Canal," *Michigan History*, 39 (Sept., 1955), pp. 257–80. Some authorities assert that Harvey claimed too much credit for building the canal and that actual construction was completed largely through the efforts of John W. Brooks. See Ernest H. Rankin, "Lake Superior—1854," *Inland Seas*, 19 (Winter, 1963), pp. 311–17.

23. Philip P. Mason, ed., "The Operation of the Sault Canal, 1857," *Michigan History*, 39 (March, 1955), pp. 69–80.

24. Manitou County, consisting of the Manitou, Beaver, and Fox islands, was organized in 1855. In 1895, however, the county was dissolved and these islands were attached to Leelanau County.

25. John Van Oosten, "Michigan's Commercial Fisheries of the Great Lakes," *Michigan History*, 22 (Winter, 1938), pp. 107–43.

26. George A. Cuthbertson, *Freshwater: A History and a Narrative of the Great Lakes* (Toronto, 1931), and Walter Havighurst, *The Long Ships Passing* (New York, 1942), are among the numerous books that deal with Great Lakes shipping history.

27. Reber, *History of St. Joseph*, p. 65.

28. *Ibid.*, p. 69. The quotation in the preceding paragraph is found in *ibid.*, p. 67.

29. Alvin F. Harlow, *The Road of the Century: The Story of the New York Central* (New York, 1947), pp. 218–20.

30. *Ibid.*, pp. 220–23; Arthur S. Hill, "The Romance of a Railway," *Michigan History*, 23 (Winter, 1939), pp. 53–75.

31. Charles Hirschfeld, "The Great Railroad Conspiracy," *Michigan History*, 36 (June, 1952), pp. 97–219. The article was published as a book, under this same title, in 1953.

32. Harlow, *The Road of the Century*, pp. 245–80.

33. John T. Percival, "Railroads in Ottawa County," *Michigan Pioneer and Historical Collections*, 9 (1886), pp. 270–79.

34. Thomas D. Brock, "Paw Paw Versus the Railroads," *Michigan History*, 39 (June, 1955), pp. 130–31.

35. Stanley B. Smith, "Notes on the Village of Schoolcraft in 1850," *Michigan History*, 40 (June, 1956), pp. 146–47.

36. Hirschfeld, "The Great Railroad Conspiracy," *Michigan History*, 36:216–17.

37. Edmund A. Calkins, "Railroads of Michigan since 1850," *Michigan History*, 13 (Winter, 1929), pp. 5–25.

38. Harriet Martineau, *Society in America*, 1 (London, 1837), pp. 245ff.

39. Robert L. Thompson, *Wiring a Continent: The History of the Telegraph Industry in the United States, 1832–1866* (Princeton, 1947).

40. Ralph R. Tingley, "Postal Service in Michigan Territory," *Michigan History*, 35 (Dec., 1951), pp. 447–60; Alvin F. Harlow, *Old Post Bags* (New York, 1928).

41. Stocking, "Prominent Newspaper Men in Michigan," *Michigan Pioneer and Historical Collections*, 39:155–68; Justin E. Walsh, "Radically and Thoroughly Democratic: Wilbur F. Storey and The *Detroit Free Press*," *Michigan History*, 47 (Sept., 1963), pp. 193–225.

42. McMurtrie, *Early Printing in Michigan.*

43. Kistler, "The German Theater in Detroit," *Michigan History,* 17:289–301.

CHAPTER 14

1. Exactly how much each man contributed has been a matter of some controversy. See John C. Patterson, "Marshall Men and Marshall Measures in State and National History," *Michigan Pioneer and Historical Collections,* 38 (1912), pp. 220–44.

2. Ellwood P. Cubberly, *The History of Education* (Boston, 1920), pp. 687–88. Dain, *Education in the Wilderness,* covers the entire period of Crary and Pierce's educational activities.

3. For a brief biographical comment on Crary, see O. C. Comstock, "Hon. Isaac E. Crary," *Michigan Pioneer and Historical Collections,* 14 (1890), pp. 280–83.

4. George W. Knight, *History and Management of Land Grants for Education in the Northwest Territory, Papers* of the American Historical Association, vol. 1, no. 3 (New York, 1885).

5. R. Clyde Ford, "The Life and Work of John D. Pierce," *Michigan Pioneer and Historical Collections,* 35 (1907), pp. 295–308; Charles O. Hoyt and R. Clyde Ford, *John D. Pierce* (Ypsilanti, 1905). Cubberly, *The History of Education,* devotes several pages to Mann and Barnard but does not mention Pierce.

6. John D. Pierce, "Origin and Progress of the Michigan School System," *Michigan Pioneer and Historical Collections,* 1 (1877), pp. 37–45.

7. Francis W. Shearman, *System of Public Instruction and Primary School Law of Michigan* (Lansing, 1852), pp. 23–37.

8. *Ibid.,* pp. 32–33.

9. *Ibid.,* p. 32.

10. Willis F. Dunbar, "The University and Its Branches," *Michigan Alumnus Quarterly Review,* 46 (July 20, 1940), pp. 303–15.

11. Archie P. Nevins, "The Kalamazoo Case," *Michigan History,* 44 (Mar., 1960), pp. 91–100.

12. Van Buren, "The Log Schoolhouse Era," *Michigan Pioneer and Historical Collections,* 14:283–402.

13. Charles T. Perry, *Henry Philip Tappan* (Ann Arbor, 1933).

14. Egbert R. Isbell, *A History of Eastern Michigan University, 1849–1965* (Ypsilanti, 1971).

15. Madison Kuhn, *Michigan State: The First Hundred Years* (East Lansing, 1955); Paul W. Gates, "The Morrill Act and Early Agricultural Science," *Michigan History,* 46 (Dec., 1962), pp. 289–302.

CHAPTER 15

1. Gilbert H. Barnes, *The Antislavery Inpulse, 1830–1844* (New York, 1933), emphasizes the importance of Finney's role in the reform movements of this period. Streeter, *Political Parties in Michigan,* and Ronald P. Formisano, *The Birth of Mass Political Parties: Michigan, 1827–1861* (Princeton, 1971), the principal sources for the politics of this era, discuss these reform impulses in the context of Michigan politics.

2. A. D. P. Van Buren, "Temperance in Pioneer Days...," *Michigan Pioneer and Historical Collections,* 5 (1884), pp. 426–32, and Van Buren, "Our Temperance Conflict," *ibid.,* 13 (1889), pp. 388–407.

3. Floyd B. Streeter, "History of Prohibition Legislation in Michigan," *Michigan History*, 2 (April, 1918), pp. 289–308; John Fitzgibbon, "King Alcohol, His Rise, Reign, and Fall in Michigan," *ibid.*, 2 (Oct., 1918), pp. 737–80.

4. Charles R. Starring, "Lucinda Hinsdale Stone: A Pioneer in the Education of Women in Michigan," *Michigan History*, 42 (March, 1958), pp. 85–97.

5. John and Audrey Cumming, "The Saints Come to Michigan," *Michigan History*, 49 (March, 1965), pp. 12–27.

6. Milo M. Quaife, *The Kingdom of St. James* (New Haven, 1930). See also George S. May, ed., *James Strang's Ancient and Modern Michilimackinac, Including an Account of the Controversy between Mackinac and the Mormons* (Mackinac Island, 1959); and Mark Strang, ed., *The Diary of James J. Strang* (East Lansing, 1961).

7. N. Gordon Thomas, "The Alphadelphian Experiment," *Michigan History*, 55 (Winter, 1971) pp. 205–16. Several other communitarian projects were launched in Michigan after 1860. The Ora Labora community existed in the Thumb area from 1862 to 1868. The Hiawatha Association maintained a community near Manistique in the 1890s, and the Sunrise Co-operative Farm Community existed in the Saginaw Valley in the 1930s. See Carl Wittke, "Ora et Labora, A German Methodist Utopia," *Ohio Historical Quarterly*, 58 (April, 1958), pp. 129–40; David C. Byers, with the assistance of Willis F. Dunbar, "Utopia in Upper Michigan," *Michigan Alumnus Quarterly Review*, 63 (Mar. 2, 1957), pp. 168–74; and Joseph J. Cohen, *In Quest of Heaven* (New York, 1957).

8. Mildred A. Danforth, *A Quaker Pioneer: Laura Haviland, Superintendent of the Underground* (New York, 1961); Merton L. Dillon, "Elizabeth Chandler and the Spread of Antislavery Sentiment to Michigan," *Michigan History*, 39 (Dec., 1955), pp. 481–94; Larry Gara, *The Liberty Line: The Legend of the Underground Railroad* (Lexington, 1961). An example of the post-war reminiscences concerning underground railroad activities in Michigan is found in May and Brinks, eds., *A Michigan Reader*, pp. 279–82.

9. The best account of the Crosswhite Case is John H. Yzenbaard, "The Crosswhite Case," *Michigan History*, 53 (Summer, 1969), pp. 131–43. For another fugitive slave case, see Benjamin C. Wilson, "Kentucky Kidnappers, Fugitives, and Abolitionists in Antebellum Cass County," *ibid.*, 60 (Winter, 1976), pp. 339–58.

10. In addition to Cass and Ford, other Michigan residents besides Birney have been candidates for President on third party tickets; for example, E. Harold Munn of Hillsdale ran on the Prohibition party ticket in 1964 and 1968.

11. Andrew C. McLaughlin, *Lewis Cass* (Boston, 1919), pp. 213–15; Willis F. Dunbar, *Lewis Cass* (Grand Rapids, 1970), pp. 58–59.

12. At this time and until 1913, United States Senators were elected by the legislature, not by popular vote.

13. Frederick D. Williams, "Robert McClelland and the Secession Crisis," *Michigan History*, 43 (June, 1959), pp. 155–64.

14. For brief biographical sketches of the governors, see Fuller, *Messages of the Governors*. For Zachariah Chandler, see Sister Mary Karl George, *Zachariah Chandler: A Political Biography* (East Lansing, 1969). On Stuart, see Anne McCain, "Charles Edward Stuart of Kalamazoo," *Michigan History*, 44 (Sept., 1960), pp. 324–35.

15. Alan R. Richards, "The Traditions of Government in the States," *The Forty-Eight States* (New York, 1955). For the convention proceedings see *Report of the Proceedings and Debates of the Convention to Revise the Constitution of the State of Michigan, 1850* (Lansing, 1850). The text of the 1850 Constitution may be found in Streeter, *Political Parties in Michigan*, pp. 316–50.

16. Formisano, *The Birth of Mass Political Parties*, pp. 213, 215, 270, 287–88,

discusses in more detail the intricacies of the "colored suffrage" issue, as Formisano calls it, using the terminology of the period, not modern usage. See also Ronald P. Pormisano, "The Edge of Caste: Colored Suffrage in Michigan, 1827–1861," *Michigan History,* 56 (Spring, 1972), pp. 19–41.

CHAPTER 16

1. Joel J. Orosz, "Lincoln comes to Kalamazoo," *Chronicle: The Magazine of the Historical Society of Michigan,* 14 (Summer, 1978), pp. 13–18, 25–30.

2. T. Maxwell Collier, "William H. Seward in the Campaign of 1860, with Special Reference to Michigan," *Michigan History,* 19 (Winter, 1935), pp. 91–106; Alan S. Brown, "Southwestern Michigan in the Campaign of 1860," *Michigan Heritage,* 2 (Winter, 1960), pp. 67–74; Streeter, *Political Parties in Michigan, 1837–1860,* pp. 283–92.

3. At this time, a voter had the opportunity to pick and choose among the six electors pledged to support each of the Presidential candidates rather than having to vote for an entire slate of electors as in more recent elections. Thus there was considerable variation in the vote totals of the candidates for electors for each of the parties on the 1860 ballot. The popular votes given for the Presidential candidates represent the average vote cast for the electors pledged to support these candidates in the subsequent vote of the electoral college.

4. George S. May, "Ann Arbor and the Coming of the Civil War," *Michigan History,* 36 (Sept., 1952), pp. 241–43.

5. John Robertson, comp., *Michigan in the War* (Lansing, 1880), pp. 17–21. For the chronology of these and other wartime developments, see George S. May, *Michigan and the Civil War Years, 1860–1866: A Wartime Chronicle* (Lansing, 1964).

6. May, "Ann Arbor and the Coming of the Civil War," *Michigan History,* 36:248–50; Dunbar, *Kalamazoo and how it grew,* p. 91.

7. Computations of the exact number of men from Michigan who served in the armed forces in the war vary greatly. The War Department in 1865 reported the number to be 90,048. The Michigan Adjutant General in 1882 computed the number as 90,747, but stated that this total did not include Michigan men who enlisted in the regiments of other states.

8. Irving I. Katz, *The Jewish Soldier from Michigan in the Civil War* (Detroit, 1962).

9. There is little agreement as to the exact number of Michigan men who lost their lives in the war. A "Roll of Honor" compiled by legislative order in 1869 contains the names of 14,855 men, but an authoritative compilation by Frederick H. Dyer in later years placed the number of fatalities at 14,753. See May, *Michigan and the Civil War Years,* p. 77.

10. Minnie Dubbs Millbrook, *A Study in Valor: Michigan Medal of Honor Winners in the Civil War* (Lansing, 1966).

11. George S. May, "The Adventures of John C. Pemberton on Mackinac Island," *Michigan History,* 49 (June, 1965), pp. 108–22.

12. Ida C. Brown, *Michigan Men in the Civil War,* Michigan Historical Collections *Bulletin 27* (Ann Arbor, 1977), lists 502 such collections containing an estimated 6,000 letters, diaries, and other papers of soldiers that are found in the Michigan Historical Collections. Numerous other collections of soldiers' materials are found in other Michigan depositories.

13. Betty Fladeland, "Alias Franklin Thompson," *Michigan History,* 42 (Dec., 1958), pp. 435–62; Betty Fladeland, "New Light on Sarah Emma Edmonds, Alias Frank Thompson," *ibid.,* 47 (Dec., 1963), pp. 357–63.

14. Michigan has no official state song, but "Michigan, my Michigan," to the tune of "O Tannenbaum," is the one most widely sung. In 1902, the poet Douglas McCulloch composed new words for the familiar tune, and these are the ones most generally used today. A different tune was widely promoted, but never caught on, partly because its range was too great. See Frederick Schneider, "'Michigan, My Michigan': Origin and History of This Noble State Song . . . ," *Michigan Pioneer and Historical Collections,* 35 (1907), pp. 155–69, for the story of the original song and a copy of all its verses.

15. Mrs. Raymond H. Millbrook, ed., *Michigan Women in the Civil War* (Lansing, 1963).

16. Richard H. Sewell, "Michigan Farmers and the Civil War," *Michigan History,* 44 (Dec., 1960), pp. 353–74.

17. *Ibid.,* p. 357.

18. Gates, *Michigan Copper and Boston Dollars,* pp. 15–18.

19. Herbert Brinks, "The Effect of the Civil War in 1861 on Michigan Lumbering and Mining Industries," *Michigan History,* 44 (March, 1960), pp. 103–105.

20. *Ibid.,* p. 106; Martin D. Lewis, *Lumberman from Flint: The Michigan Career of Henry H. Crapo, 1855–1869* (Detroit, 1958), p. 122.

21. Sidney Glazer, "The Beginnings of the Economic Revolution in Michigan," *Michigan History,* 34 (Sept., 1950), p. 194.

22. The constitutional question was resolved in November, 1866, when the voters, by a margin of 86,354 to 13,094, approved an amendment to the state constitution authorizing a soldiers' vote in future wars. May, *Michigan and the Civil War Years,* p. 74.

23. Blair's career is covered in a series of four articles by Jean Joy L. Fennimore that appeared in *Michigan History,* 48 (March, 1964), pp. 1–17; 48 (June, 1964), pp. 130–60; 49 (Sept., 1965), pp. 193–227; and 49 (Dec., 1965), pp. 344–69.

24. George S. May, "Parker Pillsbury and Wendell Phillips in Ann Arbor," *Michigan History,* 33 (June, 1949), pp. 155–61.

25. John C. Schneider, "Detroit and the Problem of Disorder: The Riot of 1863," *Michigan History,* 58 (Spring, 1974), pp. 5–24.

26. Harlan Hatcher, *Lake Erie* (Indianapolis, 1945), pp. 240–46.

CHAPTER 17

1. A board foot is a measure denoting a piece of wood one foot square and one inch thick.

2. *Michigan, A Guide to the Wolverine State,* p. 369.

3. See Clifford Allen, ed., *Michigan Log Marks* (East Lansing, 1941), and Ralph W. Stroebel, *Tittabawassee River Log Marks* (Saginaw, 1967).

4. Stewart Edward White's *The Riverman* (1908) is a novel that vividly portrays this phase of lumbering.

5. Rolland H. Maybee, *Michigan's White Pine Era, 1840–1900* (Lansing, 1960), pp. 37–43; Hudson Keenan, "America's First Successful Logging Railroad," *Michigan History,* 44 (Sept., 1962), pp. 292–302. Actually, although Gerrish probably deserves credit for popularizing the logging railroad, others had experimented with the technique earlier, including the logging activities of the Whittemore family in the Tawas City area as early as 1855. See Ruth B. Bordin, "A Michigan Lumbering Family," *Business History Review,* 34 (Spring, 1960), p. 70. This article is reprinted in Robert Warner and C. Warren VanderHill, eds., *A Michigan Reader, 1865 to the Present* (Grand Rapids, 1974), pp. 34–44.

6. *Portrait and Biographical Album, Mecosta County, Michigan* (Chicago, 1883), pp. 572ff. Hartwick Pines State Park includes a partial reconstruction of a lumber camp, along with other materials relating to Michigan lumbering.

7. Carl A. Leech, "Deward: A Lumberman's Ghost Town," *Michigan History,* 28 (Jan.–Mar., 1944), pp. 5–19; Ferris E. Lewis, "Frederick: A Typical Logging Village in the Twilight of the Lumbering Era," *ibid.,* 32 (Dec., 1948), pp. 321–39; 34 (Mar., 1950), pp. 35–49.

8. Stewart Holbrook, *Holy Old Mackinaw: A Natural History of the American Lumberjack* (New York, 1938). E. M. Beck, *Songs of the Michigan Lumberjack* (Ann Arbor, 1941), and *Lore of the Lumber Camps* (Ann Arbor, 1948), represent the fruits of the many years that Beck spent in collecting lumberjack ballads.

9. Holbrook, *Holy Old Mackinaw,* pp. 119–24.

10. See James Stevens, *The Saginaw Paul Bunyan* (New York, 1932).

11. John I. Bellaire, "Michigan's Lumberjacks," *Michigan History,* 26 (Spring, 1942), pp. 173–87; George B. Engberg, "Who Were the Lumberjacks?" *ibid.,* 32 (Sept., 1948), pp. 238–46. See also John W. Fitzmaurice, *The Shanty Boy, or Life in a Lumber Camp* (Cheboygan, 1889), reprinted in 1965 by the Central Michigan University Press.

12. Sections from biographies of Crapo and Sage and the article on Whittemore by Ruth Bordin are in Warner and Vanderhill, eds., *A Michigan Reader,* pp. 26–56.

13. Bob Boelio, "Muskegon Remembers Hackley," *Michigan Living/Motor News,* 61 (Aug., 1978), pp. 20–21, 36.

14. Utley and Cutcheon, *Michigan: As a Province, Territory and State,* 4:77–85; Douglas Griesemer, "American Red Cross in Michigan," *Michigan History,* 22 (Winter, 1938), pp. 5–18; Stewart H. Holbrook, *Burning an Empire: The Story of American Forest Fires* (New York, 1943), pp. 94–107.

CHAPTER 18

1. Samuel W. Durant, *History of Ingham and Eaton Counties, Michigan* (Philadelphia, 1880), p. 493.

2. Fuller, ed., *Centennial History of Michigan,* 2:44–45; Michigan Department of Natural Resources, *Mineral Industry of Michigan,* 1974 (Lansing, 1977), p. 17.

3. Fuller, ed., *Centennial History of Michigan,* 2:49–50; Dorr and Eschman, *Geology of Michigan,* pp. 125–26; *Michigan Statistical Abstract, 1978,* pp. 773–74.

4. Fuller, ed., *Centennial History of Michigan,* 2:17–24; William L. Webber, "Discovery and Development of the Salt Interest in the Saginaw Valley," *Michigan Pioneer and Historical Collections,* 4 (1883), pp. 13–22; *Mineral Industry of Michigan, 1974,* pp. 9–10; *Michigan Statistical Abstract, 1978,* pp. 773–74.

5. *Mineral Industry of Michigan, 1974,* pp. 10–13; Fuller, ed., *Centennial History of Michigan,* 2:27, 45–48; Darrell H. Pollard, "Michigan Oil and the New Deal," *Michigan History,* 43 (June, 1959), pp. 212–13; Lew Allan Chase, "Silver and Gold in Michigan," *ibid.,* 30 (Apr.–June, 1946), pp. 255–62.

6. Alfred B. Lindley, "The Copper Tariff of 1869," *Michigan History,* 35 (March, 1951), pp. 1–31; Charles B. Lawrence, "Keweena Portage," *ibid.,* 38 (March, 1954), pp. 45–64. Gates, *Michigan Copper and Boston Dollars,* provides the best over-all coverage.

7. Chaput, *The Cliff,* p. 76.

8. Pyne, "Quincy Mine: The Old Reliable," *Michigan History,* 41:219–42.

9. Willis F. Dunbar, "The Opera House as a Social Institution in Michigan," *Michigan History,* 27 (Oct.–Dec., 1943), pp. 661–72.

10. Murdoch, *Boom Copper,* pp. 153–59, reprinted in May and Brinks, eds., *A Michigan Reader,* pp. 247–52; William A. Sullivan, "The 1913 Revolt of the Michigan Copper Miners," *Michigan History,* 43 (Sept., 1959), pp. 294–314; William Beck, "Law and Order During the 1913 Copper Strike," *ibid.,* 54 (Winter, 1970), pp. 275–92. In the late 1950s, R. Allen Good, professor of history at Michigan Tech in Houghton, felt that the intense feelings regarding the 1913–14 strike still existing among residents of the Copper Country made it politically unwise for him to publish anything about this event.

11. Charles R. Cobb, "Ho! Gogebic County!" *Michigan History,* 6 (No. 2–3, 1922), pp. 328–45; Philip P. Mason, *Iron Ore Mining in Michigan Past and Present* (Lansing, 1958), p. 5; *Mineral Industry of Michigan, 1974,* p. 16.

12. Mason, *Iron Ore Mining in Michigan,* p. 8.

13. Clint Dunathan, "Fayette," *Michigan History,* 41 (June, 1957), pp. 204–208.

14. James Fisher, "Michigan's Cornish People," *Michigan History,* 29 (July–Sept., 1945), pp. 376–85. John Rowe, *The Hard-Rock Men: Cornish Immigrants and the North American Mining Frontier* (New York, 1974), is the best full-scale study.

15. Lindley, "The Copper Tariff of 1869," *Michigan History,* 35:4–5; Murdoch, *Boom Copper,* p. 121.

16. Pyne, "Quincy Mine: The Old Reliable," *Michigan History,* 41:228–29.

CHAPTER 19

1. Utley and Cutcheon, *Michigan: As a Province, Territory, and State,* 4:52–58. Much of the material on railroads in this chapter is based on Dunbar, *All Aboard: A History of Railroads in Michigan.*

2. Robert S. Henry, "The Railroad Land Grant Legend in American History Texts," reprinted in Vernon Carstenson, ed., *The Public Lands* (Madison, 1963), p. 135.

3. Calkins, "Railroads of Michigan since 1850," *Michigan History,* 13:5–26.

4. Brock, "Paw Paw Versus the Railroads," *Michigan History,* 39:129–83.

5. Lee Alilunas, "Michigan's Cut-over Canaan," *Michigan History,* 26 (Spring, 1942), pp. 188–201.

6. In the case of the Village of Elberta v. City of Frankfort (*347 Michigan Reports,* pp. 173–85), the Michigan Supreme Court, on December 6, 1956, upheld Elberta's contention that the land on which the carferry docks are located is within the village of Elberta.

7. See George W. Hilton, *The Great Lakes Car Ferries* (Berkeley, 1962).

8. "Historical Address, Delivered July Fourth, 1876, by the Hon. S. P. Ely of Marquette," *Michigan Pioneer and Historical Collections,* 7 (1886), p. 168.

9. Calkins, "Railroads of Michigan Since 1850," *Michigan History,* 13:8–10.

10. Havighurst, *Vein of Iron: The Pickands Mather Story,* pp. 95ff. Milo M. Quaife, *Lake Michigan* (Indianapolis, 1944), p. 167; Havighurst, *Long Ships Passing.*

11. Hatcher, *A Century of Iron and Men.*

12. Havighurst, *Vein of Iron: The Pickands Mather Story,* pp. 90–99.

13. Lew Allen Chase, "Michigan's Upper Peninsula," *Michigan History,* 20 (Autumn, 1936), pp. 327–28.

14. Daniel Drake, quoted in J. A. VanFleet, *Old and New Mackinac* (Ann Arbor, 1870), pp. 157–63.

15. *Marquette Centennial* (Marquette, 1949).

16. *The Tourist and Investor: An Illustrated Guide to the Lake Superior District* (Hancock, 1895).

17. *The Standard Guide, Mackinac Island and Northern Lake Resorts* (n. p., 1904).

18. Grand Rapids *Press,* 1 July 1912.

CHAPTER 20

1. Quoted in George S. May, *A Most Unique Machine: The Michigan Origins of the American Automobile Industry* (Grand Rapids, 1975), p. 81.

2. Harold H. Dunham, "Some Crucial Years of the General Land Office, 1875–1890," reprinted in Carstenson, ed., *The Public Lands,* p. 192. Sister Mary Karl George's *Zachariah Chandler: A Political Biography* was a long-awaited biography of this major politician.

3. Utley and Cutcheon, *Michigan: As a Province, Territory, and State,* 4:217–18. See also Earl D. Babst and Lewis G. Vander Velde, eds., *Michigan and the Cleveland Era* (Ann Arbor, 1948); John W. Lederle and Rita F. Aid, "Michigan State Party Chairmen: 1882–1956," *Michigan History,* 41 (Sept., 1957), pp. 257–68; and Robert Bolt, *Donald Dickinson* (Grand Rapids, 1970).

4. Charles R. Starring, in his "Hazen S. Pingree, Another Forgotten Eagle," *Michigan History,* 32 (June, 1948), pp. 129–49, depicted Pingree as a figure who had been unjustly neglected by historians. Melvin G. Holli, *Reform in Detroit: Hazen S. Pingree and Urban Politics* (New York, 1969), helped to put Pingree in better perspective.

5. Charles D. Rhodes, "William Rufus Shafter," *Michigan History,* 16 (Autumn, 1932), pp. 375–83.

6. Jaspar B. Reid, Jr., "Russell A. Alger as Secretary of War," *Michigan History,* 43 (June, 1959), pp. 225–39.

7. Thomas Powers, *Bolita mula Maynila (News from Manila),* Michigan Historical Collections *Bulletin No. 19* (Ann Arbor, 1971). The materials on the Philippines at the Michigan Historical Collections of the University of Michigan are the most extensive of any American research center.

8. Fuller, ed., *Messages of the Governors of Michigan,* 4:310. The message is reprinted in Warner and VanderHill, eds., *A Michigan Reader,* pp. 85–96.

CHAPTER 21

1. The manufacturing statistics from 1850 to 1900 are summarized in the *Twelfth Census of the United States, 1900,* vol. VIII, *Manufacturing,* Part II, p. 411. For a discussion of these statistics, see Glazer, "The Beginnings of the Economic Revolution in Michigan," *Michigan History,* 34:193–202; and Fuller, ed., *Centennial History of Michigan,* 1:526–30.

2. Farmer, *History of Detroit,* pp. 776–77.

3. "Gale Manufacturing Company," *Headlight, Albion Edition* (Chicago, 1895), pp. 18–20; "The Advance Thresher Co." and "The Nichols & Shepard Co.," *Headlight, Battle Creek Edition,* 2 (May, 1895), p. 36; Sidney Olson, *Young Henry Ford: A Picture History of the First Forty Years* (Detroit, 1963), pp. 23–24. *Headlight,* a railroad promotional magazine, is an invaluable source of information on business activities in a number of Michigan communities in the mid-nineties.

4. Gerald Carson, *Cornflake Crusade* (New York, 1957); Richard M. Schwarz, *John Harvey Kellogg, M. D.* (Nashville, 1970); Horace B. Powell, *The Original Has This Signature—W. K. Kellogg* (Englewood Cliffs, N. J., 1956).

5. Donald C. Thompson, "Grand Rapids—A furniture legend," *Chronicle, The Magazine of the Historical Society of Michigan,* 11 (Third Quarter, 1975), pp.

3–10; James S. Bradshaw, "Grand Rapids Furniture Beginnings," *Michigan History,* 52 (Winter, 1968), pp. 278–98; James S. Bradshaw, "Grand Rapids, 1870–1880: Furniture City Emerges," *ibid.,* 55 (Winter, 1971), pp. 321–42.

6. Report on the carriage industry in *17th Annual Report of the* [Michigan] *Bureau of Labor,* p. 65.

7. Carl Crow, *The City of Flint Grows Up* (New York, 1945), pp. 24–37; Lawrence R. Gustin, *Billy Durant: Creator of General Motors* (Grand Rapids, 1973), pp. 17–48.

8. Dunbar, *Kalamazoo and how it grew,* pp. 99–101, 118–19, 133–38.

9. George W. Stark, *The Huron Heritage: Fifty Years of Concrete Achievement by the Huron Portland Cement Company, 1907–1957* (n. p., n. d.), pp. 10–11.

10. Don Whitehead, *The Dow Story: The History of the Dow Chemical Company* (New York, 1968).

11. Esther R. Railton, "Marlborough," *Michigan History,* 48 (Sept., 1964), pp. 233–41; Stark, *The Huron Heritage.*

12. *Mineral Industry of Michigan, 1974,* p. 8.

13. Woodford and Woodford, *All Our Yesterdays,* pp. 206, 242. Detroit did not support its championship baseball team, however, and Stearns sold it in 1888 to buyers who moved it elsewhere.

14. Farmer, *History of Detroit,* p. 823; Reuben Borough, "Saturday Afternoon Town," *Michigan History,* 48 (June, 1964), pp. 120–22.

15. Leonard Engel, *Medicine Makers of Kalamazoo* (New York, 1961); Grand Rapids *Press,* 21 May 1978.

16. Arthur Pound, *Detroit: Dynamic City* (New York, 1940), pp. 236–42.

17. *Michigan and Its Resources* (Lansing, 1893), pp. 51, 187–91, summarizes the data for Michigan shipyards. Actually, although the Wayne County shipyards built more ships than any other area in the country, the tonnage of the ships produced in the Bay County shipyards exceeded that of the Detroit area shipbuilders.

18. Catlin, *The Story of Detroit,* pp. 493–99.

19. Woodford and Woodford, *All Our Yesterdays,* pp. 207–209; Dunbar, *Kalamazoo and how it grew,* p. 139–40; "The Round Oak Stove Works," *Headlight, Dowagiac Edition* (Chicago, 1895), pp. 13–20.

20. Frank B. Presbrey, *The History and Development of Advertising* (Garden City, N. Y., 1929), p. 388.

CHAPTER 22

1. This paragraph, and much of this chapter, is based primarily on May, *A Most Unique Machine: The Michigan Origins of the American Automobile Industry,* and the same author's *R. E. Olds: Auto Industry Pioneer* (Grand Rapids, 1977).

2. George S. May, "William O. Worth: Adventist Auto Pioneer," *Adventist Heritage,* 1 (July, 1974), pp. 43–53.

3. Henry Ford, in collaboration with Samuel Crowther, *My Life and Work* (Garden City, N. Y., 1923), p. 22.

4. *Ibid.,* pp. 22–23.

5. Gustin, *Billy Durant: Creator of General Motors.* A new biography of Durant, by Bernard Weisberger, entitled *The Dream Maker,* was published in 1979.

CHAPTER 23

1. Robert M. Warner, *Chase Salmon Osborn, 1860–1949,* Michigan Historical Collections *Bulletin No. 10* (Ann Arbor, 1960), is a brief biographical sketch of this important figure.

2. Robert M. Warner, "Chase S. Osborn's 1910 Primary Election Campaign," *Michigan History,* 43 (Sept., 1959), pp. 349–84, portions of which are reprinted in Warner and VanderHill, eds., *A Michigan Reader,* pp. 96–102.

3. In accordance with his policy of economy, Osborn in 1911 vetoed a bill appropriating state funds to the Michigan Pioneer and Historical Society. Since the inception of that society in 1874, the legislature had annually provided a sum vary- ing from $500 to $4,000 to publish the volumes known as the *Michigan Pioneer and Historical Collections.* Osborn's action was in part motivated by doubts concerning the legality of giving state funds to a private organization. Therefore, in 1913, during the administration of Governor Woodbridge Ferris, the legislature passed an act creating the Michigan Historical Commission, an official state agency, to receive funds for various historical programs. The old Pioneer and Historical Society con- tinued, later changing its name to the Historical Society of Michigan. However, society members continued to receive benefits from the state. From 1917 to 1978, the quarterly magazine, *Michigan History,* published by the Michigan Historical Commission and its successor, the History Division of the Michigan Department of State, was furnished free to society members, until Attorney General Frank Kelley, belatedly following Osborn's line of thinking, ruled that the gift of this state- financed publication to members of a private organization was an inappropriate use of state funds. Thus, beginning in 1978, *Michigan History* became available strictly on a subscription basis, while the Historical Society of Michigan, deprived of the publication which had been a main incentive for individuals to join the organization, beefed up its own publication program.

4. Robert M. Warner, "Chase S. Osborn and the Presidential Campaign of 1912," *Mississippi Valley Historical Review,* 46 (June, 1959), pp. 19–45.

5. The only other occasion in which the Republican candidate failed to win all of Michigan's electoral votes was in the election of 1892 when a Democratic- inspired change altered the method of choosing electors and enabled the Democrats to pick up five of the state's electoral votes, with the remaining nine votes going to the Republican candidate.

6. The other Democratic governor in this period was Edwin B. Winans in 1891–92. The other non-Republican governor, Josiah W. Begole, governor in 1883–84, was elected on a combined Greenback-Democratic ticket. In earlier years Begole had been connected with the Republican party.

7. Catlin, *The Story of Detroit,* pp. 420–22; David B. Davis, "The Movement to Abolish Capital Punishment in America, 1787–1861," *American Historical Re- view,* 63 (Oct., 1957), pp. 23–46; Edward W. Bennett, "The Reasons for Michigan's Abolition of Capital Punishment," *Michigan History,* 62 (Nov.–Dec., 1978), pp. 42–55; Harold M. Helfman, "A Forgotten Aftermath to Michigan's Abolition of Capital Punishment," *ibid.,* 40 (June, 1956), pp. 203–14.

8. W. F. Hopp, *The Michigan State Prison, Jackson, 1837–1928* (Jackson, 1928).

CHAPTER 24

1. James D. Wilkes, "Van Tyne: The Professor and the Hun!" *Michigan History,* 55 (Fall, 1971), pp. 183–204; John Carver Edwards, "Ann Arbor's Maverick Patriot: Professor W. H. Hobbs' Search for National Security, 1915–1918," *Detroit in Perspective,* 3 (Fall, 1978), pp. 32–52.

2. Frank B. Woodford, *Alex J. Groesbeck: Portrait of a Public Man* (Detroit, 1962), pp. 94–100. The number of Michigan men who served in the war has in the

past been given as 135,485, but the current volumes of the *Michigan Manual* have now increased this figure to "about 175,000." *Michigan Manual, 1977–1978,* p. 8.

3. *The 32nd Division in the World War* (Milwaukee, 1920).

4. Richard M. Doolen, *Michigan's Polar Bears: The American Expedition to North Russia, 1918–1919,* Michigan Historical Collections *Bulletin No. 14* (Ann Arbor, 1965).

5. Allan Nevins and Frank Ernest Hill, *Ford: Expansion and Challenge, 1915–1933* (New York, 1957), pp. 23–24; Harry Barnard, *Independent Man: The Life of Senator James Couzens* (New York, 1958), pp. 99–100.

6. The Ford Peace Ship venture has been the subject of numerous books and articles, the latest being Barbara S. Kraft's *The Peace Ship: Henry Ford's Pacifist Adventure in the First World War* (New York, 1978).

7. Nevins and Hill, *Ford: Expansion and Challenge,* pp. 116–24, covers the Ford-Newberry contest. Spencer Ervin, *Henry Ford vs. Truman H. Newberry: The Famous Senate Election Contest* (New York, 1935), is a massive study.

8. Bald, *Michigan in Four Centuries,* p. 316.

9. Quoted in Karolena M. Fox, "The Movement for Equal Suffrage in Michigan," *Michigan History,* 2 (Jan., 1918), pp. 90–109.

10. Woodford, *Alex J. Groesbeck, passim.*

11. Barnard, *Independent Man,* pp. 101–92.

12. C. David Tompkins, "Profile of a Progressive Editor," *Michigan History,* 53 (Summer, 1969), pp. 144–57. Vandenberg's books on Hamilton were: *Greatest American: Alexander Hamilton* (1921), and *If Hamilton Were Here Today* (1923).

CHAPTER 25

1. Amos H. Hawley, *The Population of Michigan, 1840 to 1960: An Analysis of Growth, Distribution and Composition* (Ann Arbor, 1949).

2. George Bush, *Future Builders: The Story of Michigan's Consumers Power Company* (New York, 1973), pp. 35–50.

3. Z. Z. Lydens, ed., *The Story of Grand Rapids* (Grand Rapids, 1966), pp. 131–32.

4. Woodford and Woodford, *All Our Yesterdays,* pp. 278–81.

5. Allan R. Treppa, "The 'Ypsi-Ann'—Michigan's First Interurban," *Detroit in Perspective,* 1 (Spring, 1973), pp. 191–201.

6. Philip P. Mason, "The League of American Wheelmen and the Good-Roads Movement, 1880–1905," unpublished doctoral dissertation, University of Michigan, 1957; Roger L. Morrison, *The History and Development of Michigan Highways* (Ann Arbor, 1938).

7. Frank B. Woodford, *We Never Drive Alone: The Story of the Automobile Club of Michigan* (Detroit, 1958), pp. 26–28.

8. Carl B. Franks, "Marker to First Mile of Concrete Road," *Michigan History,* 43 (March, 1959), pp. 109–14; George S. May, "The Good Roads Movement in Iowa," *The Palimpsest,* 36 (Jan., 1955), p. 34.

9. Woodford, *Alex J. Groesbeck,* pp. 201–22.

10. J. H. Brown, "How We Got the R. F. D.," *Michigan History,* 6 (Nos. 2–3, 1922), pp. 442–59.

11. Robert L. Kelly, "History of Radio in Michigan," *Michigan History,* 21 (Winter, 1937), pp. 5–19; Cynthia Boyes Young, "WWJ—Pioneer in Broadcasting," *ibid.,* 44 (Dec., 1960), pp. 411–33. The latter article is reprinted in Warner and VanderHill, eds., *A Michigan Reader,* pp. 183–95.

12. The Consumers Power Company and Detroit Edison have, since 1948, furnished plaques to mark farms that have been owned by the same family for a century or more. This Centennial Farm program, inaugurated by the Michigan Historical Commission and carried on by its successor agency, resulted in a total of over 3,000 farms being so designated by 1979.

13. Kuhn, *Michigan State: The First Hundred Years,* chapters 2 and 3.

14. Philip Dorf, *Liberty Hyde Bailey: An Informal Biography* (Ithaca, N. Y., 1956).

15. *United States Census of Agriculture, 1964,* vol. I, Part 13: *Michigan.*

16. Gates, *Michigan Copper and Boston Dollars,* p. 145.

17. Fuller, ed., *Centennial History of Michigan,* 2:29–33; *Mineral Industry of Michigan, 1974,* pp. 18–21; preliminary production figures for 1978, as given in Ann Arbor *News,* 4 March 1979.

18. Post-war auto industry developments are summarized in John B. Rae, *The American Automobile* (Chicago, 1965), pp. 73–104. For another, more critical view of Sloan's contributions, see Emma Rothschild, *Paradise Lost: The Decline of the Auto-Industrial Age* (New York, 1973).

19. For an example of the articles on Detroit by outside reporters, see Warner and VanderHill, eds., *A Michigan Reader,* pp. 133–43.

20. See the article on "The New Laborer," in Alfred D. Chandler, Jr., ed., *Giant Enterprise: Ford, General Motors, and the Automobile Industry* (New York, 1964), pp. 181–94.

21. Robert C. Maday, "An Historical Geography of Hamtramck Township: An Attempt at Explaining the Origins of the City of Hamtramck," unpublished master's thesis at the University of Michigan, 1977; George P. Graaf, *The People of Michigan* (Lansing, 1974), pp. 85–90.

22. Harold B. Fields, "Free Negroes in Cass County Before the Civil War," *Michigan History,* 44 (Dec., 1960), pp. 375–83.

23. John C. Dancy, *Sand Against the Wind: The Memoirs of John C. Dancy* (Detroit, 1966). *Michigan Challenge,* 8 (June, 1968), pp. 9–63, includes a series of articles on numerous topics relating to the Negro in Michigan.

CHAPTER 26

1. Barnard, *Independent Man: The Life of Senator James Couzens,* pp. 194–96.

2. Rae, *The American Automobile,* pp. 109–21; Gustin, *Billy Durant,* pp. 223–61.

3. As noted earlier, Grover Cleveland, the Democratic Presidential candidate in 1892, had won five of Michigan's fourteen electoral votes, the only Democrat to gain any of the state's electoral votes between the election of the Democrat, Franklin Pierce, in 1852, and the election of Franklin Roosevelt in 1932.

4. Because of the crucial role played in the developing bank crisis by Couzens and Ford, their biographers have devoted considerable space to this event. See, for example, Barnard, *Independent Man,* pp. 213–52; and David L. Lewis, *The Public Image of Henry Ford: An American Folk Hero and His Company* (Detroit, 1976), pp. 238–41.

5. *Annual Report* of State Banking Commission (1949), p. 10.

6. Home-rule cities could levy an additional tax under the provisions of this amendment. It also provided that voters of any assessing district might authorize the collection of additional millage. The original provisions were somewhat modified by subsequent amendments.

7. As late as the 1960s, Democratic legislators angrily—and successfully—demanded the removal of a label that had been attached to the portrait of Comstock in the state capitol that linked the Democratic governor with the introduction of the sales tax.

8. For a brief biographical sketch of Murphy by Sidney Fine, see Warner and VanderHill, eds., *A Michigan Reader,* pp. 205–12. Fine is the author of a definitive biography of Murphy, with two of the three volumes that will comprise this work published by 1979. For articles on the campaign of 1936 and the 1938 Murphy gubernatorial campaign, see Richard D. Lunt, "Frank Murphy's Decision to Enter the 1936 Gubernatorial Race," *Michigan History,* 47 (Dec., 1963), pp. 327–34; and Samuel T. McSeveney, "The Michigan Gubernatorial Campaign of 1938," *ibid.,* 45 (June, 1961), pp. 97–127.

9. Sidney Glazer, "The Michigan Labor Movement," *Michigan History,* 29 (Jan.–Mar., 1945), pp. 73–82; Doris B. McLaughlin, *Michigan Labor: A Brief History from 1818 to the Present* (Ann Arbor, 1970), pp. 3–49.

10. See Warner and VanderHill, eds., *A Michigan Reader,* p. 135.

11. Sidney Fine, *The Automobile Under the Blue Eagle* (Ann Arbor, 1963), gives the background of the labor movement in the auto industry before the Depression and the impact of the Depression on the growth of union support.

12. Sidney Fine, "The General Motors Sit-Down Strike: A Re-Examination," *American Historical Review,* 70 (April, 1965), pp. 691–713, indicates that union leaders circulated the report in order to create support for a strike which would close down the Flint plant's operations. A shortage of certain supplies would have caused the company to close the plant in a few days. For complete details of the Flint sit-down strike see Sidney Fine, *Sit-Down: The General Motors Strike of 1936–1937* (Ann Arbor, 1969).

13. For the Ford labor problems and the final labor settlement, see Allan Nevins and Frank Ernest Hill, *Ford: Decline and Rebirth, 1933–1962* (New York, 1963), pp. 133–67.

14. James K. Pollock, "Civil Service Developments in Michigan," *Good Government,* 58 (1941), pp. 27–28.

15. For production figures, see Motor Vehicle Manufacturers Association, *Automobiles of America* (Detroit, 1974), pp. 107–14. Alan Clive's *State of War: Michigan in World War II,* is scheduled for publication by the University of Michigan Press in 1979.

16. Nevins and Hill, *Ford: Decline and Rebirth,* p. 174.

17. Marion F. Wilson, *The Story of Willow Run* (Ann Arbor, 1956); Lowell J. Carr and James E. Stermer, *Willow Run: A Study of Industrialization and Cultural Inadequacy* (New York, 1952).

18. These events are covered in detail in Nevins and Hill, *Ford: Decline and Rebirth.*

19. Dancy, *Sand Against the Wind,* pp. 21–34; Kenneth G. Weinberg, *A Man's Home, A Man's Castle* (New York, 1971).

20. Quoted in Robert Shogun and Tom Craig, *The Detroit Race Riot: A Study in Violence* (Philadelphia, 1964), pp. 6–7. This is the most extensive treatment of the 1943 riot. See also Alfred McClung Lee and Norman D. Humphrey, *Race Riot* (New York, 1943).

21. "Detroit is Dynamite," *Life,* 13 (17 August 1942), pp. 15–23. The title of this remarkably prophetic article was perhaps a play on the old chamber of commerce promotional motto which had referred to "Dynamic Detroit," and as Arthur Pound had also done in his book, *Detroit: Dynamic City,* published only two years before the publication of the *Life* article.

22. In a review of Shogun and Craig's *The Detroit Race Riot,* in *Michigan History,* 50 (Sept., 1966), pp. 271–74, Broadus N. Butler, a Negro official at Wayne State University, detailed the system that had arisen in Detroit which Butler felt had largely negated the possibility of another large-scale race riot from developing in that city.

23. Portions of Vandenberg's speech are reprinted in Warner and Vander-Hill, eds., *A Michigan Reader,* pp. 249–53.

CHAPTER 27

1. Charles T. Pearson, *The Indomitable Tin Goose: The True Story of Preston Tucker and His Car* (Minneapolis, 1974). Rae, *The American Automobile,* pp. 161–77, deals with the period of post-war adjustment in the auto industry.

2. Richard M. Langworth, *Kaiser-Frazer: The Last Onslaught on Detroit* (New York, 1975).

3. Barton J. Bernstein, "Walter Reuther and the General Motors Strike of 1945–1946," *Michigan History,* 49 (Sept., 1965), pp. 260–77.

4. Robert L. Tyler, *Walter Reuther* (Grand Rapids, 1973), is a good brief biography.

5. For problems that resulted in Michigan labor circles from the A.F.L.-C.I.O. merger, see Jacqueline Brophy, "The Merger of the AFL and the CIO in Michigan," *Michigan History,* 50 (June, 1966), pp. 139–57. The article is reprinted in Warner and VanderHill, eds., *A Michigan Reader,* pp. 253–67.

6. Bald, *Michigan in Four Centuries,* pp. 450–51.

7. Woodford, *Alex J. Groesbeck,* pp. 306–18.

8. Stephen B. and Vera H. Sarasohn, *Political Party Patterns in Michigan* (Detroit, 1957), p. 55. Much of the political discussion in this chapter is based on this perceptive, brief study of Michigan politics in the first half of the twentieth century.

9. Frank McNaughton, *Mennen Williams of Michigan: Fighter for Progress* (New York, 1960), is the only adequate source for Williams' career through his gubernatorial period.

10. Woodford, *Alex J. Groesbeck,* pp. 229–34; C. W. Shull, *Legislative Reapportionment in Michigan* (Detroit, 1961).

11. Democrats, like Republicans, however, favored the retention of county lines, because party organization was by counties. Apportionment strictly according to population could not be achieved without laying out districts that cut across county lines. In the areas that could be most affected by strict reapportionment, the issue of whether or not to support change was to a considerable degree a non-partisan one. Many Republicans in the Detroit area supported the granting to that area of its fair share of legislative representation, while Democrats in the Upper Peninsula, who had dominated elections there since the Depression of the thirties, tended to favor the status quo as much as did Republicans in other outstate areas because of the power that the existing apportionment system gave them in the legislature.

12. Michigan Department of Revenue, *19th Annual Report,* p. 10.

13. Prentiss M. Brown, *The Mackinac Bridge Story* (Detroit, 1956), is a good brief account of the efforts that culminated in the building of the bridge. Brown remained the chairman of the Mackinac Bridge Authority until his death in 1973.

14. The Mackinac Bridge is the longest suspension bridge in terms of the distance between the cable anchorages at either end of the bridge. Supporters of the claims to pre-eminence of San Francisco's Golden Gate Bridge argued that the length of the span between the bridge's towers was the important statistic, in which

case the Golden Gate Bridge, with a span of 4200 feet, was four hundred feet longer than the Mackinac Bridge. However, in 1964, with the opening of the Verrazano-Narrows Bridge in New York with a suspension span sixty feet longer than that of the Golden Gate Bridge, the California and Michigan bridges were demoted to second and third places in this record category.

15. Although the use tax was thrown out by the court, the state had already collected about $13,000,000, of which amount applications were received for the refunding of only $900,000, leaving the state treasury some $12,000,000 richer from a tax that should never have been levied in the first place.

16. See Neil Staebler to G. Mennen Williams, June 27, 1957, in the Neil Staebler Papers at the Michigan Historical Collections, University of Michigan, quoted in J. Bradford Freeman, "The Influence of the Michigan Delegation to the 1960 National Convention of the Democratic Party," seminar paper written under George S. May at Eastern Michigan University in 1969.

17. While he was serving as Assistant Secretary of State for African Affairs, Williams acquired a large collection of African art objects. Much of this collection was subsequently donated to the Detroit Institute of Arts.

18. Quoted in Bald, *Michigan in Four Centuries,* p. 486.

19. The assumption was, apparently, that any voter who did not vote on the issue of constitutional revision while voting on other matters on the ballot in the same election must not feel very strongly on the issue and was, in effect, indicating his or her satisfaction with the existing constitution.

20. See Albert L. Sturm, *Constitution-Making in Michigan, 1961–1962* (Ann Arbor, 1963), for the movement for calling a convention and for a discussion of the activities of the convention itself.

21. The Constitutional Convention Preparatory Commission arranged for the necessary facilities required by the delegates and supervised the preparation of eighteen detailed background reports on the major issues with which the delegates would have to deal. All but one of the reports were published.

22. Remarks made by Pollock before a University of Michigan Alumni meeting in Lansing in the winter of 1961–62, a meeting attended by George May.

23. T. George Harris, *Romney's Way: A Man and an Idea* (Englewood Cliffs, N. J., 1967), is a campaign biography prepared for Romney's abortive Presidential bid in 1968. The fact that Romney had been born in Mexico raised the question as to whether or not he would meet the Constitutional stipulation that only "a natural-born citizen" is eligible to become President. Romney's contention that he did qualify, since his parents were American citizens, is discussed in *ibid.,* pp. 197–200. Romney's withdrawal from the Presidential race in 1968 left the issue unresolved.

24. Tom Mahoney, *The Story of George Romney: Builder, Salesman, Crusader* (New York, 1960), is a more complete discussion of Romney's automotive career than the politically-oriented biography by T. George Harris.

25. Paul W. McCracken, ed., *Taxes and Economic Growth in Michigan* (Kalamazoo, 1960); William Haber and others, *The Michigan Economy: Its Potential and Its Problems* (Kalamazoo, 1959).

26. See *The Autobiography of Malcolm X* (New York, 1964), pp. 3–11. These pages are reprinted in Warner and VanderHill, eds., *A Michigan Reader,* pp. 311–19.

27. See *Report of the National Advisory Commission on Civil Disorders* (New York, 1968). Racial disturbances erupted in Detroit and several other cities in Michigan on the weekend following the assassination of the Rev. Martin Luther King, Jr., in April, 1968. Fortunately, violence did not reach the level that it did in Washington, D. C., and other large cities in the nation.

28. The interview was widely covered in the nation's press. See, for example, *Time*, 90 (15 Sept. 1967), p. 22. Romney's actual words were: "When I came back from Viet Nam, I had just the greatest brainwashing that anybody can get when you go over to Viet Nam."

CHAPTER 28

1. Nevins,"The Kalamazoo Case," *Michigan History*, 44:91–100; Willis F. Dunbar, "The High School on Trial: The Kalamazoo Case," *Papers of the Michigan Academy of Science, Arts, and Letters*, 45 (Part II) (1960), pp. 187–210.

2. State Department of Education, *Annual Report, 1966–67*, II-27.

3. Dewey was a member of the faculty at the University of Michigan from 1884 to 1894.

4. Donald W. Disbrow, *Schools for an Urban Society* (Lansing, 1968), pp. 138–45, 271. The faculty strike at Eastern Michigan University gained national notoriety in 1979 with the publication of an article by an ex-faculty member who had chosen not to participate in the strike. See Ronald L. Trowbridge, "I Crossed a Picket Line," *National Review*, 31 (16 Feb. 1979), pp. 222–23. The Hutchinson Act of 1947, while establishing a procedure for public employees to organize and present their grievances, had included punitive provisions that were to be applied against any public employees who went out on strike. The Public Employment Act of 1965 greatly strengthened the collective bargaining power of the employees and, although still prohibiting strikes by public employees, eliminated the punitive anti-strike provisions of the Hutchinson Act.

5. Douglas W. Johnson, Paul R. Picard, and Bernard Quinn, *Churches and Church Membership in the United States: An enumeration by region, state, and county* (Washington, 1974), p. 5. Unfortunately, membership in most Negro churches and in all non-Christian religious groups, which was included in the Census Bureau's survey of 1936, was not included in this 1971 survey.

6. Information supplied by the Rev. Martin Luther Simmons, Presiding Elder, Northern District, Michigan African Methodist Episcopal Church.

7. The line between black Baptist and white Baptist churches is no longer a clear one since many Negro Baptist churches are now affiliated with the American Baptist Churches, USA. Blacks comprise about twenty percent of the membership of this organization nationally, with the percentage probably much higher in Michigan.

8. Irvin, I. Katz, "Jews in Michigan," *Family Trails* (a publication of the State Library), 4 (Spring, 1974), p. 6.

9. See Fuller, ed., *Centennial History of Michigan*, 2:611–37, for extensive discussion and notes on fraternal groups and other private organizations.

10. The Michigan Department of the American Legion received its charter August 1, 1920. Much of the effort of the Legion was directed to the relief of the disabled. The first tuberculosis hospital to be operated by the American Legion for treatment of servicemen was built by the Michigan Department at Fort Custer and was dedicated November 7, 1921, by Marshal Ferdinand Foch, the French military hero of World War I. See Emil L. Carlson, "The American Legion in Michigan," *Michigan History*, 23 (Winter, 1939), pp. 15–21. See also Fuller, ed., *Centennial History of Michigan*, 2:632–33.

11. *Ibid.*, 2:634–35.

12. The association is still active and its building still in use. See Mrs. George E. Foote, *History of the Ladies' Library Association* (Kalamazoo, 1941).

13. William W. Lutz, *The News of Detroit: How a Newspaper and a City Grew Together* (Boston, 1973).

14. Mott, *American Journalism*, pp. 635–37. Aside from the Detroit *Free Press*, which had a circulation of around 600,000, the only other morning newspapers published in Michigan in 1979 were the Mt. Pleasant *Sun*, with a circulation of around 8300, and the *Michigan Daily*, the University of Michigan student publication, which has a circulation of about 8,000 in Ann Arbor. See the 1979 edition of the annual *Ayer Directory of Publications*. In addition, however, the evening Detroit *News* began publishing a morning edition in 1977.

15. Edson H. Mudge, "The Old-time Country Newspapermen," *Michigan History*, 30 (Oct.–Dec., 1946), pp. 754–58. The 1979 *Ayer Directory of Publications* listed 244 weeklies in Michigan, plus twenty-three other newspapers that were listed variously as being published on anywhere from a semi-weekly basis to ten times a year.

16. John L. Kolehmainen, "Finnish Newspapers and Periodicals in Michigan," *Michigan History*, 24 (Winter, 1940), pp. 119–27; Mark O. Kistler, "German Language Press in Michigan: A Survey and Bibliography," *ibid.*, 44 (Sept., 1960), pp. 303–23; Georges J. Joyaux, "French Press in Michigan: A Bibliography," *ibid.*, 36 (Sept., 1952), pp. 260–78.

17. Norma Lee Browning, *Joe Maddy of Interlochen* (Chicago, 1963). Van Cliburn contributed an introduction to this book which is reprinted in Warner and Vanderhill, eds., *A Michigan Reader*, pp. 268–72.

18. See Kit Lane, *Saugatuck's Big Pavilion* (Saugatuck, 1977), for one of the most famous of these dance pavilions in western Michigan. Although it burned to the ground in 1960 and has not been rebuilt, picture postcards showing the Big Pavilion continue to enjoy a brisk sale among the tourists visiting Saugatuck.

19. An article on Gordy and Motown, originally published in the New York *Times Magazine*, is reprinted in Warner and VanderHill, eds., *A Michigan Reader*, pp. 273–84.

20. For details on the Ann Arbor art fair and the differences between the three separate fairs that are held in various parts of the city, see the July, 1977, issue of the *Ann Arbor Observer*.

21. Henry Ford Museum Staff, *Greenfield Village and the Henry Ford Museum* (New York, 1972).

22. See Eugene T. Petersen, *Michilimackinac: Its History and Restoration* (Mackinac Island, 1962), and some of the other publications of the Mackinac Island State Park Commission for details of that agency's historical program.

23. The 1978–79 edition of the Historical Society of Michigan's guide, *Historical Museums in Michigan*, listed 144 such museums in the state.

25. Dunbar, "The Opera House as a Social Institution in Michigan," *Michigan History*, 26:661–72; Elaine E. McDavitt, "The Beginnings of Theatrical Activities in Detroit," *ibid.*, 31 (March, 1947), pp. 35–47.

25. Richard L. Tobin, "Ring Lardner, the man with the perfect pitch," *Chronicle, The Magazine of the Historical Society of Michigan*, 14 (Spring, 1978), pp. 11–18. See also Jonathan Yardley, *Ring: A Biography of Ring Lardner* (New York, 1977).

26. Royce Howes, *Edgar A. Guest: A Biography* (Chicago, 1953).

27. E. W. Erickson, "Johan G. R. Banér: Michigan's Viking Poet," *Swedish Pioneer Historical Quarterly*, 24 (April, 1973), pp. 73–93.

28. Kathleen I. Gillard, *Our Michigan Heritage* (New York, 1955), attempts to survey Michigan literature. See also Arnold Mulder, "Authors and Wolverines,"

Saturday Review of Literature, 19 (4 March 1939), pp. 3–4, 16; and Albert G. Black, *Michigan Novels: An Annotated Bibliography* (Ann Arbor, 1963).

CHAPTER 29

1. Michigan's first Presidential primary, authorized by the legislature in 1912 but too late to be used until the Presidential campaign of 1916, was repealed in 1931. A second primary was adopted in time for the 1972 campaign, at which time the Democratic leadership in the state was humiliated by the overwhelming plurality of Alabama's Governor George Wallace over the favorites of the two major factions in the state, George McGovern and Hubert Humphrey.

2. U.S. Department of Labor, Bureau of Labor Statistics, *Employment and Earnings,* 26 (Mar., 1979), pp. 115–19. Local wage averages vary greatly from month to month due to seasonal labor requirements, but in general, few cities anywhere in the country approach or exceed the average production worker's wage in the three Michigan cities.

3. Detroit *News,* 25 Feb. 1979.

4. Ann Arbor *News,* 25 March 1979.

5. Grand Rapids *Press,* 17 Sept. 1978.

SUGGESTIONS FOR FURTHER READING

1. See Bruce Catton, "The Real Michigan," originally published in the August, 1957, issue of *Holiday,* and reprinted in both volumes of *A Michigan Reader.*

2. For a still younger audience, Ferris E. Lewis, *My State and Its Story* (Hillsdale, 1937, reprinted in numerous editions since that year), has been the most widely used junior high text, while Russel B. Nye, *Michigan* (New York, 1966), though far less comprehensive, is the best written.

INDEX

(This index includes names of towns, cities, and counties not followed by the name of a state. All such entries are names of places in Michigan.)